SOCIOLOGY THE HUMAN SCIENCE

ELBERT W. STEWART

McGraw-Hill Book Company

New York   St. Louis   San Francisco   Auckland
Bogotá   Düsseldorf   Johannesburg
London   Madrid   Mexico   Montreal
New Delhi   Panama   Paris   São Paulo
Singapore   Sydney   Tokyo   Toronto

To Justin, Monica, and Mia

SOCIOLOGY
The Human Science

1234567890VHVH 78321098

This book was set in Souvenir Light by Black Dot, Inc.
The editors were Donald W. Burden, Lyle Linder,
Helen Greenberg, Natalie M. Talbott Blaney, and Susan Gamer;
the designer was Wladislaw Finne;
the production supervisor was Leroy A. Young.
The photo researcher was Inge King.
The drawings were done by J & R Services, Inc.
Von Hoffmann Press, Inc., was printer and binder.

Cover: A detail from *The Fourteenth of July.*
Montmartre, 1901, by Pablo Picasso. Justin K.
Thannhauser Collection. Courtesy of the
Thannhauser Foundation and the Solomon R.
Guggenheim Museum, New York.

Library of Congress Cataloging in Publication Data

Stewart, Elbert W
    Sociology, the human science.
    Bibliography: p.
    Includes index.
    1. Sociology. I. Title.
HM251.S78   301   77-16595
ISBN 0-07-061295-1

Contents

Contents

Contents

Contents

Contents

ix

Contents

Contents

xi

Contents

Preface

A knowledge of society and its trends is necessary for the mental health of its people. Conversely, the people's interested concern is essential to the health of the society. It is this conviction that has prompted me to write a text that will help students see themselves and their particular social groups in a new and expanded context, to broaden students' knowledge of the larger society in which they live, and to increase their concern for and awareness of the problems and viewpoints of other people. I have prepared this text to enable students to take with them a broader perspective and more discriminate outlook on society as a whole. This is ambitious by any standards, but not impossible. In writing this text, I have drawn on my many years of teaching experience as well as the real excitement I feel about the study of sociology. But my experience has taught me that this is often not enough. Students, like the rest of us, need road signs, maps, and reinforcements. They need to learn how to assimilate their new knowledge one step at a time. And this book contains the tools that make this type of learning possible. One of the most important of these tools is organization.

Organization

The organization of subject matter in the following pages is centered on the themes of the foundations of social life, diversity and strain, social institutions and organization, and the types of changes brought about by population growth and urban-industrial ways of life. The topics and concepts included by nearly all instructors in introductory sociology and the major theorists are all given their place. It will be noted, however, that certain topics are given more space than is usual: stratification by sex and age, for example, and the sociology of work and leisure. A special chapter on total institutions is also included. It seemed that there could be no better way of carrying out the objective of acquainting the student with societies within societies and special types of social interaction than to look into prisons and mental institutions. The final chapter is also somewhat innovative in that it attempts to relate sociological concepts to the world as a whole, particularly to the developing nations. This chapter is also a device for reviewing many of the social trends previously presented.

Learning Objectives

This text introduces the students to a new way of looking at the world around them. It is important that these new ideas be presented as clearly as possible so that the very instrument of learning does not present an obstacle to it. Every chapter begins with learning objectives. These objectives are stated briefly but provide the student with a guide to important key areas in the chapter. If referred to often, they can help the student organize and assimilate the new material.

Summary

A summary of the most important elements discussed concludes each chapter. The summary acts as a reinforcement to the text material in conjunction with the learning objectives.

Glossary and Bibliography

An introductory text requires clear explanations and examples that are meaningful to the student. In this text, new terms are carefully defined both in the text and in the glossary at the end of the book. A current bibliography is also included at the end of the text.

Inserts

Concepts are related to real-life situations. Each chapter contains a number of articles and case studies from current newspapers or journals, or from works of sociologists. These serve to reinforce and illustrate the discussion by using current events familiar to the student and relating them to the topic being studied. These cases were selected on the basis of appropriateness and student interest.

Study Guide within the Text

Reading a text and listening to lectures are not sufficient to round out the learning process. Facts and ideas must be reinforced by such methods as review, discussion, testing, and further reading. In this text, a built-in Study Guide follows every chapter and contains additional devices aimed at reinforcing learning: lists of important concepts and names of important people; thirty objective-type questions; projects to be carried out singly or as a class; and suggested readings. The list of suggested readings has been chosen mainly from journals and popular magazines that should be available in any college library. They are generally quite readable and interesting. Since there is always a time problem in the teaching of any course, it will not be possible to follow through on all suggestions contained in the built-in Study Guide. However, it is hoped that at least some time will be devoted to discussion questions and projects. Learning is much more meaningful if there is an exchange of ideas and an application of thought to the facts and theories that have been encountered. The readings will also help fortify the learning that has taken place. All together, the teaching devices at the end of the chapters should help students in their reflections on the meaning of such learning in their own lives.

Instructor's Manual

For each chapter, the Instructor's Manual will provide: (1) an overview outlining major themes of the chapter; (2) chapter objectives; (3) lecture and discussion topics, class activities or demonstrations, and suggestions for student projects and research papers; (4) short essay questions with answers; and (5) a brief annotated bibliography. In addition, there will be a general course references section which will include readers, films, and sources, etc.

Test Bank

The Test Bank will include alternative test sets for each chapter. Each test will be made up of multiple choice and true-false questions and can be easily duplicated for convenience. There will also be additional questions that the instructor can use in making up a new test or as supplementary quiz questions. A 50-item short-answer midterm test and a 100-item short-answer final test will be included. All materials are designed so that they can be used in the personalized system of instruction.

Board of Consultants

I was particularly fortunate in the preparation of this text to have the combined input of an advisory panel. This panel consisted of Stuart L. Hills of St. Lawrence University, Canton, New York; Norman K. Denzin of the University of Illinois, Urbana, Illinois; Richard Rosell of Westchester Community College, Valhalla, New York; Norma Zane Chaplain, Development Associates, Inc., Washington, D.C.; and Raymond P. Cuzzort of the University of Colorado,

Boulder, Colorado. It is obvious that from such a group of advisors came far more good ideas than could be realized in one text, but I have profited greatly from their suggestions. My thanks go particularly to Stuart Hills, who suggested many of the inserts found in all parts of the book. He and the editors, Lyle Linder, Helen Greenberg, and Natalie M. Talbott Blaney, were also very helpful in suggesting the design of student self-tests and other learning devices for the Study Guide within the text.

I would also like to thank Thomas E. Drabek, University of Denver; Frank Clemente, Pennsylvania State University; Irving Elan, Middlesex County College; H. Roy Kaplan, State University of New York, Buffalo; Peter Kott, Manhattan Community College, City University of New York; and John Maniha, Social Security Administration, Department of Health, Education, and Welfare, Washington, D.C., for their very thorough reviews and helpful suggestions.

One must always apologize for not being able to follow through on all suggestions, but time and deadlines make such an accomplishment impossible. Let me express my regrets that not all good ideas could be followed, and my thanks for so many improvements brought about by the suggestions of reviewers.

Elbert W. Stewart

FOUNDATIONS OF SOCIAL LIFE

This chapter gives a preliminary explanation of the nature and interests of sociology. After reading it, you should be able to:

1 Better understand the relationships between social disturbances and the existing social order.

2 Define sociology and society and describe the general areas of sociological concern.

3 Describe sociological points of view and compare them with those of the other social sciences.

4 Explain different ways in which one can look at society: unitary versus conflict models, evolutionary and symbolic-interactionist models.

5 Give an example of the type of work done by research sociologists.

6 Give an example of the use of theory in sociology.

1

THE SOCIOLOGICAL SCENE

Since sociology deals with all of social life, its interests include the unusual and dramatic as well as the ordinary. The ordinary routines of life make society appear stable, predictable, and understandable. Dramatic interruptions, however, force sociologists to deal with the results of changes that were not clearly observed and foreseen—changes in attitudes, in positions of power and influence, in levels of frustration, and all the other factors that prevent society from being dull and even-keeled. Two examples of the developments that shatter confidence in the steady flow of social events can be drawn from the Republic of South Africa and the United States.

After thirty years of control by the National Party and very few disturbances, the all-white regime of Prime Minister John Vorster of South Africa felt secure in its policies of extreme racial segregation known as *apartheid.* The Prime Minister had stated that he understood the thinking of the blacks and knew how to control them. Then, in June 1976, in the huge, ugly, poverty-stricken satellite suburb of Johannesburg known as Soweto, black high school students began to gather by the thousands to protest government policies. They gathered in the sports arena, shouting their hatred for the Dutch-descended Afrikaaners, for their government, and even for their language. The students raised banners and armed themselves with rocks. Antiriot squads, with attack dogs and tear gas, were called out by the government to put down the demonstration. Approximately a hundred were killed and a thousand injured before it was over. The crowd threw stones at the police,

who responded by firing point-blank into the crowd. Fleeing the firing, the crowd broke up; they gathered in groups along city streets, pelted buses with rocks, overturned and set fire to cars, smashed windows of public buildings, and looted stores. One white official was dragged from his car and clubbed to death by the angry mob.

As in all such actions, accounts vary as to how the violence started. The police tell of attempts to quiet the mob without violence, of pleas to break up, and of the use of tear gas to prevent the use of bullets. Students report that the crowd was quieting down and offering to talk reasonably when the police opened fire (*Time*, 1976).

Details will never be agreed upon, but certain outcomes are beyond dispute. As shown by later racial riots in other South African cities and by demonstrations of sympathy from white students at the University of Witwatersrand, the myth of a happy and stable social order in which the blacks were complacently content was shattered for all time. The first minor retreats from a strictly segregationist society began later in the year, with less exclusion of blacks from sports. Foreign investments dropped sharply, as did business profits and general prosperity, and the voices of opposition parties became louder than they had been for thirty years.

This was the Republic of South Africa in 1976. A parallel—and classic—American example takes us back to the 1960s. The scene is Chicago; the time, August 1968.

The decade of the 1960s had been a period in which the seemingly impossible happened. President John F. Kennedy and Dr. Martin Luther King had both been assassinated. Riots rocked

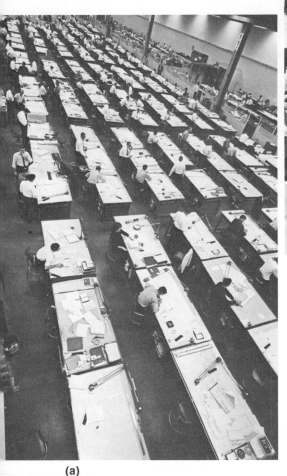

(a)

(b)

Figure 1-1 (*a*) The stable, predictable functions of a society contain the potential for dramatic, sometimes violent change, as (*b*) the 1976 racial struggles in South Africa show. Sociologists are concerned with both types of events and with determining the relationship between them. [(*a*) *Wide World;* (*b*) *Elliot Erwitt, Magnum*]

American cities, bringing widespread death and destruction and shouts of "Burn, baby, burn," as rioters set fire to buildings. There were also demonstrations and riots on many campuses, as young people did the unexpected and refused to fight for a dubious cause in a distant war in Vietnam. Tradition-bound Americans were angry over the students' activities and wondered what madness had radicalized American youth.

The social unrest came to a climax at a political confrontation in Chicago in the summer of 1968, when the Democratic party met to select a candidate for President. The National

Mobilization Committee to End the War in Vietnam and the Youth International Party (called the *Yippies*) had arrived in Chicago to make known their opposition to the war in Vietnam. They also wanted the people to know about the way in which President Lyndon B. Johnson and Vice-President Hubert Humphrey had put down dissenters at home. According to one reporter, James Ridgeway, they came "to demonstrate that America was a police state." The confrontation ended, Ridgeway continues, "as a full-blown insurrection of middle-class people against that state" (Ridgeway, 1968).

As protesters faced the police sent into Chicago's Grant Park to keep order, anger rose on both sides. Shouted slogans of "Hell no, we won't go!" "Dump the Hump" (Humphrey), and "Here come the pigs, oink, oink, oink" gave way to screamed obscenities. Frustrated policemen came back with similar obscenities, tear gas, and clubs. Police violence, first aimed at the Yippies and others with long hair, soon went out of control in what has been called a "police riot." Eventually, more moderate demonstrators and even bystanders became victims of police fury.

Fleeing the park, which had become a battleground, the crowd tried to regroup in front of the Conrad Hilton Hotel. Heavy police reenforcements arrived to move the crowd away from the convention site, but by this time any orderly police action, or any orderly movement at all, had become impossible. Some of the crowd, backed against one of the Hilton's plate-glass windows, were pushed by the police and by other frightened demonstrators until the window burst inward, cutting people with jagged glass. The crowd fought back against police clubs and tear gas with broken cobblestones, wood, bottles, and metal pipe. Trash cans, set on fire and rolled at the police, became eerie weapons in the Chicago night.

This confrontation, now a street fight, raged wildly for hours. Police and police cars were attacked; 600 people were arrested; and scores more, including reporters, were badly beaten before being hauled off in paddy wagons. By midnight the hysteria died down and the protesters, now numbering three or four thousand, settled back into the park, where they shouted, chanted, and listened to speeches before breaking up.

During the riots, according to a government commission report, there was extreme violence on both sides. Of the police, one on-the-scene reporter observed:

> The police began picking people off. They would pull individuals to the ground and begin beating them. A medic wearing a white coat and armband with a red cross was grabbed, beaten and knocked to the ground. His whole face was covered with blood. (Walker Commission, 1968)

Many radical demonstrators showed just as little restraint. One officer, hit by a piece of concrete, fell to the ground, while the crowd chanted, "More" and "Kill the pig."

This conflict made a disaster of the Democratic National Convention. A cloud was cast over Hubert Humphrey's candidacy and many voters turned to Richard Nixon, whose demand for "law and order" seemed to promise an end to such disorder. The effects of this major social disruption were felt for months after the riot itself had ended. Seven of the leaders who had first called for the demonstration, "The Chicago Seven," were tried on charges of conspiracy. They used their trial to expose and publicize inequities in the American justice system, and the disruptions they created in the Chicago courtroom ran a close second to the disorder which had earlier ripped through Chicago's streets.

The events which disrupted the American political system in the 1960s and South Africa a decade later were neither orderly nor predictable. But they were not individual acts of insanity. The events just described, though bizarre, are clearly social events, shaped by the attitudes and values of the American social system and affecting the entire society. On the personal side, the Chicago riots were set off by the actions of particular individuals: demonstrators, police, reporters, and even curious bystanders. Sociologists believe that these complex social events may be understood only through the thorough and systematic study of both large social structures and the actions of small groups and individuals within them.

Sociology is concerned with both unusual events—as in Chicago in 1968—and everyday life. Sociologists know that the ordinary and extraordinary events are closely related. Although much of the time society seems to work fairly well, little-noticed forces are at work, sometimes coming together to cause serious disturbances in the social balance. A major task of sociology is to understand society in both its routine and its unusual aspects.

WHAT IS SOCIOLOGY?

The word *sociology* means literally "the science of society." While this definition is simple to remember, it fails to describe clearly just what sociologists study. In *What Is Sociology?*—a classic book—Alex Inkeles examines both early and modern views of the discipline (Inkeles, 1964). According to Inkeles, *sociology* is concerned with three major subject areas: society as a whole, social institutions and social organizations, and social interaction and relationships. Following Inkeles, then, we will define sociology as the scientific study of society: of groups, institutions, and organizations and of the interrelationships between members of societies. Definitions of a complex field like sociology need a good deal of comment and explanation. Our definition actually contains four ideas that need to be explored: (1) scientific method, (2) society, (3) social institutions and organizations, and (4) human interrelationships.

Scientific method

Scientific method will be described much more fully in Chapter 2, but a preliminary definition is needed here. *Scientific method* is a methodical way of going after knowledge; it calls for the collection of facts by observation, experimentation, or both. To be scientific in the pursuit of knowledge, one must be willing to work carefully, step by step; avoid hasty or wrong conclusions; and accept findings even if they go against one's earlier ideas. This acceptance of the plain, untwisted facts is known by another term: *objectivity*. As human beings, scientists naturally have opinions. However, good scientists do not allow personal opinions or biases to distort the subject matter or the conclusions of their research. Also, science is slow and painstaking, accepts no shortcuts to knowledge, and accepts the idea that any conclusion may one day have to be changed.

The study of society

Everything that is studied in sociology fits under the heading *society*. But we will divide sociology into three levels: (1) the study of entire societies, (2) the study of organizations and institutions, and (3) the study of interaction among circles of friends or between rivals and enemies. *Societies* are organizations of people or other forms of life, living within a particular territory, persisting through generations, and more or less independent of other societies. A society is the largest distinct group to which the individual belongs; the United States constitutes a society, as do France, Germany, and Thailand. Further, the members of a society are interdependent, with some people doing one type of work and others another but all bound together by common rules, customs, loyalties, traditions, and patterns of interaction.

To examine what we mean by *patterns of interaction*, let us contrast a closely organized form of insect life, that of the honeybees, with human societies. In beehives, there is no individuality, no choice of life-style. The bees have a built-in genetic program that determines how they will work and when they will mate. Only a natural catastrophe can disturb the hive. Human societies, however, show much more variety. Their members are individuals, many of whom accept the rules only grudgingly or incompletely. Nevertheless, behind all the complexity, each society displays a type of patterned behavior that makes it different from other societies—customs of speech and dress, gestures, salutations, manners, beliefs, attitudes, skills, and work habits. *Patterned behavior*, in other words, refers to behavior that is repeated often enough to be characteristic of individuals or societies under a given set of circumstances. Human societies display patterned behavior, although the patterns are far less rigid than those of bees and are subject to constant change.

When studying a society, sociologists want to know how one aspect of that society affects others. How, for example, does industrialization affect education, employment, or the distribution of wealth? Does a particular economic structure, such as capitalism, promote crime and delinquency? Do changing sex roles place a strain on marriage and the family? What role can religion play in a society that stresses science and materialism?

The study of society as a whole, however, cannot give a complete view of the subject matter. Sometimes the sociologist must "change lenses" and "zoom in" for a closer view of certain parts of society. The study of social institutions and organizations becomes the first step in this close-up look at society.

The study of institutions and organizations

The major social institutions most often studied in any introductory sociology course are the educational system, family, economy, government, and religious organization. The term *institution* as used in this way refers to an organized pattern of behavior, thought, and customs designed to meet certain basic needs of a society. A type of behavior is considered to be institutionalized when it is widely accepted by members of the society and becomes a habit, honored as a tradition and slow to change.

The concept of the institution is applied in both broad and narrow senses. Thus, the educational system is considered an institution, as are individual schools within the system, each with its own customs and ceremonies. Law, as a part of government, is considered an institution, as are courts of law, police, jails, prisons, and legal procedures. The family is an institution, and so are weddings, showers, and honeymoons.

Although nothing in society is completely static, institutions are among a society's more lasting features. While institutions in the narrow sense may change or fade away, institutions in the broad sense persist for long periods of time.

Particular politicians, for example, come and go, but the institution of government remains more or less the same. Reformists protest against the economic system, promising to break up the giant corporations, but the corporations continue to merge and grow. For more than a hundred years, there have been crusades for prison reform, but Chief Justice Warren Burger has reported that some prisons built in the 1830s are still in operation today (Burger, 1971). Many fundamentalist churches flourish while more "modern" churches flounder. Marriage is denounced as an outdated institution, yet most people still marry, many with all the traditional ceremonies. Probably no institution has attracted more reformers than education—reformers who call for child-centered teaching, challenge and excitement, and preparation for the future. Yet the educational system is slow to change. Émile Durkheim, one of the founders of sociology, used education as an example of the most consistent and stable social institutions. Although written in 1895, his words sound surprisingly up to date:

> Considering the facts as they are and as they have always been, it becomes immediately evident that all education is a continuous effort to impose on the child ways of seeing, feeling and acting which he could not have arrived at spontaneously. . . . The aim of education is, precisely, the socialization of the human being; the process of education, therefore, gives us in a nutshell the historical fashion in which the social being is constituted. The unremitting pressure to which the child is subjected is the very pressure of the social milieu which tends to fashion him in its own image, and of which parents and teachers are merely the representatives and intermediaries. (Émile Durkheim, *The Rules of the Sociological Method*, ed. by George E. G. Catlin, Macmillan, New York, copyright © 1938, p. 19.)

Human societies exist in a wide variety of forms, from such tiny groups as the primitive Tasaday to the vast societies of India, China, the Soviet Union, and the United States.

9

The final line of Durkheim's description of education is noteworthy: "Parents and teachers are merely the representatives and intermediaries." Durkheim is really describing part of the *socialization* process—the subject of Chapter 4. This can be defined briefly as the process by which the individual is enabled to take part in society—is given information and taught skills, rules, customs, and attitudes. In other words, each generation of individuals is molded, by the institutions of a social system, to fit into the system and carry it on.

This discussion, of course, puts too much stress on the persistence of institutions. Disruptions and changes certainly do occur, as the Chicago riots demonstrate. However, while we constantly speak of the rapid pace of change in modern society, *major* changes are quite rare. The institutional machinery often creaks and groans, but it neither stops nor falls apart. In looking at society, then, sociologists try to explain how institutions both persist and change.

Organizations of all types are part of the subject matter of sociology, whether or not they appear in institutionalized form. An *organization* is any social unit that coordinates the activities of its members. In a formal organization, rules and duties are officially prescribed and enforced. In an informal organization, members are expected to behave in a particular way, but there are no formal rules and the expectations are usually more flexible. Corporations, banks, insurance companies, and government bureaus are examples of formal organizations. In these types of organizations, procedures become quite routinized and hard to change. However, these organizations are not quite as time-honored and rooted in tradition as institutions are.

Associations are organized groups of any kind, either formal or informal. The term *voluntary associations* is applied mostly to clubs, lodges, public service groups, and groups serving some cause, such as the Society for the Prevention of Cruelty to Animals. However, whether we are studying institutions, associations, or other parts of society, social interaction is always involved—between person and person, between person and group, and between group and group.

The study of human interaction

Social interaction, as the term implies, is the process by which people influence one another, whether by talking, teaching, helping, changing attitudes, or rousing emotions. For example, it is easy to find societal and institutional causes for the Chicago riots, but they were actually touched off by the rising anger between individuals. The actors in the Chicago drama could all be viewed as social types—demonstrator or policeman, radical or conservative—but they were also persons with their own identities, feelings, and motivations.

The courtroom drama which followed the street action also showed this human interaction. Two members of "The Chicago Seven," Abbie Hoffman and Jerry Rubin, became the "stars." They interrupted court proceedings, called Judge Julius Hoffman a "pig" and a "fanatic," came to court dressed in judicial robes, and tried to make a circus of the trial. The judge was a person of equally strong opinions. He became furious, made judicial blunders, and called defense attorney William Kunstler "perhaps psychotic."

It is in studying how humans interact that sociology comes down to the level of individuals and interprets their behavior in relation to that of others. Interaction patterns arise between child and parent, between friends, between lovers, in the classroom, on the playground, in the club, the bar, the workplace—anywhere that people gather, act, and react to each other.

Sometimes we present ourselves honestly. At other times, however, we may act a false part, either to serve our own purposes or to please others—or, as stated by T. S. Eliot, "to prepare a face to meet the faces that you meet." Erving Goffman, a sociologist who views interaction as

(a)

Figure 1-2 (*a*) In interacting with another person, we often show only one aspect of our personality. (*b*) This actress making up is deliberately doing what many people do unconsciously: putting on "a face to meet the faces that we meet." [(*a*) *Sybil Shelton, Monkmeyer;* (*b*) *George W. Gardner*]

a series of almost theatrical performances, mentions doctors who give placebos—or neutral substances, not medicines—to patients with imaginary ills. He also speaks of salespersons in shoe stores who lie to the customer about the shoe size, saying that it is exactly what the customer wishes it to be. He even tells of cases in which "sympathetic patients in mental wards feign bizarre symptoms so that student nurses will not be subjected to a disappointingly sane performance" (Goffman, 1959). In these as in other interaction situations, the actions often reflect what others expect rather than the actor's true feelings.

This interactionist approach to the study of society recognizes that people are not merely cogs in a huge social machine or robots acting out rigidly programmed social roles. According to the interactionist view, Julius Hoffman was not merely a judge but also a human being reacting in a personal way to a particular situation.

Interaction differs greatly depending on whether it occurs between equals or unequals or whether it takes place within one's own group or with an outsider. For example, an insult exchanged between friends may be passed off as a joke or may provoke an insult in return. But when a defendant insults a judge, the reaction will be quite different.

(b)

The sociological scene

11

Interaction may take the form of cooperation, competition, rivalry, or even conflict, whether for individuals or for groups. It is in looking at individual and group interaction that sociology takes on some drama. Sociology relates the individual to the social system and shows that people influence society just as society influences people.

THE SOCIOLOGICAL PERSPECTIVE

So far, we have defined sociology purely in terms of its own interests, without setting it apart from the other social sciences. All people are interested in the ways society affects their lives or confirms or disturbs their ideas and prejudices. People's views of society differ greatly, depending in part on their places in the system—rich or poor, powerful or powerless. Attitudes, convictions, and personal and professional interests also play a part.

The points of view we adopt in looking at society are called *perspectives*. The clergy, for example, may have seen the Chicago riots in terms of the morality of violence and the war which sparked the protests. Politicians were concerned with the probable effect on politics: How would the riots damage the chances of the Democrats? Would the riots force the next administration in Washington to give up the war? Many conservatives could see only the outrageous conduct of the demonstrators; many liberals could see only the brutality of the police.

Social and behavioral scientists also saw the riots from special perspectives. Political scientists were concerned about the breakdown of normal political processes. Economists wondered about the effect on the economic system of increasingly radical views, especially the view of the war as a capitalistic venture in empire building. Psychologists were interested in the personalities of the activists—their home lives and other factors that had led to antiwar idealism and violence. All these social scientists tried to study their particular subject matter as objectively as possible, but

their points of view differed depending upon their particular field of study.

Patterned social relationships

Sociologists are interested in almost all the questions other social scientists raise. Like other social scientists, they look for repeated *patterns* in ways of behaving. Regarding Chicago in 1968, they asked: "What similarities or differences can be found in periods of peace and war, in periods of social upheaval and social calm?" "Are there similarities between the Vietnamese war and other wars in which major powers fought against insurgent forces?" (In connection with this last question, see the insert "Patterns in Fighting Insurgents.") Are there certain things about the police that would lead us to expect reactions in other cities similar to those in Chicago?

Breadth of interests

The social sciences all stress careful research methods and a concern with patterned behaviors. But one special aspect of sociology is its breadth of interests. Economics, in brief, focuses on wealth and income—where they come from and where they go. Political science is interested mainly in power—who has it and how it is used. Psychology deals with personality traits—how they arise and grow. It is also concerned with emotionality, aggressiveness, and the individual's ability to deal with reality. Sociologists are interested in all that economists, political scientists, and psychologists have to say, but they do more than borrow material from those fields.

Sociology is a *synthesizing* science, bringing together many types of findings and fitting them into a coherent whole. For example, economists view an economic depression in terms of the stock market, profits and losses, and government policy about money supply. Political scientists look at the same event from the viewpoint of political control and government actions. Psychologists want to know whether the economic

Patterns in fighting insurgents   STUART C. MILLER

One American officer said: "I want no prisoners. I wish you to kill and burn; the more you kill and burn, the more you will please me. I want all persons killed who are capable of bearing arms."

[The war brought] a peace movement with "teach-ins" at universities and a more activist radical faction; rumours and finally evidence of American atrocities; complaints of rain seasons, hidden jungle entrenchments and clandestine enemy soldiers who blended with the peasants after ambushing and booby-trapping American soldiers; talk of getting our native allies to assume the burden of fighting; and finally a scandal involving one officer and seven top sergeants who pocketed commissary funds.

The officer quoted above was not Lieutenant William Calley, tried on charges of slaughtering civilians in the town of My Lai, and the war was not in Vietnam. The events belong to 1900 and the Philippine uprising against the United States led by Aguinaldo at the end of the Spanish-American War.

Excerpted from "Our Mylai of 1900," Stuart C. Miller. Published by permission of Transaction, Inc., from *Trans-Action*, vol. 7., no. 15, copyright © 1970 by Transaction, Inc.

---

depression will bring increased psychological depression, alcoholism, and suicide. Sociologists are interested in all such matters but also in how they affect the total society and all its institutions. What are the effects of a depression on education, crime rates, family relationships, class-consciousness, and disadvantaged minorities? What changes come about in attitudes, public morale, ideologies, and reform movements? To say, then, that sociology synthesizes means that it takes the findings of many disciplines, adds many findings of its own, and looks at them in the light of its own interests in the total field of social relationships.

Concentration on social conditions

The above example of an economic depression is typical of the way in which sociologists analyze social conditions. Sociologists have always tried to draw conclusions about social conditions and social trends: the consequences of the industrial revolution, the status of the working class, the effects of moving from the farm to the city, the

new educational needs of industrial societies. Depending on the problems of the times, attention has turned also to the conditions of minority groups and women, to changing sex roles and family patterns, and to crime and deviance. Such episodes as the racial struggle in South Africa or the Vietnam war, with which this chapter began, are further examples of sociologists' concern with social conditions. To say that sociology concentrates on social conditions is not to imply that other social sciences do not; it is simply to note that their fields are more limited.

Sociology and anthropology compared

It is somewhat easier to tell sociology from economics, political science, and psychology than it is to set it apart from anthropology. Both these disciplines are interested in the total range of human societies. Both are also concerned with all kinds of social groups—families and friends, tribes, classes, and nations. Many of the ideas introduced in one discipline are used in the other. Émile Durkheim is considered one of the founders of both anthropology and sociology.

Despite the similarities, however, there are important differences. Sociologists concentrate on modern industrial societies, while anthropologists focus on preindustrial societies and on the development of the human species. Anthropologists rely heavily on trained observation "in the field." Sociologists have, of course, used the same method, since observation is the beginning of learning. But sociologists also use questionnaires and opinion research, since they deal largely with people who can read and write.

Anthropologists focus their attention on culture even more than do sociologists. (Culture, or the total pattern of life of a society, will be discussed at length in Chapter 3.) Anthropologists study such cultural traits as languages, art forms, tool making, decorations, and rites and ceremonies more than sociologists do. Sociologists, on the other hand, focus more sharply on social organization, social class, minority problems, deviant behavior, and the general concerns of modern society.

WHAT IS SOCIETY LIKE?

Perspectives, as we have seen, are points of view from which studies are made. We have already talked about the perspectives of economists, political scientists, psychologists, and sociologists. Another idea, closely related to the notion of perspective, is that of the model. A *sociological model* is a simplified picture of society. It is a useful tool. An engineer, for example, may construct a small-scale replica of a bridge, dam, or canal system under study. This model helps the engineer to understand the task at hand and emphasizes major features. It may also have the flaw of stressing some aspects at the expense of others—a drawback the engineer must keep in mind. Similarly, while a sociological model provides a simple picture of complicated things, it may exaggerate some aspects and omit others.

Sociologists have developed several models of society, the differences depending on their viewpoints and on the major social problems of the times. For example, an emphasis on social conflicts like the Chicago riots leads to a model of society as a minefield in which many explosions can be expected. An opposite view would picture society as working fairly well and binding its members together regardless of their different interests. This second view, which can be called a *unitary* or *solidary model*, stresses a common core of beliefs and traditions which hold society together. Without being unrealistic, this second view stresses the positive aspects of society. This is the view of an old woman interviewed during the American Bicentennial. She complains about changes and injustices she cannot understand but believes that society is basically good (see the accompanying insert "Social Solidarity: The Patriot").

Unitary models

The organismic model Since sociologists try to be analytical rather than emotional, they are less eloquent than Mrs. Stevens. Yet a number of them hold, as she does, that society is basically good and entitled to the strong support of the individual. The English sociologist Herbert Spencer (1820–1903) developed what is called an *organismic* model of society—a unitary model that compares society with a living organism in which all parts tend to serve the whole. In such a view, every person, or cell, is important to the health of the whole society, or body. To Spencer, the mugger who attacked Mrs. Stevens would have been a cancerous cell to be weeded out in the long process of social evolution, a concept discussed further on page 18.

Mechanical solidarity Émile Durkheim (1856–1917), one of the founders of sociology, held that human beings need close relationships with each other and with society as a whole. Durkheim's major studies—on suicide, on religion, and on the division of labor in industrial-

Social solidarity: The patriot AL MARTINEZ

The frail old woman, her back still bent by a mugger's beating a year before, pushed unsteadily to her feet and began moving her arms in tune to a rhythm she was hearing in her head.

"Damned right I'm a patriot," she said, moving to the center of her third-floor apartment. "God bless America."

She kept the rhythm for a moment longer then began to sing, slightly off key but determined. "Oh say can you see by the dawn's early light. . . ."

When she had finished, she looked around proudly and stood as straight as she could, the noise of a jackhammer drifting up from the street below.

"Not everything is perfect," the old lady said firmly, leaning against the edge of a table, "But don't tell me the American dream is dead!"

Helen Stevens is 82 and lives alone on the west side of Los Angeles in what she calls "my crackerbox apartment." Last July a mugger beat her, broke her back, and choked her into unconsciousness.

She is hard of hearing, can't see well, and is sometimes lonely. When she walks, it is with a slow shuffling gait, and she is fearful of being alone on the streets after dark. . . .

"You know what it's all about?" she said, chain-smoking cigarettes. "It's about making this country better than it is, back to where it used to be when it cared about people. . . ."

"No one gives a damn about old people." She snuffed out her cigarette angrily and shuffled to the kitchen. "You want a Hires root beer?"

She opened the bottle and turned. "Old people can't work and they don't have enough money. Coffee just went up 35 cents a pound. Where the hell do they think we're going to get the money to buy those things?"

Mrs. Stevens drank her root beer and fumed for a moment. Then she smiled at her own anger.

"But I'm still a patriot," she said, "It's a wonderful country. If I didn't think so, I'd be awfully sorry."

She settled gingerly in an overstuffed chair, where she sleeps at night since her back was broken. It's the only place she can be comfortable now.

Then she said, "The American dream," thinking about it. "I've had a hard life but a good one. No one ever achieves everything. My marriage lasted only three years, but I raised a good son. I did it all myself. I used to sing on stage and was pretty good, too."

She tried a verse of Brahms' Lullaby but gave it up. "One thing I wish," she said, "is that there was justice. The man who tried to kill me will be out in three or four years." She nodded her head, "And he's going to do it again to someone."

But still . . . "I'm going to go to Washington, D.C., if I can. I'm going to go to the White House and see my country's capital. . . ."

From Al Martinez, "The American Dream — Has It Survived?" *Los Angeles Times*, July 2, 1976, pp. 1, 3, 24–25. Copyright Los Angeles Times.

ized societies—all reflect his concern with the need to band together. In *Suicide*, one of his most famous books, Durkheim tried to show that suicide rates reflect the degree to which members of a society band together. Societies whose members did not feel strong ties to one another and to the larger group showed the highest rates of suicide.

In his writings on religion (Durkheim, 1965), Durkheim argued that the main function of religion has always been to unite people by offering them one point of view for understanding the gods, themselves, and their world. Thus, religion helps bring people closer together. In studying the division of labor (Durkheim, 1947), Durkheim pointed out that this *bringing together*, or *social solidarity*, once could have been called *mechanical solidarity*, since it depended on making people as much alike as products of a machine. The newer way of life which was developing with the industrial revolution was leading to what Durkheim called *organic solidarity*. This is based on the fact that people are becoming more and more dependent on each other, since they follow specialized lines of work and must turn to others for the goods and services they no longer provide for themselves. This new order would at first cause stress and strain, but eventually, Durkheim believed, there would evolve a better social order based on people who are individual and different but are still united by their need for each other.

Structural functionalism In considering religion, Durkheim asked a basic sociological question: "What does religion accomplish?" Another way of asking this question is: "What is the place of religion in society?" Durkheim's thinking laid the groundwork of a perspective that is now called *structural functionalism*.

Social structure refers to the total pattern of organization of a society, including established customs, laws, and institutions. The results of these structures, or the purposes they serve, are called their *functions*. Sweatshops, for example, are part of the social structure of economics.

Their functions are to keep down the price of goods, increase profits, and discourage foreign competition. This type of analysis merely records what is happening; it does not try to determine whether sweatshops are good or bad.

Some sociologists, and others such as labor-union organizers, see this approach as no more than a way of ignoring injustice. Thus, the structural-functionalist perspective has sometimes implied the idea that "Whatever is, is right." Actually, such an interpretation of the structural-functionalist view is not quite fair. One can analyze functions in a number of ways, showing how policies fail to function, function in a manner opposite to that intended (dysfunction), or produce unobserved and often unwanted results (latent functions) (Merton, 1949). For example, sweatshops might cause so many strikes that they lower profits instead of increasing them, thus becoming dysfunctional for management. For an example of latent function, it can be argued that a high divorce rate is a latent function of a strong belief in the right to individual happiness. If people are not happy in marriage, they divorce. Thus an attitude that society admires (the right to happiness) becomes a cause of divorce, which is not admired. We will turn later to an analysis of the latent functions of corrupt city bosses in serving many legitimate interests.

Nevertheless, structural functionalism seems a more useful model for a stable society than for one undergoing rapid change. This model was very popular in the United States in the 1950s, when society seemed far more orderly than it was to appear a decade later. In the stormy 1960s, many sociologists turned to a model stressing the conflicts that shake society. The first and perhaps most famous conflict model was developed almost a hundred years earlier by Karl Marx.

The Marxist conflict model

As the term suggests, a *conflict model* is a model of society that stresses internal conflicts and disagreements rather than unity and that sees the basic character of society as the outcome of such conflicts. Marx saw society as an economic battleground. He interpreted history as a struggle between social classes to control the means of making a living, using the term *dialectic* to describe the process. Originally, *dialectic* had referred to an intellectual exchange in which opposite ideas are eventually reconciled. Marx, however, defined *dialectic* as the clash of opposing forces, called *thesis* and *antithesis*, that arise at each stage of history. Specifically, the Marxian dialectic consists of a clash of economic interests between workers and owners. Eventually, a new social order or *synthesis* develops, and the whole process begins again. To Marx, in the heyday of the industrial revolution, a new dialectic was emerging between capital and labor. This struggle would eventually end with the overthrow of business interests and the triumph of the workers, or "proletariat" (Marx, 1906). "Workers of the world, unite," said the Marxian *Communist Manifesto* of 1848. "You have nothing to lose but your chains!" (Marx and Engels, 1955).

During the 1800s, working conditions were miserable and the gap between rich and poor was very wide. A Marxist might have asked: "How is it possible to talk about social unity and common values when those at the bottom have nothing in common with those at the top?" A sociologist using the Marxist conflict perspective today would ask the same questions: "How can a black person in South Africa, a coal miner from Appalachia, and a Chilean peasant identify with a system that exploits them?" The views of one Marxist advocate, Sandor Fuchs, are examined in the insert on page 18: "A Marxist's Conflict View."

Non-Marxist conflict models

Marx was responsible for only one of many conflict models of society. Lewis Coser, a leading sociologist today, combines conflict theory with a structural-functionalist analysis by stressing the functions of conflict within society. If a system works smoothly, either because of clever design or because of police rule that squashes the opposition, then the system becomes stagnant. According to Coser, a social system needs a certain amount of internal conflict:

> The clash of values and interest, the tensions between what is and what some groups feel ought to be, the conflict between vested interests and strata and groups demanding their share of power, wealth and status, have been productive of vitality. . . . (Coser, 1957)

As examples of creative conflict, Coser mentions the struggle of organized labor and racial and other minority groups for recognition. The views of Muskogee Indian Jack Haikey, described in the insert "A Non-Marxist Conflict View" (page 19), are another case in point.

Social change: The evolutionary models

The industrial revolution helped create a set of theories in biology, anthropology, and sociology that had many points in common. The naturalist Charles Darwin (1809–1882) developed the *theory of evolution*, which maintains that animal species *evolved*, or *changed*, from relatively simple to more complex forms. In this process of evolution, species were forced to compete with each other for survival. In this struggle, the less fit died out. A similar theory of *social evolution* was developed by the early anthropologists. They held that human societies evolved in a series of stages, moving from "savagery" to "barbarism" to "civilization." The last of these stages they saw as the most highly developed form of social life. According to the theory of social evolution, human societies will continue to evolve.

Auguste Comte (1798–1857), who is generally regarded as the founder of sociology, did not use the term *evolution*. However, his writings do imply that societies evolve from mythological to scientific ways of thinking and learning. Herbert

A Marxist's conflict view   AL MARTINEZ

To Sandor Fuchs, a "red-diaper baby" of Communist parents, a Berkeley radical student of the 1960s, a Marxist and a would-be lawyer, the American dream will be fulfilled in social revolution.

Not violent revolution, for Fuchs can say with a laugh that he is not suicidal, but a gradual recognition across the land that the country belongs to the people within the framework of democracy.

He envisions an American society that is cooperative rather than competitive, and he believes he shares that wish with the majority of people.

But the dream will not come true soon, Fuchs says. It will involve a long and careful process of political consciousness-raising, of which he is presently a part.

"It doesn't include the type of dramatic confrontation," he says, "that leads to the drum."

Fuchs is 32, long-haired and bearded—"fulfilling the student fantasy to continue to be a political maverick."

He passed the bar exam and is waiting to be admitted into practice, meanwhile acting as a volunteer for the People's Law Center in Echo Park.

The place where he works, a home turned into a series of small offices, has a kind of radical-pad look about it. There are posters on the wall that say, "Viva la revolución" and "Countries want independence, nations want liberation, people want revolution."

A third depicts a woman with a rifle in her upraised hand and the words, "A woman's work is never done."

Yet, for all of his Marxism and revolutionary zeal, Fuchs admires the American system and doesn't want to see its basic concepts altered. He doesn't know if that's a contradiction but says he will have to come to grips with it sooner or later.

"The men who created our society were clever and dedicated," he said thoughtfully. . . ." They thought for a long time, then came up with a political framework that is rational and that works. . . . You may be cynical about politics," he finally said, "but not about democracy."

Al Martinez, "American Dream — Has It Survived?" *Los Angeles Times*, July 2, 1976. Copyright Los Angeles Times.

Spencer (1820–1903) of England and William Graham Sumner (1840–1910) of the United States were two leaders of a movement called "social Darwinism." This movement, as the name implies, adapted Darwin's concepts of evolution, struggle, and the "survival of the fittest" to human societies. It held that through a competitive struggle, superior persons rise to the top and become the upper classes of society, while the "unfit"—the poor, weak, or disabled—die out. Social Darwinism was extremely popular among the conservative businesspeople and the upper classes of the nineteenth century, since it justified their position while blaming the "undeserving" poor for their misery.

This is not to say that all social evolutionists accept Spencer's view of individual struggle and competition or of the poor as the "unfit." Many early American sociologists, most notably Lester Frank Ward (1841–1914), in contrast, believed in progress through reform. In such a view, social evolution could result from better labor laws, education, and extensions of democracy and equal opportunity.

Another model of society that developed first

A non-Marxist conflict view   AL MARTINEZ

Any submerged group trying to gain a place in the sun, or a dominant group trying to maintain its dominance, could illustrate a non-Marxist conflict view. The viewpoint of an Indian leader has been chosen here.

His name is Jack Haikey and he was born in Claremore, Oklahoma, a full-blooded Muskogee, which the Anglos came to call Creeks. It was one of the five "civilized" tribes that roamed the southeast—a term given them, Haikey says dryly, because they were the first to "assimilate" and lose their culture.

He regrets that deeply.

Haikey is editor of *Talking Leaf*, an Indian-oriented newspaper published once a month in Los Angeles. He is a quiet and unsmiling man, and his bronzed good looks make him appear younger than 34. . . .

"I want to see change among my people," he said solemnly "I want to see them uplifted, proud of themselves and their culture. The American dream means the good life, but it means more."

"It means blending the modern and traditional, as the Jews have done, maintaining their own culture while prospering and becoming powerful in politics and the professions."

"I want that for my people too. I want them to have impact."

Haikey admits that to achieve this dream will require a change in attitude among America's Indians.

"We will have to begin thinking of ourselves more positively. We will have to become first-class people in whatever we do. We must not accept anything shoddy. We deserve that and must work for it."

Haikey considers himself militant in working to achieve the present-day dream of the first Americans, but not radical.

He looks back on the Indian occupation of Alcatraz Island as important, igniting interest in the movement, and says that even though dramatic confrontation is past, the movement goes on.

"We are working through the courts and among the tribes. We have revived enterprises that have lain dormant for years. We are working at it, building a foundation."

"Here and there, things are happening."

Al Martinez, "American Dream—Has It Survived?" *Los Angeles Times*, July 2, 1976. Copyright Los Angeles Times.

---

among American sociologists is one that focuses more on the individual than on social systems. This model is known as *symbolic interactionism*.

Symbolic interactionism

Whereas an evolutionary theory views society from the top down, symbolic interactionism sees it from the bottom up. *Symbolic interaction* is the process of interaction between people through symbols, mainly language. As a model, symbolic interactionism stresses the idea that the ability to interact in symbols leads to the development of human intellect and the growth and transmission of culture. Unitary models, structural functionalism, and conflict models of society all start with major forces and then show their effect on the individual. Symbolic interactionism, on the other hand, starts with interactions between individuals, who are seen as the building blocks of society. George Herbert Mead (1863–1913) and Charles Horton Cooley (1864–1929), considered to be the originators of symbolic interactionism, used this approach to describe how the young are socialized. An interactionist view, however, is more broad. It applies not only to socialization but also to social relationships in general.

This view holds that interaction between individuals, in fact the life of society itself, is possible only as a result of shared meanings. Most shared meanings, in turn, arise out of our ability to deal with symbols. A *symbol* is anything that stands for or represents something else. Every word we use is a symbol, and so is every gesture and facial expression, whether loving and kind, amusing, angry, or vulgar. None of these words, phrases, gestures, or facial expressions has any meaning in itself but only the meaning given it by its users. These meanings can be conveyed from one person to another, and the other responds to them. However, the response to symbols received from another person cannot be represented simply as message = response but rather takes the form of message + interpretation = response (Blumer, 1962). The same word is subject to many different interpretations. It is only through trial and error in the interaction process that the shades of meaning of any symbols are gradually learned. For sociological purposes, the interpretation of meaning is more important than the intent of a statement or action. As the American sociologist W. I. Thomas pointed out, what is believed to be true is more important in its social consequences than is objective truth. If a well-meant statement is interpreted wrongly, it can destroy a friendship. Mistakes in interpretation are bound to occur unless people share the same symbols, and to say that they share symbols is essentially to say that they belong to the same society.

Interaction can occur on many levels. In the Soweto riots, for example, interaction was between group and group. Each side interpreted the actions of the other as those of an enemy. The two groups were unable to interact in symbols that were clear and beyond dispute. Did the rioters wish a truce? If so, according to one witness's report, their intent was misinterpreted by the police, who claimed that they fired into the crowd in self-defense.

In symbolic interactionism, a social system is, above all, a system of shared symbols and shared meanings. If a breakdown in meanings occurs, the system has lost some of its solidarity. On a level close to a unitary model of society, such solidarity can be said to exist if people interpret the symbols (flags, banners, slogans, emblems, leaders, and the like) in the same manner. A conflict perspective would coincide with a symbolic-interactionist perspective in stating that some groups within a society share one set of symbols and meanings, while other groups share a different set. In all cases, however, the distinction between symbolic interactionism and other social models is that symbolic interactionism starts at a basic level of person-to-person interaction.

Now that sociology has been defined and various views have been explained, it is time to turn to the subject of sociologists at work. What are some of their typical activities?

SOCIOLOGISTS AT WORK

What, exactly, do sociologists do? Do they deal simply with explanations and theories, or do they "get into the field" and talk to people, trying to find out what worries, excites, or disturbs them? The answer is that they do both. And although all sociologists are interested in both theories of society and human interaction, some are known mainly for one approach and some for the other. Two well-known contemporary sociologists who use these different approaches are Mirra Komarovsky and Robert K. Merton.

Figure 1-3 The changing patterns of relationships between men and women have been traced by Mirra Komarovsky. (*Chester Higgins, Jr./ Rapho/Photo Researchers, Inc.*)

Mirra Komarovsky: Male-female relationships

Mirra Komarovsky has always worked directly with people. During the Great Depression, she studied the problems of the unemployed. Not content with merely gathering statistics, she also interviewed many unemployed men. This involved a study of family relations which, in turn, led her to an increasing interest in the roles of men and women. In *Blue-Collar Marriage* (1962), Komarovsky reported that large numbers of working-class families seemed to be completely immune to the movement for equality between the sexes. Since that time, however, she has seen some movement toward sexual equality in working-class families, especially if both husband and wife have had at least a high school education.

Komarovsky did not pursue the subject of male-female relations in a single study, as a reporter might do. Instead, she has stayed with her subject, striving for the deep understanding that sociologists want. In her 1973 inaugural address as president of the American Sociological Association, she reported her most recent findings. This time, she focused on the problems of college men caught in the conflict between changing traditions: the dominant versus the egalitarian male. The same conflict, or role strain, also involves college women, who speak of equality but are sometimes uncomfortable with a man who does not take the lead. Of the troubled men, Komarovsky writes:

> [They] not only felt inadequate but felt that they violated their own or their partner's role expectations. It is generally believed that the ideal of masculinity has been changing among undergraduates. . . . Studies, including my own, show that the male ideal of masculinity now includes some qualities hitherto largely defined as feminine, such as sensitivity, patience, and artistic appreciation. Nevertheless, the comparison of the . . . check lists filled out by the seniors for "my ideal" man and "my real self" reveal that the feminine virtues have not so much replaced as have been added to the familiar masculine stereotype. For most of these seniors the ideal man was still "assertive," "strong," "courageous," "aggressive," and "masculine." . . .

> That the role strain in question was not merely the result of an unfulfilled desire for greater power in interpersonal relationships was especially clear when the pressure for the

traditional masculine behavior came from women friends.

"She likes to be dominated," remarked one man about his current friend, "and she wants me to be more decisive. When I become pushy she does yield. But I believe in more equalitarian relationships and I would prefer one in which neither party had to hassle."

"One thing that bothers me," declared another youth, "is the way they always picture men as having to be dominant and strong. That puts a strain on a man. I'd like to share things, and you cannot dominate and share at the same time. But girls like a hard exterior in a man."

A small minority of the troubled men yearned to play the traditional role even though they were intellectually committed to an equalitarian ideology. These seniors experienced a double strain: low self-confidence vis-à-vis women and guilt over their psychological need to dominate them. One such senior explained perceptively:

"Despite my egalitarian proclamations, tugging at my psychic strings is the thought that I am really most comfortable when I maintain a margin of dominance over a woman. My basic insecurity conflicts with my liberated consciousness, making me feel like a double-talking hypocrite." (Komarovsky, 1973, pp. 655–656)

This is just one among many possible examples of sociological work based on a study of human interaction. Komarovsky's approach, though, provides more than mere description. It interprets human problems against a background of social change. This study might be seen as pointing to a conflict model of society as

women struggle for full equality. However, the attempt to redefine male and female roles could also been seen as a way of maintaining stability in what Durkheim would have called a society based on *organic solidarity*.

Robert K. Merton: Latent functions

Although Robert K. Merton has also done research, he is best known as one of the leading theorists in the field of sociology. In a later chapter on deviance, we will deal with his very influential theory of crime. At this point, however, we will explore a concept mentioned briefly on page 16: latent functions (Merton, 1949).

Merton has observed that our institutions, laws, and customs usually have intended and obvious results which he calls *manifest functions*. The dominance of a city government by a crooked political boss, for instance, has the obvious results of making the boss and his friends richer and of cheating city taxpayers. But what are the unnoticed, unplanned consequences—the *latent functions*? Merton noticed that while many American cities have been dominated by corrupt political machines, there have also been many reformists trying to clean up the government. Until quite recently, however, bosses have always survived. Merton be-

Figure 1-4 Carmine De Sapio, for years the boss of New York City's political machine, Tammany Hall. The latent functions of the machine have been studied by Robert K. Merton. (*Wide World*)

Foundations of social life

lieved that if bossism persists in spite of opposition, democratic elections, and reform parties, it must be serving some necessary social functions. What functions do city bosses serve?

Merton's analysis led to the conclusion that bossism has survived because it has served the interests of many people besides the boss and his cronies. The typical city machine has played something of a Robin Hood role. It was graft-ridden and robbed the taxpayers, but its precinct captains did everything they could to keep people in the ward loyal to the party. When Mrs. Jorgan's husband was injured, the political machine helped her out and found a job for her son. No forms were filled out; no means test was needed. There were no humiliations, no delays or red tape, just a friendly helping hand. On election day, what needy person would not return the favor by voting for such a friendly machine?

The political machine also served a latent function for legitimate business interests. Businesses want special franchises, favorable tax setups, and freedom from investigations when they may have skirted the law. The boss could arrange all such matters quickly and quietly. The machine, in turn, could count on the support of practical businesspeople, who believed that nothing would ever get done if all the usual bureaucratic rules were followed.

The poor and powerless were also served by the political machine. Immigrants entered the country by the millions, often without friends or money. It was the machine politicians who welcomed them. In Upton Sinclair's novel *The Jungle* (1905), the Lithuanian immigrants to Chicago are greeted, shown how to mark a ballot, and paid cash for their votes. According to Merton, the Irish, who entered the country faced with hunger and hatred, found their first chance for success in working for the machine. Many later immigrants of other nationalities would learn the same lesson.

Finally, in any large city there are also illegitimate business enterprises—gambling houses,

houses of prostitution, the narcotics trade—and, previous to the time of Merton's study (1949), the bootleg liquor trade. The racketeers who ran these businesses paid off the city bosses, who, in turn, closed their eyes to shady goings on within their precincts. A fourth latent function of city bossism, then, was the official toleration of crime.

The facts that Merton analyzed in his essay on city bosses were not entirely new. Reformers had long realized that many seemingly honest business interests tolerated or even supported the bosses and that poor people and immigrants voted for the machine. However, they had tended to moralize rather than to explain. They attributed the actions of business interests to wicked indifference and the votes of the poor immigrants to ignorance or stupidity. What was new about Merton's analysis was that it tried to explain the facts. Merton combined (synthesized) existing information about a variety of groups and came up with a new explanation: latent function, or the unnoticed results of bossism in terms of the interests of many different groups.

It should also be noted that Merton's type of analysis is not designed just to find embarrassing "kinks" in the social system; it can also be used to improve the system. The only way to replace a corrupt but useful institution like the city machine is to understand its secret links and its latent functions. If there are fewer poor persons, if welfare and other agencies are more human and less bureaucratic, if businesses can be handled honestly and efficiently, if minorities can find legitimate ways of getting into the mainstream of American life, if sex becomes a private matter rather than one regulated by law, and if legitimate channels for gambling open up, then the machine's economic basis is greatly weakened. True, we do, today, have fewer immigrants, social security, better welfare systems, the repeal of Prohibition, and—in a few cases—more honest city governments and therefore fewer city bosses. However, as Merton observes,

1. **Auguste Comte** (1798—1857) of France is often called the "Father of Sociology." He coined the word "sociology," advocated the application of science to society, and theorized that a great era of order and progress would result as we change from mythological and philosophical thinking to scientific thinking. (The Bettmann Archives, Inc.)

2. **William Graham Sumner** (1840—1910) of the United States was a strong advocate of the free enterprise system and believed that social evolution depends upon a competitive struggle for survival. Although a number of Sumner's concepts, such as folkways, mores, and ethnocentrism (see Chapter 3), are useful in sociology, his strongly conservative views are no longer in vogue. (Culver Pictures, Inc.)

3. **Lester Frank Ward** (1841—1913) was originally a botanist and geologist. Ward became interested in the application to human societies of some of the principles of biological science. In sharp contrast to Sumner, Ward looked upon the development of sociology as a path to greater human welfare and social planning. He became the first president of the American Sociological Association in 1906. (Brown Brothers.)

4. **Émile Durkheim** (1858—1917) of France emphasized the need for social solidarity, particularly in his books on suicide and on religion. His *Division of Labor in Society* describes new bases for social solidarity as people become more varied in their occupations and interests. Durkheim has had a strong influence on many contemporary sociologists. (The Bettman Archives, Inc.)

5. **Karl Marx** (1818–1883) of Germany advanced a theory in sharp contrast to the social-solidarity theme of Durkheim or the economic conservatism of Sumner. To Marx, society was seen as in a state of struggle between working class and owning class—a struggle that the working class would eventually win. Although a revolutionary advocate more than a sociologist, Marx directed the attention of sociologists to the importance of social-class divisions. (Culver Pictures, Inc.)

6. **Max Weber** (1864–1920) of Germany studied the ideas of Marx, but feared a Marxist society would represent the triumph of officialdom, not of the working class. Weber concluded that modern societies are moving in the direction of productive efficiency, bureaucracy, and "disenchantment," with rational-scientific ideas encroaching on the fields of mythology, philosophy, and religion. Weber continues to grow in importance in modern sociology. Some of his ideas are presented in Chapters 14 and 15. (Culver Pictures, Inc.)

7. **Charles Horton Cooley** (1846–1929) of the United States studied the relationship between individuals, small groups, and society as a whole, rather than looking for the long-range social trends that preoccupied most European sociologists of the time. Cooley can be thought of as a forerunner of modern social psychology. Like many early American sociologists, he took an interest in social reform. (American Sociological Association.)

5

6

7

25

to try to change society without first understanding what is going on "is to indulge in social ritual rather than social engineering" (Merton, 1949).

We have looked at the works of two contemporary sociologists, Komarovsky and Merton—limited examples indeed. Even these, however, should show that both types of analysis are important. No science can progress without both facts and insights into the meaning of these facts. In Chapter 2, we will examine in much more detail some of the methods used and comment on the importance of theory in sociological studies.

SUMMARY

Chapter 1 opens with scenes of riots in South Africa and with reminders of riots a decade earlier in the United States. These episodes illustrate sociology's concern with social crises as well as daily routines. They show that there is a strong link between a society's habits of thought and action and its more explosive events. They also show how emotions and violence can build up during hostile interactions.

Sociology, called *the science of society*, tries to use scientific methods in studying entire *societies*, their *institutions and organizations*, and *human interaction*, whether that interaction is cooperative, competitive, or one of conflict.

All the *social sciences* deal with many of the same subjects, but from different points of view. *Economists* focus attention especially on wealth and its creation and distribution; *political scientists*, on power; *psychologists*, on individual behavior and the emotional forces behind such behavior. *Sociologists* are interested in all these areas of study, since a science of society must be a very broad field, concerned with all social conditions and social problems. *Sociology* is a synthesizing science, drawing conclusions from the findings of all the social sciences but with its own special fields of social institutions and social interaction.

In their analysis of society, sociologists draw up simplified pictures, or *models*, of how society works. Since societies depend upon many common customs, traditions, and beliefs to hold their people together, some sociologists have stressed *unitary* or cohesive models of society. Durkheim contended that unity was once achieved by making people as much alike as products of the same machine (*mechanical solidarity*). But modern societies, he said, depend upon dissimilarity and interdependence for cohesion (*organic solidarity*). Spencer also advanced a unitary model of society, called *organismic*, in which he compared society with a living organism and the people with cells in that organism. Later followers of Durkheim developed what is called a *structural-functionalist* model of society. They stressed the interdependence of parts of a society and the tendency of societal institutions to adjust to needed change.

In opposition to the models described above is the *conflict model*. Karl Marx, who originated this model, held that social systems are constantly torn between opposing forces and that all history can be seen as a class struggle. Many others (Lewis Coser, for example) think of society in terms of conflict but—unlike Marx—not exclusively between social classes. Coser believes that conflict—between regions, ethnic groups, capital and labor, and various business and industrial interests—is needed to avoid social stagnation.

A third model of society focuses on social change. Spencer and Sumner both compared social evolution with biological evolution. They expected societies to advance only through a competitive struggle in which the less able people would die out. Comte, the founder of sociology, believed that all knowledge advances in stages. He felt that a stage of scientific direction of society was about to be reached, with a promise of continuous order and progress. The American sociologist Lester Frank Ward also expected progress, but through social reform, not necessarily as a result of either science or evolutionary principles.

A fourth model of society is that of *symbolic interactionism* (developed from the ideas of Cooley and Mead). This view pictures society as the product of interaction between individuals. The symbolic-interactionist model focuses more on the individual than do the other models, recognizing individuals as sources of creativity and change.

A very brief description is given of some of the work done by modern sociologists. Some do survey research with very little theorizing. Mirra Komarovsky's study of male-female relationships among young people in college is given as an example. Others are thought of primarily as theorists. Robert K. Merton's essay on the functions of political bosses in American cities is given as an example of theoretical analysis. Both research and theoretical analyses have an important place in the growth of sociology.

Study Guide

Terms to know

Sociology	Synthesizing	Social structure
Society	Economics	Function
Patterned behavior	Political science	Structural functionalism
Social institutions	Psychology	Conflict model
Socialization	Anthropology	Dialectic
Organization, formal and informal	Model	Symbolic interactionism
Associations	Unitary model	Social evolution
Social interaction	Organismic model	Social Darwinism
Objectivity	Mechanical solidarity	Manifest function
Perspectives	Organic solidarity	Latent function

Names to know

Émile Durkheim	Lewis Coser	George Herbert Mead
Erving Goffman	Auguste Comte	Charles Horton Cooley
Herbert Spencer	William Graham Sumner	Mirra Komarovsky
Karl Marx	Lester Frank Ward	Robert K. Merton

Self-test

Part I. Multiple Choice. Select the best of the four alternative answers:

1 The riots at Soweto in South Africa, demonstrated that (**a**) white rulers understand the blacks, (**b**) the police fired only in self-defense, (**c**) complacency of blacks regarding the social system is a myth, (**d**) no further demonstrations seem possible.

2 The demonstrations in Chicago in the summer of 1968 (**a**) could best be described as "insane," (**b**) were shaped by the attitudes and values of the American social system, (**c**) were caused entirely by communist agents, (**d**) involved excessive violence only on the part of the demonstrators.

3 *All but one* of the following are true of scientific method: (**a**) procedures are systematic; (**b**) conclusions, once reached, are no longer subject to revision; (**c**) findings are accepted even if they conflict with previous views; (**d**) no shortcuts to knowledge are accepted.

4 An aggregate of people constitute a society only if they (**a**) are organized, (**b**) persist through time, (**c**) display considerable interdependence of members, (**d**) all the above.

5 Which of the following is the best definition of *institution* as the word is used in sociology? (**a**) an organized pattern of behavior, thought, and custom; (**b**) a legally established organization; (**c**) a public building used for governmental purposes; (**d**) a subdivision of government.

6 Analyzing the Chicago riots in interactionist terms, it can be said that (**a**) violence is mainly the result of violent personalities, (**b**) police "keep cool" regardless of provocation, (**c**) interaction situations can escalate anger and violence, (**d**) all the above.

7 Which of the following social sciences would have been most interested in the Chicago riots from the viewpoint of personality traits of participants? (**a**) economics, (**b**) psychology, (**c**) political science, (**d**) sociology.

8 Which of the following social sciences shows the broadest interests and synthesizes findings from many areas? (**a**) economics, (**b**) psychology, (**c**) political science, (**d**) sociology.

9 Which of the following is more typical of anthropology than of sociology? (**a**) great attention to primitive or preliterate societies, (**b**) interest in society, (**c**) concern with all kinds of social groups, (**d**) a conflict model of society.

10 When Mrs. Stevens says, "It's a wonderful country," she comes closest to agreement with which model of society? (**a**) the unitary model, (**b**) the Marxist conflict model, (**c**) the structural-functionalist model, (**d**) the non-Marxist conflict model.

11 Durkheim said that older societies, in which people were very much alike, were held together by (**a**) mechanical solidarity, (**b**) organic solidarity, (**c**) synthesis, (**d**) structural functionalism.

12 Lewis Coser's views on conflict within society are that (**a**) such conflict must be eliminated, (**b**) no society can long exist with internal conflict, (**c**) only social-class conflict is of any real importance, (**d**) none of the above.

13 An essential viewpoint of symbolic interactionism is that (**a**) society is possible only through a system of shared symbols, (**b**) symbols are interpreted in the same way by all people, (**c**) interaction can be correctly diagramed as message-response; (**d**) all the above.

14 Mirra Komarovsky found that (**a**) college women consistently want men to treat them with full equality, (**b**) college men never feel a need to be dominant, (**c**) such traits as sensitivity and patience have replaced the older masculine stereotypes, (**d**) much inconsistency and uncertainty exist about male-female roles and relationships.

15 Robert K. Merton found that city political bosses were traditionally supported by (**a**) the underworld, (**b**) certain legitimate business interests, (**c**) the poor and the immigrants, (**d**) all the above.

Part II. True-False Questions

1 Although sociologists are concerned with the patterns and routines of daily life, they also study such dramatic events as riots and revolutions.

2 The Chicago riots of August 1968 arose from opposition to the Vietnamese war.

3 The three subject areas that Inkeles considers central to sociology are society, institutions and organizations, and social relationships.

4 The members of a society are almost completely independent of one another.

5 Banks and insurance companies are examples of formal organizations.

6 *Social interaction* refers to the processes by which people influence one another.

7 Cruelty in fighting the Philippine insurgents in 1900 was a unique event, not fitting any type of general pattern.

8 Sociologists have always given their attention to the same social conditions regardless of the times.

9 Sociologists are interested in the study of culture, but anthropologists are not.

10 A sociological model is a simplified picture of society or an aspect of society.

11 An organismic model compares society with a machine that fails to function.

12 Karl Marx looked upon the dialectic of his times as a struggle between capital and labor.

13 In the social-Darwinist views of Herbert Spencer, the poor were considered among the unfit.

14 Komarovsky generally uses a sociological method of direct investigation through interviews and questionnaires.

15 Merton's essay on political bosses is an example of the collection of data rather than theoretical analysis.

Questions for discussion

1 Show the close connection between crisis situations such as labor unrest, racial disturbances, or energy shortages and the daily routines and customs of society.
2 Give some examples of the difficulties of changing established institutions or such formal organizations as government bureaus.
3 Analyze any problem, such as unemployment or crime, from the viewpoints of economists, political scientists, psychologists, and sociologists.
4 Three implied models of society were given in the quotations from Mrs. Stevens, Mr. Fuchs, and Mr. Haikey. Which of their views would you consider the most useful interpretation of society? Why?
5 Contrast the social policies you might expect from a society of social Darwinists (such as Spencer or Sumner) with those of a society that believes the condition of the poor can be improved.

Projects

1 Since information of the type presented by Mirra Komarovsky becomes rapidly outdated, conduct interviews or give questionnaires to other students to see if they display the same uncertainties about male-female interaction in dating as Komarovsky found.
2 Attempt a latent-function analysis of some aspect of college life (grading system, athletic competition, or fraternities and sororities, for example). Pool ideas to see how many unobserved consequences can be discovered.

Suggested readings

Becker, Howard S.: "Whose Side Are We On?" *Journal of Social Problems*, vol. 14, Winter 1967, pp. 239–247. Is it possible to be a sociologist and completely avoid commitment to certain principles, groups, and people? Read the answer to this question by a distinguished sociologist in the field of deviant behavior.

Hauser, Philip M.: "The Chaotic Society," *American Sociological Review*, vol. 34, February 1969, pp. 1–19. Why does modern society seem chaotic and unpredictable? Hauser analyzes the causes of chaos and makes a plea for an increased role for sociologists in understanding society and providing a degree of "social engineering."

Horton, John, "Order and Conflict Theories of Social Problems," *American Journal of Sociology*, May 1966, pp. 701–713. If we look at such problems of society as racial inequality, can we understand them in organismic or structural-functionalist models of society? See why Horton answers in the negative.

Kelly, J. R.: "Everyman as Sociologist: Scribner's Publication of Selected Writings of the Founders of Sociology," *America*, vol. 132, June 7, 1975, pp. 441—442. "For better or worse, we are all sociologists now," says Kelly. "Everyman has become a data seeker." But can we make any sense of the data? Can such theorists as Karl Marx, Herbert Spencer, and Max Weber help?

Schrag, Peter: "America Needs an Establishment," *Harper's Magazine*, vol. 251, December 1975, pp. 51–54. "The absence of a ruling class gives rise to aimless rebellion," says Peter Schrag. He believes liberal democracy thrives best when there is a definite "establishment." Schrag's is one version of a unitary view of society discussed in this chapter.

Time magazine, staff: "The New Sociology," *Time*, vol. 95, pt. 1, January 5, 1970, pp. 38—39. Is sociology mainly for professors and statisticians, or can it be made useful to the public? *Time* finds a noticeable trend toward involvement by sociologists in social issues and in the problems of the "underdogs" of society.

Key to questions. Multiple Choice: 1-c; 2-b; 3-b; 4-d; 5-a; 6-c; 7-b; 8-d; 9-a; 10-a; 11-a; 12-d; 13-a; 14-d; 15-d. True-False: 1-T; 2-T; 3-T; 4-F; 5-T; 6-T; 7-F; 8-F; 9-F; 10-T; 11-F; 12-T; 13-T; 14-T; 15-F.

2

THE PURSUIT OF SOCIOLOGICAL KNOWLEDGE

This chapter outlines the problems and techniques of sociological method. After reading it, you should be able to:

1   *Recognize better than before the unfounded statements that are often made about society, groups of people, and social problems.*

2   *Recognize barriers in the way of scientific knowledge and—by recognizing them—partly overcome them.*

3   *Understand what is meant by* scientific method *and be able to formulate and test simple hypotheses.*

4   *Use such statistical tools as measurements of central tendency but also know their limitations.*

5   *Understand the meaning of correlations and not confuse them with proof.*

6   *Recognize some of the ethical problems involved in research.*

7   *Understand experimental procedures and the need for controls.*

8   *Recognize the relation between the gathering of information and the formulation of theoretical explanations.*

The bartender and his customers were deep in a discussion of a murder that had occurred in a local service station the day before. Armed burglars had emptied the cash register and shot the station's owner.

"You know," said Sam to his friends at the bar, "things of that kind didn't happen when we were kids. The world's just getting worse. More crimes every day. F.B.I. figures prove it."

"Yeh," Arnie chimed in, thumping his empty beer mug for emphasis, "and you know why? It's because they did away with the death penalty. If they'd just hang a few of them, there wouldn't be no more murders like that."

"And another thing," his friend George added, "if that service station man had just had a gun of his own, it wouldn't have happened."

"Get Arnie and me another one," said Sam to the bartender. "I think you guys are right, but there's another thing that's happening nowadays, and that is that parents don't raise their kids right. Those burglars were a couple of long-haired young freaks, probably the kind whose folks never cracked down on them. If they'd just had the hell knocked out of them when they were kids. . . ."

"You mean they already know who did it?" asked George.

"Oh sure, they've already arrested a couple of young punks up the road a few miles. They didn't have the money on them but probably hid it someplace. They wouldn't have been hauled in by the cops if they weren't guilty. One of them looks like an Indian, and you know what they're like. Can't trust 'em an inch. I ought to know. Had one of them working for me once. You know one of them and you know 'em all."

The bartender, entering the conversation for the first time, observed that you can't always be sure until there's a trial.

"Don't tell me I don't know," growled Sam. "You can judge guys of that kind pretty well just looking at 'em. They're the killer type. Anyway, I'm good about figuring these things out. I was right about the Corey kid in that rape case last year, wasn't I? You don't need to be an expert on these things. All it takes is good common sense."

There were murmurs of agreement as the bartender nodded, "Yep, I guess you've got it figured out."

"You damned well know it!" said Sam, draining his mug triumphantly.

BARRIERS TO SOCIAL KNOWLEDGE

There are many reasons why scientific knowledge of society is hard to achieve. One reason is the feeling that we already know the traditional answers to common problems of everyday life. Other reasons have to do with our limited experience, our emotional attitudes or biases, or deliberate attempts at deception. A final problem regarding scientific knowledge is that not all fields of human interest and concern are open to scientific investigation.

Traditional barriers

Sam, George, and Arnie feel sure they know the answers to questions about crime because those answers have been handed down to them by their parents and neighbors who, in turn, inherited many of their ideas about the world in the same way. Sam calls these views "common sense" because they are shared or held in common by the people. Common-sense explanations are a kind of folk wisdom, based on knowledge from the past and supported by limited personal experience. However, they are not put to the rigid types of tests demanded of scientific knowledge.

Today we are not satisfied with common-sense answers to questions about either the natural world or the social world. Instead, we look for explanations from experts who have a thorough scientific grasp of their particular fields. Sometimes, however, the results of science are hard to accept, especially when they go against our common-sense notions or traditional values. This resistance to new ideas sometimes keeps government policy makers from using data gathered by social researchers, as the insert "Private Research and Public Policy: An Uncertain Marriage" shows.

Cognitive barriers

Outmoded life-styles change and "old-fashioned" ideas and opinions are discarded. But it might still be argued that we learn what we need to know about the social world by looking around us and doing a bit of thinking. Sam has actually known an Indian and found him to be irresponsible. Arnie has never known a violent criminal but assumes that all people think as he does: the threat of execution would stop such a person from committing a murder.

Cognition refers to the process of gaining knowledge, both through observation and through reasoning. While Sam's observation about the one Indian he knew may be correct, his conclusion about *all* Indians is not because it

---

Private research and public policy: An uncertain marriage   GARY GREGG

Each year the government finances social research to the tune of nearly a billion dollars and, according to critics, pays little or no attention to results. Academics have a host of theories to account for the nonuse of the data. But University of Michigan psychologist Nathan Caplan's study of 204 high level federal policymakers suggests that the situation is bad but not grim.

Caplan found the vast majority highly receptive to social-science information. He collected 500 specific cases in which research influenced policy, including such major decisions as the volunteer army, the Headstart program, and intensified funding of cancer and sickle-cell anemia research. "Researchers have cause for feeling modest staisfaction." Caplan says, "rather than the cynicism and despair so prevalent in the literature on public policy."

Yet he also found some disturbing trends. Policymakers rarely used research that wasn't conducted by their own agency. Even then, they used resluts mainly to double-check their intuitions. They quickly accepted expected results, but viewed unexpected ones with suspicion, especially if they ran against one of society's sacred beliefs. While officials rarely misused data for political ends, they frequently rejected relevant findings because they implied politically unfeasible solutions.

Caplan urges the formation of a Council of Social Science Advisors to the President, along the lines of the present Council of Economic Advisors.

Gary Gregg in *Psychology Today*, August 1976, pp. 13–14. Reprinted by permission of *Psychology Today* Magazine.
Copyright © 1976 Ziff-Davis Publishing Company.

---

is based on only one example. Most of our social observations are too limited to let us make sweeping generalizations based on them. We generally see and understand clearly only people like ourselves—members of our own social class, work group, or ethnic group. If we are religious, for example, we assume that all good people agree with our religious views. If we are not religious, we are surprised that some of our contemporaries follow very strict faiths. People seek the company of others with similar ideas and life-styles, thus cutting down their chances for gaining a broader view.

Cognition may be limited, and it may also be inaccurate. The memory of things seen and heard is very faulty. Trial witnesses, for example, often have great difficulty identifying their alleged assailants. Different people may remember the same event in different ways. The memory is a faithful servant that gradually distorts reality to serve its master. Logic, like memory, may be distorted by emotions and desires.

Emotional barriers and biases

The most important emotional barriers to knowledge derive from our *attitudes*, or likes and dislikes. During World War II, for example, American dislike for Germany and Japan spread to all people and things German and Japanese. Japanese cherry trees were chopped down in Washington, D.C., and travel books describing the beauty of the Japanese countryside and Japanese gardens disappeared from the market.

The intense emotions generated by World War II show how hard it is to either gain or popularize accurate sociological conclusions. For military reasons, it was important to know what the Japanese fighting force was like: for example, were their leaders rational enough to surrender in the face of overpowering odds? Rather than investigate this question, many American strategists reverted to emotional thinking. They pictured the Japanese as insane fanatics who would stop at nothing short of mass suicide. As a result, not one but two atomic bombs were dropped on Japan, on the theory that Japan would continue to fight until the nation was destroyed. The theory of Japanese fanaticism continued to shape American military strategy even though surrender negotiations were under way before the second bomb was dropped (Cousins, 1954).

Another type of emotional barrier to scientific knowledge results from a desire to believe that things in general turn out for the best. This point of view is referred to as the "just-world" theory. It holds that poor people deserve to be poor, prisoners deserve to be in prison, mental patients are best off in the institutions that house them, and lucky people deserve their luck. Two sociologists have gathered evidence that shows the popularity of this view. In their staged experiments, they found that a majority of people were inclined to rate the winner of a contest as "most deserving," even when winning depended purely on luck and when there was no logical reason for preferring any particular contestant. Obviously, people who have convinced themselves that everything in the world is as it should be are not going to engage in research which could upset this conviction. They will not try to discover, for example, why specific groups in the population are poor, whether prisons rehabilitate prisoners, or whether mental institutions do anything to cure the mentally disturbed. While this point of view is comforting to many people, it is not conducive to scientific knowledge of people.

Intended deceit

Sometimes barriers to scientific knowledge are imposed on purpose. In advertising and in politics, the truth is at times obscured or completely hidden while half-truths or outright lies are presented to the public. Cigarette manufacturers, for example, print health warnings in their ads, but these warnings appear in small print below pictures of healthy- and sexy-looking men and women who puff away happily, without fear for

Figure 2-1 *Above:* Attitudes and emotional biases are barriers to the rational, objective study of society. (*Jan Lukas/ Rapho/Photo Researchers, Inc.*)

Figure 2-2 *Right:* How harmful to society is pornography? In the United States, the answer must be determined by the local community. (*Magnum*)

their health. Scientific facts tell us that smoking leads to lung cancer; advertisers would have us believe that cigarettes lead to virility and sex appeal.

More alarming than the distortion of truth in advertising are the distortions of truth which occur in politics. During the Vietnamese war and later, during the Watergate scandal, high government officials issued statements which proved, under investigation, to be completely false. At other times, government officials have held back the spread of knowledge by ignoring reports from social scientists. For example, when the National Advisory Commission on Obscenity and Pornography turned in its report to President Richard Nixon in 1970, he felt that the wisest political course would be to reject its findings and bury the report. The report had recommended that adult Americans should be allowed by law to see or hear anything they wanted to, even if it was considered obscene. However, the Supreme Court ruled in 1974 that the definition of obscenity and policies regarding obscenity should be decided by local communities. In 1972, the Commission on Population Growth and the American Future had recommended that abortions be made readily available to women who wanted them. Like the recommendation on pornography, this one was rejected by President Nixon. Experts—including lawyers, psychologists, sociologists, and physicians—had served on both commissions and had prepared their reports with great stress on truth and scientific objectivity. High-ranking politicians, however, could neither accept nor endorse these reports. They were afraid that if they even spoke about them, it would cost them votes. The politician's "truth" is sometimes determined by political expediency. The advertiser's "truth" consists of whatever sells the product. But the sociologist's "truth" must be judged by more severe criteria than these. In the case of population policy, however, the Supreme Court made rulings in line with the commission's views. State and local laws were forbidden to interfere with a woman's right to abortion during the early months of pregnancy.

PROBLEMS OF OVERCOMING THE BARRIERS

Not all barriers to knowledge can be overcome. Science, obviously, cannot give the answer to certain types of philosophical or religious questions, such as the meaning of existence. Science limits its work to *empiricism*—the study of observable facts and of things as they are. For this reason, much of the realm of *values* (the realm of "what ought to be") is outside the field of science. Social scientists might study how competition affects society, but as scientists they could not rate it "good" or "bad."

Even the problems of overcoming the previously discussed barriers to knowledge are not easy ones. However, scientists are constantly aware of the problems of accepting traditional answers without testing them. Therefore they continually work to develop more refined methods of observation and analysis. Sociologists try to recognize their own emotional biases so that they do not interfere with the proper interpretation of data. This is difficult, because social scientists are products of the very society they are studying. They share its traditions and biases, and they are trained to see the same things others see and ignore the same things others ignore. The best sociologists are those who can free themselves from cultural habits of perception. Once freed from these cultural straitjackets, the innovative sociologist is able to look beneath the surface to find new facts and new explanations for the social environment.

The Swedish social scientist Gunnar Myrdal warns that even the most careful social scientists often ignore many subjects that deserve study, either because they are unaware or because exposing the facts would bring blame rather than praise (Myrdal, 1969). For example, Myrdal points out that although nineteenth-century theorists showed great interest in the new study of economics, they had no interest in studying unemployment. Unemployment was a flaw in an economic system that everyone wanted to praise. More recently, the problems of poverty, minority rights, and the position of women have received too little attention. Now, however, sociologists and other social scientists are catching up with these formerly neglected areas of investigation.

SCIENTIFIC METHOD

In the previous chapter, scientific method was given a partial definition as a systematic pursuit of knowledge, faithful to facts and cautious about conclusions. A more detailed definition of scientific method includes also the steps in the procedure for acquiring verifiable knowledge. A scientific study typically begins with a *hypothesis*, which is a tentative idea about the relationship between phenomena. For example, in the study *Tally's Corner*, about to be presented, we will see that the investigator had questions in mind about the relationship between extreme poverty and attitudes toward work and toward marriage and family.

Next, scientific method calls for a *research design* or plan of procedure. Alternative methods of procedure in sociological studies can be used: direct observation through living and working with people or less direct observation by simply asking questions of people, studying the statistics that are already available or designing social experiments. The next step is the interpretation of the facts that have been discovered. The old saying that facts speak for themselves is only partly true. In making his studies for *Tally's Corner*, the researcher found inconsistencies between statements about marriage and family and what actually happened. Therefore, he had to reconcile what people said and what they did.

Scientific method does not end after a hypothesis has been formed and tested and the results interpreted. The results must be *publicized* and submitted to the *critical comments of others*.

Sometimes the studies will be duplicated by others as a further test of the *validity* of the conclusions—for, as was noted in Chapter 1, scientific conclusions must always be revised if conflicting information and new interpretations are found.

Observational studies

All knowledge depends upon direct or indirect observation. The term *observational study*, however, generally refers to research through direct observation of people rather than through answers to questionnaires or response to experimental conditions. Such studies are useful for finding out about groups of people whose lifestyles are unfamiliar to most members of society: ethnic minorities, the very poor or rich, inmates of mental institutions or prisons, homosexuals and lesbians, youth gangs, vagrants, and skid-row alcoholics. *Tally's Corner*, a good observational study by Elliot Liebow, illustrates many of the advantages of this method (Liebow, 1967). Liebow did not make the mistake of drawing superficial conclusions based on only a few interviews. He spent eighteen months living in a section of the black ghetto in Washington, D.C., which provides the setting of his book. His research shows that good studies cannot be done hastily; they call for care, attention to detail, and the establishment of *rapport*—the ability to be accepted by others as trustworthy and understanding.

Tally's Corner shows the advantages of a long observational study over questionnaires or interviews. Liebow's subjects were adult black men, all poor, who hung around a carry-out lunch counter that the author calls Tally's Corner. (The book is named for one of the subjects of the study, not the actual name of the corner.) Liebow points out that the men of Tally's Corner are suspicious of interviews, would not answer questionnaires, and are often not even found and recorded by the U.S. Census Bureau. These men are not criminals, but they are generally

Figure 2-3 John Griffin (*left*) the author of *Black Like Me* (1961). Griffin, a white man, darkened his skin to investigate black society. (*New American Library*)

unattached, uneducated men who go unnoticed by the rest of society. Liebow enters into the thoughts and feelings of these "anonymous" people. As a result, the reader is able to develop empathy with them—that is, to see things from their point of view. As depicted by Liebow, the men of Tally's Corner are neither the best nor the worst of people; they are simply human and understandable.

An observational study must add enough to sociological understanding to make it worth doing. In this respect, too, Liebow's study meets the requirements. It begins to answer certain questions regarding attitudes toward work and family. Most of the men of Tally's Corner hold jobs most of the time, but they do not value their jobs and move on frequently. A handful avoid work entirely. Similarly, most of these men do not stay with their wives and children. After seeing many examples of this type of behavior, the researcher began to understand its causes. The only jobs available do not pay enough to support a family. Put in this situation, the men of

Tally's Corner believe that to try to support a family but fail is worse than simply to abandon them and live alone. Leaving also makes it easier for the wife and children to get welfare money, although this does not appear to be the major motive for abandonment. Family obligations are simply impossible to fulfill.

Most of the men of Tally's Corner steal while on the job. The reason is rather simple. Employers assume that the workers *will* steal and, therefore, pay low wages to cover their expected losses. Under the circumstances, not stealing would be foolish. An honest man would not be able to support even himself on his take-home pay. The case of the man called Tonk is typical:

> Tonk's employer explained why he was paying Tonk $35 for a 55–60-hour workweek. "These men will steal," he said. Although he keeps close watch on Tonk, he estimates that Tonk steals from $35 to $40 per week. What he steals, when added to his regular earnings, brings his take-home pay to $70 or $75 per week. (Liebow, 1967, p. 97)

If we ask why the street-corner man places no value on his work, the answer is simple: Society in general rates his work equally low. If we

The pursuit of sociological knowledge

39

decide that these men live only in the present and do not think of the future, our conclusion, according to Liebow, is wrong. The street-corner man does think about the future, and that is the very reason why he lives only in the present. His future "is a future in which everything is uncertain except the ultimate destruction of his hopes and the eventual realization of his fears" (Liebow, 1967, p. 66).

Marriage customs as well as the attitude toward work can be explained in terms of the general hopelessness of meeting obligations. The men of Tally's Corner all view marriage as a bad deal, although they all accept it as a social ideal. Nearly all of them have been married, and the younger men all intend to get married eventually. They are not coerced into marriage; they enter it willingly. Marriage is a coming-of-age ceremony for the street-corner man, a sign of manhood and adulthood. However, it creates economic responsibilities that are impossible to meet. Marriages must then be broken up and, older but wiser, these men will say in later years, "Never again!"

Their statements, however, avoid mention of the inability to meet marriage obligations; rather, they blame the failure on the interpersonal problems involved. Said one informant:

> From now on I'm playing the field. A man's better off in the field. I lived with her five years and every day, as soon as I walked in the house, I'd hear nothing but nagging. Mostly money. I got tired hearing all that shit. (Liebow, 1967, p. 128)

The reader probably wonders how the sociologist-observer manages to relate to the subjects and gain their confidence. Liebow was a white college graduate working for a doctorate, whereas the street-corner men were black high school dropouts. There are obvious drawbacks

to such a situation, but also a few compensations. A complete outsider is not seen as a threat or a rival, either for women or for prestige. Liebow was able to run around with the crowd and join in at dances and parties far more than he had hoped, but he was always aware of being an outsider. Only once did he feel completely accepted: In a local bootleg joint, he met a soldier who stared at him long and hard and asked what he was. "I told him I was Jewish. 'That's good,' he said, 'I'm glad you're not white!'"

Participant-observer studies

Although Liebow was surprisingly well accepted by the street-corner crowd, he could never fully belong to it. A *participant-observer* study, on the other hand, is one in which the observer actually becomes part of the group under study. Erving

Figure 2-4 Elliot Liebow's observational study *Tally's Corner* deals with black "street-corner" men. (*Ronald S. Goor, Black Star*)

Goffman wrote his famous book *Asylums* (1961) after having worked in a mental hospital as a staff member. Reporters sometimes use this technique to get a story about a particular group. The novelist John Steinbeck lived in the camps of the migratory laborers he was describing in *The Grapes of Wrath* (1939).

There are two ethical problems involved in participant-observer studies. The researcher who keeps his or her real identity and goals hidden becomes a kind of spy, watching, taking part, and then reporting on the group under study. Ethical regulations of the American Sociological Association require that no report be published that damages the people being studied and that all names be kept confidential. Nevertheless, some sociologists feel that too many reports have been done on groups that would not like to have their activities discussed, even anonymously (Erikson, 1967; Galliher, 1973). The second objection to participant-observer studies is that groups with little power, such as the poor and deviant, are more likely to have their lives exposed than are the rich and powerful. While many sociologists have entered mental hospitals incognito, no sociologist could be disguised well enough to enter the inner councils of West Point, much less a Pentagon meeting of the Joint Chiefs of Staff.

There are many advantages to participant-observer studies, however. The participant-observer gains insight into customs and attitudes that are otherwise difficult to understand. For example, Jean L. Briggs studied an Eskimo family of Canada by having herself adopted into it as a daughter. At first her Eskimo parents felt honored at having her, but eventually she found herself regarded as an uneducable child or even compared with the only feeble-minded woman in the village. Although full grown, she was completely inept at gutting fish, chewing boots in the morning to soften the frozen leather, or mending a kayak. Worse yet, she had not learned unquestioning obedience to her father. She even made suggestions and gave her opinions—inexcusable conduct for a daughter (Briggs, 1970). Eventually, she achieved full participation and ceremonial membership without deception, and the experience, although not always pleasant, gave her new insights into interpersonal relations among the Eskimos.

Participant-observer studies are helpful in reaching a full understanding of the lives and viewpoints of many occupational groups, such as assembly-line workers, migratory laborers, or coal miners. In nearly all such cases, the primary aim is to add to the fund of sociological knowledge; the secondary aim is one of reaching sympathetic understanding.

The observational studies discussed above are useful for understanding the life-styles of fairly small groups. Other kinds of studies are more effective for learning about larger groups of people. The major tools for these large-scale studies are census reports, opinion polls, and questionnaires; all are very useful.

Opinion research

The late George Lundberg, a strong advocate of the scientific study of society, once said, "The time may come when the reliable polling of public opinion will be a science comparable to meteorology. Charts of all kinds of social weather, its movements and trends, whether it be anti-Semitism, anti-Negro sentiment, or mob-mindedness will be at the disposal of the administrators of the people's will in every land" (Lundberg, 1961).

This statement may sound overly optimistic, but it indicates the importance of opinion polls, both for sociological information and for public policies. Today, polls on interracial attitudes are taken frequently; they generally show a long-range trend toward acceptance of the idea of racial equality. Opinion polling on such controversial subjects as abortion, the legalization of marijuana, environmental issues, and criticisms of tax laws helps to keep legislators informed of the feelings of their constituents.

Polling, even more than demonstrations, gradually brought our government to realize the unpopularity of the war in Vietnam. Most public-opinion polls are conducted by professional polling organizations, such as those of George Gallup and Louis Harris, rather than by sociologists. However, both types of pollsters have had to learn the same techniques and principles.

Public-opinion polling has been both condemned and praised; most of the criticism is directed at election polls. It is argued that pre-election polling creates a bandwagon effect because everyone wants to back a winner, and undecided voters may support whomever is ahead. A second criticism has to do with the accuracy of polls. In 1936, a prominent magazine, *Literary Digest*, made one of the biggest boners of the century by predicting that Alfred Landon would defeat Franklin D. Roosevelt for President. (Landon actually carried only two states.) The *Literary Digest* had made the mistake of using a polling technique that overrepresented the wealthy voters; they took names from telephone directories. Poor people did not have telephones during the Depression, but they did vote—for Roosevelt. In 1948, a mistake of only a few percentage points was made, but the mistake was crucial: most polls predicted that Thomas Dewey would defeat Harry S. Truman. This error shook the public's confidence in opinion polls. Predictions of presidential elections in the 1960s and 1970s were generally quite accurate, however, although in two very close elections the major pollsters refused to predict: Kennedy versus Nixon in 1960 and Carter versus Ford in 1976. Final polls indicated that the 1976 election would be even closer than it actually was.

Polling techniques have improved greatly since the 1930s, especially in the development of a *representative sample*. To be representative, a sample of public opinion must include a mix of all segments of the population: rich and poor, black and white, male and female, urban and rural, Democrat and Republican, and in some cases Catholic, Protestant, and Jewish. In addition, these groups must be represented *in proportion to their actual numbers in the population or in their proportion to the total number of people taking part in the activity being studied.*

An alternative to using a representative sample is to use a *random sample*. As the term implies, a *random sample* is a sampling of public opinion which is done by selecting subjects of the study at random. The assumption is that the right percentage of each category of people will be polled. In a community survey, every tenth house might be polled, or every tenth, twentieth, or hundredth name in the city register. In this case, the sampling procedure would probably be satisfactory. Since random sampling operates by the rules of chance, a fairly wide sampling must be made to avoid the chance that a disproportionate number of persons of one income level, race, or political party is polled. It is for this reason that the street interview, often used in televised news reports, is subject to great error. The one or two people questioned might have highly unusual opinions on the issue under study.

The last alternative is to poll the entire population. While this may be possible for a school or a small community, it is too costly for a large city, state, or nation.

Questionnaires

People generally think of politics, elections, and ballot issues when the term *opinion polls* is used. For this reason, a slight distinction is being made between opinion polls and questionnaires of the type often used by sociologists. The second type includes, in addition to political issues, a wide variety of topics such as job satisfaction, child-rearing methods, or current attitudes about welfare programs, violence on television, or gasoline rationing. Regardless of the types of questions asked, certain precautions must be taken in using questionnaires. First, fairly large samples should be taken, either at random or else aimed

(a)

(b)

Figure 2-5 A questionnaire dealing with the cost of living would be answered very differently by the wealthy and the unemployed. To be accurate, such a questionnaire must be sent to all representative groups in the population. [(a) Ken Heyman; (b) Benyas Kaufman, Black Star]

The pursuit of sociological knowledge

43

at reaching a certain segment of the population.

A second problem, especially with a mailed questionnaire, is that many people—over half in actual studies—don't return them. It is always possible that the people who do answer questionnaires differ in their opinions from those who do not. They may, for example, hold extreme opinions, or believe in their opinions very strongly. In reading the results of such a survey, then, tabulators should know how many questionnaires were sent out and how many answers were obtained. When the study is published, the total number of responses received is noted as $n =$ ———. It is always a good idea to see how many people were actually contacted in a survey, since a large number of responses makes the conclusions more valid.

One group of researchers has succeeded in getting returns of from 69.7 to 75.2 percent (Dillman et al., 1974). This group credits its high rate of return to an improved questionnaire format. They send out an attractive package in booklet form—with clear, simple questions—together with a covering letter emphasizing the importance of the questionnaire. Finally, they send out follow-up postcards and even replacement questionnaires for those who are slow in responding. This technique involves quite a bit of work, but it is much less costly than sending research teams from door to door.

The wording of questions can make or break the questionnaire. First, questions must be phrased clearly, so that the respondents can understand them. Second, the questions must be carefully worded to draw out precisely the information desired. For example, if a researcher wants to learn what people think about gasoline rationing, he or she must consider the circumstances under which rationing may be imposed. Simply asking, "Are you in favor of gasoline rationing?" will confuse the respondent and will not give the researcher very much information. A more effective way of posing this question would include a series of alternative answers of this type:

a. As long as we have to depend upon foreign imports of petroleum
b. If it is the only alternative to raising prices to $1 or more per gallon
c. Only in case of a national emergency, such as war
d. Whenever the supply becomes so scarce that we cannot be sure of getting gasoline
e. Under no circumstances
f. Comments . . .

Such a question will give more information about opinions and will be useful in gauging how responses change with changing economic or social conditions. The comments are sometimes difficult to tally; however, they yield very useful and often unexpected information about public opinion.

Sometimes researchers want to determine how strongly people feel about a certain issue. In this case, they will use the following type of question:

"On the average, there is no difference in mentality between men and women."
Express your degree of agreement or disagreement with the above statement, marking A for strong agreement, B for mild agreement, C for undecided, D for mild disagreement, and E for strong disagreement.
A———, B———, C———, D———, E———.

People who mark such a questionnaire "D" are probably open to persuasion regarding female equality. If the population of a country, region, or ethnic group overwhelmingly marks "E" on the question, it seems unlikely that their opinion would change easily. In this way, the shades-of-opinion type of questionnaire gives more information than one calling for a simple "agree" or "disagree" answer.

Interviews

Interviews of the type used in sociology are guided conversations between researchers and people who make up a random or representative sample of the public. The interviews are designed to answer particular questions, but the procedures are more flexible than in a written questionnaire and often more successful in eliciting information. If questions are not understood, the interviewer can restate them in different terms. The interviewer can also coax information out of an uncertain or reluctant respondent, as this one does:

Interviewer: Mrs. Hummel, what do you think of the idea of young couples living together for a while without getting married?

Mrs. Hummel: I just don't know what to think.

Interviewer: Could you make any more comments? For instance, are there some circumstances under which it's all right and others in which it's wrong?

Mrs. Hummel: Well, I guess. If they're really in love, and if he'll promise to marry her in case she has a baby by him. The trouble is, it's hard to depend on men that way.

If Mrs. Hummel were responding to a questionnaire, she probably would have checked the "no opinion" column. Face to face with a persistent interviewer, however, she worked out her opinions on this issue. Although tallying interviews is more difficult than tallying questionnaires, it is certainly not impossible. Eventually, many similar responses are received and the researcher can set up categories that can be compiled into a table. Mrs. Hummel's response would probably fall into a category labeled "approval with strong reservations."

The same precautions must be taken in interviewing as in other kinds of opinion polling. Interviewers must cover a reasonably large segment of the target population in a variety of locations. Further, they must be aware of how different *variables*, or factors, influence people's opinions. On living together without marriage, it would be interesting to know the effects of education, age, and place of residence (urban, suburban, or rural) on the question. Researchers might also want to know how the opinions of men differed from those of women, how married respondents differed from single persons, and whether church members favored a particular viewpoint.

COPING WITH STATISTICS

Sources of statistics

Many government bureaus, banks, insurance companies, and other organizations gather and publish statistics on a wide variety of topics. Many government findings are presented in the *Statistical Abstracts of the Bureau of the Census*, which can be found in any library. The *Statistical Abstracts* presents tables and graphs on such subjects as population, health, law enforcement, government finance, employment, income, prices, transportation, agriculture, forestry, manufacturing, and commerce. However, while such sources are often helpful to sociologists, they cannot always provide just the information that is needed. Using the techniques described earlier, sociologists often have to collect their own statistics. Most major universities have departments of social research which gather statistics for a particular project. In addition, research projects are often financed by private foundations or by the Department of Health, Education, and Welfare.

Possible misrepresentation

Once statistics are gathered, they are arranged into easy-to-read tables. However, such tables must be prepared carefully. As Darrel Huff points out in *How to Lie with Statistics* (1954), graphs and charts can be used to distort facts as well as to reveal them. Statistics can be misleading if they are based on too few cases or on a biased sampling. Graphs can be distorted to make the trends they reveal seem much more startling than they actually are.

In the following hypothetical example, Mayor Doyle's opponent, a "law-and-order" candi-

Table 2-1 "Normal" Graph

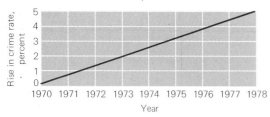

Table 2-2 Distortion of Scale

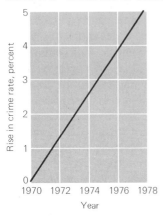

date, has charged that during Doyle's administration, the crime rate has grown steadily. Actually, the increase is not very great, as revealed in Table 2-1. Doyle's opponent, however, prepares a graph which looks like Table 2-2. Tables 2-1 and 2-2 present the same information, but Table 2-2, by a technique called *distortion of scale*, makes the crime rate appear to skyrocket. No scientific researcher would create such a deliberate distortion, but this kind of trick is not unknown in campaign literature or even in newspapers to make a dramatic point.

The researcher—and the reader—must always know just what statistics do and do not indicate. For example, it is easy to err in thinking about crime rates, since many types of crime (especially automobile theft) are committed mainly by people in their teens. The higher crime rate of a particular area may be due to an increase in the number of teenagers living there rather than a rising level of crime among the entire population. Errors in population statistics are also easy to make, as shown by the insert "The Case of the G.E. Babies" (page 48). The large number of unexpected G.E. babies in the account shows not only statistical error but also failure to consider people's motives.

Measurement of central tendency

Central tendency is the tendency for quantitative data to cluster at or near one point rather than being dispersed at random. For example, in the population of the United States, heights tend to cluster in the range of about 5 feet 2 inches to about 6 feet 2 inches; they are not distributed evenly in increments from 4 feet through 7 or 8 feet.

A common but far from perfect measurement of central tendency is the *average* or *mean*, a figure found by adding the total quantities being considered and dividing by the number of cases. For example, if 25 farmers produce 50,000 boxes of oranges, the average production per farmer equals 50,000 divided by 25 or 2,000 boxes. However, such an average might hide as much information as it reveals. If three or four farmers have produced nearly all the 50,000 boxes of oranges and the others have very small production, the average would not give a very accurate picture of the distribution of orange production or of the likely income to be derived from it.

Another way to figure central tendency is to note the point that divides the distribution curve (the line along which the cases are distributed) so that there are as many cases above as below it. This point is called the *median*. The median is used in many types of statistics, such as median income, median age, or median hours of the work week. It is easier to compute than the average and frequently gives a more accurate picture of distribution. Another possibility is to look at the point on the curve that includes the largest number of cases—a point called the *mode*. In Table 2-3, which shows family income distribution in a community, the mode most accurately indicates income distribution, showing that most families earn less than $7,000 per year.

Median, mean, and mode are all honest, reliable ways of presenting central tendency. The differing views they sometimes provide, however, show that all three concepts must be understood and also that one should take into consideration total distribution (all the cases on the distribution curve) as well as central tendency. Often the cases of greatest social concern are those near an extreme of the curve, as in Table 2-3.

Correlation

Correlation is the tendency for two phenomena to go together, as in the case of size and weight or of drunken driving and traffic accidents. Since variables that correlate seem to be somehow related, it is logical to ask if one is the cause of the other or others. Actually, correlation does not prove a cause-effect relationship, and to assume that it necessarily does can lead to serious errors. For example, in the days when hippie clothing and long hair were offensive to many middle-class people, it was assumed that there was a correlation between hippie dress and use of marijuana. However, it would take strange reasoning to conclude that particular hairstyles or dress styles *cause* the use of marijuana. On the other hand, a series of correlations between heavy cigarette smoking and lung cancer finally led to government-imposed warnings on cigarette packages, with the implication that there is a causal link between cigarette smoking and lung cancer. In other words, there are cases in which one of two correlates might be causally connected with the other.

Independent variables are phenomena that appear to be causes or partial causes of one or more other phenomena. Since lung cancer increases with increased use of cigarettes, and since no other variable has been found that could explain the increase, a causal relationship is highly probable. In this case, cigarette smoking is the independent variable, or probable cause, and lung cancer is the *dependent variable*, or effect. To be absolutely safe, however, correla-

Table 2-3 Family Income Distribution

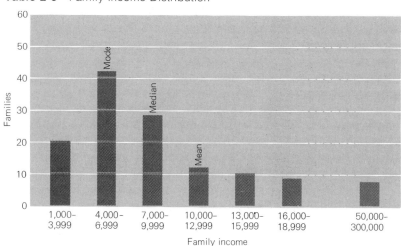

Note: Since the median is the central point, it pertains to family 68 of the 137 families represented.

The case of the G.E. babies

The perils and complexities of birth forecasting were encountered last year, in rather extraordinary circumstances, by General Electric. Last January 14, G.E. announced that it would award five shares of its common stock to any employee who had a baby on October 15—the latter date being the company's seventy-fifth anniversary. Originally the company said it expected about thirteen winners. It arrived at this figure by applying a daily U.S. birth rate to its own 226,000 employees. This computation actually yielded a prediction of fifteen births; but a G.E. public relations man thought it might be nice to trim the figure to thirteen, since the latter was the number of original G.E. investors.

The mathematics suffered from more than public relations, however. G.E. employees, since they included no children and no one over sixty-five, are obviously a much more fertile group than the population as a whole. When this fact sank in, a company statistician made a new assault on the problem. He estimated that the size of an average G.E. family was 4.2. This meant that the total number of people in the G.E. families was close to a million. Applying the crude annual birth rate to this group, and dividing by 365, he came up with a new prediction of seventy-two births on the big day.

As it turned out, there were not thirteen, fifteen, or seventy-two babies born to G.E. employees on October 15. There were 189.

Subtracting the company's highest expectation from 189 gives 117 "extra" babies. Where did G.E. go wrong? Well, among other things, the company made no allowance for the incentive provided by its own stock. This oversight, remarkable in a company that has had a lot to say about capitalist incentives, was apparently rectified by the employees. The latter not only enjoy having children, but, it appears, they rather enjoy the idea of becoming capitalists. . . .

From *Fortune Magazine*, January 1954, p. 95.

---

tional findings are stated as probabilities, not certainties.

Often two variables go together because of a *spurious* relationship—a superficial relationship appearing on the surface to be real but not coming from the right source. Mark Twain once provided an outrageous example of spurious cause by warning against going to bed. More people die in bed, he said, than anywhere else, implying that going to bed is a cause of death. In this case, both going to bed and dying (dependent variables) are related because they are the results of sickness or injury (the independent variable in the case). Unless a logical reason can be found for assuming a cause-effect relationship between two variables, one must be extremely cautious in assuming that such a relationship exists, no matter how closely the variables are associated.

Usually a number of variables are present in any subject of sociological interest. Variables in school success, for example, could include encouragement from home, hope for the future, freedom from heavy work responsibilities, freedom from worries, academic intelligence, good study habits, and many more. It is easy to make a mistake by attributing too much influence to only one variable.

(a)

(b)

Figure 2-6 Statistics can be misleading. If the income of (*a*) the mansion owner and the income of (*b*) the shack owners were averaged out, a distorted view of the community's general well-being would emerge. [(*a*) *Newport County Chamber of Commerce; (b) George W. Gardner*]

The importance of statistics

Statistics are most useful for revealing trends, or changes in behavior or opinions over a period of time. Statistics gathered over a period of years, for example, can show whether crime rates are

rising or falling, how fast the population is increasing, or whether patterns of income distribution are changing. Without carefully gathered statistics, information on society can be only impressionistic, based on possibly faulty personal observations. When a police officer says, "I've had to investigate more cases of arson this last year than ever before. There must be more kooks who like to set fires than there used to be," what does this statement actually mean? Probably it means only that, by coincidence, he happens to know about more cases of arson than usual. His observation is too casual and based on too few cases to provide proof of a trend.

Adults have always complained that adolescents are hard to understand, that they are moody, and that they lack direction. Many theorists have tried to explain their behavior. According to the sociologist Kingsley Davis, the adolescent is faced with the difficult task of bridging the gap between physical maturity and social immaturity (Davis, 1944). However, while everyone knows some troubled teenagers, no one knows the extent of adolescent problems. A statistical study seemed to be needed to find out the actual facts. Had psychologists, for example, drawn general rules from only a few cases? Just what psychological problems are typically met with in the teen years?

A statistical study of adolescence

In 1973, a team of three researchers made a statistical study of adolescence (Simmons et al., 1973). Their work shows how such a study can test casual impressions that might be based on too few cases. Their work also produced results that suggest directions for further study.

The problem The problem to be investigated was this: Is it true that the period of adolescence is accompanied by disturbances in the self-image? Four dimensions of self-image were used. The first dimension was self-consciousness. Do adolescents become more self-conscious and uncomfortable in personal interaction than younger children do? The second dimension, stability, asks whether the adolescent is as sure of what he or she is like and has as stable a definition of self as does the child. The third dimension, self-esteem, includes the "perceived self": that is, do adolescents think that others view them unfavorably? Self-esteem was measured in particular areas (sports, popularity, and good looks) of interest to the age group and

Table 2-4 Disturbance of the Self-Image among Twelve-Year-Olds in the Sixth or Seventh Grade, by Race, Social Class, and Marks in School

Self-image disturbance	Race				Social class				Marks in school			
	Blacks		Whites		Middle class		Working class		A's and B's		C's and below	
	6th grade	7th grade	6th grade	7th grade	6th grade	7th grade	6th grade	7th grade	6th grade	7th grade	6th grade	7th grade
Percent low self-esteem (global)	18% (106)	33% (27)	30% (61)	47% (32)	14% (21)	44% (16)	21% (119)	36% (39)	20% (49)	37% (30)	23% (104)	42% (24)
Percent low self-esteem (specific)	33% (92)	46% (26)	19% (58)	45% (31)	48% (21)	41% (17)	26% (108)	44% (36)	17% (47)	39% (28)	29% (91)	50% (24)
Percent high self-consciousness	28% (109)	32% (28)	27% (62)	52% (33)	24% (21)	53% (17)	29% (122)	38% (40)	22% (50)	37% (30)	29% (106)	58% (26)
Percent high instability of the self-image	31% (104)	50% (28)	26% (53)	56% (32)	35% (20)	71% (17)	27% (112)	44% (39)	30% (47)	52% (29)	28% (96)	54% (26)

also in a "global" dimension of general self-image (the fourth dimension).

The sample From each of twenty-five schools in Baltimore, 105 children were randomly selected, ranging in school level from third grade to twelfth grade. The sample included more working-class members than the national average and represented more blacks (63 percent) in proportion to whites (37 percent) than the national average. Since race and social class could easily be important variables, the researchers made a study of them, as shown in Table 2-4. Their conclusion was that, in general, the same findings "hold for blacks as well as whites, for middle-class as well as working-class respondents, and for students with high as well as low grades." If race, social class, or grades had made a significant difference, it would have been necessary to select a sample in which each of these "variables" was represented in proportion to the national average as a means of controlling variables. (See page 54 for discussion of controls.)

Measurements For each of the dimensions of self-image studied, a number of questions were asked and the answers were tallied. The following sample questions were used to measure self-consciousness and stability of self:

> If a teacher asked you to get up in front of the class and talk a little about your summer, would you be very nervous, a little nervous, or not at all nervous?
>
> A kid told me: "Some days I like the way I am. Some days I don't like the way I am." Do your feelings change this way?

Tables 2-5, 2-6, 2-7, 2-8, and 2-9 present the data compiled from the answers to questions such as these. This series of line graphs shows a sharp increase in all types of negative feelings in early adolescence which reach a peak at about age thirteen or fourteen, followed by an unsteady decline in later years. In some cases, there

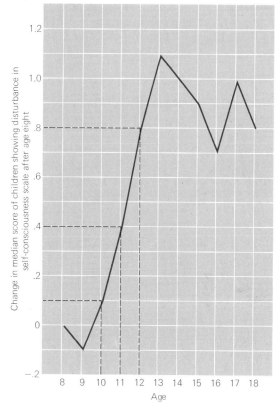

Table 2-5 Increase in Self-consciousness by Age

Source: Roberta G. Simmons, Florence Rosenberg, and Morris Rosenberg: "Disturbance in the Self-image at Adolescence," *American Sociological Review*, vol. 8, no. 5, October 1973, pp. 553–568.

are sharp dips and secondary peaks in the uncomfortable feelings, revealing the changing moods that accompany adolescence.

Conclusions This study concludes that problems of self-image do indeed arise in adolescence and that these problems are seen across all four dimensions of study: self-consciousness, self-image, self-esteem in areas of special concern, and general (global) self-image. Other data from this study show a rapid rise in feelings of depression from ages ten to twelve, along with a further unsteady rise in such feelings until about

The pursuit of sociological knowledge

Table 2-6 Increase in Instability of the Self-image by Age

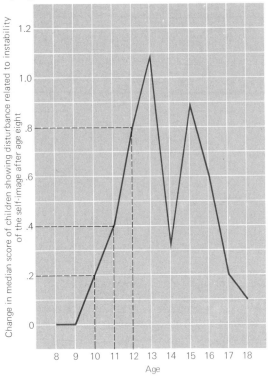

Source: Simmons et al., 1973.

Table 2-7 Increase in Depression by Age

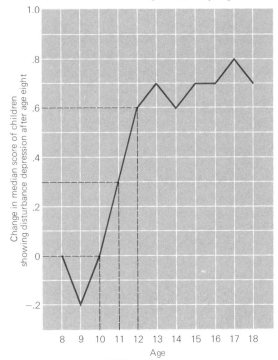

Source: Simmons et al., 1973.

age seventeen, with a slight downturn in depression by age eighteen.

Another problem was uncovered in the course of compiling the statistics: The transition from grade school to junior high school was important in increasing tension along all four dimensions. Children of twelve or thirteen who were still in grammar school had fewer problems of self-image than twelve- or thirteen-year-olds who attended junior high school. Probably the change in schools made the children recognize that childhood was being left behind and a more mature self had to be developed.

Since the age of puberty (the time of life when physical reproductive maturity is reached) varies considerably, using the same ages does not show an adolescent change in all children of that age. However, it does indicate a correlation between age and the types of adolescent disturbances described above.

SOCIOLOGICAL EXPERIMENTS

In 1969, when a great deal of hostility existed between the police and the Black Panthers, a militant black civil rights group, student members of the Panthers at the University of California at Los Angeles complained of getting traffic tickets for little or no reason. All of them displayed brightly colored Black Panther bumper stickers on their cars. The sociologist F. K. Heussenstamm decided to test one variable in this situation: Was it true that the bumper stickers alone could account for the many traffic tickets?

Table 2-8 Increase in Low Self-esteem by Age

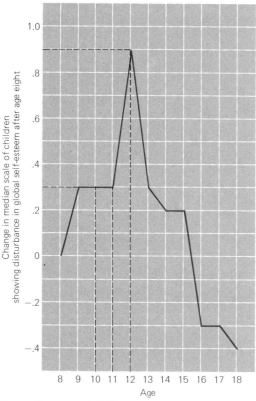

Source: Simmons et al., 1973.

Table 2-9 Increase in Unfavorable Content of the Self-image by Age

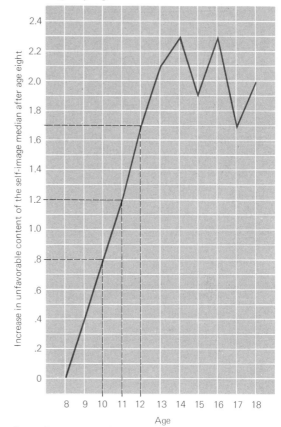

Source: Simmons et al., 1973.

Heussenstamm chose fifteen students with perfect driving records, all of whom drove about 20 miles per day and promised to maintain their usual driving habits during the experiment. To control for possible racial or sexual biases, five white, five black, and five Mexican-American students were chosen. In each group of five, three were men and two women. The one new variable introduced was the Black Panther bumper sticker on each car (Heussenstamm, 1971). The results?

Bumper stickers in lurid day-glo orange and black, depicting a menacing panther with large BLACK PANTHER lettering were at-

tached to the rear bumpers of each subject car and the study began. The first student received a ticket for making an "incorrect lane change" on the freeway less than two hours after heading home in the rush hour traffic. Five more tickets were received by others on the second day for "following too closely," "failing to yield the right of way," "driving too slowly in the high speed lane of the freeway," "failure to make a proper signal before turning right at an intersection," and "failure to observe proper safety of pedestrians using a crosswalk." On day

The pursuit of sociological knowledge

three, students were cited for "excessive speed," "making unsafe lane changes," and "driving erratically." And so it went every day.

One student was forced to drop out of the study by day four, because he had already received three citations. (An accumulation of four or more could lead to revocation of license.) Three others reached what we had agreed was the maximum limit—three citations—within the first week. Altogether, the participants received 33 citations in 17 days, and the violations fund was exhausted. (Heussenstamm, 1971, p. 33. Published by permission of Transaction, Inc., from *Trans-Action,* vol. 8, no. 4, copyright © 1971).

These statistics indicate that a single variable—the Black Panther bumper stickers—was enough to cause a great increase in traffic arrests.

Controls

In describing the Black Panther experiment, a new term has been used—*control.* A *control* is a technique for eliminating or minimizing the effect of all variables except one in an experimental situation. Heussenstamm made sure that his results would not be influenced by generally bad drivers or by great increases in the amount of driving done. Just in case members of one sex or one race are more likely to be stopped by the police than others, the ratio of these groups was kept constant as a means of control.

Often in an experimental situation, two groups will be used, one called the *experimental group* and the other the *control group.* All variables in the two groups will be alike except for the one variable being tested, which will be introduced in the experimental group but not in the control group. For example, Albert Bandura and S. A. Ross (1961) conducted an experiment on two groups of children. The experimental group witnessed an adult showing aggressive behavior toward one of the children's dolls, hitting it and

kicking it. The control group witnessed no such behavior. After the event, the children in the experimental group showed far more aggression than those in the control group. Only one variable accounted for the difference—the aggressive behavior of the adult. In this way, an experiment was able to arrive at definite cause—imitative behavior—of increased aggression. Although experiments are often difficult to design and carry out, they can have the advantage of establishing cause to a degree that correlations cannot.

Ethics in experiments

The Black Panther experiment obviously presented difficulties for the students who participated in it. However, its purpose was explained to them in advance, the fines were paid for them, and the experiment was stopped before they lost their licenses. Sociologists have drawn up a code of ethics which demonstrates their concern for experimental subjects. A further code of ethics has been devised by the Department of Health, Education, and Welfare. This is in sharp contrast to the past, when experimenters violated the human rights of their subjects. In 1973, for example, an Alabama committee on civil rights discovered that the U.S. Public Health Service had knowingly and purposefully withheld medical treatment from a group of black men suffering from syphilis (see the insert, "Syphilis Study of 600 Blacks Called Racist"). It is to be hoped that violations of human life and dignity are a thing of the past. It is the goal of sociologists to respect the rights and welfare of their subjects regardless of race or economic status.

THEORIES AND RESEARCH

Long before the age of modern science, the relationship between factual knowledge and reasoning was well stated by Confucius:

Knowledge without thought is labor lost;
Thought without knowledge is perilous.

Gathering data for the sake of knowing unrelated facts is neither personally rewarding nor socially useful. On the other hand, reasoning without knowledge is dangerous, since it can lead to false conclusions and to useless or even harmful practices. A combination of research to gain knowledge and reasoning to find the principles to which that knowledge leads is the best means known for arriving at acceptable theory.

The need for theory

Theories are logically consistent and scientifically acceptable general principles that explain the known facts and the relationships between them. They are the end product of the scientific method—the conclusion to which hypothesis, data gathering, and testing lead. A good theory should not only explain the known facts but also provide a logical basis for further investigation and in some cases for action. In medicine, for example, the theory that many diseases are caused by germs and viruses provides a much more logical basis for investigation and treatment than did the belief that evil spirits cause disease. William Howells (1962) tells of a few cases in which the belief in evil spirits led to the practice of heating the patient over a slow fire calculated to be just painful enough to get rid of the offending spirit without killing the patient.

Can we say that theoretical explanations in the social sciences have also helped bring about changes in ways of investigating and in social practices? In many cases the answer is "yes." On

---

Syphilis study of 600 blacks called racist

A federal study of 600 syphilitic black men in which the survivors were left untreated for more than 20 years after a cure was discovered was a racist violation of human rights, the Alabama advisory committee to the U.S. Commission on Civil Rights said today.

The U.S. Public Health Service has canceled the project and offered free, lifetime medical care to the 114 survivors of the experiment. But the committee reported that an official had said normal treatment for syphilis in such advanced stages could endanger the lives of the men, most of whom are over 70 years old.

Most of the men who took part in the study, which began more than 40 years ago, had contracted syphilis before the government project began; uninfected men were included as a control group.

In the report . . . the committee said earlier treatment "might have forestalled some of the later sufferings of some of the men who had syphilis. But it was not done."

The study, intended to explore the long-range effects of untreated syphilis, began in Tuskegee, Alabama, in 1932. None of the infected men was treated with penicillin after it was discovered in 1946 to be a cure for venereal disease.

"The committee grieves that again and again such violations of basic human rights as those contained within the Tuskegee study continually have to be viewed only in retrospect," the report said. "It can be said in this light that racism was there, human insensitivity was there, and we hold that this was evil."

The report said the use of black subjects for the research "can only be called a racist decision. It appears inconceivable to the members of this committee that such a study could have been conducted on a white population group. . . ."

UPI Dispatch in *Los Angeles Times*, May 13, 1973, part 1A, p. 6.

---

a small scale, Merton's theoretical explanation of political bossism, related in the previous chapter, shows a similar type of advance over an older explanation that bossism was due to mere ignorance on the part of voters. In theoretical explanations of a much more general type, the social sciences have made great progress. In Chapter 3 we will elaborate upon the idea that cultures, or peoples' patterns of living, account for the behavioral differences that were once attributed to race or different types of minds. Deviant behavior, similarly, was once attributed to "bad blood" or to diabolic possession, and cures were fairly similar to the previously mentioned medical treatment of roasting the patient alive. More recent explanations are rather complex, centering on environmental and social influences or unequal opportunities for winning approval by socially accepted means. Similarly, the old idea that only upper or middle classes show real mental ability has been replaced by the theory that innate ability is much more evenly distributed than had ever been supposed possible in the past.

SUMMARY

Chapter 2 begins by illustrating the type of unfounded opinion so often substituted for scientific knowledge of sociological events. Next, we consider some of the *barriers* to scientific knowledge: lack of experience and knowledge (cognition problems), emotional bias, the desire to make events seem justified, and the problem of intended deceit. Not all barriers to scientific knowledge can be overcome, because there are certain areas—such as moral or esthetic values—that are not verifiable by science. Yet another problem is that social scientists tend to pick and choose the conditions they investigate, depending on their own interests and the difficulties involved in such investigations.

Scientific method begins with a tentative explanation, or *hypothesis*, to be tested and a *research design*. Research methods can consist of *direct observation*, as in the case of *Tally's Corner*, which is given as an example. In such a study, a close view of the lives of others can be gained, along with an understanding of their attitudes and feelings. Sometimes the observer actually joins the group and becomes a *participant-observer*, as in the case of Jean L. Briggs.

Public-opinion research and various kinds of *questionnaires* are appropriate means for some kinds of studies. In such cases, a *representative sample* or a *random sample* must be used to make sure that no segment of the population being investigated is overrepresented or underrepresented. *Interviews* can also be used, with the advantage of fewer cases of misunderstanding, but they are more difficult to complete.

Sometimes the *statistics* needed for a study are already available through such agencies as the U.S. Census Bureau, but in other cases the statistical information must be gathered by sociologists through the questionnaires or interviews just mentioned. Care must be used with statistics to avoid *distortion* of scale or the drawing of *false inferences* (the latter illustrated by "The Case of the G.E. Babies"). Important in statistics is the measurement of *central tendency* by *average* (or *mean*), *median*, or *mode*. Although each of these measurements is useful, none tells the whole story, for extreme cases as well as central tendency may be of great importance.

To illustrate the importance of statistics, a study of adolescence is used. Only by a statistical study based on many cases can one determine how universal adolescent disturbance is. Otherwise, incorrect conclusions might be derived from a few cases that do not represent the general picture of adolescence.

Correlation is the tendency for variables to go together but does not necessarily prove a cause-effect relationship between the variables. If cause-effect relationship can be established, the variables that appear causative are called *independent variables* and those that appear to be effects are called *dependent variables*.

In experiments, attempts are made to control all variables but one—that is, to set up conditions in which all variables are identical except the one factor being tested for. In this way, an experiment can establish cause better than a correlational study can do. The case of the Black Panthers is given as an illustration. Arrest rates for U.C.L.A. students increased if they had Black Panther bumper stickers on their cars, even though such variables as driving habits and distance driven were held constant. In a group experiment, the group being experimented on is the *experimental group*, while the group that is comparable in all ways but the variable being tested for is the *control group*.

In scientific studies of people, research ethics must be taken into consideration, as the Black Panther study and the insert dealing with syphilis patients show. All investigators must attempt to ensure confidentiality and informed consent.

Theories are the culmination of research; they draw conclusions that interpret and synthesize research findings. Correct theory serves as a guide to further research and often as a basis for policy formation.

Study guide

Terms to know

Cognition	Participant-observer study	Correlation
Just-world theory	Representative sample	Independent variable
Empiricism	Random sample	Dependent variable
Values	Distortion of scale	Spurious relationship
Scientific method	Central tendency	Experiment
Hypothesis	Average, or mean	Controls (in experiments)
Observational study	Median	Theory
Rapport	Mode	

Names to know

Gunnar Myrdal
Erving Goffman
Elliot Liebow
George Lundberg

Self-test

Part I. Multiple Choice. Select the best of the four alternative answers:

1 In the barroom conversation at the beginning of the chapter, the only opinion expressed that a sociologist would accept was (**a**) the world is getting worse; (**b**) we need to hang more people; (**c**) if we all kept guns, there would be no more robberies; (**d**) it would be best to wait for a trial before deciding who is guilty.

2 Nathan Caplan found that the majority of federal policy makers (**a**) are receptive to sociological information, (**b**) are not influenced by what government agency sponsors research projects, (**c**) accept ideas even if they are contrary to their own opinions or those of the public, (**d**) frequently and deliberately misuse data for political purposes.

3 The process of gaining knowledge, both through observation and reasoning, is called (**a**) cognition, (**b**) common sense, (**c**) socialization, (**d**) cognitive dissonance.

4 The text argues that the most common reason for biased opinions is (**a**) deliberate cruelty, (**b**) seeing too much of the world and becoming disillusioned, (**c**) hearing too many opposing viewpoints, (**d**) very limited social observation and knowledge.

5 The National Commission on Obscenity and Pornography had its report to the President rejected because its conclusions were (**a**) proved to be false, (**b**) considered narrow-minded and puritanical, (**c**) considered to be losing issues in politics, (**d**) already recognized by the majority of state laws.

6 Liebow's study *Tally's Corner* is an example of what kind of study? (**a**) statistical, (**b**) observational, (**c**) experimental, (**d**) correlational.

7 Liebow's study (**a**) is based on only a few interviews, (**b**) gives less information than a questionnaire would have done, (**c**) shows a capacity for relating to the thoughts and

feelings of others, (**d**) is good description but fails to answer any questions.

8 Tentative explanations that are being put to a test by an experiment are called (**a**) correlations, (**b**) dependent variables, (**c**) theories, (**d**) hypotheses.

9 George Lundberg considered the most important function of public-opinion research to be (**a**) predicting outcomes of elections, (**b**) keeping public officials informed of the public mood, (**c**) serving as self-fulfilling prophecies, (**d**) helping politicians get themselves reelected.

10 The prediction based on the *Literary Digest* poll of 1936 was such an outstanding failure because (**a**) the magazine had been bought out by the Republicans, (**b**) too few people were polled, (**c**) well-to-do people were overrepresented, (**d**) people changed their minds at the last minute.

11 A sample of public opinion planned to represent all groups in the right proportion is called a (**a**) representative sample, (**b**) random sample, (**c**) legitimate sample, (**d**) total sample.

12 A statistical study of adolescence (**a**) found no correlation between age and self-image, (**b**) concluded that social-class differences make general conclusions impossible, (**c**) found generally more negative self-images than in the previous years, (**d**) found more positive self-images than in earlier childhood.

13 The main reason for using interviews rather than printed questionnaires is (**a**) to save the costs of printing, (**b**) to prevent the subjects from "putting on" the questioners by giving ridiculous answers, (**c**) to make sure both the questions and the responses are fully understood, (**d**) to make the job easy.

14 In "The Case of the G.E. Babies," a substantial error was made because (**a**) the G.E. statistician did not know the birthrate for the United States, (**b**) the birthrate of the United States increased suddenly, (**c**) motivation was not taken into account, (**d**) the statistician misplaced a decimal point in his calculations.

15 The method by which it can sometimes be demonstrated that a particular variable is the cause of a phenomenon is (**a**) experimentation, (**b**) correlation, (**c**) participant observation, (**d**) all the above.

Part II. True-False Questions

1 The best possible way of getting at the facts is to ask an eyewitness.

2 Although people would like to believe in a just world, they do not let their wishes interfere with the facts.

3 The only reason the men of Tally's Corner were irregularly employed was laziness.

4 The men of Tally's Corner had found it impossible to make a success of marriage.

5 John Steinbeck's *Grapes of Wrath*, although a novel, had some characteristics of a participant-observer study.

6 Jean Briggs found that by having herself adopted into an Eskimo family, she was able to teach them her viewpoints.

7 Using a random sample is one way of trying to prevent surveys from overrepresenting any one segment of the population under study.

8 U.S. Census Bureau statistics are a valuable source of information for many sociological studies.

9 A correct measurement of central tendency such as the average, or mean, gives just about all the information that is needed.

10 A statistical study can be used to test conclusions based on offhand observation.

11 A study of adolescence cited in the text concludes that in the early years of adolescence, one's self-image suffers and feelings of depression increase.

The pursuit of sociological knowledge

12 Correlation between two variables proves that one is the cause of the other.

13 Professor Heussenstamm's experiment "Bumper Stickers and the Cops" demonstrated that Black Panther stickers on cars could increase the arrest rate regardless of driving habits.

14 The experimental study of syphilis reported in the text is cited as a model of good experimental procedure.

15 According to the text, theories are of very little importance compared with empirical facts.

Questions for discussion

1 What offhand opinions have you heard that are similar to those of the barroom conversation at the opening of the chapter? Do you agree with the text that such opinions are mainly the result of lack of information? What other explanations are possible?

2 Why are such words as *lazy* and *shiftless* completely inappropriate for describing the men of Tally's Corner?

3 We are all observers, whether we are sociologists or not, but why do most of our observations of other groups of people have little validity?

4 Think of other cases besides the text example in which statistics can be used for deceit—for example, in advertising or politics.

5 The President proudly announces that the United States has by far the highest levels of production and consumption of any country in the world. What kinds of information about individual income and consumption are not revealed by the President's statement?

6 What examples can you think of in which ethical questions would be involved in investigations, either observational or experimental?

7 In the previous chapter, a conflict interpretation of society was spoken of as a model; yet Karl Marx considered his interpretation of economic conflict and class struggle a scientific theory. Argue the case for and against calling the Marxist position scientific theory.

Projects

1 Make your own observational study of a social group. Since you will not have the time or the training to do a professional job, it would be advisable to start with a group with which you are already familiar (club, sports group, religious group, political group, or followers of a cause) and to try to test only the following hypothesis: "Status and acceptance in a voluntary association demand a high degree of conformity to group points of view and customs."

2 Use a questionnaire to see if you can find correlations between certain variables in your school population. Do liberal views correlate with humanities and social science majors? Do conservative views correlate with business and engineering majors? Give the following statements to equal numbers of social science or humanities majors and business or engineering majors; ask each subject, "Do you agree or disagree with the statement?" Tally the results. (You may wish to add items to the questionnaire, depending upon what seem to be important liberal versus conservative issues at the time of the questionnaire.)

	Agree	Disagree
The use of marijuana should be legalized.	——	——
The women's liberation movement has helped bring justice to this country.	——	——
Women should have the right to abortions.	——	——
Cohabiting for a while before marriage is a good idea.	——	——

We should not use capital punishment
regardless of the crime.

People should not be expected to serve
in a war unless they consider the cause just.

Racial intermarriage should be encouraged.

3 Examine three or four articles in sociological journals (*American Journal of Sociology*, *American Sociological Review*, *Social Forces*, or *Social Problems*) and see what methods have been used for validating hypotheses. Do the conclusions seem valid to you? (Warning: Some of the articles will be unreadable for a person who has not studied statistics. First read the summary at the beginning of the article; this will give you a clue as to whether the article is interesting and comprehensible to you.)

Suggested readings

Magazine articles

Bruyn, Severyn: "The Methodology of Participant Observation," *Human Organization*, vol. 22, no. 3, Fall 1963, pp. 224–235. What is the difference between mere impressions and the work of a careful participant-observer? Bruyn outlines the steps for good results in observational studies.

Rieslow, Harry W.: "Social Experimentation," *Society*, vol. 12, July–August 1975, pp. 34–41. Why are many government programs of a social-experimental type abandoned? Rieslow explains the need for more follow-up on such programs by sociologists. What good is an experiment if its results are not measured?

Rivlin, A. M.: "Social Experiments: Their Uses and Limitations," *Monthly Labor Review*, vol. 197, June 1973, pp. 28–35. "The new social experiment is a systematic field trial of a social policy under reasonably controlled conditions," says Rivlin. To what extent can such experiments be relied upon? Are there ethical problems involved? Are there alternatives?

Wiseberg, Laurie S.: "The Statistics Jungle: Measuring War, Plague, Fire and Famine," *Society*, vol. 12, July–August 1975, pp. 53–60. How honest are the government statistics available for sociological use? If they are collected for political reasons, says Wiseberg, be cautious. "When former President Nixon was worried about unemployment, he changed its definition and thereby deflated its numbers."

Books

Liebow, Elliot: *Tally's Corner: A Study of Negro Streetcorner Men*, Little, Brown, Boston, 1967. Although this book has been discussed in the text as a good example of observational work, much more can be learned from reading it. A short, well-written, kindly, and rather amusing treatment of the subject.

Milgram, Stanley: *Obedience to Authority*, Harper & Row, New York, 1974. An ingenious and rather chilling experiment to answer the questions: "How far will people go in obeying orders from a person holding scientific authority?" "Will they inflict pain on others?" "Risk lives?" Milgram concludes that they will, and he even draws the comparison with Nazi atrocities committed in obedience to authority.

Key to questions. Multiple Choice: 1-d; 2-a; 3-a; 4-d; 5-c; 6-b; 7-c; 8-d; 9-b; 10-c; 11-a; 12-c; 13-c; 14-c; 15-a. True-False: 1-F; 2-F; 3-F; 4-T; 5-T; 6-F; 7-T; 8-T; 9-F; 10-T; 11-T; 12-F; 13-T; 14-F; 15-F.

This chapter looks upon the great variations found within cultures and between cultures and explains them in sociological terms. After reading it, you should be able to:

1 Explain the meaning of culture and show how cultural capacity has allowed humanity to dominate the earth.

2 Understand how cultures change and how they influence one another through cultural diffusion.

3 Understand the importance of languages as conveyors of culture and present the case for and against the point of view that linguistic differences help account for differences in perception and thought.

4 Understand norms and normative conflicts and their importance to cultures.

5 Recognize that many elements of culture are not clearly seen by the conveyors of the culture itself.

6 Understand the conflicting viewpoints of ethnocentrism and cultural relativism.

7 Be more perceptive about subcultural differences within our own society.

3

CULTURE AND DIVERSITY

All societies produce a variety of people with different character traits, habits, temperaments, and attitudes. Yet, within any society, there are basic similarities among people despite these personality differences. Some Americans are happily married and others are not, but none of them are likely to accuse their spouses of witchcraft—a fairly common ground for divorce in many societies of the past. Some women insist on equality and others do not; but even "unliberated" wives do not walk behind their husbands with bowed heads. Nor do they feel obligated to kill themselves if their husbands die, as women belonging to certain Indian religious groups did in the past. If an American farmer sees an owl near his barn, he may try to protect his chickens, but he does not think the owl has come to steal his soul, as a Senegalese farmer would do (Simmons, 1971, pp. 1–10).

As these examples show, the varieties of attitudes, beliefs, and behaviors that are found within a society are limited by a historically derived pattern of life generally referred to as *culture*. Culture is a very broad concept, including almost all socially learned behavior. The anthropologist Edward B. Tylor defined culture as "that complex whole which includes knowledge, belief, art, morals, law, custom, and any other capabilities and habits acquired by man as a member of society." A simpler definition of culture as "the pattern of life shared by the members of a society" is also satisfactory if certain qualifications are kept in mind. Some elements of the pattern may be shared generally throughout the culture, but other elements vary among different members of society. Considerably different behavior is often expected of men and women, of upper- and lower-class people,

and of people who belong to different age and occupational groups (Murdock, 1971, p. 320). Even language, the cultural element shared by all members of a society, varies to some degree. There are regional accents and also different ways of speaking determined by social class. Thus, language is like other fundamentals of culture: It is understood and shared by all members of the culture, but it is modified by the people who use it.

In addition to language, the cultural pattern includes rules of conduct, values, marriage systems, child-rearing practices, religious beliefs, and approved ways of achieving prestige, as well as customs regarding manners and styles of dress. Each culture has customs that seem very strange to the uninitiated. In the insert "Peculiarities of the U.S.A. Culture" (page 64), Weston LaBarre imagines how a total stranger might view two ordinary American activities—cocktail parties and football games.

Cultures are patterns for human survival; they are complexes of rules and regulations, and they become major determinants of personality. They display enough stability so that patterned ways of life are visible. Parents transmit these patterns to their children, but cultural patterns can and do change. All these characteristics of culture must be examined before the concept is fully understood. Let us turn first to the idea of culture as a pattern for human survival.

CULTURE AND HUMAN SURVIVAL

Many species have adapted to the natural environment by developing particular traits such as physical strength, protective coloring, sharp hearing, or acute sense of smell. Some

Peculiarities of the U.S.A. culture   WESTON LABARRE

Many of the characteristics of American culture would seem odd to a stranger completely unfamiliar with them. The anthropologist Weston LaBarre attempts to describe certain American ceremonials as seen through the eyes of a ficticious Professor Widjojo, who interprets them as rites of self-torture.

"Of course," mused Professor Widjojo . . . "the natives of the U.S.A. have many strange and outlandish customs; but I must say that the drinking rituals of the Usans impressed me most. These rituals occur yearly during an extended period in the calendrical round, beginning at the time of harvest rites of Thanks-for-Blessings and ending largely at the drinking bouts at the New Year. This is called The Season, after which those who can afford it usually leave their home entirely and flee southward into retirement for recuperation.

". . . At all of them (the *koktel partis*) the natives receive the same ritualized drink called *aignawg*. Everybody hates it and freely says so in private, but they must drink some of it so as not to offend their hostess. Despite the superficial phonetic resemblance, *aignawg* has no connection whatever with eggs. It is really skimmed milk, made commercially and thickened with seaweed jelly; and the cream, if any, is whipped and placed on top of the handled cup they must drink it in.

"The ordeal aspect of the ritual is indicated in the fact that the hostess presses more and more cups upon her guests, who must pretend to praise the virtues of the drink—but even more so in the fact that they sprinkle *nutmaig* powder on top, which, in large quantities, is a violent poison inducing fainting, convulsions and death. But this *aignawg* has only enough *nutmaig* on it to make the people ill for several days. The Usan natives pride themselves on 'holding their liquor' so that this ceremony is plainly a contest between a hostess and her guests.

"But I am getting ahead of my chronology. Really, the drinking season of the Usans begins in the fall of the year . . . at the time of the *futbol* games. The purpose of the Usan colleges is to collect young men by competitive subsidies to engage in these mock battles, during which they rush ferociously at one another, wearing padded armor, and ritually kill one another. It seems to be some sort of contest over a sacred pigskin, and everyone gets up alive after each act in the ceremony. Rarely is a young man killed. However, the warriors are often 'punchdrunk' (an odd phrase because they are not allowed to drink, in contrast with the spectators) and they may suffer broken legs, or faces mutilated by the nailed shoes of their opponents. . . ."

Excerpted from Weston LaBarre, "Professor Widjojo Goes to a Koktel Parti," *New York Times Magazine*, December 9, 1959, pp. 17, 42, 44, 47. © 1959 by The New York Times Company. Reprinted by permission.

---

animals—such as the bat, which navigates by using a built-in radar system—have developed unusual physical traits. These traits are called *adaptive* because they make it possible for the animal to adjust well to its own particular environment.

The human species is able to adapt to many environments. Some of humanity's adaptive traits are physical, such as upright posture and good hand-and-eye coordination. Other traits are mental and communicative—a large, complex brain and organs of speech. A final group of human adaptive traits derives from the preceding groups of traits; it consists of the ability to make tools and to work cooperatively with other people—all parts of the culture-building capacity.

Many human traits do not seem at first to be useful for survival. A long period of pregnancy, a long period of helplessness for the infant, the lack of thick body hair or fur, the lack of claws, and the lack of instinctive behavior patterns would seem to make human survival in prehistoric times difficult, if not impossible. These very traits, however, turned out to be beneficial. They made the development of society necessary, since people had to depend upon each other for survival and to learn rather than trust to instinct. Also, because human beings have a continuing

sexual capacity and an affectionate nature and because of their need for mutual cooperation, care, and protection, our ancestors became highly social. Mothers and infants were protected; huts, fires, and animal skins were used to compensate for lack of fur; and the development of tools and weapons more than made up for the lack of claws. In addition, the development of language made it possible to pass skills and knowledge from parents to children. As time passed, the patterns of life called *cultures* grew more complex and became ways of adapting to a wide variety of environments.

Figure 3-1 Marriage customs differ with the culture. (*a*) In India, marriages are usually arranged by families. (*b*) In the United States, most men and women have the freedom and the responsibility to find their own spouses. [(*a*) *Marilyn Silverstone, Magnum,* (*b*) *Mimi Forsyth, Magnum*]

(a)

(b)

65

FROM ADAPTATION TO LIMITED CONTROL

Clothing and shelter came into use during the last hundred thousand years. Consequently, when the last great period of the Ice Age came, people remained in Europe rather than retreating, as they had done in earlier periods, since their steadily accumulating culture gave them the means to survive (Bordes, 1961, pp. 803–810). Eventually, humans began to use animals to aid them in adapting to their environment, to build shelters, and to farm.

Today humans use culture not only to adapt to their environment but also to alter it. In Pakistan, northern China, and the western United States, for example, huge dams harness rivers, making water available for farming land that was once too dry for agriculture. We have built giant pipelines to carry oil from wilderness areas like Alaska and the Arabian desert to more heavily populated areas. Geodesic domes and scientific laboratories now appear in the frozen Arctic, and scientists dream of building research centers on the moon and even of controlling the weather.

However, while we have made great progress in controlling the environment, we have come to realize that the environment continues to set certain limits on cultural possibilities. Practices that pollute the environment, wear out the soil, or exhaust raw materials or sources of energy before substitutes can be found remind us that the geographic environment must be taken into consideration. As in earlier times, nature continues to limit cultural possibilities.

CULTURE AND GEOGRAPHY

People have always tried to explain differences between cultures, but because every society tends to view its own culture as superior (an attitude called *ethnocentrism*), such explanations have generally been biased. Differences in climate or geography became a popular way of explaining cultural differences in early societies, and the explanations reflect the society's ethnocentrism. The ancient Greeks believed that the barbarians who lived to the north of them were brave and vigorous, but that their cold environment kept them mentally dull. The North Africans, on the other hand, were held to be clever and shrewd but lacking in energy because of their hot climate. According to this self-serving view, only people who lived in moderate climates—like that of Greece—could build superior civilizations.

Ellsworth Huntington (1876–1947) was a more recent advocate of climatic explanations for cultural differences. Huntington proposed that a relatively cool climate was vital to creative energy and that the people of northern Europe and the northern United States had developed a superior culture because of their cool climate (1959). He ignored the fact that important civilizations have developed in some of the very warm climates of the world—in Egypt, India, and Pakistan; in Mesopotamia, Cambodia, and Indonesia; in Peru, Mexico, and Guatemala; and in the kingdoms of the Ashanti and Hausa in West Africa.

When people had to live by hunting, fishing, and gathering grains and herbs, climate influenced culture far more strongly than it does today. Even then, however, very different cultures arose in nearby areas. The Pueblo Indians of Arizona and New Mexico learned to build adobe houses and to plant crops in an area that other tribes could use only for hunting and raiding. These neighboring agricultural and hunting tribes developed different patterns of culture, including gods, philosophies, family systems, and forms of tribal organization. Modern industrial nations display many cultural differences even though they have similar environments. For example, the island nations of Great Britain and Japan share many geographic and climatic similarities, but they differ greatly in such cultural traits as art, literature, music, and philosophy; in religion; in styles of emotional expression; and in the organization of family systems. Clearly then, geography can influence the course of a culture. However, sociologists reject the idea of *geographic determinism*, or the theory that the course of a culture is *determined* by geography.

As societies around the world become modernized, the ways in which the natural environment is used change, and culture becomes less limited by geography. In many developing countries, the changes first come about in the economy and then gradually in other parts of the culture. In many places, the traditional culture coexists with a more modern culture, showing that a great deal of cultural diversity is possible in the same geographic setting.

CULTURAL DYNAMICS

The term *cultural dynamics* refers to cultural change and the reasons for and results of change. Cultures change over a period of time, partly through individual variation. Since people are all slightly different from each other, they add their own personal variations to the cultural patterns they have learned, rearing their children and carrying out other tasks in different ways. In addition, some individuals are inventive, helping to bring new ideas to a culture in art, music, poetry, science, and other fields.

There are also other factors that work almost independently of the individual to create cultural change. George P. Murdock describes the major sources of change as "increases or decreases in population, changes in the geographical environment, migrations into new environments, contact with people of differing culture, natural and social catastrophes such as floods, crop failures, epidemics, wars, and economic depressions, accidental discoveries and inventions . . ." (1971, pp. 319–332).

The first of Murdock's sources of cultural change, "increases or decreases in population," is part of the study of population (called *demography*), which will be discussed in a later chapter. We should note, however, that in the past, population increases resulted either in starvation, emigration, or major changes in life-styles. Hunting people could support larger populations only if they gave up their wandering, hunting life-style and adopted a simple form of agriculture. Today, environmentalists are aware that excessive population growth can lead to shortages of food and natural resources and also to increased pollution. Such factors can have a profound effect upon cultures.

In the highlands of eastern Africa, for example, overpopulation has led to shortages of land for grazing cattle, so that pastoral people have had to abandon their old ways of life and look for new jobs in the cities. In the United States, the population is not crowded compared with many countries. But we are beginning to wonder whether such a population can be supported in its accustomed style. Shortages of heating fuel have led to more careful regulation of thermostats; gasoline shortages often cause a reduction in driving; and water shortages in the Southwest have led to water rationing for homes and drastic reductions in cattle and crop production.

Changes in geographic environment which influence culture include major climatic changes—such as ice ages. They also include less far-ranging but equally disruptive changes in weather patterns such as too much rain (which causes floods) or too little rain (which causes droughts). The Indians who built the great cliff dwellings of Mesa Verde in Colorado were apparently the victims of a long drought that wiped out their civilization and forced them to migrate. Droughts in parts of Africa in the 1970s have forced many of the camel-herding Tuareg of the Sahara and the cattle-herding Masai of Kenya to abandon their nomadic life-styles and become farmers.

MIGRATION AND CULTURAL CHANGE

Acculturation is the process by which people from different cultures borrow each other's cultural traits. When Latin Americans become interested in baseball or Anglo-Americans learn to enjoy bullfighting, they are experiencing acculturation. When people migrate from one country to another, acculturation always occurs; the cultures of both the immigrants and the residents of their new home become modified and changed.

In the history of the United States, immigrants learned to adjust to a new culture with its regional variations. Those who settled in the South, in the seventeenth and eighteenth centuries, generally looked upon the plantation and slave system as a necessity. The larger numbers who migrated westward adopted the values of the frontier, including a zest for frontier fighting and a fascination with rifles. In parts of Latin America where Indian populations remained large, a blend of Spanish and Indian cultures occurred. Spanish culture dominated, but Indian village life, Indian products such as corn and potatoes, and Indian foods, pottery, medicinal herbs, art designs, and even legendary heroes became part of the new culture.

Many immigrants to the United States who had originally resolved to keep their traditional culture pure have found that this was impossible. The Greeks, Chinese, Japanese, and many others have built special schools so that their children could learn the traditional language and culture. However, the original culture inevitably becomes mixed with the general American culture. A process of acculturation to the new environment goes on as new cultural traits are adopted and old ones are gradually modified or dropped. Stanley F. M. Fong (1965, pp. 265–273) describes the process among Chinese-Americans, whose pattern of living in close-knit communities has slowed the acculturation process. Despite efforts to resist acculturation, subtle changes do occur. Fong has discovered that Chinese-American children have adopted new

Figure 3-2   The popularity of (*a*) meditation in the United States and (*b*) motorcycles in Nigeria are examples of cultural diffusion. [(*a*) *Ray Ellis Photo Researchers, Inc.;* (*b*) *George Gerster/Rapho/ Photo Reasearchers, Inc.*

(a)

(b)

ways of expressing their emotions and interpreting the expressions and gestures of others. Traditionally, Chinese girls are warned, "Do not show your unhappiness easily and do not smile easily, and do not let your teeth be seen when you smile" (Fong, 1965, p. 266). Children who are taught to be emotionally restrained have trouble understanding the American language of mannerisms, gestures, and facial expressions. The final changeover to the new culture is symbolized by an understanding and adoption of American ways in expressing emotions, using popular slang, far less formality in boy-girl relationships, more use of first names, and "Mom" and "Dad" rather than "revered parents." This process is not the result of imitation; it is "an inner transformation" to suit the new cultural environment. Eventually, the American-born Chinese find it difficult to relate to the new immigrants from Hong Kong, whom some describe as being too "Chinafied" or too "Chinese."

Cultural diffusion = diffusion in this book

The process by which cultural traits are transmitted from one culture to another is called *cultural diffusion*. Cultural diffusion is usually a two-way process. Early white settlers learned from the native Americans how to grow tobacco and corn and potatoes, and the Indians borrowed horses, rifles, and whiskey from the whites. Even the most inventive cultures have gained more by cultural diffusion than from their own inventions.

Many sociologists and anthropologists refer to the smallest details of a culture as *traits*, such as eating corn, tobacco, a dance step, or even a particular word. An interrelated set of such cultural traits is called a *cultural complex*. For example, when the Indians borrowed horses and rifles, they developed a new hunting and warfare complex based upon them, with new rules and regulations, new leadership (hunting chiefs and war chiefs), and a system of prestige and wealth depending upon horses. In the general American

culture, a football is a trait, while all the things that go with football games—including bands, cheerleaders, and stadiums—make up a cultural complex. Cultural diffusion usually consists of borrowing cultural traits, which are often integrated into a new type of cultural complex.

In scientific and technological fields, cultural diffusion is often intentional and planned. Scientific researchers in many countries keep in touch with each other's work through professional journals, personal meetings, and international conferences. Sometimes they coordinate their research, and their findings—especially in medicine and biology—are shared. If, for example, researchers in the United States, France, England, the Soviet Union, or Germany should develop an effective cure for cancer, they would share their knowledge immediately. Cultures are always ready to borrow useful ideas and inventions from each other. Use of the bow and arrow spread over the entire world in prehistoric times, and Indians of the Great Plains quickly adopted horses and rifles, introduced by European settlers. In modern times cultural diffusion has become very common. Automobiles and airplanes, birth-control pills, cooling and heating systems, Coca-Cola, blue jeans, "Mac burgers," and Kentucky fried chicken can be found throughout the world.

Ordinarily there is more resistance to the diffusion of ideas than to the diffusion of material goods. The sociologist Paul Cressey (1945, pp. 595–604) lists hundreds of items borrowed by Westerners from China over the centuries, including silk, peach and apricot trees, orange and lemon trees, tea, playing cards, dominoes, kites, lacquer ware, sedan chairs, goldfish, azaleas, chrysanthemums, tree peonies, camelias, papier-mâché, the burning of coal, firecrackers, the magnetic compass, grapefruits, soybeans, Chinese elms, and Chinese cabbage. In spite of all these material borrowings, the wisdom of Chinese philosophers such as Confucius, Mencius, and Lao Tzu was ignored until the eighteenth century, when a number of European intellectuals became discontented with their own social systems.

In many cases, foreign ideas and ideologies have spread only among the alienated or dissatisfied members of a culture. People who are well off in a capitalist system are unlikely to become interested in foreign ideologies such as communism. In India, upper-caste people were much harder to convert to Christianity than were the untouchables, who had nothing to lose. High-caste Hindus would have had to give up the Hindu myths that "proved" their own superiority. Two principles regarding the diffusion of ideas are evident. First, ideas spread when they are compatible with the ideology of the receiving culture, as with the spread of a new discovery or theory from one scientific culture to another. Second, incompatible ideas may spread to a receiving culture, but mainly among the discontented. If we think of the current vogue in America for the religions of Asia (variations of Hinduism, Buddhism, or Sikkhism, for example), we can see that they spread among those who are somehow discontented with their traditional religion and are seeking new answers.

Cultural diffusion of material goods and behaviors influences us constantly. The anthropologist Ralph Linton shows how the life-style of a "solid American citizen" depends on inventions borrowed from many civilizations—ancient and modern—in the insert on page 72.

Discovery and invention

Ever since the Old Stone Age, people have gradually improved their tools and weapons and discovered new sources of food, shelter, and protection. *Discovery* consists of finding new objects or ideas or of finding new uses for those already in use. *Invention* consists of combining objects or ideas in new ways. Someone who learns that a particular herb can cure a stomach ache has made a discovery; someone who mixes the juices of several herbs to make a new medicine has become an inventor. Inventions can be material, such as tools and appliances, or nonmaterial, such as new or better ways of doing things. The social security system, for example, is an invention because it provides a way of financing the support of people who are unable to work.

The amount and type of cultural inventiveness depend partly on cultural values and partly on what is called the *cultural base*. The *cultural base* is the state of development of a culture at the time under consideration. Bali has a large cultural base in art and drama. The United States has a very large cultural base in technology. If a culture places a high value on dance, drama, and art, it may invent many new dances, plays, and other artistic expressions, as in the case of the culture of Bali. But it would not develop any of the mechanical devices that Americans generally associate with the term "invention." Cultures tend to invent in proportion to their present cultural base. This is especially true of mechanical inventions, since one invention paves the way for another. Automatic transmissions and power steering, for example, followed the invention of the automobile.

In the past, most discoveries and inventions were probably accidental. Today, however, discoveries and inventions are promoted largely by governments and corporations to meet new societal demands. Scientists are hired and told precisely what type of weapon, computer, antipollution device, or insecticide to develop.

Catastrophes

Catastrophic events, both military and economic, have always been sources of cultural change. When the Roman Empire was taken over, through a series of invasions, by tribes that were less advanced, it seemed that Western civilization had been lost. But after a period of 400 years, a new feudal society grew up. The catastrophic Great Depression created drastic changes in American culture, including an expansion of the role of government, the beginnings of the

Figure 3-3 The nuclear age has brought many cultural changes, including a new vocabulary and a stress on technology. (*NASA*)

social security system, and a decline in the American belief that an individual can control his or her financial future. In the late 1960s, the war

in Vietnam spelled ruin for President Lyndon B. Johnson's social welfare programs and caused a decline in the belief that the United States should take on the task of supervising the entire world.

Catastrophic wars have shattered empires and caused the fall of one major power and the rise of another. International tensions also change cultural patterns by forcing governments to concentrate on the production of military equipment, often at the expense of consumer goods and social services.

LANGUAGE AND CULTURE

Despite the strongly discriminatory policy of *apartheid* (racial separation) practiced in South Africa, decades passed without serious rioting. Then, in June 1976, as noted in Chapter 1, Johannesburg and other South African cities were torn by riots. Years of resentment, combined with increasing hope for change, undoubtedly supplied the background for these riots, but the immediate issue was language. Black African students rioted over the requirement that they should learn Afrikaans, the language of the ruling white South Africans of Dutch descent. These students did not want to learn the language of the people who oppressed them, but their anger also had deeper sources than a dislike of Afrikaans. Because language and culture are so closely connected, these students saw an attack on their native languages as an attack against their entire culture.

Language is the means by which culture is shared and transmitted; most of our learning takes place through language. Language reflects the special interests of a culture and varies as the culture changes. Complex vocabularies develop to express the special interests and needs of a culture. The Eskimos have many words for *snow*, whereas we have only a few; and the Arabs are said to have a thousand words for *sword*. The head-shrinking Jivaro of the eastern slope of the Andes in Peru, who are constantly concerned with the spirit world, have many different words

Culture and diversity

From "The study of man"   RALPH LINTON

Our solid American citizen awakens in a bed built on a pattern which originated in the Near East but which was modified in Northern Europe before it was transmitted to America. He throws back covers made from cotton, domesticated in India, or linen, domesticated in the Near East, or wool from sheep, also domesticated in the Near East, or silk, the use of which was discovered in China. All of these materials have been spun and woven by processes invented in the Near East. He slips into his moccasins, invented by the Indians of the Eastern woodlands, and goes to the bathroom, whose fixtures are a mixture of European and American inventions, both of recent date. He takes off his pajamas, a garment invented in India, and washes with soap invented by the ancient Gauls. He then shaves, a masochistic rite which seems to have derived either from Sumer or ancient Egypt.

Returning to the bedroom, he removes his clothes from a chair of southern European type and proceeds to dress. He puts on garmets whose form originally derived from the skin clothing of the nomads of the Asiatic steppes, puts on shoes made from skins tanned by a process invented in ancient Egypt and cut to a pattern derived from the classical civilizations of the Mediterranean, and ties around his neck a strip of bright-colored cloth which is a vestigial survival of the shoulder shawls worn by the seventeenth-century Croatians. Before going out for breakfast he glances through the window, made of glass invented in Egypt, and if it is raining puts on overshoes made of rubber discovered by the Central American Indians and takes an umbrella, invented in southeastern Asia. Upon his head he puts a hat made of felt, a material invented in the Asiatic steppes.

On his way to breakfast he stops to buy a paper, paying for it with coins, an ancient Lydian invention. At the restaurant a whole new series of borrowed elements confronts him. His plate is made of a form of pottery invented in China. His knife is of steel, an alloy first made in southern India, his fork a medieval Italian invention, and his spoon a derivative of a Roman original. He begins breakfast with an orange, from the eastern Mediterranean, a cantaloupe from Persia, or perhaps a piece of African watermelon. With this he has coffee, an Abyssinian plant, with cream and sugar. Both the domestication of cows and the idea of milking them originated in the Near East, while sugar was first made in India. After his fruit and first coffee he goes on to waffles, cakes made by a Scandinavian technique from wheat domesticated in Asia Minor. Over these he pours maple syrup, invented by the Indians of the Eastern woodlands. As a side dish he may have the egg of a species of bird domesticated in Indo-China, or thin strips of the flesh of an animal domesticated in Eastern Asia which have been salted and smoked by a process developed in northern Europe.

When our friend has finished eating he settles back to smoke, an American Indian habit, consuming a plant domesticated in Brazil in either a pipe, derived from the Indians of Virginia, or a cigarette, derived from Mexico. If he is hardy enough he may even attempt a cigar, transmitted to us from the Antilles by way of Spain. While smoking he reads the news of the day, imprinted in characters invented by the ancient Semites upon a material invented in China by a process invented in Germany. As he absorbs the accounts of foreign troubles he will, if he is a good conservative citizen, thank a Hebrew deity in an Indo-European language that he is 100 per cent American.

Ralph Linton, *The Study of Man: An Introduction* © 1936 and renewed in 1964, pp. 326 and 327. Reprinted by permission of Prentice-Hall, Inc., Englewood Cliffs, New Jersey.

to describe different types of souls. In the United States, we have developed specialized and elaborate vocabularies to talk about such subjects as sports, cars, and television programs.

Language and thought

A dispute has raged for years over whether language actually helps to shape the thought patterns of a culture. Benjamin Lee Whorf (1956), who studied the Hopi and other desert Indian tribes of the Southwest, was the first to suggest the idea. He concluded that language causes people to conceptualize nature and the world in different ways. The Hopi and Navajo languages differ from European languages in the way they express the relationships between human beings and nature. The Indian languages depict people as pawns in the hands of nature, whereas most European languages depict people as active and nature as passive. For example, in English, we would say, "John is drowning." In Navajo, the same statement would translate as, "Water is overcoming John." In English, the person, "John," is the subject of the sentence— the phrasing portrays drowning as an activity performed by John. In the Navajo language, John is seen as the victim of active natural forces. In Whorf's opinion, a general tendency to see nature as active or passive can make a considerable difference in a culture.

To see nature as passive is to imply that people can master nature, at least to a great degree. This has been the usual attitude of European and general American culture, according to Whorf (1956). Languages that express a passive relationship between person and nature, as in the Navajo example above, are more likely to see human beings as destined to live in subservience to nature. This viewpoint is constantly expressed in Navajo religion as well as in the religions of the Southwestern Pueblo Indians.

Differences in language, according to Whorf, also create differences in attitudes toward time.

The Hopi language is not time-centered in the way ours is and lacks tenses for expressing past perfect, past, present perfect, and future. Past events are "remembered" events; those of the future are "anticipated" events.

Some opponents of Whorf's hypothesis think that thought patterns influence language, rather than the reverse. Others contend that if there is a relationship between language and thought patterns, it is very slight. They point out that since the ideas expressed in one language can be translated into another, thought patterns must not be too rigidly bound to one particular language. Whorf's supporters, however, could reply that meanings are often distorted or entirely lost in translation. (For an example of this, see the insert on page 74: "The Great Boss Is My Shepherd.") Opponents note that people with very similar cultures have extremely different languages and even that people with the same languages have very different cultures. Residents of France and Haiti share the same languages but exhibit very different cultures, with French culture more active toward nature and more time-oriented than Haiti's. Whatever the powers of language, grafting a new language onto a culture does not make that culture the same as the culture in which the language developed. The supporters of Whorf demonstrate a number of points to support their side: Languages with rich color vocabularies, for example, seem to make people more sensitive to subtle variations in color hues and values.

Hajime Nakamura has shown how language affects philosophy and religion by tracing changes in Buddhism as it moved from India, its land of origin, to China (1968). The Indian version of Buddhism is characterized by abstract ideas, renunciation of material values, and the seeking of altered states of consciousness. Nakamura believes that the languages of India could have influenced Buddhism in this way, since they concentrate on broad, abstract terms. Negative statements are also very common in Hindu languages; morality becomes the denial of ordi-

Culture and diversity

73

The great boss is my shepherd LOWELL D. HOLMES

Although it is possible to translate from one language to another, ideas and imagery often change greatly in translation. An interesting example is the following interpretation of the Twenty-Third Psalm by a Khmus of Laos, as reported by a missionary:

The Great Boss is the one who takes care of my sheep;
I don't want to own anything.
The Great Boss wants me to lie down in the field.
He wants me to go to the lake.
He makes my good spirit come back.
Even though I walk through something the missionary calls the valley of the shadow
   of death, I do not care.
You are with me.
You use a stick and a club to make me comfortable.
You manufacture a piece of furniture right in front of my eyes while my enemies
   watch.
You pour grease on my head.
My cup has too much water in it and therefore overflows.
Goodness and kindness will walk single file behind me all my life
And I shall dwell in the hut of the Great Boss until I die and am forgotten by my
   tribe.

Such a translation leads to the question of whether our interpretations of the wisdom of the East are not equally faulty.

From Lowell D. Holmes, *Anthropology: An Introduction*, The Ronald Press Company, New York, © 1965, p. 236.

nary desires for such things as wealth, luxury, and pleasures of the flesh. The Chinese language, in contrast, emphasizes the positive, saying more about what to do than what to avoid and showing less aversion to earthly pleasures. Consequently, when Buddhism spread to China, it lost much of its abstract nature and became, among the educated, a religion of rules for harmonious living. Among the peasants, it became a religion of ancient spells and charms, which Buddhism in India had rejected.

George Leonard points out that our own language and thought patterns have characteristics which make it difficult for us to understand some of the thinking of Asia (1974). Acupuncture, which we cannot explain at all, is clearly explained in Chinese terms of opposite but equal forces called yin and yang and conditions of body and spirit. Leonard tells of an American woman who had a mystical experience, suddenly becoming aware that in some sense "We are all one." On the advice of her relatives, she went to a psychiatric hospital for treatment. In India her experience would be viewed positively, as the first step in a process of religious enlightenment. We have very few terms to describe altered states of consciousness, and the terms we do have are negative ones. The psychologist would say that this woman was having a "hallucination"; in slang terms, she would be "spaced out." In India, terms used to describe her experience would include *enlightenment, realization,* and *purification.*

In discussing the relationship between language and thought patterns, how do we tell cause from effect—that is, decide whether language is an independent or a dependent variable? The important question becomes: "Does language shape people's thought patterns, or do their special interests and viewpoints cause them to develop particular types of languages?" As we have seen, different researchers have taken different positions on this issue.

Besides written and spoken languages, there are languages of gesture and other types of nonverbal communication. Styles in nonverbal communication express cultural attitudes (see the insert "Languages of Time, Space, and Bodily Movement") and probably also help to shape people's thinking. For example, in a society in which gestures and motions are slow and graceful, one would expect a leisurely life-style to be valued.

CULTURE AS A NORMATIVE SYSTEM

Techniques for survival, inventions, and communications systems are necessary parts of culture, but they do not make up all of culture. Cultures also include normative systems, which in modern societies are very complex.

Languages of time, space, and bodily movement

EDWARD T. HALL AND ELIZABETH HALL

In his books The Silent Language *and* The Hidden Dimension, *Edward T. Hall has noted that the communication systems of cultures include ideas about time and space as well as eye and body movements. The Latin American business person does not mean to be impolite in keeping a client waiting; in the "language" of Latin Americans, being too prompt would seem pushy. Arabs have a very different sense of space from Americans, and even within the United States there are differences in other types of language, such as eye contact. These differences are illustrated in the following excerpts from a conversation between Edward Hall and a writer for* Psychology Today.

PT: You said earlier that each culture also has its own way of dividing up space.

Hall: With space, of course, one has to mentally shift gears. Space is a communication system, and it's one of the reasons that many North Europeans and Americans don't like the Middle East. Arabs tend to get very close and breathe on you. It's part of the high sensory involvement in a high-context culture. If an Arab does not breathe on you, it means that he is consciously withholding his breath and is ashamed.

PT: For the Arabs, then, this part of culture doesn't operate outside awareness.

Hall: For us, much of it does—for the Arabs it's different. They say, "Why are the Americans so ashamed? They withhold their breath." The American on the receiving end can't identify all the sources of his discomfort but feels that the Arab is pushy. The Arab comes close; the American backs up. The Arab follows, because he can only interact at certain distances. Once the American learns that Arabs handle space differently and that breathing on people is a form of communication, the situation can sometimes be redefined so the American relaxes.

PT: In *The Hidden Dimension*, you wrote that each of us carries a little bubble of space around with us and that the space under our feet belongs to us. [*Continued on page 76.*]

[*Continued on page 76.*]

Culture and diversity

Hall: Again, the things that we take for granted can trip us up and cause untold discomfort and frequently anger. In the Arab world, you do not hold a lien on the ground under foot. When standing on a street corner, an Arab may shove you aside if he wants to be where you are. This puts the average territorial American or German under great stress.

[*Later, the conversation turns to cultural differences within the United States.*]

PT: What about the feeling many black people have that they are "invisible men"?

Hall: That's another cultural difference. Depending upon the part of the country he's from, a white on the street looks at a person until he's about 12 to 16 feet away. Then, unless they know each other, whites automatically look away to avoid eye contact. This automatic avoidance on our part seems to give blacks the feeling of invisibility, because they use their eyes very differently than whites. . . . They're more involved with each other visually and in every other way. . . .

Blacks also pay more attention than we do to nonverbal behavior. I once ran an experiment in which one black man filmed another in a job interview. Each time something significant happened, the watcher started the camera. When I looked on those films, I couldn't believe my eyes. Nothing was happening! Or so I thought. It turned out that my camera operator was catching—and identifying—body signals as minor as the movement of a thumb, which foreshadowed an intention to speak. Whites aren't so finely tuned.

From "How Cultures Collide," Edward T. Hall and Elizabeth Hall in *Psychology Today*, July 1976, pp. 66, 68–74, 97. Reprinted by permission of *Psychology Today* Magazine. Copyright © 1976 Ziff-Davis Publishing Company.

Norms: Statistical and moral

The term *norm* has more than one meaning. Sometimes it refers to a type of statistical average, what "everyone does," and at other times to rules of right and wrong. In sociology, the second meaning is used more often, but the first meaning cannot be ignored. For example, at a social club it might be the norm to drink heavily at every party, but none of the members would argue that heavy drinking is a sign of virtue. In this case, the norm is the usual, or expected, behavior in a particular context. Used in the second sense, norms are connected with beliefs and values; they have a moral meaning.

Norms concerning murder provide a good example of how complex and variable moral norms can be. Although different societies do not always agree on what legally constitutes murder, they all have some type of moral norm against random killing. Murder is considered a very serious crime in the United States and is severely punished. In wartime, however, an American soldier can be imprisoned for *not* killing. At still other times, society seems to turn away when murders are committed. Until the 1950s, for example, it was almost impossible to convict a white person of killing a black person in many states, regardless of the evidence. Murder was not exactly approved, but racist whites considered it safer to ignore the murder of blacks than to risk their belief in white supremacy—an idea that had become a moral norm for them.

Norms prohibiting stealing are fairly universal except among certain societies where there are few goods to steal or where hiding stolen property is difficult. In the United States, stealing goes against the moral norms and is strongly condemned. Yet, as we observed in our earlier discussion of *Tally's Corner*, a certain amount of petty stealing was expected among members of the street-corner society, and employers paid low salaries partly because they thought their workers would steal from then anyway. Norms against stealing in our society are not always consistent. Mugging, pickpocketing, and burglary, are more strongly condemned than graft, embezzlement, or bribery perpetrated by "white-collar" criminals.

Sometimes people respond to norms by consistently breaking them. Perhaps all the members of the fraternity that consumes cases of beer would agree with the observation, "We drink too much"; but the member who fails to join in the nightly drinking ritual is, nevertheless, condemned as a "wet blanket." In this case, the moral norm is moderate drinking, but the actual heavy drinking is a *norm of evasion*. A norm of evasion can be defined as a custom or type of behavior that is widely accepted even though it defies the stated moral norms of the society.

Another way to describe the contrast between moral norms and reality is to call the stated social norms *idealized norms* and the actual behavior followed *real norms*. Idealized norms are similar to rules one might list in New Year's resolutions: Be good, kind, considerate, work harder, and avoid smoking and drinking. Real norms are more like the behavior we return to shortly after New Year's Day.

Despite their complexity and contradictions, norms are obviously necessary for the functioning of a culture, and a culture can be described to a large extent in terms of the norms it holds.

Norms of protection and reciprocity

Many social norms have a protective function. Norms against murder and theft, for example, function to protect the community from these crimes. In simple hunting-and-gathering societies, norms of reciprocity have the same function. Members of the tribe must share food with one another when they have food; otherwise some members of the tribe may die of starvation. In our society, many of the rules of give and take

function to make social life more pleasant. We smile, for example, when someone smiles at us, we return a greeting, and we give presents to people who have given them to us. We also have protective norms similar to the food-sharing norms of the primitives. People are expected to give to charity; both government and private organizations send aid to disaster areas; and welfare measures are designed to protect the poor. However, even these protective norms may become controversial. In a large, impersonal society like ours, people seldom see the recipients of their aid, and they tend to resent welfare and other public assistance programs paid for by their taxes. The norms of charity and reciprocity are often challenged by those of self-interest.

Sexual norms

Almost all cultures try to regulate the sexual behavior of their members to some degree. In Victorian times, England and the United States held extremely rigid norms about sexual behavior, although these norms were frequently broken. Today, our cultural norms relating to sexual behavior are quite different. The message we receive from popular novels, movies, and manuals on sexual techniques seems to be that more and freer sex leads to health and happiness. The traditional cultural norms against homosexual, premarital, and extramarital sexual activities are considered to be obsolete and even harmful. Other societies, past and present, have held very different norms regarding sex. Hoebel (1960, p. 84), for example, tells us that the Cheyenne Indians were very restrained sexually. A man who fathered a son feared that he might weaken his son's spirit by having sexual relations with the mother during the first two years of the boy's life. One of Hoebel's informants, a respected and prestigious Cheyenne leader, had carefully observed the rule. Differing levels of knowledge influence norms. Since no medical evidence would support the Cheyenne viewpoint, it seems strange to us. For us, science can change sexual norms. The American "sexual revolution" occurred only after knowledge of the birth-control pill and other effective methods of contraception became widespread.

Norms and the spirits

All cultures have practical norms which regulate behavior and keep society running relatively smoothly. In addition, they have spiritual norms which refer to religious, philosophical, ethical, or even superstitious beliefs.

Some spiritual beliefs contain explicit rules. The religious doctrines of Christians, Jews, and Moslems, for example, call for charity, peace, and other forms of ethical behavior. Other spiritual beliefs are more subtle and hardly noticed by members of the culture. For example, many Indian tribes avoid finishing their artwork. They do not complete or perfect a pattern in a woven blanket because completion or perfection would imply the end of life. The idea of destiny is important to many peoples. Members of American Indian tribes believed that great leaders were informed of their future greatness by the spirits they met during their *vision quests*—lonely journeys in search of spiritual guidance undertaken in their youth.

In most cultures, certain foods are sanctified or considered to be very special. Unleavened bread and wine in Christian ceremonies, corn or the sacred peyote among American Indians, rice in Bali, and bear meat among the ancient Lapps and Ainu have all been considered spiritual objects and treated with great respect.

Sacred and dreaded numbers are prominent in nearly all cultures. In America many apartment buildings and hotels do not have floors with the number 13 because people would consider it bad luck to live on the thirteenth floor. When playing games or betting, people often select "magic" numbers: three, four, and seven are the most common. According to Alan Dundes (see the insert opposite), in America

our sacred number is three. As these examples show, beliefs of a spiritual or supernatural nature pervade all cultures, including our own, although they are often unconscious or are even denied.

Values

Whereas norms are rules for behavior, *values* are attitudes and standards of judgment about what things are important, desirable, and right. For example, popular American values stress individual freedom, the sanctity of life, and the importance of personal honesty. Although we usually assume that normative rules come from the values people hold, the opposite relationship between values and norms may hold true. Judith Blake and Kingsley Davis (1964) show that values can be interpreted as the reasons we give ourselves for following the rules. As children, we may be punished for lying and rewarded for telling the truth. If so, we will probably not tell lies very often. To explain why we do not lie, however, especially as we begin to mature, we will not say "for fear of being punished." Instead, we will say that we believe in (place a high value on) honesty. Obviously, a society will run much more smoothly if people believe in its social norms and if they can speak about the values that justify the norms by which they live.

Whether norms are the result of values people hold or whether, as Blake and Davis argue, values arise from norms, contradictions occur in the feelings people have about both norms and values. To return to a previous example, the failure to punish a white person for killing a black would violate a norm (murder is forbidden) and also a value (the sanctity of human life) which explains the norm. But to find a white person guilty of murdering a black would violate another norm (blacks must be kept "in their place") and a value (white supremacy) which accounts for the norm.

Cases of *normative inconsistency*, situations in which two conflicting norms or values are both

Magic in American culture: The number three ALAN DUNDES

Alan Dundes notes that several people have written about the general tendency for American Indians to repeat the number four in their artwork and in their stories, although a few use the number five. Several ancient civilizations in the Near East and India centered their stories and their mythologies on patterns of three. Do we also have a sacred or magical number? It is implicit in our culture, says Dundes, that the number three is a good luck sign, a religious symbol, and an integral part of our thinking, but one we have never noticed because it is too obvious. The following are some of his examples, of which he presents hundreds:

In American folksongs there are numerous examples of trebling, and it is doubtful whether many singers are fully conscious of it. For example, in many songs the verse consists of a line that is repeated three times before being followed by a final line. Typical examples include "John Brown's body lies a moulderin' in the grave . . . but his soul goes marching on"; "John Brown had a little Indian . . . one little Indian boy"; "Polly put the kettle on . . . we'll all have tea"; "Go tell Aunt Nancy . . . her old grey goose is dead"; "Lost my partner, wha'll I do? . . . skip to my Lou, my darlin'"; . . . "Joshua fit the battle of Jericho, Jericho, Jericho. . . ." [Several more are given.]

Folk expressions are also organized into patterns of three: beg, borrow, or steal; bell, book, and candle; blood, sweat, and tears; cool, calm, and collected; hither, thither, and yon; hook, line, and sinker; hop, skip, and jump; lock, stock, and barrel; me, myself, and I; ready, willing, and able; signed, sealed, and delivered; tall, dark, and handsome; Tom, Dick, and Harry; and wine, women, and song. . . .

The occurrence of three-symbolism in American religion is almost too obvious to require mention. Christian examples include the three Magi, Satan's three temptations of Christ, Peter's three denials of Christ, the three crucifixions at Calvary, the three Marys, the three nails, the three days intervening between burial and resurrection, and Christ's age of thirty-three [as well as the Holy Trinity].

From this point, Dundes goes on to show how the principle of three structures our thinking: Government must have three branches; history is divided into ancient, medieval, and modern periods; and everyone must have three square meals a day. Dundes concludes: "Trichotomy exists but it is not part of the nature of nature. It is part of the nature of culture. At this point, if anyone is skeptical about there being a three-pattern in American culture, let him give at least three good reasons why."

From Alan Dundes, "The Number Three in American Culture," in Alan Dundes (ed.), *Every Man His Way: Readings in Cultural Anthropology*, © 1968, pp. 401–424. Reprinted by permission of Prentice-Hall, Inc., Englewood Cliffs, New Jersey.

held, are fairly common. As a general rule, when norms compete, people are inclined to follow the norm that best serves their own interests. Up to the 1950s, it seemed to be in the interest of Southern whites to maintain white supremacy at all costs. Now, federal laws and changing attitudes make many kinds of gross discrimination illegal and difficult to practice. Today, in legal proceedings, the norm of equal justice is likely to outweigh the desire to uphold the belief in white supremacy.

As another example of normative inconsisten-

Figure 3-4 The belief in technology and progress has sometimes led to environmental damage. The aerosols in these household items can weaken the ozone layer of the atmosphere, which screens out harmful ultraviolet radiation from the sun. (*Martha McMillan Robers, Photo Researchers, Inc.*)

cy, consider the use of marijuana. Most states have laws making it a felony; other states consider it a misdemeanor—a less serious type of crime. *Laws* are more formalized rules than norms and always carry the threat of enforcement, which norms do not necessarily do. In the case of marijuana, laws and norms have been in agreement until recently. The reasoning supporting the norms is: "The state has the duty of protecting people against their own bad habits and possible dangers from the bad habits of others." However, recent research suggests that marijuana may be no more harmful than alcohol. Yet alcohol is legal, while the use of marijuana remains illegal in most states. The reason given for the use of alcohol is our belief in freedom of choice: People should have the right to decide for themselves whether to drink something that might be dangerous. Obviously, our belief that society should protect people from themselves conflicts with our belief in freedom of choice.

Perhaps logical legal arguments will bring about more reasonable laws concerning marijuana and alcohol. Alternatively, the use of marijuana may become as common as the use of alcohol, and laws will change as social customs change. Often changes in norms emerge from the struggles of organized social groups or from major changes in social conditions. We will discuss some of these changes in norms in later chapters dealing with the problems of racial, ethnic, and sexual equality. For now, it should be noted that contradictions between norms and values can be found in many areas of social life: We value peace, but we fight wars; we value equal justice under the law, but we often give poor people inadequate legal representation; we value equality, but we practice racial, ethnic, and sexual discrimination.

Values are sometimes used for making an overall characterization of a people and their culture. Cora Du Bois (1955), for example, characterizes the basic values of the American people as those of equality (despite contradictions in actions), individualism, and what she calls "effort-optimism." This value consists of the belief that if we try hard enough, we can overcome all our problems. According to this value, people are able to master the world in which they live. Recent concerns over environmental pollution and energy shortages may have weakened our belief in this value, but it still remains rather strong in the United States.

Francis L. K. Hsu (1972) contends that American culture stresses individualism and success so strongly that these values come before many others. We fail to grant equality to women and minority groups, Hsu says, not because we do not believe in equality but because we believe in individualism even more strongly. And our belief in individualism implies a belief in the right of the individual to excel by any legal means possible. As a result, if majority groups and men find customs that give them an edge, the belief in individualism encourages them to use them as much as they can. Not all sociologists would go quite as far as Hsu in emphasizing individualism and striving for success. Most of them, however, recognize that these values play a very active role in shaping our culture. In Chapter 9, which

Large modern cultures contain many subcultural groups, some of which are seen so little as to warrant the term "invisible subcultures." Such groups include the Gypsies, migratory farm laborers, and such religious communities as the Hutterites and the Amish.

(a)

(b)

Figure 3-5 (a) Ethnocentrism, as shown by this Pulaski Day parade in New York City, is a healthy expression of pride in one's cultural heritage. (b) In its extreme form, it can be harmful to the rights of others. [(a) Katrina Thomas, Photo Researchers, Inc.; (b) George W. Gardner]

deals with deviance, we will discuss Robert K. Merton's theory of deviant behavior. It also emphasizes the results of placing too much stress on striving for success.

Folkways and mores

The customs and norms of society were given the names *mores* and *folkways* by William Graham Sumner (1960). Mores are the rules that are considered essential to the survival of society, such as rules against murder and treason. Folkways are customs which are considered normal or right simply because people are used to them. In our society, for example, it is customary to eat with knives, forks, and spoons. In China, however, it is traditional to eat with chopsticks. While members of these cultures would not consider each other's styles of eating immoral, they would probably find them a little odd and awkward. There is a wide range of mores and folkways, and many customs fall somewhere in the middle. To one American, a failure to salute the flag would be a violation of mores. To another, it would be merely a violation of a custom, or a problem of folkways.

Sumner observed that some folkways are definitely harmful. The Australian Aborigines, for example, burn the dead person's hut and his or her few worldly goods as part of the funeral service. This custom is not unlike the American practice of holding such costly funerals that families must go into debt to pay for them. Sumner also found some food taboos harmful. Food taboos are found in many older and contemporary societies. Plains Indians avoided eating coyotes, while Hindus will not eat cattle. And most Americans eat horsemeat only if they are starving. Such customs may have their origin, as Mary Douglas suggests (1966, pp. 41–67), in ancient ways of looking at nature. For example, the ancient laws of Leviticus in the Old Testament held that animals that chew their cud and have a cloven hoof—cattle and goats, for example—are clean and may be eaten. But those that are not cloven-hoofed or do not chew the cud—such as pigs, horses, and camels—are unclean and must not be eaten. Similar thinking, Douglas reasons, made grasshoppers and locusts edible, while insects that look like them but do not leap were taboo. Douglas concludes that these laws favored the most familiar creatures of a class and ruled out the ones that seemed somewhat "out of character." Another possible explanation of food taboos is presented by Frederick Simoons (1961), who finds a number of cases in which a particular food was avoided because it was the food of the enemy.

Entire sets of mores and folkways center on such important points in life as birth, childhood, coming of age, marriage, and death. All these periods are marked by rituals, which are often as difficult to make sense of as are food taboos. According to Sumner, these rituals were sanctified by tradition and were probably based upon some ancient philosophy, but their origins have become lost with the passage of time.

Ethnocentrism

Since all people believe in the superiority of their own mores and folkways, Sumner reasoned, it is inevitable that they will all be *ethnocentric*—that is, that they will see and judge all things from the viewpoint of their own culture. Ethnocentrism is both good and bad. It often functions in a positive way to reinforce a society's belief in its own worth. Ethnocentrism can arise in local areas—such as cities, states, and regions—as well as in nations and multinational cultures. The complete reversal of ethnocentrism would probably be destructive to group morale; a culture could hardly exist if it found no source of pride in its existence. Ethnocentrism carried to an extreme, however, is a threat to intergroup relationships, international goodwill, and even world peace. An alternative to ethnocentrism is *cultural relativity*, which refers to the practice of looking at other people and customs through *their* eyes, rather than judging them according to the viewer's standards. Cultural relativism recognizes that values and practices that suit one culture may not work well for another. The cultural relativists avoid judging cultures as either superior or inferior. They would agree with this statement by Melville Herskovitz:

> With the possible exception of technological aspects of life, the proposition that any one way of thought or action is better than another is exceedingly difficult to establish on grounds of any universally accepted criteria. (Herskovitz, 1964, p. 55)

Just as one may hold that cultures cannot be rated as better or worse, so one might say that it is useless or even harmful to judge other people by one's own cultural standards. As Edward Tylor, one of the founders of modern anthropology, observed, "Do not measure other people's corn by your own bushels." Most social scientists would agree that a cultural relativist viewpoint is needed to achieve harmony between different social groups and different societies.

COMPLEX CULTURES AND SUBCULTURES

If we were describing the culture of a primitive Australian Aborigine tribe, we could provide a complete description of its rules and customs, since the culture is homogeneous—it exhibits little variation. The culture of a major country such as the United States is much more difficult to describe because the styles of life differ greatly on many bases, such as social class, ethnic group, region, occupation, and age. The various groups within a society which define their norms somewhat differently are called *subcultures*. Subcultures are thought of as belonging to the main culture despite differences in norms, although some subcultures differ from the main culture more than others. Navajos who live on a reservation, speak no English, and avoid outside contacts represent the extreme in difference from the main culture. At the opposite extreme,

the word *subculture* is sometimes used to describe such minor variations on the cultural pattern as youth subcultures, occupational subcultures, and regional subcultures. Such subcultures are closer to the main culture than is the culture of the Navajos.

A religious subculture

Most religious groups are not distinctive enough to be described as subcultures, but a few (including the Old Order Amish and the Hutterites) have gone to great lengths to keep themselves separate from the outside world. The Amish regard the outside world as a Satanic kingdom that they must avoid at all costs, even at the cost of rejecting most modern conveniences. The Hutterites (see the insert "Tilling the Soul") are more willing to accept modern inventions, but they strictly avoid luxuries, and they own goods and property communally.

As the insert shows, the Hutterite subculture has its own distinctive values, norms, life-style, and means of supporting itself. It has very strong *boundary maintenance mechanisms*—means of keeping its own people separate from outsiders. For the Hutterites, these mechanisms include a high degree of physical separation from the rest of society (especially from public schools) as well as a distinctive dress style that makes its members highly visible to each other and to outsiders. In spite of its isolation, the Hutterite culture does slowly change, adopting some of the inventions of the outside world.

An invisible subculture: The migratory poor

Near Yuba City, California, in the winter of 1971, the unidentified body of a farm worker was found, buried in a shallow grave. A search began for other hidden graves, and eventually twenty-five bodies were unearthed, all of them migratory farm laborers. The murders had gone unnoticed for a number of years because no

Tilling the soul   ELAINE SCIOLINO

In Central Europe nearly 200 years ago, the Hutterite sect was nearly exterminated for its nonconformist religious views. Now, however, 22,500 Hutterites are thriving on communal farms in Montana, the Dakotas and the western provinces of Canada. Recently *Newsweek*'s Elain Sciolino visited the 5,000-acre Rosedale colony in South Dakota and filed this report on old-fashioned life in a modern world:

In many important respects the clock stopped for the Hutterites in 1536 when their Moravian founder, Jakob Hutter, was burned at the stake. At Rosedale and dozens of other communities in the New World, they still practice pacifism and communal farming. They eschew private property, smoking, dancing, television and radio (but not drinking) and they have little regard for anything more than rudimentary book-learning. Women are still second-class citizens and first-class childbearers (Hutterite families have an average of 6.7 children). The faithful still speak a Tyrolean German dialect and keep very much to themselves. Among all the 130 people at Rosedale there are only three family names—Waldner, Stahl, and Kleinsasser. Their religious creed, an offshoot of sixteenth-century Anabaptist heresy, has changed not a whit. They still believe in adult baptism and literal adherence to the commands of the gospels. "We don't believe in modernizing Christianity," says Michael Waldner, Rosedale's minister. "If it was a sin in Christ's day, it's a sin today."

But the twentieth century has not been held entirely at bay. Although the women still have no voice in running the colony, some of them are beginning to practice birth control, usually after they have had several children. The rhythm method is preferred, but the pill is not unheard of. The decision, however, is not the woman's and only partly her husband's: it must be ratified by the community's minister. John A. Hostetler, a sociologist and anthropologist at Temple University in Philadelphia and a student of Hutterite ways, reports that on a commune near Rosedale the minister decided on sterilization for his wife after the birth of their eighth child. "He didn't ask for her opinion," says Hostetler, "and she was furious when she found out. . . ."

missing persons had been reported. All the victims were apparently "invisible" men, without families or close friends, who drifted anonymously from place to place and from job to job. *Social invisibility* refers to not being noticed by the rest of society and being known by very few other people. Often such men live in labor camps located some distance away from major towns—camps that go unnoticed by the townspeople. A few miles from Bakersfield, California, for example, Sunset Labor Camp, made famous in Steinbeck's *The Grapes of Wrath* (1939), continued in existence until the late 1960s, but very few residents of Bakersfield knew about it.

To them it was a creation of the 1930s—of Steinbeck's imagination.

Dorothy Nelkin (1972, pp. 36–41) investigated the invisibility of farm laborers in the northeastern United States and found a similar situation. One small town was surrounded by fifty migrant labor camps, but just about no one in town knew anything about life-styles or cultural patterns within the camps. Ten percent of the town's residents said they knew of no labor camps in the area.

Part of the reason for this invisibility is that camp operators like to avoid public exposure of the very bad living conditions in their camps.

Culture and diversity

The migrants themselves also have reasons for seeking invisibility. For many families, the only way to make a living is to have underage children working in the fields. These families do not want to be caught by government inspectors. Even more important is the fact that the migrant workers see themselves as an outcast group. Many of them belong to minority ethnic groups and most of them lack the education and skills which other Americans gain through public education. Their sense of being outcasts is made worse by the fact that they are not usually covered by union contracts and therefore work under conditions that federal labor laws do not allow. These people can hold onto a sense of worth only by banding together and avoiding contact with outsiders who are richer and more comfortable than themselves. Invisibility protects their feelings and helps to make life bearable in a culture of poverty.

An invisible subculture: The gypsies

The Gypsies have a longer cultural tradition and a more highly organized social structure than migratory laborers, but they are even more invisible (Sutherland, 1975, pp. 27–33). Many Americans think that Gypsies died out years ago, but the fact is that their numbers are growing. Although they are often forced to settle down for months at a time and even send their children to public schools for short periods, they still spend nearly half their time on the road. This mobility increases their invisibility. The Gypsies, like the migrant laborers, find that invisibility makes them more comfortable. In the eyes of the *gaje* (non-Gypsies), they are untouchables; in their own eyes, the Gypsies are the followers of *Romany*—the regulations, customs, and beliefs that make them a superior people.

The Gypsies have always proved their superiority to themselves by making fools of the *gaje*, by outwitting them in fortune-telling, by stealing from them, or by being shrewd traders. The Gypsies view the *gaje* exactly as the *gaje* view

them, and they trust no outsiders; to mix with outsiders is spiritually polluting. To be separated from their own people is the worst thing that could happen to them; it brings isolation and disgrace. They control their members by threatening to expel those who have broken the ways of *Romany*. They maintain their separateness from the outside culture by keeping their own language, using special signs and signals, and respecting the aged and their traditions. Old men who have always been true to *Romany* are considered to be powerful; old women are considered to be wise in the ways of the spirits. Thus, partly by choice and partly because of the attitudes of outsiders, the Gypsies continue a centuries-old cultural existence, independent, proud, and invisible.

Small, partly detached groups—such as the migratory laborers, the Gypsies, and others—develop and preserve cultures within cultures, sometimes through choice and sometimes as the only way of surviving. These groups show how patterns of life become a means of coping with the world, how norms for dealing with members and outsiders create social unity, and how cultural patterns increase the sense of self-worth and give a group a reason for being.

SUMMARY

Although a great variety of personalities is produced in any society, they all share enough of the general culture to have some traits in common. *Cultures* are socially transmitted patterns of living within societies; they include rules and regulations, customs of all kinds, and basic beliefs and values. Other species have adapted to the environment largely through such physical traits as speed, adaptive coloration, or a keen sense of smell. But human beings have created cultures to help them in the struggle for survival. Culture—with its hunting, farming, and building techniques—does more than help people adapt to many environments. To a limited extent, it helps them control the environment. To a degree, cultures are influenced by the geographic environment. However, human ingenuity is great enough that quite different cultures are possible within the same geographic setting. Geography influences culture but does not set its course.

Cultures *change* with the passage of time, partly because of individual variation among people but also for other reasons: increase or decrease in population, changes in geographic environment, migration, contact with other peoples and their cultures, natural catastrophes, wars, and discoveries and inventions. In the course of immigration, people gradually become *acculturated* to a new way of life—i.e., they take on many of its traits.

Cultures grow and change by *discovery* and *invention*, and by borrowing traits from one another. Usually practical traits spread rapidly, but conflicting ideas from a foreign culture are usually not adopted unless there is discontent with one's own cultural beliefs. Ralph Linton presents a classical study of cultural diffusion, showing that even the most inventive cultures borrow much more than they invent.

Languages transmit cultures. In the opinion of some students of the subject (particularly Benjamin Lee Whorf), languages influence the way people see reality as well as their ways of thinking. Whether or not Whorf's ideas are entirely right, it is often difficult to translate ideas from one language to another without weakening them. A Laotian rendition of the Twenty-third Psalm is given as a case in point. Verbal languages grow with and reflect a culture, and so does the "silent language"—as Hall calls it—communication through gestures, eye contact, conversational distance, and timing.

Cultures are *normative* systems, defining what is proper and customary and also what is considered morally right. The term *norms* is used to apply to rules of right and wrong; it also has a statistical meaning: the most commonly encountered behavior. Most norms are followed often enough so that those who break them are disapproved of or even punished. Occasionally, however, there is a wide gap between what people consider the norm and what they actually do. In this case, the stated norms are referred to as *ideal norms* and the actual behavior as the *real norms*.

Normative behavior is obviously necessary, since many norms call for protection of the members of society and for fair treatment as well as give and take. On the other hand, some norms are hard to explain on purely rational grounds. Food taboos, for example, are probably rooted in ancient religious and philosophical ideas that are only poorly understood today. There are also cultural norms that are obscure or not even admitted—especially superstitions among modern peoples, such as the supposedly magical properties of numbers. The beliefs from which norms are derived are called *values*—although Blake and Davis argue that the norms may have developed first, with values then being used to explain them. William Graham Sumner used the terms *mores* and *folkways* to describe social norms. Mores are rules of conduct that are considered inviolable, such as those against murder and treason. Folkways are customs that can be violated without moral blame.

Because people are rooted in their own cultures, they become *ethnocentric*; that is, they regard their own ways as right and those of others as wrong. A more objective point of view is that of *cultural relativism*, the belief that people and their actions should be judged in terms of the culture that produced them.

Complex modern societies contain many variations within them. When a group of people (ethnic, religious, regional, or occupational) develops a way of life quite apart from the general cultural pattern, it is spoken of as a *subculture*. Examples are given of the very religious and isolated Hutterites and their communal life-style, of the depressed and migratory farm workers, and of the Gypsies, who maintain many of their customs and beliefs in spite of the inroads of modern society.

Culture and diversity

87

Study guide

Terms to know

Culture
Adaptive traits
Ethnocentrism
Geographic determinism
Cultural dynamics
Demography
Acculturation
Cultural diffusion
Cultural trait
Cultural complex
Discovery

Invention
Cultural base
Catastrophe
Apartheid
Norms
Statistical norms
Moral norms
Norm of evasion
Idealized norm
Real norm
Reciprocity

Vision quest
Values
Normative inconsistency
Folkways
Mores
Cultural relativism
Subcultures
Hutterites
Boundary maintenance mechanisms
Social invisibility
Romany

Names to know

Edward B. Tylor
Ellsworth Huntington
George P. Murdock
Ralph Linton

Benjamin Lee Whorf
Hajime Nakamura
Edward T. Hall

Self-test

Part I. Multiple Choice. Select the best of the four alternative answers.

1 *All but one* of the following are included in the concept of culture: (**a**) language; (**b**) beliefs; (**c**) laws, morals, and customs; (**d**) biological heredity.

2 Certain biological traits of human beings have helped make culture possible; among them are (**a**) total physical adaptation to specific environments, (**b**) unusually acute sense of hearing and smell, (**c**) continuous sex interest, (**d**) complex instinctive behavior patterns.

3 To a considerable degree, the human species has been more successful than others at (**a**) mutating rapidly so as to adjust to environment, (**b**) adapting the environment to its own needs, (**c**) preserving the natural environment, (**d**) avoiding destructive fights among its own members.

4 It is very likely that agriculture as a way of life became necessary in human history because of (**a**) sudden climatic changes, (**b**) growth in population, (**c**) inadequate hunting skills, (**d**) discovery of new crops.

5 A synonym for cultural diffusion is cultural (**a**) borrowing, (**b**) invention, (**c**) accumulation, (**d**) loss of distinctive traits.

6 In the process of cultural diffusion, foreign ideas and ideologies are most likely to be adopted by (**a**) the rich, (**b**) peasants, (**c**) the discontented, (**d**) military leaders.

7 An example of a nonmaterial invention is (**a**) the hot-air balloon, (**b**) the internal combustion engine, (**c**) the burning of natural gas, (**d**) social security.

8 The process by which people from different cultures adopt the cultural traits of a country they move to is called (**a**) socialization, (**b**) acculturation, (**c**) diffusion, (**d**) cultural dynamics.

9 Whorf concluded that languages (**a**) are of rather recent origin, (**b**) are quite similar in the way they conceptualize reality, (**c**) are present among some nonhuman species such as porpoises, (**d**) conceptualize nature and reality differently.

10 Nakamura finds that the typical idea of morality in India as the negation of ordinary desires (**a**) spread from China to India; (**b**) shows that hot, moist climates promote pessimistic views; (**c**) is the outgrowth of languages that stress negative statements; (**d**) indicates a higher level of intellect in India than elsewhere in Asia.

11 The insert titled "The Great Boss Is My Shepherd" illustrates the idea that (**a**) ideas and imagery are often weakened in translation, (**b**) the Khmus people are not very religious, (**c**) missionaries do a poor job of teaching, (**d**) the Khmus language is inferior to English.

12 According to Hall, black Americans differ from white Americans in nonverbal expression. Blacks (**a**) pay more attention to nonverbal communication, (**b**) avoid eye contact more than do whites, (**c**) ignore other people's concept of space, (**d**) are more particular about grammatical rules.

13 Rules of behavior on which members of societies agree fairly well are called (**a**) statistical norms, (**b**) moral norms, (**c**) prohibitions, (**d**) inhibitions.

14 Dundes gives many examples to demonstrate that the most sacred number in our culture is (**a**) two, (**b**) three, (**c**) seven, (**d**) thirteen.

15 A subculture is so called because it is (**a**) a divergent pattern continued within the larger culture, (**b**) inferior to the major culture, (**c**) superior to the major culture, (**d**) substituted for a real culture.

Part II. True-False Questions

1 Superstitions are eradicated in modern, scientifically oriented cultures.

2 *Culture* as used in sociology applies only to the most educated and high-class members of a society.

3 The fictitious Professor Widjojo interpreted cocktail parties as a type of contest between hostess and guests.

4 Geography determines the course of a culture.

5 Fong indicates that in traditional Chinese culture, girls were expected to hide their emotions, whether of unhappiness or pleasure.

6 Finding a new use for such a product as Coca Cola would be an example of discovery rather than invention.

7 The South African riots of June 1976 started over the issue of requiring black students to learn Afrikaans, the language of the Dutch-descended people of South Africa.

8 Cultural diffusion is the process of borrowing cultural traits from another culture.

9 In the process of cultural diffusion, ideas, values, and ideologies are the first things borrowed.

10 In Arabic society, it is extremely impolite to breathe directly on another person.

11 In a stable society such as ours, real norms and ideal norms are the same.

12 Some primitive tribes are quite restrictive and moralistic about sex.

13 Table manners are better examples of folkways than of mores.

14 Because of their strict religious beliefs, the Hutterites forbid any alcoholic drink.

15 The Gypsies think that following the way of *Romany* makes a superior people.

Questions for discussion

1 The text has stressed the advantages of the human species over other species. Can you think of ways in which human cultural traits and inventiveness might also prove the undoing of our species?

2 Using your own example of a cultural trait that has diffused into American culture, show how it has affected the culture. Try to use a recent example.

3 From the experience you have had in trying to learn a foreign language, think of examples of linguistic differences and how they might affect thought: idioms from the language you studied, words for which there is no exact equivalent, or traditional sayings in the other language.

4 The text gives examples of cultural traits that are not always noticed by the bearers of the culture (the magical quality of the number three is one example). Try to think of other examples of unnoticed cultural traits, such as superstitions or gaps between what we say and what we do.

5 Argue the case for, and the case against, calling the salute to the flag a folkway rather than a more.

6 Imagine a world in which no one is ethnocentric but all have accepted a cultural-relativist point of view. What difference would you expect to see?

7 Try to describe distinctive norms and values in a subculture with which you are familiar. (You have an advantage if you belong to a distinctive ethnic group, but the concept of subculture can be stretched to include almost any occupational, religious, regional, or age group.)

8 Show how ethnocentrism helps to keep such invisible groups as the migratory laborers and the Gypsies isolated from the rest of society. Be sure to note that both the larger society and the excluded groups have ethnocentric attitudes.

9 Try to interpret one of our customs in the manner used by Professor Widjojo.

Projects

1 Make a study of a minority group that exists in your community. Gather some background information on them. Then increase your knowledge by interviewing members of the group and discussing differences in attitudes and customs.

2 Try an experiment in violating our usual "silent language" customs by standing too close during conversations, staring, breathing on people (as Hall says is the Arab custom), or violating the usual conventions with regard to being on time. (Use a little caution in your experiment.)

3 One difficulty in dealing with the problem of norms and values is that there is less than complete agreement among the followers of a culture as to what those norms or values should be and which ones take priority. Try an interview or questionnaire technique to find in what order people would rate the values listed below.

Instructions: All the following are considered important values by most Americans, but are some more important than others? Rank in order from one to ten the values you consider most important, one being the highest and ten the lowest.

Personal independence	Sense of humor
Obedience to the law	Social conscience
Honesty	Belief in God
Striving to get ahead	Patriotism
Personal happiness	Intellectual interests

Suggested readings

Bohannon, Laura: "Shakespeare in the Bush," *Natural History*, vol. 75, August–September 1966, pp. 28–33. Can such a great work of literature as Shakespeare's *Hamlet* speak to people despite cultural differences? Anthropologist Laura Bohannon tells the story to her Tiv friends in Nigeria as they sit drinking and shooing the chickens away from their beer. The story is lost in cross-cultural confusion, and Bohannon is told to go home, consult the old men, and "learn wisdom."

Gmelch, George J.: "Baseball Magic," *Trans-Action*, vol. 8, June 1971, pp. 39–41. What kind of magic ensures success in professional baseball? "After each pitch, ex-major leaguer Lou Skeins used to reach into his back pocket to touch a crucifix, straighten his cap, and touch his genitals," says Gmelch, as one illustration of subcultural magical rituals designed to control luck. Rituals, taboos, and fetishes are discussed.

Hall, Edward T., and William F. White: "Intercultural Communication," *Human Organization*, vol. 19, no. 1, Spring 1960, pp. 5–12. In which cultures are people expected to mean what they say and in which ones will they give only the expected answer for the sake of politeness? To show that one is really sincere, should one gesture excitedly, weep, jump up and down, shout, and snarl? The answer, in some cultures, would be "yes."

Kochman, Thomas: " 'Rapping' in the Black Ghetto," *Trans-Action*, vol. 6, February 1969, pp. 26–34. Can you distinguish between "rapping," "shucking," "whupping the game," and "signifying"? These are only parts of the language of the black ghetto, the symbols of a distinctive subculture. Read especially about the repartee known as "putting on whitey."

Lee, Richard Borshay: "Eating Christmas in the Kalahari," *Natural History*, vol. 78, December 1968, pp. 14, 16, 18, 21–22, 60–63. An anthropologist living with the Kalahari Bushmen decides to give them, for Christmas, the biggest meal they have ever had. How can good intentions fail to cross cultural barriers? How do the Bushmen put down boastfulness? Read an amusing and bewildering account of cultural misunderstanding.

Miner, Horace: "Body Ritual among the Nacirema," *The American Anthropologist*, vol. 58, no. 3, June 1956, pp. 503–507. (Reprinted in large numbers of reading books in both sociology and anthropology.) Read of a strange culture, with its water shrines, medicine men, holy-mouth men, and "listeners," who seem to believe that mothers bewitch their own children. Gradually you come to realize that Nacirema is American spelled backward—a truly strange culture.

Key to questions. Multiple Choice: 1-d; 2-c; 3-b; 4-b; 5-a; 6-c; 7-d; 8-b; 9-d; 10-c; 11-a; 12-a; 13-b; 14-b; 15-a. True-False: 1-F; 2-F; 3-T; 4-F; 5-T; 6-T; 7-T; 8-T; 9-F; 10-F; 11-F; 12-T; 13-T; 14-F; 15-T.

This chapter discusses the process by which the individual personality develops and relates to society, stressing interrelationship between the two. After reading it, you should be able to:

1 Recognize some of the reasons for wide variety in personality.

2 Understand why Freudian theory emphasizes the conflict between individual and society but has nevertheless helped free people from some types of psychological repressions.

3 Understand how the individual acquires a creative personality along with concern for the views of others and the norms of society.

4 Recognize that the socialization process continues throughout life, and, as outlined by Erikson, is characterized by a number of important turning points.

5 Develop greater awareness of the roles you play in life and of the roles you will play in the future, together with the types of role strain that can develop.

6 Recognize the situations that account for adult socialization, for resocialization, and even for what is called "brainwashing."

7 Be aware of some of the cultural changes that are affecting the socialization process and the personalities being produced.

4

SOCIALIZATION: A MUTUAL PROCESS

From the study of culture in the previous chapter, it is clear that all cultural groups try to preserve their own way of life. Methods of raising children reflect the desire to preserve culture and cultural values and are a part of *the socialization process*, which will be further defined below. As a transition from the subject of culture to that of socialization, let us consider a few examples of child-rearing methods and their relationship to teaching cultural values:

In *Israel*, children are treasured and indulged as torchbearers of the Jewish culture and Israel's bulwark against assimilation or genocide. Small children may get spanked, but severe punishments are rare. But clinical psychologist Dr. Pessah Ben Horin notes that discipline comes in the form of "withholding love" as a sign of parental disapproval, or by instilling a sense of guilt for unacceptable behavior. . . .

In *Japan*, mothers do not spank; they scold. They tell a child that by misbehaving he will be laughed at, suffer shame, or be made a fool of. A mother will pamper a preschool child and at the same time inculcate the importance of saving face. . . . By the time a child is old enough to question the significance of shame, it is already too late. A fear of shame has become part of his mentality by then.

France. Said Christine Dauart, a consulting psychologist in Paris: "Discipline is so much part of a French child's life—from the earliest age of strictly regular feeding, through a military routine at nursery school, and certainly until the beginning of secondary education—that it is generally accepted. I think it is very bad."

Corporal punishment and curtailment of work privileges enforce diligent work habits. A French survey showed that only 4 out of 100 French children do not help with household chores. . . .

In *Buenos Aires*, the middle-aged father of a teen-aged boy and girl made things perfectly clear to his children, who are attractive youngsters, ultra mod in dress and hair style:

"I want you to realize that I am not your friend, I am your father. I'm the man who gives you love, protection, backing and security, not his confidence. You'll deal with me as a father, and don't ever forget it.

The father, a polished, congenial man . . . was asked about the youngsters' mod appearance.

"Hair length and dress styles are peanut issues," he said. "They're not important. What counts is respect for family and responsibilities, and my children have it." (Torgerson, 1973a, pp. 1, 18, 19; copyright Los Angeles Times)

By pride in tradition and desire for parental love, fear of shame, respect for work and diligence, or respect for family and responsibilities, children are introduced to the ways of their culture—an important part of socialization.

THE MEANING OF SOCIALIZATION

Socialization is the process which links together the individual and his or her culture. It is often

Socialization: A mutual process

defined as the process by which the individual absorbs the values, mores, and folkways of the society, making them part of the self. In the ideal world, the aim of socialization is to achieve perfect harmony between the individual and society. In the real world, however, this does not happen; in fact, it is neither possible nor desirable. This perfect fit would create a social order that resembled an ant colony; we would be mere insects in a rigidly structured and unchanging "hill." More realistically, we can view socialization as the way an individual personality is developed in keeping with societal or subcultural values. This definition makes it clear that the growing child is not an object into which the older generation pours culture as one might pour water into a jug. Each new baby is an individual. Although he or she may look and act like all other babies at first, a unique personality begins to emerge as the child grows and matures. From the first day of life, the infant lets us know that it is active, not passive. With its first loud cry, it has let the world know that its socialization is going to be a two-way process. The parents will teach the child, but the child will also teach the parents. The older generation will reward, threaten, punish, bargain, and plead with its children, but it will not get its own way all the time. No amount of effort can make people all alike or even make all people conform well enough to be thoroughly acceptable to society.

It must be realized, too, that socialization is not completed in childhood, with an unchanging set of personality traits. People grow and change. Childhood socialization is sometimes called *primary socialization*, the kind of socialization that comes first. Later changes—including the learning of new occupations and responsibilities, ideas and attitudes—can be called *secondary socialization* or *adult socialization*. Later in the chapter we will note cases in which types of secondary socialization can bring drastic changes. These later changes, as well as the fact that primary socialization in the home differs widely,

help account for the great varieties of personalities encountered in any society—in that of Israel, Japan, France, Argentina, or the United States.

Social origins of individual differences

Many of the differences between individuals can be explained by the life experiences they have had. However, some important differences are so basic that they may determine or even create different life experiences. Being born male or female, for example, is vital in shaping the life experiences we will have and in influencing our identity and personality. Other physical factors also affect life experiences. Whether they are short or tall, fat or thin, and attractive or plain may influence both the way people see themselves and the ways in which others respond to them. A handsome man or a beautiful woman may be able to glide through life on the strength of good looks, while someone less attractive may have to work harder for achievements. In societies with racial discrimination, skin color is an asset or a liability in the socialization process.

Temperament also contributes to differences in life experiences and socialization. Shy people, for example, may find it hard to relate to others,

Figure 4-1 A variety of socialization patterns results from differences in genetic inheritance and the environment in which the child is raised. (*Ron Sherman, Nancy Palmer*)

while extroverts can breeze through interpersonal activities like dating, job interviews, and public speaking.

Besides physical and temperamental differences, subcultural differences, such as those discussed in the previous chapter, affect the socialization process. The child of European immigrants has a socialization experience that differs from that of a native American. The Chicano, the black, or the American Indian child will not experience the same socialization process that a white child will. There are also regional and social-class differences in customs and attitudes which alter the socialization process. Among families of the same social group, differences arise; and within the family, parents may treat their children differently, perhaps being severe with a first child and more relaxed with later children. Whether a child is clever, average, or dull, intellectual or athletic will also affect his or her treatment both at school and at home.

Many factors, then, help to account for the wide differences in personality that develop in the same general culture. All these factors fall into two broad categories: heredity and environment. Sociologists and other social scientists have long debated which of the two is more important—"nature" (heredity) or "nurture" (environment). However, since it is impossible to separate the two, such arguments are futile. The important thing to remember is that both heredity and environment contribute to the socialization process, and both interact in subtle ways to influence the development of personality.

Although, ideally, children who are loved and cared for should have a great advantage over those who are neglected or abused, individual differences in temperament are so great that some people manage to do well in life in spite of a poor beginning.

VIEWS OF SOCIALIZATION

Many different perspectives can be used to investigate personality development and socialization. Various questions may be asked: "What is the relationship between the individual and society?" "In what ways does society influence the individual, and how does the individual respond to these influences?" In the following pages, we will consider the ideas of several theorists who offer a variety of answers to these questions.

Socialization as repression: Sigmund Freud

Sigmund Freud (1856–1939) was an Austrian neurologist and the discoverer of a method of treating emotional disorders. Freud formulated theories concerning the relationship between the individual and society and how, during the socialization process, society generally establishes its control over the individual.

Repression and the unconscious Freud's method of treating emotional disorders, later known as *psychoanalysis*, consisted of listening to his patients as they expressed whatever ideas, thoughts, or fantasies came into their minds and encouraging them to relate their dreams. From this free-flowing stream of thoughts and dreams often came ideas of which the patients themselves had been unaware or unconscious—and about which they usually felt guilty. One patient, for example, had feelings of relief upon the death of her sister because she secretly loved her brother-in-law and realized that her sister's death made it possible for her to win him. Her guilt was so great that she eventually managed to *repress* the thought, driving it from her memory. While interpreting his patients' dreams, Freud was often able to bring their repressed thoughts to the surface. Particularly important for Freud's later theories about personality development was his discovery of the degree to which thoughts of sex and aggression were repressed. Furthermore, the repression of such thoughts, Freud concluded, was strongest among people of high ideals and conscience—those who could be called most civilized.

Sexual and aggressive nature Freud became convinced that a frequent source of trouble for the emotionally disturbed person was the repression of sexual and aggressive urges, which he called instincts. Modern behavioral scientists are much more cautious than was Freud in using the term *instinct*, which means an unlearned behavior pattern that is universal to the species. In Freud's analysis, though, both aggression and sex met the criteria of instinct. In the case of aggression, he wrote:

> Men clearly do not find it easy to do without satisfaction of this tendency to aggression that is in them; when deprived of satisfaction of it they are ill at ease. There is an advantage, not to be undervalued, in the existence of smaller communities, through which the aggressive instinct can find an outlet in enmity towards those outside the group. It is always possible to unite considerable numbers of men in love towards one another, so long as there are still some remaining objects for aggressive manifestations. . . . (Freud, 1949, pp. 89–90; copyright © 1949 by Hogarth Press)

Regarding sex, Freud formulated a theory about stages of human development which he assumed to be universal and instinctive. One Freudian hypothesis about psychosexual development is called the *Oedipus complex*. This term is derived from the name of the tragic King Oedipus of Greek mythology, who unknowingly killed his father and married his own mother. The Oedipus complex hypothesizes that the male infant loves his mother and hates his father out of jealousy over the mother's love.

The Oedipus complex is particularly important because it was one of the Freudian ideas that could be tested. Bronislaw Malinowski, an anthropologist who made studies in the Trobriand Islands, applied the techniques of psychoanalysis

Figure 4-2 "Double scotches for me and my superego, and a glass of water for my id, which is driving." (*Drawing by Handelsman; © 1972 The New Yorker Magazine, Inc.*) According to Freud, the mind consists of three interacting parts: the id, which expresses primitive urges; the ego, or conscious, rational element; and the superego, or social conscience.

to Trobriand boys. He found they had no resentment whatever of their fathers, whose roles in Trobriand society were gentle and nonthreatening. However, they hated their mothers' older brothers, who were the disciplinarians in that culture. A likely conclusion of Malinowski's finding is that the Oedipus complex was not so much a matter of jealousy over the mother's love as resentment of a stern, disciplining father. Such fathers were characteristic of Freud's culture but are not typical of all cultures.

Freud's theory of instincts remains controversial; it is generally rejected by sociologists and psychologists. Regarding the sexual nature of human beings, there is much doubt as to whether it always develops in the manner outlined by Freud. Much social learning takes place in the development of sexual expression, and there may be greater variety within the range of "normal" than is allowed for by Freudian theory (Simon and Gagnon, 1969, pp. 9–17).

Despite controversy, however, Freud helped to free the subject of sex from the silent treatment it had generally received in Western culture before his time. Freud made it possible for respectable people to talk about sex and sexual fantasies and found that many neurotic disorders were a result of repression of sexuality. Partly as a result of his work, fear of infant and childhood sexuality, described in the insert "Dangerous Infancy," began to decline.

Society versus the individual Stressing his findings on the repression of sex and aggression, Freud arrived at a social theory that pits society against the individual. Since no society could exist if everyone could freely express all sexual or aggressive wishes, Freud reasoned, the individual must be restrained. Consequently, all societies regulate the expression of aggression and sex, not only by law but also by building internal controls within the individual—controls that produce strong guilt feelings if they break down.

Freud saw the human personality as having three aspects: *id*, *ego*, and *superego*. The *id* is raw vital energy and the center of such drives as sex and aggression.

The *ego*, meaning literally the self, is actually the intelligent, adjusting part of the self. The *superego* is the aspect of the personality that has internalized the norms of society and will feel guilt if they are violated. In Freud's scheme, the id is compared with a horse pulling a carriage (pure energy); the driver with the ego (intelligently giving directions); and the superego with the laws of the road. Only strong restrictions built into the person through the development of a superego or imposed by force can keep society functioning.

Because of his view of human nature as driven by instinct, Freud tended to be pessimistic about the perfectibility of humankind. To Freud, human nature was potentially dangerous. However, two American social psychologists of the same period arrived at very different conclusions.

Dangerous infancy: Advice from the U.S. Children's Bureau, 1914

. . . The conception of the child's basic impulses has undergone an extreme transformation since 1914. At the earlier date, the infant appeared to be endowed with strong and dangerous impulses. They were notably autoerotic, masturbatory, and thumb-sucking. The child is described as "rebelling fiercely" if these impulses are interfered with. The impulses "easily grow beyond control" and are harmful in the extreme: "children are sometimes wrecked for life." The baby may achieve the dangerous pleasures to which his nature disposes him by his own movements or may be seduced into them by being given pacifiers to suck or by having his genitals stroked by the nurse. The mother must be ceaselessly vigilant; she must wage a relentless battle against the child's sinful nature. She is told that masturbation "must be eradicated . . . treatment consists in mechanical restraints." The child should have his feet tied to opposite sides of the crib so that he cannot rub his thighs together; his nightgown sleeves should be pinned to the bed so that he cannot touch himself. Similarly, for thumb-sucking, "The sleeve may be pinned or sewed down over the fingers of the offending hand for several days and nights," or a patent cuff may be used which holds the elbow stiff.

From Martha Wolfenstein, "The Emergence of Fun Morality," *Journal of Social Issues*, vol. 7, no. 4 (1951), pp. 15–25, an excerpt.

THE CHALLENGE TO FREUD: COOLEY AND MEAD

Charles Horton Cooley (1864–1929) and George Herbert Mead (1863–1931) were leaders of the symbolic-interactionist school of sociology. They held very different views from Sigmund Freud on the relationship between the individual and society. Freud pictured the individual and society as enemies, with the individual yielding only reluctantly to the greater power of society. Cooley and Mead, on the other hand, saw the individual and society as partners. In fact, according to symbolic interactionists, the individual can develop only through social relationships—that is, through interaction with others. All our behaviors, our attitudes, even our ideas of the self arise from our interactions with other people.

According to the symbolic interactionists, social forces—rather than genetic inheritance—shape the individual. This was a revolutionary idea. The writings of such social Darwinists as Spencer and Sumner had assumed that some people are inherently superior to others. Cooley and Mead implied instead that such traits as intellectual abilities, social skills, feelings of self-worth, and even the ability to love and hate are the results of the socialization process.

Charles Horton Cooley: The looking-glass self

How do we know who we are? Cooley believed that we gain and maintain our ideas of ourselves through what he called the *looking-glass process* (Cooley, 1964). That is, when we interact with another person and become aware of ourselves (the "looking-glass self") in the process, we act as though we were looking into a mirror. We use the other's response to us as we use the reflection of a mirror: to establish a self-concept or an idea of what we are like. Of course, because we are looking at another person and not really at a mirror, our image is based not on an actual reflection but on our *interpretation* of the other's response to us. Distortions may occur in this process because our interpretations (which are sometimes only guesses) may be incorrect.

This looking-glass process begins in infancy as the baby looks to its parents for kindness and care. If the parents respond with love, the infant will perceive himself or herself as being worthy of love and will develop a positive self-concept. Such a child will be able to give as well as to receive love and will be establishing the foundations for satisfying love relationships later in life. The infant or child deprived of love may react very differently. The looking-glass process, begun in infancy, continues throughout life and becomes reciprocal. No one is merely a mirror or viewer; we all become mirrors for each other and viewers of each other as we interact in daily life.

Significant others and reference groups

Cooley did not assume that all people affect us equally; some "mirrors" are more important than others. Following his ideas and those of Mead, the term *significant others* has come to be used to describe those who have an important influence on our thoughts, emotions, and actions. Early in life, our parents and other family members are our significant others. As we grow older and our experience with the world expands, this group grows to include outsiders. Adults in positions of authority—teachers, the clergy, the police—may become significant others whom we value. Other children (the peer group) also become significant others to the child. (Cooley used the term *peer group* almost exclusively to describe children's play groups, although it can be used to describe any group of status equals.) The peer group, like the family, becomes a *reference group*—a group to which we look in shaping our patterns of socialization.

One point not stressed by Cooley is important: There is no guarantee that every significant other in the child's life will teach positive social values. Influence works independently of social values, and some forms of influence may go against the

(a)

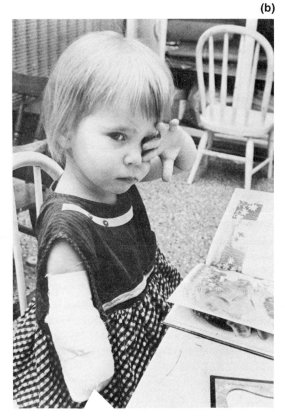

(b)

Figure 4-3 Family life is important in developing the childs's self-concept. (*a*) This child is given affection and support. (*b*) This child's arm was mutilated by her father. Which child is more likely to grow up with a positive self-concept? [(*a*) *Charles Gatewood*; (*b*) *United Press International*]

norms and values of society. In some neighborhoods and under some conditions, for example, gang leaders or numbers runners may become significant others for the child.

Identification and internalization *Identification* is the process by which a person imaginatively places himself or herself in the role of someone else and takes on the traits of that person. Children playing house or nurse or doctor make believe they have taken the roles of others. They may also pretend they are actors, important athletes, or other admired persons. In some cases, adults also identify with others. Strong leaders of great causes may attract some followers who identify with them completely. The more usual type of identification, though, takes place in childhood and is closely allied with the learning of sex roles. The small boy who tries

to shave because his father is shaving is identifying with the father; the girl who stumbles around the house in her mother's high-heeled shoes is identifying with her mother. Identification with the parent of the same sex aids sex-role development. In families having only one parent, therefore, sex-role identification can become a problem. Because children of divorced parents generally live with their mothers, many boys in our society grow up without an adult male model. More research has been done on the problem of

Socialization: A mutual process

99

fatherless boys than that of motherless girls. But now that many women have careers of their own, courts are increasingly awarding custody of children to their fathers—about 1 million children to date. The insert "Fathering" tells of the problems faced by the father of a three-year-old daughter and also contains insights into the roles of both mothers and fathers.

Internalization means absorbing attitudes and beliefs and making them one's own. At first glance, internalization would seem to be the highest goal of the socialization process; however, for a number of reasons, this is not necessarily true. First, the internalized attitudes can be those of prejudice and hatred. Second, internalization, although deeply rooted in the personality, is not always permanent. Prejudiced attitudes may change in the face of later experience, but so may norms of honesty and dependability. Further, the internalization of a norm is no guarantee that it will be applied in all cases. In 1976, West Point was embarrassed when some cadets, who presumably had internalized the norm of honesty, cheated on exams. The particular situation helps to decide whether internalized norms will indeed be upheld. One contemporary sociologist, David Riesman, has argued that norms in our society are not as strongly internalized today as they were in the past. We shall consider his ideas later in this chapter. For the moment, we may say that internalization helps to make norms and attitudes part of one's personality and more or less permanent; but in human affairs, permanence is only relative.

Feelings of inferiority Cooley's explanations of human development could account for feelings of inferiority in those who have been rejected by their parents or other people who are important to them. Since the self-image is derived largely from others, it is not surprising that

---

Fathering KENNETH WOODWARD AND PHYLLIS MALAMUD

It was 1 o'clock in the morning when Richard Robbins, 25, gently woke up his three-year-old daughter, Lauryann, who was fast asleep on the baby-sitter's couch. Together they went home to his four-room apartment in suburban Atlanta, Ga., where Robbins heated a simple supper of soup and crackers for the two of them before finally turning in at 3 A.M. It is an abnormal life-style—even for a single father—but one in which Robbins, who works the late shift at a nearby grocery, is finding more company. "If you set your values on going to the beach all the time, it's a hassle," says Robbins, who accepted custody of Lauryann when he and his wife were divorced two years ago. "Otherwise you grow up with your child and enjoy it.". . .

Still, many men are discovering that the act of becoming the sole parent can be devastating. When journalist Robert Minor, 34, took custody of his two small children five years ago, his life turned into a nightmare. "I became bitchy, resentful, unkempt and shrill," he recalls. "I became a guerrilla fighter in the supermarkets among all the other housewives." He also encountered a society that does not cater to fatherhood. "Men's restrooms don't have a shelf for changing diapers like women's do," he points out. Still, it was an experience he would not have missed. "Children break down the male facade," says Miner, who is writing a novel on fathering. "You discover a capacity for intimacy and emotion."

From Kenneth Woodward and Phyllis Malamud, "The Parent Gap," *Newsweek*, September 22, 1975, p. 54. Copyright 1975 by Newsweek, Inc. All rights reserved.

---

one who is generally treated as inferior begins to feel inferior.

According to some research (Reckless and Dinitz, 1956, pp. 744–747), a favorable self-image is a strong barrier against juvenile delinquency, whereas a self-image of inferiority is not. A study of boys attending school in a high-delinquency area revealed that one of the most significant differences between those who had not been in trouble with the law and those who were often arrested was that the former thought of themselves as good and law-abiding types. The others held less normative self-images, ranging from "tough guy" to "failure."

George Herbert Mead

Like Cooley, Mead was interested in the interaction between self and society. To learn about this, he studied the way in which the self uses symbols and role playing in the process of socialization (Mead, 1934).

Mead used the words *I* and *me* to stand for parts of the individual personality. "Me," the objective side of the person, is made up of all the training, habits, conventions, attitudes, and behaviors that the individual internalizes. Each person, however, has another aspect to the self, the "I"—the subjective and creative part of the personality. While the "me" reflects what society has shaped, the total person is more than merely the sum of these inputs. Mead's "I" represents the part of the personality that creates meaning. It is for this reason that a child whose early life has been emotionally or economically disadvantaged can still manage to create a meaningful and satisfying life. According to Mead, the "I" is always more important than the "me."

An implication of Mead's thinking is that a child brought up in a fairly free atmosphere would develop more of the constructive, independent, and imaginative side of his or her personality than one with rigid, directive parents. This view is supported in the accompanying insert, "Some People's Children."

Since it constantly organizes, synthesizes, and creates, the self—in Mead's analysis—is to be thought of as a process rather than as a finished product. The self has new experiences, weighs new ideas, puts older ideas to the test, and

---

Some people's children

All gifted children have great potential for achievement, but not all of them fulfill their promise. Many researchers believe that the difference lies in the way parents treat bright children. Psychologist Ralph D. Norman of the University of New Mexico is particularly interested in the impact that the "model parent," the one of the same sex, has on the gifted child (*Journal of Psychology*, Vol. 64, 1966). He used the Gordon Survey of Interpersonal Values which deals with how highly one values being treated with kindness, doing what is socially acceptable, being recognized and admired, being free to make one's own choices, doing things for other people, and being a leader. Norman gave this test to the parents of 49 Albuquerque schoolchildren with IQ's over 130 who did well on an achievement test, and to parents of 40 equally intelligent classmates who did badly on the same test. He found this significant difference: the fathers of boy achievers and the mothers of girl achievers give independence values a higher score and conformity values a lower score than the counterpart parents of the non-achieving children.

Published by permission of Transaction, Inc., from *Trans-Action*, vol. 4, no. 3, copyright © 1967 by Transaction, Inc. From "Roundup of Current Research" section.

Socialization: A mutual process

Figure 4-4 While role playing, the child learns the values and attitudes associated with the role. (*Lew Merrim, Monkmeyer*)

the "me," all the symbols must be defined, interpreted, and organized by the "I." The meaning of a gesture, for example, is not always clear. A waved hand can be a friendly greeting or a signal that says, "Hello, but don't come over to talk to me." The "I" must decide how to interpet this message. Language, as well as gesture, is never entirely clear and simple but full of subtleties, idioms, and figures of speech. It is the "I," the creative part of the self, which interprets language.

Games, roles, and the generalized other   The socialization process depends on learning *roles* and internalizing the values that go with those roles (i.e., the parts people play in society). It is a point stressed by Mead more than by Cooley. Much of the socialization process, according to Mead, involves playing roles and games. Small children enjoy playing roles. Unless the parents are quite sophisticated in their interpretation of sex roles, the children will divide their roles along traditional lines; boys will play with trucks or take the role of cowboy or Indian, while girls play house and take the role of mother or nurse. Certain attitudes that go with these roles are also learned in childhood. In traditional homes, girls learn to take care of dolls and dishes much as they will later, as mothers and homemakers, care for their babies and households. Boys play with tool kits, learning to be the reliable "handyman" around the house. In less traditional homes, boys and girls are more likely to engage in imaginative play together, perhaps imitating the work roles of both parents. They may pretend, for example, to be two lawyers discussing a difficult case over peanut-butter sandwiches. In all instances, they construct an imaginative view of the adult world.

When they are older, children learn to play games which have specific "positions" and rules. These games are important partly because children change positions while playing them; they play the position of batter at one time and the position of pitcher at another time. In this way,

adapts to new situations. The idea of process can be applied to both the "I" and the "me," because both societal influences and personal organizing and synthesizing continue throughout life. For example, even in old age, although society insists on retirement, the individual can decide whether those years will bring enjoyment or emptiness.

Both parts of the personality are deeply involved with symbols, which were discussed in Chapter 1. Words are our primary symbols, but we also make symbolic use of flags, banners, uniforms, badges, wedding rings, and many other things whose meanings are shared by members of a culture. While these symbols form part of the collection of social inputs which create

they learn not only the roles they are playing but the roles the others are playing as well. Thus they begin to understand other people and their roles. Learning to play by rules introduces the child to what Mead calls the concept of the *generalized other*, the society that makes certain demands on the individual. This voice of society, or social conscience, is internalized in the socialization process. As he or she grows older, the child learns that parents are not the only sources of authority, the only judges of what is right. The child learns that there are certain rules laid down by society, by the generalized other.

Rules will be discussed further later in the chapter. At this point, let us look at the work of two other theorists who have explained socialization somewhat differently from Freud or the symbolic interactionists. Jean Piaget is particularly concerned with the development of a moral sense. Erik Erikson has developed a theory that carries socialization into "stages" of adolescence, adulthood, and even old age. From this perspective, he gives a more complete analysis of the totality of life than did any of his predecessors. Piaget—like Freud, Cooley, and Mead—focuses his attention mainly upon childhood.

Jean Piaget

Piaget presents a developmental theory of personality that builds on the views of Cooley and Mead regarding internalized norms. Piaget is concerned with the rate of development of the social conscience (Mead called this the *generalized other*). According to Piaget (1938), children begin to reason by seeing rules as external to themselves, to be obeyed only for the sake of such rewards as love or to avoid punishment. In the second stage, beginning at the age of about four or five, children whose socialization has gone well become more obedient without always thinking of rewards and punishments. But these children still see rules as more or less natural forces to be reckoned with but not understood. At the third stage, reached at about

the age of twelve, the child begins to act in terms of "the spirit of the law," rather than merely the letter, and understand the reasons behind it.

Piaget concluded, however, on the basis of careful observation of children, that social norms are accepted quite differently depending on the source from which they are learned. Children who are taught by authoritarian adults may be slow to reach the third stage of development or may never reach it at all. If children learn the rules through interaction with their age mates, as in the playing of games described by Mead, they will see social norms as rules created for the mutual benefit of all.

Piaget also analyzes the gradual emergence of a concept of justice. At first, justice is seen as whatever serves the child's own purpose. Later, concepts of justice begin to emerge bit by bit. Children apply concepts of justice to things with which they are familiar, and they want their own actions to be judged by intent—"I didn't mean to hurt you." In unfamiliar situations, on the other hand, actions are judged solely by their results, not by intent (Macoby, 1968, pp. 235–240). The difference is partly related to increasing maturity, but Piaget still finds an advantage among children who have learned through interaction and cooperation with their peers. "In short," said Piaget, "in order to really socialize the child, cooperation is necessary, for it alone will succeed in delivering him from the mystical power of the world of the adult" (1948, p. 409).

Erik Erikson

Erik Erikson (1902–) began as a psychoanalyst in the tradition of Freud, but he eventually developed a theory of personality that differs from Freud's in many ways. Whereas Freud stressed instinctive drives that show themselves similarly in all societies, Erikson gives more weight to cultural difference. Whereas Freud was pessimistic about the improvement of humankind, Erkison is optimistic. Finally, Freud almost ignored adolescence and adulthood, whereas

Successful socialization involves love and care, imitation, role learning, teachings by family, peer group, and church, and a variety of life experiences. Socialization equips one generation to launch the next generation.

(Myron Wood/Photo Researchers)

(Shirley Zeiberg)

(Myron Wood/Photo Researchers)

105

Erikson emphasizes adolescence and later stages (Hjelle and Ziegler, 1976, pp. 59–77; Erikson, 1959).

Erikson thinks of life as a series of *identity crises*, a term he uses to refer to turning points in life, not necessarily times of peril. In infancy, the crisis is one of finding basic trust, and in early childhood that of achieving a sense of individual autonomy, as opposed to being a helpless baby. Although Erikson does not use the same terms as Cooley or Mead, his framework is similar. Erikson's developmental stages of childhood (four in number) are concerned with favorable self-image, imitation, and internalization, similar to the phonemena described earlier.

Erikson has shown greatest concern with the adolescent years. If the adolescent crisis, or turning point, is met satisfactorily, a strong sense of identity is developed; failure results in role confusion. The development of identity in adolescence means having confidence that an inner unity and dependability exist and will be recognized by others. The ability to achieve a strong, positive identity at this stage is to a large degree culturally determined. Erikson notes that before the present era, which offers the choice of women's liberation, a positive identity was more difficult for women to achieve than for men. To some extent, it still is. The adolescent examines and criticizes society, plans for the future, and tries to make sense of a confusing world. The adolescent must also grow into an appropriate adult sex role and develop socially acceptable sex interests.

Failure in meeting the adolescent identity crisis and resultant role confusion often result in the inability to select a job or career, in overidentification with popular heroes or a counterculture, or sometimes in a clinging to concepts developed in childhood. To Erikson, failure at this stage of life will make later psychological success more difficult but not impossible. Erikson recognizes human resiliency, an ability to overcome false starts and to change and improve.

The stage of young adulthood is the time for reaching intimacy. The most common form of intimacy is achieved through marriage and the establishment of a family. However, intimacy is not impossible for the single person who relates well to others or has a general love of humankind. The opposite course at this turning point is to become too self-absorbed to establish meaningful, intimate relations with others.

The next phase, the middle years of life, includes the period from about twenty-five to sixty-five years of age. According to Erikson, this period is characterized by *generativity*, a concern for the next generation and for society in general. Those who fail in this crisis pursue their own selfish ends, fail to become concerned parents or citizens, and begin to think of life as empty and meaningless.

Old age, the final phase, is also a turning point. The person who, at this stage, has moved through the preceding stages successfully can look back over life with a feeling of satisfaction and can face approaching death calmly. In contrast, according to Erikson, much of senility is a result not only of physical impairment but also of the psychological failure to have coped successfully with life.

SOCIALIZATION AND ROLE

Ralph Linton, an anthropologist, proposed that socialization—as well as society itself—can be explained in terms of role and status (Linton, 1936, pp. 113–131). A *status* is a position one holds in society, and a *role* is the behavior expected of the person who occupies that status. There are two forms of status: ascribed and achieved. An *ascribed status* is one we are born into or assigned to at various stages in the life cycle. Examples of ascribed statuses include male or female, son or daughter, or—in aristocratic societies—peasant, gentleman, duke, or king. An *achieved status* is attained through effort; examples include occupational statuses such as doctor, lawyer, secretary, schoolteacher, member of Congress; social statuses such as married man or woman; and educational statuses such as high school graduate or college student. Much of the aim of socialization is to prepare a person for holding achieved roles. However, even in the case of ascribed roles, a certain amount of socialization is necessary. For example, we are born male or female, but people vary in the ways they perceive and act out these sex roles. For one person, being a female might mean being a good cook and a homemaker as well as a loving wife and mother; for another it might mean being a swinging single; while for a third, it might mean being a dedicated and skilled doctor.

While it is easy to define *status* and *role*, the picture gets quite complicated when sociologists apply a role analysis to society. For one thing, all of us fulfill many different roles at the same time: son or daughter, husband or wife, employer or employee, student, citizen, club member, friend, brother or sister. Sometimes these roles interfere with each other. The man who puts in a ten-hour day as a restaurant manager may not have the time or energy to fulfill his role as a father.

Role distance

Although people prepare for occupational roles, they like to feel—and they like others to know—that they are more than merely the occupants of these roles. One young woman who used to work for an airline felt liberated when she could use her own name instead of being known as a stewardess:

> I had much more status when I was working for the airlines than I have now. I was always introduced as Beryl Simpson, who works for the airlines. Now I'm reduced to plain old Beryl Simpson. I found this with boy friends. I know one who never dates a girl with a name. He never dates Judy, he never dates Joan. He dates a stewardess or a model. He picks girls for the glamor of their jobs. He never tells you their names. When I was with the airlines, I was introduced by my company's name. Now I'm

just plain old everyday me, thank God. (Terkel, 1974, p. 83; by permission of Pantheon Books, a division of Random House, Inc.)

Erving Goffman has coined the term *role distance* to describe this desire for a personal identity apart from the identity given by a role (Goffman, 1961b). While we may feel proud of the statuses and roles we have worked to achieve, we like to feel that, apart from our social roles, we are unique. Fortunately, one doesn't have to quit a job to gain a sense of personal identity. Many creative individuals exert their own influence on particular roles, playing them slightly differently rather than becoming the "typical cop" or the "typical schoolteacher." Many people establish a comfortable balance between their occupational and personal identities, becoming "John Keating, who works as a sound engineer."

Role strain and role conflict

No matter how well one is socialized into role performance, problems arise in coping with roles—a situation sociologists call *role strain*. One type of role strain results from conflicting demands of a particular role—it is called *role conflict*. For example, a high school counselor is expected to be a friendly adviser to students at certain times and a disciplinarian at others. As a disciplinarian, he or she could well weaken the friendly relationship needed for rapport with students.

Sometimes role strain results merely from competing demands on time, as in the case of a student who must hold a full-time job while going to college. At other times, role strain arises from the effort to cope with a role that is unwanted or that fails to measure up to its promise. The actor Rip Torn told an interviewer that he decided on an acting career because he feels things strongly—he angers quickly and saddens quickly. He thought that he could use

Socialization: A mutual process

these strong emotional responses to build a satisfying career as an actor:

> So I guess that's why I became an actor. But I found that's not what they want. They want you to be their Silly Putty.
>
> Actors have become shills [salesmen]. I remember doing a show, oh, about ten years ago. I haven't worked on network television for about eight years. I was smokin' a cigar. I was playing a [character for whom it seemed appropriate] so I had a long Cuban cigar. I got up on a horse and we had to charge down a hill. It was a long shot. The director and the producer both hollered, "Cut! Cut! What're you doing with that cigar in your mouth?" I said, "I don't naturally smoke cigars, but I'm doin' it for the role. They didn't have cigarettes during the Civil War." They said, "You don't understand." I said, "Oh, now I do understand. But this isn't a cigarette program." The sponsor was Pontiac. But this show has resale value. They didn't want a Civil War character smoking a cigar because they might resell it to a cigarette company and my act might damage their commodity. They insisted I get rid of the cigar. We're nothin' but goddamned shills.
>
> An actor is used to sell product primarily. . . . (Terkel, 1974, p. 124; by permission of Pantheon Books, a division of Random House, Inc.)

Nearly everyone experiences some sort of role strain at one time or another. The young mother who can barely cope with her baby; the teacher who has nightmares about controlling his classes; the secretary who must take orders from two different bosses and still try to remain pleasant with clients; the lawyer who imagined himself engaged in dramatic court fights but spends his life plea bargaining in back rooms; the telephone operator who likes to chat but is limited to only seven or eight phrases—all of these people are experiencing role strain.

Reciprocal roles, role taking, and role sets

As we grow up, we learn about roles from watching and interacting with people around us. Early in life we learn about *reciprocal roles*— roles that depend upon one another for definition and fulfillment. Our first models of reciprocal roles include those of mother-child, teacher-student, and husband-wife. The success of these roles depends upon the agreement of both parties as to what the roles should entail. Many divorces, for example, occur when the husband and wife cannot agree on their reciprocal roles. The failure to adjust to reciprocal roles can also be described as a failure in role taking. *Role taking* is the imaginative taking of a different role so as to reach a sympathetic understanding of that role. It tries to answer the question, "What would I do if I were in his or her shoes?" Role taking is important in promoting harmony in the next type of role relationships to be considered: role sets.

Even when roles are not as strongly reciprocal as the ones just mentioned, they are not acted out alone. *Role sets* develop in relationship to a number of other people. This sometimes happens among people working together in an office, on an assembly team, in a combat crew, or in more complex relationships. Role sets which develop in work or social groups often require compromises if they are to be successful. In the acting situation described by Rip Torn, the role set includes not only actors, directors, and producers but also sponsors. In this situation, Torn became frustrated because he had to give in to the demands of the sponsor—the compromise was entirely one-sided. As we grow older and become involved in more complicated role sets, we realize that childhood preparation is not enough; we must learn more about fulfilling the roles forced upon us in the adult social world. As a result, role learning is not limited to childhood or youth but continues throughout life.

Roles and sexism

Older descriptions of role learning in childhood are strongly sexist, depicting girls as learning to cook and sew and boys as going to work outside the home. Today, many traditional masculine-feminine role distinctions are being erased. In school, girls can take courses in woodwork while boys can take cooking classes. Occupational roles that were once open to only one sex are now open to both. Women as well as men are now being urged to use their minds and fulfill their potential. In an opinion poll conducted in 1974, Yankelovich found a majority of both college and noncollege youth agreeing that "men and women are born with the same human nature; it's the way they're brought up that makes the difference" (Yankelovich, 1974, p. 98). However, while changing attitudes and behaviors open up new occupational possibilities for both sexes, they also produce cases of role strain. A woman in a supervisory position may have to cope with the resentment or hostility of subordinates who can't accept a woman in the role of a boss. Similarly, the man who becomes a kindergarten teacher, housekeepr, or nurse must adjust to his new role and must also cope with the negative attitudes of more traditional co-workers.

Agencies of socialization

Sociologists see the family, the school, and the church as the "official" agencies of socialization. In real life, however, the process of socialization is not as simple or as clear-cut as this official portrait seems to imply. First of all, these agencies of socialization sometimes work at cross-purposes, conflicting with each other. Some families, for example, are hostile to the school, the church, or both. A father who has worked his

Figure 4-5 The increasing freedom to assume nontraditional roles is shown by (a) the female roustabout and (b) the male airline steward. [(a) *Wide World*, (b) *Trans World Airlines*]

(b)

(a)

way up in life without much formal education may oppose a child's desire to go to college. "Why spend thousands of dollars on education," he asks, "when lots of college graduates can't get jobs? The only way of learning is by doing." Sometimes families and churches band together to attack schools. Textbooks have been seized and schools closed when traditional families and fundamentalist churches opposed the teaching of controversial subjects such as sex education. Similar conflicts can be seen within a single agency of socialization. Conflict within a family may disrupt the process of socialization. A child who is treated one way by a strict mother and entirely differently by a permissive father may become confused as to the behaviors and responsibilities expected.

A second factor which complicates the process of socialization is the fact that these agencies of socialization perform more than the "official" functions we expect of them—they have many latent functions as well. Officially, for example, the school functions to further socialization and learning. Unofficially, however, the school becomes a stage for status games and popularity contests and the breeding ground for youth subcultures and even antisocial gangs. We like to believe that the school offers equal opportunities for socialization to all students, regardless of their economic backgrounds, but evidence suggests that the school is more helpful to children from middle-class homes than those from lower-class homes. One study (Yee, 1970, pp. 10–12) conducted in thirty-two Texas and California grammar schools found that teachers whose classes were composed mainly of middle-class children were more warm, friendly, and encouraging than teachers of lower-class children. Probably the reasons for this are that the middle-class children are already better prepared for school and present fewer behavior problems. The study indicated, however, that the lower-class children were more sensitive to their teachers' opinions and more dependent upon their approval than were the middle-class children.

Socialization is further complicated by the fact that these three "official" agencies of socialization are not the only ones in operation. Other, unofficial forces are at work, and they sometimes function to confuse—or even to subvert—the influence of the home, church, and school. The media—television, the movies, magazines, and advertisements—often become influential agencies of socialization. By the age of fourteen, most American children have seen several thousand murders on television. Even if these murders are not condoned, even if the murderer is caught and punished, the dramatic settings of these crime shows portray violence as being glamorous and exciting—a view which no parent, teacher, or church supports. The treatment of sex by the entertainment media is similar. Television, movies, and magazines portray (and may seem to support) sexually "liberated" people for whom morality equals enjoyment: "If it is fun, it's good." Even the media's portrayal of "reality"—the evening news—features violence, crime, corruption in high places, and the sexual activities of famous people, implying increasing acceptability for such behavior. The values, behaviors, and life-styles presented by the media are quite different from those taught in the traditional home, church, or school. As a result, a set of confused messages enters the child's mind. The force of these conflicting inputs varies at different ages. In childhood, the voice of the family may remain strong, blotting out the messages issued by television and other media. In adolescence, many influences from outside the home intrude, introducing conflicts and making the process of socialization extremely complicated.

Prolonged adolescence

In Erikson's analysis of turning points in life, adolescence is given more attention than any other. As we look at inconsistency in agencies of socialization, adolescence can be seen as a period in life when contradictory influences are at work. While adolescence is marked by physical changes—it is the time when a person reaches physical maturity—it is also a time of social growth, when a person prepares for work, marriage, and social roles. In some societies, children begin working at a very early age. In these societies, adolescence is only a matter of physical maturing, as evidenced by the insert "Where There Is No Adolescence." In affluent countries, where young workers aren't needed—where, in fact, they are purposely kept off the labor market—adolescence becomes a prolonged and uncertain period of life.

Since the body is mature long before the end of this period, the term *adolescence* makes little sense physiologically. But as applied to all the years of preparation for work or a career, it is quite correct sociologically. One result of a longer "waiting" period before holding a permanent job is often a feeling of alienation, of not being part of the social system. Frequently, adolescents who feel themselves aliens or outsiders respond by criticizing and attacking "the establishment," as many did in the 1960s. Ideally, a period of prolonged adolescence gives people more time to look around, see what sort of work there is, and explore their interests and abilities. But, Bennet Berger (1972, pp. 277–286) notes, young people receive contradictory advice from the older generation: (1) Enjoy your youth as a

---

Where there is no adolescence DIAL TORGERSON

Adolescence is a luxury, a syndrome of the overcivilized. It is scarcely known in some places, where childhood ends abruptly in instant adulthood. In many parts of the world, responsibility comes early. . . .

In Thailand, rural boys of 5 or 6 go to work tending the water buffalo which represent a farm family's wealth and social standing. The buffalo, essential for plowing time, must not be allowed to run away, eat poison fodder, or fall into a pit. If it is hurt, the boy will be harshly punished.

In Italy, law forbids child labor until 14. But the Labor Ministry estimates employment of under-14 children at 450,000 in industry and commerce, plus 100,000 beggars and sidewalk entertainers and 500,000 working on peasant family farms.

Earlier this year, 12-year-old Romeo Longhi went to work at a Milan construction job at the end of the school year, and was struck and killed by a loose beam on his fourth day at work. His father makes $253 a month, an older son $69 more. The big family had needed Romeo's meager salary.

Among the Amharas of Ethiopia, boys begin collecting firewood and shooing chickens from drying grain at 4, or even 3. By 6 they are herdsmen, by 9 can sickle and winnow, by 11 they can plow.

Amharic girls are learning to cook, sew, and manage a house by 10, and at 12 or 13 are ready for marriage. The Amharas have no word for "adolescent." Soon after puberty a child passes into adulthood.

A Bedouin girl living in the Jordanian Desert learns very early what her place in life will be: At 8 she is relegated to the cook tent with her female relatives. For a Bedouin boy, life is better: At 8 he joins the men drinking tea around the fire.

From Dial Torgerson, "Parental Pressures Differ around World," *Los Angeles Times*, Jan 4, 1973, Part I, pp. 1, 18. Copyright Los Angeles Times.

Socialization: A mutual process

111

time in which to explore, grow, and understand yourself but also (2) make an occupational choice immediately and prepare for it thoroughly. Berger is also concerned with the fact that young people who aren't yet fully part of the social system are often recruited for social movements. The youth movements of the 1960s worked for civil rights and peace, but youth movements in the past have rallied around less admirable causes—the Nazi party in Germany and the Facist party in Italy.

Any period of life in which status change occurs or in which status becomes indefinite can become a turning point in socialization: adolescence, the entry into college, marriage, the first permanent job, or even moving to a new city or getting a job promotion. At retirement (a subject we will discuss in a later chapter), a person suffers a sudden loss of the usual roles, and a feeling of alienation similar to that experienced by adolescents may arise.

ADULT SOCIALIZATION

The term *adult socialization* refers to changes in learning and attitudes that take place after the adolescent years. Sometimes the changes are gradual; for example, political or religious attitudes may change. At other times, changes in thinking take place as a person changes roles. Marriage and parenthood can bring about changes in interests and attitudes as well as in life-styles. Changes in status can also lead to new experiences and attitudes. A worker who is promoted to supervisor, a management position in which orders must be given, may complain about slow workers rather than grumble about the boss. Such a worker may begin to turn against the union as a closer identification with management develops. Finally, an overwhelming change may result from an even more basic shift in identification. One example of this type is a change in sexual identification, as with a sex-change operation or when one publicly ad-

mits to being a homosexual or lesbian. (See the insert "The Case of the Gay Sergeant.")

Resocialization

Resocialization differs from other types of adult socialization in that it points to a rapid and drastic change, usually one that is forced upon the individual to some degree. Military service involves resocialization, since it is a deliberate attempt to remold a person's life and personality in certain respects. The recruit is stripped of previous status and gains a new status only by meeting the demands of the military. A more extreme case is that of religious conversion, in which the person may feel completely reoriented—a sense of rebirth into a new personality or of having been "born again." Both the military recruit and the religious convert experience a change from an old life-style to a new one that is willingly accepted and not seen as a matter of abandoning old loyalties.

Brainwashing

The term *brainwashing* is used to describe an attempt to change major views or ideologies against a person's will. When Patricia Hearst was tried in 1976 for taking part in bank robberies as a member of the Symbionese Liberation Army, she pleaded not guilty by reason of brainwashing. Although some psychiatrists agreed with her position, her plea failed. Others held that no total brainwashing could have taken place in the short time—a few months—that she had been held captive.

Brainwashing is a translation of an expression used by the People's Republic of China for purifying the mind of any beliefs in the old order that existed before the communist revolution. Theoretically, the old, mistaken ideas are washed away and the "right" viewpoints put in their place. During the Korean war (1950–1953), attempts were made to convert American captives to communist viewpoints by brainwashing. At first it seemed that new and mysterious processes were at work. But eventually these processes proved to be intensive resocialization techniques, applied along with torture and threats. The person to be "purified" was cut off from old friends and the outside world. Often, he was treated brutally at first and not accepted as a human being. Then, when the prisoner despaired of being part of a human community, a new glimmer of hope was given him. A seemingly understanding prison official talked to him in a kindly manner. As one prisoner recalls the experience:

> The government doesn't want to kill you (He said). It wants to reform you. We don't want to punish you at all, we just want to re-educate you." . . . It was my first glimmer of hope. I felt finally there might be a way out. I wasn't feeling so hopelessly alone anymore. (Lifton, 1961, p. 73)

To this soldier the promise of human contact seemed like a promise of rebirth. In Chinese

---

The case of the gay sergeant   MARTIN DUBERMAN

If there has ever been a son of midAmerica, it was Leonard Matlovich, tech sergeant, Langley Air Force Base, Hampton, Va. Matlovich believes in God, duty, his country, monogamy, competition and hard work. He volunteered for three tours of duty in Vietnam because "that's where my nation needed me." He erected an 18-foot flagpole in his front yard. He voted for Goldwater. He always did more than his share on the job, pushing himself to excel—and then took on additional jobs. He was never comfortable with sexuality; in his conservative Catholic family, "anything relating to sex was not discussed." His politics were right-wing: when the Air Force became integrated, he protested being housed with "niggers"; he considered Walter Cronkite a "flaming liberal."

That is, until two years ago when Leonard Matlovich, aged 30, lost his virginity—to a man.

One doesn't want to claim too much for the transforming power of sex—or even of self-acceptance—but if the causes can't be neatly charted, Matlovich today is clearly a different man from the superpatriot of a few years back. He is now deeply ashamed of the stand he took against integration, and his eyes water when he notes the irony that blacks at Langley have formed his chief support group since he publicly came out as a homosexual seven months ago. A sign on his apartment wall reads, "Legalize Freedom." On his front door the placard says, "Trust in God—She will provide."

Some of his values have been modified, not transformed. . . . Seemingly comfortable now with his sexual orientation, he admits that had he the choice—and he is adamant that homosexuals never have the choice—he would rather be straight. . . . He still loves the Air Force and is sure that he will be allowed to serve in it, but not if it means "living a lie." . . .

From Martin Duberman, "The Case of the Gay Sergeant," *New York Times Magazine*, November 9, 1975, pp. 16–17. © 1975 by The New York Times Company. Reprinted by permission.

Since the above article was written, a court-martial decided that Sergeant Matlovich could not remain in the Air Force. Sex orientation was deemed more important than competence, devotion, or even heroism.

Socialization: A mutual process

reeducation centers during the Korean war, the process achieved only partial results. Few American soldiers became converted to communism, but many felt quite disturbed and disoriented. Although thousands of Americans were captured, only twenty-one elected to stay in North Korea after the war, and all eventually changed their minds and returned home. The so-called brainwashing techniques are powerful, but they are neither magical nor infallible. In a later chapter, we shall discuss resocialization attempts in prisons and mental institutions but will note that drastic changes do not always come about.

CHANGING PATTERNS OF SOCIALIZATION

Such theorists as Cooley and Mead stressed the degree to which our behavior is shaped by those around us through symbolic interaction. However, they assumed that the socialization process would eventually develop personalities with strong feelings about the norms of society. Family and peer groups, they believed, worked with a certain consistency to bring about an internalization of moral values. Certain later theorists, in contrast, stress the many other influences that touch the individual and the shorter time spent with parents, family, neighbors, and friends. People spend more years in school before completion, and after completion they often go back for retraining programs or recreation. They enter into many voluntary associations, such as clubs, fraternal orders, business groups, and labor unions. They join causes—religious, environmental, pacifist, and many others. They move from place to place, seldom sinking deep roots, and they are under pressure to succeed and gain status in the eyes of new groups of associates.

David Riesman: The other-directed personality

A constantly changing society creates a demand for a new type of personality. To cope with the changing situation and shifting social groups, the individual must be able to adjust easily and quickly. In *The Lonely Crowd* (1953), David Riesman has suggested that the development of this new personality has become the most common method of coping with change today. According to Riesman, in America in the seventeenth, eighteenth, and nineteenth centuries, the image of the father was strongly internalized. That is, people accepted their fathers' moral standards as their own. They became *inner-directed*—convinced that their attitudes, values, and standards of behavior were "right" and likely to feel guilty if they failed to live up to them. Today, however, we are influenced by larger numbers of people and our socialization

Figure 4-6 Resocialization is often rapid and intense, as in the training of this Marine recruit. (*Burk Uzzle, Magnum*)

patterns stress cooperation and conformity. Therefore we have become highly responsive to the patterns set by the peer group. Looking to others rather than ourselves for standards of right and wrong, we have developed an *other-directed personality.*

Today, according to Riesman, instead of being guilt-driven, we are anxiety-driven. Our anxiety arises from fear of being rejected and disapproved by the groups to which we belong rather than because of doing something we regard as wrong. It is considered important to know how to manipulate others and get along with them. Conscience has not disappeared, but it is less important than it was to the inner-directed person. The employee caught stealing from the company, for example, may not suffer as much from guilt as from embarrassment over having been caught and exposed. In the mid-1970s, many of the people who were part of the widespread government corruption known as Watergate later wrote of their experiences. Many of them stated that they were following the lead of others; they were, in short, other-directed. The other common theme was that of being seduced by ambition, power, and luxury rather than feeling the guilt that might have come from an examination of conscience.

Riesman does not contend that inner-direction no longer exists or that other-direction is totally lacking in value. The inner-directed personality was no doubt often narrow-minded; the other-directed person is, on the surface, more pleasant and easier to deal with. However, Riesman ends his book with a plea for greater independence of personality, feeling uneasy about a society of people who are weak in self-direction.

Robert J. Lifton: Protean man

Proteus, a minor god in Greek mythology and a servant of Poseidon, god of the sea, was able to change form instantly from human to animal, bird, fish, or even fire or water. From the name of Proteus we derive the word *protean*, meaning

"able to change forms." Robert J. Lifton has adopted this term in describing people of the modern world (Lifton, 1970). Like Riesman, Lifton recognizes the need to adapt rapidly to changing conditions. However, he feels that too deep a gulf has opened between modern people and their cultural tradition. Well-defined and culturally transmitted standards of right and wrong have become less important. Families, ideologies, and religions have declined in meaning, creating a void and a search for new meanings.

As evidence of rapid personality change in the modern world, Lifton notes the grasping of new ideologies, loss of the hope that science can build a better world, demand for rapid innovation in music and the arts, growing fascination with the absurd and the violent, and an interest in mystic experiences through meditation or drugs. While Riesman sees personality change as a needed adjustment to social change, Lifton sees it more as a psychological reaction to fear of impending doom. Against such a gloomy background, however, he sees a strong urge for renewal. He sees the rapidly changing ideas and enthusiasms of protean beings as a search for new possibilities. He does not believe it is yet time for the funeral of humankind.

Lifton's ideas, although rather different from Riesman's, point to an unquestioned fact about socialization: It is not a process that develops a fixed and unchanging personality. Personality always changes as cultures change.

SUMMARY

All societies try to preserve their way of life by passing it on to the next generation through the process known as *socialization.* However, because no two individuals are ever exactly the same, the socialization process also includes the development of unique personalities.

There are theories to explain how the child develops into a reasonably well-adjusted member of society. Sigmund Freud was impressed by the pressure on the maturing individual to repress certain impulses, especially sex and aggression. He therefore developed a theory of socialization that stresses basic conflict between the individual and society. He also considered the sex drive and aggression to be instinctive forms of behavior—a belief strongly questioned by a majority of sociologists and psychologists. Despite his ideas regarding repression, Freud was in some respects a liberator, since he insisted that sex should not be a secret matter, impossible to talk about.

Cooley and Mead, forerunners of modern symbolic interactionism, viewed the relationship between individual and society very differently from Freud. They stressed the harmony between the individual and society, pointing out that the individual could develop a human personality only within society and through interaction with others. In this perspective, they stressed the importance of environment over heredity—an unusual point of view for their time.

Cooley called the individual personality the *looking-glass self*. As we look to others, we guess at their appraisal of us and react to that appraisal, so that our self-concept is actually derived from others. The loved and protected child thus develops a favorable self-image, while a neglected child often develops a negative self-image. Under favorable conditions, Cooley contended, the child follows the social norms in order to be approved by others.

Mead thought that much of the process of accepting the norms was a result of childhood play, first in imitating adult ways and then in playing games by the proper rules. To play the game, one must learn the concept of rules as well as anticipate what others will do. Anticipating the actions of others is possible only for one who can imagine his or her way into their roles. This understanding of roles, and the social expectations connected with roles, helps promote the internalization of norms and values. The resulting internalized voice of society Mead called the *generalized other*.

Mead also saw the personality as having two separate facets, the "I" and the "me." The "I" represents the original and creative side of the personality, the "me" the person's response to the expectations of others.

Jean Piaget has added to the conclusions of Mead regarding the internalization of norms. Piaget found that the child who learns the rules only from an authoritarian adult tends to think of them as being external. On the other hand, children who play and learn to cooperate with one another see rules as being made by people for their own mutual benefit.

Erik Erikson, originally a close follower of Freud, has become much more optimistic about societal-individual harmony. Like Freud, he believes in a number of developmental stages in the maturing process, including those of adolescence, young adulthood, the middle years, and old age. Each of the latter periods, as well as earlier phases of childhood, are looked upon as important turning points in life, or *crises*. Adolescence must meet its crisis by developing a sense of adult identity, young adulthood by achieving intimacy, middle-age by generativity, old age by ego integrity. Erikson sees a failure at one stage as making later stages more difficult—but not impossible—to move through successfully.

Much of socialization takes place through the learning of *roles*—the behavior expected of a person holding a particular social position or *status*. Roles may be *achieved* through effort or *ascribed*—given—by birth or society. Although achieved roles are very important to people, Erving Goffman points out that we develop a certain amount of *role distance*, wanting to be thought of as more than merely a role or set of roles.

Many roles lead to the development of *strains*, or problems involved in living up to their expectations, either because they make competitive demands on time, include conflicting expectations, or because they are otherwise unsatisfactory. Many roles are *reciprocal*, as in the case of husband-wife or mother-child. Such roles can give rise to strains if the two individuals do not interpret them the same way.

Socialization is complicated by the fact that competing agencies of socialization tend to pull people in different directions. For example, the church, school, and family may suggest one type of behavior, whereas the advertising media, television, and the peer group may suggest another.

Since adolescence—the period between childhood and full social and economic maturity—is prolonged in modern industrial society, socialization is made difficult by a long period of indefinite status. Such status conflicts, combined with very real moral conflicts within society, help to account for the radicalization of youth in the 1960s.

Adult socialization refers to fairly important changes in views and life-styles that may develop after full maturity, through job change, marriage, new associates, and new ideas. A relatively sudden and drastic change is spoken of as *resocialization*; examples are the change from civilian to military life and religious conversion. Extreme resocialization against the individual's will is known as *brainwashing*.

As a result of rapid social change, patterns of socialization also change, and so do the personalities that result. David Riesman analyzes the change as moving from an *inner-directed personality*, with a strongly internalized conscience, to an *other-directed personality*, motivated more by peers than by internalized norms. Lifton, in his description of *protean man*, concludes that modern people find it unusually easy to switch from one commitment to another. He holds that this is the result of lack of assurance and the absence of deep roots in a cultural tradition.

Study guide

Terms to know

Socialization	Peer group	Role conflict
Unconscious mind	Identification	Reciprocal roles
Repression	Internalization	Role sets
Instinct	"I" and "me" (Mead)	Agencies of socialization
Id	Generalized other	Adult socialization
Ego	Crisis (Erikson)	Resocialization
Superego	Role and status	Brainwashing
Looking-glass self	Ascribed status	Inner-directed personality
Looking-glass process	Achieved status	Other-directed personality
Self-concept	Role distance	Protean man
Significant others	Role strain	

Names to know

Sigmund Freud	Jean Piaget	Erving Goffman
Charles Horton Cooley	Erik Erikson	David Riesman
George Herbert Mead	Ralph Linton	Robert J. Lifton

Self-test

Part I. Multiple Choice. Select the best of the four alternative answers:

1 The socialization process can be described in *all but one* of the following ways: (**a**) a process of internalizing social values, (**b**) the development of an individual personality, (**c**) a perfect adjustment of the individual to societal demands, (**d**) a mutual process.

2 Sigmund Freud (**a**) thought that many people suffer psychological problems because of repression of the sex drive, (**b**) repudiated the idea of instincts, (**c**) put his ideas to experimental tests, (**d**) was optimistic about human perfectibility.

3 In Freudian terminology, the word that most closely resembles *conscience* is (**a**) id, (**b**) ego, (**c**) superego, (**d**) libido.

4 The process by which ideas and beliefs become part of the self is called (**a**) conformity, (**b**) internalization, (**c**) imitation, (**d**) obedience.

5 Freud stressed the idea of a struggle between the self and society; Cooley and Mead (**a**) agreed with Freud, (**b**) believed the individual should be thoroughly subordinated to society, (**c**) believed society should in no way restrain the individual, (**d**) stressed the view that the individual and society gain from each other.

6 Cooley and Mead both considered the chief source of personality development to be (**a**) social and environmental, (**b**) genetic, (**c**) racial, (**d**) an outgrowth of struggle between superego and id.

7 The essence of the looking-glass process is that people (**a**) are so conceited that they

constantly look at themselves, (**b**) are highly introspective, (**c**) develop their self-image according to how they think others see them, (**d**) see only a faint reflection of reality.

8 People whose opinions are most important to one's self-image are spoken of as (**a**) peers, (**b**) secondary groups, (**c**) significant others, (**d**) generalized others.

9 Jean Piaget concluded that the need for norms is best understood if learned from (**a**) parents, (**b**) teachers, (**c**) religious authorities, (**d**) the peer group.

10 The only theorist of socialization mentioned in the text who carries the socialization process all the way from infancy to old age is (**a**) Freud, (**b**) Mead, (**c**) Piaget, (**d**) Erikson.

11 In Erikson's developmental scheme, the "crisis of middle age" is one of developing (**a**) autonomy, (**b**) identity, (**c**) intimacy, (**d**) generativity.

12 The school as a leading agency of socialization (**a**) invariably reinforces the teachings of the home, (**b**) is more helpful with children from middle-class homes than with those from lower-class homes, (**c**) finds that lower-class children are indifferent to teacher approval, (**d**) is more influential than the home.

13 Adolescence in the United States is characterized by *all but one* of the following: (**a**) feelings of alienation in many cases, (**b**) conflicting advice about occupational decisions, (**c**) often critical attitudes toward the "establishment," (**d**) encouragement of a feeling of social and economic utility.

14 In the insert called "The Case of the Gay Sergeant," once the sergeant admitted to being "gay," many other new attitudes developed, including (**a**) a strong fellow feeling for black people, (**b**) support of right-wing causes, (**c**) a desire to leave the Air Force, (**d**) antagonism toward the women's liberation movement.

15 According to David Riesman, an important personality change has come about in modern America, making us generally more (**a**) inner-directed, (**b**) tradition-directed, (**c**) other-directed, (**d**) psychologically autonomous.

Part II. True-False Questions

1 "The process by which a person internalizes the values of society" is an adequate definition of socialization.

2 Differences in appearance and race affect socialization mainly because society shows a preference for some types over others.

3 Martha Wolfenstein's study of the advice of the Children's Bureau in 1914 indicates an easy, "liberated" attitude toward sex on the part of the bureau.

4 Freud's beliefs about the Oedipus complex were experimentally confirmed by the studies of the anthropologist Malinowski.

5 In their belief that human personality is a social product, Cooley and Mead disagreed with the social Darwinists.

6 Cooley believed that we could not develop a self-concept except in relation to others.

7 Rules are said to be internalized when we follow them mainly out of fear of punishment.

8 The study titled "Some People's Children" concluded that the high-IQ children who best measured up to their potential had parents who placed a high value on independence training.

9 In Mead's analysis, very little value is gained through childhood play.

10 An ascribed status is one that has been attained through great effort.

11 The roles of husband and wife are good examples of reciprocal roles.

12 The type of role strain in which a person is expected to do incompatible tasks in the performance of the roles (such as being both friend and disciplinarian) is called role conflict.

Socialization: A mutual process

13 Brainwashing is a drastic type of resocialization, generally into ideas incompatible with those of the person being brainwashed.

14 Piaget found that children develop consistent ideas of justice by the age of seven or eight.

15 Lifton's concept of protean man implies that modern people are more changeable in ideologies, norms, attitudes, and tastes than were people of the past.

Questions for discussion

1 What distinctive points of view, customs, or personality traits have you gained from your own family? What aspects of your childhood socialization have you discarded?

2 What arguments could you make in agreement with Freud's view, stressing conflict between the individual and society? In other words, what are some of the duties and norms that are very hard to abide by?

3 Try to apply Cooley's concept of the looking-glass self to your own personality. As a child, were you sensitive to glances from others that seemed to denote praise or blame? Can you think of any ways in which others' judgment of you, in the form of praise or criticism, has influenced your interests and abilities?

4 How does childhood play help with the internalization of norms? Can you think of any cases in your own learning experiences?

5 Describe cases of role strain with which you are familiar. (You should be able to find these in the role of student, of son or daughter, and of employee.)

6 Analyze, in terms of role strain, the occupational role you intend to follow after completion of college.

7 Why are the periods of adolescence and of old age and retirement particularly difficult periods of life, as seen either in terms of role analysis or from the position of Erikson?

8 Can you think of experiences that would lead you to believe Riesman is right about the drift toward the other-directed personality? Can you think of any reason for viewing Riesman's ideas with caution?

9 To what types of people does Lifton's idea of protean man best apply—educated or uneducated, young or old? In other words, what types of people are likely to change their minds easily and move from one interest or ideology to another?

10 In Goffman's analysis of role distance, he describes how people are at first totally absorbed in their occupational roles and then learn to look at them from a distance, separating their personalities from them. Have you ever had this experience in your work or in other types of role you must perform?

Projects

1 Do an observational study of children playing at adult roles at home, in the neighborhood, or at a child-care center. What conceptions of the roles are basically correct? Erroneous? From your observation, would you say that role learning through playing at roles is definitely helpful to the socialization process?

2 Analyze a popular television show as an agency of socialization. Does the show seem to teach that violence is necessary for the triumph of the right? Do police obey the law? Does the show tend to promote liberal or conservative viewpoints?

3 Make a tally of class opinion regarding Riesman's inner-directed and other-directed personalities, asking: (a) Do you think Riesman is right in saying we are becoming other-directed? (b) If you had to characterize yourself, would you say you were closer to the inner-directed or the other-directed type? [You are likely to find that students' views of others (the society in

general) and of themselves do not coincide.]

4 Make a survey of a number of intelligent and successful students at school to see whether you can duplicate the findings reported in the insert "Some People's Children." Ask the most successful students whether their parents have rated independence training quite highly.

Suggested readings

Erikson, Erik H.: "Identity and the Life Cycle, *Psychological Issues*, vol. 1, no. 1, Spring 1959, pp. 18–164. How does the problem of identity change from period to period in life? Erikson answers this question according to his psychoanalytic theory, and he explains the consequences of success and failure in meeting these problems.

Kohn, Melvin L.: "Social Class and Parent-Child Relationships," *American Journal of Sociology*, vol. 68, June 1964, pp. 471–480. How does socialization differ on a social-class basis? If you are born of a working-class family, will your learning experiences at home equip you for success in a middle-class society? Kohn explains how the background experiences of families tend to cause them to socialize children for approximately the same occupational roles as the parents have pursued.

Morris, Marian Gennaria: "Psychological Miscarriage," *Trans-Action*, vol. 3, January–February 1966, pp. 8–13. What causes some mothers to hate and neglect their babies? What are the consequences to the self-image of both mothers and children?

Simon, William, and John Gagnon: "Psychosexual Development," *Trans-Action*, vol. 6, March 1969, pp. 9–17. Does the developing human being inevitably go through certain biologically fixed stages in psychosexual development, as Freud maintained, or are sociocultural factors more important than biological factors in determining what course psychosexual development will take?

Simpson, Ida Harper: "Patterns of Socialization into Professions: The Case of Student Nurses," *Sociological Inquiry*, vol. 37, Winter 1967, pp. 47–54. Are the processes of childhood socialization repeated when an adult masters a new role? Simpson outlines three comparable phases: the shift from generalized cultural attitude that led to career choice, the steps to proficiency, and then the adoption of new reference groups.

U'Ren, Richard C.: "West Point: Cadets, Codes, and Careers," *Society*, vol. 12, May–June 1975, pp. 21–29. How the "beasts" (new cadets) are resocialized. A story of status deprivation, tension, and hazing, but with the promise of a new and highly desired status in the future. The discussion considers why the resocialization process works with some and fails with others.

Waters, Harry F.: "What TV Does to Kids," *Newsweek*, Feb. 21, 1977, pp. 62–70. "I don't relate to my family much because we're all too busy watching TV," said one fourteen-year-old. Another comments, "I've seen so much violence that if I saw someone really get killed, it wouldn't be a big deal." Does television viewing isolate the young from their families? Do violent programs create a "mean-world syndrome"? These are some of the questions pursued in this many-faceted analysis.

Key to questions. Multiple Choice: 1-c; 2-a; 3-c; 4-b; 5-d; 6-a; 7-c; 8-c; 9-d; 10-d; 11-d; 12-b; 13-d; 14-a; 15-c. True-False: 1-F; 2-T; 3-F; 4-F; 5-T; 6-T; 7-F, 8-T; 9-F; 10-F; 11-T; 12-T; 13-T; 14-F; 15-T.

5

GROUP INTERACTION

This chapter explores the types of groups to which the individual belongs and the importance of group membership. After reading it, you should be able to:

1   Recognize the individual's need for sociability and for membership in groups.

2   See the possible psychological consequences, as demonstrated by Durkheim, of isolation from social groups and their norms as well as the consequences of extreme group commitment.

3   Recognize the tendency for many people to give up their own judgment in favor of the group's but also to strengthen their morale through group membership.

4   Distinguish between primary and secondary groups and understand the significance of each.

5   Understand the importance and possible dangers of ingroup versus outgroup conflict.

6   Reach a sympathetic understanding of the problems of conflict groups within a society.

7   Be more aware of your own reference groups, both positive and negative.

As we have seen in the last two chapters, personality development occurs within cultures, subcultures, or both. It results from the interactive process of socialization. Our cultures and subcultures may be thought of as the largest meaningful groups to which we belong, and the families that start us along the road to socialization as the smallest groups. Throughout our lives, we become involved with many other groups—sometimes intentionally, as enthusiastic members, and sometimes unintentionally, almost in spite of ourselves.

Individuals need not be mere pawns in the groups to which they belong. They may be part of an interactive process, both influencing the group and being influenced by it. Groups themselves interact with each other, sometimes competitively, sometimes cooperatively. Occasionally their interests conflict with each other.

Sociologists have defined different types of groups, but while the definitions are useful, they only begin to answer our questions. In this chapter, we investigate the importance of social groups to the individual and to society. Belonging to a group makes certain demands upon us. It limits our freedom in certain ways, since we cannot associate with others without caring about their desires as well as our own. Can we, then, be freer and happier by staying away from others, or does our psychological well-being depend on relating to others in groups? Do we have to associate with intimate groups, or are the casual friends we make at school and at work enough? In some societies, groups are centered almost entirely on the family, the neighborhood, and the church. Our society contains these groups—and many others. Business organizations, labor organizations, political committees,

and semipolitical groups abound. It is not for nothing that we have been called "a nation of joiners."

How do groups influence a person's sense of identity? Can identification with a group cause the loss of a sense of self? Many of the groups we will be discussing become small societies themselves and perform many of the same functions as the larger society—providing protection, a source of identity, and a focus for loyalty. At the same time, the group makes demands on the individual. In many ways, the group becomes a go-between, linking the individual to the larger society.

THE GROUP DEFINED

Group is generally defined as a body of two or more persons who are held together by a common focus of interest and interaction. In some cases, the bond uniting group members is mutual concern and affection; in others, it is devotion to a common cause. In still other cases, members of the group take part in group activities mainly to advance their own personal goals. Let us note that a number of people who all happen to be at the same place at the same time—a bus station, for example—do not constitute a group, since they share no common focus of interest or sense of belonging. A statistical category of people, as well, is merely a statement of one common characteristic—such as all those sixty-five years of age or more. They do not constitute a group unless they unite to form some kind of organization.

Total societies and subcultures, insofar as they provide a sense of common identity for their members, can be thought of as groups. On a smaller and far more temporary scale, the same is true of persons who band together to form social movements. As long as they share a sense of identity—as "war protesters," say, or as "feminists"—they may be considered a group. Groups may be temporary or persist in time; individual members may change while the group continues. Most of our discussion of groups will center on groups that are small in size, fairly long-lived, and closely integrated. As with other sociological phenomena, differences are not always clear and distinct, so that concepts of group, community, and society merge into one another.

IMPORTANCE OF GROUP MEMBERSHIP

Personality, as we have noted, arises partly through group interaction. Individuals learn to identify with others, to take on new values, and to try to see themselves as others see them. The ways in which group membership functions for the individual differ from one society to another. In some societies, group membership is stressed, while individualism is considered unimportant or harmful. In ancient China, for example, the individual was constantly reminded of his or her

Figure 5-1 Basic to social life is a desire to belong to a group. (*Katrina Thomas, Photo Researchers, Inc.*)

obligation to the family, the province, and the empire. A person did not exist, it was repeated, except as part of a family whose members included long dead ancestors as well as the living. Modern Japan, another tightly knit society, also stresses the importance of the group. Japanese employees rarely change jobs. In the course of working for a particular company, they become part of a closed group. Leaving the company might be seen as an insult to their employers and fellow workers. In the United States, in contrast, such social pressure would be considered an infringement on personal freedom.

Sociability needs

Groups often exist mainly for the sake of sociability, the interaction with others for the sheer pleasure of their company and for the fulfillment of certain psychological needs. Very few people like to live in isolation for any length of time; for most of us, a certain amount of sociability is a necessity of life. Robert S. Weiss (1969, pp. 36–43) has analyzed the psychological needs filled by sociability. His study is based on observations and interviews with members of an organization called Parents without Partners, whose members are mainly divorcees with children. These people were chosen for study since they were looking for new friendships to make

up for the loss of their spouses. When asked what they gained from belonging to the group, they replied that it was very helpful for relieving boredom and for temporary fun and diversion, but it did not make up for the loneliness that resulted from divorce. Marriage provides an intimate form of sociability which the members did not find in this social club.

Weiss next tried to discover whether married people with no friends outside marriage also felt lonely. After questioning couples who had recently moved to a city, he found that wives who didn't work and therefore couldn't make acquaintances on the job were very lonely. Weiss concluded that both casual friends and an intimate partner are essential to fulfill needs for sociability. Before ending the study, Weiss identified five needs for sociability. They are related to each other but are different in emphasis.

1 The need for intimacy, including a chance to express feelings freely and to give and receive trust and understanding. Sex is not necessarily involved, although Weiss notes that for people who are potential mates, it is difficult to maintain an intimate relationship without sexual involvement.
2 Social integration for the sake of belonging and sharing concerns. This can be done by cooperating for the same objectives or by the exchange of information, ideas, and experiences.
3 Nurturant behavior—that is, the need for someone to care for. "We suspect," says Weiss, "that the absence of this function may be signaled by a sense that one's life is unfulfilled, meaningless, and empty of purpose" (p. 32).
4 The need for a reassurance of worth that depends on being accepted.
5 Assistance in time of need.

Many *voluntary associations* are organizations formed to fulfill the sociability needs identified by Weiss. Some organizations, like Alcoholics Anonymous, are formed so that their members can help each other solve a common problem. Often the unofficial functions of an organization turn out to be more important than its official purpose. The organization described in the insert on page 126 was formed to help "little people" cope with employment discrimination and medical problems. More importantly, it turned out to be a place where they could meet friends, find mates, and gain self-confidence.

Belonging and the hold on life

Durkheim's *Suicide*, published in 1897, was one of the first books to explore the importance of the link to other people and groups (1966). By analyzing suicide statistics, Durkheim found that the people who are most likely to commit suicide are those who are isolated from or who have the weakest ties to others: the unmarried, widowed, divorced; those without children; and those with no strong attachments to religious, social, or community groups. Durkheim called the suicide committed by isolates *egoistic* suicide. A second type of suicide Durkheim called *anomic*, meaning "separated from the norms." This group includes people who do not feel bound to the moral order or who do not feel obligated to others. The term *anomic* was also applied to people who feel confused after moving to a new community or acquiring a new status—people who are unable to adjust to new surroundings or to a very different way of life.

A society that is becoming industrialized, with large-scale movement to urban areas, creates changes which can disturb or disorganize an individual's personality. Durkheim worked at the turn of the century, when the pace of industrialization was increasing in both Europe and the United States. He viewed anomie as a characteristic of industrial societies that affected some people more than others. Recently, the feeling of anomie seems to be most intense among people in their teens and early twenties, as evidenced by rising suicide rates in this age group (Table 5-1). As the insert "The Youthful Suicides" indicates

Little people of America

Martin S. Weinberg of Rutgers University has made a study of an association formed by little people to help them deal with their problems (*Journal of Health and Social Behavior*, March 1968). There is an analogy, he feels, between the way the life of a little person changes when he joins others to become a member of a "minority group" and the situation of other stigmatized people in our society.

The Little People of America, an organization of dwarfs and midgets, was formed in 1960. It currently has 750 paid members, and a mailing list of an additional 1500. Officially, the L.P.A. is concerned with the employment and medical problems of little people, but for most of its members its most important service is the opportunity it offers for little people to meet one another. This, Weinberg found when he interviewed members at the 1965 convention, is the reason why most little people (65 percent of Weinberg's respondents) joined the organization.

When Weinberg asked the members what they got from belonging to the group, the answers usually concerned social relationships. "Friends," said one member simply. "I found my husband," said another. Others referred to their increased feelings of security. "Knowing I am not alone." And, "I have learned not to be afraid of other people because they are bigger." The L.P.A., at annual conventions and monthly district meetings, introduces members to a wider field of possible friends and marriage partners than they have ever encountered before.

. . . Members told Weinberg that sometimes when they try to visit the home of a little person who is not a member, they are barred from the house—usually by the little person's parents. There are little people on the mailing list of the organization who are not members of it. Like members of other stigmatized categories, Weinberg believes, these little people have assimilated the values of the big people's world so thoroughly that they find their own kind grotesque. The parallels with the experience of other minorities are striking.

(page 128), anomie leads to hopelessness, inability to communicate, and extreme loneliness.

Durkheim also observed that suicide was common in many countries with very close-knit societies, such as Japan. In these countries, the reason for suicide is quite different. According to Durkheim, people feel they must take their own lives if they have somehow disgraced the group to which they belong, for life outside the group would be intolerable. Durkheim called this type of suicide *altruistic* suicide—an act performed for the sake of others. One form of altruistic suicide is the Japanese ritual of *hara kiri*.

Durkheim's analysis of suicide implies that people should be committed, to a certain degree, to social groups, norms, and responsibilities. Too little commitment is as bad as too much. Isolated or uncommitted people show a higher-than-average suicide rate. The same is true for those who are so strongly committed to the group that their lives have little meaning except as they serve the group.

Although Durkheim's work was published more than seventy years ago, the ideas of egoistic, anomic, and altruistic suicide continue to be influential. Durkheim's followers do point out, however, that a single case of suicide might involve more than one of the causes he outlined.

Foundations of social life

Table 5-1 Suicide Rates

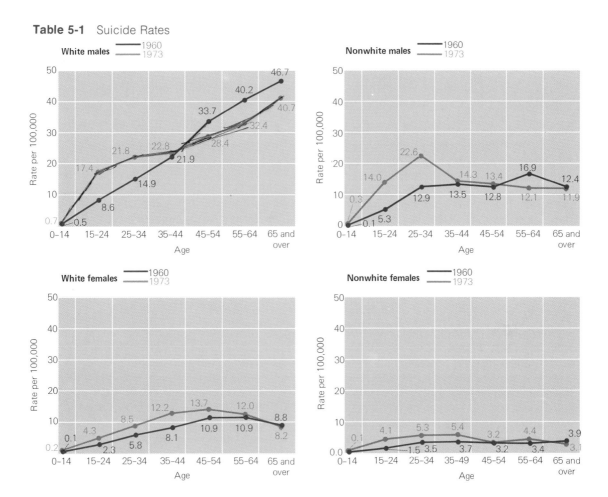

Source: *U.S. Fact Book, The Statistical Abstract of the United States*, Grosset and Dunlap, New York, 1976, p. 155.

Note: If Durkheim's explanations of suicide are correct, the period 1960–1973 showed an increase in alienation of youth, especially young men.

For example, a man who has suddenly lost all his money will have to make great changes in his life-style—a possible cause for anomic suicide. At the same time, his changed status may cut him off from his friends and family—a possible cause for egoistic suicide. Finally, this man may feel that in losing his money he has disgraced his family—a possible cause for altruistic suicide.

Groups and individual autonomy

In thinking about groups, sociologists have to answer a central question: "Should a group be thought of simply as a collection of individuals, as an entity equal to the sum of its parts? Or should a group be considered something new or different, greater than or different from the sum of its parts?" The first point of view is referred to as *nominalism*: the group exists in name only. The second point of view, that of Durkheim, is that the group has a life of its own; it cannot be understood in terms of the psychology of its individual members. This point of view is called *realism*. It holds that a group has a real existence, an identity of its own (Warriner, 1956). A third approach to groups, the one we will stress in this

Group interaction

127

The youthful suicides

At 19, Steve seemed to be a normal, healthy teen-ager. His grades as a sophomore in a Los Angeles college were average, his home life was apparently happy, and he had no overt psychological hang-ups. True, he was somewhat retiring. He regarded his schoolmates as "crude" and he never had a date so far as anyone knew. But his acquaintances merely put that down to shyness or sensitivity. Then one day Steve went into his mother's bedroom, took the gun kept to protect against intruders and put a bullet through his head.

In the past, Steve's suicide would have been regarded as a tragic incident, puzzling but on balance an isolated phenomenon. Now, however, . . . an increasing number of young people seem to be turning to suicide. . . . From a rate of 12.2 per 100,000 population in 1960, suicides among 20- to 29-year olds had nearly doubled, to 23.3 per 100,000 in 1968. [Statistics mainly for the Los Angeles area.]

Why are so many young people increasingly willing to do away with themselves? At present the answers are speculative. . . . One emotion apparently shared by most of the young suicides is an intense fear of pressure from their parents. Many also harbored feelings of hopelessness, which they seem to project onto society in general. But perhaps the most common factor is an intense feeling of loneliness. "I could certainly generalize that most youngsters in a suicidal state would have fewer contacts with others," said Peck [Director of the Los Angeles Center for Suicide Prevention]. "My guess is that we have more conditions that lead to that today—a lack of responsiveness among people and institutions." Thus one major problem appears to be that suicidal youngsters, unlike older people in a similar state, become so cut off and uncommunicative that no one really gets to know what is troubling them. "With older people in trouble, you don't usually find such intense isolation," explains Peck. "Older persons give a lot more overt indication of internal troubles."

Newsweek, February 15, 1971. Copyright 1971 by Newsweek, Inc. All rights reserved. Reprinted by permission.

text, is a compromise position called *interactionism*. According to this perspective, the group has a reality of its own which accounts for actions, attitudes, ideas, and emotions that the individual might not otherwise hold. However, most group members can still maintain *autonomy*, or a sense of self. They are also able to influence the group. Conformity to the group varies from person to person.

Conformity to group opinions

The most famous study on conformity to the group was conducted by Solomon Asch (1955, pp. 31–35). Asch asked his subjects to tell him which of three lines on a card matched the length of a fourth line on another card. The correct answer was so obvious as to make mistakes almost impossible. Also present with the actual subjects of the experiment were five other people, Asch's co-workers, who were also judging the length of the lines. All the co-workers had been told to give the same *wrong* answer to the question. In this case, would the subject give the correct answer as he or she saw it or give in to group opinion?

The setting was as follows. All participants sat in booths isolated from each other and transmitted their answers to the researcher. However, the real subject's equipment was so wired that he or she heard all the other responses before replying. The result: One-third of the subjects gave in to the majority opinion and chose the incorrect answer. In repeating the experiment several times, Asch found that the size of the group didn't matter. Whether the group was large or small, the real subjects found it difficult to stand up against unanimous opposition. However, most subjects would stand by their own judgment if at least one other person gave the right answer or even a different wrong answer. The same type of reaction can sometimes be seen in a class discussion. If several very vocal people all speak up on one side of a debatable issue, it takes a lot of courage for someone to support the opposite side. Discouraging as Asch's experimental results may seem, it should be noted that most of the subjects (two-thirds) did *not* give in to group opinion.

Winning group approval

A stronger argument for the importance of group influence comes from an experiment conducted by Charles Kissler (1967, pp. 32–35). Kissler asked small groups of people to judge several works of art, which each person did alone in the first phase of the experiment. Kissler and his colleagues then interviewed the people assigned to different groups, asking their opinions of the others in the group. After that, the researchers repeated back to group members what the others had said about them, actually giving them false statements.

The experimenters wanted to find out whether those people who thought they had been rated highly by the others would be flattered and therefore willing to agree with group opinions about the works of art. The result was as expected: Those who believed themselves to be liked by the others were easy to convince and often changed their opinions to coincide with those of the group.

But what about the people who believed that their groups had rated them badly? Would they stand by their original opinion? Would they oppose the group just to show their anger? Or would they also change opinions in the direction of group conformity? The answer depended on whether they thought they would work with the same group throughout the experiments. If they thought they would work with the group only once, they defied the group and held to their original opinions. However, if they thought they would remain with the group, many changed their opinions to conform. They seemed to want to be accepted by the group, regardless of the loss of independent thinking.

The wish to be liked and to gain prestige can have very important results. It can often lead to socially unapproved behavior. Consider the insert "The Religious Delinquents" (page 130), which deals with boys who, in spite of their religious upbringing, engage in delinquent acts at the suggestion of others.

Co-workers tend to have similar concerns and problems, and everyone wants to be accepted by others. Therefore people who work together for a long time tend to take on similar attitudes, share the same feelings, and engage in close teamwork. As time passes, their self-concepts come to depend on the views of their co-workers. According to a famous study by Shills and Janowitz (1948, pp. 280–294), the German army in World War II held together remarkably well during defeat after defeat. This was true especially among old units that had trained and fought together through the years, while "deterioration of group solidarity . . . was most frequently found in hastily fabricated units" (1948, p. 288). The older units had become close-knit; their members would not abandon each other or make individual decisions to surrender. Their self-concepts depended on how they were viewed by their comrades. They could not bear to think of themselves as deserters of the group. In the final days of the war, decisions to surrender were made by squads, not by individuals.

The religious delinquents

Juvenile court judges are fond of telling a delinquent youngster and his parents that if the boy went to church more often, he wouldn't get into so much trouble. But Thomas M. Gannon of Loyola, a sociologist and priest, has put this platitude to rest: after interviewing 150 teenaged Catholic boys coming into the Cook Country juvenile detention home, he is forced to conclude that religion is not of much use as a restraint upon delinquency. (*Sociology and Social Research*, July 1967.)

Most of the boys in the study were, by any standard, religious; 53 percent attend mass once or twice a month and 27 percent go every Sunday. . . . They are aware of the doctrines of the Catholic Church in regard to sex, stealing, and gang fighting, and most agree that these doctrines are right.

Despite their evident religious commitment, the gap between what these boys do and what they know their church says they should do is very wide. . . . Of those who agreed strongly that sexual intercourse outside of marriage is wrong, 20.3 percent had nevertheless fornicated a few times and another 26 percent had fornicated a number of times. Most of these boys agree with the church that stealing is wrong; yet 69 percent admitted they had stolen on a number of occasions.

What matters to these boys, when it comes to action, is what their friends say and not what their church teaches: If the gang wanted to go out and steal, for instance, only 26 percent of these boys would refuse to go along.

"The Religious Delinquents," published by permission of Transaction, Inc., from *Trans-Action*, vol. 5., no. 2, copyright © 1967 by Transaction, Inc.

[*Note: Father Gannon was not convinced that religion has no effect but felt that the religion involved was "commitment by default" rather than religious convictions the boys had contemplated deeply.*]

PRIMARY AND SECONDARY GROUPS

Charles Horton Cooley, whose ideas on socialization were introduced in the previous chapter, used the term *primary group* to describe the family, children's peer groups, and the neighborhood—groups involving strong feelings of belonging and intimacy. Primary groups are the source of what Cooley held to be the best human feelings—concern, love, generosity, and cooperation. These groups are considered primary because they are the first groups a child enters and also because they are vital to the socialization process. In adult life, the people who work together closely or who form intimate friendships find primary relationships outside the home or neighborhood. Primary groups are different from other groups in that their members are emotionally close, engage in face-to-face interaction, and identify with one another. Within a well-integrated family, for example, identification may be so close that the success of one member becomes a success for all, and a failure for one is felt as a failure for all. In primary groups, we learn not only to care about one another but also to take on each other's values, to arrive at group decisions, and to see the world in the same way. Primary groups give moral support in many ways. They can save members from feeling alienated and purposeless. They give us our first experience in the give and take of social interaction and teach us to cooperate to achieve shared goals.

Kingsley Davis (1949, pp. 52–61) has described the conditions that usually exist in primary groups—physical closeness, small size, and stability. But all these traits are not necessarily present at the same time. An affectionate family can maintain primary-group feeling even though some of its members have moved away. Emotional feelings of closeness, then, are more important than either physical nearness, small size, or stability. On the other hand, physical closeness is not enough. Prostitution involves a type of intimacy; but because it is entered into for pay rather than because of affection, it is not a primary relationship.

Members of primary groups or people involved in primary relationships work together for their common good. A primary relationship can also be thought of as an end in itself; it is not used to achieve outside goals. We value our friends simply because they are friends. The primary relationship is also inclusive; the total personalities are involved. Such a relationship is personal and special; no other person can take the place of a particular friend or family member.

Davis points out that the criteria of primary relationships listed by Cooley and himself are somewhat idealized. If they really existed, we would all belong to tight little cliques. Society calls on people to relate in many ways and actually opposes exclusive primary-group ties. "But if organized society is opposed to the full expression of primary relationships," Davis concludes, "it is also friendly to a partial expression of them" (1949b, p. 58). Friendships, close family relationships, and neighborly feelings are all praised, even though the demands of the outside world cut in on them.

Moral neutrality of primary groups

Although Cooley saw primary groups as the source of all good feelings, these groups can develop in both socially acceptable and unacceptable forms. Since the group members are very sensitive to the opinions of other members, they try to conform in order to win approval, whether in a law-abiding manner or not.

Synanon House, a self-help rehabilitation center for drug addicts, provides a good example of how primary-group relationships may be used to promote socially approved values and behavior. The insert "Joining Synanon" (page 132) shows how one young man reversed his criminal values to gain status (a "rep," or reputation) at Synanon. The Mafia, ironically, also relies on the qualities of a primary group: mutual understanding, loyalty, identification, and close cooperation to bind its members together. As the insert "The Mafia Family" (page 133) shows, the Mafia was modeled on the European extended family.

As the Mafia organization became larger and wealthier, the family-style structure began to give way to a business structure. Formal rules replaced unwritten family understandings, and relationships between people became regulated by contracts. Despite these changes in organization, Mafia members are still bound together into very tight, mutually dependent groups with primary-group characteristics. Robert T. Anderson (1965) has published a list of some of the rules that unite them:

1 To help one another and avenge every injury of a fellow member.
2 To work with all means for the defense and freeing of any fellow member who has fallen into the hands of the judiciary.
3 To divide the proceeds of thievery, robbery, and extortion with certain considerations for the needy as determined by the *capo* (chief).
4 To keep the oath and maintain secrecy on pain of death within twenty-four hours.

Secondary groups

Even in his time (1846–1929), Cooley recognized a major drift of the world away from primary groups, especially at the neighborhood level. With the decline of small towns and villages, as people moved to the cities, new types of groups, called secondary groups, became important. *Secondary groups* can be defined as groups created for specific purposes and interested in their members mainly for their contributions to those purposes. Business corporations, government bureaus, the Armed Forces, and colleges and universities are secondary groups. The corporation or government bureau hires people for the services they can perform. Colleges and universities give their students an education, awarding diplomas and perhaps recommending them for jobs. In all these groups, people must measure up to the mark. If they do not, the corporation or bureau will fire them, the Armed Forces will punish them, and the college or university will expel them or withhold their diplomas. The roles, and the criteria for membership and reward, are more formal and impersonal than in primary groups.

There are other differences. In primary groups, people work together for their mutual benefit. In secondary groups, people also accomplish tasks by working together, but each person is working to achieve his or her own goal—such as a paycheck—rather than to benefit the group. Politics, for example, is highly competitive, and while politicians may support each other, they always weigh their own interests. Politicians know that favors will be repaid; votes delivered to a friend in one election will earn a return in the future.

Alienation in the secondary world

To be *alienated* is to have no sense of belonging, meaning, power, or emotional attachment. People can be alienated from their jobs, their families, their societies, or life itself. Durkheim used the word *anomie* to describe alienation, but the

---

Joining Synanon   LEWIS YABLONSKY

The fact that Frankie was exported from New York to Los Angeles was a significant force in keeping him at Synanon, as he stated it: At times I felt like splitting (leaving), then I thought it will be hard to make it back to New York. I didn't know Los Angeles and was afraid to make it out there—'cause I didn't know the people. Synanon was better than anything else I could do—at the time.

Also, Synanon House was on the beach. The meals were good. In the evening many ex-addict top musicians would play cool jazz. Also there were, according to Frankie, "broads to dance with and get to know." But highly important in this antiaddiction, antidelinquency society there were others who understood him, had made the same "scenes" and intuitively knew his problems and how to handle him. He respected people he could not con. He belonged and was now part of a "family" he could accept. . . .

Frankie found that "rep" was acquired in this social system (unlike ones he had known) by truth, honesty, and industry. The values of his other life required reversal if he was to gain a "rep" at Synanon. These values were not goals *per se* which someone moralized about in a meaningless vacuum; they were means to the end of acquiring prestige in this tough social system with which he now intensely identified.

Most important, Frankie began to get some comprehension of what others thought in a social situation. The fact of empathy or identifying with the thoughts and feelings of others became a significant reality.

From Lewis Yablonsky, "The Anticriminal Society: Synanon," *Federal Probation*, Vol. 26, September 1962, pp. 50–57.

The Mafia family   ROBERT T. ANDERSON

In organizational terms, the Mafia is a social group that combines the advantages of family solidarity with the membership flexibility of a voluntary association. . . .

Family ties often bind members of the Mafia together. . . . The Mafia of the Madonie included two sets of brothers, as did the core membership of the Grisafi group. Not only are members of the Mafia frequently concealed and aided by their families, but their relatives commonly speculate on their activities and profit from them so that a clear line cannot be drawn between the criminal band on the one hand and the circle of kinsmen on the other.

Family ties have a certain utility for organizing social action. Brothers are accustomed to work together. . . . [but] the family has one major drawback as a functioning group: its members vary in interests, capabilities, and temperaments. While this may be of little consequence for running a farm, it can constitute a serious handicap for the successful operation of a gang. . . .

Throughout Europe a technique is available for the artificial extension of kinship ties. The technique is that of fictive or ritual kinship. Godparenthood, child adoption, and blood brotherhood make it possible to extend kin ties with ease. . . . The Mafia constitutes an unusual social unit of this general type so that the fictive bond is that of godparenthood, elsewhere used for allying individuals, but only rarely for forming groups.

. . . In Sicily it [godparenthood] is usually taken very seriously. An indissoluble or lifetime bond, it is often claimed to be equal or even superior to the bond of true kinship. . . . Above all, the relation is characterized by mutual trust.

The Mafia of nineteenth-century Sicily practiced a formal rite of initiation into the fictive-kin relationship. Joseph Valachi underwent the same rite in 1930 in New York. In addition to the "baptism of blood," the chief at the first opportunity normally arranges to be the baptismal godfather of the [newly initiated members] newborn child. Lacking that opportunity, he establishes a comparable tie to one of the numerous other [ceremonial kindred] relationships. The members among themselves are equally active, so that the passing of years see a member more and more bound to the group by such ties. . . .

From Robert T. Anderson, "From the Mafia to Cosa Nostra," *The American Journal of Sociology*, Vol. 71, November 1965. Reprinted by permission of the University of Chicago Press.

meaning was widened to include a sense of having no roots, of belonging nowhere. Different reasons for alienation have been found. Karl Marx blamed the alienation of the workers on the capitalist system. This system, he said, brought workers into factories they did not run, to work with tools and materials they did not own, and to turn out products in which they had no interest. Durkheim held that anomie or alienation was due to the modern industrial system, which moves people from their villages to the cities and constantly forces them to face new situations.

Erich Fromm, in his book *Escape from Freedom* (1941), dealt with the theme of people torn away from their village and family roots and forced into a shifting, anonymous society. In many respects Fromm differs little from Durk-

Group interaction

heim except that he relates anomie to a particular society and time—Germany at the time of the rise of Adolf Hitler. Fromm attributes much of the rise of nazism to the sudden collapse of belief in the old traditions of the Germany of the kaisers. Along with the shift from a strong monarchy to a weak republic (the Weimar Republic of 1919–1933), people had lost social ties to villages and local regions and to the symbolism of flags, ceremonies, and military parades. They were looking for binding forces and new meanings, which they found in nazism.

Does the decline of primary relationships and the rise of secondary relationships lead to alienation from work, from other people, and from society in general? Certainly the structure of human relationships has changed. In the older order, people were firmly bound to social groups and knew their place in society, even if that place was at the bottom. Peter Laslett (1962, pp. 86–93) gives a good description of the primary-secondary blend in social relationships that was common before industrialization. He describes a bakery in London, in 1619, where thirteen people worked: the owner, his wife, four paid journeymen, two apprentices, two maidservants, and the owner's three children. They all lived and ate in the same house, followed the orders of the owner (or master, as he was called), and were considered part of the family. The apprentices were regarded as adopted children. Everyone had a place. Group bonds were so strong that an apprentice would be fired only if he did not work at all, although the master felt free to beat him for other offenses. All the household members had a sense of identity, stability, and permanence.

With the rise of industrialism, as people moved to cities to find work, the close bonds

Figure 5-2 Although a one-to-one encounter, the relationship between prostitute and client is on the secondary level. (*Burt Glinn, Magnum*)

among people and between people and their work began to loosen. People worked in large, impersonal factories, where work was broken down into small, specialized parts that quickly became boring and meaningless. Many people complained of feeling no sense of worth or achievement or of belonging to a stable world.

Primary groups in secondary settings

Although we have defined primary and secondary groups and given a few examples of each, the distinctions between the two are not always clear. Sometimes it becomes impossible to label a particular group, and sometimes groups which seem to belong in one category show the characteristics of the other. There are families whose members do not maintain close bonds but instead are indifferent or hostile toward one another. On the other hand, some business firms seem

Figure 5-3 In addition to the responsibilities and rules on the job, there exists an informal structure, or network of friends. (*Franklynn Peterson, Black Star*)

to care about their employees and maintain a friendly atmosphere on the job. The college or university is a secondary group, but the friendships made within it are primary groups.

Informal structures

A factory, bank, or government bureau seems to be highly organized, with strict rules enforced and every person pegged neatly into place on an organization chart. Actually, against this background of the secondary-group structure, we can always find an *informal structure*. This informal structure is a group in which social relationships lack formal rules and authority but are bound by primary characteristics and informal rules. Usually, the informal rules are developed among the workers to help lighten the workload, make the work more efficient, or simplify bureaucratic procedures.

For example, in a study of mail carriers, Harper and Emmert (1963, pp. 216–225) found an elaborate rule book that was largely ignored. The rules require all mail carriers to work the same number of hours each day. They cannot walk on lawns, they must complete one side of the street before crossing over, and they must cover the blocks in a rigid one-two-three order.

What actually happened was that carriers and supervisors worked together to form their own unofficial rules. These violate the formal rules in order to make the work more efficient. By following the unofficial rules, the carriers finish an hour or two earlier, which leaves them some free time in the afternoon. However, inspectors are never supposed to know about free time for fear they would increase the workload. As a result, a carrier "'embellishes' his work performance when he is being timed. These embellishments consist of following the official work rules. The carrier . . . violates them at other times."

The mail carriers' unofficial work system shows that sometimes the only way to be efficient is to violate the rules. It also shows the workers' decision to set limits on the amount of

Group interaction

135

work they will turn out in a single day, as well as their fear that the work will be increased and the free time eliminated. Most work groups bind together in similar ways, making up new rules and developing unofficial status systems based on competence, helpfulness to others, and the ability to beat the system.

Sometimes relationships between workers and management are hostile or antagonistic. When this happens, workers develop unofficial norms to beat management by resorting to such devices as slowdowns, sick-outs, and "inadvertent" errors. One office worker tells of "accidentally" leaving a line out of some typing her boss wanted her to finish quickly. She worked in a government office where no one liked the bosses, where the atmosphere was hectic and everyone was supposed to be busy all the time. Despite all this, she reports, "Oh, we love it when the bosses go to those long meetings, those important conferences (laughs). We just leave in a group and go for a show. We don't care. When we get back, they roll their eyes. They know they better not say anything 'cause they've done nothing when we've been gone anyhow. We do the work that we have to . . ." (Terkel, 1974, p. 461; by permission of Pantheon Books, a division of Random House, Inc.). Usually the work does get done, but the staff works out unofficial rules that preserve good relationships and humanize the job.

Between primary and secondary

Many organizations fall midway between primary and secondary. People who join lodges are usually joining nationally based organizations that are too big for the face-to-face interaction required of primary groups. Yet the purpose in joining the lodge might be entirely primary, and in local chapters, primary relationships are usually maintained. Members join to gain a feeling of belonging and to make friends. Service clubs, such as the Rotary Club or various ladies' leagues, are usually friendly organizations with

Figure 5-4 Fraternal groups, such as the Rotary Club, are among the many types of secondary groups in our society. (*Charles Harbutt, Magnum*)

certain primary-group characteristics, even though many members might have the ulterior motive of making business contacts. Churches are often too large and formal to act as primary groups. However, the feelings inspired by church membership are strongly primary, and small primary groups often grow up within a larger congregation. Associations like the Sierra Club and Friends of the Earth are formed for the sake of environmental protection, but they often have local chapters whose members become very close. In these organizations, the thrill of working for a common cause is added to the other pleasures of friendship.

Recent community studies have shown that many friendship and kinship ties can be found even in big cities. Kasarda and Janowitz (1974, pp. 328–339) found that people living in large urban areas have more extensive social ties than those living in rural areas. Community size and population density were found to have almost no relation to the strength of social ties, but length of residence was found to be very important. According to Kasarda and Janowitz, social class affects the types of social ties which arise rather than the number of these ties. People who belong to higher social classes are more likely to belong to associations (secondary groups) and less likely to have close friends and relatives within their own neighborhoods than people who belong to lower social classes. In other words, people who are well-to-do have a wider choice of associates and depend less on friends and relatives. People who must move frequently in connection with their jobs are likely to have associates who are merely contacts rather than friends.

Types of secondary groups

Some of the secondary groups we have discussed are called *voluntary associations*. Lodges, clubs, charitable organizations, committees formed for particular purposes, the Boy Scouts and Girl Scouts, and health clubs are all examples of voluntary associations. Such associations may be set apart from *formal organizations*, such as corporations and government bureaus. While associations are formed for sociability or for serving causes, formal organizations are formed for production, commerce, or carrying out government policies. Formal organizations differ from voluntary associations in many other ways. Rules and jobs are officially prescribed. There are different levels of authority, and rules are usually enforceable by force or threat. Clubs and lodges often have official rules and positions, too, but they can be enforced only if the members wish to accept them. Formal organizations

usually have bureaucratic structures, a topic we will discuss in later chapters on work and the political system.

GROUPS AND EMOTIONAL INVOLVEMENT

We have noted that psychological ties are stronger in primary groups than in secondary groups. There are, however, other types of organizations which are not primary groups but which become sources of very strong identification. This often happens in associations or movements that are dedicated to fighting for causes—such as civil rights, antiwar activities, and the women's liberation movement. Feelings of identity and belonging are also very strong in many religious groups and political organizations. If these groups are competing with other similar groups for a particular goal, the feeling can run quite high: strong group ethnocentrism, willingness to give generously for the cause, and strong hostility toward opponents.

Ingroups and outgroups

Any of the groups already discussed can be thought of as *ingroups*, which are any groups to which we belong. Outgroups are those to which we do not belong. However, the ingroup-outgroup contrast is used to describe groups between which tension exists. In many factories, workers and management become conflicting groups. For workers, their own group is the ingroup and management the outgroup. For management, the situation is reversed. In a lighter vein, the concept of ingroups versus outgroups applies to rival schools, cities, and athletic teams. In its most serious application, the concept applies to nations at war or to opposing sides in a civil war.

Many examples of hostility between ingroups and outgroups can be found within a particular country or society. The racial and ethnic tensions in American society and in other societies with

(a)

(b)

similar problems will be discussed in Chapter 7. Two examples are the conflict between Protestants and Catholics in Northern Ireland and between blacks and whites in Rhodesia and the Union of South Africa.

On the political level, hostility between groups can be found after almost any hard-fought political campaign. Here, though, the game is played by the rules, and no open conflict breaks out. The American Civil War can be seen as a conflict in which rival political and regional factions were unable to resolve their differences. In the course of the war, old friends and sometimes even close relatives became enemies. At the beginning of the war, there was some cooperation between the two groups. General Robert E. Lee and his supporters were allowed to leave the U.S. Army in order to serve the Confederacy. But by the end of the war there had arisen between the North and the South a bitterness that lasted for generations.

Not all types of hostility between ingroups and outgroups result in bitter conflict. Football teams of different schools can compete with each other as friendly rivals. Sometimes when we refer to people as being part of the ingroup, we simply mean that they are at the center of community affairs. In other cases, the meaning implies a certain exclusiveness, as in the old prayer: "God bless John and his wife, and me and my wife—we four, no more."

In the insert "Belonging: The Officer Corps" (page 140), the ingroup is the army, the outgroup the civilian world. The ingroup in this case is the loyal servant of the outgroup but still regards it with some suspicion and contempt. The excerpt is taken from an article by a journalist who spent a lot of time interviewing colonels

and generals, not lower-ranking officers or enlisted men. Thus, the description could be called a view of the core of an ingroup—that part which holds the group attitudes most completely.

Conflict groups

Conflict groups are groups whose norms differ from those of the larger society and which struggle for cultural survival within the larger society. In some cases, this very struggle helps unite the conflict group and to maintain its will to cling to its traditions. The Molokans, a nonconforming religious group, survived in Czarist Russia despite years of persecution. A group of them were then allowed to move to the United States in search of religious freedom. In the more tolerant climate of the United States, it was difficult for the elders to impress on their young the need to remain separate and distinct. Thus some of the elders were led to conclude, "America . . . by her very tolerance, is a more

Figure 5-6 *Below:* In some cases, an ingroup implies a certain exclusiveness. Members of this ingroup enjoy a prestigious role and limited membership. (*Mimi Forsyth, Monkmeyer*)

Figure 5-5 *Opposite page:* In reaction to *(a)* the hurried, often impersonal daily routine, many people are turning to *(b)* encounter groups in an attempt to improve the quality of their lives. [*(a)* Charles Gatewood; *(b)* Ken Regan, Camera 5]

Belonging: The officer corps   LEWIS H. LAPHAM

Usually when I first met a general, he would take the trouble to explain that the Army was just like anywhere else, that it really wasn't so different from business, or law, or the electronics industry. At the end of a few months I came to understand that few generals believed that. Most of them take pride in the distinction between the Army and civilian society, the latter commonly referred to as "the outside" and thought to be inferior. An officer obliged to live away from an Army post is said to be "living on the economy"; the customary inflection of the phrase implies foraging in a hostile country. The distinction rests upon the premise that civilian society is dominated by "the commercial values" (i.e., money and greed) whereas the Army is seen as being governed by the ideals of honor, duty, and country. The expression of the prejudice takes various forms. I remember Galloway talking about the Army's system of promotion, a subject to which he'd given considerable thought.

"A man's got to be ambitious and aggressive," he said. "He wouldn't be worth a damn if he wasn't. But the competition isn't vicious or cut-throat like it is in business."

Or it was Hunt in a more rhetorical style, making wide sweeping gestures and declaiming about the sense of mission in the Army.

"I could run a drive-in, but so what? What is that? Where is the satisfaction in coming home to announce that you've served 5,000 hamburgers that day?"

Or it was another general addressing a class of young lieutenants at Fort Benning and telling them that unless they measured up, they might as well go back to farming or selling toilet paper. . . .

Those men who are deemed valuable to the system receive the additional advantages of servants, cars, aides, and white-pillared houses. Also, they discover a great many people who laugh at their jokes, and seldom do they hear anybody disagree with them. The women share the rank with their husbands, and the wife of a commanding general rules by divine right. . . .

Whenever I talked to officers about the rewards of Army life, they inevitably mentioned "a sense of belonging." Their offices were always crowded with memorabilia—signed photographs, plaques, models of tanks, ceremonial swords, and ornamental spurs. Those things are talismans; like the ribbons on a man's uniform they provide a substitute for the continuity of place, and establish tenuous connections in a society of nomads.

But if that society offers the comforts of a small town, it also insists upon the moral rectitude (or at least the appearance of moral rectitude) proper to a small town. The code is puritanical, and if a man is discovered in his wickedness he can expect the traditional punishment. No aspect of his conduct escapes judgment, and he is exposed at all times to the scrutiny of his peers and the gossip of their wives. "It isn't like working for Macy's," Hunt once said. "You're in the Army twenty-four hours a day."

insidious danger to sectarianism than the most relentless persecutions known to Europe" (Young, 1932, p. 274). The same feeling is occasionally found among Jewish leaders; they fear that if their people are totally assimilated, ethnic identity and religious traditions will die out.

Conflict groups do not purposely stir up conflict with outside groups; the reverse is more likely to be true. The term *conflict group* also includes many groups which have not been persecuted but have had to establish very tight group bonds in order to remain separate and distinct. The Mormons showed this behavior from the time of their founding, in 1830, until they gave up polygamy in 1890. However, they are now so well accepted that the term *conflict group* hardly applies. The Amish and Hutterites are two religious groups that keep their distinctive cultures by isolating themselves from the rest of society. They can be called conflict groups in the sense that many of their norms conflict with those of the larger American society.

Conflict groups often develop *boundary maintenance mechanisms*—ways of keeping the group separated from other groups. Ceremonies and rites of initiation are to some extent boundary maintenance mechanisms, binding the new member more closely to the group. The study of special doctrines serves the same purpose. A more obvious mechanism is the physical separation of the group from the rest of society, as with the Amish in the United States and, formerly, the Jews in the ghettos of Europe.

In many cases, boundary maintenance mechanisms are used by organizations or cliques which are not conflict groups but wish simply to maintain a sense of "we-ness." In fraternities and sororities, initiations, pins, and jackets serve this purpose. Lodges often have ingroup greetings and special handshakes for members. In the 1960s, during the hippie movement, one had to look like a hippie to be accepted by the group.

Reference groups

The groups we refer to as guides for our own standards or sense of identity are called *reference groups*. In most cases, they are groups to which we belong or would like to belong. Reference groups can be of a positive type. They may include professional groups, athletic teams, rock-and-roll groups, or social cliques. Reference groups can also be of a negative type; they can become models of how *not* to act. The changing attitudes of black Americans toward white Americans provide a good example of how a positive reference group became negative. Up to the early 1960s, white society served as a positive reference group for black people. Blacks used burning lyes to straighten their hair. And the lighter the skin of a black person, the more important he or she became, both sexually and socially (Frazier, 1957).

During the civil rights movement of the 1960s, especially among more militant black groups, a complete reversal took place. White culture was avoided as a search for black identity began. White society, then, became a negative reference group, something to avoid and react against. The hippies of the same period became a negative reference group for the "straight" members of society. The hippies felt the same way about their negative reference group, the straights, and used long hair, scruffy clothes, drugs, and obscenity as boundary maintenance mechanisms. A good way to learn what people value is to discover their positive and negative reference groups.

Socialization, cultures, and groups are important because they are the building blocks of society. The importance of primary and secondary groups, formal and informal structures, ingroups and outgroups, and reference groups will become clearer in the following chapters, as we discuss social class, deviant behavior, racial and ethnic groups, and political and economic systems. The study of humankind is essentially the study of groups.

SUMMARY

We are all born as members of groups, ranging in size from family to total society. As we mature, we become social beings. In some societies, belonging is largely a family and village matter.

Modern industrial societies also have large numbers of formal organizations and associations.

Groups consist of people with a common focus of interest and interaction. Since we learn through imitating and identifying with others, group membership is vital to personality development and psychological maturity. The importance of the group varies with the society. In Japan, for example, group loyalties, especially to the work group, are considered more important than in the individualistic United States.

Sociability, the need to associate with others for pleasure, is important for almost all people. It fills our need for intimacy, a sense of belonging, caring for others, a feeling of worth, and aid in time of need.

Durkheim, in a study of suicide, concluded that a sense of belonging is closely linked with the hold on life. Isolated people are more prone to suicide than those with social ties to others. The type of suicide stemming from social isolation Durkheim called *egoistic* suicide. The type of suicide among people who do not adhere to the norms or whose norms don't fit into their time and place is *anomic* suicide. Finally, *altruistic* suicide occurs in some cultures that expect individual sacrifice for the group or in which life is almost unbearable for the person who is out of favor with the group.

Groups have a reality apart from the individual psychology of their members. Attitudes and actions arise and grow in the group itself. In many cases, as shown by Asch, people feel unable to trust their own judgment against that of the group. Kissler has also shown that people will often give up their own opinions to win group approval. Close ties with friends can help to increase group loyalty and fighting spirit. This was shown by Shills and Janowitz in a study of the German Army in World War II.

Primary groups, a term first used by Cooley, are close, intimate groups that show mutual concern and cooperation as well as an identity of ends or purposes. Primary groups include families and close friends, and, in Cooley's original discussion, neighborhoods and children's peer groups as well. Although Cooley thought of primary groups as morally good, they are closer to being morally neutral. At Synanon, primary-group ties serve the constructive purpose of freeing people from drug addiction. However, some of these same features have also held the Mafia "families" together.

Secondary groups are increasingly common in modern societies. Less intimate than primary groups, they exist for more limited and practical purposes. Some people (Fromm, for example) fear that the secondary drift of society leads to a sense of alienation. However, primary groups exist within secondary groups, and many groups are somewhere in between. The informal primary groups help cement friendships and act as buffers between the individual and the impersonal organization.

Groups can be classified in other ways as well. Groups to which we belong are called *ingroups*. Those to which we do not belong are called *outgroups*. The relationship between them is usually one of antagonism, rivalry, or conflict. A group that considers itself superior and at the social center is also sometimes called an ingroup.

The term *conflict group* refers to groups whose norms conflict with the folkways and mores of the larger society. The conflict group uses certain *boundary maintenance mechanisms* to keep its membership intact and separate. The term *conflict group* does not imply that the group wishes to quarrel or fight but only that it wants to maintain its own identity.

Reference groups of a positive type are any groups with which the individual wishes to identify, whether as a member or not. There are also negative reference groups, those the individual tries to avoid or oppose.

Study guide

Terms to know

Group	Realism (of groups)	Informal structure
Sociability	Nominalism (of groups)	Formal organizations
Nurturant behavior	Interactionism	Ingroup
Voluntary associations	Autonomy	Outgroup
Egoistic suicide	Primary groups	Conflict groups
Anomic suicide	Secondary groups	Boundary maintenance mechanisms
Altruistic suicide	Alienation	Reference groups

Names to know

Émile Durkheim	Charles Horton Cooley
Solomon Asch	Erich Fromm

Self-test

Part I. Multiple Choice. Select the best of the four alternative answers:

1. Weiss, in a study of a group called Parents without Partners, concluded that people need sociability (**a**) mainly for assistance in time of need, (**b**) for reassurance of self-worth, (**c**) for sharing intimacies, (**d**) for all the above reasons and more.

2. The organization called Little People of America illustrates (**a**) the financial profitability of getting organized, (**b**) the psychological security of belonging to an understanding group, (**c**) the dangers of getting involved in too many activities, (**d**) the importance of formal rules of membership.

3. In Durkheim's analysis, it is possible for one to be so intimately involved in the group as to make life without it intolerable. In such a case, the typical suicide is spoken of as (**a**) altruistic, (**b**) egoistic, (**c**) anomic, (**d**) none of the above.

4. In Asch's experiment regarding the influence of group opinion on the individual, (**a**) the size of the group was very important, (**b**) the unanimity of the group was more important than the size, (**c**) all the experimental subjects gave in to group opinion, (**d**) matching the lines was a difficult task.

5. In studying the desire for group approval, Kissler found that the people who would strive most to be accepted by a group with which they would work for several days were those who (**a**) were best liked by the group, (**b**) feared they were not rated well by the group, (**c**) were least competent, (**d**) were very extroverted personalities.

6. The insert "The Religious Delinquents" indicates that the boys in the study (**a**) were not aware of the doctrines of the Church, (**b**) did not attend mass, (**c**) were protected against misconduct by the Church's teachings, (**d**) followed the suggestions of their friends rather than the teachings of the Church.

7. According to a study by Shills and Janowitz, the Wehrmacht held together for a long period

of time in spite of uninterrupted defeats mainly because of (**a**) devotion to Hitler, (**b**) fear of Hitler, (**c**) belief in victory, (**d**) group organization and group loyalty.

8 One of the following does not belong with a description of primary relationships: (**a**) durable, (**b**) emotionally involved, (**c**) contractual relationships, (**d**) small in size.

9 Peter Laslett's description of a London bakery in 1619 shows *all but one* of the following traits: (**a**) primary relationships, (**b**) a sense of belonging, (**c**) equality, (**d**) relative permanence.

10 A study of urban interaction indicates that the middle and upper classes are more likely than the poor to (**a**) join associations, (**b**) maintain ties with relatives, (**c**) interact with neighbors, (**d**) all the above.

11 In the study of postal employees, informal rules (**a**) violated the postal regulations, (**b**) lightened the workload, (**c**) made the system more efficient, (**d**) all the above.

12 Erich Fromm attributed the rise of Hitler and nazism in large part to (**a**) a reaction against communist subversion, (**b**) a logical outgrowth of German culture, (**c**) loss of traditions and primary-group belonging, (**d**) a failure to develop formal organizations.

13 Special types of dress, speech, or handshakes to identify members of a group and keep them separate from others are called (**a**) boundary maintenance mechanisms, (**b**) personality adjustment mechanisms, (**c**) adaptive mechanisms, (**d**) defensive mechanisms.

14 If a boy daydreams about being a baseball player, watching big-league players and trying to imitate them, the baseball players are for him a (**a**) primary group, (**b**) reference group, (**c**) ingroup, (**d**) secondary group.

15 According to the insert "Belonging: The Officer Corps," high-ranking officers (**a**) are a little contemptuous of commercial values, (**b**) do not like "living on the economy," (**c**) must abide by a special moral code, (**d**) all the above.

Part II. True-False Questions

1 As used in sociology, the word *group* refers to any aggregate of people or to categories such as "those over sixty-five."

2 In some respects the Confucian morality of China was more group-oriented than is our moral order.

3 In Durkheim's analysis, one is more susceptible to egoistic suicide if one has no ties to other people or groups.

4 Altruistic suicide is caused mainly by a lack of belonging.

5 Members of primary groups identify with one another.

6 A very important contributory cause of many of the youthful suicides (see the insert "The Youthful Suicides") is a feeling of intense isolation.

7 Because its activities run counter to normative values, a Mafia "family" does not have any of the traits of a primary group.

8 The statement "Borrow from your old friend and neighbor, The Serendipity Finance Company" represents a confusion of primary and secondary relationships.

9 Relationships with a prostitute are primary because they involve physical proximity and intimacy.

10 Large organizations and other secondary groups usually contain primary groups within them.

11 According to a study of mail carriers, they waste valuable time by not following the rules.

12 The contrast between ingroup and outgroup implies at least a measure of negative emotional feelings between the two groups.

13 Conflict groups include groups that have been excluded or persecuted by a society even if they have not fought back.

14 Reference groups include only groups to which we belong.

15 According to the insert "Belonging: The Officer Corps," high-ranking officers consider their jobs to be comparable to those of lawyers or businessmen.

Questions for Discussion

1 Groups may persist in time even if members and leaders change. What groups can you think of that change leaders and gradually change members without any drastic changes in group orientation, customs, etc.?

2 What sociability needs are met by groups to which you belong? Include both formal and informal groups.

3 Explain the three types of suicide defined by Durkheim and discuss whether he is right in relating them to degrees of group integration and normative integration. Could alcoholism and drug abuse have similar causes in some cases?

4 We are often warned not to conduct business with a relative. Explain in terms of primary- and secondary-group relationships why this might be good advice.

5 Older societies were more heavily based on primary groups than is ours. Argue the pros and cons of the idea that modern people suffer psychologically from being in a society that is oriented toward secondary relationships.

6 The concept of ingroups versus outgroups is a matter of degree. Try listing in ascending order a number of groups that illustrate ingroup versus outgroup feelings: competing schools, cities, states, political parties, countries, religions, races, or labor-management groups.

7 What do conflict groups have to offer that causes their followers to keep up boundary maintenance mechanisms and exclude the outside world?

8 Boundary maintenance mechanisms are not exclusive to conflict groups of the type mentioned in the text. Can you think of any boundary maintenance mechanisms that exist in athletic clubs, work groups, age groups, and elite social circles?

9 What are some of your own positive and negative reference groups? To what extent are you influenced by them?

Projects

1 Classroom experiment in conformity to group norms: Try to arrange in a social science classroom a situation in which class opinion appears to be unanimous on an issue. With the aid of the instructor, a student leader, or both, have a discussion period on the issue, arranging beforehand that the first five people wishing to argue the case will be called upon. These five, who are actually to be accomplices of the student leader, will all speak strongly on the same side of the issue. After their comments, the class will vote by a show of hands. Afterward, someone is to challenge the legality of such a vote and call for a secret ballot.

The question to be decided: Will class members be swayed by what looks like a unanimous opinion and fail to express their true opinions in a show-of-hands vote? If so, there will be a discrepancy between the hand vote and the secret ballot.

For the experiment, use a controversial issue on which you might expect opinion to be fairly evenly divided: capital punishment, legalization of marijuana, legalized prostitution, or some issue of current concern in your school or local community.

2 Visit a highly emotional group with intense feelings of belongingness. The most likely possibility is a revival meeting of an emotional church, but political extremist groups would be another possibility. What emotional and sociability needs seem to be fulfilled by group belonging and identification?

3 Study a case in which small, informal groups operate within a large, formal organization, developing their own rules, sometimes at variance with the official rules of the formal organization. (If you have a job, you can probably use your own workplace for an example. Otherwise talk with members of another employment group or use your own school for an example.)

Suggested readings

Brandes, Stanley H.: "Social Structure and Interpersonal Relations in Navánogal," *American Anthropologist*, vol. 75, June 1973, pp. 750–765. Was village life, with its close bonds of kith and kin, a more agreeable life-style than that of twentieth-century America? In this study of a little village of Spain, still living by its old, traditional pattern, the author shows that village life can be a type of prison—although admittedly Navánogal seems to be unique in some respects.

Clark, Dennis: "The Passion of Protracted Conflict," *Trans-Action*, vol. 7, March 1970, pp. 15–21. Nowhere can the conflict between ingroup and outgroup be described better than in Northern Ireland, where Protestants and Catholics threaten to tear each other apart. According to a report in *The London Times*: "Anywhere else the notion that an invalid youth risks being roasted alive because he can't make it over the backyard wall might be dismissed as a sadistic fantasy, but not in Belfast." Read the consequences of centuries of group conflict.

Haythorn, William W., and Irwin Altman: "Together in Isolation," *Trans-Action*, vol. 4, January–February 1967, pp. 18–22. What are the problems of membership in small groups of as few as two members, isolated in lighthouses, Arctic weather stations, or space capsules for long periods of time? Is the strain worse than isolation? Haythorn and Altman conducted an experiment to see.

Kanter, Rosabeth Moss: "Communes," *Psychology Today*, vol. 4, July 1970, pp. 55–58. Are communes a reaction against a world grown too urban and impersonal? Kanter's answer amounts to an affirmation of the great need for intimate, primary-group ties. Her study also comes to some interesting conclusions about successful and unsuccessful family types within communes, group-criticism sessions, property arrangements, and philosophical or religious beliefs.

Miller, Walter B.: "White Gangs," *Trans-Action*, vol. 6, September 1969, pp. 11–26. In order to belong, one has to adopt the code of the gang, but the need for belonging is very great. Miller, after a long period of study, describes the "Bandits" and the less delinquent "Outlaws." Membership in some such city gangs descends from father to son.

Zurcher, Louis A., Jr.: "The Friendly Poker Game: A Study of an Ephemeral Role," *Social Forces*, vol. 49, December 1970, pp. 173–186. What sociopsychological functions does the friendly poker game serve for the participants? What is its attraction? These are two of the questions posed and answered by the authors. In the course of the article, one is given a picture of a group that chooses its members with the greatest care to meet the group norms, both the obvious and the hidden.

Key to questions. Multiple Choice: 1-d; 2-b; 3-a; 4-b; 5-b; 6-d; 7-d; 8-c; 9-c; 10-a; 11-d; 12-c; 13-a; 14-b; 15-d. True-False: 1-F, 2-T, 3-T, 4-F, 5-T, 6-T, 7-F, 8-T, 9-F, 10-T, 11-F, 12-T, 13-T, 14-F, 15-F.

DIVERSITY AND STRAIN

6

STRATIFICATION, CLASS, AND MOBILITY

This chapter considers the ways in which people become stratified into social classes, with great differences in wealth, power, and prestige. After reading it, you should be able to:

1 *Explain the meaning of social class and the criteria on which it is based.*

2 *Understand how people perceive social class, and the differences between such perceptions and the actual facts of income distribution.*

3 *Be more aware of the problems of people in lower-class positions.*

4 *Explain caste, and see how some aspects of our class system have resembled the caste system.*

5 *Understand Marxist and functionalist views of social class systems.*

6 *Recognize the conditions of industrial societies that have made upward mobility possible, as well as the barriers to upward mobility for some groups.*

7 *Weigh the evidence on whether we are developing a permanent underclass of poverty and a permanent upper class of wealth and power.*

I moved into my quarters in the 88-room house on Chicago's fashionable near north side. It had two elevators, and contained three complete apartments for the married male servants. The houseman was required to live on the premises in case the heating system failed or some other emergency arose. . . . Since the chauffeur often had to be available until late at night, he, too, was provided living quarters. . . . The butler was entitled to his own apartment because he was the official head of staff. True to the tradition of English butlers, our man changed his clothes three times each day: black suit in the morning, cutaway and striped pants for afternoon, and black tie or tails in the evening. . . . The cook was French Swiss and a veritable virtuosa in the kitchen, but neither she nor other female help rated a full apartment.

In addition, the household was served by a Pinkerton's guard, two Germans—a laundress and a cleaning woman—and five Scandinavians—a parlor maid (who assisted the butler and took over the pantry on his day off), a kitchen maid, two chambermaids, and the lady's maid.

. . . I supervised the move of the entire household retinue to the country home in time for my employer's return from Europe. The retreat was a modest 35-room "cottage." . . . We had two Pinkerton's guards in the country, one to patrol the grounds and the other to watch the dwellings. (Maguire, 1977, p. 5; copyright Los Angeles Times)

The above description is by a social secretary to the widow of a wealthy industrialist. Contrast it with the following description given by a woman from the opposite end of the social ladder:

. . . Poverty is staying up all night when it is cold to guard the one fire we have; one spark striking the newspaper we have on our walls would mean my sleeping children would die in the flames. In the summer, poverty is watching gnats and flies devour my baby's tears when he cries, which is most of the time. I've never been in an air-conditioned house. I've just heard folks talk about them. Our screens are torn, but we pay so little rent that it's foolish to even talk about getting them fixed. Poverty means insects in your food, in your nose, in your eyes, and crawling over you while you sleep. Poverty is children with runny noses, even in the summer. Paper handkerchiefs take money, and you need all your rags for other things. Antihistamines are for the rich.

Poverty is being tired—dog tired all the time. I can't remember when I wasn't tired. When my last baby was born, they told me at the hospital that I had chronic anemia caused by a poor diet, a bad case of worms, and the need for a corrective operation.

When they told me about my condition, I listened politely. The poor are always polite, you know. We can't afford to offend those who might decide to be big and give us something. The poor always listen, for there really isn't much we can say. . . . (Ritzer, 1974, pp. 339–340)

THE MEANING OF STRATIFICATION

These are the words of persons at the top and bottom of a social stratification system. The extreme positions in the system are easier to see than the gradations between them. *Social stratification* means that society exists in layers of wealth and power. *Power* is the ability to cause others to do what we want, or even to help sway the decisions of industry or government. The owner of the eighty-eight-room mansion had the power to hire others to do her bidding. She had influence with important people and a life-style that earned her prestige and envy. The woman in the shack with the unscreened windows had no wealth or power. She could only be polite so as not to offend those who did.

People can be stratified, or ranked, in many ways other than by wealth. Military rank, school grade level, and social popularity are all ways of ranking. However, our concern here is with such factors as wealth, occupation, and social prestige. Max Weber (1864–1920), a prominent sociologist and economist, described the type of social stratification of interest here. Weber used three dimensions of stratification: class, status, and party. Weber's terminology is different from that commonly used in the United States, but his analysis is very thorough. By *class*, Weber means two things: (1) economic position—including wealth, goods, living conditions, occupation, income—and (2) "life chances," or the chance to live a long and rewarding life, with education, a good income, interesting experiences, and the ability to guarantee the same to one's children. Weber uses the term *status* in a more restricted way than was used in Chapter 5. To Weber, *status* refers to esteem and recognition, which takes different forms in different societies: in some societies, titles of nobility, in others military rank, family name, life-style, or the chairing of industrial boards. *Party*, in Weber's analysis, refers to the ability of prestigious groups to exercise power and influence the social and political system (Weber, 1958, pp. 181–195). His use of the word stems from the tendency to form political ties on the basis of class or status. This is the reason, according to Weber, that a person can be very rich but not reach the top of the social ladder unless he or she also has prestige and power. A later discussion of American upper classes by W. Lloyd Warner will also show that criteria other than wealth are important.

Another definition of *social class* overlaps Weber's definition of stratification. A social class is one level, or stratum, in a class system made up of people who are roughly equal (and think of themselves as more or less equal) in income, education, occupation, prestige, and social influence. In American society, *class consciousness*, the tendency to think of oneself and others in terms of class, is not very strong except among the very rich and the very poor. There is, however, a feeling of distinction between the middle class and the working class.

It is hard to evaluate social-class positions in America. First, our society has a work structure that includes many specialized jobs that are hard to understand: What is a software specialist, a space buyer, an administrative assistant? Second, most Americans think of themselves as middle class. Hodge and Treiman (1968) found that when people were asked to describe their social class, three-quarters of them called themselves "average" or "middle." When asked to describe themselves on a five-item scale as upper, upper middle, middle, working, or lower class, 61 percent rated themselves as middle or upper middle and only 34 percent as working class.

This survey would seem to indicate that most Americans have nearly equal incomes. Yet looking at income statistically, we find the distribution of family income in the United States in 1950 and 1970 shown in Table 6-1 (page 152). The breakdown is fairly consistent. In both years, the highest one-fifth of the population received 41.6

percent of the income, and the lowest one-fifth only 5.5 percent.

Not only are incomes extremely unequal, but the inequality has persisted for twenty years (and continues to do so). Middle-class people are generally aware of these extremes. They often complain about how the rich avoid paying income taxes, how the tax structure favors the rich, and how taxes and inflation are robbing them. Sometimes, they exaggerate the wealth of the richest families. However, they usually do not realize how little things have changed.

Occupational prestige ratings

The income distribution presented in Table 6-1 gives a much more accurate account of stratification than people's descriptions of their own social class. It does not, however, describe social class itself. Social class includes many factors besides income: occupation, inherited wealth, power, prestige, education, and life-style. Occupation is especially important. In some European societies, the aristocratic tradition is still influen-

tial, so that members of the "best families" have high social-class positions regardless of their occupations. In the United States, the question "What do you do?" is the means by which people classify those they meet. The answer "engineer" or "dishwasher" immediately tags a person in many ways.

In a 1947 National Opinion Research Council survey, respondents were asked to rate many occupations in order of *prestige*—standing in the eyes of others. Strong agreement was found among these rankings, and sixteen years later the results had not changed significantly (Hodge, Siegel, and Rossi, 1964, pp. 286–302). There were a few shifts in ratings; scientists went up a little, and politicians went down. However, the researchers reported: "Between 1947 and 1963 we are fully aware that many *individual* changes in occupations were under way as men advanced in their career lines, retired, or entered the labor force. Yet, despite the turnover of incumbents, occupational morphology, at least insofar as prestige is concerned, remained remarkably stable. . . ." (1964, p. 302).

If we examine Table 6-2 (page 153), it becomes clear that when people rate occupational

Figure 6-1 Life experiences are strongly influenced by class structure. Occupations are very different for (*a*) the lower and (*b*) the middle classes. [(*a*) *Wide World;* (*b*) *Mimi Forsyth, Monkmeyer*]

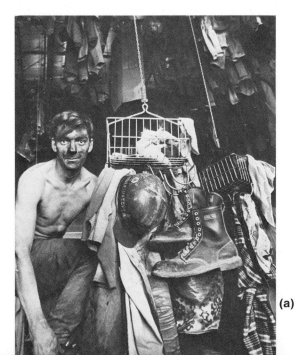

(a)

(b)

Table 6-1 Income Distribution, 1950 and 1970

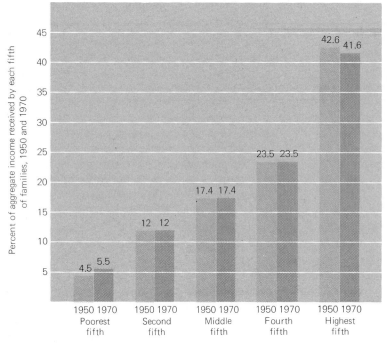

Source: U.S. Bureau of the Census, *Current Population Reports,* series P. 60, no. 80, 1970.

prestige, they are thinking of pay and educational requirements, power and influence, job interest, and feeling of accomplishment. It is also obvious that jobs involving hard physical work or unsanitary conditions rank lower than cleaner, less strenuous jobs. Although most Americans tend to see themselves as middle class, they make many distinctions in ranking other people's jobs by prestige.

Community studies

Community studies of social class show the same awareness of prestige differences as do occupational rankings (W. Lloyd Warner et al., 1960, pp. 3–58). Warner and his associates made a series of community studies, asking people who they thought ranked highest in town, who came next, and so on down the line. The researchers were able to distinguish six classes of people (in

newer communities, only five). Since their terminology is often used in studies of social class, we will sum up their findings here. It is clear that especially in describing the highest group, Warner is using the word *class* to mean about what Weber meant by *status.*

At the top of the community social system is an upper upper class. It consists of solid, reputable people who have been rich for several generations. This is the so-called old-money class. Just below them are the lower uppers, or newly rich. In distinguishing between these two classes, the amount of money is less important than how long it has been held. The old rich are usually described as being more relaxed, gracious, and conservative in tastes. The newly rich are more inclined to show off their wealth. Below the lower upper class is the upper middle class, largely a business, professional, and managerial class. Poorly paid business and professional

Diversity and strain

152

Table 6-2 Ratings of Occupational Prestige

Occupation	Score	Occupation	Score	Occupation	Score
U.S. Supreme Court Justice	94	Owner of factory that employs about 100 people	80	Railroad conductor	66
Physician	93			Traveling salesman for a wholesale concern	66
Nuclear physicist	92	Artist who paints pictures that are exhibited in galleries	78	Plumber	65
Scientist	92			Barber	63
Government scientist	91	Author of novels	78	Machine operator in a factory	63
State governor	91	Economist	78		
Cabinet member, federal	90	Musician in symphony orchestra	78	Owner-operator of a lunch stand	63
College professor	90			Playground director	63
U.S. Representative in Congress	90	Official of an international labor union	77	Corporal in regular army	62
Chemist	89	County agricultural agent	76	Garage mechanic	62
Diplomat in U.S. Foreign Service	89	Electrician	76	Truck driver	59
Lawyer	89	Railroad engineer	76	Fisherman who owns his own boat	58
Architect	88	Owner-operator of a printing shop	75	Clerk in a store	56
County judge	88	Trained machinist	75	Milk route man	56
Dentist	88	Farm owner and operator	74	Streetcar motorman	56
Mayor of large city	87	Undertaker	74	Lumberjack	55
Member, board of directors of large corporation	87	Welfare worker for a city government	74	Restaurant cook	55
Minister	87	Newspaper columnist	73	Singer in a night club	54
Psychologist	87	Policeman	72	Filling station attendant	51
Airline pilot	86	Reporter on a daily newspaper	71	Coal miner	50
Civil engineer	86	Bookkeeper	70	Dock worker	50
Head of a department in state government	86	Radio announcer	70	Night watchman	50
Priest	86	Insurance agent	69	Railroad section hand	50
Banker	85	Tenant farmer—one who owns livestock and machinery and manages the farm	69	Restaurant waiter	49
Biologist	85			Taxi driver	49
Sociologist	83			Bartender	48
Captain in regular army	82	Local official of a labor union	67	Farmhand	48
Accountant for large business	81	Manager of a small store in a city	67	Janitor	48
Public schoolteacher	81	Mail carrier	66	Clothes presser in a laundry	45
Building contractor	80			Soda fountain clerk	44
				Sharecropper—one who owns no livestock or equipment and does not manage farm	42
				Garbage collector	39
				Street sweeper	36
				Shoe shiner	34

Source: Robert W. Hodge, Paul M. Seigel, and Peter H. Rossi, "Occupational Prestige in the United States, 1925–1963," *American Journal of Sociology*, vol. 70, November 1964, pp. 286–302. By permission of the publisher, University of Chicago Press.

Stratification, class, and mobility

people are generally included in the next class, the lower middle class. This class is composed mainly of white-collar workers and skilled laborers with good jobs. Next to the bottom is the upper lower class. It consists of poorly paid semiskilled or unskilled workers who are employed most of the time and not on welfare. According to Warner's studies, the lower lower class is considered to be a dependent class. It is often spoken of by the others as "shiftless and lazy," or below the average level. This class includes many people who are willing to work and who are good workers when they can get jobs but who sometimes have to depend on welfare. Regardless of the circumstances, welfare carries a social-class stigma.

SOCIAL CLASS IN NATIONAL PERSPECTIVE

Stratification and social-class ranking are national as well as local. However, there are wide differences in awareness in each class. According to some sociologists, perhaps the greatest class unity, or class consciousness, is found among the upper upper elite.

The upper class as a national elite

Many of the rich in the nineteenth century were powerful nationally as well as locally. However, Baltzell concludes that only in the twentieth century did a national upper upper class develop (1951). Between 1900 and 1940, the very rich were forming a more and more closed society. They sent their children to the same fashionable Eastern preparatory schools, finishing schools, and universities and generally joined the same church (the Episcopal Church) and the same prestigious social clubs. Although the upper class Baltzell refers to is national, the Social Register (a list of all the people acceptable in the highest social circles, nationally or in a particular community) that distinguishes the class began in Philadelphia. The insert "The Old Upper Class

of Philadelphia" describes the typical upper-class Philadelphian of 1940, when this class had crystallized. Today, the richest families remain as rich as ever, although their life-styles have changed. There are fewer servants, chauffeurs, and social graces but more yachts and expensive recreations, more airplanes, and more jetting from place to place.

The divided middle class

The term *middle class* is hard to define. Warner divided the middle class into upper and lower sections. This scheme separates the underpaid bookkeeper or clerk from the lawyer or doctor, who are better paid and have more social pres-

Figure 6-2 Class, wealth, and power. John D. Rockefeller, a capitalist who propelled himself into the upper upper class, founded a financial empire which today influences American political, economic, and social life. (*United Press International*)

The old upper class of Philadelphia   E. DIGBY BALTZELL

In 1940, the ideal-typical Proper Philadelphian at the apex of the pyramid of social prestige and economic power in the city, may be said to have had the following attributes:

1. Of English or Welsh descent, his great-great-great grandfather would have been a prominent Philadelphian in the great age of the new republic. Somewhere along the line an ancestor would have made money, or married wisely. And along with money and social position, some good Quaker ancestor would have preferred the Episcopal Church, or have been banished from the Society of Friends for marrying "out of meeting."

2. His family would have been listed in the *Social Register* at the turn of the nineteenth century.

3. He would have been born on Walnut Street, facing Rittenhouse Square.

4. After an early education at the Episcopal Academy or some other private school in the city, he would have gone away to one of the fashionable Episcopalian boarding schools in New England.

5. Unless his parents felt an unusual loyalty and pride in local institutions, he would have gone to either Harvard, Yale, or Princeton where he would have belonged to one of the more exclusive clubs.

6. After attending the law school at the University of Pennsylvania, this young Proper Philadelphian would enter one of the fashionable and powerful law firms in the city and eventually become a partner, or enter the field of banking or finance. He would be on the board of directors of several cultural and economic institutions (Pennsylvania Railroad, a bank such as the Girard Trust Company, and perhaps the Fairmount Art Association).

7. Finally, the Proper Philadelphian would live either in Chestnut Hill or the Main Line in 1940, attend the Episcopal Church, be married, have three or four children, and walk either up or down Walnut Street to lunch with his peers at the Rittenhouse, or preferably the Philadelphia Club.

E. Digby Baltzell, "The American Metropolitan Upper Class," in *Philadelphia Gentlemen*, The Free Press, 1951.

---

tige than the other two even though they all hold white-collar jobs. Pay is so poor for many kinds of office workers that they have been called "the hidden proletariat" (*Society*, 1975, pp. 12–14). True, 75 percent of office workers are women, and women are generally paid less than men who hold the same jobs. Still, office work has higher prestige than blue-collar work and requires more education. Therefore it is generally placed, along with the job of salesperson, in the middle class.

Given the wide gap between the upper and lower middle classes, the concept of a "middle class" is stretched fairly thin. What form of class-consciousness unites the middle class? First, whether they are upper or lower, middle-class people generally consider themselves better off than working-class people, even if they earn less. They want to see their children maintain or improve their position. Also, they believe in the importance of education as a way of ensuring or bettering their children's position.

(Working-class people, too, are interested in education. However, because they are usually poorly educated, they hold low-paying jobs and have little money for books, educational toys, and outings for their children. Their children often attend poorly equipped schools. Thus, in the race for education, working-class children start with a handicap and fall further behind middle-class children. This topic will be discussed further in Chapter 13.)

The working class

Warner describes blue-collar workers as belonging to the lower middle and upper lower classes. Many other sociologists refer to these people as *working class*. According to Gerhard Lenski, the kind of work these people do is similar and is the common trait that unites them. "The resource on which each depends is a job involving a limited range of manual skills that could be performed by most other members of society after a relatively short period of training (Lenski, 1961a, p. 377). As a result, the working class finds it hard to bargain for wages. While unions protect many of them, millions of nonunionized workers are at some point laid off or unemployed. Compared with those of the middle class, working-class persons are less likely to have pleasant or even safe jobs. They are more likely to have industrial accidents and to become sick from exposure to coal dust, asbestos, and other chemical products. They usually see their status as declining in a society that values spe-

The blue collar worker's lowdown blues

. . . Workers are the Americans most affected by rapid social disruption and technological change—and least prepared for it. The workingman is angered and bewildered by what he sees happening in the nation. As psychologists and social researchers have confirmed, he believes in God and country—if not necessarily in equality for all and the right to dissent. He is convinced of the virtues of hard work, the necessity of saving and a steady, ordered way of life. He is proud of paying his own way and standing on his own feet. He is respectful toward authority but not subservient, and he still has faith in the future, even though that faith has diminished somewhat of late.

. . . His neighborhoods, formerly bastions of order, are often being transformed by the upheaval in the cities. Says Eugene Schafer, a hardhat ironworker and Democratic candidate for the state assembly from Brooklyn: "I think that I'm a forgotten American because my community is falling apart. The streets are caving in, the sanitation's lousy, the sewer system stinks, industry's gone out of the community, welfare's on the rise."

Often lacking the education to seek better jobs or the money to flee to suburbia, blue collar workers live with nagging fears of muggings, of illness or layoffs at work, and of automation. According to a recent survey by the University of Michigan, one-half of all industrial workers worry continually about their job security, and one-quarter are concerned about their safety; 14,000 were killed in on-the-job accidents last year, more than the number of U.S. servicemen who died in Vietnam in 1969. Fully 28 percent have no medical coverage, 38 percent no life insurance and 39 percent no pension beyond Social Security.

Time, Nov. 9, 1970; excerpts from "The Blue Collar Worker's Lowdown Blues." Reprinted by permission from *Time*, The Weekly Newsmagazine; copyright Time, Inc., 1970.

cialization and education. They hope their children will not follow in their footsteps. Some of them think of themselves as "forgotten Americans" (see the insert "The Blue Collar Worker's Lowdown Blues").

The lower class

The lower class, or *underclass*, includes a wide variety of people. Many are unemployed, but others are simply underemployed—either at part-time jobs or at jobs that pay too little to support a family. Often, they are alienated from society. The lower class not only has no money but also has little chance to get money. Compared with other classes, members of the lower class are sick more often and die younger. This is the class most often victimized by crime and fraud and is the most often overcharged for poor-quality housing, furniture, and appliances (Caplovitz, 1963). Oscar Lewis calls their lifestyle a "culture of poverty." It is characterized by frequent desertion and family breakup, early introduction to sex, feelings of hopelessness, and some hostility toward social institutions (Lewis, 1961). Some sociologists dislike the term *culture of poverty*. They claim it is not a culture in the sense of being a believed-in way of life. It is instead a way of dealing with the problems of survival. To a great extent, lower-class persons are the victims of an industrial system that no longer has room for unskilled people. Still, the classes above them often tend to blame them for their condition.

SOCIAL CLASS AND CASTE COMPARED

Social-class position is fairly stable in American society. Many other societies have an even more stable system of stratification—the caste system. *Caste* in its pure form is a social-class system that allows no movement at all; members of one caste cannot move to another. Stratification systems vary from caste systems at one extreme to open-class systems at the other. In an *open-class system*, ideally, there are no barriers to prevent a person from moving freely from one class to another. Actually, all social systems fall somewhere in between. Even in India, during the centuries when the caste system was in force, a few *jatis* (occupational subcastes, such as potters, weavers, or silversmiths) actually rose in rank over several generations. There was no individual mobility, but in some cases group mobility became possible. The United States is much closer to an open-class system than to a caste system. Still, poverty, poor education, and discrimination all prevent equal chances for upward mobility. At the upper levels of society, we find tax loopholes and "knowing the right people." These prevent much of the downward mobility that would occur in a completely open-class society. Even in the Soviet Union, which claims to be classless, social positions seem to persist. If either the Soviet Union or the United States were a completely open-class society, the children of the rich would be as likely to become factory workers as the children of the poor.

Caste: India and the United States

Before the legal reforms of the 1950s, caste in India was supported by law, custom, and religion. Members of higher castes feared the "pollution" that would come from marrying into a lower caste. In the United States, race relations have had a castelike quality. Close social relations, especially black-white intermarriage, were discouraged or prohibited by law.

As in India, religion was called on to justify slavery in the United States. The Old Testament revealed that the sons of Ham (one of the sons of Noah) were told they should be "the hewers of wood and drawers of water." By no logic could it be assumed that the sons of Ham were black. Still, the explanation was good enough for people looking for an excuse for slavery. Advocates of slavery decided that Ham was black.

Since the supposedly dark-skinned sons of

Ham were servants, this was the "natural" social position of all dark-skinned people. Thus was slavery in America justified, and a caste system between blacks and whites developed. In the Reconstruction period after the Civil War, upward mobility for blacks was legally possible. In practice, though, black people were kept down by "Jim Crow" laws that barred them from white schools, by discrimination in hiring that kept them poor and dependent, and by the Ku Klux Klan. This was an organization of whites who believed in "white supremacy" and wanted to keep black people "in their place." The belief that equality between the races would pollute the whites continued. One "explanation" stated that if God had meant the two races to mingle, he would not have placed them originally in different parts of the world.

"Scientific" explanations for segregation were also found. For example, it was argued that mixtures of blood would be bad for both races. The children of such matings would display the worst traits of each race. On the Western frontier, the "half-breed" was often treated worse than the full-blooded Indian. Even today, when most people say they believe in racial and ethnic

Figure 6-3 Unless changed by social upheaval or government decree, caste is a permanent barrier to upward mobility. The Republic of South Africa is a society of racial castes. This bench is for whites only. (*Paul Conklin, Monkmeyer*)

equality, racially mixed marriages are uncommon. Interracial couples have trouble being accepted in all but a few large, sophisticated cities. In India, acceptance of lower-caste members follows a similar pattern. In the industrialized cities, caste differences are hardest to see. Laws now protect the *untouchables*—those 60 million or more Indians so low in the system as to have no caste at all. In the United States, similar laws prohibit a racial caste system. Yet in both countries, these laws are hard to enforce, especially in rural areas.

Other examples of caste

In its colonies in the New World, Spain maintained a caste system. People born in Spain (the *Peninsulares*) ranked higher than all others; next came people of purely Spanish blood born in the New World. Below these castes were the *mestizos*, people of mixed Spanish-Indian blood, and below them the pure Indians. The Spanish Empire is just one example of a familiar pattern: caste differences between the colonial administrators and the natives. In such cases, racism was mingled with caste, just as it was later in the United States.

In Japan, one caste, the Eta, are seen as especially loathsome. The Eta belong to a caste that, in the Middle Ages, made leather armor. Why they should have been singled out is not clear, but leatherwork involved the tanning of hides, an unpleasant job. The insert below, from James Michener's novel *Hawaii*, deals with a mother's warning to her son about the dangers of marrying an Eta woman.

In most societies today, the rules upholding caste have been outlawed. But caste still exists in the minds of people. It makes social mingling difficult and marriage into a higher caste almost impossible. The untouchables of India still hold low class positions. Still, a certain number of them must be hired for all government jobs, as with minority groups in the United States.

In India, extremes of caste still exist in the rural villages. In many of them, discrimination is so strong that if the government tries to improve the water supply, it must put in two wells instead of one. People of higher castes allow no untouchables near their wells. If they did, they believe, the water would become polluted. This is not too

---

Avoid marriage into a low caste   JAMES A. MICHENER

. . . "There is of course one problem that every devoted son looks into before he marries, because he owes it not only to his parents but also to his brothers and sisters. Kamejiro, I said that if you married an Okinawa girl you were dead. But if you marry an Eta, you are worse than dead."

The wave of disgust that swept over Kamejiro's face proved that he despised the Eta as much as his mother did, for they were the untouchables of Japan, the unthinkables. In past ages they had dealt in the bodies of dead animals, serving as butchers and leather tanners. Completely outside the scope of Japanese civilization, they scratched out horrible lives in misery and whenever possible fled to distant refuges like Hawaii. A single trace of Eta blood could contaminate an entire family, even to remote unattached cousins, and Kamejiro shuddered.

His mother continued dolefully, "I said I could spot an Okinawan, and I could protect you there. But with an Eta . . . I don't know. They're clever! Crawling with evil, they try to make you think they're normal people. They hide under different names. They take new occupations. I am sure that some of them must have slipped into Hawaii, and how will you know, Kamejiro? What would you do if word sneaked back to Hiroshima-ken that you had been captured by an Eta?"

Mother and son contemplated this horror for some minutes and she continued: "So when it comes time to marry, Kamejiro, I think it best if you marry a Hiroshima girl." . . .

"And be careful not to marry into any family that has ever had an undertaker. Avoid city families if you can. To tell you the truth, Kamejiro, it would be best if you married a girl from right around here. . . . So when the time comes to marry, go to a letter-writer and have him send me a message, and when it is read to me, I'll find you a good local girl, and trust me, Kamejiro, that will be best."

James A. Michener, *Hawaii*, Random House, 1961, pp. 587–588.

Stratification, class, and mobility

different from certain recent American customs. For years in the American South, blacks and whites had to eat in different restaurants; use different waiting rooms, rest rooms, and drinking fountains in bus and train stations; ride in different parts of buses or trains; and attend different schools.

The isolation of classes

In both class and caste systems, it is easy for those at the bottom to be treated badly. Members of the higher classes know little about their life-styles and problems. One example of this was brought to light in California, when unionized farm workers demanded that the short-handled hoe be outlawed. For years, farm owners had insisted that Chicano laborers use these hoes for cotton, grapes, and other crops, even though they had crippling effects (see the insert "Short Handle Hoe: A History of Agony for Dubious Advantages"). This is one example of the indifference of one social class to the suffering of another, but it is not unique. It has always been assumed that one person must take out the garbage of another who is relaxing on a yacht. How can social class be explained? How does it originate, and why is it universal?

ORIGINS AND THEORIES OF SOCIAL CLASS

In 1887, Edward Bellamy published the novel *Looking Backward*, which pictured American society in the year 2000. An observer from the future looks back on the older, highly competitive, class-structured society and describes it in grim terms:

> By way of attempting to give the reader some general impression of the way people lived together in those days, and especially of the rich and the poor to one another, perhaps I cannot do better than to compare society as

it then was to a prodigious coach which the masses of humanity were harnessed to and dragged toilsomely along a very hilly and sandy road. The driver was hunger, and permitted no lagging, though the pace was necessarily very slow. Despite the difficulty of drawing the coach at all along so hard a road, the top was covered with passengers who never got down, even at the steepest ascents. These seats on top were very breezy and comfortable. Well up out of the dust, the occupants could enjoy the scenery at their leisure, or critically discuss the merits of the straining team. Naturally such places were in great demand and the competition for them was keen, everyone seeking as a first end in life to secure a seat on the coach for himself and to leave to his children after him. . . . (Bellamy, 1951, pp. 3–4)

The most striking thing about this description is the way it shows social classes as totally exploitive. True, the picture of the lower classes here is more accurate for the 1800s than for today. Still, Bellamy's novel expressed the feelings of the poor so well that it remained popular for many years.

Since Bellamy was a novelist rather than a sociologist, we will turn to others for theoretical views. First, though, let us try to learn how social-class systems begin.

The origins of social class

The Eskimos and Aleuts, the Bushmen of the Kalahari Desert, and other hunting and gathering tribes without surplus wealth had no clear-cut class differences. As we noted in the chapter on culture, such societies had to share their food to avoid starvation. Successful hunters would share with others and would be given food when their own luck was bad.

As agricultural societies and cities developed, different social classes were also formed. Not all

Short handle hoe: A history of agony for dubious advantages

ROBERT A. JONES

No one knows exactly when the short handle hoe first appeared in California, or why. Possibly it was packed in the belongings of Filipino immigrants who came to work the fields around Salinas and Fresno at the turn of the century.

The short handle hoe is about 12 inches long and to use it a man must bend at the waist, chopping at weeds or thinning the crops with a flick of the wrist and forearm. In this way the worker is placed very close to his work, and that pleased the owners, for when a man aims at a weed from a distance of one foot, he rarely misses. The Chicano workers called it the "cortito" and they stooped to its service for more than 60 years.

But though its origins are unclear, there is little mystery to the effect of the hoe on those who used it.

When it was outlawed last week by the State Division of Industrial Safety, the order said, "substantial medical evidence" had established that long-term use of the short hoe caused injuries to the back, often accompanied by great pain and suffering.

After last week's order, associations of growers and shippers asked for a stay of the ban in Orange County Superior Court saying "Costs will go up and everyone will suffer financially."

But the predictions of assocation officials have been contradicted by the experience thus far of one of the most prominent members among them. At Bud Artle, Inc., of Salinas, the largest producer of lettuce in the world, foremen discovered that after the first day of the changeover, field workers had increased production with the long handle hoe.

Robert Artle, president of Bud Artle and son of the founder, said he was "amazed" at the results.

"We fought this thing and worried over it and now it turns out not to be a problem. Frankly, I feel like a goddamn jackass," said Artle. . . .

The human back, Dr. Flanagan and other doctors testified, simply cannot withstand the strain of continuous stooping and twisting required of farm workers using the short hoe. After a term of years, the injury rate is nearly universal.

"Anybody that's been using the short hoe extensively in the field over a 10-year period has got back trouble. He's not going to make it to retirement age of 65," Flanagan testified.

Perhaps the most famous back injury attributed to the short hoe belongs to Cesar Chavez, president of the United Farm Workers of America. For 10 years in his youth Chavez worked the fields of Imperial Valley.

"I remember coming to California for the first time from Yuma," Chavez said in an interview. . . . "We didn't understand. We thought the handles had broken."

The hoes were no mistake, and 10 years later Chavez' back was permanently damaged. Today there are periods when he cannot rise from bed and others when he works under continuous pain of herniated discs. . . .

(Leonard Freed/Magnum)

(Paul Conklin/Monkmeyer)

(Bill Owens/Magnum)

In addition to differences in occupation, education, and income, social classes represent different styles of life.

(Burk Uzzle/Magnum)

(Hiroji Kubota/Magnum)

163

social-class systems arose in the same way, but Ralph Linton's description (1936) of the Tanala of Madagascar is useful. This example is interesting because it shows how a three-part class structure developed very rapidly. Until about 200 years ago, the Tanala were an egalitarian people. They hunted and planted a little rice, which was irrigated only by the rain. Gradually the Tanala learned from people to the east of them how to plant in low, damp areas and how to build terraces, dig ditches, and irrigate their rice. The result was increased production, much higher land values, and a vested interest in the land by families who saw the advantages of the new system. The Tanala changed quickly from an egalitarian to a land-owning society, with permanent villages, an owning class, a king, and eventually slaves.

Class societies have not always grown through internal development; often they were based on conquest. The royal family of England, for example, traces its origin to the Norman Conquest of 1066. Many of the titles and estates of the aristocracy can also be traced to the Conquest.

Superiority theory

Regardless of how social classes develop, some people generally rank higher than others. According to one theory, the upper classes are naturally superior to those below them. This is true not only because they are wealthy or control the military but also because their high rank is God-given. In the past, many rulers were considered divine. This divinity also touched the nobles and the priests.

The theory of natural superiority can serve to explain any social structure that exists. The upper classes have superior manners and the highest standard of living. They are served by scholars and priests and often live by complex codes of honor. The lower classes grovel before them, lie and cheat to survive, smell of sweat and dirt, dress badly, and are uneducated, coarse, and crude. What further proof of their inferiority

is needed? The same type of reasoning can be applied to different races as well.

In a weaker form, this explanation is found in a traditional view of American society: Those who do well are those who deserve to do well. Weber states that the Puritans suffered great anxiety because they believed that they were predestined at birth for either heaven or hell. The best way to prove that one was among God's elect was to be successful in the world, since it was believed that God blesses the work of those he loves. People who were poor probably lacked divine grace. Thus, they were inferior and destined for hell.

The Marxist view: Social class as exploitation

According to Karl Marx, social classes are systems by which the rich exploit the poor, working them hard and paying them little. Marx believed that most struggles of history have been class conflicts. The conflict that Marx saw emerging in his time (the mid-nineteenth century) was between the working class (*proletariat*) and the *bourgeoisie*—the owners of mines, factories, railroads, and other means of production and distribution of goods. The bourgeoisie was gradually replacing the old landowning ruling class. The new capitalist system, according to Marx, was a worse form of exploitation than the old feudal system. Under feudalism, the serfs had been attached to their land. They had a right to work it and to keep part of what they grew. Artisans owned their shops and tools and took pride in their work. Under capitalism, the workers owned nothing, had no rights, and had no economic interest in the goods they produced.

According to the early followers of Marx, the conditions that created capitalism would also lead to its overthrow. The new factory system required workers to move to the cities and work in crowded plants. Under such conditions, workers would quickly develop class-consciousness and be ready to rise up against their exploiters.

Meanwhile, the class of small shopkeepers would be destroyed by competition from giant industries and would become part of the proletariat. When society became sharply divided into a privileged owning class and an exploited working class, revolution would occur.

There *was* a huge gap between rich and poor in Marx's time. However, a revolution did not take place as he had predicted. Revolutions occurred not in the industrialized countries but in countries based on agriculture, with a large peasant class. If working conditions had not improved, Marx might have been right. But what actually happened was that the labor unions gained strength, winning better wages and working conditions. Governments were afraid of possible revolution. Led sometimes by liberals and other times by conservatives, they introduced such reforms as workmen's compensation laws and eventually social security.

Social class as social function

Kingsley Davis and Wilbert Moore have taken a functionalist perspective. Their theory is the *societal need* theory of stratification. They believe that social class serves the needs of society by giving the highest rank to those positions "that have the greatest importance for society and require the greatest training or talent (Davis and Moore, 1945, pp. 242–249). But such positions must give more than prestige. They must also bring a high income to ensure that the people chosen will work hard. There must be enough money to benefit their children. Many important jobs—such as cleaning streets or digging ditches—do not rank very high simply because many people can do them with little training. The doctor, scientist, and business executive, in contrast, hold highly trained positions for which talent is scarce. Therefore, they have high status and prestige. Since Davis and Moore were trying to apply general principles to all social systems, they were aware of the problem of inherited position. In these cases, they said, greater emphasis is placed on training the person who will someday hold that position, as with a future king or the firstborn son of a nobleman.

Many high-ranking positions not only require talent and training but are hard to fill. A doctor must work long hours and sometimes make life-and-death decisions. The Presidency of the United States is often described as a "man-killing job." Since such jobs are so difficult, high rewards must be given to attract qualified people. These rewards, say Davis and Moore, must include more than pay. They must involve high status and high social-class position as well.

Melvin Tumin (1953) is very critical of the Davis-Moore theory. He believes that it ignores both inherited wealth and extreme differences in wealth and overemphasizes the rewarding of talent. Another objection is that children from poor families have little chance to develop their talents. Thus, social class can actually decrease the amount of talent available. Other critics point out that many jobs that call for much training, such as teaching, are not very well rewarded. Finally, the higher the class one is born into, the less one need strive to achieve any position. No doubt David Rockefeller is a good banker, but he was able to become president of Chase Manhattan Bank with less effort than one of his tellers would have needed to do the same thing.

The circulation of elites

Since most social-class systems result in inherited wealth, it can be argued that they become more and more unjust. In trying to refute this charge, Vilfredo Pareto and Gaetano Mosca observe that upper classes are not permanent (Bottomore, 1966, pp. 48–67).

"History is the graveyard of aristocracies," said Pareto (1935, vol. 3, p. 2053). Sometimes aristocracies fall because of revolution or conquest, but Pareto was referring to a natural process of decline. Continued high status and an easy life, said Pareto, makes the *rentier* (landowning) class careless and lazy. This creates an opportunity for the *speculator* (enterprising business) class to displace them. The speculators, Pareto said, come up from the masses and are able to take business risks. Although Pareto tried to trace what happened when older aristocracies were replaced by the business classes in modern history, he did not find out whether the new elite actually arose from below or were already close to the upper classes.

Many sociologists have tried to account for ruling elites today. Harold D. Lasswell (Lasswell et al., 1952) argues that intellectuals today tend to lead revolutions and establish themselves in power. James Burnham (1941) used the term *managerial revolution*, stating that trained managers were taking control of industry away from the owning class. Max Weber (1947) believed that government officials and bureaucrats were the new ruling elite. Others have nominated scientists and technicians. T. B. Bottomore, a critic of many of these viewpoints (1966), believes that technicians and scientists can never rise to the top, since they depend on the wealthy elite or the government for research funds. The intellectuals, according to Bottomore, hardly make up a power bloc. They are divided among themselves and don't command much attention. Although intellectuals have prestige in some countries, they are not wealthy or powerful. Managers, according to Bottomore, have replaced owners in carrying out policy. Still, their jobs depend on pleasing the owners, and they often come from the upper classes themselves. Finally, Bottomore believes that bureaucrats merely carry out policies made by the real powers in government. If it could be proved that these were largely independent of the rich, then they could be said to make up an upper class of power, if not of wealth. It will be argued in Chapter 15, however, that most government officials must, to stay in office, please the major business interests and the rich.

Today, especially in Europe, the upper middle class has taken over the leadership role from the aristocracy. The new ruling class, however, is not being replaced by other classes. This does not mean that the societies are stagnant. A great deal of upward movement does take place, which makes the system much more agreeable than it would otherwise be. Most of the movement, we should note, is from lower to middle or from middle to upper middle class. Rarely are those at the top replaced.

SOCIAL MOBILITY

Social mobility, also called *vertical mobility*, refers to upward or downward movement within the social-class structure. A distinction should be made between *career mobility* and *generational mobility*. A man who changes from factory worker to manager has experienced upward *career* mobility. The daughter of a street cleaner

Figure 6-4 Upward mobility involves buying the goods associated with the higher class. (*Jim Cron, Monkmeyer*)

who becomes a teacher has achieved upward *generational* mobility.

American beliefs regarding mobility

The idea that anyone who really tries can succeed is considered a widespread American attitude. Joan Rytina and two colleagues (Rytina, Form, and Pease, 1970, pp. 703–716) tried testing this attitude. They hypothesized that rich people would be much more likely than poor people to agree. They also assumed that people would agree more strongly with a general statement than with statements regarding equal opportunity in specific cases. They asked respondents to agree or disagree with the statement, "There is plenty of opportunity, and anyone who works hard can go as far as he wants." The next question asked more pointedly, "Do you think that a boy whose father is poor and a boy whose father is rich have the same opportunity to make the same amount of money if they work hard?"

Of the three income groups of whites tested, over 90 percent of both rich and poor agreed with the general statement, as did 80 percent of the middle class. On the question about the two boys, the responses were quite different. Only 47 percent of the poor and 49 percent of the middle class agreed that the boys would have equal chances, as compared with 57 percent of the rich. Of the black people tested, only 11 percent of the poor and 21 percent of the middle class agreed. These opinions were probably based on their own experience with unequal opportunities. On the statement "The rich and the poor have equal influence on government," only 3 percent of poor blacks and 30 percent of poor whites agreed, in sharp contrast to 55 percent of the rich.

This survey indicates that Americans don't all agree on what has been called "the myth of equal opportunity." In all cases, a person's position in the social structure—including class and racial or ethnic status—affects his or her thinking.

A final hypothesis was tested. It was expected that Americans would rate the United States higher than the countries of Western Europe in allowing for upward mobility. Actually, a majority thought there was only a slight difference in favor of the United States. The opinion was correct, according to Lipset and Bendix (1960). Their own studies had found upward mobility patterns in Northern Europe similar to those of the United States.

Upward mobility in America: The reality

Blau and Duncan (1967) concluded, a few years after Lipset and Bendix, that the United States still has an edge over Europe in allowing for upward mobility. The difference is probably smaller now than in the past. This is not because the United States is lagging but because Europe is catching up. Another finding should be considered. During periods of recession or depression, it is easy to believe that upward mobility is becoming harder and harder. However, Blau and Duncan—and many others—have found a continued high level of mobility, tending more upward than downward. The reasons why social mobility is uneven, with more people moving up than down, have changed throughout American history.

In the nineteenth century and well into the twentieth, the United States was considered the land of opportunity. People of all nations came here to seek their fortunes. The free land in the West made it possible for many, both old residents and immigrants, to become independent farmers. The closing of the Western frontier in 1890 and the economic depression of the 1890s remind us that the road to fortune and security was not easy. Still, American farmers considered themselves luckier than those of Europe, many of whom were tilling land they did not own, living a hand-to-mouth existence with little hope for change.

Another upward path was through expanding industry. Coal, iron, and petroleum processing, as well as manufacturing, called for a huge labor force. By today's standards, the pay was terrible, but there were more jobs here than in most European countries. As the railroads and later the automobile industry expanded, and with the early development of mass education, people continued to believe that America was the land of promise.

Today, with most agriculture taken over by large corporations, the independent, family-owned farm is largely a dream of the past. Although mining and manufacturing industries continue to expand production, newer and more efficient methods require fewer and fewer workers. The same holds true in agriculture. As a result, upward mobility must occur in new fields, both in the United States and in other industrialized countries. Sometimes upward mobility results from the celebrity status of entertainers or athletes, but the great majority of upward mobility is more directly related to the industrial system.

Ours is sometimes called the "postindustrial age." This does not mean that industry is past but that the work structure is now dominated by white-collar, technical, scientific, and professional fields. It is to these areas that most people look when they seek upward mobility. It is because of opportunities in these areas that the rate of mobility has not gone down.

But, we must ask, are technicians and scientists recruited from among the sons and daughters of blue-collar workers or from the white-collar group? As will be noted in the chapter on

Figure 6-5 Sports and show business have always been means of rapid upward mobility. (a) World boxing champion Muhammad Ali and (b) entertainer Diana Ross. [(a) and (b) United Press International]

(a)

(b)

education, the school system does less to move people out of lower-class positions than was once believed.

Who are the upwardly mobile?

The upwardly mobile are generally well-educated people from well-educated home backgrounds, willing to move from their home towns if necessary. They typically come from small families and are more concerned with getting ahead than with keeping up family ties (Blau and Duncan, 1967). Long-established white American families and the children of immigrants are more likely to be upwardly mobile than nonwhites. We will discuss the reasons for this here and in the next chapter.

In determining who will move up socially, family background is important. People from poor or poorly educated families have great handicaps to overcome. Such people can experience some upward mobility. However, movement is very limited and occurs mainly because these people, being at the bottom of the ladder, have nowhere to go but up. The poor have limited information. Often, they are not aware of jobs, training programs, or the kinds of financial aid to be had. They usually do not have contact with people who could help them. They generally have more children to support than those with more money, and college is usually beyond their financial reach. Often they feel their lives are hopeless, so that they don't even try to avoid the failure they see ahead. This was especially true for black and Chicano families in the past. Their situation has recently improved because they have stressed pride in their heritage and because of an aggressive civil rights movement.

People who move from rural to urban areas tend to be more upwardly mobile than those who stay in their home towns. In fact, people who move to the city show greater upward mobility than people of the same social class who were born in the city. Their move to the city shows their willingness to cut home ties in order to benefit themselves. Others feel more strongly bound to their families and the old familiar places. They are more likely to remain in areas such as the rural South, where chances for upward mobility are poor.

QUESTIONS REGARDING MOBILITY

The rate of upward mobility in America and other industrialized societies remains high, but sociologists wonder about the future. The first question they ask is: "Are there enough high-level jobs so that upward mobility can continue until all who are able to handle them receive them?" Second: "Is there an underclass in American society that has so many disadvantages that it can't move up?" Finally: "Do the studies of mobility apply only to movement which ends in the middle class, or can people still move all the way to the top? Is the wealthy elite class so closed that few or none can enter?"

How much mobility is needed?

In 1961, Robert Faris wrote a thought-provoking article entitled, "Reflections on the Ability Dimension in Human Societies" (1961, pp. 835–843). In it, he asked whether enough talented people are produced to meet a society's needs as it grows more complex scientifically and technologically. His conclusion: Societies can produce enough talent if they give equal opportunities for all. At the same time, Faris's article shows how hard it is to predict social patterns in America. Just over a decade later, a turnabout in labor requirements occurred. The U.S. Labor Department predicted that in the late 1970s and throughout the 1980s, there would be more college graduates than jobs requiring college degrees. The Labor Department concluded that some graduates would have to settle for jobs formerly held by high school graduates. This picture, though, may change if any of the following takes place: an upturn in the economy, new industrial developments, a government decision to develop new energy sources, programs for saving the environment, and projects for improving the cities.

Is there a permanent underclass?

Earlier, we noted that the best candidate for upward mobility is a person who comes from a family that has already achieved some success. People from lower-class homes tend to maintain lower-class life-styles and income levels. Yet, except during recessions, the number of people living at or below official poverty levels has declined over the last twenty years. During the 1960s, the number of people living officially in poverty dropped from 40 million to 24 million, or from 22 percent to 12 percent, although the trend was upward again in the 1970s. These figures show the ability of groups to lift themselves out of poverty if they have the chance (Levitan, 1973, pp. 241–246).

Over half the heads of poor families work. However, they work at inadequate jobs and only one-fifth of them work full time. (Bell, 1973, pp. 253–257). Forty percent of inner-city families are headed by women who are often not trained for work outside the home. Their pay is low partly because they lack training and partly because they are discriminated against as women. Poor families are larger than middle-class families; 60 percent of all poor children come from families with four or more children. The burden of supporting many children makes upward mobility a struggle.

Poverty is most widespread in rural districts. Here, nearly 20 percent of the people are officially poor. These people do not share the general prosperity of the rest of the country. Data presented by Senator Ernest F. Hollings (1973, pp. 258–260), a Democrat from South Carolina, lead to the conclusion that a vicious circle has set in: Residents of the poorest rural areas are deprived of the things they need to break out of poverty—education, healthy food, and good medical care.

According to Senator Hollings, rural areas spend 10 percent less on education, 50 percent less on welfare and sanitation, and 33 percent less on health and hospitals than the nation as a whole. Obviously, the most important cure for these problems is money, but the existing welfare system provides so little that vital needs are neglected.

If the poor flee from rural poverty, they usually land in the crowded slums of big cities, where job opportunities are only slightly better than in the areas they left behind.

In answer to the question, "Is there an underclass of permanently poor people in America?" we can say that in an expanding economy, the answer is no. The percentage of poor people declines. Still, there are some areas where poverty seems to be both widespread and persistent. Although these areas of poverty are somewhat smaller than in the past, their existence cannot be ignored.

Social class and early death

It has long been known that infant mortality in the United States is higher than in many other developed countries. Indeed, in this respect the United States ranks fourteenth among all nations, according to United Nations statistics. A recent study by the National Center for Health Statistics of the U.S. Public Health Service sheds some light on the matter (MacMahon and Feldman, 1972), finding a strong link between infant death and low socioeconomic status of the parents. Moreover, nearly half the infant deaths in the lowest classes are preventable. (See the insert "Social Class and Early Death.")

Is there an entrenched upper class?

It is true that there are high rates of upward mobility in the United States. However, many

Social class and early death

[According to a recent study, there is a strong correlation between infant mortality and the socioeconomic status of the parents.] The findings are published in a report titled "Infant Mortality Rates: Socioeconomic Factors" (by Brian MacMahon, Jacob J. Feldman, and Mary Grace Kovar). They write: "These indexes of socioeconomic status were examined—education of father, education of mother, and family income in the year prior to the birth or the infant death. All three indexes showed a strong association with risk of infant death, the risk being between 50 and 100 percent higher than in the middle and upper classes." A particular finding was that mortality rates were "substantially higher for black than for white infants at all levels of each of the three variables."

. . . "Using education of the father as the measure of socioeconomic status," the authors write, "and considering as the minimum attainable mortality rate of 17.4 per 1,000 observed among the highest educational class, it can be estimated that 47 percent of the deaths in the lowest socioeconomic group (with a rate of 33 per 1,000) were in excess of this minimum and were, therefore, in a broad sense, preventable."

From *Scientific American*, August 1972, "Science and the Citizen: Underdevelopment in the United States," p. 45.

---

sociologists and economists believe that this movement is into the lower middle and even the upper middle and lower upper classes. The figures seem to show no movement into the upper upper class.

In 1958, C. Wright Mills introduced a useful term: the *power elite*. This group he defined as a class of people controlling the major corporations and closely linked to the government and the military. Mills tried to show that the very rich in the United States (about 100 families) were a more stable group than they had been earlier. According to Mills, in the nineteenth century, 39 percent of the country's richest people had been born poor. By 1950, this was true of only 9 percent at the top; the rest were born rich.

John Porter (1968, pp. 5–19) examined the power elite in 1968 and came to the same conclusion: "As for our time, it is safe to say that the upper-upper class is in a state of stability." Porter discusses a broader group than that described by Mills—the upper-upper-class families of Boston, New York, Philadelphia, and Virginia.

Since the money of these families is handled by expert managers, their fortunes are kept intact. Economist Robert Heilbroner (1966, pp. 23–35) also believes that those at the top are more secure than in the past. Although gift and inheritance taxes might be expected to break up large estates, there are tax loopholes, such as making gifts to heirs before death or setting up foundations, that keep the money in the family. Heilbroner finds the concentration of stock ownership to be just as great now as in 1922, before taxes aimed at the rich existed.

Ferdinand Lundberg, author of *The Rich and the Super-Rich* (1968, pp. 21–22), is even surer that great wealth has deep roots. He states that 1.6 percent of the American people owns 80 percent of all stock, 100 percent of all state and local bonds, and 88.5 percent of all corporate bonds. The public is aware of certain families—such as the Rockefellers, Morgans, Mellons, DuPonts, and Hunts—whose fortunes are very secure. There are many less famous families, according to Lundberg, in the same position.

Stratification, class, and mobility

171

Occasionally someone from a lower class suddenly becomes very rich, but no superrich families have fallen from their high positions. We can only conclude, as Mills, Porter, and Heilbroner have done, that the upper upper class is now stable.

SUMMARY

Stratification, the division of society into different layers, is most apparent when the very rich and the very poor are compared, not only in income and life-style but in prestige and power. People in middle positions are also stratified into social classes, but the lines are not always clear and *class-consciousness* is not as great as it is among the two extreme groups. *Social classes* consist of people who are roughly equal in income, education, occupational prestige, and social influence and who are accepted as such by themselves and others. These criteria of social class are about the same as those used by Max Weber in describing three types of stratification—*class*, *status*, and *party*.

In the United States, most people (61 percent) rate themselves as middle class or upper middle class, and 34 percent place themselves in the working class. Despite such self-ratings, income is very uneven, with the highest fifth of the population receiving 41.6 percent of the income and the lowest fifth receiving only 5.5 percent. Only a slight change has taken place in the last twenty years. Similarly, in ratings of occupational prestige, very little change occurred in the same period. Rankings of occupational prestige indicate stronger feelings about stratification than do self-ratings, in which nearly all people call themselves middle class or working class.

Community studies also show a strong awareness of stratification, with an *upper upper* "old money" class at the top, the *lower upper*, or newly rich, in second place, and well-paid business and professional people in third place (the *upper middle class*). White-collar workers and skilled laborers make up the *lower middle class*,

and unskilled workers belong to the *upper lower class*. Those who depend on public welfare support make up the *lower lower class*.

The term *power elite* describes an elite upper class that controls the major corporations and has strong influence in government and the military. The middle class shows a wide division between well-paid business and professional people and poorly paid office workers and salespeople. Many of the latter jobs are held by women, who are generally paid less for their work than men. The term *working class* refers to people with manual skills that usually require only a short period of training. They are in a poor competitive position to demand good pay unless they are unionized. The working class generally feels deprived because of unhealthy and dangerous jobs, few promotions, and low prestige. The *lower class* consists of people who are unemployed or underemployed. These people are often seen as victims of a system that does not have enough jobs for those with few skills. Sometimes, though, they are blamed for their troubles by the classes above them.

Although wide social-class distinctions exist, it is possible for people to change their position within a class structure. This is not true of *caste systems*, or class systems which allow no movement from one position to another. In comparing the caste system of India with the class system of the United States, one can see parallels between caste and the positions of black Americans. Attitudes about jobs, social acceptability, and intermarriage are similar. Racial caste in the United States was stronger in the past than it is now.

Caste has existed throughout history. Often, racial differences are involved. Caste isolates one group from another and reduces social concern. The castelike position of Chicano fieldworkers illustrates this point.

Social-class distinctions increase as societies change from simple hunting and gathering to advanced agriculture, when landowners begin to exploit a peasant class. Class systems also result from conquest. Regardless of their origin, a myth of the superiority of upper classes arises. Among the Puritans in the United States, upper classes were looked on as predestined for heaven.

Karl Marx, who explained social class as a system of exploitation of the poor by the rich, expected the owning class (*bourgeoisie*) to be overthrown by the working class (*proletariat*). Others (Davis and Moore, for example) have held that social class guarantees that there will be talented people to hold important positions for which talent is scarce. Pareto and Mosca contend that in the long run there is a *circulation of elites*, with upper classes being replaced by newcomers from below. Some have contended that managers, intellectuals, scientists, or bureaucrats are moving into the elite positions once held by the rich. Others state that such changes are an illusion. The rich, who pay the salaries, still hold the real power.

Social mobility, or *vertical mobility*, refers to the movement up or down the social-class ladder. America has long been regarded as the land of opportunity for upward mobility, although such mobility now seems to be only slightly greater than in Northern Europe. Public-opinion surveys show that middle- and upper-class whites generally regard upper mobility as easily possible; blacks and poor white see it as much more difficult. In the nineteenth century, growth on the frontier and industrial expansion helped make America a land of opportunity. Today, in contrast, upward mobility depends on education for advanced skills and professions. The upwardly mobile tend to be ambitious people from well-educated home backgrounds. By the 1970s, there were more college graduates than jobs to employ them.

The possible oversupply of college-trained people for the job market is one concern regarding the social-class system. Other concerns are that an underclass of permanent poverty and an upper class of permanent wealth and power now exist.

Study guide

Terms to know

Stratification *layers*
Power *have influence*
Social class *equal in money ed etc*
Life chances *long rewarding life*
Status (in Weber's analysis) *position held in society*
Party (in Weber's analysis) *power where influence*
Class consciousness *politics*
Prestige *standing in the eyes of*
Social register *others*
people in the highest social area at US or a community
Upper class
Middle class

Working class *manual labour lower mid high*
Lower class *welfare*
Warner's classifications:
Upper upper class
Lower upper class
Upper middle class
Lower middle class
Upper lower class
Lower lower class
Caste *stringent layers*
Open-class system *move to to any class you want, no restrictions*

Exploitation *rich take advantage of poor*
Proletariat *working class*
Bourgeoisie *owners of factories*
Rentier class *landowning class*
Speculator class *business class*
Managerial revolution *industry take over by managers*
Social mobility (vertical mobility *movement in social classes*
Career mobility *social change through job change*
Generational mobility *I move to be president)*
Power elite *industrialists who are close to politics (where the action is)*

Names to know

Max Weber *Party status*
W. Lloyd Warner
Ralph Linton

Exploitation
Karl Marx *Proletariet Bourgoise*
Kingsley Davis and Wilbert Moore
Vilfredo Pareto *rentier class*

Gaetano Mosca
C. Wright Mills *power elite*
Ferdinand Lundberg

Self-test

Part I. Multiple Choice. Select the best of the four alternative answers:

1. When Americans were asked to rate their social position on a five-way scale, 61 percent rated themselves as (a) upper, (b) upper or upper middle, (c) upper middle or middle, (d) working class or lower class.

2. A distribution-of-income chart comparing 1950 with 1970 shows (a) major percentage gains for the middle fifth, (b) major gains for the fourth fifth (next to highest), (c) a major loss for the highest fifth, (d) a change of not more than one percentage point for any fifth.

3. A comparison of occupational prestige as rated by the American public in 1947 and in 1963 showed (a) major changes in favor of white-collar jobs, (b) an increase in the prestige of skilled labor, (c) a very slight change in favor of scientists, (d) a wide difference in the rating of all occupations between the two dates.

4. In Warner's community studies, the factor that distinguishes the upper upper class from the lower upper class is a matter of (a) how long the wealth has been held, (b) the amount of wealth, (c) the source of wealth, (d) whether the amount of wealth is increasing.

5. In Warner's study, the lower lower class is differentiated from the upper lower class mainly on the basis of (a) prestige of the work done, (b) ethnic origin, (c) dependency, (d) ability to speak English.

6. In his description of the old upper class of Philadelphia, Baltzell comments that they generally possessed *all but one* of the following traits: (a) English or Welsh descent, (b)

membership in the Social Register, (**c**) a connection with one of the prestigious law firms, (**d**) Baptist, Methodists, or Quaker church membership.

7 Compared with the other classes, the lower class (**a**) has better health, (**b**) is able to buy goods at lower cost, (**c**) is less victimized by crime and fraud, (**d**) none of the above.

8 Caste always has *all but one* of the following characteristics: (**a**) marriage within the caste; (**b**) support of religious attitudes, myths, or both; (**c**) clear physical differences between the castes; (**d**) virtually no mobility.

9 In the excerpt from Michener's novel *Hawaii*, the Japanese mother advises her son that he would be "worse than dead" if he married (**a**) an Eta girl, (**b**) an Okinawan girl, (**c**) a city girl from Japan, (**d**) a girl from Hiroshima.

10 The description of the use of the short-handled hoe concludes that (**a**) employers had been worried about the hoe but considered it necessary, (**b**) there had been callous indifference to the matter until protests and medical reports were made, (**c**) the hoe had been entirely necessary, (**d**) many people lived into their late sixties and seventies in spite of back injuries from use of the hoe.

11 Ralph Linton illustrated one possible origin of social class in his study of the Tanala. The variable that caused the shift to a rigid class system was (**a**) conquest by outsiders, (**b**) the change to an industrial system, (**c**) the change to a wet-rice culture and permanent farms, (**d**) the change from defensive to aggressive war.

12 A theory that lower classes are morally inferior has existed in American history, stemming from the ideas of the (**a**) Puritans, (**b**) Quakers, (**c**) Catholics, (**d**) non-Christian immigrants.

13 It is argued in the text, following the thinking of T. B. Bottomore, that the wealthy elite are being replaced in modern society by (**a**) managers, (**b**) intellectuals, (**c**) bureaucrats, (**d**) none of the above.

14 A study of beliefs regarding social mobility (by Rytina, Form, and Pease) concludes that (**a**) rich people understand the difficulties encountered by the poor in trying to get ahead, (**b**) people are more realistic about generalized statements than about specific cases, (**c**) the poor and black are much less optimistic about upward mobility than are the upper classes, (**d**) the ideas of the poor and black are unreasonable.

15 Although Davis and Moore make strong arguments about the necessity for social class, Tumin finds objections to their theory, concluding that (**a**) the higher one's inherited position, the less talent is needed to stay on top, (**b**) inherited wealth makes people too lazy to try, (**c**) differences in wealth are no longer great enough to promote much effort, (**d**) people with enough talent always get ahead regardless of the class system.

Part II. True-False Questions

1 There are many kinds of stratification besides that of social class.

2 According to Max Weber, stratification ultimately depends so exclusively on wealth that such criteria as power, life-style, and prestige are irrelevant.

3 Social class is purely a matter of individual position, not family position, in such an individualistic country as America.

4 In ratings of occupational prestige, the American public apparently takes into consideration criteria other than income.

5 Baltzell concluded that between 1900 and 1940, a true national elite upper class had come about.

6 Office work generally rates lower in prestige than do unionized industrial jobs.

7 The middle class is a fairly homogeneous class of well-paid positions carrying roughly equal pay and prestige.

8 As analyzed by Lenski, the working class, unless unionized, is in a weak competitive position relative to the classes above it.

9 It has been the experience of both India and the United States that antidiscrimination laws are hard to enforce in rural areas.

10 The Indian government found it necessary to put in two wells in many villages, one for people and one for cattle.

11 The best one-word summary of the Marxist view of social class is *exploitation*.

12 Davis and Moore contend that social-class systems are found in only a few societies because they do not function well.

13 Blau and Duncan found slightly more upward mobility in the United States than in Northern Europe, but the difference is declining.

14 A study of the short-handled hoe in California agriculture indicates that, although it was hard on workers' health, it was necessary for high productivity.

15 Both Lundberg and Porter conclude that the American upper upper class is declining in permanence and power.

Questions for Discussion

1 Contrast self-ratings of social class in America with the facts of income distribution and ratings of occupational prestige. Why do so many people like to call themselves middle class?

2 Describe the upper upper class as defined by Warner. Is there such a class in your community? If so, what is the source of their wealth and how long has it been held?

3 Many office workers are not paid as well as industrial workers; yet they generally consider themselves to be in a better social-class position. Why?

4 What are the special problems of the working class that lead to discontentment, even for those who are steadily employed?

5 Compare the caste system of India with racial caste in the United States, especially as it existed before the civil rights movement of the 1960s.

6 Why is it so easy for upper-class people to think of themselves as superior in mentality as well as in class position?

7 Contrast the Marxist position on social class with that of Davis and Moore. Which theory seems a better explanation of the facts? Evaluate both theories.

8 Why is upward mobility much easier for some people than for others?

9 How has the opportunity structure in America changed since we were mainly an agricultural society?

10 What arguments can you present for or against the idea that America is developing a permanent, firmly rooted upper class?

Projects

1 To show the importance of social-class differences and the hidden nature of poverty in American communities, make a tour of your own community. Photograph a few houses in the wealthiest districts, middle-class districts, and the poorest districts.

2 Try to replicate some of the research cited in the text on public opinion regarding social class. Using a cross-section of opinion, find out whether about 75 percent of the people in your community call themselves middle class. If the question is pursued further, will they divide about 61 percent to 34 percent in rating themselves middle class or working class?

Diversity and strain

3 Try to replicate the study done by Rytina, Form, and Pease regarding differences between black and white people and between the rich and the poor in estimating the chances for mobility of a boy or girl with rich parents compared to a boy or girl with poor parents.

4 In a survey of your community, find what jobs are commonly available that involve a considerable health risk—the types of jobs mentioned in the text as being commonly held by the working class.

Suggested readings

Berreman, Gerald D.: "Caste in India and the United States," *American Journal of Sociology*, vol. 66, July 1959, pp. 120–127. How could a "land of opportunity" develop a system in some ways comparable to Indian's caste system? Even the personality expected and often developed by low-caste people of India has had its parallel among blacks in the racial caste system of the United States. Neither caste system disappears quickly, in spite of laws and public pronouncements.

Form, William H.: "The Internal Stratification of the Working Class: System Involvements of Auto Workers in Four Countries," *American Sociological Review*, vol. 38, December 1973, pp. 697–711. Karl Marx expected the workers to unite and change the social system. How well united is the working class? Form, in a study of four different countries, finds the workers to be sharply divided against themselves, lowering the possibility of a working-class movement. What are the lines of division?

Gans, Herbert J.: "The Uses of Poverty: The Poor Pay All," *Social Policy*, vol. 2, July–August 1971, pp. 20–31. Do the better-situated members of society have a vested interest in poverty? Yes, says Gans, in this functional analysis of poverty. Poverty has many uses.

Lewis, Oscar: "The Culture of Poverty," *Scientific American*, vol. 215, October 1966, pp. 19–25. Is there a common way of life among the very poor of urban civilizations in much of the world? What are the parallels between families of extreme poverty in the United States, Mexico, and Puerto Rico? Above all, Lewis describes being in a society but not belonging to it and the types of adjustments needed for survival.

Nagel, Stuart S.: "The Tipped Scales of American Justice," *Trans-Action*, vol. 3, May–June 1966, pp. 3–9. What part does social-class position play in obtaining justice? Nagel cites evidence of deprivation of justice in preliminary hearings, the setting of bail, being held awaiting trial, and the quality of defense counsel—some of the many correlates of social-class position.

Rytina, Joan Huber, William H. Form, and John Pease: "Income and Stratification Ideology: Beliefs about the American Opportunity Structure," *American Journal of Sociology*, vol. 35, April 1970, pp. 703–716. This article, mentioned in the text, gives a good description of how vested interest influences our perception of social reality. How do the poor manage to see things that are hidden from the eyes of the rich?

Schrag, Peter: "The Forgotten Americans," *Harpers Magazine*, vol. 239, August 1969, pp. 17–24. Scrag tries to explain some of the attitudes of working-class Americans. Why are many of them strong law-and-order people? Why do they display a certain hostility toward those who are even poorer?

Key to questions: Multiple Choice: 1-c; 2-d; 3-c; 4-a; 5-c; 6-d; 7-d; 8-c; 9-a; 10-b; 11-c; 12-a; 13-d; 14-c; 15-a. True-False: 1-T; 2-F; 3-F; 4-T; 5-T; 6-F; 7-F; 8-T; 9-T; 10-F; 11-T; 12-F; 13-T; 14-F; 15-F.

This chapter defines racial and ethnic minorities and examines their problems and relationships with the dominant culture. After reading it, you should be able to:

1   Explain the meaning of racial and ethnic groups.

2   Understand the origins of prejudice and how prejudiced attitudes are related to discriminatory practices.

3   See why increased interaction and the reduction of social distance are important in reducing prejudice.

4   Understand economic factors in intergroup antagonism, such as competition for jobs, a "split labor market," and marginal adjustments for minority groups.

5   Understand the complexities and inconsistencies in modern attitudes toward minorities.

6   Realize why large numbers of people have experienced discrimination and persecution.

7   See that social forces account for the close connection between race or ethnic group and poverty.

7
MINORITIES: RACIAL AND ETHNIC

In Chapter 6, we discussed social inequality in our society as well as the forces that create social mobility and the barriers that prevent it. We noted that all social classes have ethnocentric attitudes and that they often hold negatives attitudes toward one another. They often do not understand each other's problems.

Nearly all these statements could also be made about racial and ethnic groups. Often, racial or ethnic ties strongly affect one's chances for upward mobility. Further, members of these groups have ethnocentric attitudes about themselves, which are not related to their social-class positions. The failure to understand one another may be even greater between racial and ethnic groups than between social classes. Negative attitudes toward minority groups are strengthened when their members are in the lower social classes. These lower-class minorities, in turn, react by stereotyping the majority group as snobbish and insensitive.

THE MEANING OF RACE

The concept of race has become so mixed with inaccurate stereotypes that many social scientists would like to drop it from their vocabulary. However, as long as racial and ethnic prejudice continues and as long as people are treated differently on the basis of their ethnic group or color, a discussion of race cannot be avoided. *Race* refers to inherited physical differences in groups of people of different geographic origins. It was once common to divide the human species into three major races: Negroid (originating in sub-Saharan Africa), Caucasoid (originating in Europe), and Mongoloid (originating in East Asia). The American Indians were sometimes classified as a branch of the Mongoloid race. The dark-skinned people of Melanasia, New Guinea, and Australia were often classified as yet another major race. Recently it has become common to use the term *geographical race* to refer to the region of origin. This term also indicates that if people are separated from each other geographically for very long periods of time, they will evolve distinctive physical characteristics.

Race probably reflects some physical adaptation to the environment. It is believed, but not yet proved conclusively, that the Eskimos have a greater inborn resistance to cold; that desert peoples such as the Berbers have a high tolerance for dry heat; and that people whose ancestors have lived in the tropics show greater adaptation to hot, moist conditions (Baker, 1958, pp. 283–306). However, these physical differences between people are only slight. It is much more important to note that each race can live in the other's environment. An Arab could work in Alaska, while an Eskimo who moved to Mecca would make a physical adjustment to the new environment.

The differences between races are vastly outweighed by the similarities among them. All human beings belong to the same species, *Homo sapiens.* All are culture builders, all have intelligence and imagination, all tell stories and dream dreams, sing songs, and create art. All can be kind or cruel. No race has a monopoly on good or bad qualities, talents, or behaviors.

There are certain genetic differences between groups. Sickle cell anemia is a disease in which red blood cells have trouble carrying oxygen through the body. It is found among black people in certain parts of Africa and their descendants in the United States. Tay-Sachs disease is most frequent among non-European Jews, and a blood condition known as porphyry is found among people of Dutch descent living in South Africa. Such racial and genetic factors can be important in terms of medical treatment; otherwise, they are unimportant. They tell us nothing about the intelligence, character, or talents of a black person, a Jew, or someone of Dutch descent.

However, in any particular society, one race or ethnic group might be treated as superior and another as inferior. The way members of a race are treated will influence the development of their intelligence, their character, and their talents. Social experience can help decide whether their gifts will be developed or remain unused. These are the realities that make the study of racial and ethnic groups necessary.

THE MEANING OF ETHNICITY

Ethnic is a term related to culture. An *ethnic group* is a group whose culture is different enough in beliefs, values, and customs so that its members feel an ingroup identity which sets them apart from others. Ethnic groups are particularly important as they relate to unequal treatment and to the feelings people hold about ethnicity. Members of white ethnic groups from some parts of Europe have had a great deal of trouble being fully accepted in the United States. Michael Novak (1972), a writer of Slovak descent, feels that American WASPs (white Anglo-Saxon Protestants) hold negative attitudes toward Poles, Italians, Greeks, and Slavs. He uses the term *unmeltable ethnics* to show that these people have not blended into the general American population as quickly as people from northwestern Europe and are not accepted as easily. Eve Merriam makes fun of some WASP attitudes in the insert "A WASP Hymn."

Jews are considered to be a separate ethnic group because of their unique cultural history and because their religion differs from that of the Christian majority. Other religious groups have also been given special status. Before the election of John F. Kennedy in 1960, it was assumed that no Catholic could ever become President. The majority culture had ascribed a separate and distinct ethnic identity to Catholics based on their religion alone. Membership in the Orthodox Church of Eastern Europe is much smaller, but these people, too, were held to be different and strange when they first arrived in the United States.

In some cases, groups differ from the American majority both racially and ethnically. This is true of American Indians except for a handful who have moved fully into American industrial-urban society. To some extent, the same is true of Chicanos. Black people, who first came to America as slaves, were so wholly cut off from their African cultural roots that they can hardly be said to represent a foreign culture. Although their experience has caused them to develop subcultural differences of their own, these differences are still within the American mainstream. Chinese, Japanese, and other Asian people, on the other hand, have entered the United States with distinctive cultures of their own. A generation or two ago, it was assumed that these immigrants, and those from Southern and Eastern Europe, would blend with American culture until ethnic identity would no longer matter. Recently, this view has been questioned and ethnic identity reasserted. Before we discuss this "melting pot" theory of ethnic identity, we will examine some traditional explanations of racial and ethnic prejudice.

PREJUDICE AND DISCRIMINATION

Prejudice is a negative attitude toward a person or group; *discrimination* is a system of unequal treatment toward the object of prejudice. It seems logical that prejudice would result in discrimination, and this is usually the case. The

A WASP hymn EVE MERRIAM

All men are brothers:
White Anglo-Saxon Protestants   and   others.

All God's children are blessed:
White Anglo-Saxon Protestants   and   the rest.

We are all one in His sight:
White Anglo-Saxon Protestants   and   those whom the census designates as
                                          non-white.

To each of us His grace is willed:
White Anglo-Saxon Protestants   and   the traditionally unskilled.

His love is ever seeking:
White Anglo-Saxon Protestants   and   non-English speaking.

His amplitude embraces
White Anglo-Saxon Protestants   and   municipal welfare cases.

Divinely He inspires
White Anglo-Saxon Protestants   and   low-income-housing-project qualifiers.

A single omnipotence rules
White Anglo-Saxon Protestants   and   vocational guidance schools.

One Godhead hath created
White Anglo-Saxon Protestants   and   the limited credit-rated.

United we all hearken to His almighty heeding:
White Anglo-Saxon Protestants   and   those in need of remedial reading. . . .

Yes, His total glory doth infuse
White Anglo-Saxon Protestants   and   those who do not belong and therefore
                                          who do not have to pay country club dues.

Then praise Him who fathers all believers:
White Anglo-Saxon Protestants   and   socio-economico-culturally
                                          disadvantaged underachievers.

For the good Lord hath us all begot:
White Anglo-Saxon Protestants   and   not!

Eve Merriam, *The New Republic*, vol. 161, June 12, 1969, p. 24.

---

reverse, however, is also true: Discrimination can encourage prejudice. There are several reasons for this. One reason is observed social reality. *Observed social reality* refers to what happens when members of upper classes look at members of lower classes. They see them doing menial work, as being poorly educated and poorly dressed, and they take these conditions to be the result of stupidity and laziness. If particular minority groups occupy lower-class positions, it

Minorities: Racial and ethnic

is easy to see them as social inferiors and therefore to conclude that they are somehow "naturally" inferior. These attitudes become habit-forming. Alexis de Tocqueville, an astute observer of American life in the 1830s, found this to be the basis of white prejudice against blacks, both in the slave states and in the free states. In the free states, according to de Tocqueville, prejudice was even stronger than in the slave states. Part of the reason, he concludes, was cultural habit:

> There is a natural prejudice which prompts men to despise whomsoever has been their inferior long after he is become their equal; and the real inequality which is produced by fortune or by law, is always succeeded by an imaginary inequality which is implanted in the manners and folkways of the people. (1974, p. 479)

Another principle can be used to explain the link between discrimination and prejudice. If we find ourselves deliberately hurting another person through discriminatory acts, we feel forced to *rationalize*, that is, to find socially acceptable and plausible explanations, but not the true ones (Festinger, 1962). The mental process runs more or less as follows: "I am a good person, but I have deliberately injured another human being. However, I would not have done it if he had been a good, normal person. He belongs to an inferior breed and therefore deserves what he gets. Besides, if you don't let him know who's boss, he'll take advantage of you."

Thus, discrimination leads to prejudice in at least three ways: (1) It contributes to the creation of an observed reality that reinforces prejudice; (2) it becomes a firmly rooted social habit that supports prejudice; and (3) it may require a kind of rationalization that encourages prejudice. All these points of view help to explain an ongoing process, but they do not tell us how prejudice starts. We can be prejudiced against people we have never discriminated against. Although the discrimination-prejudice cycle is important to understand if we are to figure out why people treat each other as they do, there are other explanations we should consider.

Stereotyping and prejudice

Stereotypes are standardized and oversimplified descriptions applied to groups of people. Occasionally they are derived from limited experience, as when a person knows one Armenian and decides that all Armenians are just like the one he or she knows. Often the stereotype is based on no direct experience at all. Sometimes it stems from what others say or even from their facial expressions when they discuss another group. Old folktales can also create and keep stereotypes alive (Gypsies are mysterious and dangerous); so can jokes, nicknames (krauts, spiks, gooks); and biased historical accounts. Stereotypes can even find their way into great literature, as with Shakespeare's portrayal of Shylock, a Jewish moneylender, in *The Merchant of Venice*. Stereotypes pervade every culture and are picked up unconsciously. We "know" that the Scotch are shrewd but stingy and that Irish people are hot-tempered. Up to quite recently, black people were the target of racial slurs in jokes, stories, and popular entertainment. Similarly, for years nearly all Italians were shown in the movies as gangsters, most of whom looked or acted like Al Capone. Mexicans have generally been pictured as bloodthirsty bandits or stupid, amiable sidekicks.

Following the lead provided by the Jewish Anti-Defamation League, leaders of a number of racial and ethnic groups have recently fought back against these stereotypes. Thomas M. Martinez, a Mexican-American, objects to the ways his people have been stereotyped in television ads:

> Exaggerated Mexican racial and cultural characteristics, together with some outright misconceptions concerning their style of life, symbolically suggest to the audience that

such people are comical, lazy, thieving, who want what Anglos can have by virtue of their superior taste and culture. (1972, p. 95)

Martinez has made up a list of advertisements that are objectionable to Mexican Americans and has identified the racist messages carried by these ads; see Table 7-1 (page 184).

Interaction and prejudice

Unless adults or other children teach them to discriminate, children of different races and ethnic groups play together and get along as well as they would if they all belonged to the same group. When they get older, even if prejudices are only minimal, children acquire them. Then cultural attitudes will probably prevent them from making friends with people who are "different," especially when dating or thinking of marriage.

During the period of slavery in the American South, relations between masters and household slaves were often quite close, but a special type of behavior was learned. A social distance was created that clearly defined the master as boss and the slave as subordinate. Long after slavery had ended, social distance remained as part of

Figure 7-1 In the United States, the stereotype of the carefree, irresponsible black person began during the period of slavery and persisted until the 1960s. (*Library of Congress*)

the Southern cultural tradition. *Social distance* means the degree to which people are accepted or rejected in social relationships. If we feel a great social distance between ourselves and members of another group, we often try to exclude them from our neighborhoods, parties, or clubs. To this day, considerable social distance remains in American culture. An interesting case arose when Griffin Bell, in order to become United States Attorney General in the Carter administration, resigned from the exclusive Driving Club of Atlanta, Georgia. Rule 18 of the club had always allowed full membership privileges (although not actual membership) to the mayor of Atlanta. The rule was revised in 1970, when Atlanta elected its first Jewish mayor, and the revised rule held when Atlanta elected a black mayor, Maynard Jackson, in 1973. No longer does the mayor of Atlanta have automatic membership privileges in the Driving Club. The bad publicity, however, should not go exclusively to Atlanta. Many other cities have similar clubs that maintain a wide social distance

Minorities: Racial and ethnic

Table 7-1 Advertisers Promoting Racism: A Partial Listing

Name of Advertiser	Content and/or Context of Ad	Racist Message
Granny Goose	Fat Mexican toting guns, ammunition	Mexicans = overweight, carry deadly weapons
Frito-Lay	Frito Bandito	Mexicans = sneaky thieves
Liggett & Myers	"Paco" never "feenishes" anything, not even revolution	Mexicans = too lazy to improve selves
A. J. Reynolds	Mexican bandito	Mexicans = bandits
Camel cigarettes	"Typical" Mexican village, all sleeping or bored	Mexicans = do-nothings, irresponsible
General Motors	White, rustic man holding three Mexicans at gunpoint	Mexicans = should be and can be arrested by superior white man
Lark (Liggett & Myers)	Mexican house painter covered with paint	Mexicans = sloppy workers, undependable
Philco-Ford	Mexican sleeping next to TV set	Mexicans = always sleeping
Frigidaire	Mexican bandito interested in freezer	Mexicans = thieves seeking Anglo artifacts
Arrid	Mexican bandito sprays underarm, voice says: "If it works for him, it will work for you."	Mexicans = stink the most

Source: Thomas M. Martinez, "Advertising and Racism," in Edward Simon, *Pain and Promise: The Chicano Today,* Mentor Books, New York, 1972, p. 104.

from Jews, blacks, and various other minority groups (Birmingham, 1977, pp. 68–69).

Prejudiced attitudes may also be learned from the direct interaction between members of different groups. If all the interaction is between people of one group in superior positions and people of the other group in inferior positions, then it is sure to become stereotyped. It makes prejudice stronger, and a vicious circle is begun. Unfavorable stereotyping leads to prejudice, which in turn leads to discrimination, which leads back to unfavorable stereotyping. Economic stratification is linked to prejudice this way. The logic runs: Keep minorities "in their place" so as to avoid competition; then, stigmatize them as ignorant, shiftless, and lazy to justify keeping them "in their place." Laws to discourage discriminatory educational, hiring, and advertising practices have the effect of breaking this vicious circle. The term *in their place* loses its meaning if

Diversity and strain

minority-group persons are seen occupying a wide range of roles, high as well as low.

Prejudiced personalities

Even in societies in which prejudice and discrimination are strong, some people show much more hostility than others. Adorno and his associates (Adorno, Frenkel-Brunswick, Levinson, and Sanford, 1950) used the term *authoritarian personality* to describe people who not only show strong prejudice but also like to observe "pecking orders." These people tend to defer to their superiors and abuse their subordinates. They also see things in strongly stereotyped ways and cannot stand compromise or conflicting opinions. All things are seen as good or bad. These traits, the researchers concluded, frequently go together. Adorno's study, which dealt with right-wing groups, has been criticized as ignoring those of the extreme left. However, the concept of the authoritarian personality is still seen as valid; it applies to very ethnocentric people who are hostile toward anyone outside their group.

There are, no doubt, some people who have a psychological need to hate outgroups. However, patterns of prejudice and discrimination are not created by a small minority. They are shared and silently supported by the great majority of people. If this were not true, they would be much easier to change than they are.

ECONOMIC AND POLITICAL EXPLANATIONS OF PREJUDICE

Conflict and competition are basic reasons for prejudice and discrimination. When two countries are locked in war, their hatred of each other rises until each sees the other as evil. When a minority group within a country sympathizes with the enemy, that group may be hated even more than the enemy. Such was the case with Ireland. The Irish, subject to English rule in the 1600s, conspired with Spain and later with France against England. Fear and suspicion added greatly to the already prejudiced attitudes of the Irish and the English toward each other.

When a minority group is an economic or political threat to the majority, hostility between them grows stronger. Foreigners or other minority-group members are hated most when jobs are scarce and the majority is feeling the pinch. This theory of prejudice is called the *frustration-aggression theory*. It holds that aggression is always caused by frustration, or the blocking of people's paths toward their goal. In the United States, from 1882 to the 1920s, the lynching of blacks rose whenever the price of cotton fell. In this case, the economic reasons for racial violence were indirect. Black people did not cause the cotton prices to fall or take jobs away from whites. But poverty increased the frustrations of whites, which led to aggression. The blacks were a handy target for white aggression. However, more direct competition for jobs is also an excuse for violence. In the United States in the nineteenth century, the Chinese were attacked because they agreed to work for very low wages (see the insert "Anti-Chinese Pogroms" on page 188).

The split-labor-market theory of racial antagonism

Edna Bonacich (1972, pp. 547–559) has tried to explain ethnic and racial antagonism in terms of a split labor market. A *split labor market* is a condition that arises when minority groups are hired for lower pay than the majority group will accept. A split labor market also arises when minority-group members are the only people who hold certain menial jobs. When a split labor market exists, members of majority groups are kept out of particular jobs and, at the same time, begin to look down on outgroup members who hold those jobs.

In the South, in the days of slavery, there were few jobs for poor whites. They could not work without pay, as the slaves were forced to do. At

Although people the world over exhibit different physical characteristics, this difference is accentuated by culture.

Anti-Chinese pogroms HERBERT HILL

The politics of anti-coolieism was translated into direct action in the form of violence against Chinese along the Pacific Coast and in some areas of the mountain states during 1885 and 1886. The pattern of these attacks conformed to a standard patholo-gy. In 1885 the nationwide depression reached its most severe stage. As this point was reached in a given locale, white workingmen, usually under the combined leader-ship of union officials and local politicans, often formed anti-Chinese organizations and sounded the call for the physical removal of the Chinese and their belongings from the area. The expulsion of Chinese usually followed one of three patterns. Often it took place very rapidly and spontaneously. Sometimes it followed a period of agitation which saw a rather intensive involvement of white workers in the local politics of anti-coolieism. Finally, agitation to expel Chinese would lead to savage violence, as in Rock Springs, Wyoming, where some 30 Chinese were killed by white miners in 1885. Similar violence occurred in Eureka, California, and in Tacoma and Seattle, Washing-ton, where entire Chinese populations were driven out by force in 1886.

During the same period, the California state legislature and various cities subjected the Chinese to extreme legal perseuction. As early as 1870 the state legislature categorically outlawed the employment of Chinese in certain public works projects. Two years later it mounted a full-scale attack on them by prohibiting Chinese from owning real estate or securing business licenses.

Meanwhile San Francisco was imposing its own restrictions. For example, a license fee of $8.00 a year was demanded of one-horse laundry wagons. But those laundrymen who collected and delivered by foot (the Chinese) had to pay $60.00.

. . . Generally the Chinese did not register formal complaints, as they were legally prevented from testifying against whites. The most serious instance of organized violence against them took place in Los Angeles, where a mob shot and hanged 20 Chinese, pillaged homes and stores, and tortured Orientals.

From Herbert Hill, "Anti-Oriental Agitation and the Rise of Working-Class Racism," published by permission of Transaction, Inc., from *Society*, vol. 10, no. 2, copyright © 1973 by Transaction, Inc.

[*Note: Pogrom is a word meaning the destruction or massacre of helpless populations, originally used to describe massacres of the Jews in Czarist Russia.*]

the same time, they did not want to do the same type of work as the slaves, since they felt superi-or to them. To do slave labor is to lose status as a free person. Thus, although the slaves seemed to be outside a competitive labor market, they actually provided a threat to that market.

Even after slavery ended, for decades black people worked almost exclusively at jobs that gave little pay or prestige—shining shoes; serv-ing as porters, maids, or janitors; sharecropping; and digging ditches. Such jobs became stereo-typed as black jobs, and many poor whites refused to hold them.

In the Southwest, where much of the "stoop labor" in agriculture has been done by immi-grants from Mexico or by Mexican-Americans, field jobs tend to be regarded as "Mexican" or "Chicano" jobs. It could be argued, of course, that Anglo-Americans once did all kinds of field-work themselves. However, when larger farms and hired labor become the standard, cheap labor (Mexican or Mexican-American) drives

Diversity and strain

more expensive labor (Anglo-American) out of the market. It is quite likely that the racial stereotyping of jobs is just as effective as low pay in driving out the majority group. Similarly, until very recently, whenever jobs were stereotyped as belonging to women, those jobs lost status and men withdrew from the competition.

The split-labor-market theory applies best to certain minority groups in American history. Blacks and Chicanos are the most prominent, but at times poor white ethnics from Southern and Eastern Europe have worked in the mines, while the Chinese at one time had a virtual monopoly on railroad work. Some American Indians were brought into the split labor market after having been deprived of their best lands. Navajos, for example, have been hired at jobs considered inferior by many others or are hired at better jobs for less pay than their white co-workers receive. Their art objects, representing hundred of hours of work, are sold at prices so low that majority-group labor could not possibly compete. The workings of this system are shown in the insert "The Split Labor Market on the Navajo Reservation" (page 190).

Antagonism against minority groups may also be aimed at people who are not at the bottom of the social scale in the economies of the countries to which they have migrated. In the United States, Jews, the Chinese, and migrants from India have filled this middleman position.

Ethnic groups in the middleman position

The term *marginal adaptation* is used to describe the way in which people who live on the border between two cultures find a niche for themselves in the dominant culture. For certain groups, that niche has consisted of a middleman position. The middleman is one who buys goods from a supplier and then sells them to the public or one who transports goods from a source to other suppliers. Moneylending and pawnbroking are other occupations of a similar type. Bonacich (1973, pp. 583–593) notes that the types of

businesses involved are those that are easy to liquidate if necessary. The reason is that many groups of migrants have not meant to be permanent settlers but have dreamed of returning home or of finding a homeland of their own.

Although members of these ethnic groups may see themselves as permanent residents, many of them do settle down and begin to form a middle class in the adopted land. In medieval Spain, the Jews and Moors formed such a group. They were forced to leave in the late fifteenth century, and this is considered one of the reasons for the slow development of the middle class in that country. Throughout medieval Europe, the Catholic Church had outlawed usury (the charging of interest on money) as an occupation for Christians. Since, at the same time, Jews were not allowed to own land, they were forced into such fields as trade, banking, and moneylending. In much of Europe, Jews dreamed of returning to a homeland of their own. But they stayed on in foreign lands so long as to identify with them very strongly. Some of them became prominent: the British Prime Minister Benjamin Disraeli and, later, the French Premier Pierre Mendès-France are examples. Nevertheless, many Jews feel that their future is uncertain. "Anything Jewish is always apprehensive," says Bertram Gold (Karnow, 1974, p. 12), executive vice-president of the American Jewish Committee. The Jews have come to know permanence of residence, devotion to the countries they inhabit, and great academic and professional success. But they have never had absolute certainty that their world will not somehow collapse if the majority group should decide to attack them.

The Chinese have filled the middleman and business roles in much of Southeast Asia. Like the Jews, they have known hostility, lost lives and property, and been driven out of their homes (in Indonesia) by the thousands. They have not been as harshly persecuted as the Jews, however, partly because there has been no prejudice against them like the earlier Chris-

The split labor market on the Navajo reservation

In 1972, the Federal Trade Commission investigated practices on the trading posts of the Navajo Reservation. A few were honest, but many were not. Examples:

Many traders engage in exploitive practices. Weavers are paid only a fraction of the market value their rugs later bring to tourists. Even in the prestigious Two Gray Hills area, underpayment is the general rule. San Juan County social worker Carmie Toulouse testified that a rug woven by one of her clients was sold to a trader for $30. One month later, she observed the rug on sale at the same post for $250.

Exploitation is also accomplished by "losing" pawned goods, usually silver and turquoise jewelry:

In one case, a Navajo woman was informed that her pawn was "lost" when she attempted to effect redemption. She was able, however, to walk into the pawn vault unobserved, where she found the item in plain view. Upon confrontation, the trader refused to release the item and physically ejected the woman from the post. To recover the item, she returned to the post accompanied by a DNA lawyer. (DNA is the Navajo legal organization—Dinebeiina Nahiilna Be Agaditahe.)

Split-labor practices are also used in the more traditional manner of placing two different prices of labor:

Finally, the trading post is central to Navajo hiring by itself acting as employer. Trading posts are estimated to employ approximately 400 persons. Trading facilities are typically managed by a white man and wife, with additional help from children and relatives. Pressured by the Navajo tribal legal department, posts have recently commenced hiring local Navajo residents. Although half of trading post employees are now Navajo most are employed in menial positions. *Those that enjoy positions of responsibility are compensated at a lower rate than comparable white employees.*

From *The Trading Post System on the Navajo Reservation*, Report to the Federal Trade Commission, Los Angeles Regional Office, June 1973, pp. 47, 52, 54.

---

tian animosity toward the Jews. However, they have not been accpeted as full members of their host nations.

Many people have migrated from India to seek their fortunes elsewhere. However, they keep up their ties with their own people and hope to return. Mohandas Gandhi (1869–1948), for example, who became the spiritual leader of India in its long struggle for independence from England, was born in South Africa of an Indian emigré family. In most cases, as with the Jews and the Chinese, entire families migrated. However, in some communities, young men were sent to foreign lands to earn money so that they could return home and help their families. Overseas, many of these Indians worked at jobs that would have been seen as below their caste, but they became farmers or traders, sold goods on the streets, dealt in leather goods, or sometimes even worked as domestic servants.

Many of these middleman occupations antagonize people of the host country. To make a living as a middleman, one must buy as cheaply as possible and sell for as much as possible. As a result, both the wholesale supplier and the buyer of goods see the middleman as shrewd and devious. A middleman who does well may put aside enough money to make loans, but this activity does not make the middleman more popular in the new community. Occasionally the ethnic group turns instead to the professions, as is often the case with the Jews and to some extent the Chinese. These occupations do not cause as much resentment as the middleman positions, and they have probably helped to reduce ethnic antagonism in the United States. The reasons for changing attitudes toward minorities, however, are much more complex, and the new attitudes are often confused and contradictory.

CONTRASTING ATTITUDES

In 1937, the black novelist Richard Wright described his earlier experiences as he made deliveries for a hotel in Jackson, Mississippi. Each story provides a startling example to racism. The two brief excerpts given in the insert "Uncle Tom's Children" illustrate the inferior position of black people at that time.

Uncle Tom's children   RICHARD WRIGHT

One of the bellboys was caught in bed with a white prostitute. He was castrated and run out of town. Immediately after this all the bellboys and hallboys were called together and warned. We were given to understand that the boy who had been castrated was a "mighty lucky bastard." We were impressed with the fact that next time the management of the hotel would not be responsible for the lives of "trouble makin' niggers."

One night, just as I was about to go home, I met one of the Negro maids. She lived in my direction, and we fell in to walk part of the way home together. As we passed the white watchman, he slapped the maid on her buttock. I turned around, amazed. The watchman looked at me with a long, hard fixed-under stare. Suddenly he pulled his gun and asked:

"Nigger, don't you like it?"

I hesitated.

"I asked yuh don't yuh like it?" he said again, stepping forward.

"Yes sir," I mumbled.

"Talk like it, then!"

"Oh yes sir!" I said with as much heartiness as I could muster.

Outside I walked ahead of the girl, ashamed to face her. She caught up with me and said:

"Don't be a fool; yuh couldn't help it!"

This watchman boasted of having killed two Negroes in self-defense.

Yet, in spite of all this, the life of the hotel ran with amazing smoothness. It would have been impossible for a stranger to detect anything. The maids, the bellboys, and the hallboys were all smiles. They had to be.

From "The Ethics of Living Jim Crow," in *Uncle Tom's Children*, by Richard Wright, Harper and Row, Publishers, Inc., New York, 1937.

Such episodes remind us of the days of slavery, when abuse and humiliation had to be accepted without a show of hostility. This situation is also shown vividly in Alex Haley's biographical-historical work Roots *(1976).*

Modern attitudes

The old attitudes that forced the blacks into silent submission and humiliation are fading, but attitudes toward blacks today are confused and contradictory. One extensive survey of fifteen American cities found 86 percent of whites saying that they "would not mind having a qualified Negro as a supervisor on their job" (*Society*, 1972, pp. 10, 12). Approximately 68 percent agreed that unfair housing practices are used against the blacks and that black people should have the right to protest as long as demonstrations are orderly. However, about half the whites opposed laws to prevent racial discrimination in housing and almost half objected to having black neighbors living next door to them, even if these blacks were of the same educational and income level. Teenagers were slightly less prejudiced toward blacks than adults, according to this study. Churchgoing seems to increase opposition to violence against blacks, but it does not appear to make white people more sympathetic to black causes or more eager to mingle socially with them.

The busing issue

For several years, Americans seemed to support the racial integration of schools. Thomas Pettigrew (1975, pp. 3–4) quotes the National Opinion Research Center's findings of 1974 that 92 percent of whites said they would not mind sending their children to schools with a few black children and that 74 percent favored schools that were about half black and half white. A slight majority (51 percent) even approved of sending their children to schools with a black majority. As to busing to integrate the schools, however, a Gallup poll of November 1974 found 72 percent of white parents opposed. In contrast, 75 percent of the blacks polled favored busing.

Opponents of busing often argue that children should go to school in their own neighborhoods. However, slightly over half of all schoolchildren are bused to school anyway, mainly to achieve

decentralization—that is, to prevent overcrowding in certain schools. Only 7 percent are bused to achieve integration. Interestingly, busing is opposed only when it is used to achieve integration.

Pettigrew tries to explain the opposition to busing. About 20 percent of white Americans, he says, are firm believers in segregation. They can be roused to demonstrate against busing, as in Boston and in Louisville, Kentucky, in the mid-1970s. Only about 20 percent of whites firmly believe in integration and are willing to take a public stand on it. The remaining 60 percent *say* they favor desegration but don't want to pay for it or be inconvenienced by it. This majority is easily influenced by what the government does. The coolness toward busing expressed by Presidents Richard Nixon and Gerald Ford helped to encourage public opposition. Many people argue that busing is a failure and that some better means of integrating the schools should be found.

It is hard to tell whether busing can help solve the problems of prejudice and discrimination. When busing doesn't work—when it causes riots, gang fights, and school closings—it makes front-page news. However, when it does work, it

Figure 7-2 The busing of school children to end segregation based on neighborhood residence has sometimes met with violent resistance. (*United Press International*)

is accepted so quietly that we never hear about it. Further, we must consider the question: "Does busing improve the education of the students bused?" The answer may be inferred from standardized test scores taken before and after integration. Pettigrew believes that, on the basis of what we now know, busing is a moderate success:

> There is no magic in racial desegretation. If a system such as Boston's sets out to make the process fail, it can accomplish its goal. If systems such as those of Sacramento and Minneapolis set out to make it succeed, they can also accomplish their goal. Fortunately, there are more systems like those of Sacramento and Minneapolis. So there are usually some black test score gains, together with no loss (sometimes gains) in white scores. This is particularly true for schools that are predominantly middle class and attain an accepting, integrated environment. The black test gains are generally not dramatic, though they can be educationally crucial. (Pettigrew, 1975, pp. 3–4)

Critics who oppose busing and call for another solution seem to ignore one fact: School attendance is based on where the student lives, and in the United States, housing is still highly segregated. In the long run, desegregating the neighborhoods could help achieve integration. For now, though, most communities must resort to busing or continue racial segregation in their schools.

To be or not to be ethnic

Americans show the same contradictory attitudes toward ethnic minorities as they do toward blacks. During the late nineteenth and early twentieth centuries, Americans were very hostile toward foreigners who could not or would not be assimilated. The Chinese became victims of discriminiatory policies and violent mobs because of their distinctive appearance and because they were willing to work for very low wages (recall the insert "Anti-Chinese Pogroms"). The belief of the majority was that America was a great "melting pot" and that all immigrants should give up their ethnic identities as soon as possible. Further, to be like everyone else was to have "made good."

In 1945, W. Lloyd Warner and Leo Srole (pp. 285–296) published a study on how long it has taken various immigrant groups to become assimilated into American society. To a great extent, this study is a profile of ethnic, racial, and religious prejudice. Protestants were more quickly accepted than Catholics, and Catholics were accepted sooner than non-Christians. Warner and Srole discovered that the more "foreign" people looked—the less they conformed to the WASP stereotype—the longer it took them to be accepted and assimilated.

The 1960s and 1970s overturned the melting pot with a resurgence of ethnic pride. "Black is beautiful," "viva la raza," and "red power" have all become popular slogans. Michael Novak, a sociologist of Slovak descent, complains that his people and those from Eastern Europe are *hyphenated Americans*; they are Polish--Americans, Slovak-Americans, and Czech-Americans but never simply Americans. Novak's parents always told him to be proud of his identity as an American, but at the same time:

> When my family moved from the Slovak ghetto of Johnstown to the WASP suburb on the hill, my mother impressed upon us how well we must be dressed, and show good manners, and behave—people think of us as "different" and we mustn't give them any cause. "Whatever you do, marry a Slovak girl," was another advice to a similar end. "They cook. They clean. They take good care of you. For your own good." (1971; copyright 1972 by The Macmillan Company)

The contradiction was obvious: Be completely American, but marry into your own ethnic group and keep its values.

New reasons for ethnicity

Nathan Glazer and Daniel P. Moynihan (1974) have tried to find out why more people stress their ethnic identities now than in the past. Glazer and Moynihan link this recent interest to government programs and policies that aid minority groups. If special consideration is being given to blacks, then white ethnics who are not much better off—Poles, Slovaks, Italians, Greeks, and Rumanians, for example—also want their share. Culture and religion remain important for ethnic identity, but there is a new stress on economic issues and on opportunities in school and on the job.

Government policies such as hiring quotas are aimed at helping minority groups economically and making them part of mainstream American. However, if racial and ethnic groups organize to gain and continue these policies, the latent function may be to increase their loyalty to the group. This pattern of increased ethnic identification is not unique to the United States. It is growing in all multinational states, especially if people feel excluded from government services and social opportunities. Israel has the problem of Oriental as well as European Jews. Yugoslavia must try to promote Serbians and Montenegrans as well as Croatians. Western European countries have to cope with new ethnic groups— Algerians in France, Turkish and Italian laborers in Germany, and Pakistanis and Indians in England.

The desire to join ethnic organizations and to maintain an ethnic identity does not stem wholly from economic concerns, as Glaser and Monynihan have noted. People want to feel a sense of identity with a particular culture—its legends, folk art, and festivals. They need a sense of belonging in a world that seems too large and impersonal. Ethnic-group affiliation, according to Michael Novak, fills these needs: "Whereas the Anglo-Saxon model appears to be a system of atomic individuals and high mobility, our model has tended to stress communities of our own,

attachment to family and relatives, stability, and roots" (1971).

REACTIONS TO DISCRIMINATION

People react to discrimination in many different ways. One person might adjust by quietly making the best of a bad deal. Others might try to improve their educations or jobs skills, hoping to make it with hard work despite discrimination. People whose cultural traditions stress educational, business, or professional achievement often improve their social positions. People whose cultures do not stress such goals often see the struggle as hopeless.

Sometimes the feeling of oppression becomes so strong that the self-image is destroyed and a reaction of self-hatred sets in. The victim of discrimination decides that society is right: There must be something wrong with him or her. Others turn their anger outward. The riots that erupted in Watts (California), Detroit, and Newark during the 1960s are examples of group violence triggered by anger and frustration (see Chapter 11). Another common reaction to discrimination is stronger loyalty to one's own group. It is this reaction, as we saw in an earlier discussion of conflict groups, that helps certain groups survive.

Intensification: American Indians

Intensification refers to an almost ritualistic way of preserving loyalty to one's own culture, traditions, and identification group. This adjustment to stress is also known as *nativism*, meaning a strong attempt to preserve one's native culture.

Figure 7-3 *Opposite page:* Ethnic pride includes (*a*) wearing identifying symbols, (*b*) reviving traditional customs and ceremonies, and (*c*) establishing organizations to monitor discrimination and combat harmful stereotypes. [(*a*) *United Press International;* (*b*) *Vivienne, Photo Researchers, Inc.;* (*c*) *Freda Leinwand*]

(a)

(b)

(c)

Minorities Racial and ethnic

Intensification, or nativism, sometimes takes the form of spiritual revivals. The best known of these was the Ghost Dance of the Western Indian tribes in the 1870s. The Indians believed that if they performed this ceremony, the lands stolen by the whites would be returned to them. The Indians' hopes were dashed when the American cavalry, suspicious of what was going on and furious because of Custer's defeat, attacked the Indians at Wounded Knee, South Dakota. They killed more than 300 men, women, and children in the final massacre of the Western Plains.

Among American Indians today, intensification takes two different directions. First, many of the reservation chiefs and other office-holders do not want to see their people become lost in the white world. Second, the modern and more radical American Indian Movement (A.I.M.) also calls for heightening Indians' awareness of themselves as a people, but as a united people. A.I.M. appeals to Indians and part-Indians of all tribes, including those living on reservations and those living in the cities, to unite in an effort to preserve Indian lands and to find methods to raise themselves out of poverty.

Threat and intensification: The Japanese

The Japanese-Americans living on the Pacific Coast were sent to relocation centers during World War II. They responded to this in ways that surprised most Americans. They organized and ran the camps smoothly, keeping them immaculately clean. They even developed gardens in the uncultivated desert areas around these camps. By selling garden produce, they stretched the small allowances given them and even returned money to the government. Many also volunteered for work in agricultural harvests in many other parts of the country. Within a few years after the war, hostility toward them subsided. It was concluded that the Japanese had managed to live well in those camps because they had become good Americans.

Ronald A. Haak (1970, pp. 23–31) interviewed many of those who had lived in the relocation centers and found that what really sustained them was their loyalty to their cultural traditions. These people came from a culture that stresses close cooperation, uses hard work to solve problems, and does not value charity. Their feeling of exclusion increased, naturally, after they were imprisoned. This intensified the need for close cooperation and independence. The Buddhist stress on compromise and avoiding bitterness helped them adjust to their difficult position. Their young men volunteered for duty with the U.S. Armed Forces and achieved distinguished service records. Haak closes his discussion with a remark that explains most Americans' view of the Japanese experience: ". . . It is far more flattering to concede that the Japanese had been Americans all along than to entertain the suspicion that ethnicity is admirable in its unredeemed state" (1970, p. 28).

Ethnic groups tend to close ranks when threatened. During periods of oppression in the nineteenth century, Chinese-Americans remained a tight community, depending on familism, self-containment, and strong community organization to keep them as safe as possible. Today, new pressures are causing generation gaps and other problems in San Francisco and other Chinese-American centers, but the threat to survival is gone. When threat is withdrawn, tight organization is no longer necessary.

Chicano identity

Mexican-Americans have recently moved toward greater cultural loyalty. Earlier, it was hard to estimate the rate of mobility of the Chicano group because those who were successful and upwardly mobile generally called themselves Spanish rather than Mexican. Now the idea of being Spanish is no longer preferred, and the term *Chicano* is widely accepted. Fernando Peñalosa lists several changes in Chicano attitudes in recent years, all showing an intensification of loyalty (Peñalosa, 1972, pp. 72–78). The sense of Chicano community is stronger than in the past, "la raza" ("the race") has become a cause to fight for, and achieving group goals seems possible. There is a renewed interest in the history and culture of Mexico—although this interest had never entirely died—and barrio art, music, and drama have been revived on a larger scale. Greater demands are made to gain influence in institutions most important to the Chicanos themselves, especially schools. Finally, Chicano sociologists and other scholars are becoming interested in studying their own people and are increasingly critical of Chicano studies made by Anglo-Americans. Now, more Chicanos view education as the major path to upward mobility. These changes have come about not because of increased threat to Chicano communities but partly because they have seen the recent gains made by blacks. Another reason for this growing intensification is that the Chicanos are now predominantly urban and thus able to get together more easily than when they lived in rural areas. Finally, there is the growing feeling that much can be accomplished. Hope for the future can be as strong an incentive as threat in drawing people together for a common cause.

Intensification in the black community

Blacks are the only American minority group to have been brought here entirely against their will, to have been enslaved, and to have had their original culture almost totally and deliberately stamped out. The prevailing attitude of black Americans is and has been in favor of desegregation. Despite many statements from whites that blacks actually seek self-segregation, over two-thirds of blacks strongly support desegregation (Campbell, 1971). However, this does not mean a desire to imitate whites or to judge all things by white standards. The civil rights movement of the 1960s reawakened an interest in African culture and caused a decline in hair-straightening and other styles that copy whites. Black leadership has passed into the hands of blacks rather than being dominated by white liberals, as in the early days of the National Association for the Advancement of Colored People. The radical leaders of the 1960s never gained majority following, but they brought about an important change in the black self-concept, summed up in the slogan "black is beautiful." Such euphemisms as *colored* were dropped, and *black* became the preferred name for a people who had found pride in their identity.

A pattern of segregation still persists, especially in housing. Black unemployment rates in the segregated ghettos run three or four times as high as unemployment rates for whites. This problem has caused some black people to give up any attempt to enter white society. As was pointed out in the last chapter, far fewer blacks than whites believe that with hard work, everyone has an equal chance to succeed. For many of those to whom life has been only a series of frustrations, finding a new identity is more important than joining an integrated society. One religious movement, the Black Muslims, has spoken especially strongly not only of black equality but of black superiority.

John Howard (1966, pp. 15–21), in "The Making of a Black Muslim," describes two main reasons for joining the organization. Several of the men he talked with joined because they were seeking values opposed to those of the white world. The Black Muslim faith offered these. Others wanted to join a movement that would help them become financially successful. These people chose the Muslims because they are diligent and frugal, valuing hard work and a modest life-style. Many Muslim-sponsored business enterprises do very well. The Black Muslims believe that the time of the white race is running out and that the black people must separate themselves from white America. They had become a bit less fanatical in this belief even before the death of their long-time leader, Elijah Mu-

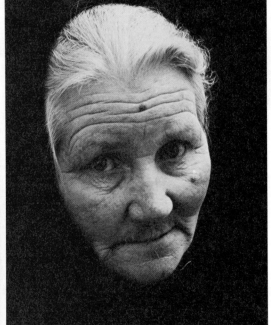

Looking at human beings, one sees racial differences but also—and more importantly—striking cultural differences within races.

hammad, in 1975. However, the Muslim doctrine was long one of absolute rejection of the whites as well as their economic system, culture, and religion. (See the insert "Things Begin to Add Up: The Conversion of Amos X.")

The overwhelming majority of black Americans do not share the Muslim view that all of American culture must be rejected. Intensification of racial pride for most blacks does not call for separatism. Instead, it involves an ideal of personal and group pride: blacks as an equal group in a pluralistic society. Most blacks wish to gain better-paying and more prestigious jobs, but they will not sacrifice group identity and

---

Things begin to add up: The conversion of Amos X JOHN HOWARD

Amos X grew up in an all-Negro town in Oklahoma and attended a Negro college. Because of this, he had almost no contact with whites during his formative years.

> One of my aunts lived in Tulsa. I went to see her once when I was in college. I walked up to the front door of the house where she worked. She really got excited and told me if I came to see her anymore to come around to the back. But that didn't mean much to me at the time. It is only in looking back on it that all these things begin to add up.

After graduating from college, Amos joined the Marines. There he began to "see how they [the whites] really felt" about him; by the end of his tour, he had concluded that "the white man is the greatest liar, the greatest cheat, the greatest hypocrite on earth." Alienated and disillusioned, he turned to professional gambling. Then, in an attempt at a more conventional way of life, he married and took a job teaching school.

> I taught English. Now I'm no expert in the slave master's language, but I knew the way those kids talked after being in school eight or nine years was ridiculous. They said things like "men's" for "men." I drilled them and pretty soon some of them at least in class began to sound like they had been inside a school. Now the principal taught a senior class in English and his kids talked as bad as mine. When I began to straighten out his kids also he felt I was criticizing him. . . . That little black man was afraid of the [white] superintendent and all those teachers were afraid. They had a little more than other so-called Negros and didn't give a damn about those black children they were teaching. Those were the wages of honesty. It's one thing to want to do an honest job and another thing to be able to.

With the collapse of his career as a public school teacher and the breakup of his marriage, Amos went to California, where he was introduced to the Muslim movement.

> I first heard of them [the Muslims] in 1961. There was a debate here between a Muslim and a Christian minister. The Muslim said all the things about Christianity I had been thinking but had never heard anyone say before. He tore the minister up.

Finding an organization that aggressively rejected the white man and the white man's religion, Amos found his own point of view crystallized. He joined without hesitation.

John Howard, "The Making of a Black Muslim," published by permission of Transaction, Inc., from *Trans-Action*, vol. 4, no. 2, copyright © 1966 by Transaction, Inc.

Diversity and strain

Table 7-2

Percent in Poverty	White	Black
Male	7.6	30.1
Female	10.3	37.1
65 and over (female)	20.6	44.1
65 and over (male)	11.3	39.4
Children under 6	11.3	42.6

Source: The *World Almanac and Book of Facts*, 1975 edition; copyright © Newspaper Enterprise Association, New York, 1974. P. 156.

loyalty for the sake of moving up. To date, substantial progress has been made. Still, most blacks remain relatively poor.

RACE AND POVERTY

Statistics show that even today, when certain government policies work to equalize opportunity, being black means being poor. A few statistics will make the point clear. The contrast between the numbers of black and white people living at poverty levels is startling; see Table 7-2.

Unemployment figures tell the same story. Unemployment among blacks is 2.21 times as high as among whites. Unemployment among people with Spanish surnames is 1.71 times as high as among other whites.

In occupational categories, the same inequality is evident in the contrast between blacks, those with Spanish surnames, and other white Americans; see Table 7-3.

Americans with Spanish surnames include mainly people of Mexican descent as well as considerable numbers of Puerto Ricans and Cubans. Of the three groups, the Cubans have the highest income and employment level. Figures for the Chicanos are considerably lower, and those for the Puerto Ricans are the lowest.

In spite of the discouraging figures on poverty, the number of black people completing high school has steadily increased in the past twenty years. In 1974, for the first time in American history, the percentage of blacks entering college equaled the percentage of blacks in the total American population, although they often entered community colleges with the intention of completing only one or two years. Chicanos have had a higher dropout rate from school than either whites or blacks, but a fairly drastic change is now taking place. As a general rule, education for minority groups has paid off, but not as well as for whites. Even a college-educated black person earns on the average only about 78 percent as much as a white with the same education.

Blaming the victim

There are two ways of looking at the problems of depressed minority groups. One is to blame the group itself; the other is to look for causes within the larger society. Those who believe that all Americans have an equal chance to succeed tend to blame these groups for their own prob-

Table 7-3

Occupation	White	Spanish-Surnamed	Black
Professional	14.4	6.5	8.5
White collar (including professional)	49.8	28.9	28.6
Service	11.7	15.8	26.4
Farm	3.7	5.6	2.7
Other	10.6	19.0	20.1

Source: The *World Almanac and Book of Facts*, 1975 edition; copyright © Newspaper Enterprise Association, New York, 1974. P. 422.

lems. White people once believed that blacks were not as intelligent as they. In recent years, this belief has declined, from 58 percent in 1942 to 22 percent in 1956, with little change since.

Despite a growing awareness of black intellectual equality, many whites continue to hold blacks responsible for their disadvantaged social position. After extensive interviews with whites in fifteen American cities, Howard Schuman found that most of them blame blacks for their generally poorer jobs and living conditions (1969, pp. 44–48). Nineteen percent of Schuman's respondents said that poor living conditions were due to discrimination; another 19 percent thought that discrimination was partly responsible. But 54 percent said that the blacks themselves were responsible for their poverty. (Four percent said blacks were just as well off economically as whites, so the questions were pointless.)

If human behavior and life-styles are determined by environment, then to blame those who do not achieve is a matter of blaming the victims of unfavorable environments. It is quite easy for well-to-do Americans to imagine how they would improve conditions if they were born into very poor families, but they often do not understand how and why improvement is so difficult. If we make the case as extreme as possible, it becomes clear that failure is almost certain in some situations. Let us dramatize this fact as follows.

Suppose you have grown up in a neighborhood in which 25 percent of the adults are out of work. There are no books in your home, only comics and one or two movie magazines. Your two younger brothers are doing badly at school, and so are you. Everything that goes on at school convinces you that no one cares about you. Your father doesn't live at home; your mother works hard to hold the family together. You are now seventeen; you want money and a car for dates. Since your mother has no money left after paying the bills, she tells you that you will have to quit school and find a job. Would you (1) drop out, (2) stay until the end of the

school year, (3) stay long enough to finish high school, or (4) tell your mother that you will stick it out, graduate from high school, and finish college? It is highly unlikely that you would choose the last answer. You might try to finish high school, but the odds are that you would quit before graduation.

If we consider human behavior as being determined by the environment, it is easy to see how circumstances rule out some of the chances for success. At the same time, it is cruel to tell someone, "I know you don't have a chance, so you might as well give up." Motivation becomes as much a part of the environment as the school one attends. Sometimes the home provides the motivation to succeed, sometimes the school or friends; sometimes there is no motivation. Fortunately, more positive self-images among minority groups have motivated many more group members to succeed in recent decades. Other recent gains for minorities include policies which outlaw hiring discrimination, opening new upward paths for them. Improved self-images and fairer hiring practices will not solve the problems of prejudice and discrimination overnight, but slowly, such advances can provide hope for more and more people. Meanwhile, it is important for members of the larger culture to realize that in blaming members of poverty-stricken minority groups, or other unfortunate individuals, they are *blaming the victims* of generations of poverty and neglect.

SUMMARY

In the previous chapter it was noted that social classes often have very little understanding of or concern for one another. What is true of social classes is equally true of racial and ethnic groups. Social class is linked with racial and ethnic groups because race and ethnicity are often strongly linked to possibilities for upward mobility in a society.

Race refers to inherited physical differences in groups of people of different geographic areas, as in the case of Europe, Asia, sub-Saharan Africa, or Australia. Racial differences may indicate small degrees of adaptation to different environments, but such differences are very slight. Every race is capable of surviving in any inhabited part of the earth.

An *ethnic group* is a group that is different enough culturally to have an ingroup identity that sets it off from the majority. Such white ethnic groups as Jews and Polish-, Italian-, and Greek-Americans cannot be told apart from the majority group on the basis of looks. On the other hand, an ethnic group can also be racially different, as in the case of American Indians or Afro-Americans.

Ethnic and racial minorities have experienced varying degrees of prejudice and discrimination—*prejudice* being a set of negative attitudes toward the group and *discrimination* a system of unequal treatment. Prejudice and discrimination can make for a vicious circle, since discrimination leads to poverty and inferior status which, in turn, are used to strengthen prejudice. The reinforcement of prejudice and discrimination has been particularly marked in the case of black Americans. Since the cultural norms praise the idea of equality, *rationalizations* or excuses are found for discrimination. These make the conflict between stated belief and actual practice less obvious. A common rationalization of discrimination is that members of the minority group are less able or potentially threatening. Minority groups are stereotyped, and often these views of them are preserved in literature, entertainment, and popular jokes.

Prejudice is learned from others. It is best preserved if the victims of prejudice are never actually seen as equals but are kept at a distance and in low social-class positions. *Social distance* refers to the unwillingness to accept others as equals or to interact socially with them. Usually increased interaction on the basis of equality tends to reduce prejudice. Some personalities, called *authoritarian personalities*, apparently are more given to prejudice than others. However, the personality explanation accounts for only a small part of the prejudice that exists in society.

Apart from stereotyping and rationalization, prejudice is also strengthened by economic problems. When two groups compete for jobs, one at lower pay than the other, the situation is called a *split labor market*. Blacks, Mexican-Americans, and American Indians have all had to compete in a split labor market—and the same is true to some degree of employed women. Competition for scarce jobs and economic recessions sometimes lead to a *frustration-aggression* pattern in which violence against minorities can explode. A few ethnic groups have found a place for themselves in the role of middlemen or by engaging in lending or pawnbroking. The Chinese have been in this position in much of Southeast Asia; the Jews were traditionally forced into such a means of livelihood in Europe. The middleman position tends to arouse antagonism, since the middleman is blamed for high prices.

Attitudes toward racial and ethnic minorities have changed in the United States, but in a confused pattern. The Jim Crow laws and abuses described by Richard Wright and Alex Haley have declined. A majority of whites now believe black people should have equal opportunities in jobs and housing, but almost half oppose laws to prevent housing discrimination and nearly as many object to black neighbors next door. Although nearly all whites advocate educational equality, a large majority oppose the busing of children to achieve integration. Advocates of busing believe it is the only way to achieve equality in education.

White ethnic minorities were once believed to want complete assimilation and loss of separate identity. In the 1960s and 1970s, more has been written about their desire for preservation of some elements of their own culture. Glazer and Moynihan suggest that one reason for a stress on ethnicity is that ethnic organizations can work for better opportunities in education and jobs. They

Minorities: Racial and ethnic

note that similar organizations to promote opportunities for ethnic minorities are encountered in many parts of Europe.

Developing pride in racial or ethnic identity (referred to as *nativism*) is often an important step in upgrading a minority group, as has been the case in the last two decades with blacks and Chicanos. A study of the Japanese-Americans who were moved to relocation centers during World War II indicates that pride in their cultural identity was intensified during the experience. Among black Americans, pride in race has sometimes taken an extreme form, as in the case of the Black Muslims. In general, though, most black Americans do not advocate complete separation from whites. They wish to maintain their separate identity in a pluralistic society.

In America, race is closely connected with poverty, the poorest groups being the blacks, the Spanish-surnamed, and the American Indians. Despite progress in interethnic and interracial understanding, there is still a tendency to blame minority groups for their own poverty. This attitude can be described as *blaming the victim* of a discriminatory system for being discriminated against. If, as most social scientists maintain, human behavior is determined by circumstances, such a point of view is completely untenable.

Study guide

Terms to know

Race	Rationalization	Marginal adaptation
Geographical races	Stereotype	Middleman
Ethnic group	Social distance	"Hyphenated American"
"Unmeltable ethnics"	Authoritarian personality	Intensification
WASP	Frustration-aggression theory	Nativism
Prejudice	Split labor market	Blaming the victim
Discrimination	Pogrom	

Names to know

Michael Novak	W. T. Adorno	Alex Haley
Alexis de Toqueville	Edna Bonacich	Thomas F. Pettigrew
Leon Festinger	Richard Wright	

Self-test

Part I. Multiple Choice. Select the best of the four alternative answers:

1 Race is defined as a matter of difference in (**a**) culture, (**b**) mentality, (**c**) physical type, (**d**) technological development.

2 A good example of a group that is both racially and ethnically different from the majority of Americans is that of (**a**) people of Eastern European descent, (**b**) Italian-Americans, (**c**) reservation Indians, (**d**) all the above.

3 In Festinger's analysis of resolving cognitive dissonance, when we are unfair to people of another race, we (**a**) don't let it bother us, (**b**) feel good about it, (**c**) feel unhappy about it, (**d**) try to convince ourselves that they deserve it.

4 Discrimination leads to prejudice through (**a**) the habit of looking down on victims of discrimination, (**b**) observing the generally inferior status of those discriminated against and accepting it as "natural," (**c**) finding reasons for cruelties against victims of discrimination, (**d**) all the above.

5 Historically, the stereotypes of races have been supported by (**a**) racial and ethnic jokes, (**b**) movies, (**c**) history books, (**d**) all the above.

6 When different racial or ethnic groups have been employed at the same job at different wages, (**a**) high-priced workers tend to drive out lower-priced workers, (**b**) unemployment is highest among black workers, (**c**) low-priced workers tend to drive out high-priced workers, (**d**) none of the above.

7 A good example of prejudice against a minority group in a middleman position is that of (**a**) Italian workers in Germany, (**b**) Chinese in Southeast Asia, (**c**) Algerians in France, (**d**) black Americans.

8 Interaction between races (**a**) always lowers antagonistic feelings, (**b**) always increases

antagonistic feelings, (**c**) makes no improvement in relations if conducted on the basis of stereotyped roles, (**d**) improves relations provided each race conducts itself as the other race expects it to.

   9 Modern racial attitudes appear to be quite mixed, with white respondents to a questionnaire seeming most favorable to black fellow workers or even supervisors on the job but least favorable to (**a**) busing to achieve school integration, (**b**) fair housing, (**c**) having black neighbors, (**d**) having black children in their schools.

   10 John F. Pettigrew explains the mixed attitudes of whites about racial policies in this way: (**a**) None are sincere in their stated belief in equality, (**b**) three-fifths are in favor of equality only if it involves no inconvenience for them, (**c**) Presidents Nixon and Ford tried too hard to force school integration by busing and thus stirred up resentment, (**d**) all the above.

   11 The Warner and Srole studies of assimilation into American society concluded that assimilation was retarded most by (**a**) religion, (**b**) foreign language, (**c**) appearance, (**d**) whether the country of origin had once been at war with the United States.

   12 In the 1870s and 1880s, discriminatory laws were passed and acts of murder and other violence were perpetrated in Western states against the (**a**) Chinese, (**b**) blacks, (**c**) Japanese, (**d**) Armenians.

   13 In Michael Novak's analysis, Poles, Czechs, and other minority groups from Eastern Europe place a higher value than do Anglo-Americans on (**a**) individualism, (**b**) material success, (**c**) community, (**d**) trying to be different from others.

   14 The percentage of black and white children being reared in poverty (**a**) is approximately equal for the two races, (**b**) is nearly twice as high for blacks as for whites, (**c**) is three times as high for blacks as for whites, (**d**) is nearly four times as high for blacks as for whites.

   15 A survey found that whites, when asked why blacks generally have poorer jobs and living conditions than whites, tended to (**a**) blame the institutions of white society, (**b**) place the blame equally on environmental factors and the black people themselves, (**c**) place the blame on the blacks, (**d**) refuse to fix blame on anyone.

Part II. True-False Questions

   T **1** The modern trend in racial classifications is toward "geographical races" rather than a classification into three very distinct groups.

   T **2** It is possible that some types of racial differences represent adaptation to different physical environments.

   F **3** It is correct to say that prejudice causes discrimination, but it is not correct to say that discrimination causes prejudice.

   F **4** By far the most common cause of discrimination is a somewhat "sick" personality.

   T **5** Thomas Martinez contends that advertising practices have given the Chicanos an unfavorable image as irresponsible and as gun-toting bandits.

   T **6** A split labor market exists when two different racial or ethnic groups are hired for different levels of work or for different levels of pay for the same work.

   T **7** A split labor market tends to increase racial antagonism, ethnic antagonism, or both.

   F **8** In the South in the late 1800s, during periods of job shortages and low prices on cotton, the black and white races became more friendly because of their mutual problems.

   T **9** According to a Federal Trade Commission report in 1973, Navajos on the reservation are cheated on prices and the pawning of goods and are given lower pay than whites for the same work.

Diversity and strain

206

10 A quotation from Richard Wright ends with the statement, "The maids, the bellboys, and the hallboys were all smiles," implying that they were naturally happy people in spite of their problems.

11 Under present conditions, integration of housing areas seems to be very practical as an alternative to busing children for the sake of racial integration.

12 John F. Pettigrew sums up many of the cases of busing and pronounces them a moderate success.

13 According to Glazer and Moynihan, a new interest in ethnicity has arisen both in the United States and other countries, although it has no practical economic advantages.

14 The Japanese who were incarcerated in American relocation centers during World War II weathered the experience better than might have been expected because of their adherence to Buddhist teachings and their other cultural values.

15 The Black Muslims have always worked for eventual integration into white American society.

Questions for discussion

1 Give examples of cases in which racial or ethnic discrimination can lead to an inferior social position that becomes the basis for prejudice.

2 The text mentions that stereotyping arises from or is perpetuated by folktales, historical accounts, jokes, movies, and advertising. Give some examples of your own of how stereotypes are perpetuated in this way.

3 Explain why a split labor market tends to increase intergroup antagonism.

4 Women generally work at lower pay than men or occupy jobs that men do not take. How does this fact seem to affect stereotypes of women?

5 How has the role of middleman and sojourner affected attitudes toward the Chinese in Southeast Asia or Indians in Africa? Can you think of other similar cases?

6 Can you think of cases in which members of other groups (ethnic, occupational, or age groups) have had to be all smiles despite working conditions—cases similar to the one described by Richard Wright?

7 What are some of the contradictory views of the white majority in America regarding the black minority?

8 What are some of the advantages of increased loyalty to one's own racial or ethnic group, particularly if it has been discriminated against in the past? Are there any possible problems that might arise from such an attitude?

9 The idea of "blaming the victim" was described relative to blaming poor minority groups for their own poverty. Can you think of any other cases of blaming the victims that frequently occur in society?

Projects

1 Nearly all members of ethnic and racial minorities are antagonized by some of the popular stereotypes of their groups. Try to interview members of a few ethnic or racial groups—Italians, Poles, Chicanos, Puerto Ricans, Chinese, or blacks. Find out what is particularly antagonizing. (If your class is racially and ethnically mixed, this would be a good topic for class discussion.)

Minorities: Racial and ethnic

2 If you know a good example of an authoritarian personality, try to engage him or her in a conservation to see whether the personality traits fit Adorno's description:

    a Strong racial and ethnic antagonism

    b Intolerance for ambiguity; that is, the view that there is only one right way to believe or to do anything

    c Respect for strong leaders

    d Contempt for people in lower positions than one's own

    e General dislike of foreigners

3 Do a content analysis of a popular movie or television show that includes racial or ethnic minorities. Are any stereotypes perpetuated? Are attempts being made to modify old stereotypes?

Suggested readings

Alter, Robert: "A Fever of Ethnicity," *Commentary*, vol. 53, June 1972, pp. 68–73. What are the dangers of clinging to ethnicity in search of personal identity? Are there alternatives to both ethnic divisiveness and a homogeneous America? Alter attempts to answer these questions in a critique of Novak's enthusiasm for ethnicity. (See Novak's article below.)

Boesel, David, Richard Berk, W. Eugene Groves, Bettye Edison, and Peter H. Rossi: "White Institutions and Black Rage," *Trans-Action*, vol. 6, March 1969, pp. 24–31. Dealing particularly with the ghetto, this article discusses the problems of white institutional structures—white employers, merchants, teachers, police—in black areas, as well as the beginnings of black countervailing power.

Fendrich, James, and Michael Pearson: "Black Veterans Return," *Trans-Action*, vol. 7, March 1970, pp. 32–36. As Martin Luther King said, "We are taking the young black men who have been crippled by our society and sending them 8,000 miles away to guarantee liberties in Southeast Asia which they had not found in Southwest Georgia and East Harlem." What resulted from the black experience in Vietnam? This story of alienation answers some of the questions as well as giving a more general insight into what it means to be black in a white society.

Garbarino, Merwyn S.: "Seminole Girl," *Trans-Action*, vol. 7, February 1970, pp. 40–46. Will a college education, competence, and good intentions necessarily make it possible for a member of an Indian tribe to help her own people? Garbarino, in his interview with a Seminole girl, finds how deep the problems of cultural divisions and misunderstandings can go.

Heller, Celia S.: "Chicano Is Beautiful: The New Militancy and Mexican-American Identity," *Commonweal*, January 23, 1970, pp. 454–458. Mexican Americans and black Americans have in common much more poverty than Americans of European descent and can use similar tactics for self-advancement. Why is it difficult for them to work together? What are the differences between these two groups in their search for a new identity?

Newsweek, editors: "The American Jew Today," *Newsweek*, March 1, 1971, pp. 56–58, 62–64. Is it possible to blend into American society, approve intermarriage, and also preserve cultural identity? How do foreign problems regarding Israel and the Soviet Union create problems and divisions among American Jews? These and other questions are discussed in this survey of success and unease.

Novak, Michael: "White Ethnics," *Harper's Magazine*, vol. 243, September 1971, pp. 17–27. Is America an ethnic "melting pot" or are the white ethnics actually unmeltable? Novak takes the latter view and explains why.

Petroni, Frank A.: "Teenage Interracial Dating," *Trans-Action*, vol. 8, September 1971, pp. 54–59. Why are interracial dates a subject of great tension among high school youth? Why do white girls go with black boys whereas white boys do not date black girls? The answers have much to say about attitudes toward race and status.

Pitt-Rivers, Julian: "Race, Color and Class in Central America and the Andes," *Daedalus*, vol. 96, Spring 1967, pp. 642–559. Are differences in color and race the real basis for prejudice? Pitt-Rivers shows how very differently the bases for the classifications of people are arranged in different societies.

Key to questions. Multiple Choice: 1-c; 2-c; 3-d; 4-d; 5-d; 6-c; 7-b; 8-c; 9-a; 10-b; 11-c; 12-a; 13-c; 14-d; 15-c. True-False: 1-T; 2-T; 3-F; 4-F; 5-T; 6-T; 7-T; 8-F; 9-T; 10-F; 11-F; 12-T; 13-F; 14-T; 15-F.

This chapter examines the degree to which women are cast into a subordinate position as well as the generally inferior position of the aged. After reading it, you should be able to:

1 See more clearly the ways in which stratification by sex and age takes place in society and the way this is justified.

2 Reexamine the socialization process and see how socialization alone accounts for many of the differences in the temperament, interests, and aspirations of the two sexes.

3 Be more aware of sex-based legal discrimination.

4 Recognize the importance of reporting cases of rape or wife-beating and see how silence perpetuates such practices.

5 Understand the possible positive effects on both men and women of a decline in sex-and-temperament stereotyping.

6 Recognize the degree to which the modern industrial system excludes the aged.

7 Understand the need for maintaining meaningful interpersonal ties with the aged and even with the dying.

STRATIFICATION: SEX AND AGE

Except in the very rare case of a person who undergoes a sex-change operation, sex is an unchangeable, ascribed status. Sex carries with it an expectation of particular roles, some for men and others for women. Men are expected to be the leaders, to be strong and aggressive, adventurous and competitive. Women are expected to follow a more subordinate role in this "man's world." This linking of sex to role is part of a pattern of prejudice and discrimination against people on the basis of their sex, called *sexism*.

It is a man's world in the sense that positions of social and political power nearly always go to men—seats in congresses and on high courts, the jobs of president, governor, and general. In industry it is also a man's world; most managerial positions are given to men. In art, music, and literature, too, works created by men have been taken more seriously than those produced by women. Space, too, has become a man's world; 13 women originally trained for the American astronaut program were later dropped even though they passed all the tests (*Cosmopolitan*, 1977, pp. 49, 179). Even in religion, it is a man's world; up to very recently, those who ordained women priests were reprimanded or even excommunicated. Our language reflects this male domination as well. We say *mankind* rather than *womankind* or *humankind*, we discuss *man's* origin, or *man's* destiny, and we use the pronoun *he* to refer to people in general.

This cultural bias in favor of men saps womens' confidence in their own abilities and tends to limit their accomplishments. It is destructive to some men as well. Many men cannot meet the high goals society sets for them and hence see themselves as personal failures. Often sex roles concerning expectations don't go with personal temperaments or abilities, but those who defy the roles too openly are criticized.

Not only is it a man's world, but it is a world for men who are not too old. The elderly of both sexes are usually forced to retire, to give up their occupational roles often long before their physical or mental condition makes this necessary. If their decline into old age is long and slow, they are often segregated from others and herded together into old-age or nursing homes.

Stereotypes about men and women, the young and the old, are created, become hardened by cultural tradition, and are imposed on the individual through the socialization process. Today these stereotypes are being challenged.

STRATIFICATION OF THE SEXES THROUGH CULTURE AND SOCIALIZATION

Both history and mythology document a long record of unequal treatment for women. In spite of medieval cults of chivalry that honored and glorified upper-class women and in spite of goddesses, earth mothers, and priestesses, the status of the average female has been vastly inferior to that of the male. The Bible depicts the creation of woman as an afterthought and tells us that Eve's disobedience caused the downfall of the human race. In traditional Chinese society, women's feet were bound, and women were subject to the "three obediences"—first to their fathers, then to their husbands, and then, if widowed, to their sons. Arabic society has veiled and secluded its women. Hindus believe that being born female is a punishment for sins committed in a previous life. The great Confucian scholar Kaibara, of Japan, wrote of woman, "Such is the stupidity of her character that it is incumbent upon her, in every particular, to distrust herself and obey her husband" (Mace and Mace, 1960, p. 74). And in the Western world, St. Paul sternly warned, "Let your women keep silence in the churches; for it is not permitted unto them to speak; but they are commanded to be under obedience, as also saith the law."

Some traditions praise women, who are often seen as self-sacrificing angels of love and virtue, with special powers to heal and comfort. These virtuous women, however, must act out well-defined feminine roles. In the roles of mother and faithful wife, they are highly praised; but if they should step out of these roles, they are strongly condemned. The inequality of treatment between the sexes is so great that an old Orthodox Hebrew prayer concludes: "I thank thee, O Lord, that thou has not created me a woman."

How culture defines the sexes

In his analysis of societies as systems of status and role, Ralph Linton points out that regardless of what role is assigned to men, it is considered superior to the roles given to women (1936, pp. 113–131). If the men of a tribe make pottery, the potter's art is considered important. If the pottery is made by women, however, pottery making is considered to be less important than activities such as hunting and fighting. Linton does not offer a theoretical explanation of why men's roles are invariably defined as superior, but his conclusions about the facts still hold true. There are a few societies, such as those of the Pueblo Indians, in which the women seem to hold superior positions, since houses and storage bins belong to them. Even such societies, however, are not true cases of *matriarchy* (rule by women). The role of priest is considered the highest role in the society, and all the priests are men.

Not only are separate roles assigned to the two sexes, but linking role to sex gradually makes each sex unfit to play the roles of the other. Men are expected to be awkward and helpless at cooking and sewing; women are expected to be equally incompetent at hunting or changing a tire.

Socialization of the sexes

Much effort is devoted to making the two sexes fit the proper stereotypes, as our earlier discussion of socialization through role learning indicates. Freudian psychologists have tried hard to explain and justify the proper traits for women. Freud firmly believed that "anatomy is destiny." He viewed women as naturally submissive and loving and felt that women shouldn't compete with men in the political and business worlds. Those who wished to compete in such ways were diagnosed as being neurotic or frustrated, perhaps suffering from "penis envy," a term that originated with Freud.

In fact, women are less able to compete because they have not been taught the attitudes and skills needed for success in the world of work. The very fact that they are not expected to have successful careers serves to discourage them from trying. Many of those who try hardest to overcome the odds become nervous and frustrated, but the reasons are social rather than biological.

Ever since Betty Friedan wrote her influential book *The Feminine Mystique* (1960), increasing attention has focused on the socialization of women into subordinate roles. Friedan opposed the idea that all women should devote most of their lives to keeping house. Her views are echoed by Jo Freeman (1970, pp. 36–43), who concludes her article "Growing Up Girlish" with the observation that if "anatomy is destiny," this is true only because society has insisted on making it true.

Freeman compares the traits that Lewis Terman found most typical of girls with those that Gordon Allport found most typical of oppressed minorities (Allport, 1954, pp. 189–204). Girls were found to be more nervous, unstable, neurotic, socially dependent, submissive, timid, emotional, passive, and lacking in confidence than boys. The traits of subordinated minorities which Allport discovered are very similar: sensitivity, submission, desire for protection, indirectness, ingratiation, compassion for the underprivileged, and identification with the dominant group's norms, accompanied by fantasies of power and revenge. If these traits are found among members of subordinated groups independent of sex, then they must be due to social position, not biological difference.

Although girls make consistently better grades in school until about the end of high school, they have a lower opinion of their intellect than boys do. Scholastically, girls get off to a better start than boys, but they end up worse. The reason, Freeman believes, is that as they get older, girls are expected to develop their feminity, which does not include being intellectual or competing with men. Girls do best in the lower grades of school because the socialization pattern makes them more responsive to their teachers' demands. Boys are more readily excused for being rebellious in their early school years.

However, as the years go by, the pattern of effort and achievement reverses itself, and boys begin to do better in school. The people who show increases in IQ, Freeman finds, are those who are competitive and aggressive, which is more often true of young men than of young women. The sons of well-placed families are encouraged to compete for good jobs. Girls, however, are encouraged to make themselves attractive so that they can make a good match and achieve a good status through marriage. If they are encouraged to work, work is often seen as a temporary activity, to be dropped when they become wives and mothers.

In a study of socialization, Barclay and Cusumano (1967) found that boys without fathers imagined that they would become successful through good luck rather than through competition. Possibly, these boys pick up this pattern of fantasizing from their mothers, having no male model to follow. In the ambitious two-parent home, boys are more likely to model their ideas

and behavior after their fathers and girls after their mothers. Fathers teach their sons to work hard for success; they tell them that effort pays off. Daughters may receive more affection from their fathers, but they are not pushed to compete in the world of work. The socialization message the girls receive will depend on how strongly the mother holds to traditional values of femininity. Mothers with jobs outside the home are more likely than full-time housewives to have daughters who are ambitious to get ahead through their own efforts (Freeman, 1970, p. 41).

The socialization pattern is changing under the impact of the demands of the women's liberation movement and the occupational demands of modern societies. The current trend toward small families makes it easier for a majority of women to enter the labor force. At present, however, women generally have to accept jobs that are below their level of competence.

WOMEN AND THE LAW

Since the mores of a culture are reflected in its laws and legal procedures, it is not surprising to find laws that place men in superordinate positions (superior in rank and power) and women in subordinate positions (of lower rank, with little or no power). In marriage, the woman takes the man's last name and the law considers the man to be the head of the household. The man's occupation and income, rather than the woman's, are considered in loan and credit applications. Moreover, the social-class position of the family is based on the husband's job and economic status, almost regardless of the wife's accomplishments. In many states, married women cannot own or sell property in their own names.

Criminal cases and civil suits

Rather than being egalitarian, the justice system discriminates against men in some respects and against women in many more. If the death penalty is a possible punishment for murder, men who are found guilty are more likely to die than are guilty women. Stuart Nagel and Lenore Weitzman (1972, pp. 18–25, 62–63) have reviewed the research on sex inequality in the courts and find that in most types of crime, men are more likely than women to be held in jail awaiting trial and to draw heavier sentences. The courts, in a fatherly role, or what is called *legal paternalism*, seem to assume that women are more childlike than men and more easily reformed. Therefore, women's cases are sometimes handled much like children's in the juvenile court. Women are less likely to be tried by jury than men; if they are poor, they are less likely than men to have public defenders. It is true that women's sentences may be less severe than those of men; but the chances of conviction, at least for the poor, are greater for women than for men. This is because judges are more likely to find defendants guilty than juries are.

There is also an interesting exception to the rule that men draw heavier sentences than women. In cases of felonious assault, since women are seen as defying their role as the "gentle sex," they are dealt with more harshly by the courts than are men.

Women bring fewer civil suits for damage or injury than do men, and the amount of money awarded them is somewhat less. When settlements are made for injuries, men win in 76 percent of the cases and women in 69 percent. In injuries involving "loss of consortium" (those involving loss of sex functioning), the rewards to men are nearly three times as high as rewards to women. This difference apparently reflects the sexist assumption that loss of sexual relations is more damaging to a man than to a woman.

Rape and battery

In cases of rape and battery, women are also placed at a disadvantage by the legal system. Courts have, until recently, assumed that rape seldom occurs, that a woman's account of what happened cannot be trusted, and that women make false accusations against men. Until recently, judges have always warned juries that rape charges are easy to make and hard to defend against, a warning that tends to bias the

---

A case of wife battery

Victim stated the first argument started over a pack of cigarettes. Victim stated accused (her husband) held her against the bathroom wall by the hair and continued to beat victim with his right hand. Victim is six months pregnant at this time. Victim stated accused kept telling victim, "Bitch, you are going to lose that baby," and then accused would beat victim in the stomach again. After the assault in the bathroom, accused told victim to cook dinner. Victim stated the accused picked up a butcher knife and put it to the victim's throat and told victim, "I am going to kill you and you know I can do it, don't you?" Victim answered "Yes," and accused laid the butcher knife down on the table and turned around and hit the victim in the face with his fist and knocked victim to the floor. . . . Victim stated she blacked out. . . . Victim stated when she regained consciousness, the accused was still beating her.

From 4.1 Assaults, Felonious, File #41, Complaint #13626, July 1974. Washtenaw County Sheriff's Department, Ann Arbor, Michigan. Reprinted in Judith Gingold, "Battered Wives," *Ms.*, August 1976, p. 51.

---

case (Saylin, 1974, pp. 2, 5). Similar warnings are not given in other assault trials; the jury is simply asked to consider all the evidence carefully. Rape cases are humiliating, and the humiliation is increased by much questioning. Although women are not ordinarily expected to fight, they are expected to prove that they physically resisted sexual assault, which is not easy if the assailant is armed. Lawyers defending accused rapists often pry into the victim's private life, trying to convince the jury that if she has had premarital or extramarital sexual relations, she is somehow responsible for the attack; she had tried to seduce her attacker.

Rape has attracted more attention than battery in recent years, even though cases of wife beating are more frequent than cases of rape. Judith Gingold (1976, pp. 51–54) finds that wife beating is very frequent and is not limited to lower-class marriages.

Gingold notes that in 1973, the F.B.I. reported 4,764 rape complaints in New York State and 14,000 cases of wife abuse. Many of these assaults are brutal, as illustrated in the insert "A Case of Wife Battery." Law officers and judges are reluctant to interfere in family fights. Wives are reluctant to report these assaults for various reasons. Some are afraid of reprisals, others feel embarrassed to make these "family problems" public, and many fear the economic insecurity that would result if the marriage were ended. One expert in the field, quoted by Gingold, believes that women have been taught to feel that it is their duty to make their husbands happy, "So they not only take the beatings; they tend to feel responsible for them." David Goldstein, an attorney in Ann Arbor, Michigan, observes, "In seven years of practice, I've never seen a husband put in jail. Never once." (Gingold, 1976, p. 52).

Divorce settlements

It is a common myth that divorce courts favor women. In part, this myth is created by headlines telling of divorces among very rich couples and settlements in the millions. Usually, however, divorce settlements do not favor women. Following cultural tradition, women are considered to be the best or most "natural" parents and are given custody of the children, although recently divorced husbands have begun to object to this sexual stereotyping. While courts order the father to pay child support, these payments are seldom made. Kenneth Eckhardt (1968, pp. 470–474) made a study of all fathers in an urban county in Wisconsin who were able to pay child support and checked on their history of payments during the period 1955–1965. Only 38 percent were found to be complying fully with the court order at the end of the first year. At the end of the tenth year, 13 percent were complying fully, and 8 percent partially; 79 percent were making no payments whatsoever. Nagel and Weitzman conclude that the cases reported by Eckhardt are typical of most of the United States (1972, p. 62). Often, these fathers simply disappear. Even if they are found, they usually manage some kind of compromise. These figures give only a partial picture of the problems connected with child support. Many other fathers simply desert their families without going through the formality of a divorce and therefore do not turn up in the statistics.

Women, juries, and judges

Nagel and Weitzman also investigated a number of sexist hypotheses of behavior based on sex differences. They asked the following series of questions: "Is it possible that a kind of chivalry prevails that causes men to decide cases in favor of women? Is it possible that opposites attract, so that women jurists rule in favor of men, especially attractive men, and men in favor of attractive women? Or is a brainwashing explanation possible? Are both sexes brainwashed into thinking more highly of the male and therefore rule in the man's favor? Or is it possible that likes attract, so that women decide in favor of women and men

Table 8-1 Summary: Women and the Law

Sexist Hypothesis	Legal Consequences
1 Women are weak, easily corrected, and require paternalistic treatment.	Fewer jury trials and assigned attorneys. Less likely to be jailed awaiting trial, shorter sentences.
2 Women have less economic responsibility than men.	Men are awarded higher damages in injury cases or property cases.
3 Sex is less important to women than to men.	In damage cases involving sex functioning, men receive nearly three times as much settlement as women.
4 Women should take care of children.	Women are given custody of children in most divorce cases.
But	But
5 Women are clever and manage to rob men in divorce settlements.	Little enforcement of child-support rulings. (Only 38 percent of men make full payment first year; only 12 percent comply fully until children are grown.)
6 The man is master in the home, and domestic affairs are no one else's business.	Wife-beating cases are rarely prosecuted.
7 Women are devious and may be partly responsible in rape cases.	Rape is extremely hard to prove and involves humiliating procedures.
8 Each sex is suspicious of the other. Men generally believe men and women believe women.	Women will be disadvantaged until equally represented on juries and in judgeships.

Adapted from: Stuart Nagel and Lenore J. Weitzman (*Society*, vol. 9, March 1972), Mary Saylin (*ACLU Open Forum*, June 1974), and Judith Gingold (*Ms.*, August 1976).

in favor of men? Finally, is it possible that all these hypotheses are wrong and there is no sexual discrimination in deciding law cases?"

These researchers discovered that as a general rule likes attract—women believe the testimony of women, and men believe other men. This informal system of sexual prejudice works to the disadvantage of women. In most states, women are more often dismissed from jury duty than are men, and there are very few women judges in local, state, or federal courts. Until there are more women lawyers and judges and until women are equally represented on juries, court decisions based on testimony of the two sexes

against each other will penalize women. As Table 8-1 shows, in legal matters women lose seven times out of eight.

CULTURAL CHANGE AND SEX ROLES

As societies become more technologically advanced, sex roles change. Even in some traditionally male-dominated societies, women are moving toward equality. An Egyptian *khatba* (marriage arranger) complains that her business is suffering because too many girls are allowed to meet men on their own: "Permitting girls to work side by side with men has reduced our chances. What makes things even worse is that men now prefer working girls in order to maintain a standard of living similar or near the one they see in movies and television" (*Los Angeles Times*, 1972, p. 17).

The *khatba* is still welcome in rural areas, especially in upper Egypt. There, suspicious fathers have been known to kill daughters who have allowed themselves to be seen by unfamiliar men. In urban areas, though, the scene is changing. One reason is that systems of gross sexual inequality are questioned by those with a knowledge of the outside world. Occasionally the leader of a very traditional country can be persuaded to adopt new views and legislate social change. In Mogadiscio, capital of Somali, these changes came quickly and were enforced by drastic measures—as indicated in the insert "Firing Squad Ends Issue of Women's Lib."

A functional approach to role inequality

Probably the aims of the women's liberation movement would have little chance of success if many conditions today did not work in favor of sexual equality. Gerald Marwell (1975, pp. 445–455) uses a functional analysis of sex roles

---

Firing squad ends issue of women's lib   DIAL TORGERSON

Usually women's liberation is accompanied by other changes in a society, in areas such as education, industrialization, and urbanization. When change in age-old customs is suddenly instituted by government in a society not conditioned for the change, enforcement is possible only through drastic use of political power:

"Since January 1975," a member of Mogadiscio's small women's liberation clique said with a slight smile, "it's funny, but no one complains much about women having equality."

In January, after President Mohamed Said Barre proclaimed equal rights for women, many of Mogadiscio's sheiks . . . spoke out vehemently against the plan.

The Koran, they pointed out, specified many times that women hold an inferior place. Some even said President Barre, head of the military government, should resign.

The government began arresting sheiks—some within a few minutes of their pronouncements. They were swiftly tried for "subverting state authority." The sentences were shockingly harsh:

Ten sheiks were executed by firing squads. Six were sentenced to 30 years in prison, and 17 received 20-year terms. Only one was acquitted. . . .

Word of the executions resounded throughout the Arab World.

Some of the more modern countries such as Egypt and Syria have taken some steps toward liberalizing the laws affecting women. But none have gone so far as the Somali Republic.

The Somali decree extended equality to inheritance. Under the law of the Koran a woman inherits half as much as her brother, and the widow's share is a carefully stipulated one-eighth.

From Dial Torgerson, "Firing Squad Ends Issue of Women's Lib," *Los Angeles Times*, March 29, 1975, pp. 1, 5. Copyright Los Angeles Times.

Stratification: Sex and age

217

which assumes that these roles change only in a society whose interests are served by such changes. He argues that in a society in which only a few work roles are needed, the easiest way to handle the division of labor is to assign jobs purely on the basis of sex. Since only women can bear and nurse children, it seems logical and efficient to limit their roles to duties that can be performed near the home and children. They may do gardening, make baskets or pots, cook, and make clothing, but to range far from home on the hunt would separate them from their reproductive and child-care roles. Since the hunting and fishing done by the men can be learned by almost anyone, and since not all the tribe is needed for such activities, the assignment of hunting and fishing to the men is highly functional.

On the other hand, the society may become more complex, developing needs for all kinds of talents that are in short supply. Then it becomes more efficient to fill work roles on the basis of achievement rather than on the basis of sex. If some of the new tasks can be performed by women and there are more skilled jobs than can be filled by men, then society functions better by letting women compete for jobs. Marwell points out that it is easy to tell who has the talent and who has not, and it is also clear that abilities are not distributed on the simple basis of sex. Marwell's conclusion is that modern industrial societies can function best if women have equal chances for employment and promotion. Although this conclusion is logical from a functionalist viewpoint, it does not mean that all discrimination against women is being ended at once.

Marwell could have dealt with another aspect of sex roles. It is no longer important that all

Table 8-2 Differences between Males and Females in Average Annual Earnings for Full-Time and Part-Time Workers

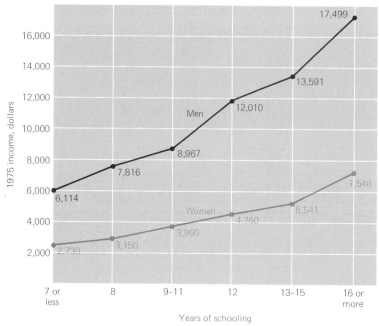

Source: Bureau of the Census.

Diversity and strain

women have children, nor do women who choose to become mothers have to spend their entire lives in reproduction and childcare. Marwell observes that societies respond more to what seems functional than to what can be defended only on normative grounds. He notes, however, that we have long been drifting away from ascription, or rigid patterns of role assignment. Increasingly, we condemn racism or caste as means of placing people in societal roles. Consistency would cause us also to reject sexism as a basis for role assignments except in the biological role of bearing children.

Marwell's functional approach raises an interesting question for sociologists. If assignment of roles purely on a basis of ability is functional for a modern society, why does sexism in occupations continue (see Table 8-2)? It is a fair assumption that the capacity to become a doctor is evenly distributed across sex lines. But in societies like the United States, where doctors have very high status, the great majority of doctors are men. In the Soviet Union, where the status of doctor is far lower than in the United States, the majority of doctors are women. The two situations would seem to prove that the capacity to fulfill the role of doctor is as great among women as among men, but that in the majority of societies, the role is usually given to men. This conclusion is consistent with Linton's observations about sex roles in primitive societies.

We could argue, as Freud did, that men achieve the higher roles because they are naturally aggressive. Or we could argue, as Marwell does, that society continues to favor men because of cultural lag. *Cultural lag* is a situation in which social change lags behind the possibilities opened by technological change. Changes in birth-control techniques and child-rearing customs and the development of household conveniences have made it easier than in the past for women to work. Modern educational systems train women's minds as well as men's. Yet in fact, most of the high-level jobs remain in the hands of men. Traditional social attitudes may account for this discrepancy. The idea that household tasks are for women and leadership roles are for men lingers on, becoming a cultural lag which prevents a realistic view of the occupational structure.

Women's liberation and cultural change

The aim of the women's liberation movement may be viewed as an effort to overcome these cultural lags. The leaders of the movement are mainly college-educated women. Maren Carden interviewed leaders of a number of women's rights group and found that about 90 percent of them held B.A. degrees and that one-third had higher degrees (1974). It is not surprising that these women would be highly sensitive to attitudes and practices that try to limit women's work roles. In the first years of the women's liberation movement, such women were often the subjects of satire and seemed to represent only a very small minority of women. In a few short years, however, they caused American society to start reexamining itself, influenced the government to pass antidiscrimination laws in hiring, and greatly increased their following.

The most immediate and practical goals of the movement are to gain job equality in pay and promotions. Present inequalities in pay are very great (see the insert "Sex Inequality in Pay," page 221). So as to move ahead in careers, many women have decided to have fewer children. Thus, they demand the right to free contraceptive information for all women, including unmarried women. This is one of the reasons why feminist leaders believe that medically safe abortions should be available for women who want them. Since only a very small minority of women want to give up all ideas of having children, it is only natural that women leaders should call for more child-care centers so that women can be free for work outside the home. These aims also require changes in the traditional family structure. Feminists believe that men should play a larger role in housework and child

(a)

(b)

(c)

Figure 8-1 Cultural lag has long kept women out of positions of power, but the situation is changing. (*a*) Margaret Thatcher, leader of the Conservative Party in Great Britain. (*b*) Juanita Kreps, Secretary of Commerce, and (*c*) Patricia Harris, Secretary of Housing and Urban Development in the Carter Administration. [*(a), (b), and (c) United Press International*]

Sex inequality in pay SHEILA B. KAMERMAN

. . . Of men and women who were income recipients in 1975, men had median incomes of $8,853 while women received $3,385. Median family income of male-headed families was $14,816; median income of female-headed families as $6,844. The significance of this disparity is underscored when we turn to wages earned by men and women in 1975. Men who worked full time all year had median earnings of $12,760 while comparable women had median earnings of $7,500.

Even when one compares women and children with the aged, a group most people recognize as deprived and likely to be poor, women and children are worse off . . . a slightly higher percentage of children live in poverty (16 percent) than elderly (under 15 percent). . . . A little over 13 percent of all families were headed by females in 1975, but such families accounted for 40 percent of the poor families and included over half of the children living in poverty.

From Sheila B. Kamerman, ''Needy American Women, Waiting for Equity,'' *The New York Times*, February 19, 1977, p. 23. © 1977 by TR. New York Times Company. Reprinted by permission.

care. These changes in family life-styles would create a more equal socialization for boys and girls and would decrease sex-role differences.

Cultural myths: The working wife

Feminists are trying to change both cultural life-styles and cultural myths. Two of the cultural myths under attack concern working women. The first is the myth that working women are not as happy as housewives. The second is that women working outside the home are less likely to have happy, stable marriages than house-wives. Recent trends seem to support the women's liberationists. In 1970, a majority of women (68 percent) polled considered taking care of a home and rearing a family more interesting than having a job (*Society*, 1974, pp. 6–7). Such a statement, however, does not really say whether women can be happy on the job while still enjoying household and family life. Another question not answered is whether the women were unenthusiastic about jobs because they felt that women usually didn't get good ones. About one-third of the women interviewed believed that women usually are given menial, boring

jobs and get very little credit for what they do.

A 1976 study of working wives is much more optimistic about job roles. Reporting her findings in the September 1976 issue of *Psychology Today* (pp. 76–80), Myra Ferree of the University of Connecticut finds working wives happier than full-time housewives. She interviewed married women who held jobs as clerks in supermarkets and department stores, waitresses, and factory workers. At the end of her study, she concluded that definite working hours, financial rewards, contact with other people, and a sense of accomplishment do much to explain the increased satisfaction of working women. Ferree's study was restricted to the Boston area and to women without children under school age at home. In spite of these limitations, the conclusions fit logically into a picture of greater expectations among women. In the past, housewives were more likely to be part of a neighborhood and kinship network that provided sociability and recognition. (In Ferree's study, the 25 percent of women who were happy with the housewife role had adequate social contacts of the neighborhood-kinship type.) There was also agreement about what activities—cooking, can-

ning, sewing—a housewife should perform. Today the housewife is both more isolated and more uncertain of the requirements of her role. The working women did not experience these disturbing uncertainties. They all said they felt self-confident and were doing their jobs well. In contrast, only one full-time housewife felt the same confidence in herself in the housekeeping role.

The second myth about the working woman is that her job has a bad effect on her marriage. A number of studies have shown that a woman who brings home pay is more nearly equal to her husband in decision making than is the full-time housewife and feels better able to express her feelings and opinions. In the past, divorce rates seem to have been higher among working women than among those who stayed home, possibly because only women in desperate economic difficulties looked for work outside the home. The latest studies, however, show slightly greater marital stability for young working women than for those without jobs (see the

Figure 8-2 The struggle for legalized abortion represents one attempt by women to gain control of their own lives. (*Sherry Suris/Rapho/Photo Researchers, Inc.*)

insert "Don't Blame the Divorce Rate on Working Wives").

The changing self-image

Like the leaders of ethnic minority groups, feminist leaders see the need for improving self-concepts among their followers. In 1968, Philip Goldberg made an experiment that shows women to hold unfavorable views of themselves and therefore to be prejudiced against other women. Goldberg had women read and rate essays, some of which were attributed to John T. McKay and others to Joan T. McKay. The women rated John's writing above Joan's on three scales—persuasiveness, profundity, and style. Actually, the same person had written all

Figure 8-3 With day-care centers to care for children, women are more free to combine marriage and family with a career. A career can thus become a long-time commitment, rather than a stopgap. (*Frederick De Van, Nancy Palmer*)

the articles. The women had given in to cultural bias that holds men to be more creative than women (Goldberg, 1968, pp. 28–30).

Have women's views of their own abilities improved since Goldberg's study, and is society's attitude toward women improving? There are a number of indications that the answer to both questions is "yes." By 1972, half the American women polled expressed approval of attempts to raise their status—an 8 percent increase in a single year (*Society*, 1974, pp. 6–7). In slightly later studies conducted by Yankelo-

---

Don't blame the divorce rate on working wives   JODY GAYLIN

The divorce rate may be rocketing, but don't blame it on the increasing number of working wives. In 1970 there were more broken marriages among young housewives than among their counterparts with jobs.

After comparing U.S. Census figures for 1950, 1960, and 1970, sociologist Elwood Carlson found that "today work for women is coming to be associated with stable rather than unstable marriages." Among women in their late teens and early twenties, 84 percent of the working wives remained married, compared with 82 percent of their nonworking peers.

Overall there are still more broken marriages among working women than among nonworkers, but the difference is narrowing. This is evident among working women born between 1926 and 1935: in the last decade the percentage of intact marriages in this group declined from 76 to 73 percent, while those of nonworking wives dropped six points, to 82 percent.

Carlson believes the original gap in divorce rates between working women and nonworking wives may have been caused by some unusual circumstances that no longer apply to employed women. People have assumed that working wives make marriages unstable, because the great increase in broken marriages coincided with a parallel increase in the number of working women. Coincidence, however, is not cause. Carlson cautions that "just because the trend shows that working wives and unstable marriages are no longer associated does not mean that a particular marriage will benefit (or suffer) from two working spouses."

From Jody Gaylin, "Don't Blame the Divorce Rate on Working Wives," *Psychology Today*, July 1976, p. 17.

Stratification: Sex and age

223

One of the stereotypes opposed by women's liberation is the view of women as depersonalized sex objects. One researcher wondered how men would react to the kind of treatment women usually receive. She visited a number of singles bars and looked the men over as though they were nothing more than potential sex objects. The results of this unusual study are summarized in the insert "Reversing Roles in the 'Meat Market.'"

The traditional stereotypes which portray women as chatty, empty-headed, frail, and dependent could be seen as insulting to men as well as women. Capable men usually prefer capable women. As long ago as the 1930s, Lewis Terman found that the more intelligent of the two partners in a marriage is less happy than the other. An empty-headed wife is no asset to a man unless he is even more empty-headed. The feminists argue that in the long run, more happy marriages will result if women are allowed to develop their minds fully. They state that greater equality for women will also improve the male role.

vich (1974, p. 102), both college women and noncollege women agreed, by 98 percent and 94 percent, respectively, that women should receive equal pay for equal work. In 59 percent of the cases, college women termed "nonsense" the idea that women are more emotional and less logical than men; 50 percent of noncollege women took the same attitude. Sixty-one percent of the college women and 55 percent of noncollege women agreed with the statement that "Men and women are born with the same human nature; it's the way they're brought up that makes them different." One measure of the increase of general.public esteem for women is reflected in changing attitudes about the acceptability of a woman for President. In 1937, only 27 percent of those polled in a national sample said they would vote for a woman for President; by 1974, the figure had increased to 70 percent (*Society*, 1974, pp. 6–7). This change in attitudes, however, does not mean that we will soon have a Ms. President; neither the Democrats nor the Republicans have shown any interest in nominating a woman.

Possible effects on the male role

The high status given by society to male roles does not necessarily mean that these roles are comfortable or easy to fulfill. The man is expected to be brave, decisive, aggressive, highly competitive, athletic, and willing to risk his life in war. Many men fail to meet these expectations or meet them only at great emotional expense, by pretending to be what they are not.

Women's liberationists argue that as sex roles become more equal, men won't have to appear so aggressive and the nonaggressive man will feel more comfortable. If men share half the responsibilities of child care and home care, the

Diversity and strain

Reversing roles in the "meat market"

Mary Jo Deegan, a University of Chicago researcher, compared singles bars to a "meat market" in which men look over and appraise all the women as carefully as would shoppers at a market. What would happen, she wondered, if the women looked over the men in the same manner, reversing the roles? She tried out the role reversal in thirty singles bars in the Chicago area.

The researcher decided to appraise men the way men in these white singles bars customarily evaluate women. One tactic was to cast a lingering glance at a subject's body, noticing his height, general physique and clothing, and then taking a pointed look below the belt. Another technique was to look over the head of a short man or to glance sidewise at a none-too-trim rear. Women, traditionally, are not flustered by being examined in this callous manner. But the men subjected to this procedure, whether they were college students or young executives, city-dwellers or country boys, had a uniquely male reaction: all were visibly embarrassed. Many blushed and several spilled their drinks.

In fact, the researcher found that when she appeared indifferent or unimpressed by her survey of male flesh, the subject under examination had to suppress his anger forcibly.

quality of childhood might be improved. Boys and girls would not see as many possible future roles closed to them because of sex stereotypes.

This transition will not be easy for many men. Although the traditional male role includes a good deal of strain for many men, this role has the attraction of high prestige. Furthermore, women who were once regarded as nonthreatening are increasingly seen as competitors in the job market. As Komarovsky's studies presented in Chapter 1 indicate, both sexes now hold ambivalent attitudes about sex roles. They want to be modern and reasonable, but they are afraid to move too far away from the traditional definitions of masculinity and feminity.

THE FEMINIST MOVEMENT AND SOCIAL CLASS

As we noted earlier, the leaders of the modern feminist movement come mainly from the well-educated middle and upper classes. Attempts to involve women from working-class families have not been very successful. One reason for this is a phenomenon often found at work in social systems: People who see real opportunities ahead but find themselves barred from them are usually the first to protest. Many women in lower-class positions, whose education is limited and whose husbands work hard at blue-collar jobs, feel fortunate just to have a home and a husband. Although many of these women work, a lack of special training often keeps them at dead-end jobs. They are more likely than better-educated women to think of their husbands' roles as harder than their own. In addition, the blue-collar class is more likely to be conservative about social changes than the middle class. This may be because economic insecurity makes them cling to what little they have and avoid change and also because these people have a more limited experience of life.

Working-class people do, however, welcome economic changes which will help them. As noted earlier, working women of all classes support the feminist call for equal pay for equal work.

Although college students and people of the same age who don't attend college agreed on many social issues about working conditions, medical care, and distrust of the establishment, this consensus broke down over the question of sexual equality. College students seem more willing than the noncollege group to accept the idea of female equality. Of the college women polled, 63 percent agreed with the statement that women are discriminated against, whereas only 42 percent of the noncollege women agreed. (Men's opinions on this question were not given.) Asked their reaction to the statement " 'Women's place is in the home' is nonsense," 64 percent of the college women but only 47 percent of the noncollege women agreed (Yankelovich, 1974, pp. 95–102). When both men and women were included in the sample polled, 47 percent of the noncollege respondents and 57 percent of the college respondents agreed that the statement was nonsense. Obviously, even among noncollege youth, support for the traditional roles is far from overwhelming and seems to be declining.

Many working-class women have been turned off by feminist leaders who devalue the role of housewife. Recently, some feminist leaders have reconsidered their views about housework and housewives and now seem to realize that some women prefer the traditional roles. Instead of comdemning housework and housewives, they ask that women who manage homes and raise children be viewed as productive and valuable workers. This change in attitudes could resolve the ambivalence which many people feel about traditional female roles. Although motherhood seems to be a sacred value in our society, the *Dictionary of Occupational Titles*, which lists 21,000 occupations with a point system for rating each, places the occupation of housewife at the very bottom of the list (Carden, 1974, p. 168).

THE STRATIFICATION OF OLD AGE

Old age is difficult to define precisely because it arrives at different times for different people and has conflicting sociological, statistical, and biological meanings. Sociologically, old age can be thought of as the time when people abandon (willingly or not) the occupational roles they have long held. Biologically, old age occurs when people are no longer capable of filling their previous occupational roles. As we shall see, the sociological and biological aspects of old age often arrive at different times. Finally, old age can be defined in simple statistical terms, as in U.S. Labor Department studies, as the period beyond sixty-five. In the following discussion, we will be much more interested in the sociological and biological definitions of old age than a

Figure 8-5 These women are protesting against the "lowly housewife" image. Their organization, Wages for Housework, stresses the dollar value—and, therefore, the importance—of the role of housewife. (*Neal Slavin*)

simple statement of a specific age in years.

Sociological and psychological factors combine with biological factors to determine the onset of old age. Studies conducted in Soviet Abkhasia, where large numbers of people live past their hundredth year, suggest a link between long life and active participation in a culture. The people who live long are those who remain active, continue to be an important part of the social system (Benet, 1971, p. 3), do not suffer total role loss, and therefore do not feel alienated from society.

Mental changes as well as physical changes occur as people age. Some types of intelligence, such as associative memory, decline with age. But the type of intelligence that depends upon experience and education declines only slightly if it is used constantly (Horn, 1967, pp. 23–31). Continued activity is important to mental life as well as physical life in old age.

Variation in the status of old age

The treatment accorded the aged has varied widely from society to society. A review of the anthropological literature was made by Simone de Beauvoir (1974), a leading writer on both feminism and age. She concludes that cultural needs help determine whether the old will be given high status or will be abandoned to die. Abandonment is most frequent in societies where food supplies are too scarce to keep the group alive and caring for the aged would mean a threat to the survival of the group. In agricultural societies, where more food is available and where at least small amounts of surplus food can be saved, old age is sometimes given high status, and the advice of the aged is held to be a great asset to the group. The Balinese tell a tale about an ancient mountain village where the people killed and ate the aged. Soon there were no old people left to keep alive their traditions or tell them how to build the great ceremonial houses they needed. One man had

hidden away his grandfather, whom he brought out after the people promised not to kill him. The old man was able to tell them all they needed to know. From that day, the old were treated with respect. This Balinese tale is a myth which shows the important role that the aged played in nonliterate societies: they were the storehouses of history and tradition.

Old age in industrial society

When we compare our own society with those reviewed by de Beauvoir, we see customs that lie midway between the extremes of killing the aged and honoring them. Modern medicine has increased the average human life-span. In the United States, about 30 million people now live past the age of sixty and 20 million past the age of sixty-five.

In the social realm, however, our treatment of the aged is less considerate. In modern societies, old age means role loss. In agricultural communities, old people have traditionally continued to perform at least part of their occupational roles. But the aged of modern societies are encouraged—often forced—to retire early and completely. This role loss can damage the mental health of people who have spent most of their lives working and who have gained a sense of worth and identity from their work. In a culture dominated by a hard-work ethnic, some people feel guilty and inadequate when they no longer have jobs. Living on a pension or social security means a drastic decline in income, and in a materialistic society, a loss of income means a loss of status (see Table 8-3). Too many of the aged end up on the bottom rungs of modern society. Although people over sixty-five years of age make up only 10 percent of the population in American society, they make up 18 percent of the poor (President's Commission on Income Maintenance, 1969, p. 14).

Even those who are fully able to work find that the labor market doesn't want them. Like other

Table 8-3 Social Security Benefits for the Aged

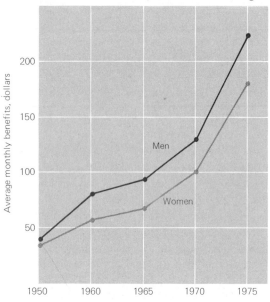

Note: One problem that makes retirement uninviting is low income. Unless other pensions or sources of income are available, people must live at the poverty level on social security.

groups we have studied, the aged as a group are stereotyped and discriminated against. They are held to be unable to perform even the most ordinary kinds of work. Yet Supreme Court justices, senators, and many other powerful leaders hold their positions for as much as ten or twenty years past the usual retirement age. This stereotyping of and discrimination against the aging is comparable to racism and sexism; hence it is known as *ageism*.

Disengagement theory

A common view of old age for a number of years has been the *disengagement theory*. Formulated by Elaine Cummings and William Henry (1961), this theory holds that loss of roles and social relationships always occurs among the aged and is agreeable to them because they wish to withdraw from too many commitments and obligations. Arlie Hoschchild, however, points out

certain flaws in the theory. First, the desire to disengage depends upon the nature of the society in which people live; such desire seemed to be minimal in older agricultural societies. If disengagement is common in industrial societies, it is probably a result of compulsory retirement and a lack of preparation for leisure activities in old age. Second, even in industrial societies, disengagement is influenced strongly by one's position. Those holding important positions (for example, business executives, judges, and senators) tend to remain active much longer than people in humdrum jobs (Hochschild, 1975, pp. 553–569). The experience of a number of small corporations and one large one (U.S. Steel) having no compulsory retirement policies is that the majority of people who hold minor jobs retire in their sixties, but a few continue well into their seventies. Even among people holding very ordinary jobs, there is great opposition to forced retirement (Shapiro, 1977, pp. 36–41).

Retirement

In the United States, the age of compulsory retirement has been moving downward. In 1870, 70 percent of those past sixty-five were employed; by 1970, only 20 percent of this age group were earning wages (de Beauvoir, 1974, pp. 220–243). The same trend can be seen in most countries of Europe, but there it is less drastic. Before the Age Discrimination in Employment Act of 1967 was passed, almost 90 percent of job ads found in American newspapers called for people of forty years of age or less.

While our society tends to regard the elderly as useless castoffs, unfit to work, the number of aged people has increased steadily. In 1850, only 2.5 percent of the population was age sixty-five or over; in 1970, the figure was 10 percent. It is only in the less industrialized countries, with high birthrates and shorter life-spans, that most of the people are young. In India, for example, the elderly make up only 3.5 percent

Diversity and strain

(a)

of the population; in Brazil, approximately 2.5 percent; in Togoland, 1.5 percent. Statistics show that while the United States now has more older people than ever before, a smaller percentage of them are employed. A stranger might suppose that the elderly in industrial societies are more feeble than they used to be, less educated, in poorer health, or less dependable. None of these statements is true. The problem stems from the nature of the industrial system which not only makes people occupationally obsolete at age sixty-five or before, but also tends to concentrate them in urban and suburban areas. There, neighborhood ties are weaker than in rural areas, and relatives are less likely to be present.

The industrial system that has created problems for the elderly is also able to provide solutions. It creates enough wealth so that the retirement incomes of the aged could be raised above the poverty level. Employment for some of the aged is also feasible. During the war years, it was shown both in England and the United States that elderly people were dependable and conscientious workers, only slightly slower than younger people at learning new routines. Changes could also be made to benefit the elderly who do want to retire. Changed attitudes

(b)

Figure 8-6 (a) Some older persons do lead a meaningful life, such as these tutors of young students. However, in a society that stresses youth and vitality, (b) many others often feel lonely and useless. [(a) Sylbil Shackman, Monkmeyer; (b) Steve Allen, Black Star]

are needed to preserve a sense of self-worth, whether or not one has a job. For those who are strongly work-oriented, tutoring children who are having trouble at school would help, or cultivating gardens, or helping the disadvantaged. For many others, school systems can (and, to a limited extent, do) provide recreational classes that bring both the mental and social stimulation that old people as well as young people need.

Above all, just as in the case of women and minority groups, we must change our thinking about the aged, to get rid of the old stereotypes. Less than 10 percent of the aged need institutional care (if we accept retirement age as our definition of aged). Most live on their own; they are neither incapacitated nor senile. They enjoy friends and recreation, breaks in the everyday routine, good food, and entertainment. In other words, the elderly continue to be fully human. People avoid thinking about advanced old age because it is too closely tied to thoughts of death. Even medical students receive little or no training about old age (see the insert "Medical Students Poorly Educated on Aging").

Death, the final phase

The approaching death of a friend or relative usually causes sincere sorrow and concern. At the same time, the thought of death is so unpleasant that we wish to dismiss it from our minds. From infancy, we are socialized to be kind to others and not to abandon them in an hour of need. In our discussion of human groups in Chapter 5, we observed that people have a great psychological need for sociability and belonging. Yet the dying are often abandoned. If

---

Medical students poorly educated on aging

Medical students are so poorly educated on aging and its illnesses that their lack of sensitivity to older people includes name calling, says the first director of the government's National Institute on Aging.

"I've heard medical students use the terms 'crock,' 'toad,' 'turkey,' and the one I heard most recently was 'dirtball'" said Robert N. Butler. . . .

Some studies show that medical students become more negative about the aged as they go through school," said Butler, a psychologist and gerontologist [a specialist in the problems of aging].

Few if any serious courses in geriatrics are required in the nation's 114 medical schools, and in only 31 are elective courses offered, he said.

In defense of insensitive medical students, Butler said, their only acquaintance with older people may be the corpses they dissect.

"Your first corpse is usually an older person, an experience you may have nightmares about. They deal with it through gallows humor or what I call Peter Panism, the idea that they themselves are not going to grow old."

Butler is on the campaign trail to persuade major medical schools of the need for improving instruction in geriatrics.

He said he wants to clear up some myths about aging, the kind that lead a doctor to tell a patient, "Well, what did you expect, you're getting old," or the idea that senility is inevitable.

UPI Dispatch from *The Bakersfield Californian*, September 18, 1976.

Diversity and strain

they die the slow death that modern medicine makes possible, they tend to become outcasts. We are taught to value life, to be horrified by cruel or careless acts that cut life short. At the same time, we don't want to watch the suffering of others. We have our pets "put to sleep" if they are incurably sick or suffering greatly. It is not, however, easy to apply the same thinking and practices to humans. Sociologists are interested in studying the conflicting values, attitudes, and practices which surround our treatment of the sick and the dying.

Abandonment Although the great majority of the aged are able to live normal lives, about 10 percent need constant care. Since there are now other ways of caring for the aged than in the family home, large numbers are sent to places called "convalescent homes" or "rest homes." While these institutions may be necessary, many of them are not pleasant (even those that are well run). Many others are very poorly run; their administrators are sometimes more interested in

making profits from government Medicaid payments than in caring for the patients (R. Burger, 1970). The quality of many rest homes would probably be improved if more relatives came to visit, but visitors are fairly rare. Many people do not visit their aged friends and relatives because they find the atmosphere in these homes depressing. Rest homes are viewed as halfway houses on the road to death, and people do not like to watch their old friends or relatives fading away. Sometimes families place relatives in rest homes before it is necessary simply because they cannot bear to see them change. Anselm Strauss tells of the resentment expressed by one man who was old and losing weight because of a chronic illness. An old friend avoided him on the street, pretending not to see him, apparently because he didn't want to see his approaching death (1973, pp. 37–40).

Because doctors are trained to save the living, not to preside over death, they have some of the same problems in relating to dying patients as do members of the family. Nurses often show the same negative attitudes toward dying patients unless they have special training, unusual insight, or much practice in the care of the dying. In one experiment designed to investigate attitudes toward the dying, researchers studied the reactions of a group of well-meaning women who had volunteered to visit patients in a hospital ward. The researchers told these volunteers that some of the patients were expected to recover, while others were going to die. It soon became clear that the visiting women tried hard to avoid the dying patients. Even in brief visits with them, the visitors avoided eye contact with these patients and found excuses for leaving them (Turbo, 1973, p. 109). Another study showed that nurses were slower to respond to calls from terminal patients than from those who were expected to recover (Turbo, 1973, p. 111). One nurse, experienced with terminal patients, explains why her colleagues avoid the dying:

Q: Do you think that the majority of girls [nurses], at least in your experience,

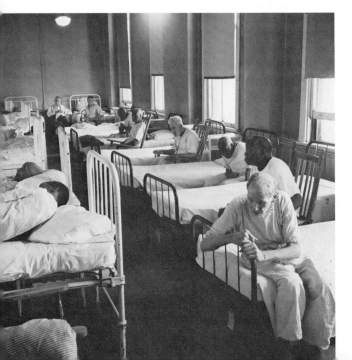

Figure 8-7 Nursing homes generally offer little intellectual or emotional support. Patients are sometimes neglected or treated as terminally ill. (*St. Louis Post Dispatch, Black Star*)

Stratification: Sex and age

231

To stereotype the aged is to overlook great differeces in physical health, vigor, and mental outlook—all of which can be strengthened by the continued sense of self-worth and usefulness.

would be averse to working with the dying?

A: Some of them. I think so. Now what has happened in our experience is that once a patient has been pronounced DNR—or do not resuscitate—that the general feeling then is push them out of the doors, because you know, what good am I going to do for them because they're dying anyway. . . .

But, on the other hand, there may be another type of patient, one comes to mind from last year who was in the unit for some time. He was married to a nurse himself, was very acutely ill for a long time, had complications after complications, all the way through the book. I mean, you could predict them all. Finally he was left in a condition whereby he was alert a certain amount, could feel pain, was kept on a machine. . . . And nothing more could be done, and no one knew quite which way to turn. So there he was, and everyone would come in and kind of wish he wasn't there, and we all built up this barrier against looking after him. (From *Vital Signs* by John Langone, copyright © 1974, by John Langone, by permission of Little, Brown and Company, Boston; pp. 200–201)

Elizabeth Kübler-Ross has become well known for her interest in and writings about death and dying. She provides another type of insight into the problems of death by summarizing the *stages* people go through when they are aware they are dying. A long period is needed for psychological adjustment to death. Hence, patients pass through a series of stages as death approaches: first they deny the fact; then they become angry. Later, they try to bargain with God. Then depression sets in before a final state of resignation is reached. In many of these states, the patients are very difficult to relate to or to comfort. As in other situations involving acute emotional stress, the person most in need of comfort is the most difficult to approach. Yet the dying need support, love, and care from friends in order to reach the final stage of resignation and peace (Kübler-Ross, 1969).

Great Britain has dealt with the problems of the dying by building a number of hospices, mainly in London. *Hospice* originally meant a place of hospitality for travelers or for the needy. It is now used in England to mean a place devoted exclusively to the care of the dying. Visitors are allowed at all times, and children are especially encouraged to come. If possible, the patients are sent home when death is near, since the familiar setting adds to their comfort and peace of mind. The hospices avoid giving the patients feeding tubes or catheters and generally avoid respirators or other "heroic" measures to keep people alive (Hendin, 1973, pp. 111–116) or, more accurately, to prolong dying. They keep patients out of pain, using heroin if necessary (heroin is illegal in the United States), and they encourage patients to communicate with each other. Needs for sociability disappear only if patients become comatose; otherwise people are social creatures to the end of life. A few days before her death, one of these patients told the doctor in charge that those last six months of her life were the only time she could remember in which she was completely relaxed and free from worry. In most cases, death does not have to be prolonged torture. Although the British hospices oppose the concept of euthanasia, their practice is similar to what American doctors call *negative* or *passive euthanasia* (see page 235).

Euthanasia Those who favor *euthanasia*, or terminating the patient's life in order to stop suffering, generally argue that people should have the right to die with dignity. The status of the dying, they say, should not be so degraded that they regress to a state of complete mindlessness, becoming mere "vegetables." Supporters of euthanasia believe it is wrong to prolong a patient's suffering. The nurse we quoted earlier felt a strong personal conflict over this issue:

We had to sit down with a psychiatrist and have a number of counseling sessions ourselves about it because we felt we just weren't doing anything for him [the patient]—that the more we did for him the more upset we became inside because it seemed as though we were prolonging his suffering. (Turbo, 1973, p. 202).

Negative or *passive euthanasia* is referred to colloquially as "unplugging the machine." This kind of euthanasia is quietly practiced in many hospitals, carried out by the instruction "DNR" ("do not resuscitate"). In the latter case, the patient is often in a state in which he or she might be pronounced legally dead by Kansas law. The state of Kansas now defines death as the prolonged failure to detect brain waves, and life-sustaining machinery can be stopped even if the heart still beats (Turbo, 1973, p. 37). To date, the Kansas definition has not been accepted in other states, which still define death as stoppage of all such vital functions as breathing and heartbeat. This leaves doctors uncertain of their legal obligations. Courts have generally ruled in favor of doctors when cases of passive euthanasia have come to light. In September 1976, the California Legislature passed an act making passive euthanasia possible if a patient, while still conscious and rational, asked not to have his or her life extended by special means. Other state legislatures have introduced such measures, and probably some will pass them in the future. Meanwhile, opponents of negative euthanasia argue that it involves shortening a life and that a patient judged hopeless might, in fact, recover.

In *positive euthanasia*, a doctor administers a drug to terminate a patient's life so as to prevent or end suffering. No state allows this practice. Among foreign countries, only Uruguay allows it if the patient has requested it. In Switzerland, a doctor can make an overdose of medicine available to a patient who requests it but cannot administer it personally (Turbo, 1973, pp. 27–

34). The arguments against positive euthanasia are stronger than those against negative euthanasia: there is a difference between withholding extreme measures to preserve life and administering something lethal. Opponents of positive euthanasia argue that it is an act of murder, not mercy. Obviously, the moral, legal, and medical issues raised by euthanasia are far from being settled.

Medical science has been able to prolong the life of the body more effectively than the life of the mind. Hence we are faced with new moral dilemmas. Is it consistent with the value we place on human life to allow a heart to stop beating when it could be kept going by a machine? On the other hand, is it consistent with the value we place on life to allow people to linger on indefinitely in states which do not seem to resemble life? This dilemma will be with us for a long time.

SUMMARY

Stratification occurs by sex as well as by age and by social-class position. At all times and in all cultures, traditions have limited the roles of the two sexes. They have nearly always given a *superordinate* role to men and a *subordinate* role to women. Proverbs and religious teachings have been used to justify this. Linton found that in the division of labor in societies studied by anthropologists, men's roles are always given higher status than women's roles. The system of prejudice and discrimination against women is called *sexism*.

In the socialization process, women have been indoctrinated into the idea that to be "normal," they should accept and like the traditonal female roles of homemaker and mother and avoid roles that place them in competition with men in business, science, and the professions. The socialization process has become a self-fulfilling prophecy, often preventing women from attempting such competitive roles. Although high school girls make better grades than high school boys, they have less confidence in their ability than boys have. Fewer go to college and far fewer go to graduate school.

A review of several studies of women and the law concludes that in most respects women are legally discriminated against, a system known as *legal paternalism*. It is true that in criminal cases women usually receive shorter sentences. But women are less apt to receive jury trials than are men—and it is generally believed that juries find them "not guilty" more often than do judges. In damage cases, women are less likely than men to win; when they do win, they collect less. The procedures in rape cases are so humiliating that women often avoid pressing charges. Courts are reluctant to interfere in cases of wife beating. Although courts usually grant custody of the children to women in divorce cases and grant them child support, full payments are seldom collected. In jury trials, men tend to believe men and women to believe women. Since men are called to jury duty more than women in most states, women are placed at a disadvantage. They are also disadvantaged in that the great majority of judges are men.

Social change is causing changes in sex roles, particularly in the industrialized Western societies, but also to some degree in urban parts of such male-dominated societies as Egypt and areas of the Arabic world. Gerald Marwell offers a *functional analysis* of the reasons for such change. In simpler societies, occupational roles were few and could be learned by anyone. Thus, the most efficient solution was to divide roles along sex lines. In modern, complex societies, it is more efficient to rely on achieved than an ascribed roles and to open competition for achievement to both sexes. Since the reproductive role of women occupies much less of their total time now than in the past, they are better able to compete for economic roles. However, because cultural attitudes change more slowly than cultural needs (a condition called *cultural lag*), women still receive less than full occupational equality.

The women's liberation movement has grown rapidly in public acceptance and political influence. Leaders of the movement attempt to change discriminatory hiring policies, discriminatory laws and legal practices, and socialization procedures. They also work for a greater role for women in politics, which the public, according to opinion polls, accepts in principle. Very recent studies support the women's liberation viewpoint by concluding that wives in the labor force are happier than those who are full-time housewives. Other studies indicate that women are beginning to develop a more favorable self-image regarding their ability to compete.

Although men have sometimes felt threatened by women's liberationists, it can be argued that changes in sex-role stereotypes can be helpful to men as well as to women—particularly changes in those stereotypes that call for extreme aggressiveness and bravado or that prevent men from expressing their true feelings.

College women support the women's liberation movement more fully than working-class women, but the latter agree completely on the cause of equal pay for equal work. College youth are generally more favorable to women's liberation objectives than are noncollege youth, but even among the latter group, 47 percent consider the statement "A woman's place is in the home" as nonsense.

The aged as well as women tend to be placed in subordinate roles, especially in modern industrial societies. This process is known as *ageism*. Early retirement results in serious *role loss* and, for all but the affluent, insufficient income. *Disengagement theory*, which holds that role loss is both inevitable and desired, is now being criticized. For the majority, retirement is sudden and comes before it is necessary. The percentage of elderly in modern society is steadily increasing, and many live until they reach an age at which care is needed. *Gerontologists* specialize in the problem of old age. Generally speaking, however, care for the aged is inadequate, especially the type of care that gives psychological support. Even medical students are given little training in the health problems of the aged.

When poor health declines into a terminal illness, there is a tendency for the aged to be abandoned. Visiting the dying is a painful experience, making it tempting to rationalize that they wish to be left alone. Terminal patients pass through various *stages* in dying. Actually, during the last stage of life, people seem to need psychological support. This makes their ordeal less painful. Much is being done in modern English *hospices*, devoted exclusively to the care of the dying, to make the last days of life serene.

Because so many people in the last days of life either lose mental awareness or suffer great pain, there is an increasing interest in *negative*, or *passive*, euthanasia—that is, allowing people to die without taking special steps to preserve life. This is fairly common practice, but it is on uncertain legal grounds. In 1976, the California Legislature passed the first law advising the medical profession to observe the wishes of people who, while still able to do so, leave instructions to be allowed to die. No state recognizes *positive euthanasia*, or mercy killing, and Uruguay is the only country to have legalized the practice.

Study guide

Terms to know

Sexism	Functional analysis of sex-role inequality	Stages in dying
Matriarchy	Cultural lag	Hospice
Superordinate	Old age	Euthanasia
Subordinate	Ageism	Negative or passive euthanasia
Legal paternalism	Role loss	Positive euthanasia
Sexist hypothesis	Disengagement theory	
Khatba	Gerontologist	

Names to know

Betty Friedan   Simone de Beauvoir
Jo Freeman   Elizabeth Kübler-Ross
Gerald Marwell

Self-test

Part I. Multiple Choice. Select the best of the four alternative answers:

1 Ralph Linton found that in the assignment of roles to the two sexes in primitive societies, (**a**) men always do the gardening, (**b**) women always make the pottery, (**c**) men's roles are always considered more important, (**d**) women's roles are always less strenuous physically than men's.

2 Statements regarding female inferiority are found in the writings of (**a**) Confucian philosophers, (**b**) Hinduism, (**c**) St. Paul, (**d**) all the above.

3 Daughters of women who are gainfully employed are more ambitious occupationally than other girls because (**a**) they model themselves on their mothers, (**b**) they resent their fathers, (**c**) they pity their mothers for having low-paying jobs, (**d**) they are apt to be maladjusted and less typically feminine than other girls.

4 In rape cases, (**a**) women often fail to bring charges because of the humiliation involved, (**b**) courts go to unusual lengths to be fair to women, (**c**) a woman's past sexual conduct has always been considered irrelevant, (**d**) all the above.

5 According to a study cited in the text, which of the following characterizes the attitudes of men and women toward one another in a trial? (**a**) gallantry, (**b**) complete impartiality, (**c**) opposites attract, (**d**) likes attract.

6 In damage cases, higher amounts are usually awarded to (**a**) women; (**b**) men; (**c**) women, but only if they are young; (**d**) neither sex, there is no bias.

7 Marwell presents logical arguments for assuming that women should gain occupational equality in industrial societies, but he says that full equality has not yet been achieved because of (**a**) cultural lag, (**b**) women's indifference to higher income, (**c**) men's academic superiority, (**d**) none of the above.

8 The Egyptian *khatba* complained that arranged marriages were going out of vogue in (**a**) Upper Egypt, near Sudan; (**b**) rural areas; (**c**) urban areas; (**d**) agricultural areas.

9 The study in which the writings of John T. McKay and Joan T. McKay were compared seems to demonstrate that (**a**) women are prejudiced against women, (**b**) women are fair in judging one another; (**c**) women are prejudiced against men, (**d**) men have no prejudices regarding women.

10 Attitude surveys show that working-class women and women's liberationists are in closest agreement on the issue of (**a**) abortion, (**b**) careers, (**c**) equal pay for equal work, (**d**) child-care centers.

11 In a survey by Yankelovich, a majority of college youth agreed to which of the following? (**a**) women are discriminated against; (**b**) the idea that woman's place is in the home is nonsense; (**c**) women should be equal to men; (**d**) all the above.

12 The aged are most likely to be abandoned or killed in societies that (**a**) fear the aged, (**b**) have insufficient food, (**c**) have no religious beliefs, (**d**) think of the next world as blissful.

13 In some ways, old age is worse in modern industrial societies than in agricultural societies because of (**a**) poor health care, (**b**) greater role loss, (**c**) too many activities, (**d**) expectations of the aged that are too great.

14 Kübler-Ross says that the typical terminal patient goes through certain stages of adjustment to death, the first being (**a**) anger, (**b**) bargaining with God, (**c**) denial of the fact, (**d**) depression.

15 Failing to take intensive measures to prolong the life of a patient who is sure to die soon is called (**a**) positive euthanasia, (**b**) negative euthanasia, (**c**) senilicide, (**d**) gerontocide.

Part II. True-False Questions

1 Languages are among the few cultural developments that show no bias in favor of men.

2 Traditional sex roles are agreeable to the temperaments and abilities of nearly all men and women.

3 Jo Freeman quotes studies showing that women develop personalities in some ways similar to those of oppressed minorities.

4 Women generally receive shorter jail sentences than do men for the same offenses.

5 Statistics compiled in New York State indicate that wife battery is even more frequent than rape.

6 In divorce settlements, women are usually given custody of the children and usually manage to collect the child support awarded by the courts.

7 In an account of women's liberation in Somali, the female leaders were exiled.

8 A 1976 study found working wives to be generally happier than those not in the labor force.

9 Compared with women of earlier generations, the modern housewife tends to be isolated and uncertain of the prestige of her job.

10 Women rated the writings of John T. McKay as better than those of Joan T. McKay, although they were actually by the same writer.

11 In a study called "Reversing Roles in the Meat Market," men were more embarrassed at being examined by women than women usually are at being similarly examined by men.

12 Investigations indicate that many people live to be more than 100 years old in Abkhasia because of special herbal medicines used only there.

13 A Balinese tale quoted by Simone de Beauvoir illustrates the idea that aged people are of value in some countries that honor traditions.

14 Because of their special training, nurses conscientiously stay with the dying.

Stratification: Sex and age

15 People sometimes avoid friends who are critically sick because they do not wish to see the change in them or to think about impending death.

Questions for discussion

1 The text states that ours is a man's world linguistically as well as in many other ways, and examples are given. Try to supply more examples of the way in which our use of language tends to favor men over women.

2 Argue the following proposition: Average temperamental differences between the sexes—such as aggressiveness, dominance, and means of emotional expression—are accounted for solely by the socialization process.

3 Based on the experiences of members of the class, what types of discrimination take place against either men or women in housing? In the use of credit? In divorce settlements?

4 The text describes a drastic method of elevating the status of women that was used in Somali. What explanations can you give for changes in policies in countries that are not as yet industrialized?

5 Some people think the rise to prominence of women is being accompanied by a fall in the status of men. Others believe that both sexes will be benefited by a redefinition of roles. What is your opinion on the subject, and why?

6 Why are working-class women less enthusiastic about many of the goals of the women's liberation movement than college-educated women?

7 What are some of the variables in societies that help determine whether old people will be honored or discarded?

8 Simone de Beauvoir lays the blame for mistreatment of the aged on our highly competitive, industrial system. Does the charge seem fair?

9 Argue the cases for and against negative euthanasia and positive euthanasia.

Projects

1 Make a survey of your own community and campus regarding prestigious jobs. How many women are on the city council or in major city administrative jobs? How many women on your faculty hold administrative positions? Try also to answer in at least one major industry in your town, the question: "What is the ratio of men to women in supervisory jobs?"

2 Do a brief opinion survey within your community, asking:
Should women have equal pay for equal jobs?
Should women have equal rights to promotion?
Should women be encouraged to seek political office?
Assuming her qualifications were better than those of any of her opponents, would you vote for a woman for governor? Senator? President?
Is there a contrast between the answers to such questions and the findings of project 1?

3 Visit two or three rest homes in your vicinity to see how well patients are cared for. Are the physical facilities good? Look and inquire particularly to see whether anything is done to keep elderly patients in touch with the outside world. Are any activities encouraged that reduce their sense of futility?

Suggested readings

Clark, Matt, Susan Agrest, Mariana Gosnell, Dan Shapiro, and Henry McGee: "A Right to Die?" *Newsweek*, November 3, 1975, pp. 58–59. When a person has suffered irreversible brain damage and can be kept alive only in a "vegetable" state, should she be allowed to die? The writers started with the case of Karen Ann Quinlan, who lived in such a state for a long time. They consulted doctors, neurologists, and others on this and similar cases.

Ferree, Myra Marx: "The Confused American Housewife," *Psychology Today*, vol. 10, September 1976, pp. 76–78, 80. The movement to jobs does not free women from housework, and other women remain full-time housewives. Why is the role much less rewarding than in the past? What has happened to "housewife networks"?

Fuchs, Victor R.: "Differences in Hourly Earnings between Men and Women," *Monthly Labor Review*, vol. 94, May 1971, pp. 9–15. An excellent illustration of the split labor market. "When sex differences across occupations are examined, one of the most striking findings is how few occupations employ large numbers of both men and women." How does this affect wages for women?

Goleman, David: "We Are Breaking the Silence about Death," *Psychology Today*, vol. 10, September 1976, pp. 44–47. Can dying patients see through the make-believe mask of smiles? Should they be deceived about their state as long as possible? How can we interpret periods of withdrawal from social contact? Goleman answers these questions, drawing heavily on the experiences of Kübler-Ross.

Gray, Betty MacMorran: "Economics of Sex Bias," *The Nation*, vol. 212, June 1971, pp. 742–744. "Who are the workers who don't make the official unemployment reports—the hidden unemployed?" Gray presents the facts and figures to show they are mainly women, teenagers, and the old, desperately seeking work but not even listed as unemployed.

Moran, Robert D.: "Reducing Discrimination: Role of the Equal Pay Act," *Monthly Labor Review*, vol. 93, June 1970, pp. 30–34. Reviews a long record of discrimination, but shows the amount of legislation on the statute books to enforce nondiscrimination against both women and the aged. What reasons have been found for subverting the intentions of such legislation? Must jobs be exactly equal or substantially equal? What about heavy lifting? Are training policies discriminatory?

Perry, Wingfield: "The Night of Ageism," *Mental Health*, vol. 58, Summer 1974, pp. 13–20. Why is the cruel and unjust discrimination against the aged so little observed or worried about? What are some of the myths that sustain discrimination against the aged? Perry answers these questions effectively.

Treiman, Donald J., and Kermitt Terrell: "Sex and the Process of Status Attainment: A Comparison of Working Women and Men," *American Sociological Review*, vol. 40, April 1975, pp. 174–200. Although the process of job achievement (through education and training) is identical for men and women, differences in pay continue. Why do women earn less regardless of experience, and why do married women earn even less than single women? The authors give the evidence and analyze the reasons.

Key to questions: Multiple Choice: 1-c; 2-d; 3-a; 4-a; 5-d; 6-b; 7-a; 8-c; 9-a; 10-c; 11-d; 12-b; 13-b; 14-c; 15-b. True-False: 1-F; 2-F; 3-T; 4-T; 5-T; 6-F; 7-F; 8-T; 9-T; 10-T; 11-T; 12-F; 13-T; 14-F; 15-T.

9

DEVIANT BEHAVIOR

This chapter examines the prevalence of deviant behavior and theories concerning its causes. After reading it, you should be able to:

1 Recognize that deviant behavior is rather general in society, not limited to certain social classes or to unusual personality types.

2 Recognize the importance of social environment in accounting for deviance.

3 Understand and be able to give examples of different adjustments to a type of anomie described by Merton's theory of deviant behavior.

4 Understand the nature and importance of white-collar crime.

5 Give examples of how labeling influences attitudes toward deviance and tends to make deviance a permanent behavior pattern.

6 Recognize the existence of organized crime and the economic base on which it rests, particularly in its profits from "victimless crimes."

News headlines provide an interesting introduction to the subject of deviant behavior. The following reports of deviant activities were found in the *Los Angeles Times* on a single day selected at random (*Los Angeles Times*, July 30, 1976). For a paper which doesn't specialize in crime stories, the list is impressive.

A first group of headlines described relatively common types of crimes. One concerned the kidnapping of a busload of children at Chowchilla, California. The other told of the shooting of two women (one was killed) by two boys, aged seventeen and eighteen, who were just out having fun with their high-powered rifles:

TWO REMAINING SUSPECTS IN
KIDNAPPING ARRESTED

TWO YOUTHS HELD IN RIFLE SLAYING

Several headlines had to do with athletes, the first with the illegal use of drugs by German Olympic competitors. The second involved a player who did not report for duty according to contract, and the third athlete was accused of perjury:

BAN ON GERMAN ROWERS SOUGHT FOR
DRUG MISUSE

DICK ALLEN FINED $2,200 BY PHILS FOR
GOING AWOL

ATTORNEY SAYS LIES CONVICTED
FOOTBALL FIGURE

Following these were a number of crimes committed in the business world: price fixing, stealing business secrets, giving false information to the government, evading disclosure-of-interest laws, and violating worker-safety laws:

FOURTEEN BOX FIRM OFFICIALS PLEAD
NO CONTEST
IN PRICE-FIXING CASE

BRITON ACCUSES U.S. OF STEALING
BUSINESS SECRETS

DUN, BRADSTREET FILED FALSE DATA,
U.S. CLAIMS

AGENCY TO PROVE BANK ABUSES OF
CONSUMER LAWS

RHODE ISLAND PLANT EXCEEDED SAFE
LEAD TOLERANCES
FOR WORKERS, U.S. CHARGES

Another group of crimes stemmed from the abuse of power. In one case a marine recruit was shackled and clubbed to death during basic training. In another, a drunken father severely beat his young children, and a third case involved the abuse of mental patients. The final item is taken from the editorial page; it protests the use of policewomen disguised as prostitutes to entrap men.

THE SHACKLING OF SANITY

MENTAL PATIENTS REPORTED ABUSED
BY SOME EMPLOYEES

Deviant behavior

243

CHILDREN, VICTIMS OF ABUSE, NEED CAMP

POLICE USE OF SEXUAL DECOYS:
EQUAL "JUSTICE" IN HOT PANTS

Next comes a category of political crime. The first headline refers to Patricia Hearst, the revolutionary Symbionese Liberation Army, and two of its leaders, William and Emily Harris. The next headline refers to the illegal burglarizing of the offices of the Socialist Labor Party by the F.B.I. A third report describes how journalist Daniel Schorr gained secret information about the government. In a fourth headline, a congressman is censured for violating conflict of interst laws:

HARRIS JURY TO BEGIN DELIBERATIONS TODAY

CAR WITH SOCIALIST PETITIONS RECOVERED

SCHORR SAID CIA PROVIDED REPORT, WITNESS TESTIFIES

HOUSE REPRIMANDS SIKES FOR FINANCIAL MISCONDUCT

A final headline refers to a crime that defies classification: A judge ordered a man to seek psychiatric help after he had killed 15 million of his neighbor's bees:

BEE POISONER GETS 120-DAY JAIL SENTENCE

The daily paper did not cover all crimes of the day, nor did it report all the other deviant behavior that had recently occurred. Covering these stories would require an encyclopedia-length newspaper. A glance at these headlines should, however, clarify several points. First, only a few of the people involved (the kidnappers and the youthful slayers) represent our usual stereotypes of criminals. Perhaps the revolutionary Harrises meet the stereotype because

they were accused of bank robbery and kidnapping, but their avowed purpose was revolution, not to gain money. The rest of these stories concern "respectable people"—businesspeople, brokers, bankers, managers, representatives of congress, athletes, fathers, hospital employees, police officers, F.B.I. agents, and marine drill sergeants.

Readers may view these cases in different ways. Opponents of government secrecy applaud Daniel Schorr; yet he is accused of violating the law. Some people would agree that the Salt Lake City Police Department should use decoys to entrap men who seek the services of prostitutes. Others would agree with the opinion expressed by the editorial writer Ellen Goodman:

> We have to consider, if we will, why we want to make victimless criminals at all. It seems that we have enough criminals—the kind who bang other people on the heads and embezzle union pensions and sell heroin to schoolchildren. There is hardly such a shortage that we must go out of our way to make more. . . . (1976, p. 4)

Nearly everyone would agree that William and Emily Harris were guilty of crimes in connection with the activities of the Symbionese Liberation Army, but some would want them to receive light sentences and others would want them imprisoned for life. Some would say the F.B.I. was doing its duty in burglarizing the offices (and possibly the automobile) of the socialists. Others would point out that lawlessness on the part of law enforcers and a government that spies on law-abiding citizens are great social dangers. Some people would shrug off most of the charges against business firms with the remark, "Business is business." Others would see crimes committed by leading citizens as particularly serious; to them, exposing workers to high levels of dangerous pollutants would be equal to intent to murder.

DEFINING DEVIANCE

Deviant behavior is behavior that varies markedly from the norms acceptable to a society. This definition assumes that there are widely accepted norms of right and wrong. Despite the differences of opinion just cited, there is widespread agreement on some types of behavior that violate the norms. Surveys conducted by a group of sociologists (Rossi, Waite, Rose, and Burk, 1974, pp. 224–237) reveal that the public perceives three types of criminal activities. The first and most serious type includes offenses against the person, such as murder, rape, kidnapping, and assault. Crimes against property, such as burglary and larceny, are seen as less serious. Sex crimes except for rape are rated fairly low. The public apparently sets crime apart from deviance, whereas sociologists think of crime simply as an illegal type of deviance.

Asked in another study to identify the "most deviant" people, respondents placed homosexuals, drug addicts, and alcoholics at the top of their lists. The activities of all these people fall into a category called *crimes without victims* (Simmons, 1965, pp. 223–232). These are crimes in which no one is preyed on by another. If there is a victim at all, it is the person committing the crime—the alcoholic, the drug addict, or the suicide.

Since norms depend on public attitudes, our definition of deviance would apply to what the public calls "serious crime" and also to "crimes without victims." In fact, violations of social norms include a broad spectrum of behaviors. A child who throws a temper tantrum, a person who hijacks an airplane, and a mental patient who claims to hear the voice of God over the radio are all violating social norms.

Certain "buts" must be kept in mind, however, in using the above definition of deviance. First, agreement is far from total, although it does exist in some areas. Second, as times change, many traditional norms lose support. Divorce,

Figure 9-1 As norms have changed, people have felt more free to express their sexual preferences. This lesbian couple has established a home together. (*Chie Nishio, Nancy Palmer*)

for example, was once considered deviant and disgraceful. Now it has become an acceptable (and widely used) way of ending a marriage. Similarly, many laws remain in effect even after they are no longer enforced. Even the police are aware that some types of laws are outmoded. Especially in large cities, many laws concerning private morals are generally ignored, as indicated in the insert "The Laws Cops Rarely Enforce" (page 246).

The definition of deviance also depends on who is doing the defining—a member of the deviant group or an outsider. In the eyes of society, for example, Patricia Hearst became deviant when she joined the Symbionese Liberation Army. From the point of view of the S.L.A., however, she ceased to be deviant when she joined them, adopted their political philosophy, and took part in their activities. Similarly, members of a neighborhood delinquent gang become deviant from the gang's point of view if they refuse to engage in petty theft, fight for the gang, and take part in other gang activities. Throughout most of the following pages, deviance will be defined from the viewpoint of

The laws cops rarely enforce

Most policemen contend that they enforce all laws when, in fact, there are many laws that they enforce selectively or not at all, in the opinion of Kenneth Culp Davis, an administrative law expert who recently completed a study of how policemen work.

Among laws that Davis and his researchers found policemen rarely enforce are those prohibiting social gambling, intercourse in automobiles or in parks, public marijuana smoking, jaywalking, spitting on the sidewalk, smoking where prohibited, curfew violations, juvenile drinking, adult drinking in parks, and attempting to bribe a police officer. . . .

Selective law enforcement, he says, is not only necessary but "entirely legal" if it is done openly. But he believes that a situation in which police pretend to enforce all laws is unhealthy. . . .

"Honesty of government agency is the best policy," Davis wrote. "I think that the man and woman who want to live together should be entitled to know that, in the absence of special circumstances, the police have not enforced the fornication statute for many decades."

[*Warning: The report is based on Chicago, which Davis considers typical of larger American cities, but may not apply to smaller towns.*]

---

the general society. But to understand deviant subcultures, it is important to see things from the viewpoint of the deviant group itself.

EARLY EXPLANATIONS OF DEVIANCE

Explanations of deviance have changed over the years. In religious communities, deviance was seen as the work of the Devil. It was assumed that everyone was tempted now and then and everyone sometimes gave in to temptation, becoming a sinner. As seen from a modern sociological perspective, this view of deviance is both inclusive and realistic: it assumes that everyone has the potential for deviance. There was another religious interpretation, however, that divided people very clearly into two groups—the good, who were filled with divine grace, and the bad, who were doomed to damnation. Such a black-and-white view appeals to the righteous because it assures them that they are a separate and

special group—that they have nothing in common with sinners.

Nineteenth-century theories of heredity

In the late nineteenth century, social scientists also subscribed to a *hereditary theory of crime*. Criminality was held to be an inherited trait, and criminals were seen as almost a different species, throwbacks to an earlier stage in human evolution. According to this "scientific" view, criminals resembled apes rather than true humans. Cesare Lomboroso of Italy was a well-known advocate of this theory. Richard L. Dugdale, who wrote a hair-raising account of a degenerate family whom he called the Jukes (Adams, 1955, pp. 48–49), was the most famous American advocate of this position. In his book *The Jukes: A Study in Crime, Pauperism, Disease, and Insanity* (1877), he tried to prove how heredity created generations of criminals and other social deviants. For years this book was widely read and quoted as proven fact, yet Dugdale's research and methodology were amazingly careless and unscientific. He ignored all cases that did not fit the theory, and he loaded his account with stories of "degenerate" people who were not even blood relatives of the Jukes family. Furthermore, he assumed that any of the Jukes accused of crimes were guilty whether or not they were convicted. Dugdale described one Juke as "thief, but never caught," and noted elsewhere, "impossible to get reliable information, but it is evident that at nineteen he was a leader of crime." Another member of the Jukes family was accused (but not convicted) of a single crime—breaking a deaf man's ear trumpet! Dugdale's research proved nothing about crime, but the popularity of his book showed that millions of people were happy to believe that all criminals are members of distinct and identifiable "criminal families."

The view that crime is hereditary would, of course, have social consequences. Society feels little responsibility to people who are identified as being biologically inferior to everyone else. These nonhumans can be locked away in prisons fit only for beasts—for, according to this viewpoint, they *are* beasts.

Today, the view that criminality is hereditary has been rejected, along with the idea of a recognizable "criminal type." Some violent, motiveless crimes might be rooted in certain types of mental or physical pathologies. However, most deviant behavior is held to be the result of environmental influence. Even the idea that particular types of mental illness cause crime is seen as a social myth. According to researchers Henry Steadman and Joseph Cocozza, psychiatrists are not able to predict who will and who will not commit violent crimes (1975).

Deviance and sociological theory

In the 1920s, Clifford Shaw (Shaw and McKay, 1942) studied delinquency in Chicago and found that the delinquency rate in some areas was twenty times as high as in others. There were only two conclusions. Either particular areas of the city drew families incapable of controlling their children, or the environment itself made normative control of the young very difficult. Shaw's study showed that over the years, as one immigrant group after another moved out and others moved in, the ethnic composition of the high-delinquency areas had changed. It made no difference where the immigrant groups came from. The delinquency rate in these areas remained high but declined among families who were able to move out. Shaw's evidence of this ethnic succession in crime seemed to show that the environment was the most important factor in socializing the young into delinquent ways. In addition to living near each other, all these families were poor, a factor which has led sociologists to study the link between poverty and crime.

Poverty and crime

Evidence taken from societies around the world suggests that poverty itself does not always produce crime. Many very poor areas have low crime rates—for example, the rural areas of India. Perhaps there is little crime there because the people feel bound by traditions which prohibit crime, or perhaps there is little to steal. However, in large modern cities, where the poor live close to the wealthy and where the ties of tradition are weak, poverty may help to cause crime, especially crimes such as burglary and pickpocketing. F.B.I. statistics for the United States tend to support this view. Contrary to public opinion, poverty is worse in certain rural areas of the United States than in the cities. Yet, crime rates there are lower than in urban areas, although the difference is declining. Sociologists have developed the concept of relative deprivation to explain this difference in crime rates. *Relative deprivation* means that people feel deprived if they have less wealth or status than those around them. Thus in a poor village of

India or in a poor, rural area of Appalachia, poverty is easier to bear than in the city, where poverty is surrounded by wealth.

Merton's theory of anomie

Robert K. Merton (1959) has devised a theory to explain how environmental and other pressures lead to a high crime rate in the United States, even though we are one of the richest countries in the world. Not only do we have poverty in the midst of plenty, says Merton, but we place more pressure upon people to succeed than do most other societies. In many poor parts of the world, poverty is the expected way of life of the majority, who were born into the lower class and, it is held, should be willing to remain there. No one is condemned for being poor. In the United States, on the other hand, the "hard work and success" ethic is very strong. People who are poor throughout their lives are viewed as failures. When old friends meet after many years, they try in subtle ways to find out how well the other is doing, and parents often play a status game of comparing their children's achievements with those of the neighbor's children. Given these attitudes, the failure to succeed brings humiliation as well as material poverty. Under such circumstances, Merton reasons, people become success-oriented, subordinating means to ends. Driven by the pressure to succeed, many people stretch the rules. They cheat at least a little to gain their goals, but some cheat in much larger ways.

All societies, Merton says, develop fairly well agreed upon norms as to what goals one should pursue in life as well as rules for reaching these goals. In some societies the goals might be military achievement, enjoyment of leisure, or merely earning enough to subsist. In the United States, however, the goal that most people believe to be proper is to earn a great deal of money. Furthermore, everyone is expected to succeed. However, there is a wide difference in people's access to the success goals demanded by society. Some are born into wealthy families; others come from homes with poverty and little education, where parents cannot help them or offer advice on how to succeed. Still others are discriminated against on racial or ethnic grounds. The result, says Merton, is that success, although expected of everyone, is not open to all by legitimate means. The result is that a state of *anomie* exists. Merton defines this as a split between societal goals and the ability to reach them. People adjust to this situation in many ways. They may reject honest means and resort to crime to achieve their goals. They may accept the honest means but fail to reach the goals. They may repudiate both the means and the goals, or they may even rebel against the system.

Merton has summarized his theory as shown in Table 9-1. In Merton's scheme, a plus (+) indicates agreement with social norms, and a minus (−) indicates disagreement. The conformist achieves societal goals by honest means; the innovator achieves societal goals by devious means. The ritualist is honest but fails to achieve societal goals. The retreatist cares neither for success goals nor for honesty. Finally, the rebel approves of some societal norms and revolts against others. According to Merton, society values the conformist most, values the innovator a little less, and the ritualist less still, does not value the retreatist at all, and sees the rebel as an enemy. A few examples will help to clarify Merton's theory.

The *conformist* is exemplified by the honest businessperson, professional, politician, or anyone else who makes a notable success of life by honest means. The businessperson is the prime

Table 9-1

Goals	Means		Resultant behavior
+	+	=	Conformity
+	−	=	Innovation
−	+	=	Ritualism
−	−	=	Retreatism
±	±	=	Rebellion

example of this social type because Merton characterizes America as a society highly oriented to financial and business success.

The *innovator* is the person who succeeds by devious means without getting caught and who is rated second in public esteem. Innovators are willing to fix prices, do industrial spying, evade business laws, and disregard the safety of workers to save costs. Participants in the Watergate affair were innovators who would have been highly regarded if they hadn't been caught. The public does not admire unsuccessful innovators.

Recent investigations of Medicaid fraud turned up a new kind of business innovation, "ping-ponging" in medical clinics. This is the practice of sending patients through a long series of expensive and unnecessary medical tests in order to collect more money from Medicaid. One clinic director, who was also in charge of a methadone program, made all his methadone patients go through long, expensive medical tests once a month to increase his Medicaid billings and profits. If the patients refused to take these tests, the doctor refused to give them their methadone (Thomason, 1976, p. 5).

The innovators, as their name implies, are highly creative and can be found in all areas of business life. In an age of computers, a new breed of "electronic" innovators has arisen. These "computer bandits," described in the insert on page 250, use their training in computer technology to make money the easy (and devious) way.

The *ritualist* is poor, gives up hope of success, but remains strictly honest. The patriotic eighty-two-year-old woman presented in Chapter 1 is a perfect example—not well off, but honest and respectable and devoted to her country. Another good example is that of an honest, hard-working garbage collector interviewed by Studs Terkel:

> I don't look down on my job in any way. . . .
>   And, yeah, it's meaningful to society (Laughs).
> I was told a story one time by a doctor. Years

Figure 9-2 (*a*) Bernard Bergman, an unsuccessful innovator, was found guilty in 1976 of abuses connected with a chain of nursing homes owned by him. (*b*) The law often deals lightly with such white-collar criminals. [*(a) United Press International; (b)* © New Yorker Magazine, Inc., 1976)]

(a)

(b)

"*Warrington Trently, this court has found you guilty of price-fixing, bribing a government official, and conspiring to act in restraint of trade. I sentence you to six months in jail, suspended. You will now step forward for the ceremonial tapping of the wrist.*"

The computer bandits ALLAN J. MAYER

For Milo, a bright young computer programmer with a habit of spending money he didn't have, things couldn't have worked our more conveniently. He had just been hired to computerize the check-handling systems at the National City Bank of Minneapolis, the same bank where he kept his personal checking account. Milo diligently designed an elaborate program that would tell the bank's computer how to process checking transactions. But in the middle of the complex program, he slipped in an extra command of his own: the computer was instructed to ignore any of Milo's personal checks whenever his account didn't have sufficient funds. Milo got away with it for months, but then the computer broke down, forcing the bank to go back to processing checks by hand—and an ordinary clerk discovered the scheme.

Milo is just one of thousands practicing what U.S. attorney Terry Knoepp calls "the crime of the 1980s"—computer fraud. By using and abusing electronic brains, a new breed of white-collar criminal, skilled in the arcane lore of computer science, is costing banks, corporations, and even the government uncounted millions in stolen goods, services, and hard cash. Just how bad things have got is hard to say, since more than 85 percent of all computer crimes may go undetected or unreported. In his recent book "Crime by Computer," Stanford Research Institute's Donn B. Parker estimates the total take at about $300 million a year. That's small change compared to the $40 billion that was lost in 1974 from conventional fraud and embezzlement. Still, with more and more companies computerizing their operations—the U.S. computer population is expected to grow from about 150,000 now to more than 500,000 by 1980—the potential for electronic fraud is enormous.

. . . A teller at New York's Union Dime Savings Bank, for example, embezzled $1.4 million over three years to pay his gambling debts. . . . A California accountant looted more than $1 million from his company by recording higher payments for raw materials than the firm actually paid. . . . In the Classic Equity Funding [insurance] swindle of 1972, to pump up Equity stock, the insurance company's executives recorded the sale of 97,000 policies in their computer, when in fact they had sold fewer than 33,000.

Finally, the computer can be used to help crooks plan routine capers. Three years ago in Chicago, a ring of burglars recruited a computer to compile lists of prosperous targets, rather like an advertiser zeroing in on a rich market. With such electronic guidance, the gang stole more than $1 million in negotiable securities from private homes.

ago, in France, they had a setup where these princes and lords and God knows what they had floating around. If you didn't stand in favor of the king, they'd give you the lowest job, of cleaning the streets of Paris—which must have been a mess in those days. One lord goofed up somewhere along the line, so they put him in charge of it. And he did such a wonderful job that he was commended for it. The worst job in the French kingdom and he was patted on the back for what he did. That was the first time I ever heard about garbage where it really means something. (1974, pp. 152–153; by permission of Pantheon Books, a division of Random House)

Diversity and strain

If society considered honest means more important than success goals, the eighty-two-year-old woman and the garbage collector would rate just below the conformist. However, says Merton, goals are rated above means; therefore, the honest ritualist trails behind the dishonest innovator in public esteem.

The *retreatist* values neither success goals nor the honest means used by others to reach those goals. Merton used tramps and hobos to exemplify this social type. A more contemporary example is that of "the cat," described in the insert "The 'Cat' as Retreatist." Like the innovator, the cat pursues his goals by illegal means, but his goals are not those which society values—he's out for "kicks" only. These "cats" grow up in a ghetto environment that almost totally denies them the means of achieving success goals by legitimate means.

The *rebel* values some social norms and rejects others. The communist, for example, is a rebel because he rejects the private enterprise system, but at the same time he supports the social value of equality. The fascist (the person who would like to see a nationalistic dictatorship and white dominance) has little quarrel with the economic system but rejects political democracy and especially the idea of equality for all races. The Ku Klux Klan claims to believe in an older, purer, all-white America and rebels against any movement toward racial equality. If Merton's analysis fits the rebel as well as the other categories, we would expect the political rebel to be a person alienated by a system that does not give all people access to success goals. Such a person would probably be willing to go to drastic lengths to make revolutionary change. Fascists and Klan members, on the other hand, would be seen as

---

The "cat" as retreatist   HAROLD S. FIRESTONE

In contrast with the "square," the cat gets by without working. Instead he keeps himself in "bread" by a set of ingenious variations on "begging, borrowing, or stealing." Each cat has his "hustle," and a hustle is any non-violent means of "making some bread" which does not require work. One of the legendary heroes of the cat is the man who is such a skillful con-man that he can sell "State Street" to his victim. Concretely, the cat is a petty thief, pickpocket or pool shark, or is engaged in a variety of other illegal activities of the "conning" variety. A very few cats are actually living off the proceeds of their women "on the hustle."

The main purpose of life for the cat is to experience the "kick." Just as every cat takes pride in his hustle, so every cat cultivates his kick. A "kick" is any act tabooed by "squares" that heightens and intensifies the present moment of experience and differentiates it as much as possible from the humdrum routine of daily life. Sex in any of its conventional expressions is not a "kick" since this would not serve to distinguish the cat from the "square," but orgies of sex behavior and a dabbling in the various perversions and byways of sex pass muster as "kicks." Some cats are on the alcohol "kick," others on a marihuana "kick," and others on a heroin "kick." There is some interchangeability among these various "kicks" but the tendency is to select your "kick" and stay with it. Many of these young drug users, however, had progressed from the alcohol to the marihuana to the heroin "kick." Each "kick" has its own lore of appreciation and connoisseurship into which only its devotees are initiated.

From Harold Firestone, "Cats, Kicks and Color" in Howard S. Becker, *The Other Side*, a Free Press Paperback, The Macmillan Company, New York, 1964, pp. 281–297. © 1964 by the Macmillan Publishing Company, Inc.

---

people who feel threatened by new competitors or people whose perferred way of life is becoming outmoded.

Today revolutionary activity occurs on an international scale. Airline hijackings and terrorist bombings are often committed in one country to promote a cause in some other country, as is the case with the terrorist activities of the Palestine Liberation Organization. These crimes continue to fit Merton's diagram in that they involve ambivalence regarding social norms. One type of norm (a law) is violated for the sake of another type of norm (the "cause"—liberation, equality, or whatever). To point out the normative conflict involved in these situations, we have included a report of a skyjacking conducted by a group of Croatian partisans who support independence for the Croatian minority in communist Yugoslavia. In addition to seizing a Boeing 727, they planted a bomb that killed an American policeman and wounded three others. Yet Croatians in the United States regarded these people as heroes. Even more amazing, however, was the response of the plane's flight engineer: " . . .They were really great guys. I want to go to their trial." (See the insert "A Skyjacking for Croatia.")

Merton's analysis stresses the moral conflicts involved in deviant behavior. Other sociologists have presented theories which focus on different aspects of deviant behavior. These are discussed on the following pages.

A skyjacking for Croatia   DAVID A. ALPERN

Passengers aboard TWA Flight 355 from New York to Chicago were being served their predictable airline dinners—steak, chicken or cold cuts—when they heard the shaky voice of pilot Richard Carey on the intercom announce that they had just been skyjacked. "The pilot came on and told us to relax, that we had a serious problem and everyone should keep cool," passenger James Perkins recalled later. Thus began a bizarre airborne odyssey in which a handful of Croatian nationalists took the medium range Boeing 727 with 93 people aboard on a 4,230-mile transatlantic mission to Montreal, Newfoundland, Iceland, and Paris. Back in New York, meanwhile, a bomb left by the terrorists exploded unexpectedly on a police range—killing one officer and injuring three others. . . .

The terrorists in this case were partisans of Croatia, now a region of Communist Yugoslavia. In recent years Croatian nationalists have initiated more than half a dozen violent episodes—including bombings, assassinations and skyjackings. "I don't believe in this hijacking, but the Croatian people are desperate and will do anything," said Dinko Suljak, head of the Croatian national council in New York. "They want independence and freedom." . . .

During a stop in Montreal, the terrorists sent word that another bomb had been left in a subway locker at Manhattan's Grand Central Terminal along with two political tracts. They wanted four U.S. newspapers and the International Herald Tribune to publish their appeal for Croatian independence. . . . The FBI officials swiftly chose to comply, passing copies of the Croatian appeal to the press—and drawing a protest from the Yugoslavian government as a result. . . .

The learning of crime: Differential association

Edwin H. Sutherland (Sutherland and Cressey, 1960) was one of the first sociologists to point out that most types of crime and deviance can best be understood as behavior learned on the basis of differential association. *Differential association* means that people associate with normative and deviant influences in different degrees. Some have strong normative support from home; others do not. Some not only lack normative support but are forced to spend most of their time with people who do not live up to the norms.

Sutherland applies the idea of differential association particularly to *white-collar crime*, which he defines as the type of crime learned by respectable people as they work for organizations that routinely violate the law. White-collar crime includes graft and embezzlement or any type of crime committed by people who generally succeed in keeping up a respectable image. Sutherland's own examples of white-collar crime include price fixing, false advertising, falsifying accounts for income-tax purposes, "rigging" weights and measures, and violating antitrust laws.

The Watergate cover-up was a special type of white-collar crime, in which men holding high positions and enjoying good reputations were violating laws as a routine part of their duty to former President Richard Nixon. In spite of all the unfavorable publicity about the Watergate affair, a Chicago *Daily News* report of April 19, 1975 indicated that 60 percent of the 238 young business managers polled believed they would have gone along with their boss under similar circumstances. Loyalty to one's boss and to the organization may require the learning and use of illegal procedures. (Illegal procedures, of course, can be used independently, as in the case of the computer bandits.)

In Sutherland's analysis, we all learn something of deviance, but for most of us, this is more than balanced by the internalization of social norms. However, if deviant behavior brings rewards, deviance gradually becomes habitual and less destructive of the individual's self-image. The deviant person begins to see the behavior as more or less normal. This is most likely to happen in the company of other people who support the deviant value system and whose views carry influence. Someone who objects to drinking alcohol, for example, can easily find his principles changing if he is surrounded by likable friends who drink and goes to their parties. In this case, a situation for learning deviant behavior has developed: There is group support for this behavior, and material or emotional rewards are available. If a person gets sick the first time he drinks, then the experience will fail to become a favorable deviant learning experience.

In their analyses of deviant behavior, Cloward and Ohlin (1961) stress the importance of *opportunities* for learning crime. They show that juvenile delinquency is most likely to turn into persistent adult crime in areas where there is an underworld from which to learn the pattern and which will give group support and help make the crime rewarding. Albert Cohen (Cohen and Short, 1971) has consistently stressed the influence of group interaction as a cause of crime and delinquency, but he views some types of delinquency as a consequence of hostility between social classes. These points of view are not mutually exclusive. Analyses of gang delinquency in our cities show that crime is a behavior which depends on learning opportunities, attitudes, and group influence.

Social class and delinquency

If it is true that criminal behavior is learned under favorable circumstances, and if feelings of deprivation exist among the poor, then we would expect crime rates to be high in crowded urban areas. These are the areas in which an underworld is most likely to exist, where markets are available for selling stolen goods, and where drugs are most easily available. In such a setting, it is not surprising that juvenile delinquency rates are high and that malicious gangs form. Cohen (1955) believes that lower-class delinquency tends to be largely malicious but nonutilitarian. That is, the boys (and girls, though in much smaller numbers) resent society in general—the school, the police, and employers—and act out their resentments by becoming vandals. They see themselves as targets of discrimination. They dress and speak differently from middle-class children and their informational backgrounds are different, but teachers don't accept these differences. Consequently, all the compliments on good work, neatness, and good manners go to middle-class children, while these lower-class children are criticized. The first acts of delinquency, then, can be seen as protests rather than as attempts to reach the success goals posited by Merton's analysis of deviance. In later years, it is quite likely that some of the delinquents will turn to such utilitarian activities as theft, gambling, or drug dealing.

Cohen does not deny that middle-class youth also get into trouble, but he believes that their deviant activities result from the effort to have fun rather than from outbursts of resentment. According to Cohen, middle-class youth do not usually destroy property. Charges against them typically deal with liquor, marijuana, automobiles, and sex. A carefully researched study of lower- and middle-class boys only partly confirms Cohen's point of view.

The Saints and the Roughnecks

William J. Chambliss studied two small cliques of boys—the Saints and the Roughnecks—in a high school in a middle-sized town (1973, pp. 24–31). The Saints were from middle-class backgrounds. They had money and cars and did well in school; their families enjoyed good reputations in the community. They were well liked by their teachers, the community, and the police. The Roughnecks were lower-class boys who attended the same high school but did less well

academically. Their manners and language were rough. They occasionally got into fights, and they spent much of their time hanging around corners in town. Teachers, the townspeople, and the police considered them a bad bunch, likely to get deeper and deeper into trouble.

The Saints were hardly saintly. Despite a good front, they were constantly being delinquent during the two years they were being studied. They used clever tricks to get out of classes and then took off for the nearby city. There was never a week during which at least part of the group of eight did not cut school, illegally and deceptively. They drove too fast even when they were sober, which wasn't often. In the city, they bought liquor illegally and managed to get into bars even though they were under age. Just for fun, they removed red warning lights from holes in the street and then watched to see who would drive into the holes. They vandalized vacant houses, wrecking them as thoroughly as they could. The only thing they ever stole was gasoline for their cars.

The Saints were clever criminals. Vandalism and other crimes were commited out of town— the local police had nothing on them. Once or twice they were caught cutting school. They acted repentant, begging forgiveness for "this one mistake." The one or two times when they were stopped by the police for speeding, their act was equally good and they got by with a warning. Four of the eight Saints graduated from high school with the highest honors.

The Roughnecks had neither cars nor money. Their school attendance was much better than the Saints', probably because they hadn't worked out effective tricks for getting away. After school, since they couldn't get away to the city, they hung around town, where people generally saw them as a "no-good lot." They drank only now and then because no one would sell them liquor. Their only contact was a local "wino" who would buy them a quart of whiskey if they would treat him, but they rarely had the cash to

(a)

(b)

Figure 9-3 The law and social class. (*a*) These lower-middle-class teenagers may be treated fairly severely by the law if they get into trouble. (*b*) Their wealthier counterparts are likely to get off more easily. [*(a) David Strickler, Monkmeyer; (b) Bob S. Smith/Rapho/Photo Researchers, Inc.*]

support his drinking. Unlike the Saints, the Roughnecks did not commit costly acts of vandalism.

The Roughnecks' delinquency consisted of shoplifting and occasional fighting. At those rare times when they drank heavily, they did so right in town, where they were almost sure to be seen. Perhaps their greatest social offense was the hostility they showed toward the teachers, police, and the general public. Their hostility was returned. The mutual dislike between the Roughnecks and the community increased.

A follow-up study made a few years later showed that all but one of the Saints went on to college. One became a doctor, one a lawyer, and several became business managers. Only two of the Roughnecks went to college. Both of them received football scholarships and both

became high school coaches. Two of the Roughnecks received long prison sentences, one for manslaughter and the other for murder. One became a bookie in town, and the other might have become a truck driver—his old friends weren't sure where he was. Of course, there is no way of knowing what would have happened if the Roughnecks had not been stereotyped in

Deviant behavior

their youth. However, Chambliss is convinced that labeling was involved in their later records.

Social class, Saints, and Roughnecks

The study of the Saints and the Roughnecks demonstrates social-class differences. Consistent with Cohen's theory, the lower-class boys were less accepted from the first and more easily condemned as delinquents. Because they were too poor to leave town, their delinquent acts were more likely to be observed by the community. Furthermore, it was much easier for their pattern of delinquency to persist. Two of the boys were rescued from the community by their football scholarships; they got a chance to leave their old reputations behind and make a new start. The others couldn't escape the labels given to them by the community.

When the Saints were occasionally caught breaking the law, their behavior was dismissed with the remark that boys have to "sow their wild oats." They were well treated by the police, by their teachers, and by the community in general. Although they never seemed to study, all but one of them graduated with an A or B average. Sometimes sympathetic teachers gave them good grades just because they were thought to be bright and capable. The Roughnecks didn't get such breaks.

Contrary to Cohen's theory that malicious mischief comes from the lower class, the mischief in this case was the work of middle-class boys. This is probably not typical, since there is more school vandalism in poor inner-city schools than in surburban schools. Chambliss concludes that in actual cost, the amount of theft committed by the Roughnecks and the amount of damage caused by the Saints was about equal.

Labeling theory

In recent years, *labeling theory* has become prominent. According to this theory, if people become thoroughly labeled as delinquents, crim-inals, or other kinds of deviants, they tend to live up to the label and take on a deviant self-identity. Police, teachers, and juvenile authorities have the power to impose labels, which differ from time to time and from social class to social class. For example, the term *drug fiend* was once applied to anyone who smoked marijuana, making such a person seem a dangerous degenerate. The word *delinquent* is applied so much more often to lower-class than to middle-class youth that it seems almost to have been invented for class stereotyping. In terms of Cooley's looking-glass self, the person who sees a reflected image of delinquency can be made to feel like a delinquent. As in the study by Reckless cited in Chapter 4, a "good" self-image is a powerful deterrent to deviant behavior. A deviant self-image helps to perpetuate deviance. Chambliss's Roughnecks were successfully labeled except for the two boys who were able to break away from the community. For the others, community attitudes became a self-fulfilling prophecy.

The Saints, on the other hand, were never stigmatized—that is, never marked and set apart in the public mind as socially unacceptable. They were always considered good, red-blooded American boys who would do well in the world. With one exception, the self-fulfilling prophecy again worked, and even the one Saint who did not go to college didn't get into trouble with the law.

Future expectation and delinquency

Nathan Caplan of the University of Michigan's Institute for Social Research made a study of 837 boys living in a high-delinquency area (1974). He found that the best way to predict which boys would get into trouble with the police during the next school year was to consider their own expectations of success or failure in school and later life. By the age of ten, most of the boys had a definite idea of their chances for success at school and for getting good jobs later in life. Interestingly, their own self-images were not too closely linked with the work they were doing in school at the time. Those who had little hope of future success became involved with the police three times as often as those who expected to succeed. Those most prone to delinquency were not too different from the rest in most other respects. They were just as likely to belong to clubs and athletic groups and to be popular with their friends. Since the study did not follow the boys after they graduated, it is not known whether later experiences will change these patterns.

The professional thief

Our discussion of deviance and theories of deviance suggests that reputations and labels are important in helping people to become and remain deviant, as are opportunities for learning deviant ways, the lack of legitimate means to success, and negative views of one's future chances for success. People who turn to stealing for a living are, like white-collar criminals, "innovators," according to Merton's system of classification, although they are not given the status awarded to white-collar innovators. In one way they are better examples of the theory than are the white-collar criminials, because the latter usually have a chance at success by legitimate means but become deviant out of a wish to achieve success on a grand scale. The *professional thief* is a person who finds crime a means to a livelihood, accepts the self-image of thief, and even rationalizes such a choice of livelihood. He hopes for the "big haul," but usually he doesn't make it.

Many youths who grow up in high-crime areas, where there are many opportunities for learning crime, commit criminal acts only now and then; they don't take up crime as a career. For others, crime becomes a persistent pattern. In the insert on pages 258–259, Bob, a professional thief, presents his view of a criminal career as "hard work." He is more philosophical than most thieves and tries hard to rationalize his way

of life. Sociologists who specialize in the study of deviance can hardly argue with Bob's conclusions. If all the information we have about deviance were fed into a computer, it could not come up with a sure answer as to which child will go "straight" and which one will go "bent." Furthermore, this kind of prediction could become a case of self-fulfilling prophecy. Deviance theory has progressed since the days of Lombroso and Dugdale, but there is still much to learn.

WHITE-COLLAR CRIME
Getting organized

Over a period of years, crime in the United States has become an increasingly well-organized business. To some degree it has always been well organized in big cities. In Chapter 1, we discussed Robert K. Merton's analysis of the latent functions of the city boss. Merton noted that city bosses are not as common now as in the past, but connections between city officials, the police, and organized crime still exist. The fact that patterns of cooperation between these three groups have changed little is well illustrated by comparing the writings of Lincoln Steffens, a nineteenth-century "muckraker," with those of the contemporary criminologist Donald Cressey.

While he was still a young and naive reporter, Steffens had an envelope full of money stolen from him on a streetcar in New York City. He reported the matter to his friend, Police Commissioner Byrnes:

> I complained to Byrnes by 'phone; he asked how much was in the envelope, how the envelope was addressed, and what lines of cars I had used to go home and to dinner. When I answered all his questions, he said, "All right, I'll have it for you Monday morning." And Monday morning Brynes handed me the envelope with the money just as I had received it from my paper. (1931, pp. 222–223)

Courage of his convictions   TONY PARKER AND ROBERT ALLERTON

Q: My first question is this: If you were to describe yourself in one word, would the description invariably be "a criminal"?

A: Yes, definitely. That's what I am, I never think of myself in any other way.

Q: And have you any intention of changing, of going straight or reforming?

A: None whatever. There's one thing, though. I'd like to make clear at the start—and that is I don't want to try and pass myself off as a master criminal or anything like that. I'm not. I've had successes and failures in life like everyone else, and I'm nothing out of the ordinary as far as criminals go. . . .

Q: The thing that I find most difficult to understand about you is that you're apparently quite undeterred by your repeated prison sentences. You've now reached the stage, with your record, that when you're caught next time it's more than likely you'll get about eight years' preventive detention. I don't understand how you can be prepared to face that.

A: I'm not prepared. This is the thing which most people like you never grasp. I'm no more "prepared" to do eight years' P.D. than you're prepared to knock somebody down in your car tomorrow. I don't think too much about the one more than you do about the other. It's an ever-present risk, but one doesn't dwell on it—so you see what I mean? I've always got this thing in my mind, and so have other criminals like me—"it won't be this time that I'll get caught." . . .

Q: You don't think, then, that there's anything wrong in not working for your living?

A: But I do work for my living. Most crime—unless it's the senseless petty thieving sort—is quite hard work, you know. Planning a job, working out all the details of the best way to do it—and then carrying it out, under a lot of nervous strain and tension—and having to run around afterwards, if it's goods, fencing the stuff, getting a good price for it, delivering it to the fence, and so on—all this needs a lot of thinking and effort and concentration. It certainly is "work," don't kid yourself about that.

But anyway this whole point's not that simple. A lot of other people don't work for their living, in the way you mean—but nobody gets on them the way they do at criminals. Quite a large proportion of "upper classes" for instance . . . and usually it's that sort who get fiercest about people like me . . . I steal from people like that without the faintest compunction at all, in fact, I'm delighted to do it. . . .
[The conversation turns to violence, which Bob opposes in a philosophical way, but for a criminal it's often the only way out. When he was a boy, Bob and his friends went to burglarize an old woman. They put her in a chair and tied her up.]

So of course she starts screaming and raving like a mad woman. Before we went it had been decided it was going to be my job to keep her quiet. I rammed my shooter against her ear and said: "Belt it, you old faggot, or I'll pull the trigger."

It made not a blind bit of difference, she just yelled all the louder for help. The other two were turning everything to bits trying to find where she'd hidden her money, and this racket she was making was really getting on their nerves, so one of them said, "Oh, for Christ's sake hit the old bag, can't you? If you don't lay her out she'll have the whole neighborhood on us."

And I just couldn't do it. All I could do was stand there bleating, "Shut up, will you! I'm warning you, I'll pull the trigger!" Naturally it didn't stop her. Finally one of the other two walked over, took the gun out of my hand, and belted her unconscious. He put the gun back in my hand, really angry, and he said: "It's her or us, you silly bastard, can't you see that?"

It taught me the lesson, and after that I was all right. But I've never been keen on the idea of hitting old women, or old men for that matter. Just a personal weakness. . . .

Q: What really made you a criminal? Do you know?

A: . . . What made me a criminal? I could reel off a whole lot of reasons, but they'd only be part of the real answer. I'm always afraid of saying circumstances made me what I am, because I don't think they did entirely at all. Seeing my father, a straight man, getting only poverty all through his life for being straight . . . living in an environment where nearly everyone I knew was dishonest, where stealing was a necessity at some times, an adventure at others, but was always acceptable whatever the reasons . . . wanting to impress other kids, getting a reputation for being a tearaway . . . seeing the terrifying dreariness of the lives of other people who were "straight" . . . not being able to face working for a living because I hated the idea of work.

These were the circumstances, but they were only part of the answer. . . .

But you know, you're asking me a question that far better people than me can't answer. Some of them get paid for sitting in chairs at universities and trying to work out the answer to this one, don't they? People like Grunhut and Mannheim and Radzinowitz. "What makes criminals?" . . . they're working on it all the time, getting paid thousands a year to try to come up with the answer. . . .

And, well, sometimes some of them get near some of the answers. But they don't know the answer, any more than Lombroso . . . did. They can tell you about conditions, environment, heredity, reactions to treatment of one kind or another— but they still can't tell you why under one set of circumstances some people go bent and others go straight.

From *Courage of His Convictions*, Tony Parker and Robert Allerton, Hutchinson Publishing Group Limited, London, 1962.

Steffens was amazed by this quick and effective detective work. Other reporters who knew the city crime scene explained to him that Byrnes had passed the word along to the man in charge of pickpockets on that particular streetcar line that a friend of his had been robbed and he wanted the money back. Otherwise, they would lose their unofficial "right" to operate in the area.

Steffens' story is almost 100 years old. Do things still work the same way? Donald Cressey reported in the late 1960s:

The "favors" police do for organized criminals are sometimes returned in kind. A city official had a prostitute in his house while his wife was away. The whore stole a fur coat and the official noted its absence. He called a trusted police official, explained the situation, and said it would be embarrassing if the coat were still missing when his wife returned. The police official called a dozen prostitutes, with no success. He then revealed his plight to a Cosa Nostra lieutenant, keeping the name of the city official confidential. The lieutenant returned the coat two days later, but the police official kept it for another two days, then explained to the city official that diligent and delicate detective work was necessary for its retrieval. (1969, p. 263)

The intermediary in this case, as noted, was a member of the Cosa Nostra, a nationwide organized criminal structure also known as the Mafia. Cosa Nostra consists of twenty-four "families," which are loosely tied to each other. They vary in size and wealth and operate in many of our biggest cities. Their enterprises still include drugs, gambling, and prostitution, but they have now expanded into hotels and nightclubs, banks and loan companies, and real estate. Because of the size of their enterprises, the organizational structure has become more bureaucratic than that of the old "Mafia families" described in Chapter 5, but these groups still have friends in high places (Cressey, 1969, pp. 8–18).

Members of the upper levels of Cosa Nostra are rarely caught and convicted. Stuart Hills describes the generous treatment given to those Cosa Nostra leaders who are imprisoned:

In 1967, Sam Giancana, reputed Chicago syndicate boss, was the recipient of steaks and cigars personally delivered to the most comfortable cell in the Chicago county jail while a federal prisoner. In 1966 in Jersey City, another notorious criminal had private accomodations in the warden's quarters and access to female companions. Vito Genovese, former New York Cosa Nostra boss, reportedly continued to transmit major policy decisions to his "family" members during his eight years of federal imprisonment and to arrange cell assignments for friends. (Hills, 1971, p. 123)

We do not mean to imply that all city officials are controlled by the syndicate or that all are corrupt. To try to control everyone would be inefficient, risky, and expensive. It is much more efficient to establish control over just a few key figures, especially political bosses who help keep elected officials in office and to whom they are indebted. The chief of police or the captain of a vice-control squad can also be key figures through which organized crime can work.

When a zealous rookie police officer investigates a suspicious-looking gathering in the neighborhood he patrols that turns out to be a gambling enterprise and finds that his reports are repeatedly ignored, that the persons he arrests are later dismissed, or that he is assigned to a new patrol beat—he and the rest of the police force are likely to "get the message." (Hills, 1971, p. 124)

Discrimination in crime

According to Merton's theory of deviance, those who have no chance to succeed by legitimate means still feel the societal pressure to succeed. This helps to explain how a person born in the slums can eventually work for the Syndicate (a large association of racketeers controlling organized crime) or for smaller rings involved in similar activities. It leaves out a few details, however.

Figure 9-4 Carlo Gambino, former "boss of bosses" of organized crime. (*Wide World*)

The Syndicate decides who can have access to profitable criminal activity. Former Congressman Adam Clayton Powell protested on behalf of black gambling interests that the Syndicate makes large profits from Harlem, but it manages to drive out gambling and other profitable rackets owned by blacks (Hills, 1971, p. 123).

Many people who have little chance of success in either the legitimate or the criminal world choose "kicks" as an alternative. Addiction rates are high in ghetto areas. The profits from drug sales go to the Syndicate, while the poor of the black community suffer the damage that comes from drugs.

Victimless crimes and the Syndicate

Lawyers and judges use Latin terms to describe two types of forbidden acts: *malum in se* (those that are evil in themselves) and *malum prohibitum* (those that are evil because prohibited). The first class includes acts such as murder, rape, assault, and robbery. The second class includes crimes without victims—prostitution, illegal gambling, alcoholism, and homosexuality or lesbianism. All these "crimes" are important to those who stress the "labeling" view of deviance. These people hold that the only airtight definition of deviance is a circular one: The deviant is a person who is successfully tagged as deviant. Such a statement obviously allows one to criticize the labeling perspective on the grounds that many people would probably have become alcoholics or criminals whether they suffered from public labeling or not. On the other hand, the labeling perspective focuses on the criteria the public uses for calling people deviants. As Erich Goode comments, no one calls oppressors, exploiters, racists, or imperialists deviants, but they do far more harm than the people so labeled (Goode, 1975, pp. 570–583).

Crimes without victims are often closely tied to organized crime. Access to three of the five types of deviance listed above is provided by the organized-crime underworld. Alexander Smith and Harriet Pollack (1971) present a number of objections to considering such acts crimes. They point out that making prostitution, drug use, and gambling illegal helps to feed organized crime and, further, that the laws concerning these activities are inconsistent and unevenly enforced. The man who patronizes a prostitute is not considered a criminal, but the prostitute is. Similarly, getting drunk on alcohol is regarded as funny, but getting high on marijuana is a crime in many states. In New York, it is legal to gamble on the state lottery or to visit a city-run Off-Track Betting office, but private lotteries like the numbers game are illegal, as are private bookies. In California, gambling on horseraces is approved, but almost all other kinds of gambling are illegal. In Nevada, gambling is legal. (Does this mean that Nevadans are deviants?)

Laws against crimes without victims not only play into the hands of organized crime but also present other problems for law enforcement. Since there are no victims to bring charges or to testify, the police must produce all the evidence. It is in these cases that the police are most tempted to take liberties with the law, to use wiretaps, and to conduct raids without the required court orders. Prostitutes, more than any other class of criminals, are constantly subject to entrapment by police.

It is hard to change public attitudes about victimless crimes. The underworld has a financial interest in keeping these activities illegal and will fight against change with all the influence at its disposal. Most people are accustomed to viewing these acts as crimes, and they tend to think that removing them from the crime list would be the same as endorsing them. There is also a tendency to believe, contrary to the evidence, that these crimes are being held in check by present law enforcement methods. Whether or not one believes in legalizing crimes without victims, it is clear that current methods of dealing with these activities are not working.

New categories

Gresham Sykes, a prominent criminologist, suggests that new trends in deviance tend to refute the validity of older theories of deviance (1971). In the past, sociologists assumed that all people are interested in more or less the same goals of wealth and prestige. Those who fail by legal means try illegal means. Those who fail by both legal and illegal means become tramps, vagrants, or addicts. These explanations, in Sykes's opinion, do not fit new types of political crimes or certain types of "crime for fun" that have become prominent in recent years.

Crime for fun Albert Cohen, writing in the 1950s, described such a thing as vandalism for fun, but he saw this fun mainly as the release of anger by lower-class boys. The description of the Saints by Chambliss presents an even more clear-cut case of crime for fun. Now, says Sykes, many quite successful middle-class people attempt certain types of crime for fun:

> At the present time, however, there is a strong possibility that crime and delinquency as sport may be on the increase. Auto theft, for example, is often a kind of game, a white-collar form of juvenile dating; and in the last ten years, according to Uniform Crime Re-

Figure 9-5 Since (*a*) the possession and use of alcohol are legal, and since the possibility of addiction is as great as with (*b*) marijuana, many argue that the illegality of marijuana is inconsistent. [*(a) Wide World; (b) Paul Conklin, Monkmeyer*]

(a)

(b)

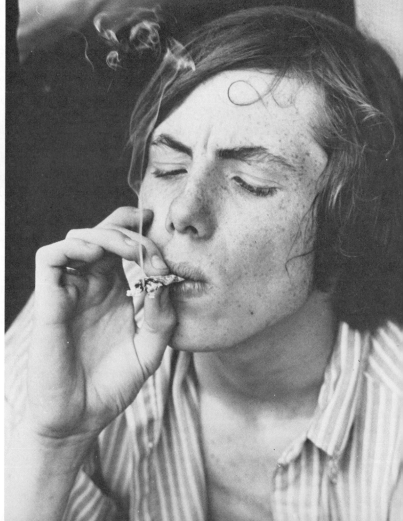

ports of the FBI, the rate has gone up 138 percent. There are also many reports that shop-lifting is showing a marked growth, not simply among the poor, but among those well up the socioeconomic scale and often by people who are stealing neither from need nor compulsion, but from a search for excitement. Secretaries in New York, for example, are reported sometimes to find stealing from Macy's far more appealing than a luncheon at Schrafft's. (Sykes, 1971; reprinted from *The American Scholar*, vol. 40, no. 4, Autumn 1971. Copyright © 1971 by the United Chapters of Phi Beta Kappa. By permission of the publishers)

Sykes goes on to suggest that the challenge of outsmarting electronic "gadgets" provides a motivation for middle-class crime. The "computer bandits" and people who devise clever ways to make free long-distance phone calls have fun trying to beat an impersonal electronic system.

Political crimes *Political crimes* are crimes against the state—either subversive, terroristic, or treasonable acts or the flagrant misuse of power. Such crimes are by no means new, but Sykes considers the possibility for abuse of political power now to be greater than in the past because of the growing role of government and secret government agencies. Terrorism also, although not new, has become more common. It is aided both by the growth of fanatical groups and by more effective weapons and techniques. Seizures of hostages, assassinations, and acts of sabotage have become increasingly common in both the United States and Europe and even more so in the Middle East.

Victims without crime

Many business corporations establish offices and plants around the world in order to conduct activities that would be illegal at home. A firm from one country can locate in another in order to escape paying taxes or in order to pay wages that are below the minimum standard in the United States. Some American companies sell goods in foreign countries that would not pass inspection at home. If these goods included only relatively harmless items, such as badly made clothing, the problem would not be too serious; but manufacturers of prescription drugs are major offenders in this area. Manufacturers of drugs sold in Latin America do not have to comply with labeling and warning regulations established by the American Pure Food and Drug Acts. Consequently, American companies that sell harmful or inadequately labeled drugs in Latin America are committing no crimes (as defined by law), but they are killing a large number of victims. (See the insert on page 264, "U.S. Drug Firms' Practices Kill and Injure Many in Latin America, Scientist Charges.")

Deviance takes many forms, changing with the times and with the schemes of the deviants. Societal reactions to deviance also change, but there is a tendency to see only what is most conspicuous and to worry about victimless crime while whole nations are being victimized.

SUMMARY

One day's newspaper accounts are used to show the prevalence and variety of the type of deviant behavior classified as crime. Stories included a killing; several violations of laws by athletes; such business crimes as price-fixing, stealing business secrets, giving false data, and violating safety regulations; such crimes by people in authority as mistreatment of mental patients and children; and such political crimes as terrorism by radicals, illegal burglarizing by the F.B.I., and financial misconduct by a member of the House of Representatives. Finally, there is a report of a man poisoning and killing 15 million of his neighbor's bees.

These reports omit such types of deviant behavior as socially disapproved sex acts, alco-

U.S. drug firms' practices kill and injure many in Latin America, scientist charges RICHARD C. PADDOCK

A University of California pharmacologist charged . . . that practices of U.S. drug companies in Latin America killed and injured many people there by not fully disclosing to foreign physicians the potential hazards of some drugs and by "grossly" exaggerating the drugs' effectiveness.

D. Milton Silverman testified before a Senate small business subcommittee that if the companies were to use the same promotion practices in the United States that they do in Latin America they would be in violation of the Food and Drug Administration regulations.

"I find great difficulty in understanding how a company can describe one of its products as dangerous in San Diego but safe a few miles across the border in Tijuana," he said.

Silverman said the drug companies claimed their promotion practices did not violate the laws of any Latin American country, and resulted from "honest differences" with the Food and Drug Administration, which regulates the drug industry in the United States.

Silverman, who said he had spent two years researching the subject, including three months in Latin American countries, testified that he found "glaring inconsistencies" in the promotion of antibiotics, oral contraceptives, antidepressants and other drugs here and in Latin American countries. . . .

According to Silverman, Latin American doctors "have told us of cases of permanent brain damage caused by excessive use of antipsychotic tranquilizers—and sometimes by tranquilizers given to control bed-wetting or nail-biting in children."

He testified that in U.S. pharmaceutical manuals the list of "warnings and possible adverse reactions is lengthy and detailed. . . . The potential hazards published in the Latin American volumes are usually minimized, glossed over, or totally ignored. In some cases not a single danger is disclosed."

Senator J. Glenn Beall, Jr. (R.-Md.), acting subcommittee chairman, said that the government could not act in the matter because FDA regulations did not cover companies that bottle and label drugs outside the United States.

By Richard C. Paddock, *Los Angeles Times*, May 27, 1976, Part I, p. 5. Copyright © 1976, Los Angeles Times. Reprinted by permission.

holism, drug abuse, and mental illness. What is particularly striking is that so many of the stories involve supposedly respectable people—bussinesspeople, F.B.I. agents, caretakers of the mentally ill, athletes, and politicians. Equally important, not all people would agree on the seriousness of the alleged crimes. The public generally lists as "most serious" such acts of violence against the person as murder and rape and such acts against property as burglary and theft. In the public mind, *deviance* refers more specifically to homosexuality and lesbianism, drug addiction, alcoholism, and mental illness.

Deviance refers to any behavior that varies markedly from the norms acceptable to a society. Although the definition is generally valid, not all people agree about the norms and norms change over time. Even the police rarely enforce some types of laws that seem out of date relative to the norms.

Diversity and strain

Deviance, especially serious crime, was often explained in the nineteenth century as the result of bad heredity. This hereditary theory of crime, now rejected, helped to widen the feelings of difference between "good" and "bad" people, hardly recognizing any stages in between. In more recent times, theories of deviance have focused on the environment. Clifford Shaw, for example, described the *ethnic succession of crime*—that is, that certain parts of cities remained high-delinquency areas regardless of which ethnic groups occupied them.

Merton's *theory of deviance* maintains that American society has a high crime rate because there is no clear connection between the success goals imposed by society and access to the legitimate means to reach these goals. Many are denied legitimate means for success, either because of discrimination or social-class background, and our society judges people by financial success. Therefore, there are strong temptations to succeed by deviant means. Merton speaks of those who succeed by socially approved means as *conformists* and those who succeed by devious means as *innovators*. He also classifies the *ritualists*—those who try honestly but fail; *realists* who give up the struggle; and *rebels* against the system.

Sutherland's theory of *differential association* also sees the reasons for deviance as social in nature. We learn illegal ways by association, just as we learn much of our other behavior by association with others. Sutherland is particularly interested in *white-collar crime*, or crime committed by politicians, businesspeople, and others who appear to be respectable. His theory also offers an explanation for the learning of other types of deviance in areas where there are models for such learning—drug abuse, theft, or gang violence, for example.

Since lower-class boys are apt to be reared in high-delinquency areas, it is not surprising that they are arrested for delinquency more often than middle-class boys. Albert Cohen explains lower-class delinquency as partly the result of hostility against middle-class norms. A study by William Chambliss, however, seems to show that lower-class boys may not be more delinquent than others—they simply tend to receive a "bad press."

The case described by Chambliss illustrates the *labeling theory* of deviance—the idea that society labels people in certain ways and causes them to think of themselves as deviants. The self-image is very important in determining whether delinquency will persist. Caplan, in a study of boys in a high-delinquency area, found that the trait most predictive of delinquency is the expectation of failure in school and in later life—the result of a negative self-image.

Many delinquent youths eventually give up their deviant ways, but some do not. Some become *professional thieves*. An excerpt from an interview with a professional thief (more philosophical than most) shows the full acceptance of a deviant self-image and also considerable rationalizing of deviant behavior.

Many criminals are protected by crime organizations, collectively referred to as the Mafia, the Cosa Nostra, or the Syndicate. Organized crime often has ties with political machines and business interests, but it thrives especially on such "victimless crimes" as gambling, prostitution, and drug abuse.

Gresham Sykes notes an increase in the 1960s and 1970s in new categories of crime: political crimes (especially terrorism and abuse of power) and crimes for fun.

It is also possible to violate social norms without committing a crime if such a violation is not defined as a crime. An example is given of the drug industry. It is accused of recklessness in selling and promoting drugs overseas—especially in Latin America—where there are fewer laws against products that can endanger life and health.

Study guide

Terms to know

Deviant behavior
Crimes without victims
Hereditary theory of crime
Ethnic succession in crime
Relative deprivation
Anomie
Merton's theory of deviance:
  Conformist

Innovator
Ritualist
Retreatist
Rebel
White-collar crime
Differential association
Labeling theory
Stigmatize

Professional thief
Cosa Nostra (Mafia)
The Syndicate
Malum in se
Malum prohibitum
Political crimes
Crimes for fun

Names to know

Cesare Lombroso
Clifford Shaw
Robert K. Merton
Edwin H. Sutherland

Howard Becker
Donald Cressey
Gresham Sykes
Albert Cohen

Self-test

Part I. Multiple Choice. Select the best of the four alternative answers:

1 Besides such common crimes as theft, deviant behavior includes (**a**) abuse of power by officials, (**b**) white-collar crime, (**c**) strange behavior resulting from mental illness, (**d**) all the above.

2 In a survey, the public rated which of the following as most deviant? (**a**) murder and rape, (**b**) homosexuality, (**c**) felonious assault, (**d**) revolutionary activities.

3 A study in Chicago indicates that the Chicago police are not likely to enforce laws against (**a**) social gambling, (**b**) petty larceny, (**c**) prostitution, (**d**) all the above.

4 Poverty and crime are most apt to be associated together in cases (**a**) of generally poor countries, (**b**) of poor rural areas, (**c**) where absolute deprivation is present, (**d**) where relative deprivation is obvious.

5 In Merton's analysis, the person most respected by society is the conformist; just below this person in esteem is the (**a**) innovator, (**b**) retreatist, (**c**) ritualist, (**d**) rebel.

6 The computer bandits described in an insert would be classified by Merton as (**a**) innovators, (**b**) retreatists, (**c**) ritualists, (**d**) rebels.

7 The main aim in life of the "cat" described in the text is (**a**) monetary success, (**b**) "kicks," (**c**) getting even with "whitey," (**d**) finding a girl to marry.

8 Sutherland's differential association theory attributes crime to (**a**) evil intent, (**b**) learning, (**c**) abnormal chromosomes, (**d**) social-class deprivation.

9 In Albert Cohen's theory of delinquency, more delinquency is found among lower-class boys

Diversity and strain

than others because of (**a**) learning illegal behavior at home, (**b**) association with the underworld, (**c**) resentment of a middle-class world, (**d**) none of the above.

10 A follow-up study of the Saints and the Roughnecks several years later illustrates (**a**) the self-fulfilling prophecy, (**b**) "The first shall be the last and the last, first," (**c**) the advantages of studying hard in high school, (**d**) the principles of justice.

11 The labeling theory of deviance is consistent with (**a**) Cooley's idea of the looking-glass self, (**b**) the self-fulfilling prophecy, (**c**) the good-boy study by Reckless mentioned in a previous chapter, (**d**) all the above.

12 Norman Caplan found that the most important factor in predicting freedom from delinquency was (**a**) grade in school, (**b**) expectation of future success, (**c**) belonging to school clubs, (**d**) being other-directed.

13 Donald Cressey tells of a case in which a politician's wife's coat was stolen by a prostitute. To recover the coat, the politician had to depend on (**a**) the police, (**b**) a private detective, (**c**) a madame, (**d**) a Cosa Nostra lieutenant.

14 Crimes without victims (**a**) are a fruitful ground for organized crime, (**b**) are generally not organized, (**c**) are cases in which both the supplier and the patron are defined as criminals, (**d**) are ignored by law-enforcement officials.

15 An account of the practices of drug firms accuses them of (**a**) monopolistic practices, (**b**) failing to warn doctors in the United States of the possible hazards of their drugs, (**c**) failing to warn Latin American doctors of the possible hazards of their drugs, (**d**) bribing Latin American officials to get more markets.

Part II. True-False Questions

1 Only under dictatorships can some types of behavior be described as political crime.

2 Acts that are deviant from the point of view of the majority are not necessarily deviant from everyone's point of view.

3 The famous study of the Jukes family is cited as a case of improper methodology.

4 Modern sociologists place little or no credence in theories that crime is due to heredity.

5 Merton's theory of deviant behavior contends that society believes in certain success goals but has no norms regarding the means by which they should be achieved.

6 The retreatist follows neither the goals nor the means subscribed to by society.

7 The Croatian terrorists whose skyjacking is described in the text were hated by the air crew and passengers.

8 Types of criminal activity can be learned in some businesses as standard operating procedures, even in businesses that are considered legitimate.

9 In the study of the Saints and the Roughnecks, the delinquent behavior of the lower-class Roughnecks was more easily observed than that of the Saints.

10 Somewhat at variance with Cohen's theory, the middle-class Saints committed many acts of malicious mischief.

11 Although Bob, the professional thief, was a thief all his life, he liked to rationalize that he was not really a criminal.

12 Bob, the thief, went to great pains to rationalize away the accusation that he did not work for a living.

13 Bob was convinced that his poor home background had made him a criminal.

14 It is hard to corrupt a police force without corrupting every member.

15 Attempts to prosecute crimes without victims, such as illegal gambling, are more likely than other types of prosecution to lead to illegal police methods.

Questions for discussion

1 Argue the case for and against the police's use of decoys who pretend to be prostitutes in order to entrap men. Who is deviant in this case, the men being entrapped or the police?
2 Why is it difficult to define deviance simply as the violation of social norms?
3 Why were hereditary explanations of crime so popular in the nineteenth century? What appeal did they have for righteous people?
4 Explain the concept of relative deprivation and how it applies to the connection between poverty and crime. Can you think of other applications for the concept of relative deprivation? For example, does it apply to male-female relationships or to minority groups?
5 Give as many examples as you can of the innovator and the rebel in Merton's theory.
6 Sutherland's theory of differential association applies to all people. What learning experiences and associations have you had that would make you inclined to violate norms? What learning experiences and associations have you had that would make you uphold the norms?
7 After reading the account of the Saints and the Roughnecks, can you think of any similar cases in your own experience in which some people have been stigmatized for delinquent behavior and others have not?
8 The labeling theory obviously applies to other types of cases than those mentioned in the text. How would labeling make it difficult for a mental patient to be reintegrated into society? An ex-convict?
9 Can you think of other cases of "victims without crimes"—that is, situations in which the public is victimized by practices that do not actually violate laws?

Projects

1 Interview managers of local department stores regarding shoplifting—kinds of people involved, problems of detection, problems of getting convictions, and whether any such conduct seems to be "crime for fun."
2 Interview a young person who has spent considerable time at juvenile hall. From the story he or she tells, does it sound as though the problems are best summed up as:
   a Resentment, as Albert Cohen would assume.
   b Ability to succeed only by deviant means, as Merton might expect.
   c The result of differential association, or of too much association with delinquent attitudes and practices and not enough with normative attitudes and practices.
   d Partly the consequence of labeling and adopting a deviant self-image.
   e The feeling that life holds no acceptable future, as in the cases studied by Caplan.
   f Other explanations. Specify.
3 Follow newspaper accounts for one week and pick out good examples of Merton's five types of adjustment to goals and means: conformists, innovators, ritualists, retreatists, and rebels.

Suggested readings

Bowers, Faubion: "Homosex: Living the Life," *Saturday Review*, vol. 55, February 12, 1972, pp. 23–28. As mentioned in the text, a survey of public opinion placed homosexuality at the top of the "deviance" list. Will this attitude change now that gay organizations are fighting for their rights? This article discusses various explanations of homosexuality, explains the stigma, and explodes many popular myths.

Fannin, Leon, and Marshall Clinard: "Differences in the Conception of Self as a Male among Lower- and Middle-Class Delinquents," *Social Problems*, vol. 13, Fall 1965, pp. 205–214. Does a he-man definition of maleness lead to the undoing of many lower-class boys? How does the middle-class delinquency pattern allow an easier return to social respectability?

Goode, Erich: "On Behalf of Labeling Theory," *Social Problems*, vol. 22, June 1975, pp. 570–583. Labeling theory may not explain all cases of deviance, but it focuses attention on society's strange ways of labeling people, such as calling a lower-class heavy drinker a "drunkard" and an upper-class heavy drinker a "problem drinker." Goode also asks, why, for example, are oppression, exploitation, racism, and imperialism not labeled as deviant?

Lipset, Seymour Martin, and Earl Raab: "An Appointment with Watergate," *Commentary*, vol. 56, September 1973, pp. 35–43. Two distinguished sociologists write on the connection between characteristics of American society and the Watergate crimes, finding connections between the Nixon administration, the Ku Klux Klan of the 1920s, and McCarthyism—all explained partly as cases of paranoia over radicalism.

Newsweek, editors: "Living with Crime, U.S.A.," *Newsweek*, vol. 80, December 18, 1972, pp. 31–34. Is fear of crime helping to create some of the conditions that escalate crime rates? Of what help is the Legal Assistance Administration? Why is rape the least-punished crime? *Newsweek* tries to deal with all these questions and the general trends in crime.

Szasz, Thomas S.: "The Ethics of Addiction," *Harper's Magazine*, vol. 244, April 1972, pp. 74–79. Thomas Szasz may seem extreme in his position, but read what this nonconforming psychiatrist has to say about removing all laws against the use of drugs. He would remove one type of crime from the long list of victimless crimes.

Verlarde, Albert J., and Mark Warlick: "Massage Parlors: The Sensuality Business," *Society*, vol. 71, November–December 1973, pp. 63–74. An article describing the massage parlors that give "locals" and other types of sexual pleasure. It is more than mere description, however. It notes the close connection between a highly respectable clientele and a business that is frequently harassed by police forces and self-appointed guardians of public morals.

Wellford, Charles: "Labeling Theory and Criminology: An Assessment," *Social Problems*, vol. 22, February 1975, pp. 332–345. Is the labeling theory an adequate tool for explaining a deviant self-image and therefore the perpetuation of deviance? No, says Wellford, after a thorough analysis of its assumptions. Situations have more to do with deviant acts than does self-concept. (Goode's article, mentioned above, gives the opposite side of the argument.)

Key to questions. Multiple Choice: 1-d; 2-b; 3-a; 4-d; 5-a; 6-a; 7-b; 8-b; 9-c; 10-a; 11-d; 12-b; 13-d; 14-a; 15-c. True-False: 1-F, 2-T, 3-T, 4-T, 5-F, 6-T, 7-F, 8-T, 9-T, 10-T, 11-F, 12-T, 13-F, 14-F, 15-T.

This chapter examines types of institutions that are not well known to the outside world, particularly prisons and mental institutions. After reading it, you should be able to:

1 Understand the principles behind the forms of punishment given to prisoners and sometimes to the mentally ill.

2 Understand the meaning of total institutions and see the problems such institutions have in trying to rehabilitate or resocialize inmates.

3 Understand in terms of interactionist analysis how the role of guard can have a brutalizing effect, which is made worse if prisoners are used as guards.

4 Understand the problems in trying to relate sentence length and rehabilitation.

5 Explain and criticize the methods being used in prisons to resocialize inmates, particularly new behavior modification techniques.

6 Be aware of cases where persons are placed in mental institutions for a long time without therapy and of present laws to prevent this.

7 Recognize the problem of stigmatizing former prisoners or mental patients.

10

TOTAL
INSTITUTIONS

In the last chapter we observed that society likes to draw clear distinctions between the good and the bad, the deviant and the nondeviant. One function of the system is to divide the law-abiding from delinquents or criminals. In ancient and some contemporary societies, criminals were maimed or disfigured. This practice served three functions: (1) it widened the gap between them and law-abiding people; (2) it made them easy to identify, warning others of them; and (3) it made it impossible for criminals to return to any society but the criminal subculture. In modern societies, we imprison criminals rather than maiming them, but prisons work in a similar way. They set the good apart from the bad. Sometimes they have the latent function of making it impossible for inmates to adjust to the outside world.

Mental institutions have changed considerably from the times of Old Bedlam Street, London, where passersby entertained themselves by watching and teasing the mentally ill inmates. Today, the treatment is different. In many institutions, it is both conscientious and somewhat effective. However, some institutions resembling the original "Bedlam" hospital can still be found. In these institutions, patients are mistreated and don't receive therapy, records are lost, and sometimes the wrong people are institutionalized. In the following pages, we will move from a discussion of penal institutions, such as jails and prisons, to a discussion of mental hospitals, stressing the similarities between them.

THEORIES OF PUNISHMENT

The earliest known system of written laws is that of the Mesopotamian ruler Hammurabi, of about 1700 B.C. These laws were based on the idea of *retribution* or *revenge*. According to this legal code, society should treat the criminal as the criminal had treated the victim:

> If a man has knocked out the *eye* of a patrician, his *eye* shall be knocked out. (Law 196)
> If he has broken the limb of a patrician, his limb shall be broken. (Law 197)

The laws of Moses, preserved in the Old Testament, also propose retribution as the proper punishment for a criminal:

> . . . Thou shalt give life for life, eye for eye, tooth for tooth, hand for hand, foot for foot, burning for burning, wound for wound, stripe for stripe. (Exod. 21:23–25)

Societies sometimes think of punishment in terms of *atonement*. This means a chance for the individual to repent and make himself or herself acceptable to a god or gods. In medieval Europe, this rationalization was used in the burning of witches and heretics: only if they had undergone great suffering could they be purified.

Another social view is that punishment should serve as a *deterrent*. In this view, the punished criminal is an example of what can happen to anyone who breaks the law. The punishment is a warning to others, to restrain them from crime. To this day, the principle of deterrence is a rationale for long sentences and the death penalty.

Yet another justification for punishment is that of protecting the public by *disabling* the offender, so that he or she will commit no more crimes. If offenders are killed, they are no longer dangerous to society. If they are locked up for life, the same is true.

Durkheim suggested that societies punish lawbreakers not for revenge but for *reaffirmation of the norms*, to prove to themselves that their ways are right. If the wicked are punished and the innocent are freed, people see justice in operation, the value of laws is confirmed, and the system appears to work well.

The concept of justice may serve as a means of retribution, atonement, deterrence, disablement, or a reaffirmation of norms. It varies somewhat from the idea on which our present penal system is supposedly built—the idea of *rehabilitation*. Rehabilitation theory assumes that a person can be changed and made an acceptable and functioning member of society. Ideally, rehabilitation does not depend on imprisonment. Sometimes probation or a suspended sentence are used instead. The usual way of rehabilitating criminals, though, is to lock them up in jails or prisons, where punishment still plays a large role in the treatment. In the prisons, attempts are made to change the prisoners' behavior, either by teaching them new skills that will help them on the outside, by giving them group therapy, or by using drugs, electric shocks, or even psychosurgery to change their personalities. A few of the same techniques are used for mental patients. The difference is that in mental hospitals these procedures are seen only as means of rehabilitation, not as punishment.

What are the special characteristics of such institutions as prisons and mental hospitals? What social relationships develop there? Do these places really cure people of crime or of mental disorders? Can the problems causing crime and mental illness be found in social systems rather than in individual pathology?

CHARACTERISTICS OF TOTAL INSTITUTIONS

Erving Goffman (1961a) defines *total institutions* as those that totally control their inmates' lives, regulating all their activities without their consent or even their knowledge of what will happen to them from day to day. Their aim is that of drastic resocialization. In his investigations of total institutions, Goffman uses a method called *ideal-*

type analysis. That is, the sociologist conducts observational studies of many institutions and groups of people and then identifies the most important traits they share. The institutions and people will vary to some degree, but on the whole they will reveal a typical or "ideal" pattern. Doctors use a similar method to diagnose and treat disease. Children with measles do not always display identical symptoms, but the doctor's knowledge of the "ideal" form of the disease helps the diagnosis. In the case of total institutions, no two of them are identical, but the sociologist's *ideal type* increases our understanding of what we are looking at as we enter a particular prison, mental institution, or military boot camp.

In ordinary life, we sleep and eat at one place, work at another place, and go out to yet other places for recreation. All these activities are shared with different groups of people. In total institutions, these activities are restricted to one place. They are organized by a central authority, and the same groups are involved. All activities are designed by the institution itself to carry out its own purpose. The individual inmate has no control over his or her life and does not know when release will come. Inmates who are mental patients do not know their labels or diagnoses.

Inmates and staff

Total institutions include distinct groups of people: inmates, who make up the larger group, and staff, which is usually much smaller. Each group regards the other as being made up of very different types of people. Their relationship to each other is usually hostile. In prisons, inmates stereotype the guards as high-handed, arrogant, and potentially brutal. The guards see the inmates as untrustworthy, potentially dangerous, and deserving of their punishment. As a result, two separate social systems develop, both of which must be learned by the new inmate (see the insert "Cons and Fish").

In the mental institution too, antagonistic ster-

Cons and fish   DAE H. CHANG AND WARREN B. ARMSTRONG

Upon entering prison one is told that if he breaks an institutional rule, he will be given a ticket or a report by an officer and if one has too many tickets he will not make parole. The institutional rules are so broad they encompass everything from not wearing socks to masturbation. The prison officials are using the inmates' desire for freedom to force conformity. By this they are putting the inmates under pressure. This is not the only source of pressure.

Upon entering prison, the "fish" (new inmate) is put under pressure by the older "cons" to conform to the convicts' code of ethics, which consists of rules such as not telling on other inmates, not talking to the officer unless he speaks first, etc.

If the "fish" is young, white and good looking, pressure will be applied by the older "cons" to make him a "queen." If a new inmate shows any sign of fear, pressure will be applied for his commissary [things he can buy at the commissary].

The institutional rules and the convict's code of ethics are in direct conflict with each other. The inmate is in the middle with both sides trying to claim him.

Each day I hear officials ask why? Why did this model inmate suddenly explode? The answer is simple—pressure or tension.

The prisons are nothing more than bomb factories. Through pressure they are creating "human time bombs" which will either explode in prison or on the streets once an inmate is released.

Writings of Prisoner No. Eight.

From Dae H. Chang and Warren B. Armstrong, *The Prison: Voices from the Inside*, Schenkman Publishing Co., Cambridge, Mass., 1972, pp. 157–158.

---

eotypes develop. The staff view patients with pity or contempt, and patients fear the staff. Social distance between the two groups is very great. This distance is maintained by limiting communication not only between staff and inmates but also among the inmates themselves. Limiting communication applies especially to withholding knowledge about the inmate's fate. It also includes trying to suppress rumors or gossip about it. "Whether the official grounds are military, as in concealing travel destination from the ranks, or medical, as in concealing diagnosis . . . such exclusion gives staff a special basis of distance from and control over inmates" (Goffman, 1961b, pp. 19–20).

Mortification and will breaking

Since the goal of the total institution is to change the inmate's behavior, the inmate's original self is broken down by what Goffman calls the *mortification process*. In this process, the institution strips inmates of self-respect and status to create a complete break with the past. Visitors may come only when allowed. Defiant inmates find themselves in a will-breaking contest in which they are bound to lose. (One example of how this works is provided by *One Flew Over the Cuckoo's Nest*, first a novel by Ken Kesey and then a movie.) Along with their old status, the inmates lose their personal property and anything else that would mark them as different or distinct. All inmates wear the same uniforms. They are given regulation haircuts, and even the smallest possessions, such as combs, are taken from them.

Communication also becomes a mortifying experience. Inmates are forced to hide their feelings in conversation and must submit to verbal abuse without reacting—either verbally or

Figure 10-1 Prisoners are routinely stripped of their clothes and personal property. Obedience to guards and all other authority figures is stressed. (*Danny Lyon, Magnum*)

by gesture. Conversations between inmates and staff do not involve give and take. They consist of what Goffman calls *contaminative exposure*—the dredging up of all the inmate's secrets. This information is put in the files and may be used later on. David Rosenhan describes the limits on conversation and privacy which he and his associates found. In 1971–1972, they paid several visits to a mental hospital, posing as patients.

> [The inmate] is shorn of credibility. . . . His freedom of movement is restricted. He cannot initiate contact with the staff, but may only respond to such overtures as they make. Personal privacy is minimal. Patient quarters and possessions can be entered and examined by any staff member for any reason. His personal history and anguish is available to any member . . . who chooses to read his folder. . . . His personal hygiene and waste evacuation are often monitored. The water closets may not have doors. (1973, pp. 250–258. Copyright 1973 by

the American Association for the Advancement of Science)

There are many physical examinations. Normal sexual activity is usually prohibited. This leads to frustration and homosexual episodes. The sense of identity and worth as a man or woman is eroded. Regarding total control over lives, Goffman notes that on the outside, people decide for themselves when to get up, when to eat, when to exercise, to shower, to make the bed, and what to say in greeting others. Only children have these decisions made for them. All these actions become regulated in total institutions, and the inmate loses the right to act like an adult.

The privilege system

The inmate who follows the rules carefully gains access to a few privileges which seem very minor but which stand for the outside world. Cigarettes, newspapers, candy, and extra coffee or time off from working assignments become great rewards, valued far more highly than an outsider could ·ever imagine. The privilege system is the chief means by which an institution provides positive reinforcement for change in behavior. (*Positive reinforcement* is any reward or desired experience that helps strengthen desired behavior.) Ironically, these reinforcements often teach the inmate how to be a good inmate rather than how to function in the outside world. The privilege system also gives the inmate a little control over his or her world.

In many cases inmates try to gain control over their environment through an inside black market. They deal in drugs, cigarettes, and other desired items that are stolen from the institution or smuggled in from the outside. An informal organization grows up, complete with a system of rules and means of punishing squealers. The inmate system may have its own pattern of ingroups and outgroups. Accounts of prison life published by Chang and Armstrong (1972) describe a three-part social system which includes guards, white inmates, and black inmates. In most of these systems, the black prisoners outnumber the whites and have the highest positions of power and prestige.

Total institutions interest sociologists for a variety of reasons besides their outward functions of rehabilitation or cure. They become miniature societies of their own. They are separate and invisible to most people unless government investigations or inmate riots attract attention. They are totalitarian societies within a democratic society. In prisons, especially, people are thrown together in new combinations: embezzlers with murderers, auto thieves with rapists, drug peddlers with pickpockets.

Is Goffman's analysis, which pulls together the characteristics of many institutions, exaggerated? Experimental evidence based on a study by Philip Zimbardo, of Stanford University, would indicate that the answer is "no," at least for prisons.

A SIMULATED PRISON

In a 1973 study of American prisons, William Nagel examined new prisons that presumably were more humanitarian than older prisons. Nagel found that regardless of their good intentions for reform, all these prisons showed some of the characteristics of total institutions noted by Goffman. Dehumanization and corruption existed even in prisons that were originally administered by good, decent people. Nagel concluded that the prison experience eventually becomes degrading both to those who are guarded and those who guard.

A year earlier, Philip Zimbardo conducted an experiment in what he called "prisonization" (1972, pp. 4–8). He set up a simulated prison on the Stanford campus and hired twenty-four young men. At random, he gave some of the men the role of prisoner and others the role of guard. This random assignment kept him from choosing "guards" who preferred that role be-

cause they liked to dominate others. In the experiment, guards were expected to keep prisoners under control and prevent escape, but they were not to use physical punishment. All the subjects were screened for physical and mental health, and those who showed antisocial behavior or attitudes were dropped. All were college students from Stanford or nearby.

The experiment began as mock police officers arrested the students, charged them with suspicion of armed robbery, booked them, searched them, handcuffed them, and read them their rights. When they got to the prison, the subjects were stripped, sprayed with a delousing agent, photographed, and ordered to remain silent. Part of the mortification process was accomplished by making all the prisoners wear uniforms consisting of a sort of nightshirt decorated with prison numbers. Prisoners were allowed three meals per day and three supervised visits to the toilet. They were also supposed to have reading time and movie privileges, but some of their rights were ignored after a few days. The discouraging results of the prison experiment were described by Dr. Zimbardo in the insert on pages 276–277: "Pathology of Imprisonment."

Simulated prison compared with real prison

Zimbardo's prison experiment would lead us to believe that brutality is inevitable for prison guards. It develops in the prison itself, even if it was not a character trait before the person became a guard. Goffman's analysis and Nagel's study support this conclusion.

However, there are also certain traits of prisoner-guard interaction that were not developed in the simulated prison but are often found in real prisons. These traits both soften the harshness of the prison system and lead to its corruption (Sykes, 1967, pp. 175–186). In real life, prisons do not always conform to the ideal pattern of a total institution. Prisoners are not completely docile. Since the guards are in con-

Pathology of imprisonment   PHILIP G. ZIMBARDO

At the end of only six days we had to close down our mock prison because what we saw was frightening. It was no longer apparent to most of the subjects (or to us) where reality ended and their roles began. The majority had indeed become prisoners or guards, no longer able to clearly differentiate between role playing and self. There were dramatic changes in virtually every aspect of their behavior, thinking and feeling. In less than a week the experience of imprisonment undid (temporarily) a lifetime of learning; human values were suspended, self-concepts were challenged and the ugliest, most base, pathological side of human nature surfaced. We were horrified because we saw some boys (guards) treat others as if they were despicable animals, taking pleasure in cruelty, while other boys (prisoners) became servile, dehumanized robots who thought only of escape, of their own individual survival and of their mounting hatred for the guards.

We had to release three prisoners in the first four days because they had such acute situational traumatic reactions as hysterical crying, confusion in thinking and severe depression. Others begged to be paroled, and all but three were willing to forfeit all the money they had earned if they could be paroled. By then (the fifth day) they had been so programmed to think of themselves as prisoners that when their request for parole was denied, they returned docilely to their cells. Now, had they been thinking as college students acting in an oppressive experiment, they would have quit once they no longer wanted the $15 a day we used as our only incentive. However, the reality was not quitting an experiment but "being paroled by the parole board from the Stanford County Jail. . . ."

About a third of the guards became tyrannical in their arbitrary use of power, in enjoying their control over other people. They were corrupted by the power of their roles and became quite inventive in their techniques of breaking the spirit of the prisoners and making them feel they were worthless. Some of the guards merely did their jobs as tough but fair correctional officers, and several were good guards from the prisoners' point of view since they did them small favors and were friendly. However, no good guard ever interfered with a command by any of the bad guards; they never intervened on the side of the prisoners, they never told the others to ease off because it was only an experiment, and they never even came to me as prison superintendent or experimenter in charge to complain. In part, they were good be-cause the others were bad; they needed the others to help establish their own egos in a positive light. In a sense, the good guards perpetuated the prison more than the other guards because their own needs to be liked prevented them from disobeying or violating the implicit guards' code. At the same time, the act of befriending the prisoners created a social reality which made the prisoners less likely to rebel.

By the end of the week the experiment had become a reality. . . . The consultant for our prison, Carlo Prescott, an ex-convict with 16 years of imprisonment in California's jails, would get so depressed and furious each time he visited our prison, because of its psychological similarity to his experiences, that he would have to leave. A Catholic priest who was a former prison chaplain in Washington, D.C., talked to our prisoners after four days and said they were just like the other first-timers he had seen.

But in the end, I called off the experiment not because of the horror I saw out there in the prison yard, but because of the horror of realizing that *I* could have easily traded places with the most brutal guard or become the weakest prisoner full of hatred at being so powerless that I could not eat, sleep or go to the toilet without permission of the authorities. *I* could have become Calley at My Lai, George Jackson at San Quentin, one of the men at Attica or the prisoner quoted at the beginning of this article. [The quote referred to was from a very embittered prisoner who had spent 37 months in solitary, along with beatings, sprayings with chemicals, and having to sleep naked on a cold concrete floor.] . . .

With regard to prisons, we can state that the mere act of assigning labels to people and putting them into a situation where those labels acquire validity and meaning is sufficient to elicit pathological behavior. . . . The prison situation, as presently arranged, is guaranteed to generate severe enough pathological reactions in both guards and prisoners to debase their humanity, lower their feelings of self-worth and make it difficult for them to be part of a society outside of their prison.

Philip G. Zimbardo, "Pathology of Imprisonment," published by permission of Trans-Action, Inc., from *Society*, vol. 9, April 1972, pp. 4–8. Copyright © 1972 by Trans-Action, Inc.

---

stant contact with the prisoners, they are placed under pressure to be "good joes." Some of them, like some of Zimbardo's guards, try to be decent. Guards also realize that the convicts could attack them. They know that riots occur in prisons, that sometimes the inmates seize hostages, and that some of the most hated guards are murdered. In addition, some guards feel more kindly toward certain prisoners, especially those convicted for being bookies or for other activities not too offensive to guards. Further, guards who can't keep order are seen as inept. A guard's reputation depends upon his block's being orderly. For all these reasons, a little compromise helps to keep things quiet and under control. Consequently, minor violations of the rules are sometimes overlooked.

Prisoners as guards

Sometimes the more trusted inmates are allowed to help with routine jobs around the prison. At its best, this policy can help both the prison staff and the prisoners by giving them roles more like those found on the outside. In the worst prisons, however, some inmates who are given special privileges become ruthless. The more powerful swindle and steal from the others. Usually there are "gorillas" in the prison who prey on the weaker inmates, beating them or assaulting them sexually. In some of the worst institutions, older, hardened criminals have been used to supervise labor details. Tucker Prison in Arkansas became known for this practice. Conditions there have improved, partly because of newspaper publicity:

> The state's prison system had been operated on fear for a century, and most of the traditional methods had been used: beatings, needles under the fingernails, stompings, the "hide" (a leather strap 5 inches wide and 5 feet long), starvation, and an electric device whose terminals were attached to the genitals of the inmate. . . .
>
> The power of the inmate guard was so absolute that when Governor [Lawrence] Rockefeller first visited the prison he was not allowed in until his bodyguard had surrendered his gun to an inmate at the front gate. (Murton, 1970)

Despite their many bad traits, prisons are obviously necessary: they house people convicted of serious offenses. Many such people would be dangerous to society if left on the streets. The hope is that by the end of their terms, inmates' behavior will be changed enough so that they no longer pose a threat to life or property. Is this hope realistic? What changes come about in the convicts? Do prisons really rehabilitate people, or do they only punish them and keep them put away for a while?

SERVING TIME

As we noted in discussing labeling theory, the tagging of a person as deviant or criminal tends to strengthen the deviant self-concept. The person tends to live up to the reputation. If this is true, then arrest and imprisonment may have an opposite effect from what is intended. The convict's view of himself or herself as deviant would be strengthened, and chances for rehabilitation would decrease. At first glance, the arrest records of juvenile delinquents seem to confirm this hypothesis. Young offenders who are referred back to their own homes are much more likely to reform than those who are sent to juvenile homes. However, there are many variables at work. Delinquents from homes that courts consider helpful and supportive are more likely than others to stay out of further trouble. These are the delinquents referred back to their parents. It is possible, too, that social class makes a difference. Those from lower-class backgrounds seem to experience more pressure toward delinquency than those from middle-class backgrounds.

Also, these poorer offenders are less likely to be returned to their parents.

Anthony R. Harris has studied the effects of imprisonment on young offenders who were not returned to their parents (1975, pp. 71–87). His sample consisted of 105 white and 129 black prisoners, all with previous records, with a median age of twenty-two years. The median age for first arrest had been fifteen, and the prisoners had served an average of two years before the study. They had, on the average, ten years of education and came mostly from the lower classes. The prisoners were asked to answer a number of questions about what they expected when they were released. Did they consider it possible to find acceptable jobs and to stay out of further trouble? According to the labeling hypothesis, once the men had been imprisoned, they would see little hope of going straight. They would accept the labels society had given them, and the prison experience would have no rehabilitation effect.

Effect of length of sentence

Contrary to the labeling hypothesis, the prisoners' answers indicated that at first, for six months to a year, the effect of imprisonment was to reform them. During the early part of their

Table 10-1 U-curve of Expectations for a Law-abiding Career after Release from Prison

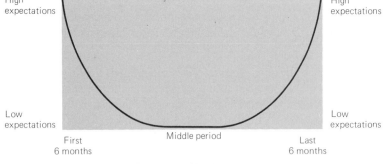

High expectations

Low expectations

High expectations

Low expectations

First 6 months

Middle period

Last 6 months

Total period of imprisonment

sentences, the prisoners told Harris and his associates that they wanted to get legitimate jobs, and they hoped that an honest future was possible. However, after serving time for over a year (after six months in some cases), their view changed. They felt that going straight would either be impossible or not worth the effort. It is hard to tell whether this change in attitudes resulted from the labeling effect, from the tendency of prisons to act as schools for crime, or from some other cause.

The U-curve in rehabilitation expectation

The Harris study does not tell us how much *recidivism* (repeated convictions for crime) would occur among those men who saw no legitimate future, since it concerned only men imprisoned at the time. Several studies have suggested that prisoners' attitudes follow a U-curve. At the beginning of their terms, they hold conventional norms. Their belief in these norms declines during the middle of the sentence and then rises again as the date of release approaches (Glaser and Stratton, 1961, pp. 381–392). (See Table 10-1.) That is, as a rule, first-time offenders, when first imprisoned, resolved to go straight after release. In the middle of their sentence periods, they accepted inmate views and doubted they could succeed on the outside. In their final months, they again identified with the outside world and hoped to succeed in that world. This pattern supports greater optimism about the effects of imprisonment than the pattern Harris found. Sociologists explain the U-curve pattern by saying that inmates come to share the norms of the prison population during their confinement. However, during the early part of their terms and again at the end, the outside world functions as their frame of reference. The effect of the *convict* label can be reversed if the institution and the inmate's home support a new self-concept. This, at least, is the belief of many authorities on rehabilitation who favor small prisons in the community (Clinard,

1963, pp. 630–631). In the insert "Rehabilitation or Dead End," page 280, a young inmate contrasts an institution that promises hope with the juvenile home he was later sent to.

PRISON CRITICISM AND NEW EFFORTS

Outcries against the prison system are often heard today. These protests come not only from liberals but also from conservatives such as U.S. Supreme Court Chief Justice Warren E. Burger (1971, pp. 8–10). In an address before the American Bar Association, Burger painted a dismal picture of the typical American prison. It is from fifty to one hundred years old and contains very limited work-training facilities; the job training there usually involves obsolete trades. The typical American prison lacks other services, too. There are almost no psychiatric services, no transitional facilities or halfway houses, and the medical service is poor. No research studies are made to improve or change prison conditions, and guards are paid so little that the job cannot attract qualified people.

Prison size and custodial function

Reforms have made federal prisons less brutal than they once were, but state prisons and county jails remain very rough (Goldfarb, 1975). County jails are often understaffed, crowded, and filthy (see Table 10-2, page 281). Some are so bad that to be held in them may be seen as "cruel and unusual punishment." Even worse, they often house juvenile delinquents as well as adults. The president of the Crime and Delinquency Council says:

> It is ironic that although no jail is designed to hold children, 100,000 kids a year wind up in jails. It is more than ironic, however. It is a disaster. Drunks, drug addicts, prostitutes and troubled youngsters need professional help, not jailing. (*U.S. News*, 1975, p. 56)

Rehabilitation or dead end   DAE H. CHANG AND WARREN B. ARMSTRONG

I was shocked to find out that this new institution was not like the rumors and tales I had been told. In the two and a half months I was there . . . I completed my fifth and sixth years of grade school. The detention [seemed] a place where rehabilitation is possible. Rehabilitation may be sought there, but it seldom lasts when a person returns to his old milieux. The speed limit increases on this road as one gets closer to the end. After three trips I was quickly promoted to two "camps." Both of these camps have great merit as far as helping youth goes. They taught me the meaning of trust, how to work and earn money (one dollar a day). There are limits, however, in that they take a child out of his home environment, where his problems exist and cure him in a new environment. Then they place him back where his problems began. . . .

I reached the end of my road as a delinquent, when I arrived at Kampell. This is the state's institution for the hardest juvenile offenders. The conditions there were the worst I have ever encountered in a state run institution. If you broke the rules of this institution you were put in the hole. The hole consists of two doors, one of bars and the other of plate steel, and walls and floors and ceiling of concrete. There were no lights. You were stripped naked and given one blanket. The guards would throw water on you if you acted wrong, or if they just happened to feel like throwing water. The officers were mostly middle-aged and weak. To compensate for their weakness they gave special privileges to big and strong inmates (a goon squad). These inmates would beat the hell out of other inmates in the hole. . . . The conditions and institutional rules of this prison are beyond belief. Sexual assault is so common it is to be observed by anyone who wishes to observe it. . . .

Every aspect of this prison and this warden is a hindrance to rehabilitation. Corruption walks hand in hand with inefficiency, and the road the inmates follow to get here—that well-worn road to dead end—leads them here again and again and again.

[*The inmate states that the warden was eventually fired and some improvement took place.*]

From Dae H. Chang and Warren B. Armstrong, *The Prison: Voices from the Inside*, Schenkman Publishing Company, Cambridge, Mass., 1972, pp. 162–164.

As for the prisons, even the best of them still fall far short of being rehabilitative institutions. Better recreational facilities, exercise yards, and reading rooms have been added, along with "behavior modification" systems which give inmates privileges in return for good behavior. However, recidivism rates continue to be high. Gresham Sykes states that nearly 60 percent of all prisoners return to prison sooner or later (1967, p. 66).

Why can't prisons rehabilitate the inmates? One reason lies in the very nature of total institutions. These institutions must not only perform the functions assigned them but also keep order before they can operate at all. Therefore it becomes easy to allow the secondary function—maintaining order—to take precedence over the primary function—reform or cure. Guards and other prison personnel are not paid, promoted, or otherwise rewarded according to how well their prisoners do after release but on how well they keep order. Thus, the custodial function is usually most important, both in the prison and in the mental institution.

Table 10-2 Percentage of City and County Jails with Undesirable Characteristics

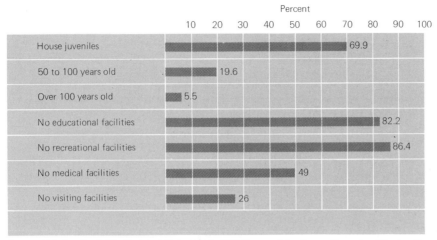

Source: *U.S. Fact Book: The Statistical Abstract of the U.S. Bureau of the Census.* Grosset and Dunlap, New York, 1976, p. 167.

The Swedish example

The recidivism rate in the United States of approximately 60 percent is much greater than that of Sweden—a mere 15 percent. This difference reflects major differences in the two countries' treatment of prisoners (*Time*, 1971, pp. 46–55). Swedish prisons are small, with an average of 120 inmates, and inmates are allowed to visit their wives and families. The average sentence is about five months. This is partly because Swedish law is more lenient than American law on almost all offenses except drunk driving. Prisoners receive diagnostic tests and are given psychotherapy if it is needed. After release, those who have served time for serious offenses are urged to change their names and start new lives in places where they are not known. That way, the stigma of prison will not continue to follow them. Because Sweden's population is smaller and less varied than that of the United States, its prisons don't have the problem of keeping order between antagonistic racial or ethnic groups. This allows the Swedish system to concentrate more on rehabilitation and less on keeping order. Although prison conditions vary between the two countries,

Swedish methods have been tried successfully in some parts of the United States. Kansas prisons, for example, provide good psychiatric care. Several prisons in other states allow the wives of married prisoners to visit them overnight, and visits by family members and friends are also encouraged. A few prisons give inmates passes to attend nearby colleges. These innovations reduce the custodial and punitive functions of prisons. They also give inmates a link to the outside world, giving them a sense of identity and helping them prepare for constructive futures on the outside.

The indeterminate sentence

An *indeterminate sentence* is a sentence giving a maximum and minimum number of years for a particular offense. If the convict is considered ready for release at the earlier date, the minimum sentence will apply. The indeterminate sentence was used first in California, where prison officials had the greatest leeway. For example, at one time, selling marijuana drew a sentence of from five years to life (Mitford, 1971, pp. 45–52). The indeterminate sentence was

Total institutions

281

designed to treat cases individually so that inmates who seemed on the road to rehabilitation could receive relatively light sentences. However, the overall effect of this policy was to greatly increase the power of the guards and prison officials and to make first sentences longer, on the average, than in any other state (Mitford, 1971, p. 45–52). Prisoners often say that they should be treated as individuals. On the other hand, they also believe in the same sentence for the same crime. The indeterminate sentence is hated by most prisoners and was drastically modified in California in 1976, partly at the recommendation of Governor Jerry Brown.

BEHAVIOR MODIFICATION

A major new idea in treating prisons is *behavior modification*. This form of treatment rests on the theory that human behavior can gradually be changed, or modified, in socially approved directions. It works through a system of rewards, called *positive reinforcements*, and punishments, called *negative reinforcements*. Positive reinforcement is believed to give the best results. In fact, B. F. Skinner (1972), a major supporter of behavior modification, sees a future society where punishment will not even be needed. However, behavior modification is by no means a cure-all. The idea that it can work miracles is criticized in the book (and later, the movie) *A Clockwork Orange*. In it, a criminal is so completely cured of violence that he cannot survive in a violent world. He is constantly beaten and finally attempts suicide. The government that had "cured" him had to remodify his behavior, bringing back his old violent self.

Abuses of behaivor modification

A Clockwork Orange, though a parody, has some parallels in real life. For many years, attempts to change behavior included electroshock therapy, drugs, frontal lobotomies (operations that detach part of the frontal lobe of the

Figure 10-2 Rehabilitation often includes teaching prisoners a trade to earn a living. On the whole, such programs are not successful. (*Marvin Lazarus, Photo Researchers*)

brain), and such old standbys as beatings and solitary confinement. Frontal lobotomies often caused loss of intelligence, convulsive disorders, or even death. They are now a thing of the past, although more refined techniques are sometimes used. In January 1973, a convict who showed no signs whatever of aggressive and uncontrollable behavior would have had his brain operated on had it not been for an outcry from the *Detroit Free Press* (Lowinger, 1974, pp. 17–19).

Actually, there is a legitimate use for *neurosurgery*, or operation to remove tumors or other physical abnormalities within the brain. *Psychosurgery*, on the other hand, refers to operating on the brain for the purpose of altering behavior. Such a practice is much more controversial.

Vernon Mark of Boston City Hospital thinks there are a few cases of extreme, uncontrollable violence in which psychosurgery should be used (1973, pp. 1–5). Peter Breggen, a Washington, D.C., psychiatrist, opposes such surgery on any grounds whatever, contending that it is most often used on young people, blacks, and radical prisoners (Nelson, 1974, p. 5). Wayne Sage states that many cases of psychosurgery are performed in prisons on a diagnosis of aggressive epilepsy, although the condition is actually very rare (1974).

Other types of therapy are much less extreme, ranging from traditional occupational training, counseling, and group discussions to drug therapy and the behavioral modification techniques previously mentioned. Unfortunately, no techniques have been very successful (Martinson, April 1, 1972, pp. 13–16).

The new therapy techniques, which some authorities hoped would be a breakthrough in changing behavior, are usually resented by the prisoners. One problem is that the prisoners are urged to see themselves as mentally ill—a stigma they resist. Another problem is that the new techniques are often administered by guards who are not trained in behavior modification. Jessica Mitford states, "The convicts see themselves trapped in a vice between, as one put it, 'the punitive nineteenth-century guard and the 1984 headshrinker'" (1971, p. 47). The psychiatrist Thomas Szasz, a critic of scientific attempts at behavior control, states:

> Most of the legal and social applications of psychiatry . . . are actually instances of despotism. The thesis that the criminal is a sick individual in need of treatment . . . is false. . . . [The deviant] is first discredited as a self-responsible human being, and then subjected to humiliating punishment defined and disguised as treatment. (Mitford, 1971, p. 48)

Aversive therapy

According to Wayne Sage (1974), much of what passes for behavior modification is based on *aversive therapy*. This therapy is a systematic attempt to change behavior to acceptable patterns by deprivation or punishment. At their

Figure 10-3 This progressive prison in Walla Walla, Washington, houses both male and female prisoners. Meeting here in group therapy, they work out their problems in a supportive atmosphere. (*Bob Peterson, Life Magazine*)

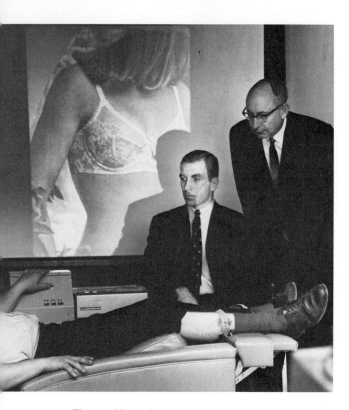

Figure 10-4 Aversive therapy is a controversial behavior modification technique. Here, the man with the electrode strapped to his leg is given an electric shock every time an unacceptable picture appears on the screen. The shocks will continue until he changes the picture. (*Bernie Cleff*)

best, such programs are aimed at preventing certain types of behavior. Sometimes, however, the goal seems to be the destruction of the subject's character structure. One common approach, according to Sage, is that used at the federal penitentiary at Marion, Illinois:

> The prisoners' report describes a . . . nightmare in which troublemakers are isolated and observed. Their personalities are then ripped apart during attack session by 10 to 12 of Gorder's gorillas [Gorder is the psychiatrist who instituted the program], a

group of convicts trained to search out vulnerable points of entry in a prisoner's character structure. A few of the tactics listed include . . . techniques of character invalidation, e.g., humiliation, revilements and shouting to induce feelings of guilt, fear and suggestibility; this coupled with sleeplessness, an exacting prison regimen and periodic interrogational interviews. (Sage, 1974, © 1974 by *Human Behavior* Magazine)

The technique seems to break the prisoners' will and leave them in a "psychic straitjacket," compliant and rather stupefied but in no way prepared to exist in the outside world.

Sage charges that the new behavior-modification techniques (1) cross the narrow line between aversive therapy and plain torture, (2) are used to keep order in the prisons rather than to rehabilitate inmates, (3) are aimed particularly at black militants and others who are perceived as radicals and rebels, and (4) are useless. He believes that the treatment center at the Soledad Prison in California has had the effect of converting criminals into revolutionaries, as in the case of some members of the Symbionese Liberation Army. Sage maintains that the radical behavior of "graduates" of prisons like Soledad can best be explained as a reaction against behavior modification programs. The use of the drug Anectine in behavior modification programs has raised a great deal of controversy. Anectine has such powerful aversive effects that its use was outlawed in the Vietnamese war as a war crime. Nevertheless, it is used in prisons, particularly on prisoners diagnosed as criminally insane in the prisons at Atascadero, Vacaville, Soledad, and San Quentin—all in California.

Positive reinforcement

Not all prison programs consist of aversive therapy. Some prisons have successfully used positive reinforcement. In Colorado Closed Adolescent Center No. 18, Sage notes, inmates can earn tokens for good conduct. These tokens can be saved, like money, to buy privileges such as cigarettes, snacks, and better rooms in the prison. As the Colorado center shows, positive reinforcement can work. However, when programs are badly designed or carelessly used, they can be dangerous. Because prisons are hidden, closed societies and because prisoners are often seen as enemies, it is easy to regard any means of keeping order as good—even if those means are useless, discriminatory, or cruel.

MENTAL PATIENTS AND SOCIAL NORMS

Many traits of prisons are found in mental institutions. Mental illness, like crime, is a type of deviant behavior. Like crime, it can take many forms. It may be minor, as with the neuroses, taking the form of headaches, extreme nervousness, or depression. Neurotics are people who might get some help from psychiatric care, but they have not lost their grip on reality and are not institutionalized. The more severe illnesses are called psychoses. The symptoms usually include seeing and hearing things that are not there, loss of contact with reality, delusions of grandeur or of threat and persecution, feelings of bewilderment and confusion, or withdrawal into a shell to avoid the world.

Society and the care of mental patients

As with criminals, society likes to make a sharp distinction between the normal and the mentally ill. After all, it is a comfort to believe that mental problems are limited to certain types of people. Part of the result of this sharp distinction is to stigmatize the mentally ill. The parallel with criminals is clear. If a former convict or a former mental patient commits a crime, it makes the headlines. This helps to maintain the old stereotypes of deviance. In 1968, Senator Thomas Eagleton was nominated to run for Vice-President of the United States. After it was found

that he had been given electroshock therapy for depression, he was forced to withdraw. The public is apprehensive about emotional problems of this type. The concern reflects doubt as to whether such problems are ever completely cured, but it also reflects a tendency to stigmatize those who have sought psychiatric help.

As with criminal convictions, commitment to mental institutions is more common among lower- than middle- or upper-class people (Hollingshead and Redlich, 1953, pp. 163–168). It is possible that admissions figures are a little misleading. Wealthy people usually go to private psychiatrists before their problems become serious enough to make a mental hospital necessary. But even allowing for this, admission rates would probably be greater for the lower classes. They are exposed to more stress and are therefore more likely to become mentally ill.

As we've noted in discussions of delinquency and criminal rehabilitation, people tend to live up to the predictions made about them. Norman K. Denzin found a similar pattern of self-fulfilling prophecies in the treatment and release of mental patients (1968, pp. 349–358). In mental institutions, patients who impress the authorities most favorably are the ones most likely to improve. Does this mean the authorities are very accurate in their diagnoses? Denzin offers a different explanation. Those who are judged most likely to improve are also the ones given the most attention and care. Therefore, the prediction itself might be the indirect cause of the improvement. It would follow, then, that those patients who are seen as being hopeless are given little or no attention. In fact, many mental institutions have been accused of neglecting severely disturbed patients.

Mental illness and legal norms

It is not a crime to be mentally ill, but the mentally ill are often treated like criminals. The difference is that mental patients do not necessarily receive the same legal protection as accused criminals. One can be convicted for a crime only if criminal intent can be established, and criminal intent is possible only for those who are *legally responsible*. Very young children are not considered criminals even if they set fire to a house, since they cannot be held legally responsible. The concept of legal responsibility is also used in cases of mental illness, but it hinges on the legal definition of insanity. The law follows the M'Naghten Rule of 1843, which says that a person must be incapable of distinguishing right from wrong in order to be absolved from legal responsibility for his or her actions on grounds of insanity. A philosopher might wonder whether

any of us is always sure of the distinction between right and wrong, but this question does not bother the law. The distinction *does* bother psychiatrists, however. The very word *insanity* is a legal, not a psychiatric term. Still, the psychiatrist must often rule, often after only a brief observation, on whether a suspected criminal is legally insane. If judged guilty, a defendant could be given a sentence of perhaps two years. If judged innocent by reason of insanity, however, the same defendant could be sent to a mental institution until cured—which could conceivably amount to a life sentence. In 1966, a U.S. Supreme Court decision was passed to improve the legal treatment of the criminally insane. The Court ruled that a person could not, without proper judicial review, be held in a maximum-security hospital for the criminally insane longer than the length of a prison sentence for the same

Figure 10-5 The dayroom of a typical state mental institution. As with prisons, the custodial function often takes precedence over rehabilitation. (*Jerry Cooke, Photo Researchers*)

On being sane in insane places

It has been known for some time that the traditional modes of psychiatric diagnosis of mental illness are not very reliable. Some members of the psychiatric profession (such as Thomas S. Szasz in his book *The Myth of Mental Illness* and R. D. Laing in *The Divided Self*) have challenged the entire concept of mental illness on philosophical, legal and therapeutic grounds, alleging that the term is useless, misleading, and harmful to patients.

A new attack on the assumption that psychiatrists can distinguish the sane from the insane comes out of an experimental project conducted by David L. Rosenhan, professor of psychology and law at Stanford University. Rosenhan and seven other volunteer subjects sought admission as patients to 12 mental hospitals by stating that they had been hearing "hollow voices." All the subjects easily gained admission. . . . None knew how long it would take to get discharged. The length of hospitalization ranged from seven to 52 days. Even though the pseudopatients stopped simulating any symptoms of abnormality immediately on admission, hospital staff members did not discover, or apparently even suspect that they had entered the hospital under false pretenses.

"It is clear," writes Rosenhan in *Science* [vol. 172, Jan. 19, 1972, pp. 250–258] "that we cannot distinguish the sane from the insane in psychiatric hospitals. How many people, one wonders, are sane but not recognized as such in our psychiatric institutions?"

The pseudopatients did not go entirely undetected. In every case, Rosenhan says, a considerable fraction of the patients in the hospital detected that the pseudopatient was somehow different. Some voiced their suspicion vigorously: "You're not crazy. You're a journalist or a professor. You're checking up on the hospital." For the first three pseudopatients, 35 of 188 real patients in the admissions wards recognized them as being pseudopatients even though no staff member did.

The volunteers used pseudonyms and those who were members of the mental health professions gave another occupation. Otherwise their life history was given factually.

offense. The decision had the effect of releasing over 900 patients from a New York maximum-security hospital to regular hospitals. Contrary to what hospital authorities feared, only twenty-six of these patients had to be returned to maximum security (Steadman and Cocozza, 1975). This example seems to imply that psychiatric diagnoses are not always accurate. An experiment conducted by David L. Rosenhan indicates that hospital staffs cannot always distinguish between the mentally ill and the normal (see the insert "On Being Sane in Insane Places").

Rationale of incarceration

Incarcerating the mentally ill is supposed to assure their protection and treatment. Some patients are dangerous to themselves or others, although most are not. Some receive treatment that helps their illness, but many do not—although the law is changing on this point. Often, as in prisons, those who run the institutions are more interested in keeping the inmates quiet and orderly than in helping them. As a result, drug therapy is sometimes used just to keep patients quiet.

Figure 10-6 Outpatient care is an attempt to treat mental patients while assuring them a normal life. Here, after a therapy session, patients attend a party. (*Marion Bernstein, Editorial Photocolor Archives*)

Although we are moving toward community care and away from large state mental institutions, the institutions are considered necessary for patients who might be dangerous. The 1966 Supreme Court ruling does not keep people from being held for a long time in mental institutions; it just requires judicial review of their cases. During these reviews, evaluations or predictions may be made as to how likely the patient is to commit dangerous or criminal acts. In these situations, preventive custody—holding people not for acts they have committed but for acts they are believed likely to commit—becomes possible. In ordinary law, people can-

not be held in preventive custody for crimes someone else thinks they might commit unless they are convicted of conspiracy. The result is that mental patients do not have the same rights as others. Not only is the system unjust, but it assumes that judges and psychiatrists can make accurate predictions. Faced with the decision of whether to commit someone who might be harmful, a psychiatrist is pressured to err on the side of safety. If the suspect is released and later commits a crime, the psychiatrist is in trouble. If the suspect is locked up, it will be assumed that the psychiatrist was right. Actually, crime rates among released mental patients are not much higher than among the general public, even when those judged "dangerous" are included (Steadman and Cocozza, 1975).

Sometimes people are committed only because their relatives find their behavior odd and don't know how to cope with them. The insert "The Case of Kenneth Donaldson" (page 290) tells how a man lost fifteen years of his life as a result of his father's fear and ignorance and shows how poorly our mental institutions function.

NEW DIRECTIONS IN MENTAL CARE

M. Brewster Smith describes three revolutions in mental health care (1968; pp. 19–23). The first revolution recognized that mental patients are sick, not criminals or possessed by devils. The second revolution was the birth of psychotherapy (the treatment of mental illness by psychological rather than physical means), as well as the introduction of such other techniques as shock therapy and drug therapy. The third revolution introduced the idea that mental disorders cannot be treated as private affairs. They must be considered within "the entire web of social and personal relationships in which the individual is caught" (M. Brewster Smith, 1968, p. 22). Despite good intentions, the large mental institutions that resulted from the second phase have not been successful. The time-consuming, expensive Freudian analysis has been available only to a few. The others are treated with drugs, shock therapy, or nothing at all. The third phase in the treatment of mental illness will, it is hoped, rely less on large institutions and more on outpatient therapy that stresses reintegration into the community.

Both legal changes and economic factors are working to release patients from large state institutions. An important legal breakthrough began when a group of employees were dismissed from Bryce Hospital in Alabama. They hired a lawyer, George Dean, in a class-action suit to regain their jobs. Dean argued in court that their dismissal made it impossible for the mental hospital to provide proper therapy for its inmates and that therapy should be regarded as a constitutional right under the Fourteenth Amendment. Federal District Judge Frank Johnson, Jr., ruled in favor of the applicants and agreed with Dean's reasoning. His ruling resulted in an investigation of the hospital, which proved to be a modern "snake pit." One patient had been in solitary confinement for six years. Another, a girl who was being broken of sucking her thumbs, was kept in a straightjacket for nine years. The institution was dirty, hot, and overcrowded. There was only one doctor with psychiatric training to care for 5,000 patients. Most of the staff was untrained and unaware of modern techniques of therapy (Offir, 1974, pp. 62–63).

Civil commitment

In recent years, lawyers have fought civil commitments which institutionalize people against their will. Kenneth Donaldson, whose case is described in the insert on page 290, was the victim of a civil commitment; he had committed no crime for which he could be detained. Many dramatic cases have been of this type. Daniel Oran (1973) describes a series of cases in which people were committed against their wills simply because they were held by others to be peculiar or to be nuisances. Those examples support the opposition to civil commitment against the patient's will.

People who argue the opposite side of the case can also support their arguments. They cite instances in which delusional patients attack their imaginary tormentors. Other patients have brought constant torment and humiliation to their families. A modern position seems needed. We must ensure legal protection against false commitment and, at the same time, retain the right to hospitalize those who are considered dangerous.

Total institutions, both prisons and mental hospitals, will probably be with us for a long time. Some improvements have come, especially in mental hospitals. It is hoped that changes

The case of Kenneth Donaldson

"They came for me at night," Kenneth Donaldson said. "Like in Russia, two deputy sheriffs, sweet and innocent. They told me they had a warrant. That I should come down to the jail. Just to talk, they said, just to talk to them."

That was on a winter's night in 1956. For the next 15 years Donaldson would be locked in a mental institution behind a 12-foot chain-linked fence topped with three feet of barbed wire.

For the next 15 years he would receive no treatment. There was no treatment to give him. For there was nothing wrong with Kenneth Donaldson. It would take Donaldson the best part of his life to prove this, and when it ended in the U.S. Supreme Court a few months ago, everyone agreed: a ghastly mistake had been made.

"They would threaten to give me shock treatments unless I behaved myself," he said. "Sometimes they would try to force me to take pills. There would be an orderly with a tray and a thousand guys lined up. He would go down the line and say, 'I haven't got your kind of pill. What color do you want?'"

Donaldson was trapped in the Florida State Mental Hospital at Chattahoochee, Fla., an institution with 6,800 patients and 20 doctors. The law said Donaldson had to be a resident of Florida to be locked up there. He wasn't. The law said Donaldson had to have a psychiatric examination before he could be committed. He never had one.

And what was Donaldson's great crime? What did he do to get locked up for 15 years? He wrote letters. Lots of letters.

Donaldson was in Florida to help his parents build a home. He told his father about the things that were happening to him. That he would write letters to all sorts of people in government and that lately he sensed there was a conspiracy of harrassment against him.

In today's post-Watergate world where government harrassment has been well documented, Donaldson's suspicions don't sound strange at all. But in 1956 it all sounded a little bit crazy. "I know it sounded paranoid," Donaldson said, with a shake of his gray hair.

It certainly did so to Donaldson's father—an elderly, frightened man. So he committed his son to Chattahoochee. And there his son stayed, trapped in a place where they locked him up in a ward with tuberculosis patients as punishment for saying he wasn't crazy. . . .

From Roger Simon, "Sane Man Trapped in Insane Web: Ghastly Error Robs Him of 15 Years," *Chicago Sun-Times*, November 2, 1975.

---

will occur in both kinds of institutions, helping them to function better as rehabilitative centers and making them useful to both society and the inmates.

SUMMARY

Throughout recorded history, various methods have been used for dealing with criminals and the mentally ill. In the ancient laws of Hammurabi and Moses, we see the law of *retribution* or *revenge*. Other theories of punishment have been those of giving offenders a chance to *atone* for their sins, *disabling* them so they cannot commit more crimes, or making examples of them in order to *deter* others. Durkheim also suggested that punishment serves the purpose of *reaffirming the norms of society*. More recently, the treatment of crime has been aimed at *rehabilitation*. These attempts are not necessarily effective.

Modern societies, when they punish, use incarceration in *total institutions*, which have complete control over inmates and attempt to resocialize them. The concept of total institutions is applicable to both prisons and mental institutions. Goffman characterizes the *ideal type* of total institution as sharply divided between inmates and staff, who regard each other with suspicion and hostility. The new inmate is subjected to a process of *mortification* and will breaking, and all facts of his life are opened to the staff in the process of *contaminative exposure*. A privilege system is generally instituted to reward compliant behavior. Compliance often becomes more important than preparation to reenter the outside world.

In a simulated prison experiment, men playing the guard role readily accepted the role; many were brutalized by it. Those playing the role of inmate tended to become submissive and even to develop negative self-images. In some respects, the experimental situation even exaggerated reality, since in actual prisons there are sometimes pressures for guards to be "good joes." Occasionally, though, guards may behave very brutally, especially when hardened convicts are used as unofficial guards.

Does serving time have a rehabilitative effect, or does the prison work only as a school for crime? At first glance, the school-for-crime hypothesis seems valid. Prisoners are more apt to want to "go straight" during their first few months in prison than after they have served a year or two. However, studies also show a new resolution to go straight as the prisoner's term comes to a close. Studies of the effect of sentence length, then, remain inconclusive.

As a rule, the larger the prison, the less able it is to rehabilitate. Most of the energy is devoted to running the institution and keeping inmates in line. Sweden, with prisons of only 120 inmates, has a much better record of rehabilitation than does the United States.

Attempts to reform prison systems are often made. California has used the *indeterminate sentence*, which gave officials firm control over inmates but was bitterly resented by most of them. Sentences were usually longer than in other states, and prison disorders were just as frequent.

Behavior modification has recently come into vogue in the prisons. B. F. Skinner expects nearly all modifications to be accomplished through *positive reinforcement* (rewards) rather than *aversive therapy* (punishment). Prisons have tended to turn behavioral modification into aversive therapy.

Mental institutions are another form of total institution. Former mental patients, like ex-convicts, are stigmatized by society. Legal norms define *insanity* as the inability to know right from wrong. This definition helps to place some dangerous people in mental institutions rather than prisons. The word *insanity* as so used, however, makes little sense to psychiatrists. Serious complaints have been made about mental institutions: It is too easy to have people committed, and often patients are not given therapy. U.S. Supreme Court decisions in the 1970s have made it illegal to hold patients indefinitely without therapy and without review of their cases. M. Brewster Smith has traced the development of mental health treatment. First, we depended on large institutions in which mental patients were treated almost as criminals. When mental patients were recognized as ill, there were improvements and new forms of therapy, but mainly in large state institutions. Today, we are moving toward much smaller institutions and outpatient care as well as a recognition that patients must be reintegrated into the community.

Study guide

Terms to know

Retribution
Atonement
Deterrence
Disablement
Total institution
Reaffirmation of norms
Rehabilitation
Ideal type
"Mortification"

"Contaminative exposure"
Privilege system
Positive reinforcement
Recidivism
U-curve
Indeterminate sentence
Behavioral modification
Neurosurgery
Psychosurgery

Neurosis
Psychosis
Aversive therapy
Legal responsibility
M'Naghten Rule
Insanity (legal meaning)
Preventive custody

Names to know

Hammurabi
Moses
Émile Durkheim
Erving Goffman

Philip G. Zimbardo
David L. Rosenhan
B. F. Skinner

Self-test

Part I. Multiple Choice. Select the best of the four alternative answers:

1 Of the various theories of punishment mentioned in this chapter, the one stressed by Durkheim was that of (**a**) revenge, (**b**) atonement, (**c**) disablement, (**d**) reaffirmation of the norms.

2 An *ideal type* analysis refers to (**a**) societal ideas, (**b**) a perfectly designed institution, (**c**) finding the typical pattern, (**d**) a study of extremist ideologies.

3 Depriving the inmate of status and any sense of dignity are part of the process of (**a**) mortification, (**b**) institutionalization, (**c**) contaminative exposure, (**d**) exorcism.

4 The privilege system serves *all but one* of the following functions: (**a**) reintegration into society, (**b**) keeping the prison system honest, (**c**) positive reinforcement, (**d**) some sense of control over one's life.

5 When Rosenhan and his colleagues posed as inmates in mental institutions, they found that (**a**) only qualifed people could see inmate records, (**b**) inmates were free to talk to the staff, (**c**) little social distance existed between inmates and staff, (**d**) none of the above.

6 In Zimbardo's simulated prison, (**a**) inmates took the matter as a joke, (**b**) some of the guards took pleasure in cruelty, (**c**) a Catholic chaplain said the inmates did not resemble real inmates, (**d**) an ex-convict said the simulated prison in no way resembled real prisons.

7 In prisons, guards often compromise to some degree with inmates because (**a**) it helps to keep all cellblocks orderly and prevent unfavorable reports, (**b**) they feel that most prisoners

are getting more punishment than they deserve, (**c**) they think of themselves as similar to the inmates, (**d**) all the above.

8 Studies of length of sentence indicate that prisoners (**a**) identify with the outside world for the first six months, (**b**) identify with the convict world after a year or more, (**c**) identify with the outside world when about to be released, (**d**) all the above.

9 U.S. Supreme Court Chief Justice Warren Burger describes the typical United States prison as (**a**) having been built within the last two decades, (**b**) having well-qualified guards, (**c**) having good medical care and fairly good psychiatric care, (**d**) none of the above.

10 Prisoners generally do not like an indeterminate sentence because (**a**) they object to equal time for equal crime, (**b**) it places too much power in the hands of prison authorities, (**c**) they do not believe in treatment on the basis of individual merit, (**d**) it increases the recidivism rate.

11 One of the charges made by Wayne Sage against behavior modification in prison is that (**a**) it is too mild to be effective, (**b**) it is discriminatory against blacks and radicals, (**c**) it relies entirely on positive reinforcement, (**d**) it is not used to gain compliance with prison rules.

12 Under the M'Naghten Rule, a person can be found innocent of a crime on grounds of insanity only if he or she (**a**) has hallucinations, (**b**) cannot tell right from wrong, (**c**) has been judged unlikely to commit further crimes, (**d**) is diagnosed as paranoid or schizophrenic.

13 Neurosis is often accompanied by (**a**) hallucinations, (**b**) delusions of persecution, (**c**) both a and b, (**d**) neither a nor b.

14 Kenneth Donaldson was held in a Florida state mental institution for fifteen years (**a**) because of a history of violence, (**b**) without a psychiatric examination, (**c**) over the protest of his father, (**d**) because he asked for mental therapy.

15 Psychiatrists who have to testify whether a mental patient is too dangerous to release (**a**) are under pressure to err on the side of caution, (**b**) generally give the patient the benefit of the doubt, (**c**) follow the legal norm of "innocent until proven guilty," (**d**) are virtually infallible.

Part II. True-False Questions

1 Old Bedlam Street in London was famous as the scene of a cruel mental institution.
2 The ancient laws of Hammurabi were based on retribution, but those of Moses were based on rehabilitation.
3 Goffman defines total institutions as those that totally rehabilitate inmates.
4 The terms "cons" and "fish" refer to older inmates and new inmates, respectively.
5 The "fish" is under opposite pressures from the institutional rules and from the "cons."
6 If a "fish" is young and good-looking, the older "cons" will try to make a "queen" of him.
7 In Zimbardo's simulated prison, the more decent guards effectively restrained those who had a desire to be cruel.
8 Tucker Prison in Arkansas was a particularly brutal prison because it used the older inmates as guards.
9 As a general rule, very large institutions seem to do less to rehabilitate inmates than do smaller ones.
10 Sweden has a much lower recidivism rate than has the United States.
11 B. F. Skinner, a leading advocate of behavior modification, believes that nearly all behavior can be modified by positive reinforcement.
12 The legal definition of *insanity* is the same as the psychiatrist's definition of *mental illness*.
13 In sociology, mental illness is considered a form of deviant behavior.
14 When Rosenhan and his colleagues entered mental institutions as patients, the staff realized they didn't really belong there.

Total institutions

293

15 The stigma against people who have been mental patients has disappeared now that the public has greater knowledge of psychology.

Questions for discussion

1 Discuss some of the implications of Durkheim's suggestion that punishment serves to reaffirm the norms. Does this mean that norms will not be upheld unless there is punishment? Does it mean that the more severe the punishment, the more confident the public will feel that its norms are being upheld?

2 Goffman describes what he calls "the mortification and will-breaking process." Have you ever encountered this kind of treatment in camp or at school? What effect does such treatment have on enforcing conformity to the rules? On adjustment to outside society?

3 Recalling Chapter 5 ("Social Groups"), comment on why those guards in the Zimbardo experiment who would like to have been decent to the prisoners were actually quite ineffective.

4 In actual prisons, what are some of the pressures that urge guards to be "good guys" to some degree?

5 Comment on the effects of aversive therapy in *A Clockwork Orange* or *One Flew Over the Cuckoo's Nest*. (Note: These are movies based on novels of the same title.)

6 The text gives objections to the policy of indeterminate sentences. Can you think of any objections to the opposite policy— having all inmates serve precisely determined sentences?

7 What is wrong with the legal definition of *insanity*? If you have taken a course in psychology, compare this definition with a psychologist's definition of *mental illness*.

8 The insert "On Being Sane in Insane Places" is quite surprising in its conclusions. What characteristics of total institutions probably blinded those in authority to the facts about the imposters?

9 For rehabilitation to occur, reintegration into society is necessary. Can you suggest any policies that would help former mental patients or ex-convicts come back into the mainstream of life?

Projects

1 Visit a local jail, prison, or mental institution. (Particularly for prisons, this will probably have to be a class project with considerable time allowed for making arrangements.) How do procedures compare with Goffman's description of total institutions? Does the institution seem to accomplish the desired resocialization?

2 In a conversation with a person you do not know very well, mention that you spent two years as an inmate of a mental institution. Note the reaction. Are you immediately stigmatized by the statement? (You should try this only under circumstances in which you will be able to explain later that the statement was a sociological experiment.)

3 Psychiatrists who have to pass judgment on whether it is safe to release a mental patient face a serious dilemma. They can make the mistake of releasing someone who is dangerous or make the opposite mistake of holding an inmate indefinitely in preventive custody. Try to find out how the public feels on such an issue. Give the following example and ask a sample of the public what they would recommend:

Karl E. was once accused of an attempt on the life of one of his neighbors, when he swung at him with a meat cleaver for no apparent reason. He was judged to have committed the act of violence but was found not guilty by reason of insanity. Since then, Karl has served ten years in a mental institution, has received intensive psychotherapy, has been a model patient, and seems to be cured. If you had to make the decision, would you (**a**) release Karl E., feeling that the injustice of keeping him longer would outweigh the risk involved, or (**b**) keep him institutionalized, feeling that the public must be defended against any risk whatever from such a person?

Suggested readings

Davis, Alan J.: "Sexual Assaults in the Philadelphia Prison System and Sheriff's Vans," *Trans-Action*, vol. 6, December 1968, pp. 8–16. The inmate subculture within the prison is often brutal. Absence of sexual outlets leads to homosexual rape, as discovered on a large scale in this study of the Philadelphia system.

Jackson, Donald: "Justice for None," *New Times*, January 11, 1974. What dilemmas must a judge face in passing sentence? Is the purpose of the sentence retribution, deterrence, setting an example, or what? Do all legally prescribed sentences make sense in any of these terms? Jackson gives cases in which any decision a judge makes has to be wrong.

Martinson, Robert: "The Paradox of Prison Reform," a series of four articles in *The New Republic*, April 1, 18, 15, and 29, 1972. Many people consider talk of rehabilitation a myth, but why does Martinson add that it is a dangerous myth? What are the dysfunctions of a public belief in the myth of rehabilitation? Martinson answers this question and also offers alternatives to present methods of treatment within prisons.

Mitford, Jessica: "Kind and Usual Punishment in California," *Atlantic Monthly*, vol. 227, March 1970, pp. 45–52. Is the California prison system, generally considered one of the best, as good as it is said to be? Definitely not, says Mitford. Prisoners serve longer sentences, recidivism rates are high, training programs are virtually useless, and filth, bad food, and homosexual problems are present.

Newsweek, editors: "The Ex-con's Unhappy Lot," *Newsweek,* February 24, 1974, pp. 84–85. Rehabilitation of prisoners has to prepare the prisoner to meet the world, but has anyone thought of preparing the world to meet the ex-prisoner? How much chance does the ex-con really have to go straight? *Newsweek* gives a few encouraging examples, but for the majority of ex-cons, life on the outside is far from satisfactory.

Oran, Daniel: "Judges and Psychiatrists Lock up Too Many People," *Psychology Today*, vol. 7, August 1973, pp. 20–22, 27–28. Is mental health a mere synonym for conformity? Are harmless eccentrics put away at heavy cost to society as well as cost in misery for themselves? Oran presents confirming evidence.

Shiloh, Ailon: "Sanctuary or Prison: Responses to Life in a Mental Hospital," *Trans-Action*, vol. 6, December 1968, pp. 28–35. What happens when a mental institution finds about 40 percent of its inmates so thoroughly institutionalized that they no longer want to leave? Why are many inmates afraid, even though care is by no means abusive? Shiloh finds the answers in a Veterans Administration hospital.

Time, editors: "Crime in America," vol. 105, June 30, 1975, pp. 10–24. Why does crime show a steady rise? What are the responsibilities of police, courts, and the public? Are there any better ways to rehabilitate offenders? What views of the justice system do the prisoners themselves express?

Key to questions. Multiple Choice: 1-d; 2-c; 3-a; 4-b; 5-d; 6-b; 7-a; 8-d; 9-d; 10-b; 11-b; 12-b; 13-d; 14-b; 15-a. True-False: 1-T; 2-F; 3-F; 4-T; 5-T; 6-T; 7-F; 8-T; 9-T; 10-T; 11-T; 12-F; 13-T; 14-F; 15-F.

This chapter examines an area of social life in which behavior develops that is not clearly directed by the culture. After reading it, you should be able to:

1 Distinguish between culturally structured behavior and collective behavior.

2 Recognize some types of mass hysteria and their results, especially during crises.

3 Understand different types of crowd behavior in social-psychological terms and also in terms of societal causes.

4 Be able to assess crowd behavior as to whether it is rational or irrational and in terms of convergence theory and emergent-norm theory.

5 Understand reasons for and possible results of the spread of rumor and know about the tensions that cause rumors to grow and spread.

6 Distinguish between fashion and fad and see why some types of fads become socially significant.

7 Understand several types of social movements and how they may affect society: egalitarian, radical, world-rejective, and revolutionary.

11

COLLECT

BEHAVIO

In the spring of 1975, the Republic of South Vietnam collapsed. With the defeat, panic spread—a panic made worse by rumors of a bloodbath to come. In the capital, Saigon, people demonstrated against the corrupt and dying regime of President Thieu. In other parts of the country, soldiers fought with civilians for places on rescue ships. In the cities, looters grabbed what money and supplies they could as insurance for the days ahead. Parents and their children fled to the countryside. Except for family protection and the efforts of a few rescue workers, it seemed that all discipline and order had collapsed.

For the North Vietnamese, this was the moment of triumph. Propaganda was spread among the South Vietnamese. Banners, slogans, parades, and public broadcasts hailed a new era. Those who had been outlaws under the Thieu regime would be the leaders of the new order. New institutions and norms would be symbolized by new uniforms, flags, and songs. The revolution was complete.

The events of this changeover in government show nearly all the traits of collective behavior: mass demonstrations, riots, rumors, looting, propaganda, the breakdown of discipline—all motivated by discontent with the old regime.

Collective behavior defined

Collective behavior can be defined as relatively spontaneous actions of groups of people to relieve feelings of dissatisfaction and anxiety. Turner and Killian define *collective behavior* simply as "the actions of groups that operate without clear-cut direction from their cultures" (1972, p. 10). The most common forms of collective behavior are mass hysteria, social movements, mobs, riots, and demonstrations.

Minor forms of collective behavior include fads, the spreading of rumors, and the outbursts of emotional religious groups or audiences at rock concerts. All these behaviors are less disciplined and less predictable than ordinary social behavior. In all these cases, people are strongly influenced by the actions of others. Collective behavior is created to a great extent by people's emotional responses. It arises as they express feelings of anxiety, fear, joy, or hostility and look for ways of handling undefined situations.

Sociologists often ask why similar situations cause collective behavior at some times but not at others. The answer seems to be that certain features of society are conducive to particular types of collective behavior. Neil J. Smelser calls this situation *structural conduciveness* (1962). The ways in which this works are described below.

HOW COLLECTIVE BEHAVIOR ORIGINATES IN SOCIETY

Collective behavior occurs most often in modern societies which are not tightly structured and in which information spreads rapidly. By a tightly structured society we mean one in which (1) most people agree on values and norms, (2) traditions are strong, and (3) there is little conflict over laws or such institutions as religion, government, family, and the economic system. Examples are peasant societies and societies with a strong central government, such as the Soviet Union. The United States is a loosely structured society, with wide differences of opinion on norms, in which the government allows the people to express themselves freely. Collective behavior is also helped by massing people together in large cities, especially people of many different racial and ethnic backgrounds. As

Smelser notes, a simple, homogeneous, agricultural society would not have had the Wall Street panic of 1929, the urban riots of the 1960s, or the women's liberation movement.

However, some types of collective behavior can occur in any society with tensions and anxieties. The Salem witchcraft trials of the 1690s took place in a tightly structured community. Here, anxiety over the devil created distorted views, false accusations, and hostile outbursts against the accused. This type of behavior is called *mass hysteria*, the most elemental and diffuse form of collective behavior.

FORMS OF COLLECTIVE BEHAVIOR

Mass hysteria

Smelser defines *mass hysteria* as a "belief empowering an ambiguous element in the environment with the generalized power to threaten or destroy" (1962, p. 84). Mass hysteria is often caused by events that seem supernatural. Even in the twentieth century, cases of this kind can be found. After the release of the movie *The Exorcist*, newspapers reported many stories about people who thought they were gripped by evil spirits. For a tragic example of this kind of thinking, see the insert "The Exorcists."

Mass hysteria and the Black Death   In the Middle Ages, mass hysteria was common in times of trouble. Hysteria swept over Europe during the bubonic plague of 1348, which killed about one-third of the European people. Since there were no medical or scientific explanations, people turned to other beliefs. Some scholars believed that the plague was caused by bad air created by the movements of Saturn and Mars (Campbell, 1931, pp. 34–37). Many people blamed the Jews, who, according to rumor, were poisoning the wells of Christians. Then as now, outsiders made good *scapegoats*—people to blame for the trouble of society. Others accused doctors of spreading the plague rather than checking it. Doctors were stoned by crowds in France (Langer, 1964).

During the plague years, ordinary customs and mores broke down. Many of the clergy died;

Figure 11-1 April 2, 1975, Nha Trang, South Vietnam: Refugees struggle for a place on an evacuation plane before the victorious North Vietnamese arrive. (*United Presss International*)

The exorcists

The voice on the tapes was that of a woman, but it was unnaturally deep and the words were incoherent screams mixed with furious profanities. The tapes recorded the dying days of a timid, 23-year-old epileptic named Anneliese Michel, and they were part of the evidence on a manslaughter case West German authorities were preparing last week against the Bishop of Würzburg, Joseph Stangl, and two priests he appointed to exorcise the Devil from the young woman. When Michel died last month of malnutrition and dehydration, she weighed only 70 pounds. One of the priests, Father Arnold Renz, maintained that six devils—including Nero, Judas, Hitler, and Lucifer himself—possessed Michel and made her refuse to eat. Her parents accepted that analysis, but more liberal German Catholics challenged it. "Possession is a question of belief, not empirical fact," said theologian Ernst Veth, Michel's tutor at the University of Würzburg. "They should have called a doctor."

others gave up their duties and even their parishes. Many people became pious in hopes of escaping the plague. Others, Boccaccio tells us, were sure that "there was no other physicke more certaine, for a disease so desparate, than to drink hard, be merry, . . . singing continually, walking everywhere, and satisfying their appetites with whatever they desired, laughing and mocking at every mournful accident, and so they vowed to spend day and night: for now they would go to one taverne, then to another, living without any rule or measure . . ." (quoted in Campbell, 1931, p. 137).

The bubonic plague produced results that sociologists look for in many other cases of mass hysteria: generalized fear and mistrust, the scapegoating of minorities and of those who are supposed to relieve the situation, and piety by some and debauchery by others.

The modern parallel: War and mass hysteria
Today, wars have become our version of the Black Death. During wars, when survival becomes uncertain, church attendance increases. At the same time, particularly among soldiers who face death, there is a greater desire to experience the pleasures that remain—"wine, women, and song" or drugs. Looting and raping may occur as all normal social restraints dissolve.

The losing side in a war looks for scapegoats, including the leaders who failed them. Drabek and Quarantelli (1967, pp. 12–17), who conducted disaster research on several tragic fires, found that people would rather blame individuals than laws and procedures. During World War II, blame fell on the American admiral who could not believe the Japanese were approaching Pearl Harbor and on British generals who could not hold back the Germans in North Africa.

Minority groups also become scapegoats during war. In World War II, Japanese-Americans were moved to "relocation camps" in the desert. Rumors circulated that they had secret signaling devices to guide Japanese aircraft to American targets. Even symbols of the enemy have suffered. During World War I, dachshunds as well as German-Americans were attacked on the streets, and several Japanese cherry trees were cut down in Washington, D.C., during World War II.

The modern witch hunt In the United States after World War II, people began to look for "subversive elements" rather than witches. Thus began a period of spy hunts, loyalty oaths, widespread feelings of fear and distrust, and the infamous "witch hunts" of Senator Joseph McCarthy. J. Edgar Hoover found America threatened by "the most evil, monstrous plot against mankind since time began." McCarthy feared "a conspiracy so immense, an infamy so black, as to dwarf any previous such venture in the history of mankind." McCarthy called the previous Roosevelt and Truman administrations "twenty years of treason" (Belfrage, 1963, pp. 119–120; Cook, 1971). He then moved against liberals, who became "commiesymps" (Communist sympathizers), and against the State Department, especially those members who correctly foresaw the triumph of Mao Tse-tung in China.

Minor cases of mass hysteria Occasional cases of mass hysteria arise over strange, possibly psychosomatic illnesses. Nearly 200 schoolgirls in Blackburn, England, were stricken with headaches, fainting, nausea, and other symptoms for which no physical cause was ever found (*Scientific American*, 1967, p. 58). Kerchoff et al. report a similar case in a Southern mill town. Many people suffered what seemed to be a nervous condition, caused, they thought, by a strange bug in some of the textiles they worked on. This insect was never found, nor could doctors find any physical cause for the epidemic (1968).

Frequently, contemporary examples of mass hysteria are related to outer space and mysterious aliens who are supposed to be nearing the earth. A famous radio program by Orson Welles, titled "Invasion from Mars," led to widespread panic. He broadcast a very realistic dramatized version of *War of the Worlds* by H. G. Wells. Many who tuned in during the middle of the program mistook the show for a news broadcast and started to flee from the monsters from outer space (Houseman, 1948, pp. 47–82).

In summer 1976, newspapers reported the discovery of a number of dead cattle, killed for no apparent reason. It was said that parts of their bodies—eyes, entrails, genital organs—had been carefully cut out. Since no good reason could be found, rumors started to fly. Some people claimed that it was the work of a witch cult that used animal organs for strange rites. Others believed creatures from outer space were responsible. As it turned out, the cattle had been killed by wild animals, and no surgical skill was involved. But the rumors spread.

The outer-space connection Sometimes outer space is seen as a source of friendly rescue. Leon Festinger made a well-known study of space cultists who expected to be rescued from this earth by creatures in flying saucers. He was concerned mainly with how his subjects rationalized their beliefs (Festinger, Riecken, and Schachter, 1956). Recently, public attention has been drawn to a couple, nicknamed Bo and Peep, who claim to be missionaries from a heavenly kingdom in outer space. They have gathered a band of fifty followers who expect to be flown to this divine realm in spaceships. At the time of this writing, the group is wandering around the country, its exact location unknown. This bizarre episode has disturbed many people, especially the friends and relatives of the followers of this strange couple. (See the insert "Invitation to an Unearthy Kingdom.")

Characteristics of crowd behavior

Sociologists use the word *crowd* in many ways. Most often it refers to a temporary, unstructured collection of people who are aware of each other and are influenced by each other. Several types of crowds have been defined and described. *Casual crowds* consist of people who happen to be present at a particular place (a beach or a park, for example) at the same time. *Conventional crowds* are audiences or people at orderly meetings. Casual crowds and conventional crowds become important to the study of collective behavior only when something occurs to cause a fight, panic, or other disturbance. Some-

Invitation to an unearthly kingdom LYNN SIMROSS

They talk of . . . Jesus Christ and UFOs. They are The Two, a couple of Texas meta-physical teachers named Marshall Herf Applewhite and Bonnie Trusdale Nettles, better known as Bo and Peep.

They travel swiftly, furtively, across the land, preaching something called Human Individual Metamorphosis (HIM), soliciting a flock to follow them to another realm. They say they have come from "the next kingdom," the same one "Christ came from."

Bo and Peep also contend that Jesus left earth "in a cloud of light (what humans refer to as UFOs)" and that they and their followers will do the same thing soon. . . .

You might think it a hoax until you learn that there are about 50 people trekking somehwere across the country, mesmerized by the HIM doctrine.

That in itself is not easy. "If the human is a good prospect," says a HIM leaflet, "he lets go of these fragments of his human foundation."

What that means is to follow Bo and Peep you must give up all your worldly possessions, your family and friends, sex, smoking, drugs, and alcohol. You must bring along some money (for the communal fund) and have means of transportation because you will be moving around a lot.

What are Bo and Peep really up to? Right now it is anybody's guess. But authorities in at least eight states—from California to Illinois—are "officially studying and looking into the case."

Hundreds of calls have come in to law enforcement agencies, and even to the FBI, from people who have lost their wives, sons, mothers, daughters, cousins, lovers and friends to the wiles of Bo and Peep.

So far, though, lawmen have been unable to find any kind of charge against the couple that would hold up in court. The people who have left their homes are all over 18 and left willingly, so they can't be classified as missing persons. And what money they did give Bo and Peep, they gave by their own choice.

Speculation on Bo and Peep's actual plans for their new cult runs a wide gamut. Some think they are "just a couple of ding-a-lings"; others are sure they are sophisti-cated con artists. A few have tried to link the pair to the recent Colorado cattle mutilations (there is no evidence of this) and many have wondered if the couple are Manson-like cultists with violent leanings. . . .

From Lynn Simross, "Invitation to an Unearthly Kingdom," *Los Angeles Times*, October 31, 1975, Part IV, p. 1. Copyright © 1975 by the Los Angeles Times.

---

times the term *expressive crowd* is used to describe people who are merely expressing their emotions in a group setting. Dancing crowds and people at ecstatic religious gatherings are exam-ples of expressive crowds.

Orgiastic crowds are a special type of disorder-ly crowd. We think of them as participants in events that have gotten completely out of hand. These groups become drunk, destroy property, disturb the peace, and may be raided by the police. In another usage, the *orgiastic crowd* may be a conquering army that is out of control, looting and raping.

The term *crowd* alone usually refers to an *active crowd*, meaning participants in a mob, riot, panic, or other social disorders. These crowds, like orgiastic crowds, have been charac-terized as irrational, spontaneous, and suggest-

(a)

(b)

(c)

Figure 11-2 Different types of crowds have been described by sociologists. (*a*) This beach scene represents a casual crowd. People are aware of each other but not organized. (*b*) A conventional crowd is described as orderly and predictable. (*c*) Participants at sports events usually comprise expressive crowds. (*d*) The people in this scene of the Wall Street panic of 1929 represent an active crowd: tense, volatile, and suggestible. [*(a) Cella, Photo Researchers; (b) Lew Merrim, Monkmeyer; (c) Michael Hayman, Photo Researchers; (d) United Press International*]

(d)

ible. Gustave LeBon studied the riots and revolutions in France which led, in 1871, to the overthrow of Napoleon III. He was the first writer to identify these characteristics of crowd behavior. LeBon, who had an aristocratic bias, viewed crowds as purely lower class and individuals in the crowd as completely controlled by a group mind. Herbert Blumer (1955) has since clarified some of LeBon's ideas and has explained the term *group mind*.

Crowd contagion

Observers looking at an angry mob might think they are seeing evidence of a group mind, a kind of mental telepathy which unites the group. More accurate terms for this phenomenon are *heightened suggestibility* and *social contagion*. Members of an active crowd are in an undefined, ambiguous situation. They may be held together by a belief that they are facing danger from communists, black people, white people, or criminals roaming the streets. In such cases, a person with a strong, commanding presence who acts as a leader can suggest a form of action, and the crowd may go along. Members of active crowds display "milling behavior": They move about, look at each other, interpret the glances of others, and increase their own anger, fear, or anxiety in response to the emotions they find in other faces. This process of *circular reaction* explains the development of crowd unity better than LeBon's theory of a group mind. It also implies that social contagion is the major cause of crowd behavior.

Convergence theory

The social-contagion explanation of crowd behavior is open to criticism. Although it is true that social contagion sometimes takes place, we must ask: "Who becomes part of the crowd in the first place?" (Turner and Killian, 1972, pp. 18–25). Do crowd members act the way they do because they stimulate each other, or did they arrive at the scene because of the kind of people they are? *Convergence theory* maintains that people take part in crowd behavior mainly because they came together as a result of personal attitudes and predispositions. In its extreme form, convergence theory would claim that people use crowd behavior as an excuse to do as a crowd what they fear to do alone. According to this theory, participants in mobs or riots could be viewed as angry, frustrated individuals. From this perspective, participants at emotional religious gatherings would be seen as people troubled by feelings of guilt, inadequacy, or other tensions which can be relieved by singing, praying, "testifying," and similar expressions of intense emotion.

Although convergence theory seems to apply to many types of rioters and demonstrators, it probably exaggerates the influence of individual predispositions. Convergence theory ignores the fact that different types of people are involved: would-be participants, curiosity seekers, others who try to stop the riot, and still others who may try to exploit the situation by looting. McPhail and Miller (1973, pp. 721–735) find that word-of-mouth communication and rumor are most likely to reach the willing participants. However, others may learn of the action, depending how close to it they are and on whether it is a sudden event or has been planned. They do not all converge for the same reason. The validity of convergence theory depends largely on how the crowd acts. Lynch mobs, for example, consist of people who share a single motive and a single goal. In urban riots, probably many onlookers are drawn in who had not intended to take part. Thus, convergence theory would account for lynch mobs better than for urban riots.

Emergent norms

The concept of *emergent norms* is a third way of explaining active crowd behavior. This theory holds that crowds develop their own norms as they form. The theory assumes that the crowd is made up of people with different opinions and motives who are drawn together by the excitement of the event. When the event is a simple matter, such as a concert, a behavioral norm quickly develops. Generations of fans have screamed and wriggled over such performers as the Beatles and the Rolling Stones.

In the case of riots, norms change as circumstances change. The incident which provokes a riot might involve a policeofficer, who would seem to be a logical focus of attack. Perhaps by the time the crowd has formed, the policeofficer has left. How can the crowd show its hostility now? In this case, we can imagine a norm energing. Any property or symbol belonging to the opposition may become a target. Someone may divert attention to a merchant who is said to be a swindler; then a quick consensus forms and the crowd attacks the merchant's store. A new, or *emergent*, norm has developed. Any enemy in the area is to be attacked. The usual norms no longer work except as they limit violent actions or are used to justify them.

The emergent norm can also act to suppress riots. After the murder of Dr. Martin Luther King, Jr., a riot was anticipated in Cleveland. Members of the black community, partly in support of Carl Stokes, the black mayor they had helped elect, took to the streets. They talked to excited groups, urging them to keep calm; Dr. King would have wanted it that way. The efforts of these counterrioters changed what could have been an emergent norm of violence to one of peace (Anderson, Dynes, and Quarantelli, 1974, pp. 50–65).

Each of the three theories of crowd behavior—contagion, convergence, and the emergent norm—is useful in explaining the actions of crowds in different situations. LeBon, we will recall, stressed the unity of crowds, or the irrational collective mind. Later theories provide better explanations, but this analysis is useful for focusing on irrationality in crowd behavior.

Are crowds irrational?

LeBon liked to say that crowds are ruled by emotion rather than reason. At first glance, this seems to be true. Yet, both the American Revolution and the French Revolution, which we celebrate today as triumphs for democracy, started with crowd actions. In Paris, there was the storming of the Bastille; in Boston, the harassment of British troops and the dumping of a famous cargo of tea. As these examples show, determining whether a crowd is rational becomes a problem. An investigator must ask: "Rational in terms of whose interests?" Those who were loyal to the British and French kings saw their own actions as rational and those of the crowds as irrational. The other problem about rationality has to do with ends and means. Our opinion is so strongly influenced by our norms and values that any answer becomes a value judgment. Was the American Revolution rational? Of course. The French Revolution? Yes. The Russian Revolution? Absolutely not—it created a communist threat to our way of life. Obviously, all these statements reflect the norms of our culture.

A look at the urban riots of the 1960s makes them seem irrational. Black people burned their own areas, making their housing and shopping problems worse. There is another side. Many black leaders saw the riots as a rational way to publicize black rage. Others tried to stop the riots. As the insert "Conflicting Reactions in Riot Areas" (page 306) shows, there was no consensus in the ghettos. Looking back, although a lot of damage was done, solid gains were made. The blacks gained integrated police forces, more black mayors, and better enforcement of civil rights acts. But the poor ghettos remain.

People who condemn violence sometimes say that a person who takes part in a riot is less intelligent than one who doesn't. Actually, this does not seem to be true. The National Advisory Commission on Civil Disorders reported that the average participant in the urban riots of the

1960s was a young black male, aged fifteen to twenty-four, a lifelong resident of the area, somewhat better educated than average although not necessarily a high school graduate, and poor but not poorer than his nonrioting neighbors. What set him apart was greater pride in his race and extreme distrust of the political system and its leaders (National Advisory Commission on Civil Disorders, 1968, pp. 128–129).

In an independent study of rioters in Newark, New Jersey, Jeffery Paige came to similar conclusions (1971, pp. 810–820). He tested the hypothesis that the alienated and apathetic would be most prone to violence. However, he found that the people who had little political information and little trust in the system were the least likely to riot. The people most likely to riot were those who were best informed about political events but did not trust the system. What seems to set off rioters from nonrioters is the degree of commitment to a cause. Studies of rioters in Paris and London during the eighteenth century, including those who stormed the Bastille, show the same combination: a fairly high degree of political information and very little trust in the system (Rudé, 1971).

SMELSER'S THEORY OF COLLECTIVE BEHAVIOR

Neil J. Smelser has tried to analyze all types of collective behavior in terms of the cultural traits associated with them (1962). He uses the concepts of *structural conduciveness, structural*

Conflicting reactions in riot areas

A Detroit survey revealed that approximately 11 percent of the total residents of two riot areas admitted participating in the rioting, 20 to 25 percent identified themselves as "bystanders," over 16 percent identifed themselves as "counterrioters," who urged rioters to "cool it," and the remaining 48 to 53 percent said they were at home or elsewhere and did not participate. . . .

[On one riot occasion in Detroit] a spirit of carefree nihilism was taking hold. To riot and destroy appeared more and more to become ends in themselves. Late Sunday afternoon it appeared to one observer that young people were "dancing amid the flames."

. . . A man threw a Molotov cocktail into a business establishment at the corner. [Fanned by winds,] the fire reached the home next door within minutes. As residents uselessly sprayed the flames with garden hoses, the fire jumped from roof to roof of adjacent two- and three-story buildings. Within the hour, the entire block was in flames. The ninth house in the burning row belonged to the arsonist who had thrown the Molotov cokctail. . . .

As the riot alternately waxed and waned, one area of the ghetto remained insulated. On the northeast side the residents of some 150 blocks inhabited by 21,000 persons had, in 1966, banded together in the Protective Neighborhood Action Committee (PNAC). With professional help from the Institute of Urban Dynamics, they had organized block clubs and made plans for the improvement of the neighborhood.

When the riot broke out, the residents, through the block clubs, were able to organize quickly. Youngsters, agreeing to stay in the neighborhood, participated in directing traffic. While many persons reportedly sympathized with the idea of a rebellion against the "system," only two small fires were set—one in an empty building.

From *Report of the National Advisory Commission on Civil Disorders*, pp. 4, 5, 7.

Diversity and strain

strain, *generalized beliefs, precipitating incidents, mobilization,* and *social control.* Smelser believes that these six factors must all be at work before hostile outbursts (mobs or riots) occur. If they are all at work, such outbursts are sure to come. Each of these concepts is described below.

Structural conduciveness

The term *structural conduciveness* describes a society structured so that it has many conflicting interest groups that make themselves heard, communicate freely with each other, and may clash. This kind of society is open to collective behavior of all types, including riots, demonstrations, social movements, fads, and crazes. Structural conduciveness is only one factor that makes collective behavior possible; it does not make such behavior inevitable.

Structural strain

Structure refers to the relationship of each part of society to another. Such parts may include a system of popular elections, free enterprise economics, monogamous marriage, and universal education. Strain occurs when parts of the system do not—or do not seem to—work properly or mesh with other parts. If groups seem unable to get anywhere by popular elections in a society with both democratic election and success expectations, or if the government becomes remote from the people, structural strain arises. If the supposedly "free enterprise" system is seen as a system of monopolies which offer nothing to the average person, social strain results. If cultural norms and educational systems call for equal opportunities but minority groups, poor people, and women feel excluded, then another source of strain develops.

Generalized beliefs

Generalized beliefs—beliefs widely held in the society—have already been mentioned in refer-

ence to hysteria. Early types of generalized beliefs concerned mysterious evil forces such as witchcraft. Generalized beliefs can also be positive, such as prophecies of a second coming of Christ. The generalized belief at the time of the urban riots was a bitter one: belief in the exploitation of blacks by white society, specifically by landlords, ghetto store owners, and prejudiced city councils and police. In a sense, this generalized belief also contained a millennial element—the feeling that the day of black equality was at hand.

Precipitating incidents

Precipitating incidents are events that touch off collective behavior. These are not the same as *causes.* The urban riots of the 1960s had many causes; but sometimes, as in the Watts area of Los Angeles, the incident that touched off the explosion—the precipitating incident—was minor. In Watts, it was the arrest of a black man on a drunk driving charge. Even wars have been started by minor incidents. Consider just the names of some of them: the War of Jenkins' Ear (between England and Spain) or the War of the Flyswatter (between France and Algeria). World War I was touched off by the assassination of the heir to the throne of Austria-Hungary.

Mobilization

The term *mobilization* as used by Smelser does not necessarily refer to the military. It includes a means of spreading propaganda, notifying potential activists, and trying to get community support. After investigating the riots of the 1960s, the National Advisory Commission on Civil Disorders found no national organization. It did find some local organization, as shown by pamphlets and an underground press.

The problem of social control

Social control means maintaining order and observing the norms of society. During the ghetto riots of the 1960s, social control took place in two ways. First, many people in the ghetto had internalized the norm of nonviolence. Second, there was the activism of counterrioters, as in Cleveland. In most tense situations, some people feel they have an interest in keeping the peace. When nonviolence norms fail, social control is possible only with force. However, police power could not stop the riots of the 1960s. In general, even if police power is increased, a society cannot continue to rely on outside force alone. Unless most of its members favor social control, society is in a weak position whenever structural strain and antagonistic generalized beliefs are at work.

Inevitability of riots?

Smelser's theory seems to imply that if the six factors described above are at work, collective behavior must occur. Actually, most of the factors at work in the 1960s are probably with us now. Why, then, have there been no riots in recent years? Seymour Spilerman (1971, pp. 427–443) questions whether riots will occur if there are problems in only one small area or city. During the 1960s, riots in one city seemed to trigger riots in others. This was not just imitation. Tensions in the society as a whole had reached the explosion point. Therefore Spilerman concludes that riots depend on events and communications running through the whole society. Those favoring Smelser could argue that generalized beliefs have changed since the 1960s, when black Americans were far more optimistic than they are now about gaining economic equality. It is true that, in recent years far more black people have moved up in politics, entertainment, and the business and professional worlds. But most ghetto residents are not much better off. At the same time, however, civil rights legislation, an increase in the number of black mayors, and better integration of police forces have probably all worked to reduce tension in

the black communities (Spilerman, 1971, pp. 427–443).

Rumors and collective behavior

Riots and lynchings sometimes stem from unconfirmed rumors or exaggerated and twisted versions of actual events. *Rumor* is a form of communication that arises whenever people want to know what is happening but can get little dependable information. Most rumors are spread by word of mouth. Sometimes contradictory rumors are spread. In these cases, rumors that seem easiest to believe last longest. The insert "Where Rumor Raged," from a study of Detroit, shows that fear stimulates rumor. In this case, white people were afraid for their children and black people feared that they might be put in concentration camps or become victims of mass murder.

In the summer of 1967, Detroit had been hit by race riots, and the city was haunted by fear. As the summer ended, rioting was brought under control, but all through the winter of 1967–1968 more riots were anticipated. Rumors spread in all major cities, but in Detroit the situation became worse because of a newspaper strike that made it hard to get accurate news. As is usual in a conflict situation, extremists on both sides spread rumors that helped to keep the city on edge. Two small right-wing newspapers spread the message that the black riots were part of a communist conspiracy. On the other side, an extremist black newspaper fed the rumor that plans were being made to set up concentration camps for black leaders and that whites were planning to wipe out the black race.

To stop the rumors, the city of Detroit set up a rumor control center. People could phone in to ask about the accuracy of stories they had heard. The most common rumors were tabulated and analyzed, as described in the insert "Where Rumor Raged."

Rumors, as this insert shows, not only rein-

Where rumor raged   MARILYN ROSENTHAL

The first rumor received by the center went like this: "Mrs. H. heard from her neighbor who heard from her aunt, who heard from a lady in Birmingham (Michigan), who heard from her neighbor who heard from her cleaning lady that the riot was to start July 1st. The lady in Birmingham had asked her cleaning lady to work on July 1st, and the cleaning woman had responded by saying she could not work on July 1st as this was the day the riot was to start."

That first day the center received 96 calls; there was to be a day when it would receive 1600. The calls generally fell into three categories: rumors of irrelevance, rumors of incidents, and rumors of fear.

[Irrelevant rumors consisted of crank calls, or "I hear the mayor is running around with. . . ." Rumors of incidents were reports of actual happenings but greatly exaggerated. A protest at school turned into a school being looted and burned. The overwhelming number of rumors were rumors of fear.]

The overwhelming number of rumor calls were of a much less specific nature. The callers seemed to need to have their fears allayed. There was fear of a black invasion of the suburbs; fear that the water systems were going to be blown up or poisoned; fear of violence directed at a specific suburb such as Grosse Pointe or Dearborn; fear that violence would begin on a specific date. "I heard from a man who works in a plant in Livonia that the riots will start on June 20th"; "On July 4th"; "On Easter Sunday." A specific date seemed to give the rumor an air of authenticity.

A rumor that appeared again and again in the center reports concerned the killing of white children. Blacks were going to kidnap and kill a young boy from every subdivision in the suburbs; school buses would be attacked; children would be shot on street corners. In one Jewish neighborhood, the rumor took the quasibiblical form that a young Jewish male from each street would be shot. Many rumors concerned policemen, and how their families and homes would be attacked and destroyed. It was feared that each policeman's family was to be killed one by one.

By the time the rumors faded away, more than 10,000 calls were recorded, and the great majority of rumor callers were thought to be white. The center developed an elaborate classification system, but one especially frightening rumor defied the usual classifications.

The Castration Rumor

The castration rumor seems to erupt at many times of crisis in history, and it has cross-cultural variants, appearing in Egyptian mythology and elsewhere. While castration rumors were much more frequently heard in whispered private conversation, they did make their way to the center. Although they appear to have had no basis in either fact, incident, or statement, they are of such a special, highly charged nature that they must be examined separately.

The essence of the rumor was this: A mother and her young son are shopping at a large department store. At one point the boy goes to the lavatory. He is gone a long time, and the mother asks a floor supervisor to get him. The man discovers the boy lying unconscious on the floor. He has been castrated. Nearby salesclerks recall that several teenage boys were seen entering the lavatory just before the young boy and

(Continued)

Collective behavior

leaving shortly before he was discovered. If the story is told in the white community, the boy is white and the teen-agers are Negro. If it is told by Negroes, then the mother and the boy are black and the teen-agers white. . . .

[The same type of rumor appeared in other cities and has accompanied wars.]

The anxiety triggered deep emotional response. Every person is to some extent responsive to castration anxiety, as a current problem or as a vestigial remnant of childhood development. Some in the community experienced this current stress as a spontaneous eruption of castration anxiety manifesting itself in the castration rumor. This was the only explanation of the castration rumor that anyone had to offer.

Barring proof of a specific incident, this explanation would appear convincing. However, one other element can't be neglected: the reality of historical memory. While there may have been no racial incidents of castration in Detroit, old stories of white castration of blacks in the South are not unknown, nor untrue. Individuals may not recall specific cases, but vague memories and hazy recollections of hearing or reading of them linger in the black community's historical memory. So the psychological dynamics suggested by psychiatrists are given added probability as they operate within a context of a plausible historic event.

From Marilyn Rosenthal, "Where Rumor Raged," published by permission of Trans-Action, Inc., from *Trans-Action*, vol. 8, February 1971, pp. 34–43. Copyright © 1975 by Trans-Action, Inc.

---

force the fearful images conflicting groups build up about each other but also express fear for those things people value most highly—their homes, children, freedom, and life itself. Ordinarily, rumors are a form of gossip, sometimes malicious but rarely leading to crowd actions.

FASHIONS AND FADS: COMMERCIALISM OR COLLECTIVE BEHAVIOR?

Fashions are widely accepted customs in dress, speech, music, art, and other areas. But fashion often seems so manipulated by business that it does not appear to be part of collective behavior. Hemlines go up or down, while hula hoops, surfboards, and skateboards come and go. However, the public has something of a veto. Men can rebel against tight-fitting jackets. Women can fight the "new look" for the season. In exercising this veto, consumers add an element of collective behavior to fashion. It is also true that some groups take up the extremes of style, making them more successful than even the designers had expected. These extremes of style, usually called *fads*, are quickly adopted and just as quickly dropped. *Fad* is a somewhat belittling word; we think that young or foolish people follow fads, while more responsible members of "the establishment" follow fashion. Actually, in many cases young people wear comfortable clothes, while middle-class businessmen dress in suits and ties even in hot weather. Fashion is respectable and approved by tradition; fads are not.

Fads also include new ways of having fun: packing phone booths or Volkswagens, the "streaking" of the early 1970s, Frisbies, and idolizing popular singers or musicians. In all these cases, the groups which adopt the fads are doing so without clear-cut directions from their cultures. It is not clear, however, whether following fads makes people less discontented and anxious, as suggested in the earlier definition of collective behavior. The drastic changes in music and hairstyles that occurred in the 1960s provide good examples of major cultural fads.

Music

Singers and popular songs come and go, but for many years most popular musical lyrics dealt with love themes—or blues themes when love went wrong. In the 1960s music changed: Lyrics protested social and political wrongs, folk songs became more popular, new tempos were used, electronics was added to instruments, and the music itself became more inventive. The Beatles, the Rolling Stones, Bob Dylan, and Joan Baez created music very different from earlier jazz or other types of popular music. Several writers have viewed this music not merely as a new style or fad but as a social phenomenon symbolic of a new generation (Gleason, 1967; Rosenstone, 1969, pp. 132–144). Robert Rosenstone sums up briefly what the new music was saying:

This, then, is the portrait of America that emerges in the popular songs of the 1960s which can be labeled as "protest." It is, in the eyes of the song writers, a society which makes war on peoples abroad and acts repressively toward helpless minorities like Negroes, youth, and hippies at home. It is a land of people whose lives are devoid of feeling, love, and sexual pleasure. It is a country whose institutions are crumbling away, one which can presumably only be saved by a sort of cultural and spiritual revolution which the young themselves will lead.

Whether one agrees wholly, partly, or not at all with such a picture of the United States, the

Figure 11-3 Chile in 1976 was the scene of political chaos. Many protested against the involvement of the United States in Chile. Folk singers Pete Seeger and Joan Baez appeared at a benefit for "the cause of human rights in Chile." (*United Press International*)

major elements of such a critical portrait are familiar enough. . . . (p. 141)

Rosenstone's essay was written in 1969. Since then, the music he describes has changed. The protest theme has become less marked with the end of the war in Vietnam and the end of the stormy 1960s. Musical innovation, however, has not disappeared. As with the social movements to be discussed later, music has often influenced the culture. In some countries, protest songs now raise more concern than in the United States. (See the insert "Folk Singers: A Thorn in Spain's Side.")

Hair

"Until the Beatle revolution, American men were probably the most clean-shaven, short-haired men in the world" (Brown, 1970). Ac-

cording to Warren Brown, short hair usually symbolizes men and long hair, women. To reverse the symbols, then, becomes a sign of protest. Liberated women as long ago as the 1920s wore short hair. Liberated men of the 1960s started letting their hair grow longer. To the conservative older generation, long hair and beards symbolized revolution. Since the days of Karl Marx, with his long hair and full beard, political cartoons have portrayed bomb-throwing anarchists as long-haired, full-bearded men. Many conservative regimes, Brown tells us, have always perceived long hair and beards as a threat. (See the insert "That Threatening Hair.") However, longer hair—though shorter than in the 1960s—has now become the custom and may be seen on conservative businessmen. The one-time symbol of protest has become part of the establishment.

Folk singers: A thorn in Spain's side   STANLEY MEISLER

Long live the light of your eyes;
Long live your heart so great;
Long live your words, comrade of my blood.

—*Spanish folk singer paying tribute to a Communist party leader.*

Under the dictatorship of Francisco Franco, singing this lyric would have meant certain imprisonment. Today, with Franco in his grave, Spanish singers are no longer likely to be arrested, but such songs can still irritate the government, which often bans their concerts and fines the men who organize them.

The songs that irritate are known simply as folk. They are protest songs, somewhat like the music made popular in the United States by Joan Baez and Bob Dylan. In Spain, special rhythms, like flamenco, are sometimes used and the songs are often sung in regional languages. In whatever languages, the words of folk are words of protest—against poverty and exploitation, against authoritarianism and the denial of rights, against centralism and suppression of minorities.

Although Spain has a new freedom of assembly law, Spanish officials seem to be confused about how to handle the protest singers. Some authorities permit the concerts; some ban them. It is easier, for example, to obtain a license for a folk concert in Barcelona than in the Madrid area. . . .

Diversity and strain

That threatening hair WARREN BROWN

"The connection between beards and freedom," writes Reginald Reynolds, "is . . . a long one." No wonder that nowadays, when we think of hairy men, we think of Karl Marx, Bernard Shaw, Garibaldi, Fidel and his followers, anarchists, wobblies, Sinn Feiners [Irish revolutionists]—not to overlook hippies, yippies, and the New Left, Allen Ginsberg, the former Jerry Rubin, and the former Abbie Hoffman.

Tyrants have therefore always trembled at the thought of the hirsute. In the 1830s, Turkey, by imperial decree, banned beards; the King of Bavaria outlawed mustaches. In Naples, according to one nineteenth-century observer, men were being "dragged daily into the barbershops by the police and their beards trimmed according to the political creeds of the authorities." In 1967, the military dictators of Greece announced that long-haired tourists would no longer be allowed into the country, and barbershops would be set up at all entry points to turn Cavaliers into Skinheads. (The ban was soon lifted because of travel-industry protests.) Modern-day Cuba, having had its revolution, wants no more truck with revolutionaries, and in 1968 the Cuban military banned long hair and mustaches from Havana University. As for the United States, our official position was taken in 1968 also, when the Supreme Court refused to overturn the explusion of three long-haired students from a Dallas high school. [Since changed to some degree by school-district regulations and custom.] The lone dissenter was that honorary Cavalier William O. Douglas, who stated that he believed that a country founded upon the Declaration of Independence could permit "idiosyncrasies to flourish, especially when they concern the image of one's personality and his philosophy toward government and his fellow men."

From Warren Brown, "Why Hair Has Become a Four-Letter Word," *Avant Garde*, May 1970.

SOCIAL MOVEMENTS

The *social movement*, the longest-lasting form of collective behavior, is designed to create or resist changes in attitudes, behavior, and institutions. If social movements are successful, they are no longer a form of collective behavior. They become part of the culture.

Patterns in major social movements

The women's liberation movements of the nineteenth and early twentieth centuries show a strange pattern. When one major demand of the movement was met, people thought the fight was over. That is, when women gained the vote, many women felt the problem of women's rights had been solved. The women's liberation movement of the 1960s came as a shock to many people, who had never thought about all the grievances discussed in Chapter 8.

Both the earlier and the present women's liberation movements show another trait of social movements. In the beginning, the leaders are generally seen as silly or fanatic. They chain themselves to railings of the governor's mansion or burn their bras. Surely they couldn't be taken seriously! Sometimes, there is strong opposition or persecution. Eventually, such movements become more respectable and better organized and start to cooperate with the establishment. Lawyers are hired, publicity is organized, and lobbyists move to Washington and state capitals. Finally, the movement becomes institutionalized.

Collective behavior

Figure 11-4 (a) This march in Selma, Alabama, was part of a mass movement in the mid-1960s to gain equal rights for black Americans. (b) In the late 1960s, women used the same means to publicize the aims of the women's liberation movement. [(a) Bruce Davidson, Magnum; (b) Ginger Chih]

In our times, permanent groups such as the National Organization for Women and the Women's Political Caucus have been formed. Antidiscrimination laws have been passed. The Equal Rights Amendment has been drafted and sent to all state legislatures for ratification.

The civil rights movement had a characteristic common to social movements—charismatic leadership. Charismatic leaders are leaders who possess personal magnetism, command personal loyalty and respect from followers, and help formulate the basic ideology of the movement.

Diversity and strain

Until his death, Dr. Martin Luther King played this charismatic leadership role. Like so many movements, the civil rights movement went through a period of struggle and violent opposition. Its greatest leader was murdered. Eventually, though, many of the goals of the movement became official government policy; and a more quiescent period followed. The present situation may prove comparable to the women's rights movement. Much has been gained, but remaining grievances, such as housing segregation and economic inequality, might cause a more active phase of the movement again in the future.

Egalitarian movements

The two women's rights movements and the civil rights movement are examples of movements which try to gain equality for their groups. Other movements for equality have been prominent in the 1960s and 1970s. Chicanos and Indians, like women and black people, stress pride in their heritage. They are trying to improve opportunities in school and work for their people as well as to obtain equal rights. Among the handicapped, organizations have been formed to promote the types of facilities and hiring policies that would give them greater equality. The elderly have formed a similar rights organization called the Gray Panthers.

Other American social movements have worked for equal opportunities. The free public education movement of the nineteenth century and the labor union movement of the nineteenth and twentieth centuries are examples. During the Great Depression of the 1930s, social security and old-age pensions won some equality for workers and the old. The Welfare Rights Organization is such a movement today.

Radical movements

A distinction is being made here between radical movements and revolutionary movements. Not all radical movements call for revolution—the overthrow of existing institutions. The word *radical* refers to all people who want basic changes in the social system. Some radicals expect change to come about gradually. Communists and socialists are both radicals in the sense of wanting basic change in the economic system, but socialists try to make changes within the existing democratic governments. Communist parties advocate the overthrow of the capitalist system along with the government and social classes that profit from capitalism. Even here, though, there are differences. The Italian and French communist parties often cooperate with the government. Those of Thailand and the Philippines do not.

Movements of world rejection

In their early phases, many religious movements have been movements of world rejection. Feeling discontented with an imperfect world, the followers of these movements turn away. They decide to prepare for a better world to come or otherwise shun society. Some nonreligious movements show a similar pattern. In some respects, the hippie movement of the 1960s was based on the rejection of the present world.

Hippies rejected the norm of economic success. They saw American society as a gigantic "rat race" of people pressuring themselves to get ahead. However, like runners on a treadmill, these people never really made progress. They worked hard for possessions, only to find that they had to work even harder for still more possessions.

It is possible to argue that the hippies didn't really reject the world. Instead, they became perfect examples of the American norms of individualism, freedom, democracy, egalitarianism, and peace. Even so, they rejected present-day affluence in favor of a simpler past.

Sociologists who study communes find many different attitudes toward norms and values among their members. As a rule, however, commune members reject much of the modern world and support the values of the past. Rosabeth Kanter, in studying communes, finds nostalgia to be the prevailing attitude:

> Throughout the commune movement is found nostalgia for the small town, for the farm, for crafts and hand work, for natural foods, and for the dress styles, hair styles, toys, herbal medicines, and equipment of the nineteenth century. The folksy down-on-the-farm tone of *The Mother Earth News*, which publicizes communes and back-to-the-land technology, expresses this nostalgia. Also involved is a longing to return to the more recent past, a nostalgia for the innocence, simplicity, playfulness, and lack of obligation of childhood; the flower child image of the hippie movement symbolizes this tendency. Judson Jerome characterized these phenomena as part of a movement to create "Eden" rather than "utopia." (1972, p. 168)

These communes look back to an old-fashioned America for their values. Although communes arise as part of a counterculture in protest against many traits of the modern world, they are not organized revolutionary movements designed to remake society.

Revolutionary movements

Revolutionary movements are those that try to overthrow existing political and economic systems and power structures. Using the Puritan Revolution of England, the American Revolution, and the Russian Revolution as models, Crane Brinton has looked for certain similarities in the successful revolutionary movement (1938). He found that there must be many people distributed throughout the social structure who are discontented with the old regime. Along with the discontentment, there must be leaders who formulate a new ideology, who promise the beginning of a new age for humani-

ty. (An *ideology* is a system of ideas that gives a reason for a particular way of life or social system, such as democracy or dictatorship.) Brinton found that the leaders of revolutionary movements do not come from the most alienated and dispossessed segments of the population. Leaders arise as a new class of people comes to power. In the countries he studied, Brinton identified that new class as the middle class.

Brinton found that despite setbacks from time to time, there was a long period of rising prosperity before these successful revolutions took place. Especially for the middle classes, this prosperity created frustration; people felt that much more could easily be accomplished. Therefore the middle class pressed against their ineffective governments for change. In each case, the ruling monarchy, deeply in dept, tried to levy higher taxes and succeeded in alienating the people. Dissension grew up within the ruling class and the armed forces. The final collapse came with the failure of the armed forces to defend the old regime, either through inability or because they had swung to the insurgents.

After analyzing these and other revolutionary movements, James Davies has added another important element to Brinton's analysis (1962, pp. 5–19). In all the cases he studied, Davies found that the discontented classes had achieved a good deal of economic progress, but this progress was suddenly blocked—by inept governmental actions, financial crises, crop failures, or econonic depressions. According to Davies, the most explosive revolutionary situations arise when people's hopes for the future have been greatly raised over a long period of time and then are suddenly dashed.

If Brinton and Davies are correct, we should expect the world today to be quite explosive. People are aware of more possibilities than in the past. Revolutionary ideologies of nationalism, racism, and communism are easily available, as are the products of the industrialized world. Living conditions are very poor in much of the underdeveloped world. But death rates are declining because of improved medical care, and increasing industrialization promises economic improvements. At the same time, government regimes are often inept, and they are becoming more vulnerable to such worldwide economic conditions as depressions and fuel shortages. All the ingredients for trouble are at hand, helping to make ours an unsettled and dangerous age.

SUMMARY

The collapse of the Republic of South Vietnam is used as a drastic example of many kinds of *collective behavior*. During the collapse of the South Vietnamese government, panics, riots, looting, and orgies of killing and rape took place. The field of collective behavior includes such events and many others of a more or less spontaneous nature that take place in society— mass hysteria, rumors, mass movements, fads, and the extremely emotional behavior at some types of political rallies, religious observances, and rock concerts.

Collective behavior is associated with societies that have rapid communication, subcultures with different ways of life, and freedom of expression and action. However, some types of collective behavior occur even in societies without mass communications. The mass hysteria that accompanied the Black Death in the fourteenth century is one example. The Salem witch hunts are another. In these cases, fear spread and innocent people were made scapegoats. In our time, scapegoating has affected black people in the South and in the McCarthy era, political liberals. Minor cases of hysteria have involved supposed visitors from outer space.

There are different types of crowds: *casual, conventional, expressive, orgiastic,* and *active.* In the last three cases, *heightened suggestibility* and *social contagion* are found. The crowd is very responsive to the behavior of others, especially the leaders. There are many theories about active crowds engaged in riots. One such is

Figure 11-5 A parade on the ninth anniversary of the founding of the People's Republic of China. The revolutionary movement that created this new state obliterated the political, social, and economic life of the old regime. (*Cartier-Bresson, Magnum*)

convergence theory, which holds that people who are ready to riot converge at the scene. It has been pointed out, however, that many participants start out as bystanders. An alternative to the convergence theory is the *emergent-norm theory,* which holds that decisions are made as the crowd gathers and decides what to do. There are also arguments over whether crowds are irrational. What seems rational to some people or societies does not seem so to others. Not all onlookers take part in riots; some actually try to stop them.

Neil J. Smelser is famous for a social-structure theory of collective behavior. Smelser says that six conditions are necessary for riots: *structural conduciveness, structural strain, generalized beliefs, precipitating incidents, mobilization of the rioters*, and *weakness in social control*. All these conditions existed in black ghettos before the riots of the 1960s, and they still exist now. Today, however, there are no riots.

Rumors are common to active crowds (mobs and rioters). They spread and grow as they are passed along by antagonistic people.

Fashions and *fads* are also considered part of collective behavior, although fads are a much better example than fashions. Since fashions are promoted by business, they can be said to have clear-cut direction from the culture. Fads are more spontaneous. They often arise among young people or minority groups and serve the purpose of fun and variety. Fads become most important to collective behavior when they symbolize social protest, as with the hairstyles and music of the 1960s. These styles often cause a struggle between conservatives and radicals.

Social movements are also part of collective behavior. They include *egalitarian movements, radical movements, movements of world rejection*, and *revolutionary movements*. Revolutionary movements attempt drastic change in the social order by destruction of the present power structure. Two theories, those of Crane Brinton and James C. Davies, are presented. Both say that revolutionary movements are led by classes that have made a certain amount of progress and have high expectations for the future. Davies adds that for a revolutionary movement to develop, something must occur to suddenly thwart those expectations.

Study guide

Terms to know

Collective behavior
Tightly structured society
Loosely structured society
Mass hysteria
Scapegoats
Crowd
Casual crowd
Conventional crowd
Expressive crowd
Orgiastic crowd
Active crowd

Crowd contagion
Convergence theory
Emergent-norm theory
Counterrioters
Smelser's theory of
collective behavior:
Structural
conduciveness
Structural strain
Generalized belief
Precipitating incident

Mobilization
Social control
Rumors
Fashions
Fads
Social movements
Egalitarian
Radical
World-rejecting
Revolutionary
Ideology

Heightened
suggestibility
Social contagion
Milling behavior
Circular reaction

Names to know

Gustave LeBon
Herbert Blumer
Neil J. Smelser

Crane Brinton
James C. Davies

Self-test

Part I. Multiple Choice. Select the best of the four alternative answers:

1 One characteristic of collective behavior is that the actions involved are relatively (a) well organized, (b) institutionalized, (c) spontaneous, (d) communist-inspired.
2 The most basic and disorganized form of collective behavior, as analyzed by Smelser, is (a) a riot, (b) mass hysteria, (c) scapegoating, (d) a fad.
3 In the Black Death of 1348, Jews were made scapegoats and so were (a) priests, (b) licentious people, (c) government officials, (d) doctors.
4 Modern warfare produces certain behaviors resembling those of the Black Death, including (a) scapegoating, (b) increased piety, (c) increased debauchery, (d) all the above.
5 In a Southern mill town, many cases of hysterial illness were attributed to (a) anthrax in the wool, (b) the bite of a strange insect, (c) a lubricant used in the machinery, (d) chemicals used in the dye.
6 The account entitled "Invitation to an Unearthly Kingdom" can be attributed to anxieties about (a) the devil, (b) political revolutionaries, (c) outer space, (d) earthquake predictions.
7 LeBon's description of crowd actions that seems *least* plausible is (a) spontaneity, (b) suggestibility, (c) little reflective capacity, (d) a group mind.
8 Both riots and mobs are included under the term (a) *active crowd*, (b) *expressive crowd*, (c) *orgiastic crowd*, (d) *casual crowd*.
9 Studies of urban riots of the 1960s indicate that the majority of people living near the area (a) joined the riot, (b) became counterrioters, (c) stayed home, (d) took part in looting.
10 A study of urban rioters in Newark found that those who took part were (a) nonpolitical and

apathetic, (b) distrustful and nonpolitical, (c) political and distrustful, (d) political and trustful in the system.

11 In Smelser's theory of collective behavior, a loosely structured society with conflicting interests and ability to organize and communicate easily is referred to as having (a) structural conduciveness, (b) structural strain, (c) generalized beliefs, (d) mobilization capacity.

12 In her article "Where Rumor Raged," Rosenthal found that the most common rumors could be called (a) rumors of irrelevance, (b) rumors of incidents, (c) rumors of fear, (d) rumors of hope.

13 In the article "That Threatening Hair," Brown implies that William O. Douglas was the only Supreme Court justice to uphold the right of Dallas high school students to wear their hair long because Douglas was (a) something of a rebel, (b) very conservative, (c) old and senile, (d) antagonistic toward the other justices.

14 Most social movements of the 1960s and 1970s could be characterized as (a) radical movements, (b) egalitarian movements, (c) movements of world rejection, (d) revolutionary movements.

15 Brinton and Davies would agree that revolutionary movements (a) are led by the poorest elements of society, (b) occur after long periods of hopeless poverty, (c) occur only if there appears to be hope for the future, (d) occur only if promoted by outside interests.

Part II. True-False Questions

1 Although the collapse of South Vietnam resulted from war, most of the traits of collective behavior were present in the final days.

2 Turner and Killian define *collective behavior* as "actions of groups that operate without clear-cut direction from their culture."

3 During the Black Death, all the people became much more pious and restrained than before.

4 In a modern, scientific age, there are no more hysterical cases of fear of devils, possession, and the like.

5 The "witch hunt" of Senator McCarthy's time fits the text description of mass hysteria quite well.

6 A classic case of mass hysteria resulted from a radio broadcast of a story about an invasion from Mars.

7 Herbert Blumer has provided much better explanations than did LeBon of how crowd contagion takes place.

8 Convergence theory holds that all people at the scene of a riot or mob action will inevitably be drawn in.

9 Emergent-norm theory assumes that after a crowd gathers, decisions are made.

10 People who take part in riots are less intelligent than the general public.

11 Rumors are most likely to spread if they fit the existing ideas of the people who hear them.

12 A common rumor about a little boy being castrated was spread in Detroit by whites about blacks and by blacks about whites.

13 Many fads could be described as new ways of having fun.

14 Fads and fashions become important when they seem to symbolize an important change or a threatening opinion.

15 Only in a few recent cases have the leaders of social movements been called fanatics.

Questions for discussion

1 In your experience, what types of group interaction have led to the greatest social contagion?
2 How is social contagion accounted for by Gustave LeBon and by Herbert Blumer? Do either of them relate social contagion to the conditions that might have caused it?
3 Draw a parallel between the scapegoating of Jews and doctors during the Black Death and more recent examples of scapegoating. (Try to think of examples other than the ones given in the text, involving other minority leaders, or social movements.)
4 Which, in your opinion, better accounts for race riots—convergence theory or emergent-norm theory? Answer the same question with regard to student antiwar demonstrations and lynch mobs.
5 Taking the role of an English Tory, comment on the irrationality of the crowd at the Boston Tea Party.
6 What are the differences between Smelser's theory of collective behavior and those of LeBon and Blumer? Which is more sociological? Why?
7 From your own experience or from your reading, analyze a case of rumor, distortion of the facts, and conformity to the preconceptions of the rumor spreaders.
8 Why is our society more likely to have social movements than some other societies?
9 If the theories of Brinton and Davies are correct, what societies today would be likely to have revolutionary movements?

Projects

1 Attend a college football game and analyze it in terms of structured behavior and unstructured behavior. That is, which events are called for by regulations and norms and which are not? In either case, is crowd contagion present?
2 Recordings have been made of the famous Orson Wells radio program "Invasion from Mars." Get a copy to play for the class and consider why it led to mass hysteria when it was presented in 1938. (This question is discussed in an article by an associate of Orson Welles, John Houseman, in *Harpers Magazine*, vol. 197, December 1948, pp. 74–82.)
3 If you are interested in music or literature, analyze the connection between fashion and fad in those areas. For example, look into the lives of certain innovators in those fields (Stravinsky or Schoenberg in music, Whitman in poetry, and James Joyce in prose). Why is someone considered an upstart or faddist at one time and a genius at another?
4 Analyze a current fad. Where did it start? What is its appeal? How does it spread? Does it symbolize new social attitudes, or is it strictly for fun?

Suggested Readings

Conant, Ralph W.: "Rioting, Insurrection and Civil Disobedience," *American Scholar*, vol. 37, Summer 1968, pp. 420–433. What are the preconditions of riots and what are the stages in their development? These questions are analyzed by Conant. Also, using traditional American values as his guide, Conant lists six conditions justifying nonviolent protest.

Drabeck, Thomas E., and Enrico L. Quarantelli: "Scapegoats, Villains, and Disasters," *Trans-Action*, vol. 4, March 1967, pp. 12–17. Why do some people make better scapegoats than others? Why do we blame people rather than inadequate laws for disasters? What happens when we blame people rather than laws and regulations? Drabeck and Quarantelli examine these questions in a review of some of the greatest fire disasters in American history.

Dynes, Russell, and Enrico L. Quarantelli: "What Looting in Civil Disturbances Really Means," *Trans-Action*, vol. 5, May 1968, pp. 9–14. Why is looting rare in natural disasters but common during civil disturbances? Dynes and Quarantelli find a great difference in attitudes toward protecting private property.

Gusfield, Joseph R.: "Social Structure and Moral Reform: A Study of the Women's Christian Temperance Union," *American Journal of Sociology*, vol. 61, no. 3, November 1955, pp. 221–232. What phases can a social movement go through? Why do such slogans as "Drink is the curse of the working man" appeal to one age and not to another? Gusfield's discussion, both scholarly and amusing, covers not only the WCTU but has much to say about movements in general.

Houseman, John: "The Men from Mars," *Harper's Magazine*, vol. 197, December 1948, pp. 74–82. Why did a radio program describing an invasion from Mars cause mass hysteria? Was the reaction influenced by the historical period in which it was produced? Why did Welles himself think the program was going to be a failure? Houseman answers these questions in "The Men From Mars."

Kerckhoff, Alan C., Kurt W. Back, and Norman Miller: "Sociometric Pattern in Hysterical Contagion," *Sociometry*, vol. 28, March 1968, pp. 2–15. Why did a group of workers in a Southern textile mill all develop the same types of physical symptoms even though no physical cause could be found? Who is most vulnerable to such types of hysterical contagion? The authors arrive at an explanation. (This is a short version of the research work, mentioned in text, done for the book *The June Bug*, Appleton Century Crofts, New York, 1968.)

Schneier, Edward V.: "White-Collar Violence and Anti-Communism," *Society*, vol. 13, March–April 1976, pp. 33–37. How did the public mood—a type of mass hysteria—make McCarthyism possible? How did HUAC (House UnAmerican Activities Committee) continue the work of McCarthy after his time? A story of how mass hysteria over communism led to mass fright on the part of liberals.

Key to questions. Multiple Choice: 1-c; 2-b; 3-d; 4-d; 5-b; 6-c; 7-d; 8-a; 9-c; 10-c; 11-a; 12-c; 13-a; 14-b; 15-c. True-False: 1-T; 2-T; 3-F; 4-F; 5-T; 6-T; 7-T; 8-F; 9-T; 10-F; 11-T; 12-T; 13-T; 14-T; 15-F.

SOCIAL INSTITUTIONS AND ORGANIZATIONS

This chapter explores trends in marriage and family, compares family systems on a cross-cultural and social-class basis, and looks at some of the present alternatives to marriage. After reading it, you should be able to:

1 Recognize that marriage in some ways makes heavier demands today than it did in the past.

2 View family and marriage as being questioned and challenged by alternative life-styles, but still the way of life of the majority.

3 Understand some of the variations in family systems in order to realize that families adjust to meet cultural demands.

4 Recognize social-class differences in marriage and family regarding child rearing, sex, and egalitarianism as well as different rates of family breakup and reasons for breakup.

5 Analyze the changing functions of the family that help make it less stable than in the past.

6 Understand the arguments for communal living but also recognize the problems of communes.

7 Present arguments for and against cohabitation without marriage.

8 Make some reasonable predictions about family trends in the future.

12
MARRIAGE AND FAMILY

Not long ago, nearly all Americans saw our marriage and family system as the only "civilized" way of life. Marriage and motherhood were sacred. True, some marriages broke up or ended in divorce, but this happened only to the "wrong" people. Respectable people were expected to marry once and to be happy in marriage. If unhappy, they were to make the best of it. They were also expected to have several children and to socialize them as they saw fit. Neither children nor the "experts" would tell them what to do.

It is easy to exaggerate how far we've come; these beliefs and practices have not changed completely. Most people still marry and say they are happy in marriage. Most parents still teach their children their own norms and values. Most husbands still dominate the marriage. The important change is not so much in the present majority of families as in the direction marriage is taking. A rapidly increasing minority is out of line with tradition.

A survey by the U.S. Census Bureau in 1975 (Associated Press, 1976) found that those between twenty-five and thirty-four years of age who had never married had increased by about 45 percent since 1970, from 2.9 million to 4.2 million. Many of these people—28.5 percent, as compared to 21.2 percent five years earlier— were living in households of their own. Divorced people also remarried fairly soon—in 1970, all but 7 percent. By 1975, 10 percent of all persons aged twenty-five to fifty-four who were divorced or widowed had not remarried.

In 1970, 85 percent of all children under eighteen were living with both parents. By 1975, this had gone down to 80 percent. The change in the last five years has been more rapid than usual. The trend is expected to level off in the near future because of the continued high regard for family life in American society. Still, no one

can be sure. For the moment, let us examine the things that make marriage look better to some than it does to others.

CHARACTERISTICS OF MODERN MARRIAGE

In modern societies, people expect more gratification from marriage than they did in the past. It is not enough that the husband be an honest, decent man and a good provider or that the wife be a good homemaker and mother. Especially in the educated middle-class family, love has become more important. Both partners look for personal fulfillment. They want to have their own special interests, activities, and work roles. No longer is the wife expected simply to take care of the house and put her interests second to her husband's. This does not mean that companionship and the sharing of life goals are no longer important, but it does mean that new demands have been placed on marriage. Couples have to try harder to mesh their personal and outside interests. These are some of the reasons why young people hesitate to marry, sometimes preferring first to live together and see whether they get along. They feel that marriage should free them, not tie them down. Given these heavy demands, it is not surprising that many marriages are broken up by divorce.

Society always has a stake in marriage and sets up rules to govern it. Modern attitudes, though, make marriage more and more an individual and private matter. To compare society's and the individual's views of marriage, let us compare modern marriages with those of more traditional societies. In older forms of marriage, the bride and groom were often strangers. The marriage was *arranged* to benefit the two families. Individual satisfaction was not important and often not considered. Today, families and societies still put some pressure on young people to marry within the same class, racial, ethnic, or religious group, but they no longer arrange marriages.

Built-in supports for marriage

People who remain single even a few years past the usual marriage age are aware of society's pressure on them to marry. Parents are anxious about their plans. First, they encourage children not to marry too young. Then, if the children are still single in their mid-twenties, the parents begin to worry. Unmarried people face discrimination in the tax structure, in renting or buying apartments or homes, and in getting credit. Married friends also put pressure on single people. In the big cities, the pressures are less strong, and there may even be a special status in avoiding marriage. For most rural and suburban people, though, the pressure to marry continues.

A type of romantic myth continues to support marriage, although today it is becoming weaker. The romantic tales of medieval poets were of passion flamed by separation—of a dream that could not come true. In the modern myth, dreams come true, love can overcome all obstacles, there is an ideal mate for every person, and the emotions are a sure guide to happiness. The myth helps to make sure that almost everyone marries. Of course it is exaggerated, but it works. It supports the idea of free choice in marriage, and that is necessary in a society which, like ours, places a high value on the individual. It also helps ensure a high marriage rate in a society with very few arranged marriages.

Societal attitudes toward sex have also helped to ensure marriage. Although these attitudes are more permissive than they once were, society still stresses sex within marriage. Sexual relations between unmarried teenagers are frowned on and, in some areas, may be grounds for arrest. If a society could prevent all premarital and extramarital sex, then the sex drive itself would ensure that most people would marry. No society has

ever been able to do this, but society's pressures to marry are very strong even today.

Marriage is an important turning point in the lives of people. Unless they are very young or have married someone outside the approved group, most people are congratulated when they marry. The older generation hopes to see them "settle down" and become responsible adults. The newly married achieve a new status. Jobs and apartments, housing loans, and credit are easier to get. The couple feel that they have now "arrived" at an important life goal. If the romantic myth has worked its magic, each of them takes great pride in the marriage.

Built-in problems of marriage

Even happily married people jokingly speak of "the ball and chain," admitting that in marriage, freedom is reduced. This is true. Whenever we are close to another person, whether in marriage or in friendship, we have to take the other person's needs into account. In our type of

Figure 12-1 Young people increasingly see marriage as a liberating partnership of equals. (*Ron Sherman, Nancy Palmer*)

society, which values individual freedom, people may resent this. At the same time, they learn that complete freedom also brings loneliness and alienation. Still, many newlyweds find it hard to learn the art of give and take.

The roles of wife and husband are new ones, which must be learned slowly. Especially now, when sexual equality is a major social issue, people are not sure what the "proper" roles are. Yankelovich (1974, p. 99) found that most college students did not agree that a woman's place is in the home. In contrast, a slight majority of noncollege youth still agreed with this traditional norm.

Even if two people agree on what their roles are, making decisions is not always easy. Conflicts are sure to arise. In these situations, it is easy for the person who cares most about the marriage to become the loser, feeling that he or she must always "give in" to keep the peace. Often the relationship can be viewed in "exchange terms": one partner gives up a goal or desire in exchange for more peace in the family or love from the other partner. There are dan-

gers, however, that if the same person constantly gives in, resentments will build up.

When setting up a new household turns out to be more expensive than was expected, arguments about money may arise. In fact, arguments over money are among the most common conflicts in marriage. The romantic myth may also lead the partners to expect greater harmony than is usually possible between people.

In American society, the family is often an isolated unit, located far from relatives and without strong neighborhood ties. In less mobile societies, the extended family (relatives) provides strong support to marriage and family life. Anthropologists have noted the contrast between the two types of society and see isolation as a particularly severe problem for American families. The insert "Alone in the Suburbs" gives an insight into the problem.

In spite of all these problems (plus many more that develop as the family grows), most families still hold together. In spite of rising divorce rates, a large majority (88 percent) of Americans polled in 1974 by the Roper organization felt that society could not "do just as well without the institution of marriage." Of all the young people surveyed, 84 percent expected to marry and have children (*Society*, March–April 1974, p. 7).

UNIVERSALITY AND DIVERSITY IN FAMILY PATTERNS

In the United States, family patterns vary with social class, ethnic background, race, and age. Throughout the world, and especially in non-Western societies, the differences in family patterns are much wider. In all societies, however, the family performs similar functions. The basic family functions have been described by Murdock (1947): legitimizing sexual relations and reproduction; feeding, clothing, and sheltering family members; and socializing and educating children. Minor exceptions can be found. For example, not all births are seen as legitimate by society. But many couples, especially among the lower classes, live together without legal or religious sanction. There are also many exceptions to providing economic support and socialization for the young. In some communes, the task is taken over by the group rather than the family. Generally speaking, though, in all societies a *nuclear family*—consisting of a father, a mother, and their children—can be found. The family lives alone or in an *extended household* with other families related by marriage. In spite of these similarities, the variations in family systems are great. The family form depends on whether it is an independent unit or part of a larger kinship group as well as on the number of spouses permitted. The variations make sense in terms of cultural relativity—that is, they fit neatly into the societies in which they are found.

The consanguineal family

The modern American family is an *isolated nuclear type*. This means that parents and children alone make up the family unit and nearly always live in their own separate household. The opposite model is called a *consanguineal family*, from *con*, meaning "with," and *sang*, meaning "blood." This model refers to a family that includes "all people of one blood." Actually, the consanguineal group usually includes just the father's relatives or, in fewer cases, just the mother's, but not both. Until modern times, the family ideal in China was the consanguineal model that is also *patrilineal*—tracing descent through the father's line. Grandparents, their adult sons, their sons' wives, and their grandchildren all lived in the same house or in the same walled compound. Such a family was also *patriarchal*, that is, ruled by the senior male member. This type of family structure was common in many societies of the past, especially in Asia and Africa. The Pueblo Indians of the American Southwest live in consanguineal families. Their families are *matrilineal* (tracing descent through women rather than men.) They are also *matrilocal*, since the married couple live in the household or near vicinity of the wife's mother.

Any type of consanguineal family is almost indestructible, since so many relatives are included. In China, divorce was almost impossible. When the nuclear family was broken by the death of one of the spouses, the consanguineal unit continued. The advantages of this type of family include its permanence and its provision for a large, cooperative kinship group. The grandfather was the head of the Chinese household and made all the important decisions. In this way, the consanguineal family was tightly bound to tradition. This family structure encouraged social stability. Family members were never isolated or alienated from each other or from society. Each person had a set and certain status. According to Francis L. K. Hsu (1967), this type of family could exist only among relatively wealthy people or in areas where there was plenty of good land, so that the land could support extra relatives. In China, the consanguineal family worked well in a stable, agricultural community. It tended to break up in the city.

(a)

Figure 12-2 Although the family is universal, it may take the form of (*a*) a nuclear family or (*b*) an extended family, including many relatives. [*(a) Burk Uzzle, Magnum; (b) Costa Manos, Magnum*]

(b)

Polygyny

Marriage and family patterns can also vary in the number of wives a man can have. A very common form is *polygyny*, in which a man has more than one wife. In the nineteenth century, the society of the Baganda people (in modern Uganda) was an outstanding example of polygyny. Almost all the men had more than one wife, with two or three for common men, ten or more for chiefs, and hundreds for the king. Internal warfare and frequent executions by the king killed so many men that eventually there were about three women for every man (McQueen, 1952, pp. 66–87).

In some cases, polygyny or other forms of plural marriage are necessary for survival. One example is that of the Eskimos, who sometimes practiced polygyny. Among the Eskimos, it was almost impossible for a man to live without a woman to make clothes and boots and to mend canoes. Nor could a woman live without a man who could hunt and fish. If there were too many women, some men took extra wives. When there was a (rare) surplus of men, a woman might have more than one husband. No one worried much about self-fulfillment or romantic ideals; the problem was to survive. On this level, the system worked well.

Many African tribes practice polygyny, although this is becoming less and less common. In polygynous societies, there are norms which regulate the relations between men and their wives. To ensure equal treatment for all women, men must sometimes spend one night with each wife in turn, never showing favor to any one of them (see the insert "Love in a Polygynous Marriage").

Jealousies over love and sexual relations are either uncommon or kept quiet. Problems over status do arise between the senior wife and junior wives. The women are also concerned about inheritance. Each one hopes that her children will receive at least an equal share of the cattle owned by the husband.

In the Arab world, polygynous families are less common now than in the past. The Koran lays down rules about who can have extra wives. A man must maintain a good reputation and have enough money to support his extra wives. Ideally, he should be willing to marry the widow of a friend who has died or been killed in battle. By doing so, he can take care of her and her children. This system was important in the days of constant warfare, when many men were killed. None of the polygynous family systems would be acceptable to modern feminists, although polygyny seemed to satisfy some Arab women. They thought that it would be better to share a good man than to be the only wife of an inferior man. The thinking was practical, not romantic. It also reflected an adjustment to the inevitable.

Polyandry

In another form of marriage and family, *polyandry*, a woman has more than one husband. As a preferred type of marriage, polyandry is rare in the world. It has been practiced in Tibet, in Hunza, and among a small group of herding people in southern India called the Toda. In most cases, polyandry takes on a fraternal form, as when a group of brothers all marry the same woman. Explanations for the development of polyandry vary. Among the Toda, it has served to keep herds of sacred cattle in the same families. Since a group of brothers had only one wife, their children all belonged to the same family lineage. With this arrangement, limited resources such as sacred cattle did not have to be divided among male heirs.

The minimal family

In a few cases, the family as a distinct institution has been reduced to a minimum. In such cases, the biological father has almost no role in the family. Occasionally, both parents are largely freed from duties to their children. In earlier

Love in a polygynous marriage JOMO KENYATTA

Jomo Kenyatta, the aged president of Kenya, wrote of the marriage system of his people, the Gikuyu, according to the cultural ideal:

Having described the division and distribution of labour, it is necessary to mention something about the distribution of love. No doubt some people wonder how one man is able to love many women. This is a very vital question, especially among those whose religious beliefs have taught them that to love more than one woman is a crime, and furthermore a sin against heavenly gods. On the contrary, the Gikuyu are taught from childhood that to be a man is to be able to love and keep a homestead of as many wives as possible. With this in view, Gikuyu male children are brought up to cultivate the idea and technique of extending their love to several women and to look upon them as companions and as members of one big family. The girls, too, are taught how to share a husband's love and to look upon him as the father of one big family. The idea of sharing everything is strongly emphasized in the upbringing of children, so when they grow up they find it natural to share love and affection with others, for it is said that: "To live with others is to share and to have mercy for one another," and: "It is witch-doctors who live and eat alone."

In order to avoid jealousy (*oiru*) among the wives, Gikuyu custom provides that each wife must be visited by her husband on certain days of the moon. . . . Each wife has this special privilege. The wives . . . see to it that the husband does not neglect his duty of distributing his love equally among them. Such conjugal relation is the only way in which polygamous homesteads could be kept in harmony. The three days after menstruation are considered as the most likely for a woman to conceive. For this reason the husband does not generally cohabit with her again until after the next menstruation. If by then she has conceived, the husband allows a period of three months to elapse before having intercourse again, in order not to cause an abortion.

Jomo Kenyatta, *Facing Mt. Kenya*, Vintage Books, Random House, New York, 1938, pp. 172–173.

---

times, the Nayar Taravad of India had a system which ensured the continuity of the group without marriage. Women were assigned a number of lovers who could visit them at night, but the union was not seen as a marriage (Gouch, 1959, pp. 23–24). The Nayars were a military caste, in which servants and older family members cared for children. The young men had to be available for military duty. They could not be bothered with the duties of fatherhood. Ancient Sparta, it seems, also played down the importance of marriage. Men spent most of their time in the military lodge rather than with their wives. Sons were taken from their mothers at the age of seven to start military training. In Nazi Germany, during the 1930s and 1940s, Hitler encouraged births outside of marriage to free young soldiers from family ties and responsibilities. According to anthropologist Claude Lévi-Strauss (1971, pp. 333–357), extreme militarism can be an enemy of a close-knit family.

The *kibbutz* of Israel is a widely studied and generally admired communal family system. The *kibbutzim* are agricultural communes. The children are reared mainly by women (*metapelets*) who are interested in caring for children. This frees the parents to work on the farm. The *kibbutz* movement was started by young Jewish immigrants to Israel who were rebelling against the father-dominated Jewish tradition. The result is a system in which young couples live together, with or without marriage, and have only slight responsibility for their children. Children visit them an hour or two each day. The children are raised mostly within peer groups. Unions between couples tend to be permanent, but the pair are free to separate at will.

Although not founded for military purposes, the *kibbutzim* have served this function well. Men and women are freed for military duty when necessary. Only a small minority of Israelis belong to *kibbutzim*, but they have contributed greatly to Israeli military leadership (Bettleheim, 1969).

The denigration of romance

Except possibly for the *kibbutz*, none of the family systems described above stresses romantic love. The traditional Oriental family has considered family survival too important to base marriage on passion. In polygynous families, the prestige of high-status males was more important than romance. In other cases, military needs have come first.

In such societies, though, love may follow marriage. A famous passage from the *Ramayana*, an epic poem written in India, expresses intensely romantic feelings. Rama, the hero of the epic, is sent into exile in the forest for fourteen years. His wife, Sita, begs to go with him. Her speech has provided an ideal for Indian women:

Thou art my king, my guide, my only refuge, my divinity.
It is my fixed resolve to follow thee. If thou must wander forth
Through thorny trackless forests, I will go before thee, treading down
The prickly brambles to make smooth thy path. Walking before thee, I

Shall feel no weariness: the forest thorns will seem like silken robes;
The bed of leaves, a couch of down. To me the shelter of the presence
Is better far than stately palaces, and paradise itself.
Protected by thy arm, gods, demons, men shall have no power to harm me.
Roaming with thee in desert wastes, a thousand years will be a day:
Dwelling with thee, e'en hell itself would be to me a heaven of bliss. (Mace and Mace, 1960, p. 125. © 1959, 1960 by David and Vera Mace; reprinted by permission of Doubleday and Company, Inc.)

This passage expresses a wife's love for her husband. It does not allow for love between unmarried people, which could disrupt arranged marriages. The poem also confirms the "proper" relation of wife to husband. The wife is subservient to her husband, who becomes her "guide, king, refuge, divinity."

People whose societies do not link marriage with romance may find our customs very strange. In an interview with two sociologists, Madame Wu, the wife of the Chinese ambassador to the United States, expresses her view of American marriage customs. Madame Wu speaks for Taiwan, not for the People's Republic of China, where marriage customs have changed greatly from the traditional pattern.

When Madame Wu arrived in Washington, D.C., in 1954, a reporter asked her for her views on love and marriage:

"Suppose the man picked out for you doesn't tally with your ideal?"
"My what?"
"Your ideal; all women have ideals, you know."
"I don't know that. I guess not Chinese women."
"Didn't you ever wonder what he would be like?"

"No. Chinese girls no time think about love. Before time comes think about love, Chinese girl has husband."

"Suppose you didn't like the husband picked out for you?"

"But I did. I loved him when I saw him."

"Which wasn't till your wedding day?"

"No."

"Suppose it hadn't been Mr. Wu, but somebody else—would you have loved him?"

"I would love the husband my parents choose; that is my duty. But they not choose anyone else for me. In China we believe in fate. Every couple that ought to be marry is tied together with an invisible red string. So when parents make arrangements, fate leads. Matches are made in moon. So it always is right. Fate make one certain man for each woman."

The smiling, imperturbable Madame Wu was speaking for more than two thousand years of Eastern experience. She was not impressed by Western ways.

"Americans love and marry and get divorce," she added. "We marry and love and get home and happiness and children. Which way you like?" (Mace and Mace, 1960, p. 143. © 1959, 1960 by David and Vera Mace; reprinted by permission of Doubleday and Company, Inc.)

Madame Wu spoke for an older generation. In a talk during the same year (1954) with a group of teenage students in India, David and Vera Mace explained American dating, courting, and marriage customs. They thought the young people would envy American freedom. They were surprised at the students' reactions:

When we had finished, there was a meditative silence. Concluding that they had been impressed, we decided to start a discussion.

"Wouldn't you like to be free to choose your own marriage partners, like the young people do in the West?"

They expressed strong disagreement.

Taken aback, we searched their faces.

"Why not?"

"For one thing," said one of them, "doesn't it put the girl in a very humilitating position?"

"Humiliating? In what way?"

"Well, doesn't it mean that she has to try to look pretty, and call attention to herself, and attract a boy, to be sure she'll get married?"

"Well, perhaps so."

"And if she doesn't want to do that, or if she feels it's undignified, wouldn't that mean she mightn't get a husband?"

"Yes, that's possible."

"So a girl who is shy and doesn't push herself forward might not be able to get married. Does that happen?"

"Sometimes it does."

"Well, surely that's humiliating. It makes getting married a sort of competition in which the girls are fighting each other for the boys. . . ."

One of the girls added another objection:

"But *does* the girl really have any choice in the West?" she said. "From what I''ve read, it seems that the boy does all the choosing. All the girl can do is to say yes or no. She can't go up to a boy and say, 'I like you. Will you marry me?' can she?"

We admitted that this was not the done thing.

"So," she went on eagerly, "when you talk about men and women being equal in the West, it isn't true. When our parents are looking for a husband for us, they don't have to wait until some boy takes it into his head to ask for us. They just find out what families are looking for wives for their sons, and see whether one of the boys would be suitable. Then, if his family agrees that it would be a good match, they arrange it together." (Mace and Mace, 1960, pp. 143–45. © 1959, 1960 by David and Vera Mace; reprinted by permission of Doubleday and Company, Inc.)

Figure 12-3 Computerized dating services promise to pair men and women according to compatibility of backgrounds and tastes—a service once rendered by parents and matchmakers. (*Esaias Baitel, Rapho/Photo Researchers, Inc.*)

Conclusions about family types

Family structures change to meet the needs of the culture. When individual survival depends on the family, the family cannot trust the whims of romance. In many societies, long after common people were free to marry as they pleased,

nobles and royal families continued to form arranged marriages. Their families and alliances were too important to trust to chance. As the Indian student pointed out, arranged marriage helped also in a society in which women were expected to be too shy to compete for men.

The village-type economy of the large consanguineal family has declined. The new urban-industrial society also frees the individual from reliance on the family farm. This means greater freedom in choosing a job and no urgent need to obey parents in regard to marriage.

As arranged marriage has declined, the feeling that marriage should stress personal satisfaction has increased. There is a worldwide trend toward more equal treatment of both sexes. Because of this and the decline of aristocracies, polygyny is becoming rare. Polyandry, which was always rare, is even more so now that female infanticide has been outlawed. There are now as many women as men. The only practical solution in line with the tradition of polyandry is for a group of brothers to marry a group of sisters.

Within some of the family systems described, there were considerable differences between the upper and lower classes. In most societies with polygyny, only chiefs or rich men had many wives. In East Asia, the upper classes were the ones that had large households and consanguineal families. In modern societies, too, family systems vary with social class.

SOCIAL CLASS AND MARRIAGE

The egalitarian family structure is more common in middle-class than in lower-class families. So is the idea of spouses as companions. George Levinger's 1965 study of 600 applicants for divorce in the Cleveland, Ohio, area revealed that people from different social classes make different complaints about their marriages (1966, pp. 803–807). Of the lower-class wives, 40 percent complained of physical abuse, while only 22 percent of middle-class wives did so.

Complaints about money problems showed a similar pattern. Among the middle-class applicants for divorce, complaints of lack of love were much more common. More middle-class men cited sexual incompatibility.

These figures suggest some interesting contradictions. Why, for example, is a woman who receives more physical abuse less likely to complain about lack of love? Levinger explains this by saying that more middle-class couples *expect* love. Among them, marriage without love is seen as a good reason for divorce.

Levinger also found that sexual compatibility is more important to the middle class than the lower class. It is middle-class people who buy sex manuals. A survey made by *Redbook* magazine, describing mainly white, middle-class women, indicates a strong interest in sex as well as in compatibility (see the insert on page 336: "How's Your Sex Life?").

Based on Levinger's analysis, we could say that in marriage, economic survival and freedom from physical abuse are basic needs. After these are satisfied, people begin to care more about love and interpersonal warmth, understanding, and compatibility in interests and goals. The goal of self-realization, so strongly emphasized by the women's liberation movement, is put off until the other, more basic goals are reached.

In the area of the country covered by Levinger's study (Cleveland), a marriage counselor had to be seen before a divorce could be granted. This counseling was aimed at solving the problems of middle-class marriages. It was not expected to help marriages with the basic problems of money or physical abuse.

Social class and divorce rates

When wealthy and prominent people divorce, the news hits the headlines. This leads one to think that the rich have the most divorces. Research by William Goode found that the reverse is usually true, not just in the United States but in most other societies as well (1962, pp. 507–526). The poor divorce far more often than the rich or the middle class. Goode found a divorce rate of 18 per 1,000 per year for professionals and 40 per 1,000 per year for laborers. The major exception to this rule arises when divorce is very costly. When this happens, lower-class people resort to separation without divorce. Divorce rates among all classes have

Figure 12-4 The work of the therapists Masters and Johnson has resulted in more emphasis on sexual campatibility in marriage. (*Bob Levin, Black Star*)

How's your sex life?

The white, middle-class, married woman has come a long way since her sexual pulse was last taken by Alfred Kinsey in 1953. According to a poll of 100,000 readers of *Redbook* released last week—the largest survey on female sexuality ever made—80 percent of the women had had premarital intercourse, beginning at an average age of 17, as had 90 percent of the women under 25. (The Kinsey Report found that 33 percent of women who were under 25 had premarital sex.) Almost one-third of the women had had extramarital affairs, and another 36 percent said they would like to; 90 percent of those polled have orgasms, most within ten minutes. . . .

"Our findings show that women have completely abandoned the role of passive sexual partner," said sociologist Robert J. Levin, who conducted the study. "They are now active participants in the sexual relationship"—a fact confirmed by 78 percent of the women, most of whom are white, between the ages of 20 and 34, married for the first time and working at least part time out of the home. Nearly 65 percent of the women reported masturbating occasionally or frequently, 69 percent occasionally had sex while under the influence of alcohol and 63 percent of the women under 25 sometimes smoked marijuana before having sex.

Seven out of ten wives reported sex with their husbands was "good" or "very good," and nearly 30 percent of the women who never experienced orgasm responded the same way. Strongly religious women were more likely to be satisfied with their sex lives than "mildly" or "farily" religious women, a phenomenon *Redbook* attributes to a more enlightened clergy, teaching that sexual pleasure is essential to a good marriage.

According to the *Redbook* poll, women under 25 engage in intercourse an average of twelve times a month, while women between 25 and 34 average nine times a month. And almost 40 percent of the women complain that they are not having enough sex.

Newsweek, September 1, 1975, p. 57. Copyright © 1975 by Newsweek, Inc. All rights reserved. Reprinted by permission.

risen since 1962, the date of Goode's study. But more recent evidence indicates that his findings are still valid.

Part of Goode's explanation for high divorce rates among the poor reminds us of the reason for the high rates of desertion reported in *Tally's Corner* (see Chapter 2): Unskilled men often cannot find jobs to support a wife and children. As a result, they become irritable, fight with their wives, and eventually leave them. The wife, by working or by getting welfare support, can make as much money as her husband. Thus, neither spouse has much to lose by divorce. Since the U.S. Census Bureau does not classify divorce by income or social class, it is hard to test the validity of Goode's figures today. However, a special 1974 report by the Census Bureau noted a sharp rise in the number of female-headed families between 1970 and 1974—from 5.6 to 6.6 million. This increase, the report stated, resulted from increased divorce and separation. The figures also showed that female-headed households were most common among lower-class racial and ethnic groups. Women headed one-third of all black families and one-sixth of Spanish-speaking families, but only one-tenth of white households (Mock, 1974, part I, p. 24).

High divorce rates are not limited to any one

class. U.S. Census Bureau figures show that in 1900 there were 10.3 marriages and 0.9 divorces per 1,000 population. By 1950, there were 11.1 marriages and 2.6 divorces per 1,000 population. In 1974, the figures were 10.5 marriages and 4.6 divorces per 1,000 population.

Parenthood

Regardless of social class, marriages that last show similar satisfactions and strains. Studies of marital satisfaction show a high point at the outset of marriage and a low point soon after the birth of the first child. Then a partial recovery follows as the new roles of parenthood are learned. A second serious dip in marital happiness occurs when the children become teenagers. It again increases as the children mature and begin to relate to their parents more easily than they did in their teen years (Rollins and Cannon, 1974, pp. 271–282; Russell, 1974, pp. 294–301).

Discipline tends to vary. Parents are much stricter with girls than with boys, especially in their teen years. Lower-class parents are as eager to see their children succeed as are middle-class parents. However, they are less able to supply the knowledge and money needed for college or other aids to success (Yorburg, 1973, pp. 153–186).

As was noted in the chapter on social class, people tend to remain in the social class of their birth. Some of the reasons have to do with the parents' work and other life experiences and with ways of teaching their children. Lower-class parents, for example, stress that "Work is a job, not a career; the paycheck is the only sanction for going on" (Yorburg, 1973, pp. 162–163). They do not teach resourcefulness and independent judgment, values that are needed to move up. To them, obeying orders is more important.

Attitudes toward premarital and extramarital sex

College students today are more open and easy about sex than noncollege youth. Yankelovich found that only 22 percent of college students, as compared with 47 percent of noncollege youth, held casual premarital sex to be morally wrong (1974, pp. 88–93). College students were also more optimistic about marriage than noncollege youth: 53 percent of the students and only 48 percent of the nonstudents looked forward to marriage. However, slightly more college youths (28 percent) said they would like to try living in a commune before marriage. College students also had more tolerant attitudes on issues related to abortion and sex (see Table 12-1).

Table 12-1

	College, Percent Agreeing	Noncollege, Percent Agreeing
Having an abortion is wrong	32	48
Relations between consenting homosexuals are wrong	25	47
Extramarital sex relations are wrong	60	65
Casual premarital sex relations are wrong	22	47
Swapping partners among married couples is wrong	57	72

Source: Yankelovich, 1974, pp. 88–93.

Marriage and family

The worldwide celebration and sanctification of marriage indicate that societies have considered it important for their cultural continuity.

Statements of expressed attitudes do not always match actual behavior. Alfred Kinsey (1948), who studied sexual behavior in the 1940s, found a sharp difference between social classes as measured by education. Of the twenty-year-old men, 45 percent of those in college—compared with 87 percent of those with only a grade school education—had had premarital sex relations. The inconsistency between the findings of Kinsey and Yankelovich is striking. Yankelovich concludes that college and noncollege youths are thinking more and more alike. However, he does not refer specifically to views on premarital sex.

The lower class has always had a sexual double standard. It permits and even approves of sex for men while it also condemns the women involved. The middle class shares this attitude to some extent. Still, middle-class fathers have probably taught their sons to be somewhat more careful of their girl friends' reputations. Now that the double standard has weakened and a woman's reputation is not seriously damaged by premarital sex, middle-class inhibitions have broken down. As a result, premarital sexual behavior in the two classes is more similar. One study found that the double standard had completely disappeared among seventeen-year-olds.

By that age, 35 percent of both sexes had had premarital sex relations—and all of them came from middle-class backgrounds (Vener and Stewart, 1974).

SOCIAL CHANGE AND MARITAL INSTABILITY

In our discussion of family types, we noted that consanguineal families generally succeeded in keeping marriages intact. Part of the reason was that these families had compelling economic and social reasons for staying together. The modern family performs most of the same functions as the older family types, but not to the same degree. Other social institutions have taken over some traditional family functions. Table 12-2 shows that the rate of marriages has decreased and the rate of divorces has increased over the past several decades.

Changes in economic functions

The old rural family was a cooperative unit. All members worked together to run the farm or shop. The modern family has a very different economic base. Changes in the job structure first required the father to leave home to earn an

Table 12-2 Marriage and Divorce Rates per Thousand Population

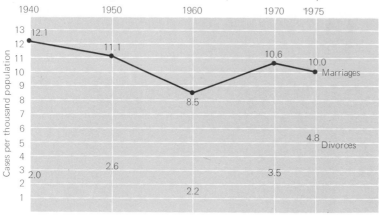

Source: *Statistical Abstract of the United States, Bureau of the Census,* U.S. Government Printing Office, Washington, D.C., 1976, p. 390.

Figure 12-5 Television has become an important socializing agent for millions of children. Many of them watch it for two or more hours per day. (*Vivienne, Photo Researchers, Inc.*)

income; then, in many cases, the mother too had to work. Parents continue to support their families, but family members no longer work together cooperatively. Wives are not as economically dependent upon their husbands as they once were. Thus, separation or divorce is easier if the wife is unhappy. With rare exceptions, the family no longer trains children for future work roles.

Changes in the socialization function

Today the family has a much smaller role in socializing its children. Child care is considered to be the work of specialists in schools and clinics. Public education—sometimes preceded by nursery school—starts earlier and continues longer. Parents spend less time with their children than they did in the past. Day-care centers, peer groups, and even television sets have become substitute parents. As a result, children are not patterned on their parents as closely as they

once were. Members of different generations become, to a degree, strangers to each other.

Parents worry and care about their children now as much as ever. They send them to doctors and dentists, and even to psychiatrists, more often than in the past. Their progress in school becomes a major family concern, but the family has little contact with the school. Because of the long period of schooling, children remain economically dependent on their parents for a long time, even after they have reached physical and sexual maturity. Adolescence is often a period of strain, since the young are strongly influenced by outside forces that the family cannot control.

Other functional changes

Although some American families plan summer outings or support Little League baseball, recreation today is highly specialized by age. Some suburban parents see themselves as chauffeurs, driving their children to activities in which the parents have no part. Television has taken over the time once spent in family talk or reading. This is true especially in less educated families. In

(a)

(b)

Figure 12-6 In our modern industrial society, the division of work separates families for most of the day. (*a*) The mother and young children generally remain at home, while the father commutes. (*b*) The results of his work are often invisible to the family. [*(a) Eve Arnold, Magnum; (b) M. Faller, Monkmeyer*]

a 1974 Gallup poll, 29 percent of those who were college-educated listed watching television as their favorite pastime in contrast with 48 percent of those who were high-school-educated and 62 percent of those with only an eighth-grade education.

In the United States, before the enactment of social security laws in the 1930s, the elderly were cared for at home. Families made a virtue of necessity and prided themselves on living up to a moral duty. Middle-aged people shared in the care of their parents and saw to it that younger children were polite and helpful toward them. Thus, the aged helped bind families together. Home care of the aged was not easy, but it served a family function.

Since, middle-aged people seldom have to support and care for their aged parents, such burdens are no longer thought of as primary family duties. As a result, children grow up without even thinking that the aged will someday be their concern. They are not drilled in the ethics of deference to elderly relatives that are part of more tradition-directed societies in which families are more powerful.

Social and geographical mobility

People often move because they want better jobs or because they are transferred by their employers. All together, at least 25 percent of the United States population is on the move in any given year. Members of the immediate family move together, but often they move away from close relatives and old friends. The drive to get ahead can also separate family members. This is especially true when the young move away from their parents' social and intellectual worlds.

Charles Hobart finds that the stress of upward mobility creates confusion in values (1963, pp. 405–412). For many, moving up on the job becomes more important than the family. Sometimes, there is more interest in the things that

Figure 12-7 The singles life is becoming a respectable alternative to marriage. This apartment house in Los Angeles is for singles only. (*Bill Ray, Life Magazine*)

show the family has "made it"—a new house, a second car, a boat—than in the family itself. Success is measured by the way the home is decorated rather than by the happiness of family life. Part of the problem, Hobart believes, lies in primary- and secondary-group characteristics. In the urban, mobile society, which emphasizes goods rather than human relationships, secondary goals often win out. Hobart's analysis may be too gloomy. Upper-middle-class families are probably more success-oriented than others, but as we have seen, they are more stable than lower-class families.

Finding the right partner

Other factors in marital success include similarity of intelligence, interests, and beliefs, and putting off marriage until the middle twenties. People generally look for mates who share their beliefs and life-style but the search is harder than it was in the past. In our complex, urban society, people are less alike than in older, rural societies. The search for the right person is sometimes made harder by ambition. We all hope to marry someone who is socially on the way up, someone who is charming, witty, affectionate, and rich; but such people are in short supply. Further, we are all limited by own assets. As Erving

Goffman said, "A proposal of marriage in our society tends to be a way in which a man sums up his social attributes and suggests to a woman that hers are not so much better as to preclude a merger or a partnership in these matters" (Walster, 1966, p. 508).

From 1900 to about 1965, people tended to marry early. This practice generally does not lead to success in marriage. One study shows that those married before the age of twenty were three times as likely to divorce as those who married between the ages of twenty-five and twenty-nine (Glick and Norton, 1971, pp. 307–317).

In the last few years, people have tended to marry later. Part of the reason is that, increasingly, young people live together without marriage. The sexual revolution and new methods of contraception mean that people do not have to marry. They can now enjoy sex without fear—though not, perhaps, without guilt. Further, the women's liberation movement has influenced the thinking of many women. They now feel freer to spend time working and living as singles, enjoying their freedom and learning who they are and what they want to do. The antidiscrimination laws covering work and housing make the singles life more attractive.

Communal living, "swinging," and cohabitation are three current trends that seem to threaten traditional marriage. Do these trends represent the marriage and family styles of the future?

ALTERNATIVES FOR THE FUTURE

Morton Hunt has studied many trends in family life that alarm traditionalists. Hunt finds them neither alarming nor socially harmful (1973). Divorce, Hunt believes, is a traumatic experience, but it does not signal the death of marriage. Divorcees may be bitter for a while, but most of them marry again. Most people need to marry, Hunt contends, because secondary relationships are not enough. People need intimate ties with another person. They may have a relationship without marriage, but their arrangement often resembles marriage. "Saint Paul said it is better to marry than to burn," says Hunt, but "today, feeling the glacial chill of the world we live in, we feel it is better to marry than to freeze" (p. 266).

Communes

Hunt looks at some current alternatives to *monogamous* marriage (one man–one woman). The first is the *commune*. This is a form of social organization resembling an extended family, in which family functions are shared. Communes were described in the previous chapter as retreats from the modern world. In his work, Hunt examines their success and failure in solving family problems. Many communes are conventional, being made up of married couples. The type which has been held up as an alternative to marriage is one in which all members are considered to be married to all other members of the opposite sex—the group commune marriage (see the insert "The Communal Alternative").

Hunt speaks of certain other customs as supplements to marriage rather than alternatives. The majority of societies have not insisted on total marital fidelity, and quite a few modern marriages do not make such a requirement

---

The communal alternative   MORTON HUNT

Group marriage offers solutions to a number of the nagging problems and discontents of modern monogamy. Collective parenthood—every parent being partly responsible for every child in the group—not only provides a warm and enveloping atmosphere for children but removes some of the pressures from individual parents; moreover, it minimizes the disruptive effects of divorce on the child's world. Sexual sharing is an answer to boredom and solves the problem of infidelity, or seeks to, by declaring extramarital experiences acceptable and admirable. It avoids the success-status-possession syndrome of the middle-class family by turning toward simplicity, communal ownership and communal goals.

Finally, it avoids the loneliness and confinements of monogamy by creating something comparable to . . . the extended family. . . . (There is a difference, of course; in group marriage, the extended family isn't composed of blood relatives.) Even when sexual switching isn't the focus, there is a warm feeling of being affectionately connected to everyone else. As one young woman in a Taos commune said ecstatically, "It's really groovy waking up and knowing that 48 people love you."

There is, however, a negative side. This drastic reformulation of marriage makes for new problems, some of them more severe than the ones it has solved. Albert Ellis, quoted in Herbert Otto's . . . *Family in Search of a Future*, lists several categories of serious difficulties with group marriage, including the near impossibility of finding four or more adults who can live harmoniously and lovingly together, the stubborn intrusion of jealousy and love conflicts, and the innumerable difficulties of coordinating and scheduling many lives.

Other writers, including those who have sampled communal life, also talk about the problems of leadership (most communes have few to start with; those that survive for any time do so by becoming almost conventional and traditional) and the difficulties in communal work sharing (there are always some members who are slovenly and lazy and others who are neat and hard-working, the latter either having to expel the former or give up and let the commune slowly die).

A more serious defect is that most group marriages, being based upon a simple semiprimitive agrarian life, reintroduce old-style patriarchalism, because such a life puts a premium on masculine muscle power and endurance and leaves the classic domestic and subservient roles to women. Even a most sympathetic observer, psychiatrist Joseph Downing, writes, "In the tribal families, while both sexes work, women are generally in a service role . . . male dominance is held desirable by both sexes."

Most serious of all are the emotional limitations of group marriage. Its ideal is sexual freedom, but the group marriages that most nearly achieve this have the least cohesiveness and the shallowest interpersonal involvements; people come and go, and there is really no marriage at all, but only a continuously changing and highly unstable encounter group. The longer-lasting and more cohesive group marriages are, in fact, those in which, as Dr. Downing reports, the initial sexual spree "generally gives way to the quiet, semipermanent, monogamous relationship characteristic of many in our general society."

Not surprisingly, therefore, Dr. Ellis finds that most group marriages are unstable and last only several months to a few years; and . . . Lewis Yablonsky . . . who has visited and lived in a number of communes, says that they are often idealistic but seldom successful or enduring. Over and above their specific difficulties, they are utopian—they seek to construct a new society from whole cloth. But all utopias thus far have failed; human behavior is so incredibly complex that every totally new order, no matter how well planned, generates innumerable unforeseen problems. It really is a pity; group living and group marriage look wonderful on paper.

Reprinted with permission of Playboy Press from "The Future of Marriage," by Morton Hunt. Copyright © 1972 by Playboy.

Marriage and family

either. In the past, wealthy men had mistresses, and sometimes their wives had lovers—often, with the knowledge of their mates. The custom worked to keep the marriage partners together even if they were bored with each other. A modern equivalent, says Hunt, is swinging.

The swingers

Charles and Rebecca Palson did a participant-observer study of swinging (1972, pp. 28–38). Swingers argue that if a married couple change sexual partners once in a while, their marriage is more interesting. Swinging is less destructive, they say, than a drawn-out love affair. In swinging, both partners are present and nothing is secret. They swing to have fun; they don't intend to fall in love. The Palsons concluded that swinging did seem to make some marriages more stable and happy. One happily swinging couple is described in the accompanying insert.

The Palsons concluded that swinging is not a custom that will sweep the country. American attitudes toward sexual freedom seem to follow a cyclical pattern. The lively 1920s were followed by the more conservative 1930s of the Depres-

Figure 12-8 Some people dislike living as an isolated nuclear family. Communes are one alternative. (*Sybil Shelton, Monkmeyer*)

sion. Permissiveness during World War II was followed by the strongly family-oriented 1950s. The Palsons expect the cycle to repeat itself, partly because a long period of economic prosperity has been interrupted. Swinging does not seem to pose a threat to marriage. (See the insert "A Swinging Couple.")

Cohabitation

Anthropologist Margaret Mead once suggested that temporary marriage licenses be issued to college students for trial marriages. Many students today have gone one step further, living together without a license—which is called *cohabitation*. Eleanor Macklin (1974, pp. 53–59) found that between 10 and 33 percent of all unmarried college students on major campuses lived with a lover of the opposite sex. In a study based mainly on Cornell University, she found that cohabitation had no ill effect on grades and that 90 percent of the students liked it very

A swinging couple   CHARLES AND REBECCA PALSON

[Paul had been married before, but had found the affair boring. The same seemed to be the case with his second marriage, to Georgia.]

Paul resorted to outside affairs, but found them unsatisfactory because they took too much time and money, and "it just wasn't worth all the lying." He suggested to Georgia the possibility of swinging with some friends of theirs, pointing out that he loved her but that "every man needs a bit of variety." Georgia initially thought the idea was crazy, but Paul persisted and finally persuaded her to try it. [Since persuading old friends was difficult,] they discovered swinging magazines and began making new contacts through them.

Neither Paul nor Georgia have any trouble with jealousy and agree that this is because "we are so good in bed with each other that no one could really compete." From time to time Paul even brings home girls he has met; Georgia doesn't get jealous "just so long as he introduces them to me first and they do their thing in my house." For her part, Georgia has discovered that she likes women too and regularly brings home girls from a nearby homosexual bar. "Men," she says, "are good for sex, but it isn't in their nature to be able to give the kind of affection a woman needs." Georgia's activities don't worry Paul a bit:

> A woman just couldn't give the kind of support I do. They just don't know how to get along in the world without a man. A lot of these lesbians she meets are irresponsible and would never be able to take care of the kid.

Swinging has affected Georgia's self-confidence as well as changing her sex habits. She now feels much more confident in social situations, a change that began after she started making her own choices about whom she would swing with. At first she had let Paul make all the decisions. . . .

From Charles and Rebecca Palson, "Swinging in Wedlock," published by permission of Trans Action, Inc., from *Society*, vol. 9, no. 4, p. 33, copyright © 1972 by Trans Action, Inc.

much. Almost all the respondents stressed the emotional benefits of sharing their lives. Both men and women felt cohabitation was successful. Most of them did not think of it as a trial marriage. In a few cases, they expected to marry their current partners eventually. In most cases, they did not.

Macklin sums up the two major arguments for and against cohabitation. Some people fear that it will cause students to avoid the commitment necessary for marriage and make them care only about their own pleasure. Others argue that they will simply put off marriage until they are ready for it. Further, they will profit greatly from having shared their lives with someone else.

A word for tradition

Despite the current interest in alternative lifestyles, most Americans still marry. Michael Novak argues that these alternatives affect only a small minority:

> Some 66 percent of all Americans remain married to the same man or woman throughout a lifetime. Considering how difficult marriage is, and how easy divorce is, this is a staggering figure. Thus the image of America we gain through television and the movies, through Time and Newsweek and the "style" and "modern living" sections of

our newspapers gives a more accurate view of the top 10 percent than of the bottom 10 percent. (1975, part IX, p. 5; copyright © 1976 by *Harper's* Magazine. All rights reserved. Reprinted from the April 1976 issue by special permission)

Novak also praises traditional marriage and predicts that it will continue as an affirmation of life:

> To marry, to have children, is to make a political statement hostile to what passes for "liberalism" today. It is a statement of flesh, intelligence, courage. It draws its strength from nature, from tradition, and from the future. Apart from millions of decisions of couples . . . to bring forth children they will nourish, teach, and launch against the void, the human race has no future—no wisdom, no advance, no community, no grace.
> Only the emptiness of solitary space, the dance of death. It is the destiny of flesh and blood to be familial. (1976, p. 46)

The probable future

The family relationships and duties described by Novak have been fulfilled by many types of families. These include extended families ruled by the aged, marriages arranged between strangers who could not divorce, and modern nuclear families. The family today has more freedom and equality than families of the past. Family planning, the growing equality of women and children, and a child-rearing pattern based more on affection than on fear have increased the freedom of family members. Authoritarian families still exist, but the trend is in the other direction. Today, most people value their own freedom and are therefore more willing to grant it to others (Goode, 1966, pp. 41–56).

Along with the growth of freedom has come a greater tendency to divorce. This is often hard where there are children. In the long run,

though, it may be less harmful than raising them in a hostile home. Whatever its problems, the family is still the best refuge from the impersonal outside world. In the family, acceptance is a right, not a privilege earned by special abilities.

The society of the future may do better than ours in rescuing children from destructive homes. Also, more child care outside the home will be available. There will probably be more childless couples, more people who live together without marriage, more people living alone, and more divorce and remarriage. A few communes might prove successful. On a large scale, though, the family will probably not be replaced. Basic institutions such as the family tend to change and adjust to new circumstances, but they do not die.

SUMMARY

The majority of people continue to marry and rear families. Still, the 1970s have shown an upturn in the number of unmarried or divorced people. There are also more children living with only one parent.

Modern marriage makes heavy demands: love, companionship, and sexual gratification. Also, there is some conflict between the ideals of sharing life goals and seeking individual fulfillment. The stress on fulfillment in work, play, and special interests causes some young people to hesitate about marriage. Society continues to expect people to marry. Marriage is encouraged by parents, by romantic myths, by feelings that sex still belongs within marriage, and to some degree by discrimination against single people in credit ratings and taxes. On the other hand, marriage means taking on new roles that are not clearly defined by society or always agreed upon by the couple. The family is more isolated from neighbors and relatives than in the past.

Marriage is part of all societies, but forms of marriage differ widely. An important contrast can be made between the small, isolated *nuclear family* of the United States and the large *consanguineal family* that was once the ideal, particularly in the Far East. The consanguineal family had great stability and favored the aged, but it gave little individual freedom to the young.

Families also differ on the number of spouses involved. *Polygynous* families have been common in many societies, especially among wealthy and prestigious men. *Polyandry* has been the prevailing practice in Toda society and in Tibet. In a few cases, families have been *minimal;* that is, parents were not closely linked or biological fathers had little connection with the family. The Nayars of India are a classic example. In the Israeli *kibbutz,* children are reared and supported by the *kibbutz* itself rather than by their parents. According to Claude Lévi-Strauss, the minimal family that plays down the father has been common in societies geared to warfare. Older societies in which marriages were *arranged* typically downgraded love in marriage. Sometimes, though, love and devotion after marriage were highly praised. In general, family systems are adapted to other aspects of the culture. As societies become more urban and industrial, polygyny, polyandry, and arranged marriages decline.

Family patterns differ with social class. Middle-class marriage favors near equality between the sexes, more companionship, and sex relations initiated by either partner. Middle-class complaints by both partners are often of a lack of love and understanding. Lower-class women are more apt to complain of nonsupport or physical abuse. Divorce figures are rising for all classes. Still, divorce and separation are more common in the lower class than in either the middle class or the working class.

Class patterns differ also in raising children. The middle class is more permissive and encourages individuality more than the working class. Middle-class children are punished less often. Working-class parents value strict obedience to orders, although discipline is inconsistent. Girls are raised much more strictly than boys, and there is still a sexual double standard. College youth are more permissive and egalitarian about sex than noncollege youth, but a majority of both groups condemns extramarital sex.

The stability of marriage has steadily declined in the twentieth century, partly because of the changing functions of the family. The family no longer work together as an economic unit, so members are less interdependent. The school now competes with the family to socialize children. Recreation is more set apart by age. Television has taken over much of the time once given to family talk, games, or reading. Social and geographical mobility moves families apart. Wives no longer depend on their husbands as much as they did in the past. Even finding compatible marriage partners may be harder today because of wider differences in attitudes and life-styles.

Instability in marriage may be part of the reason for cohabitation without marriage. The trend toward early marriage has been reversed. More people are avoiding marriage until they find the right person to marry, and until they feel mature enough.

Some people see the rising divorce rate as marking the end of the family. Others point out that marriage remains a popular institution. Although many people do not marry in the usual way, they frequently live together. Some try communal life-styles, often including group marriage. Others hold that swinging in marriage is a happy custom that permits both marriage and sexual variety. Michael Novak points out that despite divorce, cohabitation, communes, and swinging, about two-thirds of the American people make conventional marriages. The future will probably see more variety in marriage arrangements and substitutes for marriage than in the past. Probably even more children will be living with only one parent. But the common desire of people for affection, for intimacy, and for a degree of certainty and permanence ensures that marriage in some form will continue, probably becoming more egalitarian than in the past.

Study guide

Terms to know

Nuclear family
Consanguineal family
Romantic myth
Patrilineal
Patriarchal
Matrilineal

Matrilocal
Polygyny
Polygamy
Polyandry
Minimal family
Kibbutz

Egalitarian family
Cohabitation
Commune
"Swinging"

Names to know

George P. Murdock
Margaret Mead
Claude Lévi-Strauss

William Goode
Michael Novak
Morton Hunt

Self-test

Part I. Multiple Choice. Select the best of the four alternative answers:

1 A special 1975 U.S. Census Bureau report showed (**a**) an increase in unmarried people of ages twenty-five to thirty-four, (**b**) an increase in remarriages of divorced people, (**c**) the same percentage of children living with both parents as in 1970, (**d**) all the above.

2 Built-in supports for marriage include (**a**) discrimination against the unmarried in taxes and credit ratings, (**b**) parental pressures, (**c**) a romantic myth about marriage, (**d**) all the above.

3 The romantic myth of medieval times (**a**) was very similar to the present feeling, (**b**) generally told of the passion of separation, (**c**) always involved marriage, (**d**) was nearly always an account of hardship, but with a happy ending.

4 In the early 1970s, Yankelovich found that (**a**) nearly all young people agreed on an egalitarian marriage, (**b**) a slight majority of noncollege youth still agreed that a woman's place is in the home, (**c**) marital roles were agreed upon by the time people got married, (**d**) marriage roles are very easily learned.

5 Margaret Mead in the insert "Alone in the Suburbs" calls the modern American family hazardous because (**a**) there are not enough relatives and concerned neighbors around, (**b**) parents do not care for their children, (**c**) too many mothers hold jobs, (**d**) the cost of rearing children is so high.

6 The traditional ideal family in China (**a**) was a large, cooperative group; (**b**) provided permanence and security; (**c**) was usually found only among the well-to-do; (**d**) all the above.

7 The Gikuyu (or Kikuyu) marriage described by Jomo Kenyatta calls for (**a**) no restraints on

the man's sex desires, (b) equal treatment of the wives, (c) attempts at birth control, (d) long periods of solitude for members.

8 Claude Lévi-Strauss contends that the most common reason for minimizing family importance is (a) economic avarice, (b) a primitive stage of development, (c) competing military requirements, (d) immorality.

9 In the Israeli *kibbutzim*, (a) parents have no contact with their own children, (b) divorces and separations are not permitted, (c) most child care is left to the *metapelets*, (d) the family system is patriarchal.

10 A study of divorce indicates that far more lower-class than middle-class wives complain of (a) lack of love, (b) lack of freedom, (c) too little sex, (d) physical abuse.

11 Poor nonwhite families are more likely than white middle-class families to be (a) patriarchal, (b) stable, (c) headed by women, (d) headed by men.

12 More noncollege than college youth expressed which of the following? (a) expectation of a happy marriage, (b) a desire to live in a commune, (c) the view that casual premarital sexual relations are wrong, (d) all the above.

13 Finding the right marriage partner may be harder than in the past because (a) urban people are less alike than those in rural, village societies; (b) there are fewer opportunities for meeting the opposite sex; (c) parents interfere more than they used to; (d) men are not happy with wives who are as well educated as they are.

14 Hunt admits that communes have certain advantages, such as (a) permanence of relationships, (b) many people to care for children, (c) good leadership, (d) female equality.

15 The most likely future of marriage and the family will be (a) a collapse of the family; (b) greater freedom and equality; (c) a reversal of trends, resulting in more stable marriages; (d) almost universal mate swapping.

Part II. True-False Questions

1 Despite recent worries over the institution of marriage, the majority of Americans still marry and see themselves as happy in marriage.

2 More is expected of marriage now than in the past, at least in emotional satisfaction.

3 Modern ideas of romance are the same as those of the medieval troubadors.

4 From society's point of view, it is better to have most men marry, since married men seem more settled and stable than single men.

5 The modern American family is correctly called consanguineal.

6 Such different marriage systems as polygyny and polyandry seem to make no sense even in the cultures that produced them.

7 The Koran allows men to marry as many wives as they choose.

8 A quotation from the Indian *Ramayana* makes it clear that a romantic ideal of love existed.

9 Madame Wu contrasted American marriage and older Chinese customs by saying that we fall in love and marry, whereas they marry, then fall in love.

10 William Goode found that in the majority of societies, rich people are more likely to separate or divorce than poor people.

11 Divorce rates have increased in all social classes in the last half century.

12 Satisfaction in marriage is generally highest after the arrival of the first child.

13 The socialization function of the family has declined in modern industrial society.

14 The 1970s have seen a reversal of the trend toward earlier marriage.

15 According to Michael Novak, approximately two-thirds of Americans remain married to the same partner for life.

Marriage and family

351

Questions for discussion

1 Modern marriage makes many demands: companionship, love, and sexual compatibility, combined with a large measure of independence. Argue the following pro and con: Modern marriages are happier than those of the past. Therefore, the high demands on marriage are worthwhile.

2 Imagine yourself having been raised in a patiarchal, consanguineal family. How might it have changed your personality? What advantages would you have gained? What would the disadvantages have been?

3 Even in societies that permit them, polygynous marriages are becoming less common than in the past. What are the possible reasons?

4 Both Margaret Mead and Morton Hunt state that the modern family is too isolated, with few adults around to act as substitute parents for the children. What can be done about this? Do you favor child-care centers? Communes? Restructuring our communities?

5 The term *minimal family* refers to such family systems as that of the Nayars in the past and the Israeli *kibbutzim* today. Lévi-Strauss commented that military requirements sometimes minimize the father's role in the family. Explain how modern urban-industrial society also tends to minimize the father's role. What is this doing to the mother's role?

6 What are the arguments for and against arranged marriage? Since we no longer allow the elders to find marriage partners for the young, what do you think of using computers to match people for compatibility?

7 Why is it harder for lower-class people to make a success of marriage than for middle-class people?

8 If you were asked to set up rules for people about to marry, what would you suggest?

9 What do you expect the future to hold for marriage?

Projects

1 Some researchers have found that both sexes are happy with cohabitation without marriage. Others contend that women are more interested in having the arrangement turn into marriage. Interview a number of couples on campus who are cohabiting. Record their answers.
   Another possibility: Give a questionnaire to a number of classes to find out how they feel about cohabitation.

2 Invite a guest speaker to explain more fully the *kibbutz* system of Israel. Alternatively, you might invite someone who has lived on a commune, preferably a counterculture commune.

3 Working-class parents are apt to place a higher value than middle-class parents on obedience. Try testing this statement. Interview several parents from each social class. You might ask them to rate in order a number of values that most people believe children should observe to some degree: obedience, independent thinking, curiosity, religion, patriotism, friendliness, generosity, intellectual interests, diligence, respect for the law.

Suggested readings

Denzin, Norman K.: "Children and Their Caretakers," *Trans-Action*, vol. 8, July–August 1971, pp. 62–71. How has "fate control" passed from parents to teachers, counselors, and other specialists? This article, which relates both to the present chapter and the following one on education, suggests that we need more child care—that is, apart from that provided by schools and other large institutions.

Glick, Paul C., and Arthur J. Norton: "Frequency, Duration, and Probability of Marriage and Divorce," *Journal of Marriage and the Family*, vol. 30, May 1971, pp. 307–317. Much research has been done on predicting success in marriage. This study is based on the experiences of married people over a twenty-year period—those who succeeded and those who failed. What difference is made by age of marriage? Education? Income? Who is likely to remarry?

Kellogg, Mary Alice: "Counter-Culture Kids," *Newsweek*, March 29, 1976, p. 59. What happens to children reared in counterculture communes? Are they free of repressions, self-reliant, sociable, and creative, as their parents would hope? This article (a review of the book *Children of the Counterculture*, by Susan Wolf and John Rothschild) comments on both favorable and unfavorable results.

Look Magazine: "The American Family" (special issue), January 26, 1971. A series of articles deals with such topics as: "Is the family obsolete?" "Why children blame parents." "Why parents blame children." "Don't blame me, says Dr. Spock." "Happy families." "'Married' homosexuals." "Unwed couples." "The executive mother."

Mead, Margaret: "Future Family," *Trans-Action*, vol. 8, September 1971, pp. 50–53. Children, elderly relatives, and the poor, says Mead, have always been "done good to," but now they want a hand in the decisions that affect them. Can we develop communities and family living arrangements that integrate both children and the elderly, rather than putting them somewhere to be "done good to"?

Schudson, Michael: "Family Stages," *The New Republic*, February 16, 1974, pp. 27–28. Has the family of Western societies passed through definite stages of development—the agrarian stage, the "cruel" stage, the home-centered stage, and now the two-worker stage of strongly material interest? What is the relationship between these stages and social classes? See the conclusions in this review of *The Symmetrical Family* by Michael Young and Peter Wilmott, Pantheon Books, 1974.

Strauss, Murray A.: "Leveling, Civility, and Violence in the Family," *Journal of Marriage and the Family*, vol. 36, February 1974, pp. 13–29. If you are angry at your spouse, is it best to "level," "get it off your chest," yell and make a scene? Advice columns give conflicting advice. Strauss has an answer, based on a study of families of 385 college freshmen, that pleads for civility and "cooling off."

Teevan, James V., Jr.: "Reference Groups and Premarital Sexual Behavior," *Journal of Marriage and the Family*, vol. 34, May 1972, pp. 283–291. How strong is peer-group influence on sexual behavior? The answer is informative, regarding both sexual behavior and the nature of group influence (Chapter 5).

Key to questions. Multiple Choice: 1-a; 2-d; 3-b; 4-b; 5-a; 6-d; 7-b; 8-c; 9-c; 10-d; 11-c; 12-c; 13-a; 14-b; 15-b. True-False: 1-T; 2-T; 3-F; 4-T; 5-F; 6-F; 7-F; 8-T; 9-T; 10-F; 11-T; 12-F; 13-F; 14-T; 15-T.

13

THE EDUCATIONAL PROCESS

This chapter explains what the American educational system tries to do and questions how well it succeeds. After reading it, you should be able to:

1 *Explain why the United States became a leader in the development of mass education.*

2 *Understand the special role of the schools in developing an American cultural tradition—as well as the problems of emphasizing only one tradition.*

3 *Analyze how well the equal-opportunity function of education is carried out.*

4 *Examine alternatives to the schools as a means of achieving greater equality.*

5 *Understand the difficulty of fitting education to jobs and grasp the personal problems that result from a failure to match the two.*

6 *Present conflict and functional views of the educational system and explain their consequences.*

7 *Understand the meaning of latent functions of education and give a number of examples.*

Although mass education is now the rule in all modern, industrialized nations, it has come fairly late in world history. Early Americans pioneered the idea that all people should have at least basic schooling. Since a knowledge of the Bible was considered necessary for salvation, the Puritans started community schools to teach their children to read it. For reasons to be explained in the next chapter, the Puritans also held that it was each person's duty to work hard and get ahead. They were logical enough to see that education was needed to meet this goal. Then too, Thomas Jefferson and his followers held mass education to be vital if we were to have an intelligent, informed public that could govern itself.

In the nineteenth century, the rising American business and manufacturing class valued a certain amount of education. Schools could teach children basic skills such as reading, writing, and arithmetic. Equally important, they could tell children about the virtues of a free-enterprise system. Schools could also teach future workers about time schedules and save industrialists much of the cost of training (Bowles, 1972, pp. 42–49).

There have always been egalitarian sentiments in American society. Horace Mann (1796–1859) and other true believers in mass education held that education could serve as the "great equalizer." In the nineteenth century, both new immigrants and rural families moving to cities looked for equal opportunity through education. At this time, the United States had a unique problem. Since American traditions were just being formed, many people looked to their states rather than to the nation as their source of identity. It was the job of the American public schools, more so than in most countries, to link the people together into one nation with a common cultural tradition. (Table 13-1, page 356, shows our progress toward the ideal of universal high school education.)

FUNCTIONS OF PUBLIC EDUCATION

The *outward, obvious functions* of public education in the United States today are similar to those of schools in all industrialized countries. These functions include providing workers for increasingly complex industries, helping to promote equal opportunity, encouraging upward mobility, and teaching a common culture. Another function—on the level of higher education—is that of expanding scientific knowledge. Some schools have gone so far along this line as to have become research centers rather than places of learning.

In no case are all the outward functions of education fulfilled perfectly. There is never a perfect fit between the training of workers and the needs of the market. Equal opportunity can only be worked toward, since education is not the only factor. Further, latent functions develop—such as student protest movements—that were never expected to be part of the educational process. The schools must adapt to change as well as pass along the cultural traditions. Cultural traditions themselves give rise to social conflict. Such traditions as male supremacy, WASP supremacy, and "progress"

Table 13-1 Education: Four Years of High School or More Completed by Adults, 1950—1974

Percent of persons 25 years old and over

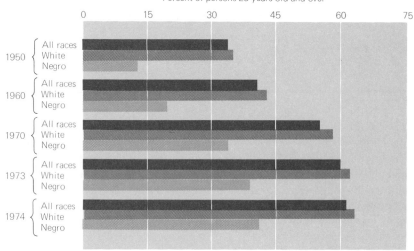

Note: The ideal of universal high school education is further from full realization than is commonly believed. The above figures also demonstrate racial inequality in education, although the gap between black and white is narrowing.
Source: *U.S. Book of Facts: The Statistical Abstract of the U.S. Bureau of the Census,* Grosset and Dunlap, New York, 1976, p. 109.

have sparked the women's liberation movement, the black and ethnic movements, and the conservation movement. We shall examine the functions of education in the United States one by one. We shall start with cultural tradition and end with an emphasis on the American ideal of equality of opportunity.

TRANSMITTING THE CULTURAL TRADITION

The cultural tradition passed along by a school system includes the country's history, its system of government, its language and literature, and its arts and sciences. Children are also trained to be good citizens. Citizenship training strengthens the cultural tradition by giving a sense of belonging to and participation in the culture. The cultural norms are taught in a very idealized way. The idea is to instill loyalty and devotion to country. This would be hard to do if children were taught that their country was sometimes unfair, cruel, or imperialistic.

The single-culture tradition

Up to the mid-1960s, the American cultural tradition was presented in a unitary framework as though we were all of Anglo-Saxon descent. This is known as the single-culture tradition. The United States, like all large, modern societies, includes many subcultures and crosscurrents as well as central characteristics. It seemed important to our ancestors, however, to weld all the people into one society. In the process, they praised the national heros (nearly all white Anglo-Saxons), justified wars and national decisions, and largely ignored the traditions of Indians, blacks, and other minorities.

The children of poor immigrants who understood little English found it difficult to compete with the children of older Americans. They were all sent to the same schools. As early as the 1820s, a New York Workingmen's Party, realizing the great problems of immigrant children in the schools, proposed that they be raised in public boarding schools. Otherwise, a few hours in school could not make up for the cultural disadvantages these children had to overcome (Lipset, 1974, pp. 57–58). The proposal was never adopted, but eventually these children or their descendants did manage to pick up the traits of American society. From the beginning, though, public schools have tended to ignore the pluralistic nature of American culture. The problem of minority cultures is still with us.

Common language and literature

It was once thought that the schools could teach what was "proper" in language and literature. Webster's spelling books of the 1780s and his dictionary of 1828 began to standardize American pronunciation of the English language. The widely used McGuffy readers of the second half of the nineteenth century determined what literature should be learned and remembered. Two problems have interfered with this neat and sure approach. First, people always disagree about "good" literature and English usage. Second, both literature and language change with time.

Part of the problem of literature and language is like that of a single-culture tradition in history

Figure 13-1 To be naturalized, immigrants to the United States must become familiar with "the American way." (*Bettmann Archive*)

versus a multiethnic approach. Should there be separate courses in black literature? In women's literature? In Chicano and Indian literature? Or should more of the literature of the minority groups become part of the established culture?

Some people argue that it is best not to interfere with a student's native tongue. It is difficult, even traumatic, to try to alter natural speech patterns. Those who disagree argue that regional and ethnic accents could eventually make it difficult for us to understand one another. Much more important, they say, is the fact that we cannot provide equal opportunity if we fail to teach standard English to all children. People whose language is considered substandard will find it hard to get good jobs or to be socially accepted by others.

Local and national traditions

In the past, educators tried to keep schools under the control of local boards of education. They reasoned that only in this way would schools reflect local interests and opinions and instill pride in the community and the state. Local schools were seen as more democratic than schools controlled by state or national governments.

At the same time, schools have become more

Niño Mexicano

Mexican Child

Figure 13-2 Some American school systems now recognize the cultural traditions of minority groups. (*Joan Roth*)

uniform nationally. Nationwide standardized tests are given to see how well children learn such subjects as reading and arithmetic. High schools use standardized tests and national norms to place their students in the most suitable classes. Colleges require standardized entrance examinations, and yet other standardized tests are needed for entry into graduate school.

Even more important, the federal government has tried hard to promote equal opportunity over the last few years. The poorest districts have been forced to integrate their schools racially in order to obtain federal aid. These efforts have varied from one administration to the next. President Lyndon Johnson's civil rights legislation, under the Great Society program, speeded up integration. Richard Nixon's "go slow" policy, and his opposition to busing, caused some setbacks. The equal-opportunity function of education is very important, but sometimes it is hard to carry out.

THE EQUAL-OPPORTUNITY FUNCTION

Some people will always do much better in school and be better prepared for careers than others. One early philosophy of education stated that those who achieved success simply worked harder than others. Encouragement to "try, try,

try again," sometimes spiced with stories about Horatio Alger, the poor boy who made good, was directed to the same conclusion: all it takes is effort. Although this kind of advice has urged people to try to succeed, it also has certain drawbacks. It implies that chances are equally good for all who try. It also assumes that *achievement motivation* (the hope, talent, and drive to reach socially approved goals) is roughly equal for all people. If it could be shown that just as many hard-working children from poor as from middle-class families do well in school and in later careers—and that the same ratio holds for men and women, blacks and whites—this view could be accepted. However, things have not worked out as planned. It is true that schools have helped improve both income and status for many people. But many recent studies have shown the shortcomings of education as "the great equalizer."

In his study in the state of Wisconsin, William H. Sewell (1971, pp. 793–809) shows how socioeconomic status (SES) and sex affect the decision to go to college and how well the students did. He based his findings on a random sample of 9,000 high school seniors, whose academic and occupational records he followed from 1957 to 1970.

Sewell found that women were less likely than men to enter college. Those who did go to college were less likely to do well, especially those of lower SES background. In the lowest SES category, men had a 58 percent better chance than women of going to college, an 86 percent better chance of continuing until graduation, and a 250 percent better chance of doing graduate work. In the highest SES category, the corresponding figures were 20 percent, 28 percent, and 129 percent. In other words, women appeared to have a greater advantage in higher than in lower SES categories. Sewell's findings are similar to those reported in other studies. Differences of opinion do arise, however, when people try to interpret the facts and suggest what to do about them.

Findings regarding college entrance

Whether or not a student goes to college depends on academic ability, motivation, and the development of certain cognitive skills. Sewell's study helps to explain the correlation between academic ability and college study. His findings show that even for those in the top quarter of school success, the higher-SES students had 1.5 times more chance of going to college than did the lower-SES students. The difference grows to 3.5 times for graduate school. In the lowest quartile, four times as many high-SES students go to college as low-SES students. Sewell's statistics raise another important question about academic performance and college entrance for women: Women's high school grades are slightly better than those of men, yet women are much less likely to go to college. Academic ability alone cannot account for this difference.

The IQ argument

Sewell's study shows the importance of socio-economic status in academic achievement. However, some people still believe that low achievement is the result of a low intelligence quotient, or IQ. Arthur Jensen (1973), of the University of California at Berkeley, and Richard Herrnstein (1973), of Harvard University, have both equated success with intelligence. They believe IQ tests can be devised that measure intelligence accurately.

Noam Chomsky attacks the reasoning of Jensen and Herrnstein from one point of view and Jerome Kagan from another. Chomsky disputes the claim that intelligence is linked with economic success. Kagan questions whether IQ tests really measure intelligence. Chomsky (1973)

points out that many very intelligent people have a low drive for wealth. Was Albert Einstein less intelligent than John D. Rockefeller simply because he was not interested in making money? Furthermore, many of the greatest minds in history, such as Galileo and da Vinci, have been persecuted rather than rewarded. Most of the scholars of the Middle Ages were monks pledged to a life of poverty. Were they, therefore, the least intelligent part of the population?

An even more important problem with the IQ argument, in Kagan's opinion (1973), is that IQ tests do not really measure intelligence. True, lower-class children usually do poorly on IQ tests. However, part of the reason is that they lack self-confidence and are afraid of the tests. Kagan tells of an experiment by Ernest Haggard in which he spent three hours explaining to lower-class children how to take tests, trying to overcome their fear of them, and motivating them by promising rewards for those who showed an improvement. The result: an average improvement of from 15 to 20 points.

Even more important, the tests measure what a person has been exposed to in his or her learning background, not innate mental capacity. Kagan shows this with five items each from the Wechsler test and from Dove's test, which is standardized on the knowledge of black ghetto children:

Wechsler test

1 Who wrote *Hamlet*?
2 Who wrote the *Iliad*?
3 What is the *Koran*?
4 What does *audacious* mean?
5 What does *plagiarize* mean?

Dove's test

1 In C. C. Ryder, what does C. C. stand for?
2 What is a gashead?
3 What is Willy Mays's last name?
4 What does "handkerchief head" mean?
5 Whom did Stagger Lee kill in the famous blues legend?

The educational process

359

(a)

(b)

People who cannot answer the question in Dove's test need not feel inferior or unintelligent, so why should people who cannot answer Wechsler's questions feel stupid? Exposure to information differs on the basis of culture and subculture. Most standardized IQ tests are based on the background of white middle-class children; therefore IQ tests provide no adequate grounds for comparing social classes and ethnic groups or for saying who is and who is not intelligent.

Motivational factors

Motivation is important in explaining why high-SES students do better in school than low-SES students. Sewell finds that differences in motivation depend on what kind of work the student hopes to do. This, in turn, is influenced by parents and close friends and—to a lesser degree—by teachers. The lower-SES student would be less likely to be urged to go to college even if money were not a problem. This student is also less likely to have a job in mind that calls for a college degree. Teachers encourage top academic students regardless of social class, but they have little influence on students' decisions about college.

Motivational factors also help explain why men do better academically in college than women. In the majority of families that had trouble sending both a son and a daughter to college, parents were inclined to favor sons. For this and other reasons—such as fear of competition or loss of popularity—daughters were encouraged to set more limited academic goals for themselves. This situation has been described frequently by women's liberationists.

Economic costs

The cost of college is one of the greatest barriers to advanced education for poor students. (See Table 13-2.) It determines not only who goes but also what college is chosen and how far college work is pursued. Although two-year community colleges offer a less expensive alternative to students who can commute from nearby areas, it is much harder to complete four years of college. Graduate work is almost impossible without some kind of financial aid.

Religious background

Religious background also has a strong influence on the decision to go to college. Jewish students are more likely to have higher educational aspirations than any other group, even if social class is held constant (Rhodes and Nam, 1970, pp. 253–267). Next in order are Catholics and members of the major Protestant denominations except Baptists. Members of smaller churches and sects are less likely to go to college. Many of these groups object to the social and scientific teachings people receive in college. Some have an otherworldly orientation that discourages striving for material success.

The Coleman report: Limitations of schools

The *Coleman report* (Coleman et al., 1966)—produced for the Department of Health, Education, and Welfare in 1966—concluded that the home is the most important factor in determining academic success. A good school is obviously better than a poor school, but even a good school cannot make up for a home that does not value education. Even in cases where schools, teachers, and teaching methods appear to be equal, students coming from deprived backgrounds do not do as well as students from homes that prize learning. Reading is less likely to be a family habit in the lower classes. Thus,

Table 13-2 Rising Costs of College

Institution	Tuition, room, board, and fees	
	1967–1968	1976–1977
Bennington College	$3,850	$6,550
Harvard University	$3,700	$7,300
Ohio State University, Columbus	$1,850	$2,975
University of California at Los Angeles	$1,850	$3,270
University of Notre Dame	$3,050	$5,310
University of Southern California	$3,250	$6,625
University of Texas, Austin	$1,610	$3,000
Wheaton College, Illinois	$2,234	$4,080

Source: From Fenga and Freyer, "Who Needs College?" *Newsweek*, April 26, 1976, p. 63. © 1976 by Newsweek, Inc. All rights reserved. Reprinted by permission.

fewer of the cognitive skills necessary in school are learned by lower-class students.

We must not go too far, however, in assuming that particular schools make no difference. The *Report of the National Advisory Commission on Civil Disorders* sums up some of the educational disadvantages of ghetto schools (1968, pp. 424–456). These schools were more crowded and usually older than the national average. In Detroit, 30 percent of the schools studied were built during the administration of President Ulysses S. Grant (1869–1877). These schools were staffed by generally less experienced teachers. Even more important, according to both the commission and James Coleman, the schools were generally regarded as inferior. As stated by the commission:

> Another strong influence on achievement derives from the tendency of school administrators, teachers, parents, and the students themselves to regard ghetto schools as inferior. Reflecting this attitude, students at-

tending such schools lost confidence in their ability to shape their future. The Coleman Report found this factor—*destiny control*—to have a stronger relationship to achievement than all the "school factors" together, [crowding, quality of teaching, books, etc.] and to be related for Negroes to the proportion of whites in the school. (*National Advisory Commission on Civil Disorders*, 1968, p. 427)

High expectations promote high achievement; low expectations, low achievement: the so-called *Pygmalion effect*. Rosenthal and Jacobson (1968) conducted an experiment showing this fact. Their study reveals the tragic effects of schools that convey a message of neglect rather than hope. (See the insert on page 364: "Pygmalion in the Classroom.") One of Coleman's conclusions was that even if schools became equally good, they could not compensate for a home background with little "know-how" of academic and economic success.

POLICIES AND PROPOSALS REGARDING INEQUALITY

At present, proposals to remedy educational inequality include controversial "tracking" programs, expensive attempts to boost children academically in their early years, and financial aid. Some people believe that nothing much can be done to change educational inequality. Others call for a sweeping change in income distribution to achieve the desired goals. We will first turn our attention to tracking, an approach adopted by many schools to cope with the different kinds of children they must teach.

Tracking

Since home background and innate ability are never equal, some children come to school better prepared than others. In kindergarten and the primary grades, these differences are not obvious to the children themselves. Also, children are generally grouped by age in the lower grades. Those who start school together stay together. Eventually, though, especially if the school is large, they become separated and are placed in different ability groupings. These groups, or *tracks*, are determined by intelligence tests, tests of reading ability, and other kinds of aptitude tests. About half the high schools in the United States, and many junior high schools, use some kind of tracking system (Schafer, Olexa, and Polk, 1970, pp. 39–46). Students on different tracks are often together for physical education but not academic instruction.

Defense of tracking The tracking system is defended as the most effective way of dealing with a wide range of academic ability. College-bound students are kept together in one class, where they compete with others of more or less equal ability. They are not held back by the constant drill and repetition needed by slower learners. Nonacademic students—those whose test scores indicate they are not likely to do well in college—compete with one another at a lower level. Finally, there are fewer discipline problems with tracking than there would be in more mixed classes.

Criticism of tracking Whatever its merits, the tracking system provokes severe criticism. Students assigned to slower classes suffer a loss of morale. Feeling left out by the system, they tend to express greater hostility, causing discipline problems to build up in the lower tracks. The class work for the lower tracks is easier and less is learned. This helps make assignment to a slower track a self-fulfilling prophecy. Later test scores may show that some students were originally misplaced, but by then they are usually too far behind to catch up. Many Hispanic children, who do not speak English well, are assigned to slower tracks mainly because of their language problems. Schafer and his associates write:

> Whatever the precise dynamics of the decision to place students at track levels, the outcome was clear in the schools we studied: Socioeconomic and racial backgrounds had an effect on which track a student took, quite apart from either his achievement in junior high or his ability as measured by I.Q. scores. (1970, p. 40)

Schafer's study showed that the test scores of upper- and lower-track students widened after students had been on separate tracks for four years. Schafer described the situation as "a case of the forecast making the weather." On the one hand, students react negatively to what they see as the stigma of lower-track status. On the other hand, teachers expect very little from these students and therefore get very little. (See the insert on page 365: "Low Expectation = Low Achievement.")

The tracking system causes trouble because it views academic inequity as a management problem. Thus it ignores the real problem: the slower student's learning difficulties. By so doing, it further widens the gap between the rapid learner and the slow learner.

Pygmalion in the classroom ROBERT ROSENTHAL AND LENORE F. JACOBSON

Note: The name Pygmalion *comes from a Greek myth of a sculptor who carved such a beautiful statue of a woman that he fell in love with it. Similarly, those children whom the teachers felt they had helped to shape became virtually cases of loving one's handiwork.*

Rosenthal and Jacobson found that when people working with animals believed the animals to be unusually bright, they were able to get unusually good performance out of them, even though in reality there was nothing extraordinary about the animals. They decided to see whether the same effect would come about if teachers believed their pupils to have an undiscovered special capacity.

In each of several classes, teachers were informed that certain of their students had been discovered by a special new test to be potential "spurters," and could be expected to show an unusual growth in IQ in the next semester. No special aid was to be given the children, but the teachers were made aware of them. Sure enough, in practically all cases, the children who were expected to show the greatest improvement actually did so. The effect was noticeable for children in the slow-learner classes, the middle-range classes, and the high-ability classes, although the greatest gain was in the middle-range classes.

About one-sixth of the school children were of Mexican descent, and they were the ones who showed the greatest improvement of all as a result of teachers' expecting them to do well. Apparently, they had suffered more than other children from having their ability underrated.

Careful examination of teacher performance made it appear that the teachers showed no grading favoritism for the children they expected to make large improvements. In fact, they tended to be somewhat more demanding on them. The fact that they expected quite a lot of the students who were rated likely to improve seems to have raised the children's self-confidence, and therefore their achievement.

One cruel result of teacher expectation appeared in the study: Those children who were labeled as "slow learners" and not given the designation "potential spurters" were looked upon unfavorably by their teachers if they showed any marked improvement. It was admirable for bright children to do even better than expected, but the intellectual outcastes were apparently expected to remain outcaste.

From Robert Rosenthal and Lenore F. Jacobson, "Teacher Expectations for the Disadvantaged," *Scientific American*, vol. 218, April 1968, pp. 19–23. Copyright © 1968 by Scientific American, Inc. All rights reserved. For a fuller account see *Pygmalion in the Classroom*, Robert Rosenthal and Lenore F. Jacobson. Holt, Rinehart & Winston, New York, 1968.

Special-help programs

Special programs have been created to promote equal opportunity in the early school years. It was the view of the Head Start program, begun during the Johnson administration's War on Poverty, that if poor children could be reached soon enough, they could be given some of the help needed to prepare them for school. It was hoped that help at an early age would prevent the bitterness and hostility that often destroy learning ability in later life. The Head Start program has generally worked well in the early

Low expectation = low achievement   WILLIAM TROMBLEY

Black and brown students in San Francisco high schools are being killed with kindness, a team of Stanford University researchers has concluded.

High school teachers, mostly white, are misleading minority students about their scholastic abilities by overpraising them, handing out good grades for poor work and by showering the students with warmth and friendliness but not demanding sound academic performance, according to the study.

"This is a study without villains," said Sanford M. Dornbusch, professor of sociology at Stanford and the study's principal researcher: "What we have found is a system in which well-meaning people are perpetuating the low achievement of black and Chicano students." . . .

[Dr. Dornbusch] speculated that "the reason this situation can be allowed to continue is because it fits what society already accepts about these kids—it's because society says, 'That's the way it is.' "

From William Trombley, "S.F. Minority Pupils Killed with Kindness, Study Says," *Los Angeles Times*, October 5, 1975, Part I, p. 3. Copyright Los Angeles Times.

---

years of schooling. Still, its benefits level off with the passing of time. They cannot compensate for poor home and neighborhood backgrounds (Williams and Evans, 1969, pp. 118–132).

Some schools use student aids who act as special friends and tutors for children who need help. These programs help children not only to learn but also to improve their attitudes toward learning. The program is expensive, making it impossible to do much remedial work. Some educators and sociologists feel that the high cost of student aids is well worth it. The investment, they say, would produce a generation who would succeed in getting jobs and would not have to go on welfare. In the long run, then, money would be saved.

Robert M. Hutchins is convinced that almost all people can learn the basic skills well enough to take care of themselves. He points out that in the Soviet Union, where 80 percent of the people were illiterate at the turn of the century, all students between the ages of seven and fifteen are now required to learn at least one foreign language and to have a good background in the physical and biological sciences

and mathematics (Hutchins, 1968, pp. 8–10). The United States, by contrast, has tried to make high school easy enough for nearly everyone to get through. Soviet schools are very severe, but they do show that students can meet heavy educational demands if necessary. In spite of the differences in policies, the dropout rate of the Soviet Union is probably about the same as that of the United States.

Financial help

Sewell, previously cited for his study on equal opportunity in education, favors far more financial aid in the form of scholarships for high school graduates who have shown they can do college work. Although this would do nothing about the earlier school years, it would help to equalize the chance for higher education. Many such scholarships have already been offered, but not by state or federal programs. Many are given by business and industry. Still, the number available rises and falls with the needs of the labor market.

Today, the college system not only favors the

middle and upper classes but even robs the poor and gives to the rich. Even though all taxpayers, including the poor, help to support our public colleges and universities, it is the rich who receive by far the greatest benefit from college. According to Ivan Illich, "Each American college graduate has had an education costing an amount five times greater than the median life income of half of humanity" (1971, p. 49). It could be argued that college education should be extended to the qualified poor. However, the cost of such a program, given the high federal and state deficits, would rule it out.

Busing and equalization

The controversy over busing to achieve integration was covered in Chapter 7. There, the sociologist Thomas F. Pettigrew was said to have considered busing a "qualified success." It had improved the work of black children while not harming that of white children. The argument for busing even under difficult circumstances is implied in the conclusions of Coleman: An isolated, all-black, ghetto school tends to be seen as a place of failure, not success. The presence of white children, whether they are liked or not, gives the school the sense of being part of the community, probably cared about by the board of education, and not isolated and neglected. Furthermore, peer-group influence is very strong in schools. The presence of students who expect to succeed can help support morale in the whole school.

Restructuring the reward system

Christopher Jencks and his associates did a study that reached approximately the same conclusions as the Coleman report. They found that school quality, equipment, and teaching methods make very little difference in achievement (Jencks et al., 1972). What really matters is social-class position, education and occupation of parents, cultural background, and genetic differences. (Genetic differences do not loom large in Jencks's study; he is by no means either a racist or a genetic determinist.) Jencks's study shows that schools alone cannot achieve equal opportunity. Because of individual differences in background, ability, and motivation, not all people will be able to succeed in playing by the rules of society. Jencks urges, therefore, that the rules be changed. He proposes more nearly equal pay for all jobs. He is shocked that the best-paid fifth of all workers earn 600 percent more than the worst-paid fifth. He is not a total leveler, but he would like to reduce such differences drastically. Although Jencks does not believe that spending more on education would do much to wipe out inequality, he still wants to see very good schools. Since people spend so many years in school, everything possible should be done to make education pleasant and agreeable.

Unequal education and equal pay: The Israeli example

Seymour Martin Lipset tells us that Israel comes closer than any other country in the world to accomplishing what Jencks suggests. The results solve one problem but create another. Minority groups (mainly Jews from Yemen and the Middle East) receive adequate pay for their work, but they must attend a school system which almost guarantees failure. Lipset explains the contrast in the accompanying insert "Education and Equality: Israel and the United States Compared."

American society will probably never go as far in achieving income equality as Israel. But it is interesting that one country has carried the equality-of-income idea at least as far as Jencks intended it, and partly within the capitalist system. The Israeli school system, however, is clearly much less egalitarian than ours. It is a source of normative strain; the high school teachers and their union oppose lowering standards in order to protect their status.

Israeli, American, and all other national edu-

Education and equality: Israel and the United States compared   SEYMOUR MARTIN LIPSET

These two emphases, egalitarianism and educational excellence have, though necessarily much modified in content, continued to inform Israeli policy. Thus, Israel has maintained one of the most narrowly spread wage and income structures in the world. The graduated taxation system there would be regarded as confiscatory by middle and upper classes in most societies. Import duties and taxation are extremely high on luxury items such as automobiles, foreign travel, and the like. Privately purchased housing costs a great deal; publicly built apartments for low income families are much cheaper. Medicine is largely socialized. Welfare benefits are high. As anyone who has visited Israel knows, the life of its educated and professional classes is difficult compared to that of equivalent strata in America or Europe. In 1971, "a family of four with 36,000 Israeli pounds per year, the average income in the top decile (roughly $7,800) . . . paid 45 percent of total income in taxes."

The lowest 30 percent of wage earners had about 15 percent added to their total income through transfer payments (government services), while "the upper 16 percent suffered a decrease from 33 to 26 percent of total income." There has been a considerable increase in the income and standard of living of those coming from Asia and Africa in the past decade. According to Schlomo Avineri, the Israeli political scientist, "The average income per standard equivalent adult among families of Asian-African origins" rose from 63 percent of the overall average for Jewish families in 1963–64 to 70 percent in 1970. . . . Much of these changes are a result of deliberate government policies. It can truthfully be said that in no other democratic country are the egalitarian emphases of socialism as real as in Israel. (In stating this, of course, I am not suggesting Israel is socialist. Clearly much of its economy is capitalist, and considerable private and corporate wealth exists and is, in fact, increasing with the growth of the economy.) . . .

Yet, although the Israeli standard of living and income is spread more equitably, as compared to other countries, the Israeli educational system does not fit an egalitarian model. Rather the original European settlers established a classic pre-World War I school structure. The Israeli high schools copied the German model, not the American common schools. From the perspective of the average American or poor Israeli youth, the high school system is impossible. An Israeli student in an academic high school has to take something like 14 subjects. Every year he studies chemistry, physics, biology, math, English, Arabic or French, history, Jewish culture, etc. He goes to school six days a week, and has four to five hours of homework every day. In this kind of system, no child from an underprivileged background, where he does not have the whole apparatus of the family to support him, can possibly do well, unless he is by some miracle supermotivated.

Israeli social scientists have documented the implications of the school system in abundant statistical detail. Thus Chaim Adler points out that as of 1969–70, only "6 out of 100 seventeen-year-olds in the population who are of Oriental parentage are fully certified academic high school graduates," as contrasted to 35 out of 100 among those of Occidental parentage.

Many Israelis, Ashkenazim and others—in government, in the universities, in the Education Ministry—are aware of this. They are consciously concerned with the prob-

(Continued)

lem, and are making important changes. But the problem lies in large part with those committed to the old system, the parents and the teachers. To suggest lowering the educational level of the Israeli high school by creating common schools threatens the status of an Israeli high school teacher, who is like the *professeur* at a French lycée. Lowering the intellectual content challenges his status, identity, and job. It is understandable that he and his union resist.

Seymour Martin Lipset, "Education and Equality: Israel and the United States Compared." Published by permission of Transaction, Inc., from Society, vol II, no. 3, copyright © 1974 by Transaction, Inc.

cational systems exist at least in part to supply workers, managers, and experts for society. Ideally, people should be trained for all the needed positions in a society, and all the positions for which people are trained should be available to them when their schooling is over.

MEETING OCCUPATIONAL REQUIREMENTS

Education prepares people to be citizens, teaches them their cultural tradition, and satisfies their intellectual and emotional needs. However, the major function of education for most people is the practical one of preparing them to hold jobs. Children begin to learn basic work skills in grade school. Although some high school students are preoccupied with sports, school events, and social popularity and others think of high school years as merely a stepping-stone to college, many students learn specific occupational skills during their high school years. For secretarial work and the skilled trades, a high school diploma may be enough. (Although today academic requirements have been increased even in these fields.) Some, of course, will get unskilled and semiskilled jobs if they have dropped out of high school or have done poorly in their high school work. Increasingly, though, our society demands credentials. The diploma is the key to success in any line of work—the admission ticket to the competitive game.

General and specific requirements

It is important, particularly for academically gifted young people, to get a sound liberal education—including philosophy, the social sciences, literature, and art—in addition to training in a special field. Nearly all educators encourage young people to get a broad academic background. It will not only enrich their own lives but also provide some of the sensitive, thoughtful people so badly needed in the world. In addition, a general education may eventually help one to move ahead professionally. In the years immediately after graduation, however, employers are interested in the specialized skills that show competence in a given field.

THE JOB MARKET

Seen from society's point of view, the schools function to supply the workers needed by society. If the schools do not fully prepare specialists for their chosen fields, they at least provide the background knowledge and experience that will help graduates develop the expertise they need. It is often claimed that the average student does poorly in written English and mathematics. But members of the elite are well trained in every

Figure 13-4 *Opposite page:* Students must develop specific skills to find work in today's specialized job market. (*The New York Times*)

area, especially those who specialize in the sciences. After the Soviet Union launched its first space satellite in the 1950s, it was feared that American schools were not producing enough scientists, mathematicians, and technical experts. Some people wondered whether modern societies in general had enough potential talent to supply the needed expertise. These fears were apparently ill founded. Today the supply-demand situation is reversed. Like the sorcerer's apprentice, the universities turn out experts who flood the market at a faster and faster rate. By the early 1970s, it became clear that the teaching field and certain other areas were oversupplied. The U.S. Labor Department predicted a surplus of nearly a million college graduates for the years 1975 to 1985, with an even greater surplus projected for the 1980s than for the 1970s. The Labor Department claimed that college gradu-

ates would in many cases have to settle for jobs that had never before demanded college education (Rosenthal, 1973, pp. 24–26).

Americans have always had faith in the value of a high school education. We believe that no one should drop out of high school, no matter how bored or academically inept he or she might be. Statistics prove that those students who finish high school do, on an average, earn more money than those who do not. It is questionable, though, whether students who drop out because of lack of interest or ability would do better if they stayed in. (See the insert "School and Earning Power for Low Achievers.") Americans also believe that the best jobs demand a college degree—and this is generally true. Two other beliefs, however, have often proved to be wrong in the 1970s: that degrees guarantee jobs and that the higher the degree the better the job.

School and earning power for low achievers

As a general rule, students who finish high school have better earning power than those who do not finish, but does this mean that all drop-outs would necessarily have done better if they stayed in school? A team of researchers from the University of Wisconsin investigated the matter. W. Lee Hansen, Burton A. Weisbrod, and William J. Scranton (*American Economic Review*, June 1970) [examined] the occupations and earnings of 2,400 men who had failed the Armed Forces Qualification Test. Some had finished high school and some had not, but all had been poor school achievers. The conclusion of the study was that length of time in school for low achievers made little difference:

> According to this study, the most reasonable advice to give to youngsters who don't seem to do well in school is not to hang in, but to:
>
> 1 Be white (the study showed an average difference of $608 a year between earnings of white and non-white subjects);
> 2 Get married (married men in the group got $459 more than the unmarried);
> 3 Get some kind of job training outside of school (training added $326 a year to the incomes of those men who had some);
> 4 Live outside the South [where wages are low].

From "Does Staying in School Up Earning Power?" Published by permission of Transaction, Inc., from *Transaction*, vol. 8, no. 4, copyright © 1971 by Transaction, Inc.

Advanced degrees can even be a disadvantage in a tight job market, as was the case with Delina Halunshka and Fred Whitehead:

Delina Halushka, 45, is a part-time Spanish teacher at a community college in Santa Monica, California. Although she holds two master's degrees and a Ph.D., she has not been able to find a full-time teaching post since 1972, when she lost her old job in a college merger. "The less education you have, the better chance you have of getting a job," she says. "That sounds crazy, but it's true."

Fred Whitehead, 32, graduated summa cum laude from the University of Kansas in 1966. After a year in London as a Fulbright Scholar, he earned a Ph.D. at Columbia and got a job teaching English at Southern Illinois University. Soon, however, he was laid off, as a result of a budget cutback. After months of futile searching for another teaching job, he finally gave up and went to a trade school. Dr. Whitehead is now a welder in Kansas City, Kansas. (*Newsweek*, 1976a, p. 60; copyright © 1976 by Newsweek, Inc. All rights reserved. Reprinted by permission.)

A conflict explanation of educational requirements

All young people must go to school, it is usually claimed, because otherwise they would not be able to get jobs. Because modern society is more technical than in the past, it is said, anyone without at least a high school education cannot function. Nevertheless, there are many jobs that require very little formal schooling. These include most kinds of assembly-line work, custodial work, and even truck driving and operating most kinds of machinery. Some of these jobs require considerable skill and training, but not the kind taught in school. At the same time, the need for engineers, scientists, doctors, nurses, accountants, and managers has reinforced the importance of school as a training ground for work. Functionalists would claim that school systems are maintained to assure a supply of trained, expert personnel.

Randall Collins (1971, pp. 1002–1018) believes that although functionalism accounts for this primary purpose of schooling, a *conflict theory of education* is even more useful. He believes that occupational groups try to professionalize themselves—that is, they set high standards to upgrade themselves socially and gain prestige. This is why, according to Lipset, Israeli high school teachers support the rigid school system of Israel (see page 367). Such groups are not the only ones that try to upgrade entrance requirements. Employers often do the same thing, since they prefer to have workers who are efficient and have the interests, manners, and habits that will make them socially acceptable.

Diplomas for the unskilled

Seventeen percent of all employers in California demand a high school education for all employees, including those working at unskilled jobs (Collins, 1971). A survey made in the 1930s indicated that only 1 percent of employers made this demand. This requirement limits potential employees to what is sometimes called a "better class of people." Collins reasons that the functional explanation of education for all is valid only in theory. It would hold true only if all unskilled jobs were to disappear. Further, functionalism assumes that education provides the skills needed for all jobs. Actually, today's unskilled jobs require no more education than did the farm and railroad jobs of 100 years ago. As for jobs requiring considerable skills, these skills are often learned on the job, not in school.

Upper-level requirements

Although higher education is necessary for the highest jobs on the occupational latter, social-class position is just as important as education.

The most prestigious law firms, banks, and business firms recruit heavily from among the graduates of ivy league colleges and elite private schools. Although these people are not necessarily more competent than graduates of other colleges, they have the social skills needed to mix easily with other members of their class. This attempt by certain occupational groups to upgrade themselves socially is called *professionalism*.

Professional efforts

In many fields, occupational groups also attempt to professionalize themselves. On the surface, their standards are educational. Basically, though, their actions stem from class-consciousness. These groups become highly protective of their members. They often adopt union-type rules and regulations to make themselves judges of their own members. Examples are the American Association of Medicine and the American Bar Association. Just as they try to protect themselves from outside interference, they also protect themselves from potential members who are not socially compatible with the group.

Collins, as noted, feels that conflict theory accounts for professionalism better than does functionalism. Each occupational group, he believes, is to some extent in conflict with the outside world. It protects its members and excludes those it considers unworthy. S. M. Miller gives a similar explanation for what he calls the "credential society." "Credentialism assures personal acceptability" (1967, p. 2). Group members can assume that potential members with the right credentials have shown that they know how to conform to the social standards of the group. Since it is hard for an outsider to judge the competence of a person in another profession, degrees or credentials are also used to prove competence to the outside world. In the field of education, for example, it is hard to establish standards for judging the competence of teachers. Thus, the whole matter is often settled on the basis of degrees. The person with the proper credentials—a master of arts degree, for example—is considered competent, and that settles the argument.

Figure 13-5 Why is it so hard to get into medical school? According to conflict theory, entrance requirements are kept high to ensure prestige and limit supply. (*Mimi Forsyth, Monkmeyer*)

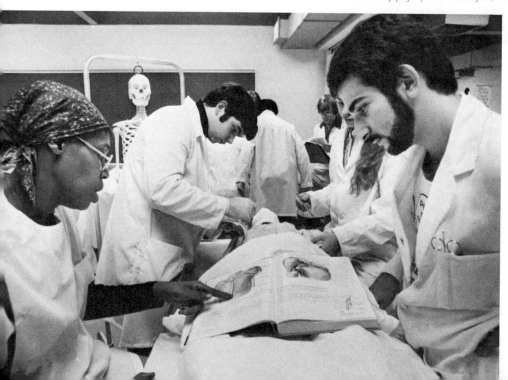

Grade inflation   DON SPEICH AND PATRICIA MCCORMACK

Grade Inflation in High Schools

More students entered the nation's universities and colleges with inflated high school grades last fall than ever before, according to a survey conducted by UCLA and the American Council on Education.

Of the more than 328,000 students surveyed, 74.7 percent had high school grade-point averages of B− to A+ compared to 72.5 percent in 1975 and 69.5 percent in 1966, the first year the survey was conducted.

Alexander Astin, a UCLA professor of education and director of the survey, believes that grade inflation—the awarding of higher grades than a student's work warrants—accounts for the bulk of the percentage increase. . . .

"When you have a measure of the achievement, which is what the tests measure . . . and it shows an absolute decline, you have to raise the question of whether students are acquiring the skills and knowledge they used to. And when you look at this in the context that grades are going up," added Astin, "it is both troublesome and ironic."

From Don Speich and Patricia McCormack, "Growing Grade Inflation in High Schools Reported," *Los Angeles Times*, Jan. 16, 1977, part II, p. 1. Copyright 1977, Los Angeles Times. Reprinted by permission.

Grade Inflation in College

A comparison of grades among college students of 1969 and 1975 gives "dramatic evidence" of grade inflation, a professor of sociology from the University of California at Berkeley reported today. Martin Trow, in a survey sponsored by the Carnegie Council on Policy Studies in Higher Education, found:

In 1969 only 18 percent of undergraduates had a cumulative grade-point average of B plus or better.

By 1975 that proportion had doubled to 36 percent. . . .

Among graduate students he also found grade inflation. Fifty-four percent of the graduate students in 1975 claimed an average of B plus or better—compared with 40 percent in 1969. . . .

Today, grade inflation is believed linked to a school's aim to help as many of its graduates as possible get into the best graduate schools. [Italics added.]

From Patricia McCormack, UPI Education Editor, "Professor Calls Inflation of Grades a Problem," *The Bakersfield Californian*, Jan. 16, 1977, p. 46. Copyright 1977, The Bakersfield Californian.

Implications of conflict theory

An optimistic conflict theorist would say that education gradually upgrades the whole society, since each group tries to protect its position by increasing entrance requirements all the time. Two less optimistic interpretations are these: (1) Although the amount of schooling may increase, the quality goes down as courses are made easier. The trend in recent years has been toward lower standards in high school and college grading. (See the insert "Grade Inflation.") (2) The system will continue to exclude almost all people at the bottom of the social-class ladder for the reasons previously discussed. In this way,

Figure 13-6 Football is more than a game. It is a ritual that creates a student subculture—one latent function of education. (*Hugh Rogers, Monkmeyer*)

education supports a certain amount of social-class stagnation. Since 1973, however, colleges and businesses have partially followed the equal-opportunity guidelines set by the federal government. Thus, they have opened their doors to minority groups and women much more than in the past. Minority groups, however, are stratified within themselves. If Collins is right, we could assume that while more minority-group people may get better jobs, only those in the middle class would make the grade.

LATENT FUNCTIONS OF EDUCATION

The *manifest or obvious functions* of education are those we have already discussed: training citizens and workers, transmitting the culture, providing a chance for upward mobility, and developing the intellect.

There are also some *latent or hidden functions* that educators are embarrassed to discuss. Higher education widens the gap between social classes and can easily increase class prejudice. One example is the resentment of intellectuals

by many working-class people, an attitude that George Wallace exploited politically in his two presidential campaigns in 1968 and 1972. Colleges have been criticized as unofficial marriage agencies, since young people often find their mates on campus. Fraternities and sororities, in particular, have made it easier for people to meet and marry others of their own class. More recently, the increasing trend toward cohabitation has become a new latent function of the colleges. The creation of youth subcultures in high school and college is still another latent function of education. Finally, many students don't want to go to school. Some of them cause school fights and discipline problems. Others become vandals, destroying school property.

One latent function that attracted attention in the 1960s was student activism. Another function, which has become more important in the 1970s, is the upgrading of academic requirements and the feeling that many ordinary jobs should require college degrees.

The critical function and student activism

The founders of the public education system probably expected college and university teachers to support the social system. Occasionally, of course, they would criticize public policies, but in a polite, restrained way. That students and professors should indulge in savage, biting criticism accompanied by demonstrations, sit-ins, and defiance of the law is quite a different matter and was clearly unintended. Still, both teachers and students have felt it their duty to point out the inconsistencies and shortcomings of society. Criticism is essential to the learning process. For this reason, colleges and universities insist on the right to academic freedom—the right to express opinions freely on all issues.

In the 1960s, social criticism saturated the academic community. Students especially were struck by the difference between what they had been taught—an idealized stress on constitutional rights, responsible government, and legal equality—and the way society actually worked. The conflict became even clearer when students focused on public issues. The most vocal and determined resistance to the war in Vietnam, especially after college students became eligible for the draft, occurred on the campus.

Even before the Vietnamese conflict, students saw the same gap between the ideal and the real. For this reason, they took part in the civil rights movement. More recently, they have demanded a voice in college decision making on such subjects as grade policies, more courses for minorities, and less dependence on the Defense Department for research money. The 1970s have generally seen a decline in college protests, but the potential is always there. Research done in Canada indicates that the longer students stay in college, the more likely they are to express hostility toward authority. (See the insert "Jobs Cool Student Protest")

EXPANSIONISM AND COMPETITION

The educational system has expanded greatly since it first began. In part, this is the result of more demanding rules for entry into various occupational groups. Employers—unless they find it too costly—are now hiring those with the most schooling. Colleges and universities have profited by the trend. It has expanded their work and provided jobs for more teachers and administrators.

Latent results have developed from this expansion. One result is resistance to the educational establishment and the development of alternatives. Ivar Berg, for example, says that the present credentialing system requires "rich man's qualifications for poor man's jobs" (1969). Berg has also written a book called *Education and Jobs: The Great Training Rob-*

Jobs cool student protest   JODY GAYLIN

The angry young lions who say nasty things about their university's administrators and trustees are likely to become lambs next fall—if they get jobs directly after graduation. Students who enter the working world lose much of their hostility towards authority, while their graduate school peers keep on scowling.

P.S. Fry tested 200 men at the University of Calgary to see if and when they changed their feelings about the powers-that-be. He gave engineering, education, and social-science students a series of psychological tests that measured their attitudes towards authority, and categorized their responses as liking, disliking, submissive fearful, self-assertive, or neutral.

During their senior year, prospective teachers, engineers, and social scientists became noticeably more tolerant and submissive to authority, curbing their previously critical attitudes markedly. Negative attitudes declined even further after they had worked six months.

In contrast, students who went on to graduate school generally clung to their negative feelings, and in some cases showed more self-assertiveness against authority as time went by. Fry compares the protective environment of the university to that of the family, suggesting that school fosters the same rebellious feelings as do the "conflicted family relationships" of adolescence. . . .

The educational process

375

bery (1970), while Caroline Bird has criticized expansionism in her book *The Case Against College* (1975). Both writers show that too many people have to stay in school, at great expense, to compete for fewer and fewer jobs. They believe that the college-for-everyone idea has been oversold.

Defenders of the educational system say that college does much more than just prepare people for jobs. They contend that college-educated persons become community leaders, join associations, work for causes, and are generally more active citizens than noncollege people. Further, they say, in the long run, those with college degrees will get better jobs than those without degrees, even if they must sometimes settle for less than they expected.

Critics of credentialism point out that there are far more middle-range jobs than professional and scientific-specialist jobs. As a result, the majority of freshman and sophomore college students now attend community colleges largely because they offer courses aimed at middle-range vocations. Private technical and business schools have also expanded, promising training in less than the four years needed for college. Even many four-year schools have become more vocationally oriented. They are trying to provide better job counseling and the practical knowledge needed for jobs.

The higher-education system now provides more in-service training for adults, more opportunity to drop out of school with the option to reenter later on, and far more variety in training programs. Meanwhile, colleges and universities do the more traditional jobs: expanding knowledge through research and providing a background in the humanities and social sciences. To these is added the duty of bringing more minority groups and women into the system.

Since schools reflect the societies that produce them, they are obviously caught in cross-pressures. In the United States, the ideal of equal opportunity clashes with the pressures of status, both familial and occupational. The goal of working to prepare for a job can conflict with the ideal of producing informed citizens. The attempt to teach everyone can thwart the goal of training an intellectual elite. For all these reasons, school programs are constantly criticized and revised. Like the larger society, they are ruled by many conflicting pressures, not by a perfect plan laid down by elite groups or by tradition.

SUMMARY

Mass education is now a feature of all industrial nations. The United States became a leader in mass education because of the Puritan stress on both religion and financial success and because of Jeffersonian ideas of the need for education in a democratic society. Early American businessmen also considered schools important for turning out efficient workers and for spreading the ideology of capitalism. Public schools also helped Americanize immigrant children and give all citizens a common cultural tradition.

In all industrial countries, educational systems now have the *manifest functions* of providing skilled workers, expanding scientific knowledge, and at least partially equalizing opportunities for people.

The pluralistic society of the United States complicates the transmission of culture. Until recently, minority cultures—such as those of the blacks and Chicanos—have been completely ignored as educators presented a *single-culture* tradition. Further, there is conflict between community control of schools and such national requirements as standardized tests and desegregating the schools.

The equal-opportunity function of education has always been considered important. Horace Mann called education "the great equalizer." Still, full equality of opportunity is almost impossible to ensure. Socioeconomic status (SES) is a better predictor of success in school and of life chances than either the quality of schools or scores on IQ tests. High-SES people have six times as good a chance of graduating from college as low-SES people. Such differences persist regardless of IQ scores.

Some experts argue that differences in academic achievement and life success are linked to differences measured by IQ tests. Others hold that many intelligent people show little interest in making money. Also, IQ tests do not really measure potential intelligence as much as environmental background. Regardless of academic ability, tuition costs strongly influence one's chances of entering or completing college. Those costs are rising rapidly.

The *Coleman report* finds that academic achievement depends more on home background than on the quality of the schools. The home determines the student's *achievement motivation*. Teacher attitudes are also considered important. The report contends that teachers favor middle-class children over lower-class children. This "Pygmalion effect" often ensures that lower-class children will fail. Both Coleman and the National Advisory Commission on Civil Disorders consider community morale and *destiny control* important to education. Achievement is difficult in ghetto schools, where a feeling of hopelessness pervades the community.

Since students differ in academic ability, they are commonly assigned to different *tracks*, or ability levels, within the same grade. Tracking makes competition reasonably fair by putting people of approximately equal ability together. It is criticized for offering weaker programs, discouraging poorer students, and creating self-fulfilling prophecies of academic failure. Special teaching programs have been suggested for making the outcomes of education somewhat more equal. The *Jencks report* states that no school policies can overcome the unequal effects of home background. Instead, Jencks advocates more nearly equal pay for all kinds of work. This policy is more closely approached in Israel than in any other democratic country.

A functional explanation stresses how schools help turn out workers for the job market. Still, there is never a perfect fit. The result is job shortages in some areas and shortages of trained personnel in others. By the 1970s, an oversupply of college graduates became apparent; it is expected by the U.S. Department of Labor to persist until the mid-1980s. There is some evidence that, for low achievers, the number of years spent in high school have little bearing on ability to earn a living.

A *conflict theory of education* may be more meaningful than a functional explanation, according to one researcher. He sees many work groups as similar to social clubs. They try to keep an exclusive membership of the right type of people, and they protect their positions by setting up high (possibly unnecessary) entrance requirements. This is called *professionalism*. Another researcher states that ours is a *credential* society. Two possible results of such policies are (1) the tendency to get more people through the system by making courses easier, or *inflating grades*, or (2) the practice of excluding people from the lowest class permanently.

According to functional analysis, many of the functions of education are latent. Examples of *latent functions* are fraternities and sororities, popularity contests, the student activism of the 1960s, and increasing class prejudice. Two researchers have gone so far as to say that one such latent function is to inflate education to the point where one must have "rich man's qualifications for poor man's jobs." Defenders of the educational system reply that expanded educational requirements benefit society. They improve the transmission of cultural tradition and help create better citizens.

Study guide

Terms to know

Manifest functions of education
Single-culture tradition
Achievement motivation
Coleman report
Destiny control

"Pygmalion effect"
Tracking
Jencks report
Conflict theory of education
Grade inflation

Credential society
Professionalism
Latent functions of education

Names to know

Horace Mann
Seymour Martin Lipset
Arthur Jensen
Noam Chomsky

James Coleman
Christopher Jencks
Randall Collins

Self-test

Part I. Multiple Choice. Select the best of the four alternative answers:

1 Horace Mann referred to public education as (**a**) industrial discipline, (**b**) the democratizing agent, (**c**) the great equalizer, (**d**) the Americanizing agent.

2 Historically, American schools have had a harder job than those of other industrializing countries in (**a**) providing industrial workers, (**b**) uniting the people in a common tradition, (**c**) training people for new types of jobs, (**d**) preventing revolutionary movements.

3 Although community control of schools is considered democratic, federal regulations have been more helpful in promoting (**a**) equal opportunities for minorities, (**b**) help for poor districts, (**c**) uniform standards, (**d**) all the above.

4 A study of inequality by Sewell found that it was harder for women than for men to enter college, especially those (**a**) of lower socioeconomic status, (b) of higher socioeconomic status, (**c**) attending community colleges, (**d**) from urban backgrounds.

5 The comparison between the Wechsler test and Dove's test shows (**a**) the superiority of the Wechsler test, (**b**) the superiority of Dove's test, (**c**) that the answers to either one are a good measure of intelligence, (**d**) that such questions measure only environment, not the ability to learn.

6 The Coleman report concludes that which of the following is most important in determining academic success? (**a**) teaching methods, (**b**) school financing, (**c**) home background, (**d**) quality of high schools.

7 Tracking is most defensible on the ground that (**a**) it makes competition fairer, (**b**) discipline problems are avoided, (**c**) slow learners are not aware of their lower academic status, (**d**) mistakes in assigning students are almost impossible.

8 According to the insert "Low Expectation = Low Achievement," San Francisco high school teachers were inclined, in relation to minority students, to (**a**) display hostile attitudes, (**b**)

make few if any demands, (**c**) give no praise for accomplishment, (**d**) show indifference.

9 Jencks considers schools incapable of achieving equality of opportunity and proposes (**a**) less schooling, (**b**) drastic reforms in schooling, (**c**) changing the family system, (**d**) giving more nearly equal pay for all jobs.

10 For the next few years, the U.S. Labor Department expects (**a**) about the right number of college graduates, (**b**) an undersupply of college graduates, (**c**) an oversupply of about a million college graduates, (**d**) an oversupply of college graduates, but only until 1980.

11 According to the insert "School and Earning Power for Low Achievers," the *least* important key to getting ahead was (**a**) being white, (**b**) getting job training outside of school, (**c**) being married, (**d**) staying in school.

12 Collins contends that many aspects of our educational system can best be explained from the viewpoint of (**a**) functionalism, (**b**) conflict, (**c**) evolution, (**d**) social solidarity.

13 Many jobs, according to Collins, are upgraded in educational requirements because (**a**) more education is needed for the jobs, (**b**) jobs are becoming more and more difficult, (**c**) an attempt is made to bring in only the "right" class of people, (**d**) college grading standards are growing more rigorous.

14 The possibility that education can increase social-class prejudice is an example of a (**a**) latent function, (**b**) manifest function, (**c**) dysfunction, (**d**) malfunction.

15 According to the insert "Jobs Cool Student Protest," a long period in college and graduate school has the effect of making attitudes toward authority (**a**) more submissive, (**b**) more hostile, (**c**) more stable, (**d**) more sympathetic.

Part II. True-False Questions

1 The Puritans had no interest in money, only in religious education.

2 Early American education gave equal treatment to the traditions of minority groups.

3 Teaching the literary tradition has become confusing because there is more than one literary tradition.

4 Noam Chomsky argues that there is an almost perfect correlation between IQ and financial success.

5 According to Schafer's research, socioeconomic status and racial or ethnic background seem to influence tracking, regardless of ability.

6 Members of the major churches are less likely to go to college than are members of some of the smaller, less traditional churches, such as Jehovah's Witnesses.

7 The logical conclusion of "Pygmalion in the Classroom" is that teacher expectation exerts a strong influence on student achievement.

8 *Tracking* refers to the practice of segregating students on the basis of their presumed ability.

9 Hutchins concludes, partly on the basis of experience in the Soviet Union, that almost all students can learn the basic skills required by modern society.

10 In the Israeli educational system, all lower-class or minority groups are able to keep up with the competition.

11 The Israeli educational system can be characterized as egalitarian.

12 The experience of two people with Ph.D. degress (Halushka and Whitehead) indicates that the higher the degree, the better the guarantee of immediate employment in a desirable job.

13 The assumption that schools ensure a supply of the workers needed by society is a functional interpretation of education.

14 Ivar Berg and Caroline Bird both argue that the idea of college for everyone has been oversold.

15 Much of the student activism of the 1960s is related to the contrast between idealized norms and real norms.

Questions for discussion

1 Pursue the issue of teacher (or counselor) expectations of student performance and how those expectations may direct students into either academic or vocational tracks. Try to draw on personal experience.

2 What are the arguments for and against developing courses that recognize more than one cultural tradition—for example, courses in black literature, ethnic music, and Chicano literature? What benefits will be gained? What expenses are involved?

3 What are the advantages of a liberal arts education as opposed to a vocational one? Should the person taking a vocational education also be expected to meet certain requirements in the humanities or social sciences?

4 Compare the academic demands on the average American student with requirements in the Israeli school system. What kind of "culture shock" might the American experience in the Israeli system?

5 What arguments can you give for and against Jencks's policy of giving more equal pay for all kinds of work?

6 Discuss the impact of vocational training in your own community. Are any jobs oversubscribed? Are there any skilled trades with a shortage of workers?

7 What might be the results of grade inflation for both academic and vocational training?

Projects

1 In groups of four or five, prepare a plan for fair scholarship distribution. The plan should include consideration of the following:
  a What criteria should be used for granting scholarships? (Need, grade average, greatest potential benefit to society, etc.)
  b What educational majors, if any, should be given preference?
  c Where should the money come from? Assuming these would be government scholarships, what alternative government expenses could be cut to pay for them, or how would additional tax money be raised?
  d Since funds are never adequate for everything desirable, where would you cut if there were not enough scholarships?

2 Visit a public and a private or parochial school. Record your observations of each visit. Based on your observations, compare the two in teaching effectiveness, racial or ethnic integration, and egalitarianism (i.e., are there chances for the economically disadvantaged in the private or parochial school)?

3 If you have not already done so, outline thoroughly the course work you will need for the occupation you intend to pursue. Do all the courses seem functional—clearly intended to improve your intellect or to prepare you for job effectiveness? Is there any evidence for what Collins calls a "conflict perspective"—that is, are some requirements added mainly to make entry into the occupation difficult and expensive?

Suggested readings

Cohen, David K.: "Public Schools: The Next Decade," *Dissent*, April 1971, pp. 161—170. Can we expect schools to provide social integration and overcome inequality? What are the problems of decentralization? Of community control? Cohen predicts an increasingly diversified educational system to meet society's demands.

Commager, Henry Steele: "The School as Surrogate Conscience," *Saturday Review*, January 11, 1975, pp. 54—57. Why is it hard for the schools to teach the idealized norms of society? Do they get support from other social institutions, or are they alone expected to train a generation that will do better in spite of the hypocrisy of society?

Hodgson, Godfrey: "Do Schools Make a Difference?" *Atlantic Monthly*, vol. 231, March 1973, pp. 37–46. Is it true, as many studies have indicated, that the schools can't do much more to promote equal opportunity? Hodgson answers the question. His fear is not that the schools have given up but that society has grown weary of such policies and is looking for excuses to abandon the effort.

Playboy, editors: "What's Really Happening on Campus?" *Playboy*, vol. 23, October 1976, pp. 28–30. What are the current attitudes toward women's demands, premarital sex, cohabitation, drugs? Are there social-class differences and male-female differences in attitudes on the campus? This survey of college students may uncover additional latent functions of college education.

Robinson, Donald W.: "An Interview with Christopher Jencks," *Phi Delta Kappan*, vol. 54, December 1972, pp. 255—257. "You shouldn't expect the schools to deal with the problems of economic inequality," says Jencks. What role does he see for the schools in promoting an integrated society and a happy childhood and youth? What institutions will be responsible for greater equality?

Schafer, Walter E., Carol Olexa, and Kenneth Polk: "Programmed for Social Class: Tracking in High School," *Trans-Action*, vol. 7, October 1970, pp. 3—46. How does a tracking system subvert its own intention of helping slow learners? These writers are convinced that tracking systems do more harm than good, and that often a policy is set of "grade floors" for college-bound students and "grade ceilings" for those in the lower tracks.

Taylor, Edwin F.: "The Looking-Glass World of Testing," *Today's Education* (Journal of the National Education Association), vol. 66, March–April 1977, pp. 39–44. After looking over a number of standardized tests for children, the author concludes that they have an Alice-in-Wonderland quality, divorced from the real world and devoid of logic. He also gives ten commandements for taking tests, such as "Thou shalt not think broadly," and "Thou shalt not be frightened." ("Don't be nervous," said the king, "or I'll have you executed on the spot.")

Key to questions. Multiple Choice: 1-c; 2-b; 3-d; 4-a; 5-d; 6-c; 7-a; 8-b; 9-d; 10-c; 11-d; 12-b; 13-c; 14-a; 15-b. True-False: 1-F; 2-F; 3-T; 4-F; 5-T; 6-F; 7-T; 8-T; 9-T; 10-F; 11-F; 12-F; 13-T; 14-T; 15-T.

This chapter examines the complex interrelationship between society and religion. After reading it, you should be able to:

1 Explain how religion has generally served to unite societies but has occasionally become a divisive force.

2 Recognize some of the similar functions of religion in modern and primitive societies.

3 Analyze the psychological functions of religion for the individual.

4 See how religion can serve both as a conservative force, supporting social institutions, and as a reforming force.

5 Understand a number of latent functions of religion, including Weber's thesis regarding Protestantism.

6 See how different doctrines and rites appeal to people of different social classes and life experiences.

7 Explain the phenomenon of conversion to a new faith such as Hare Krishna and Reverend Moon's Unification Church.

14

THE LINK WITH ETERNITY: RELIGION

I am free, free from the garbage of the world—the kind of stuff that you're a slave to. Jesus said, "Whoever commits sin is a slave to sin." I've quit taking drugs, I've quit getting it on with girls—I've changed, man! I'm free, free, free—all the time and not just for six to eight hours—all the time! I shall have problems, but I don't hassle with them, because I'm free! (Adams and Fox, 1972, p. 53)

To this young convert, religion means freedom—the freedom to leave behind the "garbage of the world" and to enter a realm of higher, spiritual truths; the freedom to escape sin and to lead a moral life; the freedom to experience life intensely, but without drugs. To others, religion means different things: belonging to a caring community or observing family traditions. To many people religion is a link to eternity—a way of transcending earthly boundaries.

Philosophers and social scientists also have many views of religion. Philosophers ask: "Why and how did religion begin?" Their answer: "In the human desire to find meaning in existence, to answer questions about life and death." Psychologists hold many different views. To Freud, religion was a wishful illusion, the "universal neurosis"; to Carl Jung, it was necessary for mental health. Anthropologists investigate the many religious beliefs and practices throughout the world. They trace the evolution of religion within a given culture and try to learn how religion functions for the individual and the group.

Sociologists focus on the interplay between religion and society. What role does religion play in social organization? How do religion and society influence each other? Does religion help bring about social change, or is it basically conservative? Can religion disrupt the establishment? A second set of questions concerns the relationship between religion and the subgroups of society. How do religious ties vary with social class, economic group, age, and sex? Finally, sociologists consider religion in America today. In a society which tries to explain the natrual world scientifically, is religion still a vital force? How are our religious institutions and practices changing? What alternative life-styles and institutions are challenging the more conventional forms of religion?

MANIFEST FUNCTIONS: RELIGION AS A UNIFYING SOCIAL FORCE

Early in the twentieth century, Émile Durkheim decided that the best way to study religion was to examine the forms of religion found in preliterate societies. Durkheim assumed that a society with a simple technology and social organization would have a primitive form of religion. This primitive religion would, in turn, provide examples of the most basic forms of religion. For his example he chose the Aborigines of Australia. However, recent theorists question Durkheim's thesis. First, technological and social development are *not* accurate indicators of religious development. The Australian Aborigines, with a primitive technology and simple social organization, had a complex and imaginative system of mythology and religion. Second, religious practices and beliefs vary greatly from one preliterate society to another. Finally, it is impossible to identify early or basic forms of contemporary religions; beliefs cannot be dug up from archaeological sites.

Although Durkheim's assumptions were wrong in some ways, his study continues to interest sociologists today. For one thing, his point of view was unique. As in his previous investigation of suicide, Durkheim saw religious ties as signs of the individual's integration into the society and its norms. Similarly, he avoided making guesses about what preliterate people thought about the universe. Instead, he concentrated on the ways in which religion becomes a kind of social cement, binding the individual to his or her society—sociologically, the most important manifest function of religion.

The sacred and the profane

For Durkheim, the key to understanding how religion works was the idea that traditional religions have divided the world into two realms, the sacred and the profane. This distinction is basic to Durkheim's definition of religion:

> A religion is a unified system of beliefs and practices relative to sacred things, that is to say things set apart and forbidden—beliefs and practices which unite into one single moral community . . . all those who adhere to them. (1965, p. 52)

Profane things are the stuff of everyday life: furniture, food, working, playing. The *sacred* world consists of spirits and mythological personalities, of magic, and of special objects or persons, all very powerful. The profane means business as usual. The sacred inspires awe and fear; it calls for reverence and caution.

To the Australian Aborigines, the most sacred objects were certain stones called *churinga.* These stones housed the souls of the clan's ancestors, the spirit of the clan's totem animal, and the spirits of the clan members themselves. The *churinga,* then, performed several binding functions. Because they were the homes of the ancestral spirits, the *churinga* gave each genera-

tion a link with the past. Therefore, they implied a link with the future—with eternity. The spirit of the totem animal in the *churinga* bound the clan to the world of nature. The *churinga* also contained the spirits of all the living clan members, making an unbreakable bond between them.

God and society

People in all societies have realized that no one can survive alone. Although preliterate people would not use the world *culture,* they understand very well what this term means. They see their way of life as the only right way, and their religions reinforce this conviction. For the Australian Aborigines, for example, the sacred objects and places, as well as the mythological beings and totems, form the core of their culture and their society. Eventually the most sacred objects, the *churinga,* become the symbols of society itself. These symbols create an amazingly strong emotional bond. Realizing this, Durkheim concluded that all gods and spirits become symbols of society. Ultimately, he said, "God and society are the same thing."

Historical evidence supports Durkheim. Ancient Egyptian, Sumerian, Israelite, Persian, Assyrian, and Hittite cultures were centered on their gods. For this reason, in war, statues of the enemy gods were often the first objects to be destroyed. Since the foreign gods were symbols of the enemy, their destruction would assure the destruction of the people themselves. Many people still feel that society should enforce religious belief. They see the nonbeliever as a threat to society. For examples of this position, see the insert, "The Compulsion to Believe" (page 387).

Religion and group feeling

For Durkheim, religion did not begin with intellectual activity. It originated in the intense emotions generated by the rites and ceremonies of early religions. These emotions, which could whip worshipers into wild ecstasy, held the

(a)

(b)

Figure 14-1 Sacred objects. (*a*) A kachina doll, which represents a supernatural being to the Hopi Indians, (*b*) the Torah of Judaism. [*(a) Photo Researchers, Inc.; (b) Hays, Monkmeyer*]

cultural group together. Eccentric, individualistic worship—or the refusal to worship at all—could not be tolerated because the whole society was based on religion. It was through religion that these people tried to understand and control the world. If children or crops died, if warriors were defeated, the people turned to rites and ceremonies that would please the gods. The flattered gods, in return, would let children recover, rain fall, and warriors triumph.

We may feel uncomfortable with the theory that religion originated in emotion, since we like to think of ourselves as rational people. It is clear, though, as the horrible deaths reserved for heretics show, that throughout human history, worshiping the gods in the right way was seen as a life-or-death matter. Disbelief or sacrilege would bring catastrophe.

THE CONTRADICTORY FUNCTIONS OF RELIGION IN MODERN SOCIETIES

Does religion in sophisticated societies today, as it did in preliterate tribes, work to hold society together? Most believers go to church, observe certain rules, and take part in religious rites, but modern, complex societies include many churches. In the United States, a national political convention may open with a prayer by an Episcopal priest and close with a benediction by a Baptist minister. Rabbis, ministers, and priests have been frequent guests at White House prayer meetings. At election time, political parties try to find a good religious balance between running mates—one way of "balancing the ticket." In addition to the three major faiths (Protestant, Catholic, and Jewish), many smaller ones—Moslem, Buddhist, and Hindu—find room in America to worship as they please. Recently, new cults have been springing up. Oranged-robed Hare Krishna people dance and chant on the streets of New York. In 1973, guru Maharaj Ji packed Houston's Astrodome with thousands of followers. Two years later, rumors

began to spread that a Korean businessman, the Rev. Sun Myung Moon, was brainwashing young people and luring them from their homes to join his Unification Church.

Most modern societies which allow religious freedom are, like the United States, complex; they are not bound together by one church. Even countries with an official religion tolerate diversity. In Sweden there is an established church which hardly anyone attends. Spain and Italy are more homogeneous, but even there non-Catholics and opponents of the Roman Catholic Church coexist with the majority. The Soviet Union, whose government tried to replace religion with ideology, has reopened churches which had been closed under Stalin.

Unity from diversity

In a society where several religions coexist with toleration and mutual respect, there seems to be a concern for religion in general. In the United States in the 1940s, a well-known poster advised, "Go to the church of your choice, but go to church." In the 1950s, a leading book on religion in America argued that all religious groups had achieved a type of unity. They had put aside their differences to support a new religion that could be called "the American way" (Herberg, 1955).

Religion as a unifying force is most apparent during national crises. During wars, an especially strong link is established between God and country. During World War I, all the major powers declared that God was fighting on their side. During World War II, these attitudes prevailed and became stronger. The government of Germany tried hard to achieve the fusion of God and country noted by Durkheim by picturing Hitler as the quasi-divine leader of a sacred cause. More recently, after the Watergate scandal and the resignation in 1974 of President Richard Nixon, many Americans felt that the country was suffering a moral crisis. The prescription: a return to religious values.

The complusion to believe

In modern societies there are no longer official, religious courts, like that of the Inquisition, which investigate people's religious beliefs and punish nonconformist or heretics, but occasionally news reports remind us that many people still insist on some degree of religious conformity. Our first example concerns the attitudes expressed by a representative of the Boy Scouts:

> A boy scout official says 16-year-old James Clark of Foster [Rhode Island] has been denied scouting's highest rank because "we cannot in clear conscience allow any boy to the rank of Eagle Scout who is an admitted atheist."*

In a second example a county judge decided that an atheist couple shouldn't be allowed to adopt a child, because of their lack of religion:

> The Burkes, who earlier adopted a boy, now $3^1/_2$, "were found to be persons of high moral and ethical standards." But Essex County Judge William Camarata ruled Friday that the Burkes "were not suitable parents for the adoption of the child because they didn't believe in God."†

In a third, case, religious discrimination is directed against a believer who practices and preaches the "wrong" kind of religion. Harry X, a Black Muslim, was imprisoned for selling a marijuana cigarette to an undercover police agent, although, following his religious belief, he does not use marijuana. In prison he was punished for preaching his religion:

> . . . Shortly after arriving at Tracy Deuel Vocational Institute in Tracy, California, Harry X was locked in solitary confinement for 60 days because he was preaching Muslim Doctrine. A year later at San Quentin, he was isolated for an additional 90 days for possession of the Muslims' newspaper, *Muhammed Speaks.* ‡

[*In 1970, the California courts ruled that Harry X had the right to preach his doctrine.*]

*From "Son of Atheist Denied Eagle Rank," *The Bakersfield Californian*, Nov. 14, 1970, p. 7
†From "Atheist Couple Vow Battle to Keep Child," *Los Angeles Times*, Nov. 10, 1970, Part I, p. 15.
‡From "The Case of Harry X," *Newsweek*, July 27, 1970, Vol. 76, p. 48. Copyright © 1970 by Newsweek, Inc. All rights reserved. Reprinted by permission.

Religion as a divisive social force

Religious wars are the most extreme examples of religion as a divisive social force. Sometimes, as in the medieval Crusades and the civil war today between the Moslems and Christians in Lebanon, members of different faiths are on opposite sides. At other times, as in the struggle between the Protestants and Catholics in Northern Ireland, wars involve different churches of the same faith.

The conflict in Northern Ireland, which has killed over 1,500 Protestants and Catholics since its outbreak in 1969, shows the complexity of religious warfare today. This war, fought mostly through terrorism, began over political and economic issues. The minority Catholics wanted equality with the dominant Protestants. Since then, the political situation has been complicated by conflicting attitudes toward British rule and the Irish Republican Army's desire to reunify the

Figure 14-3 Religious wars: tragic and destructive. Today, Protestants and Catholics are at war in Northern Ireland, and Christians and Moslems in Lebanon. (*Sygma*)

two Irelands. Religion itself was never an issue in this war, but battle has been drawn along religious lines. Allies and enemies are identified by religious affiliation—which in Ireland, much more than in the United States, provides the source of personal and social identity. In Ireland, a political scientist has observed, "Even an atheist must be a Protestant atheist or Catholic atheist in order to have status in the society" (Leo, 1974, p. 30).

The link with eternity

Philosophies concerning life after death vary from religion to religion. The Australian Aborigines and modern Hindus believe in reincranation, the return of the soul to the world in a new body. The ancient Greeks and Romans believed in a shadowy, sinister underworld. Ancient Egyptians, like modern Christians and Moslems, believed that they could look forward to a happy heaven if they lived morally.

While religions differ on personal immortality, they are all alike in one way: they are concerned for the continuity—even into eternity—of the social group. Primitive fertility rites are actually prayers for the ongoing culture. Christians refer to the "eternal Christian community." The worst curse of the Old Testament is "Thy seed shall not be planted"; the greatest blessing is to "Make of thee a great nation." Although, today, traditions are preserved in many ways, the survival of the society remains a central concern of religion.

Support for the social order

According to Durkheim, religion formed the chief support of a society's norms and institutions. It was also conservative, favoring the status quo over the new. Durkheim had studied religion in a gerontocracy, a society ruled by its elders. Only the old men were allowed to conduct the sacred rites and approach the *churinga*. Among the Aborigines, a man could reach the highest social position only after long, painful religious initiation rites. Women were subordinated to men; they had only a minor role in religious activities.

Today, our religions also tend to support the establishment. Religion sanctions marriage and family life and has generally upheld male supremacy. It was long believed that monarchs ruled by divine right. Even such practices as slavery have been justified in the name of religion. In America, this was accomplished by claiming that the black race was descended directly from Noah's son Ham, who had sinned and was punished by being made a servant. Antislavery groups whose reading of the Bible was less distorted also used religious authority to protest slavery.

Still, even though religion usually supports the social order, social structures change. Religion, which once upheld monarchy, now supports democracy. Slavery was both condoned and condemned by religion. To investigate the link between religion and social change, we now turn to a function of religion which Durkheim did not find among the Aborigines—the "prophetic function."

The prophetic function of religion

> Wash you, make you clean; put away the evil of your doings from before mine eyes; cease to do evil;
>
> Learn to do well; seek judgment, relieve the oppressed, judge the fatherless, plead for the widow. (Isaiah I: 16–17)

The prophets of the Old Testament were stern critics of their society. They condemned their people's evil ways and urged them to do good. It is from them that we derive the term *prophetic function*, which means the efforts of religious leaders to achieve moral or ethical reforms. Often, these efforts concern personal habits: drinking, adultery, dishonesty, or spotty church attendance. Sometimes, though, they deal with larger issues of social change.

Dr. Martin Luther King, Jr., leader of the struggle for black civil rights in the 1960s and founder of the Southern Christian Leadership Conference, showed how a powerful religious leader may work for social change. His marches, sit-ins, and demonstrations were met with vio-

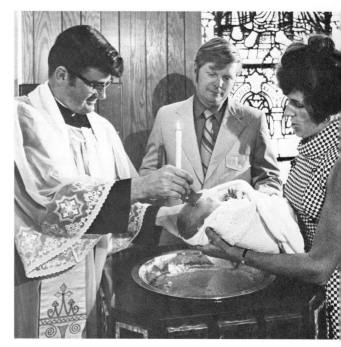

Figure 14-4 Baptism stresses the individual's new membership in the community of believers—a community for this life and for eternity. (*Rogers, Monkmeyer*)

lence by outraged Southern racists, but they led to court decisions and ultimately to profound changes in thinking among white and black Americans. Dr. King's successor, the Rev. Jesse Jackson, is continuing the struggle to achieve political and economic equality for black people.

During the 1960s, many of the clergy protested American participation in the Vietnam war. The Rev. William Sloan Coffin, then the Episcopal chaplain at Yale University, was arrested and tried in 1968 on charges of aiding draft resisters. Catholic priests Philip and Daniel Berrigan served jail terms for burning draft files. To these men, social change was more important than religious decorum. Father Philip Berrigan echoed the Biblical prophets when he told the court that had sentenced him to jail: "Our church is slowly beginning to accept our consciences, if not our actions. The priesthood is demeaned infinitely more by silence and inaction than it is by what we have done" (*Time*, 1968, p. 62).

Many religious leaders who crusade for social change are at first regarded as radicals, as threats to the establishment. Later, as with the civil rights and antiwar movements, their positions come to be accepted by the general population. Partly because of their actions, a new status quo is created.

The prophetic function of religion: A response to Karl Marx

To Karl Marx, religion was the "opiate of the people," serving as a narcotic to close people's eyes to the conditions surrounding them. Marx's argument was picked up by many radical groups. A famous rhyme circulated among American labor unionists through the 1930s:

> Work and pray, live on hay,
> You'll get pie in the sky
> Bye and bye when you die.

The message: Some religions tell people to put up with their problems, in the hope of getting a better deal in the next world. Others tell them that they are fated to suffer. This attitude of resignation keeps people from attacking social problems. Marx's charge against religion contains some truth. Slaves, serfs, and poor people in many parts of the world have been encouraged by religion to turn away from earthly problems. In considering religion and social action, then, we must remember that it can act in two ways: as a stimulant and as a narcotic.

The psychological functions of religion

Religion performs many psychological functions for both the individual and the group. For the individual, religion is a guide to the place and purpose of humanity in an immense, confusing universe. Religion helps to shape behavior by presenting moral and ethical codes. It also helps to organize life experiences. Most religions have rituals and ceremonies (baptism, circumcision, confirmation, bar mitzvah, the marriage ceremony, last rites, funerals) which mark turning points in life. For some—like the Black Muslims—religion provides a major source of identity:

> The true believer . . . casts off at last his old self and takes on a new identity. He changes his name, his religion, his homeland, his

Figure 14-5 The Rev. Dr. Martin Luther King, Jr., helped spark the civil rights movement of the 1960s. (*United Press International*)

Navajo healers WILLIAM STUCKEY

"Look, I've got a problem myself," Jack said. "Ever since I got back from Vietnam, I haven't felt right. And I've been drinking too much, way more than usual. Why do I do this? I don't know. I'm going to find out tomorrow. If you drive me over to the Arizona line, you might learn something."

We pulled up to a tar paper shack in Arizona. Answering Jack's knock was a small and tough older woman with flat, wise eyes. She questioned him tersely in Navajo, then invited us inside. Yes, gesturing to me, it's all right for the bellagana [white person] to watch.

Jack was made to sit on the floor amd take off his shoes. The woman washed her hands the way a surgeon would do before an operation, and picked up a small crystal rock. They she prayed to the Holy Ones.

Navajo religion and medicine are one and the same, and the principle mediators of both are 12 semi-deities, or saints, the Holy Ones. There is no single all-powerful God. Among the Holy Ones are Talking God, whose chant, as echoed by the Navajo healer, is "Whu, whu, whu;" Black God, "yuh, yuh, yuh;" and one with an untranslatable archaic Navajo name, Xactceoyan, "hahowa, hahowa." Illness occurs when the victim upsets the balance of nature, such as doing injury to a porcupine or snake, or violating a taboo. The healer asks the Holy Ones to correct the balance magically, by converting what is dangerous into the helpful. To reverse that process is witchcraft, the source of hexes.

At the end of her prayer, the old woman began twitching violently, her right arm jumping wildly like a newly landed fish. Strange noises, but still in her voice, came from her mouth. After some minutes, she opened her eyes and gazed calmly at Jack, giving, as he translated to me, this message:

"A neighbor who lives two miles from you has had you hexed because you served with the bellaganas in Vietnam." The hex can be reversed by a two-day chant, costing, as Jack said later, about $200. Her fee was $10. The woman was a diagnostician, not a healer.

[The healers are the *Hatathlis.*] These are the masters of the Navajo religion and medicine, beginning study at the age of five or six with an elderly *Hatathli.* They know the secret words, the prayers, the mythology and ancient history of the tribe, the dances, and the delicate art of sand painting (using natural pigments to draw pictures of the Holy Ones on the desert floor). The most complex of their chants takes nine days to perform. . . .

A closing Hatathli line in a widely used chant is a repetition of "All around me is beauty, all around me is beauty." If evil stalks the Navajos, only beauty and natural balance can stop it.

"natural" language, his moral and cultural values, his very purpose in living. He is no longer a Negro, so long despised by the white man that he has come almost to despise himself. Now he is a Black Man—divine, ruler of the universe, different only in degree from Allah Himself. . . . Now he is a Muslim, bearing in himself the power of the Black Nation and its glorious destiny. (Lincoln, 1961, pp. 108–109 Copyright © 1961 by C. Eric Lincoln. Reprinted by permission of Beacon Press)

Religion also tries to answer questions about death, suffering, and the presence of evil in the world—questions for which ordinary experience has no answers. Similarly, religion is an emotional safety net, comforting people and relieving their anxiety in times of suffering, tragedy, and death. Thus, it helps to relieve confusion and despair.

In many societies, human illness is closely connected to the spirit world. In the Navajo reservation hospitals, doctors sometimes consult with Navajo medicine men, whose treatment is considered a unique medicine for the spirit. The insert "Navajo Healers" shows how a Navajo in 1975 used traditional methods to regain his health.

Many religions allow the release of pent up emotional energy. In some religions, this release, or *catharsis*, takes place quietly, through familiar, soothing rituals, peaceful meditation, or the enjoyment of sacred music and art. In other religions, emotional release is more overt—even boisterous. Singing and dancing, testifying, and speaking in tongues are a regular part of the service. Some worshipers reach ecstatic states, losing the sense of self and reaching a feeling of oneness with the universe.

LATENT FUNCTIONS OF RELIGION

Religion and economics

To determine how society and religion influence each other, sociologists have studied the latent as well as the manifest functions of religion. One classic study, Max Weber's *Protestant Ethic and the Spirit of Capitalism*, deals with the relationship between religion and economics. Weber saw a causal relationship between early Protestant beliefs and the growth of capitalism. He stated that the concept of predestination paved the way for the development of capitalism. Predestination holds that God knows and has determined the future of every individual: salvation or damnation. Hell-fearing Puritans of the sixteenth century knew that they couldn't change this divinely determined future. Still, they tried to find signs on earth to assure themselves that they were of the elect—those to be saved. The belief developed that God blesses the work of those he loves. The Puritans decided that worldly success was a sign of God's favor, and a good indicator that they would go to heaven. Spiritual anxiety was translated into behavioral terms: be thrifty, work hard, and struggle to get ahead.

These character traits of early Protestantism—thrift and the compulsion to succeed—were just the traits needed, according to Weber, for the development of the capitalistic system. Thrift would assure extra capital for future investment. Hard work would assure success in competition. In the United States, these behaviors, known collectively as the "work ethic" or "Protestant ethic," became the norm. Consider Ben Franklin's folksy aphorisms found in *Poor Richard's Almanack*, one of the most widely read books in eighteenth-century America:

Waste not, want not.
A penny saved is a penny earned.
Money can beget money, and its offspring can beget more.

The same values and behaviors were found in Puritan England and among Protestant groups in Scotland, the Netherlands, Germany, and France.

Weber did not imply that other religious groups did not value hard work. He did, however, point up the compulsive attitude toward work in Protestantism. Weber maintained that in non-Protestant communities, a lower-class person was less likely to be held personally responsible for being poor. At the same time, a rich person was less likely to struggle to make even more money.

The link with eternity: Religion

Today, 200 years after the Puritans, the link between religious affiliation and work behavior seems to have changed. Success orientation is the same for Catholics and Protestants. One 1976 study showed that Irish Catholics in the United States are more successful financially than Irish Protestants or American Protestants in general (*Los Angeles Times*, 1976c, p. 11). These findings agree with another conclusion by Weber: That once a competitive economic system is firmly established, people become equally ambitious, whatever their religious background.

Criticisms of Weber's thesis

According to Weber, beliefs and values precede and largely determine how a religious group will organize itself economically. Weber's critics, especially Marx, argue that the reverse is true: The shape of a rising economic system is determined by the material conditions of the times. After the fact, religious beliefs are made to support or rationalize the system. Thus, the Puritans seized the chance to become rich through the new industrial system which was developing at that time. Then they used religion to justify their behavior. R. H. Tawney also argues that material economic conditions are more important than religion in forming an economic system (1928).

Other critics of Weber state that Protestantism is not a necessary part of a hard-driving, success-oriented society. They point to non-Protestant cultures whose religions also stress hard work. The most outstanding example is Japan, whose post-World War II industrial boom was achieved through an emphasis on hard work and competition so strong as to resemble a religious commandment (Bronfenbrenner, 1969, pp. 32–36).

Logical arguments may be made for and against Weber's thesis. Most sociologists today seem to prefer his position to that of his critics. First, they are impressed by Weber's scholarship. Second, they agree that although other groups may value hard work, no other religious group matched the early Protestants in their emphasis on the *moral* virtues of hard work and thrift.

A latent function: Prejudiced attitudes?

A religion that teaches one to love others would be expected to have unprejudiced followers. Yet some Christians score higher on scales which measure prejudice than do people who profess no particular religion. One of several studies on prejudice among Christians was conducted by Allport and Roos, two specialists in the study of prejudice (see the insert "Christian, Love Thy Neighbor").

Other latent functions

Robert K. Merton found that Puritanism in seventeenth-century England helped to promote science. More than either Catholics or Anglicans, the Puritans saw the study of nature as a pious undertaking, because nature was the handiwork of God. As a result, the Puritans were vastly overrepresented among early English scientists. Ironically, they helped to usher in a new age that they probably would not like (Coughlin, 1971, pp. 1–2).

Many latent functions of religion have been economic and political. When the imperialistic world powers took over smaller, less developed countries as colonies, Christian missionaries often paved the way for business interests and political absorption. On the other hand, the Christian belief that all people are equal in the sight of God has sometimes been used to oppose imperialism.

Religions can also have the latent function of alienating certain groups in society. American and English missionaries found that the most willing converts in India were the untouchables. They, with no status at all in their own religion, had nothing to lose. When the untouchables were aided by the Indian government beginning

Christian, love thy neighbor

The Christian religion bids its followers to "Love thy neighbor as thyself," but social science research has long since shown that churchgoers, as a group, are more prejudiced against strangers—Jews, Negroes, hippies, etc.—than people who don't go to church. Yet surely religion is a force that motivates some believers, from Gandhi to Martin Luther King, to extraordinary expressions of concern for all their fellow men; and studies have also shown a substantial minority of regular churchgoers who are more tolerant than the general population.

The difference seems to lie in the quality of the religious attachment: roughly speaking, people whose religious practice is motivated by extrinsic factors like sociability and conformity ("What religion offers me most is comfort when sorrows and misfortunes strike") are less tolerant than nonattenders; while people with an intrinsic involvement in religion ("My religious beliefs are what really lie behind my whole approach to life") are more tolerant than most people.

Gordon W. Allport and J. Michael Roos of Harvard wanted to probe this relationship between extrinsic and intrinsic religion and tolerance further. Working with a sample of 309 churchgoers who were members of six different Christian denominations, they asked questions designed to reveal anti-Jewish, anti-Negro, and anti-other sentiments. (*Journal of Personality and Social Psychology*, April 1967). As they read the responses, it became clear to Allport and Roos that there was a sizable group of respondents who could not seem to discriminate between intrinsic and extrinsic religious statements. About one-third of the subjects endorsed every statement they perceived as pro-religious, so that the same person could say that "Yes, my religious beliefs are what lie behind my approach to life," and "Yes, although I believe in religion, I feel there are many more important things in my life." These indiscriminate pro-religious turned out to be the most prejudiced people in the sample. . . . Their prejudice varied directly with the extent of the confusion; there seems to be a direct relationship between religious muddle-headedness and intolerance. Allport and Roos concluded that the extrinsically religious are prejudiced because they use both religion and ethnic hostility in the same way—as a means of providing security and a sense of belonging. The indiscriminately pro-religious are intolerant for another reason: they suffer from a sloppy cognitive style, characterized by an inability to make fine distinctions.

From "Christian, Love Thy Neighbor." Published by permission of Transaction, Inc., from *Trans-Action*, vol. 4, no. 9, copyright © 1967 by Transaction, Inc.

---

in the 1950s, many of them converted back to Hinduism since otherwise they could not receive aid intended for untouchables (Coughlin, 1971, pp. 1–2). In spite of government aid, however, more than 2 million untouchables have converted to Buddhism since the mid-1950s. Its philosophy seems less foreign to them than does that of Christianity (*Newsweek*, 1973, p. 88).

DENOMINATIONS, SECTS, AND CULTS

Sociologists use several terms to identify various kinds of religious groups. The distinctions are based on the size and age of the group, the nature of its beliefs, and the form of its worship. The largest and oldest churches are called *de-*

Table 14-1 Membership in Religious Faiths, United States, 1973

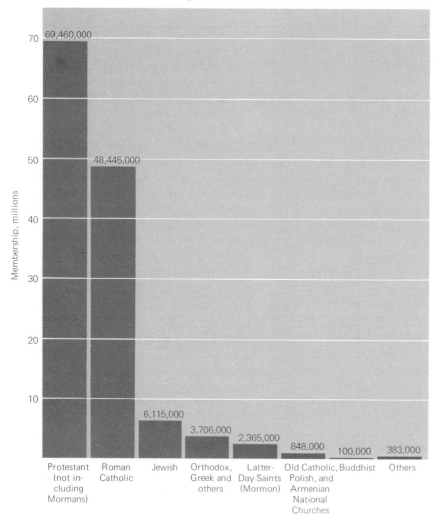

Membership, millions

Protestant (not including Mormans)	69,460,000
Roman Catholic	48,445,000
Jewish	6,115,000
Orthodox, Greek and others	3,706,000
Latter-Day Saints (Mormon)	2,365,000
Old Catholic, Polish, and Armenian National Churches	848,000
Buddhist	100,000
Others	383,000

Source: *U.S. Fact Book: The Statistical Abstract of the Bureau of the Census,* Grosset and Dunlap, New York, 1976, pp. 46-47.

nominations. In America, the major Protestant denominations include the Lutherans, Episcopalians, Presbyterians, Congregationalists, Baptists, and Methodists. (Table 14-1 shows membership in various denominations.) The smaller, more recently founded churches (which tend to be more fundamentalist in their doctrines and more emotional in their services) are called sects. The chief sects in America are the Pentecostal and the Holiness churches. The term *cult* applies to religious groups whose beliefs and practices differ greatly from those of most other churches. Recent headline-making cults include the Divine Light Mission of Maharaj Ji and the Rev. Sun Myung Moon's Unification Church.

Although some of the differences between

Social institutions and organizations

396

denominations and sects are beginning to fade, sociologists still see some characteristics peculiar to each. Liston Pope has summarized these differences as follows (1942):

Sects	Denominations
Of recent origin	Long established
Less accepting of science	Accept modern science
Otherworldly	Emphasis on this world
Emphasis on purity of belief	Accept all who wish to join
Eschatological doctrines (belief that the end of the world is at hand)	World is here to stay
Conversion as an emotional experience, often prior to joining	Members usually socialized within the church
Larger number of poor members	Members of all economic classes, but more wealthy members than in sect
Self-ordained leaders	Clergy trained in seminaries
Few, if any, community leaders among membership	Community leaders usually belong

Sect and society: A debate

Pope studied several new sects during the Great Depression of the 1930s and concluded that many sects originate among poor people. With time, some of these sects gain more middle-class members and more prestige in the community. Eventually, they may become denominations. Pope observed this pattern in the development of two American denominations, the Baptist and Methodist churches.

Ernst Troeltsch agrees that sects originate among the poor but goes further in his analysis: since sects originate among the poor, they are usually antagonistic to the establishment:

> The fully developed church . . . utilizes the State and the ruling classes, and weaves these elements into her own life; she then becomes an integral part of the existing social order; in doing so, however, she becomes dependent upon the upper classes, and upon their development. The sects, on the other hand, are connected with the lower classes, or at least those elements in Society which are opposed to the State and to Society; they work upwards from below, and not downward from above. (1931, pp. 331–332; copyright 1931, Macmillan Publishing Company, Inc.)

There is another sense in which sects may be seen as hostile to society. Many sects believe that society is evil. It is worldly and corrupt, and its members follow false religious doctrines. In this view, opposition stems from a reformist urge rather than from class conflict.

Milton J. Yinger begins with the premise that sects and cults arise among minority groups who see themselves as outsiders. In contrast to Troeltsch, he finds that these sects ultimately integrate their members into the larger society (Yinger, 1963, pp. 39–64). Yinger uses the ghost dance of the Great Plains Indians and the peyote cult of the Native American Church to illustrate his thesis. The ghost dance began in the 1870s as a reaction to the white conquest of the plains. At its core lay a dream of conquering the intruding whites. Later, the original ghost dance, which had seemed wild and threatening to the whites, turned into a quiet sacred ceremony. At first, according to Yinger, the ghost dance gave the Indians a spiritual vision that softened the bitterness of defeat. As the ghost dance changed, it incorporated some of the beliefs of the dominant white society. In this way, it created useful cultural links between the two very different societies. Changes that occurred in the peyote cult worked to a similar effect. Its followers reasoned that God gave the whites material advantages but reserved the spiritual advantages for them. Whereas whites must pray to distant God, Native Americans may take peyote and feel God's actual presence among them. A very strong current interest, among various groups, in converting prisoners indicates a hope that religion might act as a similar link between prison society and the outside world. See the insert "Religion Behind Bars."

Sects as a integrative social force have been studied by Benton Johnson, who examined the Holiness sects (1961, pp. 309–316). These sects are otherworldly in outlook. They denounce the wickedness of the world and teach their members that spiritual values are more important than money or social status. They do not take part in social welfare programs or politics. Yet, says Johnson, the values these groups preach are the same as those of a competitive society: self-improvement, hard work, reliability, moral responsibility, and disapproval of alcohol and drugs. Asked which was more important, goal-

---

Religion behind bars

Starting in the mid-1970s, there appeared to be an unusual amount of religious interest in prisons. Typically, the religion was a conversion experience and an attempt at new identity and self-concept, having characteristics of the sects, even though the major denominations were also at work in the conversion process:

"Oh man, a revival is going on right here," exults cell minister Ray Rogers of San Quentin, where a Jesus celebration featuring Pat Boone and four national wrestling champions packed the chapel last October. "They've tried dope, women, and violence. Now they're checking out the Saviour and getting zapped."

Members of established religious groups have joined the self-appointed missionaries proselytizing behind bars. The Black Muslims have a special Department of Prison Services with fourteen full-time ministers; in the last year alone, 780 prisoners have converted to Islam. Adventists conduct prayer meetings . . . Mormon families in Salt Lake City have "adopted" prisoners whom they visit each week. The Roman Catholic Church has started sponsoring *cursillos*—miniature retreats for inmates. . . .

Some Eastern cults and quasi-religious groups have also made their way behind prison walls. Scientology, transcendental meditation and "est" all have prison representatives [as do the Zen Buddhists]. . . .

Not all the reasons for the revival are purely spiritual. Overcrowding and some recent cutbacks in federally funded rehabilitation programs have led many prisoners to the relative peace and quiet of prison chapels. Some chaplains report that the lack of formal religious training in younger prisoners has also made their work easier, since they no longer have to overcome the inmates' negative preconceptions about organized religion. And a recent relaxation of prison rules has simply allowed more religious groups inside.

Con? Religious observance is not always noted in parole-board reports, but most chaplains admit that some jailhouse conversions are still pure con. "Sometimes I get fooled about conversions," says Alto chaplain Steve Doran. "But the main way you can tell is to watch the prisoner over a period of time. A man's behavior pattern changes a lot of times and his disciplinary reports stop. . . ."

---

orientation or rejecting upward mobility, nine out of ten Holiness ministers chose goal-orientation. Johnson concludes that the values of the Holiness sects are very similar to those seen by Weber as necessary to the capitalist system.

There is one area where the Holiness sects and others seem to differ from many upwardly mobile groups. Attitudes toward education in these sects are ambivalent. Most of them want their children to do well in school, but they do not stress the value of higher education. (As noted in the chapter on education, hopes for college attendance are highest among Jews, about equally high among Catholics and members of the larger Protestant denominations, and much lower in sectarian groups.) The difference is not related to income; it persists even when income is held constant. One theory is that sects disapprove of secular, scientific programs of instruction. They are also afraid that college campuses offer too many temptations to wickedness (Rhodes and Nam, 1970, pp. 253–267).

Social class and religious participation

If it were true that religious feelings are strongest among poor people, then we would expect religious participation among the poor to be greater than among the wealthier classes. On the other hand, if religious participation is just one form of full participation in social organizations, we would expect to find greater participation in the middle and upper classes. Studies by Lenski (1953, pp. 533–544) and Goode (1966, pp. 102–111) have found that religious participation varies directly with social class: The higher the social class, the greater the participation. This does not mean that the upper classes are more religious than others. They are just more active in voluntary organizations of all kinds.

A contradictory view of class and religious participation has been offered by Mueller and Johnson (1975, pp. 785–800). They conclude that religious participation is about the same in all classes. For many, they found no relationship between social class and religious participation; for women, there is only a slight positive correlation. Middle-class women are especially likely to go to church if they have young children at home. Although the preceding reports conflict with each other, one fact is clear: A poor person is not necessarily more religious than anyone else.

Community orientation and education

Wade Roof (1976, pp. 195–208) studied the relationship between commitment to one's community, educational level, and religious participation. He found that an important variable in church participation is the individual's feeling of belonging to a community. Measures of church attendance; participation in church groups; the forming of friendships in church; traditional beliefs about God, Jesus, and the Bible; and such devotional behavior as praying and Bible reading all correlate with close community attachment. They decline as the community grows.

Roof speculated that education as well as community orientation would be an important variable influencing religious participation. He thought that college-educated people would be more scientific-minded and secular in their attitudes and therefore less traditionally religious. He found this to be true of religious beliefs but not of church attendance. Those with more education were less likely to believe in church doctrine. However, their church attendance depended on their commitment to the community, not their level of education or beliefs.

CONVERSION TO A NEW BELIEF

Religious conversion sometimes follows a traumatic experience. At other times, it may result from guilt feelings about one's life-style. Whatever the cause, the decision to convert is usually made at a time of great personal stress. Some of the psychological and sociological factors in-

Figure 14-6 The Rev. Sun Myung Moon's Unification Church is controversial. While its leaders profess it to be strict but loving, some parents believe it exploits and brainwashes the youthful converts. (*Marc Rattner, Black Star*)

volved in conversion were identified in a study made of a West Coast cult which flourished in the early 1960s (Lofland and Stark, 1965, pp. 862–875). The cult originated in revelations made to a Mr. Chang, a Christianized Korean, and was brought to the United States by one of his disciples. The teachings of this cult were millennial: The world as we know it would end in the mid-1960s, reverting to the conditions found in the Garden of Eden. Cult members of course, would have favored positions in the garden.

By the time of the study, the cult had attracted about 150 followers. Most of them were young, white Protestants of lower-middle-class, small-town backgrounds. Several had had some college education. The researchers found seven characteristics which these people shared and which, they maintain, were important in their conversion: (1) Before converting, they had all experienced tension. This tension arose either from personal failure or from disillusionment with their previous religion. (2) They all had religious backgrounds and looked to religion— rather than to political change or psychiatry—for solutions to their problems. (3) Although they all felt that their previous religious experience had failed them, they believed they could find a new religious light. (4) Their conversions occurred at turning points in their lives, after they had changed jobs, left school, moved, or broken off relationships with other people. (5) They had all become friendly with other members of the cult. (6) In general, they had no close friends outside the cult who might have persuaded them not to join. (7) Before they had become totally immersed in the cult, they had become closely involved with other cult members. Eventually they were persuaded to live together in a close communal relationship, where each person's faith would strengthen the faith of the others. This constant interaction was necessary. Cult members who moved away from the group home were likely to lose their faith.

The Children of God, Hare Krishna, and the Moonies

Several cults worry parents because they take total possession of their children's lives. Some of the Children of God have left home and remain completely caught up in their highly emotional cult. The same has happened to members of the Hare Krishna cult. These young people maintain asceticism (self-denial) while trying to raise money for their organization. Members of the Unification Church of the Rev. Sun Myung Moon also spend much of their time raising money for the church. Meanwhile, Moon lives in luxury and extends the holdings of his church. These now include about $10 million worth of property along the Hudson River in New York, plus additional holdings elsewhere in the United States and in Korea (Cowley, 1975, p. 63).

According to the Reverend Moon, he has come as a new messiah to save the world from crime and communism. Since Jesus did not succeed in his mission, Moon has been sent to fulfill it. He expects eventually to be recognized and obeyed. His converts, mostly young people, live pure lives. They must be members of the Unification Church for seven years before marrying. Angry parents have formed organizations to bring their children back from the Unification Church, just as they have tried to detach them from the Children of God and Hare Krishna. In the insert "Messiah from Korea," a discussion of the "Moonies," the author opposes attempts to force young people away from the movement, since they enter by free choice. His description of the conversion of new members follows roughly the conclusions drawn by Lofland and Stark. Cults which remove people from the workaday world to isolated communities could be compared to the medieval monastic movement. Then as now, a segment of society opted out of worldly pursuits.

Many people disagree with the author's tolerant view of the Moonies' conversion program. Jean Merritt, a psychiatric social worker and a leader of a group called Return to Personal Choice, has been involved in rescuing young people from such cults as Children of God, Hare Krishna, and the Unification Church. Although they entered by their own choice, she contends, the converts had no idea what they were getting into. The Return organization has treated about a hundred members of cults, only two of whom have gone back to the cults. Ms. Merritt compares those who leave the cults to soldiers who were brainwashed in the Korean war. She states that it takes about a year before they begin to think for themselves. Much of the therapy consists of getting people to make their own decisions again. Ms. Merritt says that the cults encourage "the state of dependence of a little child. I have asked people recently out of a cult what they'd like for lunch and they can't tell me" (Cohen, 1976, p. 4). Ms. Merritt observes that another goal of her therapy is to help the returnees recognize and cope with guilt feelings: "They've had to lie to their friends and family and they have an awful lot of guilt about that. Or they were recruiters and when they see what they've done, they feel guilty" (Cohen, 1976, p. 4).

The conflicting points of view about these cults show that religious freedom is a complex issue. Treating people as religious quacks and charlatans may protect some members of society. On the other hand, it may erode religious freedom.

Messiah from Korea   BERKELEY RICE

. . . The charge of "brainwashing" deserves attention. Much of what happens to Moon's converts during the weekend and week-long initiation workshops does follow the classic steps of brainwashing: isolating them from all past and outside contacts, surrounding them with new instant comrades and a new authority figure, wearing them down physically, mentally and emotionally, then "programming" them with new beliefs and pressuring them into total commitment.

But the term brainwashing implies force and captivity, conditions that do not apply to Moon's recruits. Church members may use heavy-handed emotional or psychological pressures, but they do not force anyone to join or believe. While one might question the independence of a convert's mind, no one has proven the Church holds

(Continued)

its members against their will. It might be fairer to use the term conversion instead of brainwashing. If conversion requires the suspension of critical faculties, at least the Moonies do so willingly.

In his classic study of *The Varieties of Religious Experience*, William James described religious conversion in a manner strikingly similar to the tales told by Moonies. James wrote that conversion occurs most often among those beset by a "sense of incompleteness and imperfection," and frequently during a state of temporary exhaustion. He told how conversion brings a "new level of spiritual vitality" in which "new energies and endurances are shown. The personality is changed, the man is born anew . . . perceiving truths not known before," a sense of peace and harmony in themselves and in the world. *Instant Salvation*. Through a process of self-selection, Moon's movement probably attracts only those youths already seeking some form of total commitment. Many Moonies have been drifting from cults to communes for years, sampling the spiritual fare like diners at a smorgasbord. The Church may be capitalizing on their loneliness, but it can hardly be blamed for their vulnerability. However remarkable the experience seems to the convert and his family, James described it as essentially an "adolescent phenomenon, incidental to the passage from the child's small universe to the wider intellectual and spiritual life of maturity."

While one can commiserate with parents whose children leave home to join religious cults, it's hard to condone the desperate attempts to recover the children by kidnapping and deprogramming, a process openly based on the techniques of brainwashing. Youths of legal age have a right to practice any religion they choose. Whether or not their choice is wise has nothing to do with their right to exercise it. Eighteen-year-olds who join the U.S. Marines may be using equally rash judgment, and their boot-camp training subjects them to group discipline, exhaustion, and "brainwashing" that match anything that the Moonies endure. One could easily question the judgment of grown-ups who seek instant salvation in such socially acceptable adult cults as TM, Arica, est, primal therapy, or encounter groups.

While its critics describe the Unification Church as authoritarian, church leaders prefer to call their approach "loving and parental." They may be right. To thousands of young Americans threatened by the approach of life as an adult, Moon's Family offers the security of perennial childhood. To lonely young people drifting through cold, impersonal cities, it offers instant friendship and communion, a sense of belonging. To college students suffering the rigors of academic competition, it offers an egoless life of cooperative group spirit. To those troubled with personal problems of drugs or sex, it offers a drugless, sexless world of militant puritanism. To those troubled by our materialistic society, it offers a life of disciplined asceticism. To those who have no faith in the traditional institutions of society, it offers the comfort of belief. To those hungering for truth and meaning in a complicated world, it offers simple answers.

Critics may call Moon's movement a religious fraud, and accuse it of exploiting innocent youths, but, except for those who drop out, most Moonies seem genuinely happy in their service to Moon and the Church. In exchange for their labor, devotion and commitment, the church has given them a home, a family, and a purpose. Critics may call that exploitation or slavery, but the Moonies consider it a bargain. No more problems, no more hassles, no more doubts. Just honor thy father Moon.

Reprinted by permission of Psychology Today Magazine from the article "Messiah from Korea: Honor Thy Father Moon," by Berkeley Rice. Copyright 1975 Ziff-Davis Publishing Co.

TRENDS IN RELIGION

During World War II and for ten years afterward, church attendance in America seemed to be rising steadily. Gallup polls showed that 49 percent of the people polled attended church on a typical Sunday in 1955 and again in 1958. A decline took place during the 1960s, bringing the attendance figure down to about 40 percent, where it stayed during the period 1970–1975. Church attendance among Catholics was much higher than among either Protestants or Jews until the 1970s. It still remains higher but has fallen off sharply, from 71 percent in 1964 to 55 percent in 1974. Andrew Greeley, a noted Catholic sociologist, attributes much of the decline to Pope Paul's 1968 ruling against contraception (*Los Angeles Times*, 1976a, p. 1). His conclusion is based on extensive surveys of Catholic opinion. During the same period, there was also a decline in church attendance among Protestants. One possible reason is that ours is a secular, skeptical age in which the role of religion may be declining. However, the historical fact is that church attendance has risen and dropped before. It is risky to predict the failure of religion. There is great interest in new religions and religious experiences. Further, the traditional churches persist. These facts make it clear that religion does not disappear in an age of science.

Religious diversity

In modern America, religion has become increasingly diverse. People are offered an assortment of religious choices ranging all the way from Baptism, Methodism, or Seventh Day Adventism to Zen Buddhism or Scientology.

Interestingly, in an age that is not particularly religious, many of the churches showing gains in membership are rigidly *fundamentalist*. That is, they believe in a strict interpretation of the Bible. President Jimmy Carter's description of himself as a twice-born Christian also fits nearly one-third of all Americans. Table 14-2, covering the

Table 14-2 Change in Membership of Twelve Protestant Groups, 1958–1974

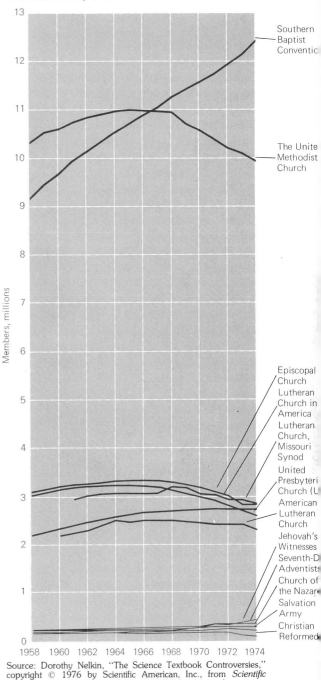

The link with eternity: Religion

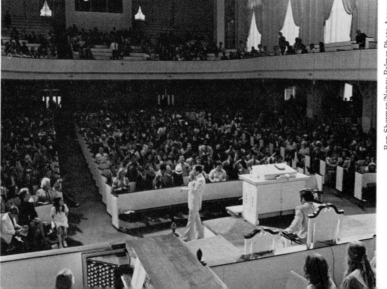

The large, well-established, and fairly affluent Protestant churches are spoken of as "denominations." Strongly emotional churches, usually smaller and less affluent, are called "sects." Those with unusual doctrines, not generally accepted by the society, are called "cults."

period 1958–1974, shows the increasing membership of the fundamentalist Southern Baptist Convention and a number of small, very strict churches—Jehovah's Witnesses, Seventh Day Adventists, and the Church of the Nazarene.

While fundamentalist churches thrive, new concerns are being heeded by other American churches. At long last, women can be ordained into the Episcopal Church's priesthood, and the first women rabbis have appeared in the Jewish faith. Priests and nuns have begun to assert a new independence by getting married. A number of churches have opened their doors to homosexuals, recognizing that they have the same spiritual needs as anyone else. In the United States, many members of the Catholic clergy are trying to relax the rules on divorced and remarried Catholics so that they can receive the sacraments of the church (Woodward and Lisle, 1976, p. 72).

While both fundamentalist and liberal trends are at work in American religion, there also seems to be an increasing interest in quasireligious groups and practices. These groups include the *consciousness movement*. This movement is a blend of psychological principles with some of the body and mind disciplines of Eastern religions. Included are Transcendental Meditation (TM), Bioenergetics, Yoga, est (Erhard Seminars Training), variations on Zen, and many more. "The movement has created a network of therapeutic outlets servicing millions of Americans who are bored, dissatisfied with their lives, or seeking a God they can experience for themselves" (*Newsweek*, 1976f, p. 57).

Since religion has come to mean many things to many people, it becomes more difficult to define. One solution is simply to accept the judgment of the practitioners. Yinger would agree that if the followers consider theirs a religious experience, then we should call their practices religion. This way of defining religion makes room for people with religious feelings and emotions but without clear religious conceptions or affiliation with a particular church. It is also the only definition that fits a society with the religious diversity of modern America.

Clearly, such a personal, subjective definition of religion is different from that described by Durkheim. In his analysis, religion is a group movement, linking the members who share a common identity. It may be that many people today are bound together by nationalism or ideology—or by social movements or causes—rather than by traditional religion. Except in times of national crisis, religions do not forge such a bond of unity that we can say "God and society are the same thing." We no longer feel compelled to make all people worship in the same way or even to make them worship at all. Modern fears center more on political and international events than on the possible evils that might stem from unbelief. Perhaps in matters of religion we have adopted an attitude a Roman philosopher expressed centuries ago:

> Why should we not all live in peace and
>   harmony?
> We look up to the same stars,
> We are fellow passengers on the same planet
> And dwell beneath the same sky.
> What matters it along which road
> Each individual endeavors
> To find the ultimate truth?
> The riddle of existence is too great
> That there should be only one road leading to
>   an answer.
>
> —Quintus Aurelius Symmachus

SUMMARY

Religion has a variety of meanings to people. To a young, emotional convert, like the one described in the introduction, it can mean salvation and freedom from sin. To philosophers, it represents an intellectual effort to answer eternal questions of life and death. Psychologists are interested in the relationship between religion and mental health, and anthropologists study the role of religion in cultural development. Sociologists study religion in terms of its effects on society.

Durkheim considered the major *manifest function* of religion to be that of providing social unity. Sacred feelings, rites, and symbols have a powerful uniting effect on the people of a society, so much so that in primitive societies it can be said at least figuratively that "God and society are the same thing." Durkheim did not look for the origins of religion in philosophical speculation but in group rites and ceremonies. A number of societies have associated their own people with a particular god, as Durkheim contended, and great effort has been expended to make all people believe alike. At many times, especially in the history of Europe and the Near East, persecution has accompanied unbelief. Three examples are given of severe religious discrimination even in the modern United States, two against athiests and one against a Muslim.

Religion appears to have a number of contradictory functions in modern societies. In most cases, a type of unity can be brought about during times of crisis, even though people have very divergent religious beliefs. In some societies, however, religion is a divisive force. Northern Ireland and Lebanon are good examples. Religion generally supports the social order, its norms and institutions; yet it also takes on a *prophetic function* of protest against the ills of the social order. Martin Luther King, Jr., was a religious leader of protest against racial inequality. Reverend William Sloan Coffin and fathers Daniel and Philip Berrigan were all arrested and sentenced because of their acts of opposition to the Vietnam war, which they considered morally wrong. Karl Marx commented only on the tendency for religion to support the social order, not on its prophetic function.

Psychologically, religion has the function of giving people answers to moral questions and also a feeling of place and importance in the universe. It answers questions that can be sources of bewilderment and despair. For many, religion provides a feeling of emotional catharsis or cleansing through prayer, confession, or emotional ecstasy. Religion can heal psychological complaints and probably thus affect one's physical health, as appears to be the case in Navajo healing ceremonies.

Religion has a number of *latent functions*. Weber contends that early Protestantism caused its followers to worry intensely over hellfire. Eventually they became convinced that the Lord blesses the works of those he loves. Therefore, emotional reassurance was to be found in working hard, saving, and getting ahead in the world, for success was interpreted as a sign of God's blessing. Robert Tawney argues, on the other hand, that the desire for business profits came first, and that religion became a justification for monetary success, since it encouraged hard work and thrift.

Other latent functions of religion include Merton's finding that Puritan love of nature as the handiwork of God led to an outburst of scientific study and discovery among English Puritans. The role of missionaries in aiding commercial interests during the age of colonialism is frequently cited as an example of the latent functions of religion.

Protestant churches are analyzed as falling into two divisions: *denominations* and *sects*. Denominations are large, long-recognized, central types of churches, attended largely by middle-class people. Sects are usually poorer, more emotional in their services, and appeal to the poor and the outsiders. Troeltsch interpreted sects as antagonistic to the social order. Two contemporary American sociologists of religion, Benton Johnson and Milton Yinger, see sects as functioning instead to integrate the lower classes and excluded ethnic groups gradually into the society. Despite the arguments of Johnson and Yinger, sects do not place as much emphasis on education as do denominations.

A third type of church is referred to as a *cult*. Cults differ from either denominations or sects in that they hold a considerably different religious doctrine. Hare Krishna and Moon's Unification

Church are cults in this sense of the word.

Religion appeals to the poor partly because it promises them a better place in another world than they have known here. Middle-class and upper-class people attend church in as large numbers (or very slightly larger, according to some studies) as the poor, but often their attendance is partly a result of a desire to take part in community affairs.

Most people are socialized into a religion, but others are converted to a new belief. Lofland and Stark found that converts to new religions are people who look to religion for solutions to problems but feel that their earlier religion has failed them. Conversion involves strong social ties to members of the new group, without interference from other friends who do not belong. These characteristics seem to hold for converts to Hare Krishna or to Moon's Unification Church.

Recent American trends in religion have included a decline in Protestant church attendance from the late 1950s till the mid-1970s. Catholic attendance is higher than Protestant, but it fell from 71 percent in 1964 to 55 percent in 1974. Catholic sociologist Greeley finds that the decline is due largely to Papal opposition to birth control by modern contraception. Although fundamentalist churches are showing growth, there is great variety in modern religion, with some groups being very far removed from traditional Christian churches. These groups include Scientology, Zen, Hare Krishna, and such quasireligious interests as Transcendental Meditation and Yoga. Above all, modern American religion has grown increasingly tolerant of diversity.

Study guide

Terms to know

Sacred
Profane
Churinga
Gerontocracy
Prophetic function
"Opiate of the masses"
Latent functions of religion

The Protestant ethic
Denominations
Sects
Eschatological
Cults
Ghost dance
Peyote cult

Navajo medicine man
Holy Ones
Hatathli
Fundamentalist
Quasireligious groups
Emotional catharsis
"Cognitive safety net"

Names to know

Sigmund Freud
Carl Jung
Émile Durkheim
Martin Luther King, Jr.

Daniel and Philip Berrigan
Karl Marx
Max Weber
Robert K. Merton

Liston Pope
Ernst Troeltsch
Milton J. Yinger
Benton Johnson

Self-test

Part I. Multiple Choice. Select the best of the four alternative answers:

1 To study and explain religion largely as a response to the human desire to find meanings is most typical of (**a**) anthropologists, (**b**) sociologists, (**c**) philosophers, (**d**) none of the above.

2 The discipline that is most interested in the dynamic interplay between religion and society is (**a**) philosophy, (**b**) anthropology, (**c**) sociology, (**d**) political science.

3 In Durkheim's analysis, all people divide the world into two realms, the (**a**) sacred and profane, (**b**) animal and vegetable, (**c**) godly and ungodly, (**d**) good and bad.

4 An insert titled "The Compulsion to Believe" tells of a couple who were required to give up their adopted baby because (**a**) they were of bad moral reputation, (**b**) they lacked the means to care for her, (**c**) they were Hindus, (**d**) they did not believe in God.

5 In modern societies, religious diversity is very great, but religion is still something of a unifying force (**a**) in times of crisis, (**b**) only in democratic states, (**c**) only in countries with an established church, (**d**) especially in urban-industrial societies.

6 In which of the following would the world's various religions be most alike? (**a**) belief in some kind of heaven and hell, (**b**) belief in return to this earth in some other form, (**c**) belief in the continuity of their religious tradition, (**d**) belief in a single god.

7 The tendency for religious leaders to seek reform in order to bring society closer to its religious ideals is called the (**a**) reformation function, (**b**) prophetic function, (**c**) eschatological function, (**d**) charismatic function.

8 Psychological functions of religion include (**a**) moral guidance, (**b**) organizing life through rituals and ceremonies, (**c**) a kind of "road map" to one's place and purpose in the universe,

(**d**) all the above.

9 In Navajo thinking, illness occurs when one (**a**) eats poisonous substances, (**b**) fails in religious observances, (**c**) upsets the balance in nature, (**d**) drinks too much liquor.

10 Max Weber believed the early Protestants had a much greater than average compulsion to succeed because (**a**) Calvin had glorified material success; (**b**) Calvinist doctrines eventually led to a belief that success is a sign of the Lord's blessing; (**c**) with enough money, they could make donations to the church that would lead to forgiveness; (**d**) all the above.

11 Allport and Roos found that the most prejudiced Christian church attenders could be termed (**a**) indiscriminately proreligious, (**b**) intrinsically religious, (**c**) nonbelievers, (**d**) irregular attenders.

12 Which of the following is more typical of sects than of denominations? (**a**) emotional conversion experiences, (**b**) acceptance of modern science, (**c**) clergy trained in seminaries, (**d**) a membership including community leaders.

13 Milton J. Yinger, in contrast to Ernst Troeltsch, contends that sects serve the function of (**a**) promoting revolutionary change, (**b**) isolating their members from the larger society, (**c**) integrating their members to the larger society, (**d**) misleading people spiritually.

14 Studies of social class and religious participation conclude that (**a**) the working class participates most, (**b**) the upper and middle classes participate most, (**c**) the impoverished are most religious, (**d**) there is little if any difference on a social-class basis.

15 A study of conversion to a strange cult concluded that the converts (**a**) were oriented to religion as a solution to problems, (**b**) had many friends outside the cult, (**c**) felt that previous religious experiences had been a success, (**d**) all the above.

Part II. True-False Questions

1 Durkheim may have been wrong in assuming that a society with one of the world's simplest technologies would also have the most primitive religion.

2 Durkheim's approach to religion was to see how religion acts as a binding force upon a society.

3 The Australian Aborigine beliefs were so primitive they could not properly be called a religion.

4 In the ancient history of the Middle East, there are many examples of gods that symbolized society to such a degree as to support Durkheim's thesis that "God and society are the same thing."

5 The Civil War in Northern Ireland began as a purely religious war and has remained such.

6 Despite some exceptions, religions tend to support existing customs and institutions.

7 Karl Marx spoke of religion as the "opiate of the people," implying that it dulls their awareness of social injustice.

8 By speaking of religion as a "cognitive safety net," the text refers to its attempts to answer questions that are otherwise unanswerable, such as those concerning death and eternity.

9 The idea of religious catharsis is that in the experience of the devotees, religious emotions have a purifying effect.

10 In Weber's analysis, the early Protestants considered the poor to be unfortunate but generally good, deserving people.

11 Weber's interpretation of the relationship between religion and economic success is the same as that of Karl Marx.

12 Eschatological doctrine holds that the world is approaching its final days of existence.
13 The Holiness sects, according to Benton Johnson, teach a doctrine that has no similarity to the Protestant ethic commented on by Max Weber.
14 Wade Roof found that college-educated people who attend church are less likely to believe in some of the church doctrines than are the less educated churchgoers.
15 Berkeley Rice contends that such a cult as that of Reverend Moon attracts only those youths who are already seeking some form of total commitment.

Questions for discussion

1 The *churinga* is said to perform binding functions among the Aborigines of Australia, and it is believed by the Aborigines to have a magic essence. See how many objects in our society you can identify that have binding functions—both religious and national. Do we have any objects that are believed to have magic powers? (Before you say, "Nonsense; we're scientific!" think about good-luck charms, amulets, and the like.)
2 Discuss the ways in which religion is a binding force in your community. Do church groups and members of synagogues get together? Are there ways in which religion becomes a divisive force in your community?
3 Get acquainted with a young person like the one quoted in the first paragraph of this chapter, who belonged to one of many groups often referred to as "Jesus freaks." What compels people to embrace faith with such emotionalism and total commitment?
4 Give examples of faiths, denominations, sects, and cults. Are all these groups represented in your community? What types of people do they draw?
5 Many social movements have been championed in the name of religion. Discuss those movements that claim to have "God on our side."
6 Is there any relationship between Protestantism and economics today? (Investigate Catholic and Protestant voting habits and partisanship, average incomes, and willingness to move away from family and relatives for the sake of upward mobility.)
7 Discuss the pros and cons of "deprogramming" people who have been converted to the "Moonie" cult or to Hare Krishna. (If no cases are currently in the news, you might look up the name of Ted Patrick in the *Readers' Guide*. He has deprogrammed many people and has been tried in court for his activities.)

Projects

1 Visit a religious group that is quite foreign to your thinking. If you are a Christian, you could try visiting a synagogue, or, if one is available in your community, a mosque or a Buddhist temple. Another possibility is to visit a highly emotional sect if you are from a major denomination or a major denomination if you are a member of a sect. Note differences in the religious group you have visited as well as similarities to your own group.
2 Try to replicate the findings of Wade Roof about community membership and church attendance. You might ask a sample of students in your school whether they attend church regularly and whether they are now living in their home town. Compare attendance between those who are living in their own communities and those who are going to school away from home. Alternatively, you might test his thesis about degree of faith in church doctrines. Compare a group of college students who attend church fairly frequently with a noncollege group. Ask them whether they accept church doctrine completely or with reservations. Note differences between the two groups.
3 It is often assumed that in an age of science, religious faith may be less important politically

than it once was. Yet Jefferson did not belong to a church, and neither did Lincoln. Find out how many people would refuse to vote for a person for President who did not belong to any church. After measuring a sample of public opinion on the issue, try to speculate on why Jefferson was accepted politically in spite of not belonging to or attending church, and whether he would be accepted today.

Suggested readings

Adams, Robert Lynn, and Robert Jon Fox: "Mainlining Jesus: The New Trip," *Society*, vol. 9, February 1972, pp. 50–56. In the conversion to a highly emotional religious commitment in the Jesus movement, members renounce all sin and live in a new fraternity of converts. Does the experience help them to achieve adulthood, or does it merely represent a psychological effort to preserve innocent childhood — and, in so doing, avoid meeting what Erikson calls the "adolescent crisis"?

Davidson, Sara: "The Rush for Instant Salvation," *Harper's*, vol. 243, July 1971, pp. 40—43. Is there a way to inner peace and enlightenment that doesn't interrupt one's life or cost too much? Will an alpha-wave headset do the trick, or must we have gurus? This is an amusing account of the writer's experience with a number of instant-salvation cults, religious and quasireligious.

Gerrard, Nathan L.: "The Serpent-Handling Religions of West Virginia," *Trans-Action*, vol. 5, May 1968, pp. 22–28. "They shall take up serpents; and if they drink a deadly thing, it shall not hurt them . . ." (Mark 16:18). This is an account of a religious sect that takes the above statement from Mark literally. Deadly snakes are handled in the course of religious meetings. What psychological functions do such practices serve for the devotees?

Nelkin, Dorothy: "The Science-Textbook Controversies," *Scientific American*, vol. 234, April 1976, pp. 33–39. Why, in an age of science, do controversies continue to arise over the teaching of evolution? Are actual threats to the development of scientific perspectives posed by a number of campaigns against science textbooks?

Roof, Wade Clark: "Traditional Religion in Contemporary Society: A Theory of Local-Cosmopolitan Plausibility," *American Sociological Review*, vol. 41, April 1976, pp. 196–208. To what degree can church attendance be attributed to belief, and to what degree can it be attributed to community integration and feelings of citizenship responsibilities? How are social class and age differences related to church attendance? What are the effects of a feeling of community belonging or the lack of such feeling?

Sinha, Surajit: "Religion in an Affluent Society," *Current Anthropology*, vol. 7, April 1966, pp. 1–5. A scholar from India draws a comparison between a small town in India and one in the United States. What are the contrasts between religious observances and their functions in an affluent American town and the town in India? How does religion help smooth the path of life in both cases? Does it have any negative effects?

Thomasson, Richard F.: "Religion Is Irrelevant in Sweden," *Trans-Action*, vol. 5, May 1968, pp. 22–28. Although a considerable majority of Swedes believe in God and about one-third believe in heaven, only 4 or 5 percent attend church. Sweden has an established church. Does the establishment of religion make it less capable of meeting modern needs than nonestablished religions can do?

Key to questions. Multiple Choice: 1-c; 2-c; 3-a; 4-d; 5-a; 6-c; 7-b; 8-d; 9-c; 10-b; 11-a; 12-a; 13-c; 14-d; 15-a. True-False: 1-T; 2-T; 3-F; 4-T; 5-F; 6-T; 7-T; 8-T; 9-T; 10-F; 11-F; 12-T; 13-F; 14-T; 15-T.

15

POLITICAL POWER

This chapter examines political power, how it is gained and exercised, and whose interests it serves. After reading it, you should be able to:

1 Better understand the process of political socialization that you have encountered and will continue to encounter.

2 Understand the influence of social class, age, and race on political affiliation.

3 Recognize the major sources of power and influence in the community and nation.

4 See how you can influence public decisions.

5 Understand the reasons for growth of government but, at the same time, view government critically.

6 Get a clearer picture of the reasons for bureaucratic organizations and their functions and dysfunctions.

Every night, the eight o'clock television news in Kinshasa begins with an image of heavenly clouds dividing. The music swells and from the clouds emerges the dark, handsome face of a man, his benign expression full of compassion and wisdom.

Slowly the bespectacled face grows larger, finally filling the screen, and the audience is given the opportunity once again to gaze on the man who casts himself as half god and half chieftain—President Mobutu Sese Seke.

His teachings—called Mobutism—have been decreed to be the national philosophy. His is the only picture that is permitted in public places—and it hangs even in elevators. His people wear badges showing Mobutu's face pinned over their hearts, sing his name in the lyrics of popular songs, and wear T-shirts bearing his likeness. (Lamb, 1977, pp. 1, 24; copyright 1977, Los Angeles Times)

Sometimes political power is concentrated in the hands of one person, as in Zaire. It has been fairly common historically for rulers to pose as blessed beings, sent by Heaven for the purpose of guiding the people. Especially for a new government uncertain of its future, such as Mobutu's, every possible device must be used for legitimizing the regime. *Legitimizing* means making a political regime seem rightful to the people and in accord with law and custom. In democratic countries, a government is considered legitimate if it is chosen by the people in an honest election. In Medieval Europe, a legitimate ruler was a king in the direct line of descent from the previous king and held to have been chosen by God. In the Soviet Union or China, the legitimate head of the state is the person recognized by the leaders of the communist party and sometimes glorified almost as much as Mobutu.

Much of this chapter will describe how power is distributed in such a democratic country as the United States. The well-known division of power between federal, state, and local governments and between executive, legislative, and judicial branches is only a small part of the division of power. Government in a democratic country can be thought of as an institution that mediates between the demands of large numbers of conflicting forces—business, labor, agriculture, minority groups, regional interests, and the like. Actually, even dictatorships must take some account of interest groups. However, there is far less open competition to gain the attention of the government in a dictatorship than in a democratic country.

Whether a governmental system is dictatorial or democratic, its leaders will try to socialize their people into the official government philosophy. Only thus can the system continue and appear legitimate to its people.

POLITICAL SOCIALIZATION

Political socialization, the process of internalizing political values, obviously differs in different political systems. While Mobutu reigns, socialization in Zaire will consist of learning respect for Mobutu and his philosophy. In the Soviet Union, political socialization consists of developing loyalty to Marxism-Leninism. In such societies as the United States, England, or Canada, or in the more socialistic but democratic country of Sweden, political socialization is more complex. Regardless of their interests, people are taught to abide by a consensus—a general area of agreement regarding rules by which decisions can be made. Beyond that, they are free to express very different opinions and interests. In the home, children may hear very sharp criticism of the government. Conservative parents will complain of high taxes, restrictions on business, and a welfare state. Radical parents will complain that big, selfish interests run the country. Some of the most alienated will conclude that all politicians are corrupt and the election process is really a farce. In schools, on the other hand, the emphasis is on consensus.

Political socialization in school

Michael Mann (1970, 423–439) maintains that in both England and the United States, one of the aims of the schools is to promote a consensus about the political system. In the United States, a belief in the Constitution, along with a sanctification of symbols such as the flag, is part of the consensus. In England, the schools promote acceptance of the royal family as a symbol of the political system. In both countries, nationalism is cultivated as a higher value than class interest. Political and legal authority are seen as basically humane. The economic and political systems are seen as giving as much equality of opportunity as possible. Conflicts of interest are given very little attention.

Political indoctrination in school does not make all people think alike on important issues. In fact, it often causes confusion. As children grow older, they become more cynical in their political and social attitudes, and they have trouble expressing their views in abstract terms (Mann, 1970, p. 437). Sometimes they vote against their own interests or become alienated and do not vote at all. Public-opinion polls of the 1970s indicate that people have less confidence

in the fairness, efficiency, and responsiveness of government than one would expect on the basis of what is taught in the schools. (See the insert on pae 416: "Evaluations of the Governmental System.")

Social class and family influence are even more important factors in political socialization than the schools, especially in determining party loyalty. Although family influence—defined as the father's political preference—has been found to be most important (Knoke and Hout, 1974, pp. 700–713), social class, race, and religion all play a part in shaping parental attitudes. The influence of social class and race is well illustrated by figures—cited in Chapter 6—from the research of Rytina, Form, and Pease (1970). They found that children from different social-class backgrounds saw the political system in different ways. A majority (55 percent) of the rich had so fully internalized the idea of the complete fairness of the system that they believed the rich and poor to have equal influence on government. Only 30 percent of the poor and only 3 percent of poor blacks agreed that rich and poor have equal influence.

Later political socialization

Which political party a person votes for is by no means settled early in life. Thomas S. Smith has explored some of the influences in the development of Democratic or Republican loyalty (1969, pp. 907–921). Although the 1950s and 1960s showed a gradual decline in party commitment and a slight increase in so-called independents, the change was not very great. Young voters are generally less partisan than middle-aged voters, but at all age levels, certain factors are associated with Democratic or Republican party preference. High income, Protestantism, white-collar jobs, white race (especially of Northwestern European descent), and education past high school are all associated with Republicanism. Low income, Catholicism, blue-collar jobs, and nonwhite race or other minority-group sta-

Figure 15-1 Consensus and dissent. *(a)* In 1976, Walter Mondale's vice-presidential campaign revealed broad areas of agreement among voters. *(b)* On many occasions, the government is sharply criticized. [*(a) Michael Hayman, Photo Researchers, Inc.; (b) Ron Sherman, Nancy Palmer*]

tus are more typical of Democratic affiliation. For example, in 1972, when Richard Nixon was reelected in an overwhelming victory, he received 68 percent of the white vote but only 13 percent of the black vote. Protestants gave Nixon 70 percent of their vote, Catholics only 52 percent. Of the college educated, 63 percent voted for Nixon; of those with only a grammar school education, only 51 percent (Gallup Opinion Index, 1974). This voting pattern can be explained in part by the different economic policies of the two parties. The Democratic party has advocated more generous programs to help the poor. The Republican party has stressed cautious economic policies that appeal to people in the higher tax brackets.

Smith finds that party loyalty increases with what he calls *structural crystallization*. Schoolchildren from poor family backgrounds who

hope to have good jobs someday do not have a crystallized, or firm, status; their status is uncertain and changing. If a man or woman has worked for twenty years at the same job, reached middle age, and sees no possibility of doing better, his or her position in the social structure is crystallized. If the crystallized status is a low one, it argues for Democratic party loyalty. If the status is high, it is more likely to lead to Republican or independent voting.

When a person's status is *inconsistent* (a

Political power

415

Evaluations of the governmental system   WILLIAM WATTS AND LLOYD A. FREE

Public evaluations of government indicate less than full confidence and also display certain inconsistencies. Whereas 71 percent of the public sampled stated either "a great deal" or a "fair amount" of confidence in the federal government's handling of domestic matters, more specific questions seemed to indicate considerable dissatisfaction. The first table below is in response to the following three questions:

First, if you had to rate our governmental system as a whole in terms of honesty, fairness, and justice, what mark would you give the system: excellent, good, only fair, or poor?

What mark would you give our governmental system as a whole when it comes to efficiency in handling the problems it faces?

And in showing consideration for and responsiveness to the needs, hopes, and desires of ordinary citizens like yourself, what mark would you give to our governmental system as a whole?

	Honesty, fairness, justice, percent	Efficiency, percent	Consideration and responsiveness, percent
Excellent	7	5	5
Good	34	33	28
Only fair	47	50	49
Poor	10	11	16
Don't know	2	1	2

Taking into account what you would like America to be like ten years from now, do you think a basic change will need to be made in the way our governmental system is now set up and organized or don't you think this will be necessary?

Change	54 percent
No change	36
Don't know	10

Excerpted from *State of the Nation*, edited by William Watts and Lloyd A. Free, pp. 244–247. © 1973 by Potomac Associates, Washington, D.C.

poorly paid female worker with a Ph.D. degree, for example; or black but rich), he or she is likely to feel stress, desire change, and consequently vote liberal. The main exceptions to this rule are *skidders*, people born in fairly high status positions who are slipping or feel their status to be threatened. These persons may long for things as they were and therefore vote conservative.

Class consciousness is weaker in the United States than in many other countries. For this reason, social position and income are not reliable factors in determining voter preference. Personalities or foreign policy issues sometimes loom larger than social class in determining the vote. Nevertheless, surveys continue to show that social-class position has an effect on voting preferences, more markedly in Great Britain than in Germany or the United States, but to some degree in all three countries (see the insert "New Determinants of Political Affiliation").

THE DISTRIBUTION OF POWER

In a democracy, the theoretical distribution of power is "One person, one vote." It would be naive, however, to assume that power is in fact distributed evenly. Some individuals and groups are in a better position than others to influence how the public votes on issues and candidates. Even more important, elected officials are under great pressure from powerful individuals and interest groups to do their bidding. To fully understand how power is distributed in our society, we must look beyond the factors influencing individual voter preference to the great sources of power outside government—big business, organized labor, and certain other influential interest groups.

New determinants of political affiliation

Most modern political commentators believe that the concept of everlasting political divisions is outdated . . . as social class differences decline. But Morris Janowitz of the University of Chicago and David Segal of the University of Michigan are bucking the trend. Their analysis of survey research data from Germany, the United States, and Great Britain has convinced them that new causes of political divisions are created when older ones cease to matter (*American Journal of Sociology*, May 1967). . . .

The class basis of party affiliation is strongest in Great Britain (where only 11 percent of high-income, middle-class respondents cross class lines to join the Labor Party); middling in Germany (where 25 percent of high-income, middle-class respondents belong to the mildly socialist Social Democratic Party); and weakest in the United States (where the Democratic Party has such broad appeal that 47 percent of high-income, middle-class respondents claim allegiance to it, as well as 61 percent of low-income, working-class people).

Along with class differences, other bases of political cleavage persist. In the United States, race is one such factor. Negro affiliation with the Democratic Party cuts across all occupational and income lines. In Great Britain, age and sex affect party affiliation; whatever their socioeconomic positions, women and old people lean toward the Conservative Party.

In both the United States and Great Britain, there is a political distinction within the upper-middle class between professional and government people on the one hand and businessmen on the other. Professional and governmental people often forsake class politics and cross over to vote Democratic (or Labor); but businessmen at the same financial level are less likely to do so.

In both the United States and Great Britain, the more conservative party has a reputation for being better able to manage foreign affairs. When concern for the international situation overrides domestic considerations, this factor may become most significant in determining party affiliation.

SOURCES OF POWER AND INFLUENCE

Power is the ability to control the actions of others or the social and physical environments in which they live. Power can be exercised in two ways: through authority and through influence. *Authority* is power that is recognized as legitimate or legal. Examples are the power of the President to sign or veto acts of Congress, the power of a law enforcement officer to make arrests, or the extremely concentrated power of dictators, previously mentioned. *Influence* is power to sway the opinions and actions of others, often subtly and without legal sanction. Influence depends primarily on knowing the right people, being persuasive, or bargaining for favors. In political economy, the political power of the government is backed by the force of authority. In contrast, the economic power of corporations relative to government is often a matter of influence. It is not always clear, however, whether government polices the activities of corporations as well as it should or how much improper influence corporations exert on government.

Corporate power

Former Senator Fred Harris of Oklahoma tells the story of a congressman speaking about seventy years ago to a group of businessmen, saying, "I believe in a division of labor. You send us to Congress; we pass laws under which you make money . . . and out of your profits you further contribute to our campaign funds to send us back again to pass more laws to enable you to make more money" (Nader and Green, 1973, p. 26). This quotation is a reminder that campaign contributions made for political or financial gain were part of our political system long before the Watergate scandal. No politican would speak as boldly today as did the congressman of seventy years ago, but election campaigns are still costly. In an effort to prevent the buying of

elections, Congress has passed tougher measures limiting the amount of money that candidates may accept. It remains to be seen how well the new laws will work.

In spring 1976, Senator Frank Church's Subcommittee on Multinational Corporations began to reveal evidence of bribes paid by officials of American corporations to foreign officials for special favors. The committee disclosed illegal campaign contributions at home as well. Although the Gulf Oil Company pleaded guilty to having paid $125,000 in unlawful campaign contributions, the Securities and Exchange Commission later uncovered payments totaling nearly $5 million. The much larger scandals involving payments to foreign officials are the clearest example of the economic power of these huge corporations. Lockheed Aircraft Corporation is believed to have given $202 million in commissions, payoffs, and bribes; Northrop, $30 million; McDonnell-Douglas, $2.5 million. Exxon admits one of its subsidiaries made campaign contributions of $27 million to seven Italian political parties (Martz, Thomas, and McGee, 1976, pp. 26–33). Giant corporations recognize almost no political boundary lines.

Besides campaign contributions and bribes, corporations exert their power by directly influencing the voting public (Nader and Green, 1973, pp. 29–34). They spend large sums of money to create a favorable image and to win the public over to their side on particular issues. They say that the corporation is the best friend the environment ever had, that it exists only to serve the public, and that it is made up entirely of good, honest, American stockholders. Often their advertisements emphasize the importance of free enterprise and the value of saving industry from too much government regulation. Sometimes their message is more specific. They may place ads in newspapers explaining why the oil companies should receive special tax benefits or freedom for tidelands exploration and drilling. Corporations' efforts to "educate" the public, it should be added, are tax-deductible expenses.

As home heating gets more expensive, we must find better ways to insulate. Alcoa® Insulated Windows are designed to help reduce unnecessary heat loss and save energy. Alcoa Insulated Windows have twin panes of welded-edge glass, aluminum-to-vinyl construction in both sash and frame, plus heavy-pile weather stripping. Flexible vinyl glazing eliminates chipping and the cost or inconvenience of periodic scraping and painting.

If your house is air-conditioned, Alcoa Insulated Windows will help reduce heat penetration in the summer. So you can save energy all year 'round.

Available in both new construction and replacement units, Alcoa Insulated Windows offer a low-maintenance, energy-saving alternative to ordinary uninsulated windows. Fortunately, Alcoa began to develop these special windows long before energy supplies became an issue. As a result, we have them today when we need them more than ever. For more information on Alcoa's Insulated Windows, write Aluminum Company of America, 403-B Alcoa Building, Pittsburgh, PA 15219.

☖ALCOA

Today, Alcoa's Insulated Windows can help reduce the heat loss in your home.

We can't wait for tomorrow.

Figure 15-2 Advertising campaigns are used to present an image of a company that cares. (*Alcoa Company*)

Since few persons or groups have enough money to argue the other side of the case, counterarguments rarely reach the public. When times are good, the public seems to accept a generally favorable image of business. When times are bad, they suspect all businesspersons, the honest and the dishonest alike.

Lobbying is another powerful source of corporate influence; its costs are also tax deductible. It would be unreasonable to deny corporations the right to meet with members of Congress or legislators when their interests are at stake. This practice, nevertheless, gives corporations a strong lever that the ordinary citizen does not have. For example, when the Lockheed Corporation was facing bankruptcy, it lobbied for and won a $250 million government subsidy. This case is more than an example of government favoritism for business, however. Large corporations like Lockheed are central to the American economy: They employ so many people that the government is obliged to prevent their failure.

Other sources of corporate influence are exec-

Political power

419

utives who shuttle back and forth, finding employment in both industry and government. High-ranking military officers, after retirement, go to work for companies doing business with the Pentagon. Corporate executives resign to accept positions in the President's Cabinet or on boards and commissions, first selling their stock in corporations with which they might have to do business. All but one member of the Interstate Commerce Commission who left that agency during the 1960s went to work for the transportation industry—the very industry they had supposedly been controlling with a firm hand. Earl Butz, Secretary of Agriculture in the Nixon and Ford administrations, had served on the boards of several agribusiness giants—Ralston Purina, International Minerals and Chemical Corporation, Stokely-VanCamp, and the farm machinery corporation J. I. Case (now part of Tenneco). Although he dissociated himself from those corporations during his government service, could he have changed the values born of a lifetime

---

Interlocking directorates THOMAS R. DYE

Richard King Mellon: Chairman of the board of the Mellon National Bank and Trust Company; president, Mellon and Sons; member of the board of directors of Aluminum Company of America, of General Motors Corporation, of Gulf Oil Corporation, of the Koppers Company, of the Pennsylvania Company, and of the Pennsylvania Railroad [now defunct]. *Fortune* magazine lists Mellon's personal wealth in excess of one-half billion dollars. He is lieutenant general in the Reserves, a member of the board of trustees of the Carnegie Institute of Technology, of the Mellon Institute, and of the University of Pittsburgh.

James R. Killian, Jr.: Member of the board of directors of the American Telephone and Telegraph Company, of the Cabot Corporation, and of General Motors Corporation; former special assistant to the President for Science and Technology; members of the Board of Visitors of the U.S. Naval Academy; a trustee of Mt. Holyoke College, of Mellon Institute, of the Alfred P. Sloan Foundation, and of the National Merit Scholarship Corporation; chairman and member of the board of the Institute for Defense Analysis.

James Stillman Rockefeller: Chairman and director of the First National City Bank of New York; member of the board of directors of the International Banking Corporation, of the National City Foundation, of the First New York Corporation, of the First National City Trust Company, of the Mercantile Bank of Canada, of the National City Realty Corporation, of Kimberly-Clark Corporation, of the Northern Pacific Railway Company, of the National Cash Register Company, of Pan American World Airlines, of Monsanto Company.

David Rockefeller: Chairman of the board of directors of Chase Manhattan Bank, member of the board of directors of B. F. Goodrich Company, of the Rockefeller Institute for Medical Research, of the Council of Foreign Relations, of the Museum of Modern Art, of Rockefeller Center, and of the Board of Overseers of Harvard College.

From Thomas R. Dye, *Power and Society*, Duxbury Press, North Scituate, Mass. (A division of Wadsworth Publishing Company, Belmont, Calif.), 1975.

---

spent in their service? His policies as Secretary of Agriculture, according to Harris (Nader and Green, 1973, p. 35), stressed the profits of large agribusiness corporations at the expense of the small farmer.

Many executives have considerable influence in several different companies. Often, they serve on the boards of directors of several corporations at the same time. They may also hold positions on boards of regents of colleges, thereby enhancing their influence in the field of education as well (see the insert "Interlocking Directorates").

All the previously mentioned types of influence have been well known by the public for years. With the exception of bribery, they are all legal. Yet, the public's attitude toward business is changing. In the past, people were generally favorable to business, perhaps partly because of persuasive advertising. In more recent years, they have become concerned over increasing size and consolidation, suspicious of the multinational corporations, and increasingly aware of corruption. Favorable attitudes toward business have declined sharply, from 55 percent in 1966 to 19 percent in 1976 (Martz, Thomas, and Krisher, 1976, pp. 36–39). This was only part of a general decline in public trust in our institutions, including government and labor unions as well as business.

LABOR-UNION POWER

Labor unions exert power by negotiating settlements on behalf of their members or, if negotiations fail, by calling strikes to force a favorable settlement. Labor unions also have strong political influence. They work through Congress and state legislatures to preserve union shops and other labor benefits. Under the Wagner Labor Relations Act of 1935, the right to collective bargaining was recognized along with the right to a *closed shop.* That is, workers could be hired in a unionized shop only if they joined the union first. The Taft-Hartley Act of 1947 outlawed the closed shop and called instead for a *union shop.* This meant that workers could be required to join the union only after being employed for a certain period of time and after a majority of workers had called for a union in an election supervised by the National Labor Relations Board. Since states are permitted to outlaw the union shop, one of the aims of labor is to defeat such "right to work" laws whenever they are proposed in state legislatures or through state initiatives.

The power of labor unions does not stop with collective bargaining or union shops, however. Since they contribute large sums of money to elect officials who will favor their cause, they often serve as a *countervailing power*—a power that counters or opposes other sources of power. For a democracy to work properly, there should be several roughly equal countervailing forces at work. Some groups—such as children, old people, the very poor, and mental patients—have very little countervailing power. Sometimes the labor unions try to serve as a countervailing force on behalf of the entire blue-collar class. However, since the leaders generally belong to the skilled unions, labor is sometimes divided. In the 1972 election, the countervailing power of organized labor was greatly weakened when George Meany, president of the AFL-CIO, and his union failed to oppose the candidacy of Richard Nixon, who already had the blessing of most of business and management. Generally, however, the labor unions endorse Democratic candidates, as in 1976. Although their financial power does not equal that of the giant corporations, the unions are politically well organized in most major industrial states. They do the vital precinct work of seeing that voters favoring them get to the polls and vote.

Shortcomings of labor unions

The powerful labor unions have been successful in gaining wage, pension, and other benefits for their members. Still, they represent only a frac-

Figure 15-3 Frank E. Fitzsimmons (*left*), nominated for president of the Teamsters Union. There was no opposition. (*United Press International*)

tion of American workers—about 21 million out of a labor force of about 95 million. However, while the unions work for minimum-wage laws, increased social security benefits, and government policies aimed at keeping up the level of employment, they also try to maintain and increase their own political power. Since some of the most vital industries in the United States are the ones most rigidly controlled by labor unions—automobiles, steel, ship loading, railroads, and trucking—they have an industrial power greater than their membership would indicate. Partly because of repeated charges of corruption, especially against the Teamsters' Union, labor unions have sometimes suffered from an unfavorable public image (see the insert "I Say to Them, Go to Hell").

The iron law of oligarchy

The AFL-CIO, the United Auto Workers, and other unions have often come under attack for entrenched leadership. Such leadership illustrates what is known in sociology as the *iron law of oligarchy*—the idea that even in organizations devoted to the common good, a leadership group becomes entrenched, resisting competition and change. Robert Michels (1949), who proposed this law, points out certain reasons why a leadership group ceases to be democratic. In the first place, leadership is a demanding and difficult role to learn. Therefore, it seems reasonable to return people with experience to office. Equally important, the rank and file tend to be indifferent to what goes on. They trust their leaders to make decisions for them. Michels also maintains that leaders enjoy the exercise of power and are reluctant to give it up. This has been true of many labor unions. Labor unions, however, should not be singled out for all the criticism. Congressional committees are often ruled with an iron hand by the same leaders for many years. The same is often true of heads of government bureaus, corporate boards of directors, and the officials of political parties. In fact, Michels based his conclusions on a study of political parties.

Members' grievances

According to Martin Glaberman, as unions have become more bureaucratic, they have paid less attention than before to members' complaints. In spite of a contract with General Motors in 1955 designed to provide grievance procedures, there were as many as 10,000 unsolved grievances in some plants: "The situation has not improved since then. GM complains that the number of grievances in its plants has grown from 106,000 in 1960 to 256,000 in 1969 or 60 for each 100 workers" (Glaberman, 1972, p. 88).

Union leaders are tempted to compromise with management too easily, says Glaberman, to make thier jobs smooth and easy. They are responsive to traditional wage and fringe-benefit demands. However, they often are not concerned with worker complaints about the speed

"I say to them, go to hell" MICHAEL RUBY, JON LOWELL, AND TOM JOYCE

Even by Teamster standards, last week's convention in Las Vegas was a show stopper. Beefy guards strutted through the hall, ejecting dissidents and confining reporters to an overhead press box. The local police obediently cleared away protesters outside the hall. President Ford's Secretary of Labor turned up to claim membership in the Teamsters' club and proclaim his belief in it, even as his own department was investigating the union's alleged abuses. There was a perfunctory tribute to the memory of vanished chieftain Jimmy Hoffa, but Hoffa's successor, president Frank E. Fitzsimmons, set the defiant tone. "For those who would say it's time to reform this organization, that it is time that the officers quit selling out the membership of their union," Fitz bellowed to the delegates, "I say to them, go to hell."

There were plenty of candidates for the journey. Fitzsimmons himself disclosed at the convention that he and other officials had been subpoenaed last month by a Labor Department task force investigating the financial dealings of the Teamsters' $1.3 billion central-states pension fund. Just last week, a federal grand jury in San Francisco charged a former union official with embezzling $2.4 million from California trust funds. A Senate subcommittee is girding for a beefed-up probe into Teamster activities later this year. And within the 2.3 million-member union itself, a dissident group continued to assail the leadership for preying on the rank and file.

The union's power amounts to "a national scandal" according to a 177-page report released last month by the Professional Drivers Council (PROD), a group of 2,000 disaffected Teamsters. Among other things, the PROD leaders charged that Teamster officials are vastly overpaid (one regional satrap drew $126,448 in 1974), that there have been repeated thefts and kickbacks from the union's vast pension funds and that rank-and-file members are kept in line by fear of bodily harm and even death. Both the Labor and Justice Departments are investigating the alleged pension-fund scandals, and Hoffa's disappearance and presumed murder last year triggered speculation he may have been about to expose further Teamster misdoings in a bid to regain the union's leadership.

of the assembly line, health standards, freedom from chemical fumes, and other problems having to do with the quality of life in the plant.

Working-class authoritarianism?

Labor unions bring important countervailing power to bear in their demand for liberal minimum-wage policies, pensions, and social security. However, they do not exert a counterforce in foreign policy. George Meany consistently supported the war in Vietnam, even after AFL-CIO union members had begun to change their minds on the issue. Conservative in foreign policy, he also opposed the opening of communications with the People's Republic of China.

During the Vietnam war, there were clashes between union members and antiwar groups that stereotyped union labor as prowar and imperialistic. In fact, some sociologists have characterized the working class as *authoritarian*. Seymour Martin Lipset (1963, pp. 87–126) contends that since working-class people are less educated than the middle class, they are more

MR. TERRELL   MR. ESTES   MR. MURPHY   MR. LUNDIN   MR. HILDER

A political system in which all views can be heard is characterized by opposing, or "countervailing," forces, of which business and labor are perhaps the best example. Not all interests, however, are able to put comparable pressure on government.

likely to follow national leaders blindly, to be suspicious of foreigners and foreign governments, and to be unwilling to hear both sides of an argument. Others, including Form and Rytina (1968, pp. 19–30), question whether working-class people are any more authoritarian in their thinking than people of other classes.

Henry W. Berger (1972, pp. 94–98) reviewed the record of American workers in opinion polls on attitudes about the Vietnam war. He analyzed statistics by Roper showing a gradual increase in opposition to the war among workers, but more among the unskilled, service workers, and common laborers than among skilled laborers. Here are the answers to one of Roper's questions in three successive years, given in percentages of those answering "yes":

Do you think it was a mistake for the United States to get involved in Vietnam?

	March 1966	February 1967	April 1968
Skilled workers	16.6	32.2	41.8
Unskilled workers	26.7	36.3	44.5
Service workers	21.5	38.5	39.2
Laborers	30.8	45.3	57.1

These statistics (from Henry W. Berger, "Organized Labor and Imperial Policy," published by permission of Transaction, Inc., from *Society*, vol. 10, no. 1, copyright © 1972 by Transaction, Inc.) show a shift of labor's opinion that paralleled the shift in the population as a whole. (Union members, perhaps influenced by their leaders, showed more belligerence than other workers.) It is ironic that if support for the war reflects authoritarianism, the common laborers were the least authoritarian of all. Berger concludes that from the earliest days of the AFL, unions have agreed with management on foreign affairs, assuming a nationalistic stand partly to assure their own legitimacy. This position has persisted due to the slow change in union leadership. It has been aided to some extent by a vested interest in the defense industry, which supplies jobs to large numbers of workers. Expressed views on the Vietnam war, then, did not show the working class to be authoritarian. They did show that union leaders cannot be depended on to act as a countervailing force in foreign affairs.

OTHER COUNTERVAILING FORCES

It is not always true that big-business interests can influence the political system at will, with only an occasional veto from labor unions. The voting public does have a choice between candidates, and a candidate with a reputation for being on the side of the rich often has a political handicap. But the two-party system, although providing alternatives, does not supply all the countervailing power needed against the power of great wealth. The campaign chests needed to run for political office introduce another important factor into the balance of political power (see the insert "Extracting Campaign Funds" on page 426). Those who make large donations to political campaigns enjoy a big advantage over the ordinary citizen. Such people often contribute to both sides in a campaign so that they will have friends in office no matter who wins. Other backers of candidates and political causes may have unselfish motives, working for what they regard as the public good.

Social movements

Social movements of the type discussed in Chapter 9 often influence the government. The Nineteenth Amendment, which gave women the right to vote, was passed largely as a result of a social movement. This was also true of the Eighteenth Amendment prohibiting the sale of alcoholic beverages. In more recent years, equal opportunity laws have been passed as a result of the civil rights movement and the women's liberation movement. Popular opposition to the Vietnam war is considered responsible for ending that war sooner than might have been

Extracting campaign funds   MORTON MINTZ AND JERRY COHEN

The aid, who was not identified, told Johnson [Haynes Johnson of the *Washington Post*] that by the time a campaign was at hand he already had drawn up a list of potential major contributions:

> It would be a list that covers everything from steamship companies to gas companies to—well, Christ, you name it. And you'd set a quota. How much you're going to raise from each group. Then you'd get alone with them in private, without any witnesses, and you'd say, "This is what I want, and this is how I want it." In cash, or whatever.
>
> Cash was always desirable, because by the time election day came around there was always money to spend—hiring poll watchers, renting cars, getting additional office help. I have made many, many trips back to my state with a briefcase full of money—in 20 or 100-dollar bills, as much as $23,000 at a time. Or, if it wasn't a cash payment that you got, you might want the contributor to pick up a certain sizable bill.
>
> I always felt the only way to operate was to talk frankly, but I was capable of being tough, of saying either they did this or they were out, of telling them if they didn't contribute they weren't going to get in this office again until _____'s in his grave.
>
> And, of course, I always said I knew they were going to play the other side of the street [by contributing to the opponent] and that was okay with me. All I wanted was our fair shake.

Morton Mintz and Jerry S. Cohen, *America Incorporated*, The Dial Press, New York, 1971, quoted from "Congressional Staffs: The Third Branch of Congress." Washington Post, Jan. 18, 1970. p. A1.

---

expected. The campaigns of environmentalists have led to important legislation designed to protect the environment. The environmentalists have lost many rounds in this fight, but they have also had victories, often in spite of opposition from industry. For example, they have gradually forced the auto industry to meet stricter antipollution standards.

Associations

Social movements often give rise to associations whose members carry on the movement's work on a voluntary basis. Associations such as Friends of the Earth and the Sierra Club are dedicated to environmental protection (the Sierra Club actually existed before the environmen-

tal movement began). The National Organization for Women, the National Association for the Advancement of Colored People, and the Urban League are all dedicated to reform causes. The League of Women Voters tries to inform voters about both sides of public issues, though it is sometimes partisan, especially on the issue of women's rights. The recently formed Committee for an Effective Congress and Common Cause are two associations that attempt to make the legislative process more open, honest, and responsive to public needs.

No one person symbolizes the effort of the private citizen to influence government more than does Ralph Nader, who is dedicated to the cause of consumers. He has worked long and hard for consumer protection against dangerous chemical additives in foods, for safety in auto-mobiles, for reasonably priced pharmaceuticals, against monopoly pricing by utilities, toward the exposure of polluters, and for the disclosure of corruption in government. Nader has found that laws are frequently circumvented rather than enforced by the commissions responsible for their enforcement. Such books as *Vanishing Air* and *The Chemical Feast*, written by members of his group, have brought pressure on officials and commissions to enforce antipollution laws and to protect the public against dangerous chemical additives. Nader works closely with other public agencies, insisting always on Americans' right to information (see the insert on page 428: "Citizen Action Materials That Can Help You").

As government grows larger and issues become more complex, associations such as those mentioned above are more important than ever before. They are needed to watch elected officials carefully, once they are in office, and to introduce issues that otherwise would never be brought to public attention.

Figure 15-4 Ralph Nader, consumer advocate. Consumer groups have recently gained political influence. (*Ron Sherman, Nancy Palmer*)

GOVERNMENT AND BUREAUCRACY

A Harris Poll taken in 1975 showed a general decline in public confidence not only in business and labor but also in government. Over a ten-year period, the number of persons expressing "a great deal of confidence" in government dropped, from 41 to 11 percent (Martz, Thomas, and Krisher, 1976, pp. 36–39). The Watergate scandal caused some of this loss, but the drop in confidence had been going on fairly steadily from 1966 to 1975. There is one recurrent criticism of government, big business, and labor unions—and this is undoubtedly a factor in the public's doubts about these institutions. They are too big, too bureaucratic, and too uncaring about the individual.

The size and cost of government are difficult issues to deal with. Since we need programs such as medical care for the aged, aid to families with dependent children, federal funds for states and cities, and social security, cuts in these areas are hard to make. In a period of international tensions, few would be willing to make drastic cuts in military spending. Heavy government spending and resultant high taxes appear to be facts of life today. (See Table 15-1, page 429.)

Increasingly complex bureaucracies and rapidly rising expenses characterize not only the United States but all modern industrialized countries. In these countries, the government is responsible for maintaining high employment and prosperity as well as meeting the biggest public health and welfare needs. Robert Heilbroner (1970, pp. 19–31) analyzes some of the reasons for this proliferation of government functions and costs in the twentieth century: controls and regulations; growth in education, welfare, and public service; and increased military spending.

Controls and regulations

Government regulation of industry began in the nineteenth century with the Interstate Commerce Commission. It tried to control rates and other policies of railroads, which had grown too large for states to regulate. The move toward monopolies invited further government control, especially for those industries vested with a public interest—transportation, telephone, electricity, and gas. The government gradually extended its controls and regulations to dangerous processes and products—automobiles, drugs, high-speed machinery, mines, airlines and airports, dangerous chemicals, explosives, and nuclear plants. Laws were also passed to prevent monopolies and price-fixing arrangements between competitors, although these regulations have not been strongly enforced. Controls have been extended to labor conditions, minimum wages, fair employment practices, workmen's compensation laws, and the employer's share of social security taxes. Today, the government plays a larger role in international business relations than it did in the past—for example, the large-scale grain sales made to the Soviet Union. Increasingly, the government regulates the quality of the environment. It controls industrial and chemical wastes, air and water pollution, strip mining, and the use of natural resources.

Education and research

As was noted in Chapter 13, the government spends a lot of money on education today. Our scientific-industrial society requires a generally

Table 15-1 Per Capita Tax Revenue by Level of Government, 1950—1973

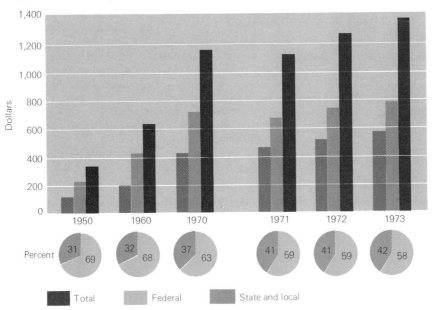

high level of education. Apart from this, spending for scientific, industrial, medical, and social research has grown so much that we can speak of an entire "knowledge industry." The cost of education, and especially of the research industry, has fallen increasingly on the federal government (see Table 15-2).

Military costs

Military costs reflect not only an uneasy world but gigantic increases in the costs of military equipment and research on new techniques, missiles, aircraft, and warning systems. In 1900, spending for United States national security made up less than one-quarter of 1 percent of the gross national product. By 1970, it amounted to 9.2 percent of the gross national product. Rapid scientific development makes ships, aircraft, and missiles partly obsolete by the time they reach full production and completely obso-

Table 15-2 Federal Government Spending for Education, 1966—1976

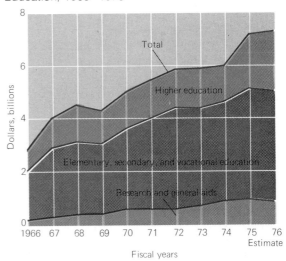

Fiscal years

Source: *The United States Budget in Brief, Year 1976*, Washington, D.C., U.S. Government Printing Office, 1976.

Table 15-3 Federal Government Spending for Defense, 1966–1976

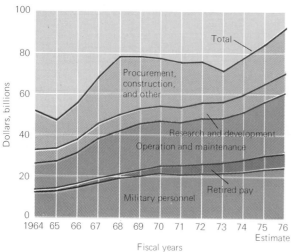

Source: *The United States Budget in Brief, Year 1976.*

Table 15-4 Federal Government Spending on Health Care, 1966–1976

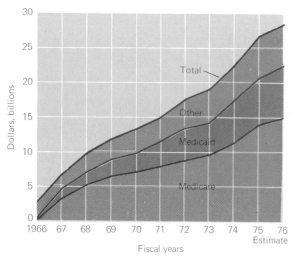

Source: *The United States Budget in Brief, Year 1976.*

lete a few years later. Even if there is no war, the pressures to keep up with other nations means that no reduction in military costs is likely in the near future (see Table 15-3).

Welfare and public services

The modern age of science and medicine has increased the human life-span. Our society now has far more elderly people than in the past who must be supported on pensions and given medical care (see Table 15-4). Furthermore, today the government has been forced to take responsibility for such problems as welfare for children, the blind, the elderly, and the unemployed—a responsibility formerly assumed by families, local communities, churches, and charitable organizations. Higher productivity has made it possible to provide more public care, but our urban-industrial society has made it harder for relatives and neighbors to care for their own people. Government has taken more responsibility for day-care centers, public health services, school lunch programs, and income supplements as well as the entire social security program and veterans' benefits (see Tables 15-5 and 15-6). Some people are uneasy about government's role in these areas. They see America as going down the road to socialism, a process summed up in the term *welfare state*. In 1900, welfare programs cost about 2.5 percent of the gross national product; now they amount to approximately 13 percent. Government responsibility for the entire welfare field shows a new scientific point of view, reflected in the term *human resources*. In Heilbroner's words, the new view "mirrors the scientific commitment to the conscious control of the environment, including the social environment—a commitment that stands directly opposed to the philosophy of capitalism which yields control over the environment to the uncoordinated and undirected influences of individual entrepreneurs and consumers" (1970, pp. 27–28). The economic system must now recognize people's needs. The dependent, the disabled, and the elderly can't just be shunted aside as they have been in the past. Simple decency requires that they be treated as human beings, not human scrap.

New jobs for government are constantly arising. Can they be done at a reasonable cost? Can they even be done intelligently and efficiently?

The big-government issue

A glance at the federal budget (see Tables 15-7 and 15-8) makes it clear why the government has grown—and why, despite political campaign rhetoric, there is little sign of its shrinking. In fact, the U.S. Bureau of the Budget projects an annual growth in federal tax receipts of about $50 billion per year (*The United States Budget in Brief*, 1976) with an increase from approximately $300 billion in 1976 to $500 billion in 1980. The federal government employs about 3 million people, and that number is slowly growing. State and local government payrolls, however, have skyrocketed, from about 3 million in 1945 to 12 million in 1975. With the growth of federal, state, and local government, several problems have developed. Businesspeople complain about crippling regulations and the masses of paper work needed to comply with rules and regulations. State and local governments make similar complaints about complying with federal regulations and administering federal programs. For example, California recently appealed to the U.S. Department of Agriculture to ban any more changes in regulations regarding the food-stamp program; there had been 500 in 1975 alone. So vast is the amount of paperwork that a new commission has been created to reduce the number of government forms (see the insert "Federal Bureaucracy and Paperwork" on page 433).

Ambivalent attitudes toward big government

In the 1960s, Lloyd Free and Hadley Cantril (1967) studied the attitudes of Americans toward government policies, particularly those involving

Table 15-5 Federal Government Spending for Income Security, 1966–1976

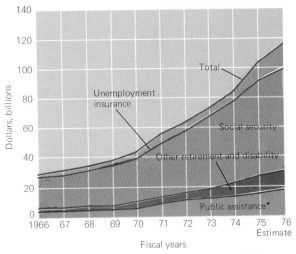

Fiscal years

*Includes other income supplements, such as food stamps and SSI.
Source: *The United States Budget in Brief, Year 1976.*

Table 15-6 Federal Government Spending for Veterans' Benefits and Services, 1966–1976

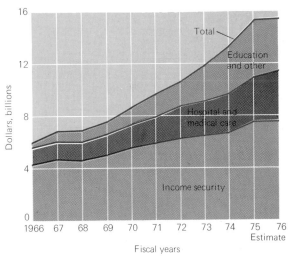

Fiscal years

Source: *The United States Budget in Brief, Year 1976.*

Table 15-7 The Budget Dollar, 1976 Estimate

Where it comes from . . .

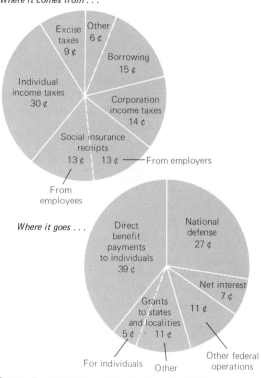

Where it goes . . .

Source: *The United States Budget in Brief, Year 1976.*

Table 15-8 Federal Government Budget Receipts, 1966–1976

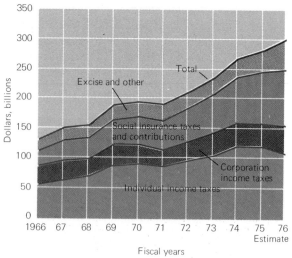

Fiscal years

Source: *The United States Budget in Brief, Year 1976.*

idea of a welfare state. Liberal policies make the political system much more responsive to the poor than it would otherwise be. However, they increase government expense and imply that today people have become more dependent on the government.

Organizations and bureaucracies

Both government and industry operate through large numbers of organizations referred to as departments, administrations, or bureaus. *Formal organizations* are defined as "large-scale, special-purpose units with explicit, impersonal goals in terms of which the members are coordinated (*Encyclopedia of Sociology*, 1974, p. 11). Formal organizations include business and industrial corporations of all types, but the term is also commonly used to refer to government departments, hospitals, penal institutions, state highway patrols, labor unions, and many more. Nearly all these organizations are *bureaucratic*—that is, they are arranged in a hierarchy of authority and control ranging from the highest to the lowest administrative levels in the organiza-

government aid in medical care, housing for the poor, reduction of unemployment, and other programs associated with economic liberalism. They found that in response to questions about specific programs, the majority of Americans were *operational liberals*, that is, liberal in their views toward the actual procedures and aims of such programs. On the other hand, when they asked questions or analyzed the findings of other researchers on generalized political sentiments—such as belief in a welfare state, government intervention in social affairs, or fear of socialistic policies—the sentiments expressed were solidly conservative. Americans, in the terminology of Free and Cantril, tend to be operational liberals and *ideological conservatives*, approving liberal policies but rejecting the

tion. Although industry is highly bureaucratized, in the public mind *bureaucracy* refers to the government—for example, the Departments of Agriculture or the Interior; the Department of Health, Education, and Welfare; the Internal Revenue Service; the Federal Bureau of Investigation; the Bureau of Land Reclamation; and the Bureau of Army Engineers. Military services are perhaps the best examples of bureaucratic structures, with a hierarchy of authority rising through the ranks from private to general or admiral.

Bureaucratic structures

The word *bureaucracy* makes us think of rule-encumbered inefficiency, red tape, and awkward procedures. In sociology, it refers to administrative aspects of organization (Blau and Scott, 1962, p. 8). Any large factory, hospital, or governmental department requires an administrative staff to carry out policy, supervise work, keep records, hire employees, and do other types of administrative work. The tendency for formal organizations to accumulate large administrative staffs has been expressed by the phrase "too many chiefs and not enough Indians," and in C. Northcote Parkinson's "laws" of bureaucracy (1957). Parkinson's first law states that bureaucracies grow in personnel by 3 percent per year whether they have any work to do or not. This law is not meant to be taken literally, but Parkinson does seriously contend that bureaucracies add more people than they need.

Max Weber described bureaucracy as the most efficient means of organizing production

---

Federal bureaucracy and paperwork   BRYCE NELSON

A Congressional Commission studying the problem of federal paperwork is headed by Representative Frank Horton (R.–N.Y.), who reports the following examples of forms required by the federal government:

In 1973, the costs of federal paperwork were more than the combined federal expenditures for health, education, welfare, environment and housing.

Government agencies print 10 billion sheets of paper a year for businesses to file, enough paper to fill a professional baseball stadium 50 times.

Harvard University spends $300,000 annually and employs 26 people full-time to fill out paperwork.

The State of Maryland refused a $60,000 HEW grant because costs of completing the forms would have taken $45,000 of the grant.

A typical small business grossing less than $30,000 annually is forced to file 53 tax forms.

A radio station in New Hampshire paid $26 in postage to mail its license application to Washington.

Horton says that the commission has already had one notable success—persuading Congress to pass legislation to allow employee wages to be reported annually rather than quarterly. When this goes into effect in two years, Horton says a national stack of paperwork two miles high and costing the economy nearly a quarter of a billion dollars will be eliminated.

From Bryce Nelson, "Citizens Protest Paperwork Avalanche," *Los Angeles Times*, Feb. 25, 1976, Part 1-A, pp. 1–2. Copyright © 1976, Los Angeles Times. Reprinted by permission.

Although much political socialization occurs at home, at school, and at work, leaders and symbols of society also play an important role.

(1947). According to Weber's definition, a bureaucratic organization consists of a hierarchy of positions, with each person doing a particular job. All jobs are carefully planned and filled; they are carried out by specialists who have gotten where they are through sheer ability. Weber also says that the ideal bureaucracy provides rules of seniority and tenure, so that people occupy their positions for a long time. Ideally, bureaucracy is no respecter of persons and plays no favorites; it operates purely on the basis of merit. Finally, Weber stressed that bureaucracy is a disciplined system, with all rules of procedure carefully spelled out.

Weber argued that in a bureaucracy, the stress on rules and expertise should produce efficiency. Gouldner (1954) finds an implied contradiction between rules and discipline on the one hand and efficiency on the other. If an organization becomes too bound up in its rules, it can become rigid and unadaptable to new situations.

As noted previously, many organizations (labor unions were given as an example) tend to develop an entrenched leadership, partly as a result of bureaucratic rules and procedures. When the organization is the government, the results become more serious. When rules become inflexible, government can become unresponsive to the needs of the people. Rigid rules and regulations and masses of paperwork do not always fit the requirements of particular cases. Furthermore, the federal bureaucracy often develops snafus when more than one bureau handles the same problem.

Although some cases require secret investigation, the need for secrecy is easily abused. The Watergate investigations found that both the C.I.A. and the F.B.I. had exceeded their authority by spying on the American public. The Internal Revenue Service is another bureau that often requires secrecy, but a person's tax records should not be exposed except in cases of legal prosecution. There are times, however, when the workings of the I.R.S. become mysterious. Philip W. Stern (1974, p. 16) reports some interesting cases of rich people escaping income taxes. Further, the I.R.S. has refused to reveal on what basis such taxes were avoided. Although Congress passed a law in 1969 allegedly to prevent the rich from taking advantage of certain tax loopholes, Stern says,

> Congress had built into even this anti-loop-hole provision some new escape hatches through which the rich and well-advised could wriggle. For in the very first year in which this "minimum tax" was in effect:
>
> Three families who had average dividend income of $2,450,000 per family had contrived to pay no tax whatever.
>
> One hundred twelve families with incomes of more than $200,000 had managed the same feat.
>
> Three hundred and ninety-four taking in more than $100,000 had been able to protect their entire incomes from Internal Revenue. (The Treasury did not reveal *how* these families were able to avoid the new "minimum tax".) (Stern, 1974, p. 16)

Bureaucracy, of course, is inevitable. It would be hard to imagine how either government or business could operate without it. Bureaus, however, need public surveillance of the type attempted by Ralph Nader and his associates. It has also been suggested that Congress review bureaucratic institutions more carefully. The aim is to make them more responsive to the people and to avoid unnecessary secrecy.

POLITICAL MOOD OF THE PUBLIC

In the 1976 presidential campaign, Gerald Ford went to great lengths to assure the public that the dishonesty and secrecy of the Watergate period had come to an end. Jimmy Carter worked equally hard to show that he was an honest person free from any secret political entanglements. Both candidates made the usual contradictory promises about lowering taxes while also combating inflation, but they were a little more restrained than usual in making promises about new and expensive programs. In fact, Carter's campaign promises had little to do with his victory. According to public-opinion analyst Daniel Yankelovich, the public mood of the late 1970s has three main characteristics: (1) financial caution, resulting from inflation and growing shortages of cheap sources of energy and raw materials; (2) a revulsion against dishonesty and unresponsiveness in government; and (3) realism about the inevitability of big government. Pledges to reduce the federal bureaucracy drastically are seen as hollow promises. Most people would like better and more honest government rather than a cut in government services. It is hard to know exactly what the public wants, since people do not all agree and moods change. Still, a public-opinion analyst is in a good position to sum up the public mood at a particular time. Some of Daniel Yankelovich's conclusions are given in the insert "What the Voters Want."

What the voters want   DANIEL YANKELOVICH

One of the striking shifts in the public mood between the 1960s and the 1970s has been the appearance of a national sense of restraint long taken for granted in private life, the realization that one's ambitions and desires more often than not cannot be gratified without compromise. It has dawned on people that governments, like individuals, must be guided by practicality. There is, then, a strong dose of realism in the public mood, the kind that calls for carefully defined, achievable goals and objectives and that recoils in disbelief from empty promises that cannot be filled.

Out of this new mood has emerged a concept of fitness consisting of three main components: a demand for greater moral leadership in government, a longing somehow to get things under control, and desire for a more compassionate, more responsive government. The dominant element among these is the first, which has been explored in depth in the Public Agenda's report, *Moral Leadership in Government.* Drawing on this study, one can define the moral leadership issue according to six basic principles:

Fairness
People are realistic enough to understand that what they want out of government requires a heavy burden of taxation. They are not trying to escape from shouldering their share of the burden. But they see gross injustices in the tax structure, and they want that changed. Likewise, the public senses that there is something fundamentally unfair in a society that emphasizes the work ethic and yet fails to provide jobs for those willing and able to work. The argument that millions of job-seeking Americans must continue to suffer from unemployment in order to control inflation simply doesn't wash.

Restoring Respect for the Law and for Moral Norms
There is a feeling that we have suffered from a serious breakdown of the norms that have governed society and kept it stable in the past. . . .

Restoring a Concept of the Public Good
As the Public Agenda's report states:

Americans fear that the country has been tending toward a psychology of self-

Social institutions and organizations

436

interest so all-embracing that no room is left for commitment to national and community interests. . . .

Involving People More in the Decisions That Affect Their Lives
. . . People have the idea that the government's approach to the public is fraught, at worst, with manipulation and outright lying, and, at best, with a lack of regard for what the public would like to see done. The only sure way to guard against this condition, it is widely felt, is for avenues to be opened which will allow people to participate more actively and continuously in the vital decisions that affect their lives.

Redressing a Perceived Imbalance between Rights and Responsibilities
It is widely believed that people have come to expect too much in the way of guaranteed satisfactions, to take too many things for granted, without feeling obliged to give anything in return. As the Public Agenda's report says, the public feels that to redress this imbalance the President "should use his unique moral authority to stress citizen obligations to the community rather than individual rights."

Trust
People today are tired of being promised one thing and seeing the opposite happen. They're fed up not just with deception but also with well-meant promises that have little chance of being kept. In recent years the bond of basic trust that ties Americans to their government has been strained to the breaking point. People hunger to have this bond repaired and strengthened, and yet, having been let down so often, they are mistrustful of those who ask for their trust without demonstrating as concretely and specifically as possible why it should be given. . . .

THE BIG GOVERNMENT ISSUE
The desire to restore a sense of control lies at the heart of the much-discussed "big government" issue. Public attitudes on this issue have for the most part been misconstrued. People are concerned not so much about the "bigness" of government as such, as with "inefficiency," its lack of responsiveness, the public belief that government and other major institutions are operating exclusively in their own self-interests without consideration of the public good. People know they cannot themselves, as private citizens, bring the economy under control, insure a strong defense, guarantee their personal safety, restore respect for the law, afford the benefits of modern medicine, preserve the environment, secure for themselves a peaceful, healthy and dignified old age, and protect themselves from that vast array of special interests that constitute so much of modern America.

Individualism in America is not dead. But it has been pushed from the public domain into the private—with emphasis on self-fulfillment, interesting work, self-education, sexuality, concern with health and nutrition, a more open marriage, a more relaxed attitude toward success and a taste of the full, rich life. These matters are still seen as being within the individual's control. The sphere of what the individual *cannot* do for himself has greatly expanded and the government's role is accepted as basic and decisive in this enlarged arena. What people are demanding, therefore, is not less government but better government.

From Daniel Yankelovich, "What the Voters Want," *The New Republic*, Vol. 175, October 23, 1976, pp. 16–19.

SUMMARY

Particularly in democratic societies, conflicting interest groups are constantly at work. They try to influence the top political institutions of state, nation, and community. Usually they work within a consensus, seeking power legally. Groups without political power sometimes resort to strikes, demonstrations, or even riots. Political leaders try to *legitimize* their power.

People are *socialized* into political viewpoints. Usually they hold common beliefs in democratic processes but conflicting beliefs regarding equality, health care, labor laws, government regulations, and many other matters. According to research by Mann, political teaching in schools tends to minimize conflicts, working instead toward conservatism and unity. Parental values strongly influence one's political loyalties, but later life experiences are also important. Despite teachers' tendencies to gloss over political differences, people do not blandly accept the idea that all is well with the government. A 1973 opinion poll in the United States found half the people thinking the government does only a fair job.

Political partisanship increases with age. This is true especially of those who reach a state of *structural crystallization*. Those of lower status generally favor the Democratic party; those of a higher status, the Republican party. Although partisanship may be declining, Janowitz and Segal found that many people in England, Germany, and the United States continue to favor one party consistently. Race, religion, and age may have a strong influence apart from social-class position.

Power is unequally distributed. Holders of office have the type of legal power called *authority*. Politically active people usually have a type of informal power called *influence*. Great wealth easily becomes a source of influence, since those with money can contribute to campaign funds, hire lobbyists to represent them, move friends into government bureaus, and help to defeat candidates who oppose their interests. Such influence becomes a political issue when corrupted, as in the case of payoffs to public officials in the United States and in foreign governments.

Power is exerted not just through government but also through corporations and financial institutions. Some executives enhance their power by serving on the boards of many corporations.

The individual worker has less influence than the businessperson. When workers organize, however, labor becomes a powerful force. Unions raise campaign funds, but they exert even more political power by getting out the vote. Unions also exert direct power in the form of strikes, threats of strikes, and boycotts. Unions, however, represent only about one-quarter of the American work force. Some of them are corrupt. Their leadership tends to become entrenched, following the *iron law of oligarchy*. Also, they are often deaf to many types of members' demands.

Arguments have arisen over whether the working class, and union members in particular, tend to be *authoritarian* personalities. During the Vietnamese war, there were several clashes between union members and antiwar demonstrators. A study by Henry Berger concludes, however, that union workers were very similar to other Americans in attitudes regarding the war. They changed gradually from acceptance to rejection. Interestingly, the least-skilled and lowest-paid workers were the most antiwar. The more highly skilled workers and union leaders were more prowar.

Business and labor are sometimes described as *countervailing forces*, each keeping the other from achieving political domination. Movements and associations can also become countervailing forces. They act against entrenched policies and institutions.' Environmentalists and consumer groups are good examples of such countervailing forces.

Government constantly grows in its functions and expenses. Its organization becomes more complex. Government growth is worldwide, resulting from government takeovers of more functions of regulation and public service. Military expenses, income security, welfare benefits, health, education, veterans' services, and many other government services constantly grow in cost. The size of government is a political issue. Many writers point out that the issue is really not size but whether the quality of service is in line with costs. Free and Cantril found that Americans are *ideologically conservative* about big government but *operationally liberal* about most of the programs that have led to big government.

The size of government leads to increasing concern about *bureaucracies*, which seem wasteful, enmeshed in red tape, and deaf to people's needs. Although bureaucratic organizations are sharply criticized, they are used by all large corporations as well as by government. Ideally, they should represent an efficient means of assigning jobs on the basis of merit, as Weber contended. However, bureaucrats are accused of becoming more immersed in rules than in solving problems.

Daniel Yankelovich tried to sum up the mood of the American people just before the 1976 election. He found that people recognized the need for big government but were very concerned over dishonesty, inefficiency, and unresponsiveness in government. They recognized a need for high taxes, but they demanded greater fairness. Above all, people wanted honest leaders and a chance to make their opinions known on major decisions.

Study guide

Terms to know

Legitimizing
Political socialization
Structural crystallization
Status inconsistency
Skidder
Power
Influence

Authority
Closed shop
Union shop
Countervailing power
Iron law of oligarchy
Working-class authoritarianism
Welfare state

Operational liberal
Ideological conservative
Formal organization
Bureaucracy
Parkinson's law

Names to know

George Meany
Frank Fitzsimmons
G. William Domhoff
Robert L. Heilbroner

Max Weber
Robert Michels
Ralph Nader

Self-test

Part I. Multiple Choice. Select the best of the four alternative answers:

1 An area of agreement on ideas within which the political power struggle can be carried on is called (**a**) democracy, (**b**) consensus, (**c**) correlation, (**d**) coordination.
2 Approximately half the public rated the federal government as only fair in (**a**) honesty, fairness, and justice; (**b**) efficiency; (**c**) consideration and responsiveness; (**d**) all the above.
3 Which of the following is (are) generally associated with voting for the Democratic party? (**a**) low income, (**b**) Protestantism, (**c**) business interests, (**d**) all the above.
4 As a general rule, status inconsistency (but not status decline) is associated with (**a**) liberalism, (**b**) conservativism, (**c**) undemocratic viewpoints, (**d**) none of the above.
5 The power of a President to sign or veto bills is an example of (**a**) extralegal powers, (**b**) influence, (**c**) authority, (**d**) bargaining.
6 Which of the following can be considered means of exerting political influence? (**a**) making large campaign contributions, (**b**) lobbying, (**c**) creating a favorable image by advertising, (**d**) all the above.
7 Labor-union power is great (**a**) in agricultural states, (**b**) because unions have more financial power than corporations, (**c**) because of good organization and precinct work in industrial states, (**d**) all the above.
8 Organized labor is weakened by *all but one* of the following: (**a**) unions represent only a small part of the work force, (**b**) the unionized industries are not very vital ones, (**c**) unions often suffer an unfavorable public image, (**d**) some unions have had a record of corruption.
9 If support for the Vietnam war can be interpreted as a sign of authoritarianism, then the most authoritarian people within labor were (**a**) common laborers, (**b**) semiskilled workers, (**c**)

skilled workers, (**d**) represented in all groups equally.

10 The person mentioned as exerting the most influence regarding consumer interests is (**a**) Ralph Nader, (**b**) Walter Mondale, (**c**) March Fong Eu, (**d**) Fred Harris.

11 Government regulation of industry to prevent unfair practices began with which industry? (**a**) shipping, (**b**) railroads, (**c**) petroleum, (**d**) steel.

12 A series of graphs on federal expenses shows the highest outlays to be in the field of (**a**) education, (**b**) defense, (**c**) income security, (**d**) health.

13 The largest federal government revenue comes from (**a**) individual income taxes, (**b**) excise taxes, (**c**) corporate taxes, (**d**) borrowing.

14 Free and Cantril found which of the following to characterize American political attitudes? (**a**) liberalism, (**b**) operational liberalism but ideological conservatism, (**c**) operational conservatism but ideological liberalism, (**d**) conservatism.

15 Which of the following would be characterized by bureaucratic organization? (**a**) industrial corporations, (**b**) penal institutions, (**c**) federal and state agencies, (**d**) all the above.

Part II. True-False Questions

1 Mann concludes that in both England and the United States, political teaching in the schools realistically shows conflicting class interests.

2 Young voters are less politically partisan than are middle-aged voters.

3 In 1972, the college-educated voters were suspicious of Richard Nixon and in 63 percent of the cases voted against him.

4 Loyalty to a political party increases with increasing social-class crystallization.

5 In both England and the United States, the upper middle class is politically divided, with businesspeople being more consistently conservative than government workers and professionals.

6 Making campaign contributions to members of Congress in an attempt to win their support is a fairly recent development in United States history.

7 Powerful business executives generally limit their activities to only one major corporation.

8 The "iron law of oligarchy" is a congressional act regulating unions.

9 Glaberman charges that labor-union leaders are too much inclined to make easy settlements with management.

10 The political worker cited in "Exacting Campaign Funds" made sure that "fat cats" contributed only to his own party.

11 Nader charges that laws are frequently circumvented rather than enforced by the regulatory commissions.

12 The size and cost of the United States government has grown in recent years, but similar growth has occurred in only a few foreign countries.

13 Max Weber saw bureaucracy as rationally organized and playing no favorites.

14 According to "Parkinson's law," the number of employees in a bureaucracy grows even if the bureau's duties decline.

15 Yankelovich found the public in 1976—1977 unrealistic about the need for big government.

Questions for discussion

1 Try to illustrate the contrast between authority and influence in your local community. Can you identify any community leaders who hold no office but exert a lot of influence? What about your local newspaper? If you cannot think of local cases, try to think of examples in state or local government.

2 Try to identify as many interest groups in your community as possible. Discuss the relative weight each seems to carry.

3 We all know that Watergate has produced major changes in the political process. Or has it? Can you think of any new regulations that have been passed because of the Watergate scandals? Any differences in government policies? Is there a new level of public awareness?

4 How would you say your parents influenced your present political perspective? Toward partisan interest? Nonpartisan interest? Or simply noninterest?

5 Review your own political socialization in school, especially through high school. Were themes of national unity stressed and conflicting social-class (and other) interests minimized?

6 Discuss the potential for a student lobby in the state legislature. What issues might a student lobby be interested in? How might it be made effective? Would it have a better chance to be effective on a state, local, or national basis?

7 The political process is influenced—and sometimes corrupted—by conflicting interest groups and their lobbies. Are there any other ways of allowing conflicting interests to be heard? Could lobbies be regulated?

8 Analyze a speech or statement made by a political figure. (In a class discussion, you will have to pick an earlier speech unless there is an election campaign in progress.) Are facts given a slanted interpretation? Is the speech heavy with symbols? Are issues faced squarely or are they dodged?

Projects

1 Try to analyze the voting patterns of state legislators or congresspersons from your state. Often the local newspapers publish voting records on political issues. Otherwise, you may be able to get the information from the League of Women Voters or local Republican and Democratic clubs or central committees. After looking over the voting record, do you see a clear partisan voting pattern? Are there any cases in which votes seem to favor special local interests?

2 As a general rule, young and old voters participate less than middle-aged voters, and young voters form the least partisan age group. Conduct a poll on your campus to see how many are Democrats, Republicans, and independents. How many who were qualified to vote in the last general election did not do so?

3 Is yours a union town? How vocal are labor unions in your community at election time? Try to interview union officials and find out what political work is being done by unions. Is there any kind of precinct organization? (Alternatively, you might consult a member of the Democratic or Republican Central Committee to see whether they are able to maintain precinct organization.)

Suggested readings

Dennis, Jack: "Who Supports the Presidency," *Society*, vol. 13, July–August 1976, pp. 48–53. How strong is public faith in the Presidency since the Nixon years? Are children still being socialized into an attitude of respect for the office? Do people feel that the office has grown beyond their control or influence?

Dibble, Vernon K.: "The Garrison Society," *New University Thought*, vol. 5, Sepcial Issue 1966–1967, pp. 106–115. Have civilian and military branches of government grown closer together until there is virtually no distinction? How strong is the tie-in between business and the military? Dibble concludes, as did C. Wright Mills, that the connection is very close.

Fairlie, Henry: "In Defense of Big Government," *The New Republic*, vol. 174, March 13, 1976, pp. 24—27. Is the issue of big government really a phony issue? Yes, says Fairlie. The real issue is whom the government should serve.

House, James S.: "Political Alienation in America," *American Sociological Review*, vol. 40, April 1975, pp. 123–147. Did political alienation in the 1960s separate older and younger generations? House concludes that government policies resulted in political alienation that cut across all segments of the population and all age groups.

Mankoff, Milton: "Power in Advanced Capitalist Society: A Review Essay on Recent Elitist and Marxist Criticism of Pluralist Theory," *Social Problems*, vol. 17, Winter 1970, pp. 418–430. Is there an identifiable ruling elite, or is power divided among large numbers of "veto" groups?

Newsweek, editors: "Big Government," *Newsweek*, December 15, 1975, pp. 34–46. Why have complaints about government steadily increased through the 1960s and into the 1970s? Proliferating programs? Overregulation? Too many forms and reporting procedures? Too much centralization? All these criticisms are examined, with numerous examples.

———: "The Embattled Businessman," February 16, 1975, pp. 56–60. Extensive criticism of business over payoffs, political influence, and tax breaks are discussed, as is the decline in public confidence.

Wilson, James: "The Bureaucracy Problem," *The Public Interest*, Number 6, Winter 1967, pp. 3–9. Do bureaucrats eventually become an "almost self-governing class whose day-to-day behavior [becomes] virtually immune to scrutiny and control?" Wilson outlines five problems of bureaucracy that must be overcome.

Key to questions. Multiple Choice: 1-b; 2-d; 3-a; 4-a; 5-c; 6-d; 7-c; 8-b; 9-c; 10-a; 11-b; 12-c; 13-a; 14-b; 15-d. True-False: 1-F; 2-T; 3-F; 4-T; 5-T; 6-F; 7-F; 8-F; 9-T; 10-F; 11-T; 12-F; 13-T; 14-T; 15-F.

This chapter explores the needs of
the worker and the work market as
well as the relationships between
work and leisure activities. After
reading it, you should be able to:

1 Recognize a number of reasons
for working besides the obvious
need to earn a living.

2 Recognize and consider what
you might do about a possible
"aspiration gap" regarding job
opportunities for college graduates
until at least the mid-1980s.

3 Realize that jobs with large,
formal organizations are not
necessarily unchallenging.

4 Understand reasons for worker
discontentment in industrial jobs,
especially assembly-line jobs.

5 Recognize the dangers to life and
health that are present in many
industrial jobs and in at least a few
white-collar jobs.

6 See relationships between types
of work and types of leisure and
recognize the need for leisure
activities at various stages in life.

7 See indications of some of the
"subterranean values" that most
people hold and often give vent to
in sports and entertainment.

16

THE SOCIOLOGY
OF WORK AND
LEISURE

For the majority of people, work provides not only income but also a sense of personal identity and purpose in life. When a cross-section of young workers were asked if they would continue to work even if they had enough money to live comfortably without working, 73 percent said they would (Yankelovich, 1974, p. 106). What is true of young workers is apparently true also of older workers. Some surveys indicate that work satisfaction increases with age. This is especially true of those whose jobs afford both good pay and prestige (Sheppard and Philibert, 1972, pp. 29–35). One study of workers in their fifties, all with high-status jobs, indicated that none of them looked forward to retirement. Without work, they feared that their lives would lack meaning and that they would die at an earlier age. They were also concerned that inflation would erode their retirement income (Distefano, 1969, pp. 127–134). Yet although they were worried about retirement, they failed to prepare for it.

Much has been written about the severe tensions caused by highly competitive work. However, a Metropolitan Life Insurance Company study of more than a thousand top executives, conducted over a sixteen-year period, found the executives' death rate to be less than two-thirds the rate of other men employed in less prestigious, less competitive jobs. The researchers concluded, "It may be that work satisfaction, together with public recognition of accomplishment, is an important determinant of health and longevity" (*Psychology Today*, 1974, p. 30).

Because of the great importance of work in our society, the unemployed person suffers not only from lack of income but also from the loss of all other job functions: status and sense of self-worth, work associates, the organization of time, and even meaningful leisure (see the insert on page 449: "Unemployment Rated Major Mental Problem"). The situation is particularly serious in view of high rates of unemployment, especially for young people and blacks (Table 16-1).

WORKERS' EXPECTATIONS

What kinds of jobs are people looking for? The young workers who said they would continue to work regardless of the need for money had some important qualifications about jobs. They gave the following percentage ratings to the qualities they would look for in a job:

Friendly, helpful co-workers (70 percent)
Work that is interesting (70 percent)
Opportunity to use your mind (65 percent)
Work results you can see (62 percent)
Good pay (61 percent)
Opportunities to develop skills and abilities (61 percent)
Participation in decisions regarding jobs (55 percent)
Getting help needed to do the job well (55 percent)
Respect for organization you work for (55 percent)
Recognition for a job well done (54 percent) (Yankelvoich, 1974, p. 104; copyright 1974, McGraw-Hill Book Company. Used with permission of McGraw-Hill Book Company)

There were slight differences between white-collar and blue-collar workers. The latter gave greater importance to higher pay. However, the differences were only slight. Although they overwhelmingly endorsed work as a way of life, young Americans are clearly looking for interest-

The sociology of work and leisure

Table 16-1 Unemployment Rates, June 1976, Seasonally Adjusted

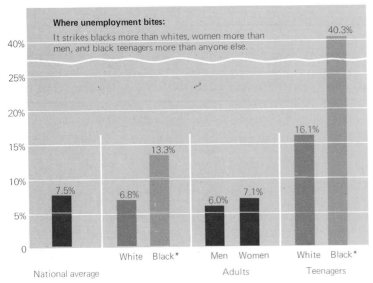

Where unemployment bites:
It strikes blacks more than whites, women more than men, and black teenagers more than anyone else.

National average		Adults		Teenagers	
7.5%					
	6.8%	6.0%	7.1%	16.1%	40.3%
	13.3%				
	White Black*	Men Women		White Black*	

*Includes other minorities.
Source: Fenga and Freyer, "The Great Jobs Debate," *Newsweek,* July 26, 1976. © 1976 by Newsweek, Inc. All rights reserved. Reprinted by permission.

ing jobs, not mere assembly-line routines. The blue-collar workers surveyed were generally dissatisfied with their jobs. They hoped, with more training and education, to find more rewarding jobs.

Unsatisfying jobs

About 25 million Americans work in low-skilled, low-paying jobs with little challenge and no upward mobility (Wood, 1976, pp. 22–31). Others hold jobs that lack social utility. Paul Goodman emphasizes the latter problem, noting how many well-educated people have jobs that involve advertising or selling products of doubtful utility or even such often harmful products as cigarettes, sleeping pills, or weight-reducing drugs (Goodman, 1960). Also, large corporations—while they may offer well-paying, high-status jobs—often stifle creativity and personal freedom. William H. Whyte made the term *organization man* famous by his book of that

title, picturing the middle- and upper-level employees of big organizations as men without freedom, spontaneity, creativity, or minds of their own (1956). They are, he implies, victims of a type of "group think." They can work well in committees but are incapable of independent decisions. As we shall see later on, though, Whyte's conclusions may apply to only a minority. First, let us examine the job market today.

OVERVIEW OF EMPLOYMENT: 1975–1985

It is never possible to predict just what the rate of unemployment will be, but the Labor Department estimates the percentage of people that will be required in various fields and also the approximate number expected to be employed and unemployed. (See Table 16-2.) Labor Department projections made in spring 1976 foresaw a gradual decline in the unemployment rate from 7.8 percent for 1976 to 4.0 or possibly 4.5

Table 16-2 Trends in the Labor Force, 1965–1975

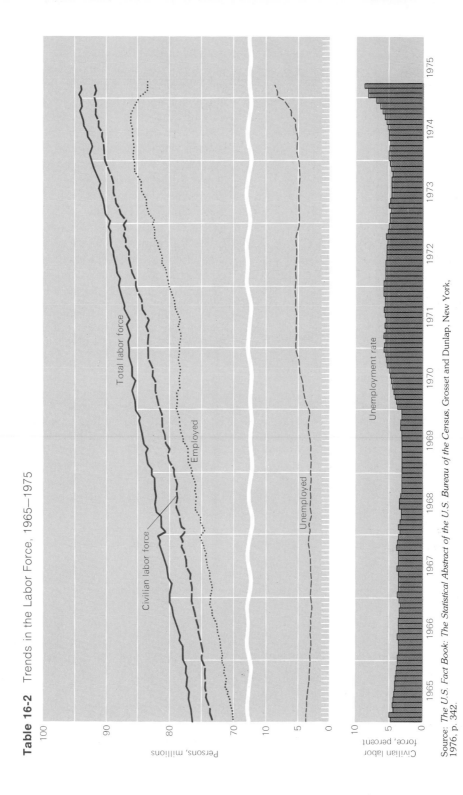

Source: *The U.S. Fact Book: The Statistical Abstract of the U.S. Bureau of the Census,* Grosset and Dunlap, New York, 1976. p. 342.

447

(a)

percent by 1985 (Bowman and Morlan, 1976, pp. 9–21). The total labor force—a more easily predictable figure than the estimate of unemployment—is expected to increase from about 89 million in 1972 to nearly 110 million in 1985. The percentage of people employed by federal, state, and local government, including the military, will rise from just over 16 percent to almost 18 percent (see Table 16-3, page 450).

A person entering the labor force needs to know what types of jobs will be in demand as well as the kinds of jobs presently available. The Labor Department's *Dictionary of Occupational Titles* lists over 35,000 occupations. In most cases, however, the Labor Department and U.S. Census Bureau list employment fields in general

Figure 16-1 (*a*) The worker, even under stress, is generally in better mental health than (*b*) the unemployed person. [*(a)Ted Spiegel, Black Star; (b) Ray Ellis, Photo Researchers, Inc.*]

(b)

categories, as in Table 16-4, which gives five major categories and predicts what percentage of people will be in each group category by 1985. The most desirable jobs are in Group I; the least desirable in Group V. The five employment categories can be described as follows: Group I consists of professional and allied jobs, including those in science and engineering. Group II includes most other white-collar office jobs and also public-service jobs, such as police work and fire fighting. Group III includes the jobs of most skilled crafts workers, mechanics, repairers, operatives in high-wage industries (such as transportation equipment and petroleum), and certain skilled service occupations—barbers and beauticians, bartenders, and practical nurses. Group IV includes a few low-level clerical occupations, such as those of shipping clerks, as well

---

Unemployment rated major mental problem   ELEANOR HOOVER

Unemployment is "America's major mental health problem," a group of social psychologists told the annual meeting of the American Psychological Association this week.

"A federal policy which still calls for 4, 5, 6, or 7% unemployment is devaluing human life," said Dr. Hannah Levin of the City University of New York, who reported on her study of the psychological effects of unemployment.

"Unemployment is a major life change—and no adult accepts it easily," she said.

"People who lose jobs and can't find work tend to feel like nonpersons. They are depressed, apathetic, disoriented and withdrawn. They feel dispossessed, helpless and often irrational. In this society, they have lost a primary source of a sense of identity, self-esteem, status, meaning and autonomy.

"In short, people who are unemployed usually suffer a loss of self and a collapse of personality."

"A man isn't a man without a job or money," she quoted a 32-year-old unemployed New York construction worker as saying.

Some of the unemployed persons Levin studied became so confused by the lack of structured time that they stopped wearing watches. Others began to drink. Some stayed off the street in the daytime in embarrassment. A few even contemplated suicide and others chose to be sick, finding that role more acceptable than being unemployed.

Most important, about 90 percent of the unemployed insisted on blaming themselves for their predicament, despite all evidence to the contrary.

"They felt," Levin said, "that if only they had gone to college, or not been late to work, or tried a little harder or shown a little more initiative, they wouldn't have lost their jobs.

"They are victims of an unspoken dominant American ideology which says they are somehow at fault for being out of work—and typically, as victims, they begin to blame themselves," she said.

The problem, she says, is even more serious where youth is concerned. "If there are no jobs for one-third of our youth, how will they continue to grow?" she asked. "The link to violence and drugs is obvious. Work should move to the top of the list of those who plan programs for youth."

Eleanor Hoover in *Los Angeles Times,* September 4, 1975, Part I, pp. 1, 22. Copyright Los Angeles Times.

Table 16-3 Projections of the Labor Force to 1985 (Numbers in Thousands)

Item	Actual 1972	Projected 1980	Projected 1985
Total labor force (including military)	88,991	103,310	109,749
Military	2,449	2,088	2,000
Civilian labor force	86,542	101,222	107,661
Unemployed	4,840	4,757	4,306
Employed	81,702	96,465	103,355
Total employment	89,251	104,441	112,097
General government	14,608	17,685	20,087
Federal (including military)	4,423	4,246	4,339
State and local	10,185	13,439	15,748
Private	74,643	86,756	92,010
Agriculture	3,450	2,750	2,300
Nonagriculture	71,193	84,006	89,710

Source: Ronald E. Kutscher, "Revised BLS Projections to 1980 and 1985: An Overview, *Monthly Labor Review,* vol. 99, March 1976, p. 5.

Table 16-4 Projections of the Experienced Civilian Labor Force by Major Occupational Status Groups: Actual, 1970; Projected, 1980 and 1985

Occupational status group	Number in millions			Percent distribution		
	1970	1980	1985	1970	1980	1985
Total (both sexes)	75.1	91.5	97.5	100.0	100.0	100.0
Group I	10.6	15.1	17.6	14.2	16.5	18.1
Group II	24.8	32.0	34.8	33.0	35.0	35.7
Group III	15.9	18.4	19.2	21.1	20.1	19.7
Group IV	15.6	17.3	17.4	20.7	18.9	17.9
Group V	8.2	8.7	8.5	10.9	9.5	8.7

Source: Harold Wood, "Future Labor Supply for Lower Level Occupations, *Monthly Labor Review,* vol. 99, March 1976, p. 27.

as painters, plasterers, roofers, and cement and concrete workers. Group V includes farm and nonfarm labor, domestic service, and laundry and dry-cleaning work. Some of the jobs in Group IV, although requiring little schooling, are fairly well paid. Those in Group V are generally very poorly paid.

The aspiration gap

At first glance, the figures on occupational change look quite encouraging. Larger percentage gains are expected in the preferred work of Groups I and II, while slight percentage losses are predicted for Groups IV and V. Yet the number of young people preparing for employment at the upper work levels is increasing faster than those jobs are becoming available. As Group I and II occupations become oversubscribed, some college-educated people are forced to take jobs that they neither want nor are prepared for.

On the other hand, Harold Wood, whose figures are cited in Tables 16-3 and 16-4, expects to see a growing shortage of laborers for Group V and some of the Group IV jobs because of the increased training of the labor force. Many lower-level jobs have been held traditionally by rural migrants, or by women and blacks. Today, immigration has been greatly reduced, and far fewer women and blacks are willing to settle for Group V jobs. They are going to school and insisting on better jobs. Thus, there could be a shortage of workers for those occupations, with possibly increased pay in an attempt to make sure they are filled.

Minority workers, women, and all college graduates seeking Group I and II occupations are finding these fields highly competitive, leading them to experience a blockage of aspirations. Women, especially, are experiencing this *aspiration gap*, since the jobs available to them are usually at lower occupational levels regardless of their qualifications (see the insert "Women in Science").

As a result of competition for Group I and Group II jobs, with disappointment for some job seekers, there may be more discontentment with work in the future than there was in the past. The student entering college would do best to consult

---

Women in science

Upper-middle-class and upper-class women can readily get quality educations, but they do not have equal access to the kinds of jobs that greet their brothers at the end of their educations. This conclusion is reached by Ruth Hubbard, writing in the March 1976 issue of *Trends in Biochemical Sciences*.

Writing on the role of women in science, Hubbard documents the paucity of women scientists. "Women chemists and biologists work primarily in educational institutions although 56.6 percent of chemists are employed by industry. In educational institutions, however, women cluster at the lowest academic ranks and in the less prestigious colleges. . . . Furthermore, women earn less than men at the equivalent faculty rank."

Hubbard writes that it is crucial to understand that women are not absent from the scientific work force any more than from other sectors that are dominated by an overwhelming male professional elite. The scientific-medical-technical work force is much more discriminatory than is usually realized. It not only excludes women from the top; it is also squarely based on women's labor at the lower levels.

Hubbard concludes, "Had women constituted half the scientific and intellectual work-force since the time Western science broke away from its medieval precursors, no doubt its structure and content would be different, as would the interpersonal relationships among scientists." But as latecomers to the scientific community, women scientists have to confront the question of whether to try to help restructure the profession along less hierarchical, competitive, and secretive lines or whether to become "female men in a male science."

Published by permission of Transaction, Inc., from *Society*, vol. 13, no. 6. Copyright © 1976 by Transaction, Inc.

---

an occupational counselor, prepare for fields with openings, and do well enough in school to be among the most highly qualified applicants. (This advice, unfortunately, ignores the traditional ideal of a broad-based liberal education.)

WORKING FOR THE ORGANIZATION

The majority of people work for large, formal organizations. These may include industrial corporations such as Ford, General Motors, or Chrysler; television networks; or the telephone company. Other possibilities are banks, insurance companies, legal firms, hospitals, penal institutions, universities, or some branch of government. Is it true that the organization eventually absorbs the personalities of the people it employs to such a degree that they no longer have independent minds? Melvin L. Kohn tried to test this theory by interviewing over three thousand men, some working for large, bureaucratic organizations and others self-employed or working for small, informal concerns.

Kohn concludes that "men who work in bureaucratic organizations tend to value, not conformity, but self-direction. They are more open minded . . . and more receptive to change than are men who work in nonbureaucratic organizations" (1971, pp. 461–474). In Kohn's study, differences between his bureaucratic and non-bureaucratic subjects are not very great, but his conclusions consistently favor the bureaucratic workers. Part of the reason is that the people most often recruited for bureaucratic positions are generally well-educated, urban people. Even when education is not considered, however, Kohn's findings still favor persons in large organizations, whether profit-making corporations or branches of government. Kohn suggests that bureaucratic jobs are more complex than comparable jobs in smaller concerns, that job security is greater, and that pay is better. The greater complexity of the work, he claims, is intellectually challenging. Greater job security makes it possible for employees to be more open and honest in their responses to supervisors. Finally, the higher pay and contact with peers in the organization help provide a feeling of self-assurance.

Professionals and bureaucrats

Far fewer professionals are self-employed today than in the past. Increasingly, doctors and lawyers become associated with hospitals and law firms. Teachers, social workers, and nurses are employed almost exclusively by large organizations. Most organizations try to create loyalty in their employees at all levels. Regardless of the organization for which they work, however, professionals often have a dual loyalty—one to the organization and another to their profession. For this reason, the professional is apt to be more independent of the organization than is a marketing expert or business administrator (Kohn, 1971, p. 465). Teachers and lawyers, for example, often think of themselves as teachers or lawyers first and as members of the law firm or college second.

Individuals vary widely in how much they become a part of the organization. The idealistic 1960s produced many professionals who wanted to avoid being swallowed up by "the establishment." Many of these reformers continue their work today (consider, for example, Ron Pollack, a "warrior for the poor," in the insert "The Hunger Lawyers"). The students of the 1970s are more worried about finding a job than students were ten years ago. Though they want interesting and socially useful work, many will undoubtedly settle for whatever is available—or possibly carve out new careers of their own.

The hunger lawyers

Ron Pollack's small New York City law firm [now located in Washington, D.C.] consistently wins the biggest money judgments in the nation. Yet Pollack and the other four young lawyers (average age 31) who work with him do not handle the traditionally lucrative kinds of cases—personal injury litigation, treble-damage civil antitrust suits, defending against corporate clients. Ron Pollack is into food for the poor. For the past six years, his Food Research and Action Center (FRAC) has successfully fought administration efforts to cut back federal spending on food for those who would otherwise have to do without. In the process, Pollack and FRAC have forced the government to free hundreds of millions of dollars' worth of congressionally approved food benefits that the White House had sought to eliminate by executive fiat. Says Pollack: "Our function is to use the law to feed the people."

The New York City-born attorney, now 32, was a student civil rights activist who went to Mississippi in the mid-60's, where he saw "in the starkest terms people who were extraordinarily hungry and needed government assistance." Only five months out of law school (New York University, class of '68), Pollack filed 26 suits in a single day against foot dragging on food programs by 26 states and the Department of Agriculture. . . . He won 25 of the 26.

From "The Hunger Lawyers," reprinted by permission from *Time*, The Weekly Newsmagazine; copyright Time, Inc., 1976.

STUDIES OF WORKER SATISFACTION

Blue-collar workers are more alienated from the organization than are white-collar workers. Their discontentment is due partly to the dehumanizing experience of assembly-line work—once considered the height of efficiency and an innovation which labor was expected to welcome. Blue-collar workers have done most of the job of organizing workers into unions and leading strikes against the employers.

The efficiency engineer

One of the most influential men in the field of labor management was Frederick Taylor (1856–1915), a manager of labor crews and an inventor. Taylor apparently wanted to benefit labor as well as management. However, his writings on industiral engineering helped to establish the monotonous assembly-line process that has plagued industrial workers ever since. Taylor believed a study should be made of all productive processes so that all operations could be broken down into the simplest possible movements. He did this task for several industries. In this way, he thought, all error could be avoided, and no matter how simple the worker, he or she could master the one or two operations necessary on the assembly line. As Frederick Herzberg describes the philosophy behind such production techniques, it was that of the mechanistic worker. "This new notion suggested that the overriding desire of the worker was to be utilized efficiently and with a minimum of effort. That man is happiest when he is 'an interchangeable part of an interchangeable machine making interchangeable parts' became an axiom" (Blau and Scott, 1962, pp. 64–69). Not only were people relieved of the responsibility of making mistakes, but they had no need to make decisions or to do any thinking whatever. That workers could adjust to such simple-minded jobs was considered proof of their simple-mindedness.

The assembly line

Unfortunately, the routine, simplified task that calls for repetition of a single operation hour after hour is not a thing of the past but the essence of assembly-line work today. This can be seen in the insert "What It's Like on the Auto Assembly Line." In this insert, note the alienating influence of the assembly-line pace, human mechanization, noise, and lack of communication. Opposed to these, however, is the fact of a steady job at good pay. In 1970, $3.77 per hour was a good wage for a job requiring little or no skill. The reporter, accustomed to more interesting work, was probably more alienated by the assembly line than the other workers. Still, no one thought of it as a good job.

The human-relations approach

Certain types of research, begun in the decades after Taylor, began to see the worker as a human, social, and intelligent being rather than a robot. In the 1920s and 1930s, a Harvard research team led by Elton Mayo conducted experiments in productivity and worker satisfaction at the Hawthorne Plant of the Western Electric Company near Chicago.

The amount of light in the plant was varied, work pauses were instituted, and temperature and humidity were regulated. The question was, "What effect would these changes have on worker productivity and morale?" The results were encouraging, but in a surprising way. When the experiments were reversed, with less light rather than more, worker morale seemed to improve just as much as it had when the

---

What it's like on the auto assembly line

What is life like on the auto assembly line, and what is the mood of the men and women working there? To find out, Newsweek's Martin Weston hired out as a production worker at the Chevrolet Nova assembly plant in Willow Run, near Detroit. Here, after four exhausting afternoon shifts on the line, is his report.

The single most important bond uniting auto workers is the never-ending physical agony of it all. On the assembly line, cars move by each work station at the rate of 50 to 65 an hour, and you sometimes have less than a minute to perform your task. "You work your ass off," one Willow Run worker summed up bitterly. "You work your ass off all day long every day you work. The thing about the job is that the line never stops. And because it's inhuman, it never takes into account the fact that sometimes human beings get tired."

On my first day, I quickly learned the impersonality of life on the line. Along with a dozen others, I stood in a circle while three foremen looked us over and then pointed out the men they wanted. It was like choosing up sides for a soft-ball game, or like a longshoreman's shapeup. The foreman didn't say a word. He just pointed.

Being the 153 pound weakling of the bunch, I got the easiest job—a job a woman was doing. Irene showed me how to install the steel shackles on the rear suspension system and grease dual mufflers for special models before throwing them on the back of the Towveyor to be installed up the line.

It looked simple, but it wasn't. The Towveyor—the conveyor system carrying front and rear ends before they are united under the car's body—moved along so fast that I had less than 60 seconds in which to install four rubber cushions (two on each side) bolt on four shackles with two bolts and two nuts. In addition to being sure they weren't on upside down (I did that once), I had to replenish my supplies continually from an assortment of boxes and bins.

No Jelly: When I first tried to do it without Irene's help I found myself running back and forth to keep up. "When I first took this job, I lost 20 pounds in three weeks," she told me. "You'll get used to it." But I never did. That first night I couldn't get to sleep; I kept putting on shackles over and over again. Even so, I fared better than another man in our beginner's crew. Charles, a tough 6-footer fresh from a job in a magnesium plant in Chicago, was put to work mounting engines on the car bodies. "The job in the magnesium plant was jelly compared to this one," he groaned after his first shift. "And in the magnesium plant we worked in real heat."

The impersonal, endless line also teaches cynicism. For a while, because bumpers weren't fitting properly somewhere up the line, I was told to hit each frame three times with a sledgehammer as it passed my station.

Obviously, many of the workers at Willow Run long to escape. Willie, a black man who installed brake controls next to my work station, hopes to "take my money and run" some day to open some sort of small service business with his brother. And for some, there is escape right on the job; both marijuana and liquor are common. Joe, a white migrant from Kentucky, was renowned along the line for his ability to drink as many as 27 cans of beer or a fifth of bourbon at a single sitting. He often came to work stoned and then drank some more on his 30-minute lunch break. "If I didn't drink," he explained, "I wouldn't ever be able to do this crap at all."

Another key to survival on the line is sneaking every possible minute away from the job. "I've been in this hellhole for six years," grunted one worker waiting to see the doctor when I stopped for the mandatory physical examination. "I'm going to have the doc look at my finger: there ain't a damn thing wrong with it, but you learn quick here never to pass up a single chance to sit down." Any distraction is welcome. . . .

For all their unhappiness with their jobs, however, the Willow Run workers showed a strange lack of union militancy. In some ways, the plant is typical of those covered by the UAW–Big Three contracts. First, the turnover is so high that it was hiring new workers in a state that counts unemployment at 9.1 percent. (I had to apply at six plants before I scored.) One reason for the turnover is that the plant is 34 miles from Detroit, and inner-city workers find it difficult to travel that far. As a result, the work force—about half black and half southern white—seemed relatively new and uninterested in UAW affairs. When I arrived, there had been a recent strike vote over safety issues; I was unable to find a single worker in my area who had bothered to vote. . . .

At the end of my fourth shift, I turned in my badge and told the guard I was quitting. Then, out in the parking lot, I saw my friend Willie and explained that I already had a day job and just couldn't handle the night job too. "You mean to say you've quit this job?" he asked incredulously.

I explained again, but somehow, Willie couldn't understand how I could give up a steady job paying $3.77 an hour and take my chances in a state where one out of eleven people is out of work. And it was only then that I realized just how important these jobs are—as miserable as they may be—to the men who have to work them.

amount of light was increased. This and other similar results led Mayo to conclude that as long as the company seemed to be showing concern for the workers, and as long as they were consulted and made part of the experiments, worker morale tended to rise. This tendency—for experimental results to be influenced by the self-consciousness of the subjects—has been known as the *Hawthorne effect* ever since (Herzberg, 1973, pp. 65–67). Negative Hawthorne effects, such as failure to cooperate or slowing down the pace of work, can also result if the workers are suspicious of the experiments.

The results of the Hawthorne experiments stress the fact that workers want to be treated with respect and that group spirit contributes to worker morale and productivity. An organization would do well to promote a feeling of common interest between workers and management and to give workers a voice in determining policies and procedures (Roethlisberger and Dickson, 1939). The human-relations approach, however, is more difficult in some situations than others. What can be done when assembly-line noise makes social relationships impossible? Can all workers be convinced that they and management share common interests? After all, management's interest in high profits and the workers' concern for better wages are sometimes incompatible. Still, Mayo's research has helped make working conditions more agreeable, even when the work itself may be boring. Considerable advances have been made during the last fifty years in the areas of leadership and supervision, the functioning of work groups, and the broadening of the concept of the worker as a human being.

Frederick Herzberg (Champion, 1975, pp. 45–50), a contemporary student of labor relations, lists several factors essential to worker satisfaction:

Freedom from too much supervision
Intrinsic interest of the job
Social cohesion of the work group

Job prestige and status
Pay
Participation in decision making

Management's awareness of these factors does not guarantee that labor's demands will be met. Some companies are interested in good worker morale and low rates of turnover. For this purpose, they have given workers a voice in policy and procedures on the job. Workers at Donnelly Mirrors (Holland, Michigan) and Kaiser Steel (Fontana, California), for example, are actively involved in the management of their companies. This is the policy of *worker participation*. Other companies give stock as a bonus or sell it at low rates to workers in order to give them a vested interest in the company. Many major industries, such as steel and automobiles, are completely unionized, and the demands of labor are negotiated. In a few other cases, companies have shown a paternal interest in workers. The opposite case of apparently total indifference to workers is illustrated in the insert "When Factories Shut Down."

CRAFT, ASSEMBLY LINE, AND AUTOMATION

In the past, the artisan was replaced by the assembly-line workers. Today, the trend is to replace the assembly-line worker with automation. In an automated plant, machinery—instructed by self-correcting computers—operates the equipment. The worker simply watches to make sure nothing goes wrong. Obviously, many workers have been replaced by automation, and even though new jobs are created, the total number of work hours is reduced.

On the positive side, automation eliminates some of the most boring and exhausting jobs, increases efficiency, and holds down production costs. Since automating plants is a very expensive process, large organizations that can afford it are more likely to automate. This is one of the

When factories shut down

"Big Dave" Masiak was once described as the strongest man at the paint factory where he worked; these days he is beset by high blood pressure, headaches, arthritis, diabetes and obesity, and he gets worse every day. He spends his days complaining about his health, or asleep. "When I sleep, nothing hurts," he says.

These ailments did not strike Dave out of the blue; they disable him now because, like many other workers in the U.S. today, he has nothing to do with his time but be a sick man. The factory where Dave had a place in the world has closed down, as do approximately seven in this country every week. According to Sidney Cobb, M.D., who directed a study of the closing of this factory and its impact on the men who worked there, Masiak is as much a cripple now as a man who has gone blind or lost the use of his legs; but for Masiak and others like him there is no disability insurance. (*Institute for Survey Research Newsletter*, University of Michigan, Winter 1970.)

When "Baker Plant" . . . closed down, there was a sharp rise in illness among the workers; half the cases studied suffered from ulcers, arthritis, hypertension severe enough to require hospitalization, alcoholism and depression that required medical help. Masiak was one of the most severely affected, but he was not unique: the plant manager retired to a remote part of Arkansas, "sick and haunted" by the closing he presided over; Baker's last production manager has not let a visitor into his house in the last two years; of Baker's seven salesmen, three died during the closing.

Clearly, the Baker management did not go out of its way to protect its men; Slote [Alfred Slote, author of *Termination: The Closing at Baker Plant*] reports a salaried employee of 33½ years' standing was not allowed to work the extra three months at another branch that would have assured him his pension; and a forklift operator with 25 years at Baker also missed his pension by a few months.

Slote and Cobb both believe that a civilized society has a responsibility to take care of people who get squeezed out when industrial technology changes. They recommend that industrial pension plans should be transferable from one job to another, that unemployment insurance should automatically provide health insurance coverage, and that plants about to close should be required to set up some sort of service to help their employees find new jobs.

Without a program of this kind, workers automated out of their jobs feel alienated from society. As one of them told Slote, "They got laws protecting rapists and murderers, but what are they doing about poor slobs like me."

---

factors that increase the concentration of economic power, as discussed in the previous chapter. From the worker's point of view, automation creates a threat to existing jobs and makes it necessary to learn new skills. Automobile assembly lines are still operating, but some are being replaced by a type of automation in which different sets of machinery take over at each station on the line. In this case, quite a few workers remain at the line watching or even helping to operate the machinery. The ultimate in automation is achieved when people merely feed raw materials automatically into a self-controlling series of machines. When this happens, human labor is reduced to tending panels. More than two-thirds of all manufacturing plants in the United States are at least partly automated (Froomkin, 1968, pp. 480–482).

Since some of the most tiring jobs, especially those involving heavy lifting, have been replaced by automation, workers who are still employed may be more satisfied in automated or semi-automated plants than in assembly-line plants. There are inconsistencies in the evidence however. Some workers complain of having even less sense of control than they had before (Champion, 1975, p. 205).

Worker integration in the automated plant

Is it true that artisans with pride in their work and with considerable independence are happier than employees in either assembly-line or automated plants? Michael Fullan (1970, pp. 1028–1039) studied 1,491 workers in the three different types of work: automobile manufacturing (assembly line), oil refining (automated), and printing (artisans).

Fullan found that 69 percent of the automated-refinery workers had stayed with their jobs for 15 years or more. Only 34 percent of the printers and 20 percent of the automobile workers had remained that long. The turnover of printers was greater because they were readily employable elsewhere. However, the printers rated satisfaction with the company almost as highly as did the refinery workers. Assembly-line workers expressed little satisfaction with their work.

Since wages were only a small percent of the total production cost in the automated plant, the refinery workers found it easier to get pay increases than did the workers in the other industries. Apparently, automation gives certain advantages to those who remain, although it results in a reduced work crew.

Industry and workers' health

The automated plant is cleaner than the assembly-line plant. There is less heavy equipment to move by hand and less physical strain. Some writers have described automation ecstatically as the dawn of a new age of clean, wholesome, pleasant work, replacing the era of sweatshops. Bernard Asbel also credits automation with relieving boredom and providing mental stimulation (1965). Walter Buckingham (1963, pp. 109–118) is more cautious in his praise, but notes that certain definite improvements have occurred. In the pottery industry, closed silos now control the silica dust that has always been a danger to lungs and life. In the petroleum and chemical industries, many toxic substances have been controlled better than in the past.

Despite improvement in some plants, the problems of worker health and safety have tended to become worse. New studies find more and more toxic and carcinogenic (cancer-causing) substances that are poorly controlled even in automated plants. High cancer rates have developed in certain stages of the production of plastics, and black-lung disease still affects over 100,000 coal miners. Franklin Wallich (1972, pp. 1–10) notes that only about 450 chemicals out of about 8,000 used in modern industries are now subject to safety limits. One U.S. Labor Department study finds health and safety hazards to be second in a list of nineteen common complaints among American workers. The Occupational Safety and Health Act of 1970 provides for a check on dangerous equipment, chemicals, and working conditions. Unfortunately, the act is not well enforced (Coles and Huge, 1969). The shocking damage to workers' health described in the insert "Chemical Death" is by no means unique.

In 1976, the University of Washington found, on the basis of a random sampling of 908 workers, that 31 percent of their diseases and medical conditions had originated at work.

Workers in the rubber industry have a 1.7 times greater chance of death from stomach cancer than the average person. Workers in steel-mill coke ovens are over 7.5 times as likely to die of kidney cancer and 10 times as likely to die of lung cancer as workers elsewhere in the industry.

Evidence from a number of fields indicates that while-collar, professional, and service workers are often in as much danger as employees in steel mills, chemical plants and other forms of basic industry.

Dentists' chronic exposure to X-rays, mercury and anesthetics contributes to their abnormally high rates of leukemia, Hodgkin's disease and suicide. Female operating room personnel, with similar exposures, have unusually large numbers of miscarriages and babies with congenital birth defects. Beauticians are extraordinarily susceptible to cardiac problems, lung cancer and respiratory diseases generally. (Cooper and Steiger, 1976, pp. 1, 22–23; copyright © 1976, Los Angeles Times)

Chemical death   RICHARD T. COOPER AND PAUL E. STEIGER

When people are sick, most turn without question to their family doctors, yet the typical family physician knows little about a worker—as employees of Life Science Products Co. in Hopewell, Va., discovered last year.

After only a few weeks of working in the plant, set up two years ago in a converted gas station, many began to suffer dizzy spells, poor vision, tremors. One man later recalled that when he stopped for a beer after work, friends had to help him hold the glass. Inevitably, workers went to their doctors.

Could it be something at the plant, some asked? Probably not, the physicians said. More likely it was overwork or nervousness. Or perhaps too many of those beers on the way home. So, worrying about mortgage payments and just getting by, they returned to work.

One man who could not stop trembling eventually went to see a young specialist in cardiology and internal medicine, a recent emigré from Taiwan named Yi-nan Chou. Chou asked what it was they made in that converted gas station. "Kepone," the man said. Kepone. Chou looked it up in a handbook of poisons.

A chlorinated hydrocarbon related to DDT, combining hexachlorocyclopentadiene and sulfur trioxide, potent in controlling ants, roaches, and banana pests. Chou took samples of the man's blood and urine and sent them to the Federal Center for Disease Control in Atlanta for analysis. Some days later Virginia health authorities arrived in Hopewell and began unraveling a major industrial scandal.

The result: Life Science Co. was shut down, 13 workers were hospitalized and about 40 others were found to have high levels of the pesticide in their blood. Federal indictments were returned against the company, its owners, and Allied Chemical Co., which had been involved in the creation of Life Science, but no way was found to cleanse workers' blood of the Kepone, which had been linked to blood cancer in laboratory animals.

From Richard T. Cooper and Paul E. Steiger, "Occupational Health Hazards—A National Crisis," *Los Angeles Times*, June 27, 1976, Section I, pp. 1, 22, 26. Copyright © 1976 by the Los Angeles Times.

Computers and white-collar jobs

For decades, the greatest growth in employment has been in white-collar and service jobs, which now make up over 60 percent of all employment. White-collar jobs include a wide range of activity, but we are mainly concerned here with secretarial-clerical work. This kind of work is less adaptable to assembly-line techniques and efficiency measurements than many kinds of blue-collar jobs. The efficiency level of this type of work is hard to rate and hard to upgrade, although many firms are experimenting with new techniques (Hyatt, 1972). One possibility for increasing productivity in office work is through the use of computers, or electronic data processing (EDP).

Electronic data processing machines are able to store and retrieve information and are not susceptible to human error. Thus, they have great potential for restructuring office work. The problem of setting up computer programs and understanding how computers work is complex and calls for a computer elite. The tasks of feeding the computer and reading the data, however, are fairly simple. The result is a widening of the gulf between the clerical staff doing routine work and the upper-level staff (International Labor Office, 1967). The long-range effect may be that many white-collar clerical workers will identify even less with management than they have in the past. On the other hand, computerizing leads to many new, specialized jobs halfway between clerical and computer engineering—systems analyst, console operator, coder, tape librarian, and optical scanner—with the number of new jobs growing at a faster pace (Toffler, 1970, p. 109).

Displacement and unemployment

Much unemployment is a result of economic downturns, and in the 1970s it is also influenced by the distribution of age groups in our population. More young people entered the labor force because of the high birthrate between World War II and the 1960s. There are also more women competing for jobs than ever before.

Automation has also affected employment. Sometimes, it results in marked improvement of products or the lowering of prices so that the products are used in much larger quantities than before. When this happens, there may be no resulting unemployment in the industry. In the telephone industry, for example, employment increased from 20,000 in the 1920s to 600,000 in the 1970s (Buckingham, 1963, p. 102). Increased efficiency and better service meant that more people used telephones, so that employment increased rather than declined. Stuart Chase states that if the telephone industry today used 1920s methods, "it would require the entire female population of the country . . . to

Figure 16-2 Automation has eliminated many jobs and created many others. (*IBM*)

handle the present volume of calls'' (1969, p. 119).

On the other hand, if an industry is not expanding but is using more automated equipment, the demand for labor decreases. This has happened in agriculture. Some industries, however, can increase production greatly without bringing about much increase in employment. The electronics industry increased its output by 325 percent in a ten-year period, but employment increased by only 50 percent (Buckingham, 1963, p. 104). The U.S. Labor Department notes that automation of the computer industry at first created large numbers of new jobs—more than were replaced—but it predicts that in the long run, this trend will be reversed (Herman, 1970, pp. 3–8).

Segmental unemployment

Regardless of level of prosperity, *segmental unemployment*—unemployment in certain sections of the country and parts of the economy—remains. This has happened in agricultural regions where hand labor is almost wiped out by machinery; in the Detroit area, where the automobile industry has attracted more workers than it can use; and, until the recent upturn in coal production, the entire region of Appalachia. Other sections of the country with much higher unemployment than average are the inner cities, inhabited largely by blacks.

Edna Bonacich (1976, pp. 34–51) notes that since about 1957, the unemployment rate of blacks has been about twice as high as that of whites. Before about 1930, black unemployment had been lower than that of whites because employers could hire blacks at lower wages. The New Deal legislation of the 1930s made it necessary for employers to pay equal wages to blacks and whites. The immediate result was a growth of unionism and the admittance of black members.

What seemed to be an advantage for the black worker, however, became a disadvantage. Since labor costs increased, industry began to seek ways to lower those costs. Employers opened plants overseas in areas where wages were lower, relocated in the United States in areas of weak unionism and low wages, or resorted to automation. All three methods have been used, and all have hurt blacks more than whites. Relocating in Taiwan, for example, means replacing cheap American labor with cheap foreign labor. Much of that cheap American labor was once black. Relocating in cheap-labor areas of the United States takes industry away from the cities, where most black people now live. Finally, automation provides either a valid reason or an excuse for hiring mainly people with higher education. Although blacks are gradually closing the education gap, whites still retain a considerable advantage. Seniority rules also help whites, and so do discriminatory apprenticeship programs in trade unions. Thus, since 1957, the ratio of unemployed blacks to unemployed whites has been about two to one, and it promises to remain about the same for the foreseeable future.

Partly because of automation, the trend toward a shorter work week and early retirement will probably continue. Many futurologists predict increasing leisure time. It is already true that the average work week leaves considerable leisure time for most workers. Also, the average person lives for many years after retirement. Under these circumstances, it is important to consider leisure as well as work.

WORK-RELATED LEISURE

Work and leisure activities are connected in a number of ways. In the first place, many leisure activities—skiing, boating, scuba-diving, or traveling—are expensive. Only people with good incomes can pursue these. Ghetto residents must rely on school-related recreation, or they may pass the time by hanging out on street corners. People often make friends where they work. Since the majority of leisure activities involve groups, workers may influence each other in their choice of pastime. Job experiences also train people for certain types of activities off the job. People whose work involves dealing with the public carry this over to their leisure and even retirement, often belonging to clubs and associations (Atchley, 1971, pp. 13–17). Also, belonging to associations is positively correlated with social-class position. It follows, then, that businesspeople and executives will spend much of their leisure time in clubs and business associations. In such cases, the distinction between work and play is rather fine. Finally, leisure can either be spent in activity that reinforces work, as in the cases just mentioned, or in reaction against work. Many people try to "get away from it all" by going to a remote mountain or island retreat. In earlier times in America, leisure activities were usually of the former type.

American ethics have traditionally stressed the value of work more than leisure. This standard derives from the Protestant ethic, discussed in Chapter 14. Work was part of the religion of early Puritanism, and it has taken on almost the same meaning in later American culture. Today, increasing productivity and the shorter work week have turned us into a society that is almost embarrassed by all our leisure. The result is an in-between situation. On the one hand, we are not all hard-driving and work-oriented. On the other hand, the work orientation remains so strong in many of us that we cannot enjoy leisure. We must often disguise it as work.

Leisure as work

Leisure is time free from work or duties. The old Puritan work ethic detests idleness. The best thing to do with leisure, then, is to make it productive—that is, turn it into work. Early Americans combined work and recreation by means of quilting bees, corn-husking bees, house raisings, and similar group activities. Modern people who cannot free themselves from the work ethic and who lack other resources some-

Figure 16-3 Some people convert leisure activities such as golf into work or goal-oriented tasks. Success at such activities is just as significant to them as success at work. To this type of person, the motorized golf cart in this picture becomes an efficient vehicle for completing a task, rather than a sports accessory. (*Fritz Menle, Photo Researchers, Inc.*)

times feel threatened by leisure. Connie O'Connor describes one such case:

He finds it impossible to enjoy the activities of family life and does not particularly like social events. He likes to have a goal to work for and attain, then set up another one and attain that. When he is forced to cease, even for a short while, in his efforts to work toward this goal, he becomes very obviously distressed. "My husband is a very hard man to live with," declares his wife. "He always has to be engaged in activities where he can grow. He never wants to share in an interest and rarely shows affection or gives of himself in any way other than sex. That is performed in a more businesslike than loving manner." (O'Connor, 1966, p. 26)

The man described above is by no means unique. His counterpart could be found in many compulsive moonlighters, who take extra jobs when they are not fully occupied by their primary jobs, or in businesspeople who can never tear themselves away from the office.

Other cases of making work out of leisure are not quite as obvious, but they definitely exist. Examples range from studying self-improvement books to eating purely for nutrition, not pleasure. Thousands of people play golf or tennis to improve their game, not for relaxation. Failure to do well in these sports is at least as frustrating as a bad day at the office. Lewis and Brissett have written an article entitled "Sex as Work," in which they argue that our many books of expert advice about sex stress not enjoyment but work, effort, and duty (1967, pp. 8–18).

A shift from work to leisure

Robert Dubin (1963, pp. 53–72) found that for most factory workers, leisure rather than work is the most interesting part of life. Professional and white-collar workers are more reluctant to retire; they still look upon their work as more important than leisure. However, they usually have a number of leisure activities and for that reason adjust to retirement better than factory workers (Atchley, 1971, p. 14). Since factory work is not rewarded by high status, it is only natural that factory workers should think of work mainly in utilitarian terms. It provides money for a home, food, clothing, and fun. For professionals and white-collar workers, the situation is somewhat different, but probably not as different as in the past. "The newer conception of the fully developed . . . man is that of a person who regards his ability to perform and enjoy leisure activities as much a reflection of his personal qualities as success at work (Winter, Rabone, and Chesler, 1968, p. 373). How the money is spent becomes almost as important as how it was earned, and much of that spending is for leisure. The executive might gain as much status

from a good golf game as from work efficiency. Social relations, community projects, educational pursuits, and home activities can give meaning to life. In fact, there is a long-running debate about human nature: Are we basically workers, fighters and strugglers, philosophers, or creatures of play? Johann Huizinga has stressed play as a means of human development, imagination, perception, and mentality in general (1955). The play ethic, however, can lead to activities that can only be called "subterranean values" in a work-oriented society.

Leisure and subterranean values

Matza and Sykes (1961, pp. 712–719) find parallels between the viewpoints and activities of delinquent gangs and a number of what they call *subterranean* (hidden) *values* of middle-class society. Delinquent gangs are contemptuous of the "square" world of work. Their goals are thrills and excitement. The most readily available source of excitement for them is in defiance of the law or sometimes in violence to maintain "rep" or to prove "heart." Teenagers who feel they have nowhere to go in any case show little interest in the work ethic. They expect a life of nonwork or of drifting from job to job.

The nonwork, adventurous attitude, Matza and Sykes point out, is not too different from the viewpoints of aristocrats or medieval knights, who disdained any work but that of the sword. Generally, illegal activities such as theft are not condoned by respectable people. Yet it is interesting to note that many middle-class people are caught shoplifting for fun. Nearly all Americans watch the violent, action-packed series that occupy many prime viewing hours on television. It should not be surprising, then, that lower-class delinquents, who live with boredom and enforced leisure, should pick up such values. Nor is such behavior limited to the lower classes. Middle-class youth also experience much leisure and considerable boredom. They, too, are frequently involved in scrapes with the law. One example is the middle-class gang, the Saints, described by Chambliss in Chapter 9.

Law-abiding Americans past their teen years may feel a similar fascination with daring and adventure. Sky-diving, ballooning, hang-gliding, scuba-diving, tearing up the terrain with motorcycles, hunting, and skiing are legitimate means of seeking thrills by people who have considerable leisure and hold jobs that are no more adventurous than sitting at a desk.

Social norms have always stressed alcohol in moderation. However, there are also subterranean values that have pictured the "hard-drinkin'" man as an admirable, robust type who can drink everyone under the table—a red-blooded American boy. Alcohol continues to be our most abused drug. Still, it is too common to provide much of a kick for people looking for new thrills. Instead, they turn to the latest fad, whether marijuana or cocaine.

Gambling has some of the characteristics of subterranean values. Gambling is exciting because it involves risks. The gambler, like the thief, is sure that this time luck will strike. Victor Barnouw (1975, pp. 291–292) says that there is more gambling among primitive people who believe in benevolent supernatural beings than among those who have threatening gods. His thesis seems to parallel the gambler's faith in "Lady Luck." For the gambler, the dream of the big haul makes success through work seem dull. Although friends at a weekly poker game don't dream of great fortunes, the risk factor is very important to their pleasure.

Jo M. Senters (1971, pp. 21–32) notes the importance of risk taking in recreation, as in other areas of life, for the aggressive business-

Figure 16-4 The subterranean values of thrill and risk make gambling popular. (*Barbara Pfeffer, Photo Researchers, Inc.*)

The assembly line takes most of the satisfaction of achievement and artistry out of work, as well as divorcing workers from the product of their labor and the tools of production.

person, politician, or military leader. Senters tests the hypothesis that in any game situation, we try to make sure that chances run about 50-50, win or lose. Otherwise, the risk factor has no attraction. In an investigation of shuffleboard teams, Senters found that team members were constantly shifted around to keep up an almost perfect 50-50 balance. As players became more expert, the stakes were gradually increased. A lot of gambling, Senters concludes, can be seen in terms of *compensation theory*. This theory holds that people who live a rather routine, boring work life, with regular pay but no chance for advancement or change, are particularly prone to create situations with uncertain conditions. The subterranean value of risk taking supersedes the "up front" values of steadiness, certainty, and dependability.

THE GROWTH OF LEISURE

The above emphasis on leisure as work and on leisure as an expression of subterranean values does not imply that all people are either "workaholics" or out for kicks. A 1974 Gallup Poll showed 46 percent of Americans listing television viewing as their favorite pastime. Millions of Americans are primarily passive viewers, watching games, television, or motion pictures. Millions more are active participants in some kind of sports. Some take part in community theater or the local symphony or get involved in popular crafts.

Americans are also tireless travelers. They drive all over their own country and take tours overseas. Figures on visits to national parks show the spirit of tourism. In 1966, to celebrate the fiftieth anniversary of the National Park Service, the national parks prepared for more visitors than ever before. Although they expected 80 million people, they actually took in 133 million (Catton, 1971, p. 105). Reasons include an interest in nature and a desire to escape city crowds at least for a while. Ironically, the popularity of such escapes to mountains or parks

makes the throng there almost as great as that of the city.

People also watch sports and play games. They do this partly for the intrinsic interest of these pursuits and partly to escape into a world where the rules are simpler than those of real life. They find such games so thoroughly absorbing that their everyday worries are blotted out—at least temporarily.

With the growth of income and leisure, it is only natural that leisure activities should expand and that the "work" component of leisure should diminish. In our "aspirin age," there is a demand for total relaxation—for television programs that make no demands on the intelligence or imagination or for jaunts to the beach or the woods. A life in which most kinds of work are routine helps to promote participant and spectator sports. The almost universal desire to gamble indicates that gambling will continue despite laws or sermons to the contrary. Whatever one's tastes or desires, there seem to be more and more channels for their expression as the leisure ethic grows stronger and the work ethic fades.

SUMMARY

Besides being a source of income, work organizes one's time and provides a sense of identity and self-worth. Friendships are made on the job, and the job influences all aspects of one's lifestyle. In a survey, young workers generally agreed that they would want to hold jobs even if they had enough money to live without working. People past middle age, especially those with prestigious jobs, are apprehensive about retirement. Work is important for people in a society such as ours, with a strong work ethic.

However, people are becoming more and more concerned with *job satisfaction*. A majority of young workers rate interesting work, friendly co-workers, and a chance to see results, to use one's mind, and to develop skills as very important. All these criteria rated as high as pay, if not higher. Still, 25 million Americans work at unsatisfying, low-skill jobs. Many others work at advertising or selling products that do little or no good.

U.S. Labor Department projections into the mid-1980s indicate that some college graduates will work at less desirable jobs than a college education has generally commanded. The result is an *aspiration gap* between work desired and work available. The aspiration gap is especially serious for women and minority workers, who, even in times of full employment, find it hard to get jobs for which they are qualified.

Most of the upper-level jobs now available are with large corporations or various branches of government. Bureaucracies are often accused of inefficiency and routinization, producing the compliant *organization man*. However, Kohn concludes that most workers in bureaucratic jobs are both well educated and open minded, and they value self-direction. Their jobs are usually demanding and complex. Some upper-level employees develop a strong identification with the organization, but professionals often identify more with their profession. Some are idealistic about the services they can perform as professionals, as in the case of lawyers championing the poor.

Studies of worker satisfaction date back to the last century, when it was assumed that factory workers would like routine jobs requiring no thought or decision making. The assembly line, devised by *efficiency engineers*, was believed to represent worker welfare as well as efficiency. But recent studies show strong *alienation* from assembly-line jobs, even if the pay is good. Modern worker-satisfaction research concludes that workers like to be treated as reasoning beings. They *see* themselves as capable of holding interesting and varied jobs, and in many cases, they like to participate in decision making. This *human-relations approach* is taken by some companies. Others are extremely callous concerning worker needs. Crafts demanding advanced skills appear to be the most satisfying blue-collar jobs. Jobs in automated plants rate

second, and assembly-line jobs are rated third.

Much industrial work is dangerous to health and safety. Coal mining involves accidents and damage to the lungs. Chemicals used in industrial plants bring similar dangers and also increase the risk of cancer. Despite new safety regulations and improvements in some industries, work health and safety show no overall improvement. A number of white-collar jobs are also risky to health.

Automation has resulted in worries about unemployment, but the job picture is mixed. Although automation replaces jobs, it sometimes results in great expansion, causing a net gain in jobs. If, however, industry does not expand, automation causes a net loss in jobs. The latter situation now affects about two-thirds of American industrial plants to some degree. Automation also affects white-collar workers, especially when computers do much of the routine office work.

For many years, unemployment has particularly affected unskilled black workers. Before the 1930s, a larger percentage of black people were employed than whites, though nearly always in low-paying jobs. Now, such factors as automation, a flight of industry to low-wage areas at home or overseas, and minimum wage laws make it more difficult for unskilled workers to get jobs.

Leisure is closely related to work in many ways. Our jobs determine how much we can spend on recreation and with whom we associate. People who like their work sometimes follow pastimes that are similar to their work. Others try to flee from any reminders of their work. Then there are people who are so firmly tied to the work ethic that they can't take pleasure in recreation. They even turn games into work.

Despite the work ethic, most people have ample time for leisure activities. Some low-status industrial workers are more interested in the status to be gained from recreation than from work. A few of them, particularly those of lower-class background, have never absorbed the work ethic. But even hard-working people with good positions usually have a number of pastimes. Such pursuits make retirement easier for these people than for those who have never developed interests outside their work.

Matza and Sykes suggest that middle-class Americans are somewhat comparable to excitement-seeking teenagers in holding a number of *subterranean values*. These subterranean values are seen in many kinds of recreation: skiing, hang-gliding, ballooning, scuba-diving, motorcycle racing, or even heavy drinking. Such values show a repudiation of the work ethic and a love of risk, as in gambling. Gambling, especially, seems to free people temporarily from too much regulation and allows them to take risks and make their own decisions. The adoption of subterranean values might be seen as a way of rebelling against an overly tense world of work.

Study guide

Terms to know

Job satisfaction
Aspiration gap
Organization man
Alienation
Efficiency engineer

Human-relations approach
Hawthorne effect
Worker participation
Automation
Segmental unemployment

Leisure
Work-related leisure
Subterranean values

Names to know

Frederick Taylor
Frederick Herzberg

Melvin L. Kohn
Johann Huizinga

Self-test

Part I. Multiple Choice. Select the best of the four alternative answers:

1 A majority of people look upon work as (**a**) a source of income, (**b**) something that gives purpose to their lives, (**c**) a source of personal identity, (**c**) all the above.

2 Workers in their fifties with high-status jobs were concerned with a sense of futility and the possibility of an early death when (**a**) quizzed about financial matters, (**b**) interviewed about their friends, (**c**) questioned about their insurance policies, (**d**) asked about their interest in retirement.

3 According to Levin, 90 percent of the unemployed (**a**) blamed themselves for their predicament, (**b**) blamed their former employers for their problems, (**c**) blamed the economic system for their problems, (**d**) placed the blame vaguely on fate or bad luck.

4 For a majority of young workers, the highest items on the list of job attractiveness were (**a**) friendly co-workers and job interest, (**b**) good pay and being able to see results, (**c**) respect for the company they worked for and a chance to improve skills, (**d**) participation in decision making and owning company stock.

5 Where does unemployment hit the hardest? (**a**) among white teenagers, (**b**) among black teenagers, (**c**) among women, (**d**) among the middle aged.

6 According to Kohn, men who work in bureaucratic organizations tend to value (**a**) conformity, (**b**) unchanging routines, (**c**) self-direction, (**d**) political futures.

7 In general, the Hawthorne effect demonstrated that (**a**) workers prefer to be left alone by management, (**b**) workers are concerned about being treated with human dignity, (**c**) a sense of *esprit de corps* has nothing to do with worker morale, (**d**) workers slow down when being observed by researchers.

8 Herzberg identified several important factors in worker satisfaction, including *all but one* of

the following: (**a**) potential for early retirement, (**b**) pay, (**c**) freedom from too much supervision, (**d**) social cohesion of the work group.

9 Approximately what portion of all manufacturing plants in the United States are at least partly automated? (**a**) one-third, (**b**) two-thirds, (**c**) one-half, (**d**) five-eighths.

10 Which of the following is *not* one of the methods used by industrial organizations to lower costs? (**a**) operating in areas of weak unionism, (**b**) operating overseas in areas of low wages, (**c**) resorting to automation, (**d**) encouraging unionization.

11 In risk taking, the values of orderliness, certainty, and dependability are superseded by (**a**) subterranean values, (**b**) reliability values, (**c**) normative values, (**d**) work values.

12 Who are *least* likely to consider television viewing their favorite pastime? (**a**) high school dropouts, (**b**) housewives, (**c**) college graduates, (**d**) high school graduates.

13 Athletic contests and games are popular because (**a**) they provide an escape into a world of simpler values, (**b**) the contests are thoroughly absorbing, (**c**) they temporarily blot out everyday worries, (**d**) all the above.

14 Barnouw concludes that gambling is most common in cultures that believe in (**a**) diligence, (**b**) stern gods, (**c**) kindly gods, (**d**) astrology.

15 Work becomes related to leisure activities because of (**a**) leisure-time expense, (**b**) friendships and group activities, (**c**) a reaction against the work pattern, (**d**) all the above.

Part II. True-False Questions

1 Neither young nor old workers would be willing to continue work if they had enough money to get by without working.

2 Work satisfaction generally tends to increase with age.

3 Well-paid workers in their fifties indicated a great interest in retiring so that they could draw their pension benefits.

4 It is usually possible to predict what the rate of unemployment will be in the next four or five years.

5 Wood expects a growing shortage of laborers in Groups IV and V.

6 Women have a greater aspiration gap than men.

7 Kohn found that the people most often recruited for positions with bureaucratic organizations come from rural backgrounds and have an average level of education.

8 More than in the two previous decades, students of the 1970s and early 1980s have to settle for whatever jobs are available rather than the jobs they aspire to.

9 White-collar workers tend to be more alienated from the organization for which they work than are blue-collar workers.

10 Studies have shown that it would be of some value to organizations to give workers a minor voice in new policies and procedures.

11 Dubin found that because they usually have a number of leisure activities, white-collar workers tend to adjust to retirement better than do factory workers.

12 A 1974 Gallup Poll found that 46 percent of Americans listed television viewing as their favorite pastime.

13 Lewis and Brisset found that sex counselors have to remind their clients that sex is not "something to work at" but rather to be enjoyed.

14 Robert Dubin found that many factory workers consider leisure activities a more interesting part of life than their jobs.

15 Traditionally, American ethics have stressed leisure more than work.

Questions for discussion

1 To what degree have the following motivated you to a college education: Education, work, athletic competition, friendship, boredom outside school, meeting the opposite sex, unemployment? Is there anything about your college experience that will help prepare you for leisure activities as well as for work?

2 Do you think the availability of leisure time contributes to drug use, crime, welfare abuse, fights, and discrimination? What proportion of such problems would you expect to be solved by full employment?

3 What measures are being taken in your town or community to lessen the aspiration gap for minorities and women? What could be done to speed up the process? Discuss your own experiences with the aspiration gap.

4 The possibility of being unemployed despite a college education must have a serious effect on optimism and various other attitudes. In your class, or among your group of friends, can you see any evidence of such a possibility affecting political attitudes, achievement motivation, or attitudes toward the role of government as employer?

5 What would you do to promote a greater degree of worker satisfaction if you were the manager of a large number of employees? Consider those things that are being done and try to expand on them.

6 Improved worker satisfaction may have many great implications for society in general. Discuss the possible relationships between improved worker satisfaction and any other social institution—for example, marriage and family, attitudes toward government and the economy, education, etc.

7 What are your leisure activities? Do you ever think of ways in which you could make a living from your hobby? For example, have you thought to yourself, "I enjoy sewing so much, maybe I could open my own boutique and sell handmade clothes"; or "Fishing is my favorite sport. I'll bet I could become a fishing guide in Canada." Discuss such ideas with others. Also consider what factors prevent these fantasies from becoming realities.

8 Do you ever experience a feeling of cognitive dissonance regarding your leisure activities? For example, do the values of work and leisure clash? Do your leisure activities seem a waste of time? Do you enjoy leisure activities that are harmful to the environment or that are more expensive than you can really afford? How do you resolve cognitive dissonance in these cases?

Projects

1 Using material available in the offices of vocational counselors, compile a list of occupational titles that might interest college students. Try especially to select unusual titles. Find out how many members of your class have thought about any of the occupations you list or have ever looked over the titles in the counselor's office.

2 Visit an assembly plant in or near your community. Talk with a few of the workers in the plant about their likes and dislikes on the job. Evaluate the results. Do these jobs produce alienation? Try to provide an explanation for your conclusions.

3 Some leisure activities are actually work in a slightly different form. Other activities are a total repudiation of the workplace, as when a very polite salesclerk likes to play a bruising game of soccer on weekends. Interview several people about the relationship between their work and leisure and try to reach a theoretical conclusion. Do some types of jobs demand more escape than others? What kinds? Why?

Suggested readings

Goldman, Ralph M.: "Life-Span Educational Insurance: A Proposal," *Educational Record*, vol. 51, Winter 1970, pp. 60–65. What is the best way to be sure people will continue to be employable at all ages? What is the best way to prepare people for recreational as well as work activities? Goldman proposes an educational insurance program that would take care of retraining needs at all times in life. He also favors a school experience that would be applicable both to work and recreation.

Kohn, Melvin L., and Carmi Schooler: "Occupational Experience and Psychological Functioning," *American Sociological Review*, vol. 38, February 1973, pp. 97–118. What are the psychological effects of having a job that calls for constant mental activity? The results are very favorable, say these two researchers of the National Institute of Mental Health. To settle for a dull job is to invite a decline in mental functioning.

Levinson, Andrew: "The Rebellion of Blue-Collar Youth," *The Progressive*, vol. 36, October 1972, pp. 38–42. Are young industrial workers increasingly discontented despite reasonably good pay? Evidence of absenteeism, high turnover rate, and shoddy workmanship leads Levinson to say "yes." This article also contains a good description of the ills of factory work.

Newsweek, editors: "A Matter of Life and Death," *Newsweek*, August 17, 1970, pp. 64–66. The trend in industrial accidents is up. During the years of the Vietnamese war, more people were killed while at work than were killed in Vietnam.

Pfeiffer, Eric, and Glenn C. Davis: "The Use of Leisure Time in Middle Life," *Industrial Gerontology*, vol. 9, Spring 1971, pp. 37–39. A number of surveys taken among middle-aged people show them to be extremely work-oriented, even more so than when they were younger, even though their retirement is growing close. Pfeiffer and Davis discuss a need for training for leisure and more flexible retirement policies.

Books

Johannis, Theodore B., Jr., and C. Neil Bull: *Sociology of Leisure*, Sage Publications, Beverly Hills, Calif., 1971. A series of research articles on leisure activities, varying from light description to attempts at theory.

Terkel, Studs: *Working*, Avon Books, New York, 1974. What do people think about their work? Read what the farmer, the miner, the heavy-equipment operator, the airline stewardess, the stone-mason, editor, barber, cabdriver, poet, occupational therapist, and gravedigger have to say. These and dozens of others were interviewed by Terkel on this extremely readable book. You will find only minimal correlation between job satisfaction and job status but considerable correlation between skill, interest, and job satisfaction.

Key to questions. Multiple Choice: 1-d; 2-d; 3-a; 4-a; 5-b; 6-c; 7-b; 8-a; 9-b; 10-d; 11-a; 12-c; 13-d; 14-c; 15-d. True-False: 1-F; 2-T; 3-F; 4-F; 5-T; 6-T; 7-F; 8-T; 9-F; 10-T; 11-T; 12-T; 13-F; 14-T; 15-F.

SOURCES OF CHANGE

This chapter examines trends in population, their social consequences, and national policies regarding population. After reading it, you should be able to:

1 Understand why population growth has become a worldwide problem.

2 Explain and argue the merits and defects of Malthus's views on population.

3 Explain demographic transition and give examples of countries in different transitional phases.

4 See the consequences of population growth in the areas of military and political power, life-styles, and human freedom.

5 Recognize the reasons for worldwide conflict of opinion as to what population policies governments should adopt.

6 Debate various ideas as to what should be done about population—pronatalist and antinatalist policies, persuasive and coercive approaches.

7 Understand the population changes taking place in the United States and their probable results.

17
POPULATION TRENDS AND CONSEQUENCES

The earth is a small planet with a little less than 200 million square miles of surface area. Two-thirds of that area is covered with water or ice, and about one-sixth of the remainder with high mountains, tundra, desert, or semiarid terrain. The remaining one-sixth of the earth supports almost all its 4 billion human inhabitants. The United States, excluding Alaska, has a population density of about 65 people per square mile and is already beginning to seem crowded. In contrast, the Netherlands, Belgium, and England have population densities of close to 1,000 per square mile, and Bangladesh has nearly 2,000.

The earth has only recently become crowded with people. The human species originated about 3 or 4 million years ago and increased in numbers very slowly. Many died of disease or food shortage; others were killed by wild animals or by each other. During the millions of years of early human life, people migrated over many parts of the world, but dense population never built up. Then, about 8,000 years ago, plants and animals were domesticated and towns began to grow. By the time of the birth of Christ, the population of the earth had increased to 250 million. Better agricultural methods and the beginnings of the industrial revolution pushed the figure to 1 billion by 1800. In a little over a century, another billion people were added, then more rapidly another, and another. At the present rate of increase, another billion will be added in about twelve or fourteen years. Each year, world population increases by about 80 million. If the entire Sahara Desert were irrigated, it could support an agricultural population equivalent to the number of people that are currently being added to the world's population every two or three years.

What caused the unprecedented population explosion of recent history, and what are its possible limits? How is the population distributed, and where are the increases most rapid? What are the present implications of population increase with regard to food supply, economic planning, government policies on family size, and the future peace, freedom, and welfare of the world? Does the population explosion concern only the rapidly growing regions of the world, or does it also affect less crowded and more affluent countries, such as the United States?

Religious norms and the most usual attitudes have generally been *pronatalist*, that is, in favor of a large number of births. Such wishes as "may your tribe increase" and such admonitions as "multiply and replenish the earth" reflect the values of the earliest human societies. In spite of pronatalist values, *infanticide* (killing of babies) has been widely practiced in a large number of societies. Newborn babies in primitive tribes were often killed if there were already too many mouths to feed. Infanticide was allowed in such ancient societies as Athens and Sparta. More recently, missionaries have tried to stop it in many parts of Africa and Asia. Since urban populations have not had as high rates of natural increase as rural populations, one can assume that various means of population control have been used, including late marriage, celibacy, contraception, abortion, and infanticide. Thus, regardless of societal ideals, city dwellers as well as primitives have held down populations when children are too much of a burden.

CONTROLS ON POPULATION

Thomas Malthus, in 1798, was the first person to write an influential essay on population. Malthus noted that in general, such "preventive controls" as celibacy, abortion, or infanticide had been far less important than "positive controls": pestilence, famine, war, and vice. As late as 1720, an outbreak of bubonic plague killed half the population of Marseilles. Smallpox was almost as devastating, and tuberculosis ran a close third. Famines occurred often in Europe and in other parts of the world, sometimes as a result of another positive control on population—war. For example, in the Thirty Years' War (1618–1648), some of the villages of Germany and Central Europe were completely depopulated, with wolves roaming the streets of what had once been inhabited places. The last of Malthus's positive controls, vice, results in veneral disease—which, before the age of modern medicine, could lead to sterilization.

Malthus contended that if the positive controls on population were removed, population would increase faster than the food supply. In fact, he developed a mathematical formula (only a rough approximation of reality) which stated that population increases by *geometric progression*; that is, it can double every 25 years (1, 2, 4, 8, 16, 32, etc.). Food supply, on the other hand, increases only by *arithmetic progression* (1, 2, 3, 4, 5, 6, etc.). If other checks on population failed, said Mathus, then starvation would stop its increase. There was one other possibility, however: the use of "preventive controls" of the type mentioned above: late marriage, celibacy, abortion, and contraception. Malthus said little or nothing about aborption and contraception, since he was morally opposed to them.

The United States, Europe, and the Malthusian principles

A glance at the United States would lead one to believe that Malthus's predictions were more wrong than right. The United States has had one of the highest rates of population increase in world history, caused by both immigration and a very high birthrate. Our birthrate once reached 50 per thousand, in contrast to the present rate of about 15 per thousand. From less than 4 million at the first census in 1790, the population grew to 206 million by 1970. Yet our food supply has grown even more rapidly than our population.

Obviously, Malthus's argument does not apply to the early history of a newly opened continent. However, would it be valid later on? Is the argument valid for Europe, which already had a fairly dense population in Mathus's day?

William L. Langer has researched certain preventive measures to control population growth in Europe (1972, pp. 93–99). One method was to deny many people the right to marry. Wealthy families had numerous servants, who were usually required to be single. On the Continent, although not in England, paupers were not allowed to marry or to live together out of wedlock. The upper classes were worried about the spread of undesirable elements. According to Langer:

> The evidence, which is admittedly sparse, suggests that among women of child bearing age in France, 30 to 40 percent remained unmarried, and that only some 40 percent of men founded families. Many unmarried men took refuge in the military or the clergy; the spinsters might take up an aunt's role in a brother's household or enter domestic service. Many writers of the time were concerned for the future of France; a modern writer speaks of the 18th century *crise de nupitalité* (crisis of marriage). (p. 95; copyright © 1972 by Scientific American, Inc. All rights reserved)

Although illegitimacy was forbidden, it was inevitable that many illegitimate children would be born. Therefore infanticide was practiced on a large scale, and some of the orphanages and hospitals maintained for foundlings were little more than slaughterhouses. Napoleon I, in an attempt to spare the lives of infants, called for the establishment of institutions for their care in all provinces, but the care there was so bad that an estimated 80 percent of them died.

Despite all these antinatalist policies, the population of Europe grew rapidly. The proportion of Europeans and people of European descent increased from 24 percent to 36 percent of the world's total (Thompson, 1959, p. 12). This increase came about partly because the bubonic plague had practically ended, inoculations for smallpox were started in the late 1700s, and sanitation and medical care were being improved. Even more important was the removal of Mathus's most important control—famine. Potatoes and corn had been introduced from the New World, vastly increasing the food supply of the poor people of Europe. Langer gives most of the credit to the lowly potato and concludes that in one way Malthus was entirely right: Food supply was the ultimate factor permitting or prohibiting population growth. Further, the newly industrialized Europe was able to live from its trade with the outside world, selling finished goods and bringing in the foods and raw materials it could not produce for itself.

This brief glance at Western history raises an important question: Can the experience of the United States and Europe be duplicated in all parts of the world? Is it possible that the world's population will continue to increase, and material well-being along with it? To answer this question, we must consider what is called "demographic transition," to see how the population facts of the late twentieth century compare with those of Europe in the seventeenth, eighteenth, and nineteenth centuries.

DEMOGRAPHIC TRANSITION

Demography is the study of population, and *demographic transition* refers to population change. Specifically, the term refers to historical changes in birthrate and death rate. *Birthrate* and *death rate* are the two most important demographic processes and are usually given in terms of births or deaths per 1,000 population per year. Population growth or decline depends upon the balance between birthrate and death

rate except in countries with significant rates of immigration or emigration.

Demographic transition consists of four phases and a possible fifth phase. *Phase 1* describes the state of survival of most of the prehistoric past. There were both high birthrates and high death rates, so that population remained fairly steady. *Phase 2* is the period just discussed in relation to Europe: a high birthrate (in spite of possible efforts at control), and a rapidly declining death rate caused by less starvation, disease, and war and the development of medicine. *Phase 3* appears when birthrates begin to decline, as they were doing in Europe and the United States by the late nineteenth century. In phase 3, however, the birthrate remains considerably higher than the death rate, so that population continues to increase. *Phase 4* is a state in which both the birthrate and the death rate have declined to very low, approximately equal levels, so that population increases very slowly if at all. Phase 4 is probably best exemplified by modern Sweden. West Germany and Poland are in approximately the same phase. It is now being approached by the United States, England, and much of Europe. *Phase 5* occurs when the death rate exceeds the birthrate, so that population declines. Phase 5 occurred in many American Indian tribes, in Ireland during the potato famine of the mid-nineteenth century, in equatorial Africa during the slave trade, and to a slight degree in France between World Wars I and II.

Industrialized and developing nations

The highly industrialized countries are in or very close to phase 4 of demographic transition today. The developing countries are in phases 2 and 3. The United States and nearly all of Europe, including the European part of the Soviet Union, are experiencing a very slow population increase. Most of Asia, the Middle East, Africa, and Latin America are in a state of rapid population increase. Since birthrates are always uncertain, future populations are predicted within general ranges rather than with precise figures. If the present trend of lower birthrates continues in the industrialized world, the population of these regions will probably increase between 30 and 60 percent by the year 2050. On the other hand, even if the developing countries manage to cut their growth rate to only 1 percent per year by the year 2000 (which is very unlikely), their populations will grow 250 percent by 2050. If no change in birthrate occurs and the death rate continues to fall, the developing world could increase its population by 1,000 percent by 2050, with ten people for every one living now! This trend would probably be blocked by starvation, if nothing else.

SOCIAL AND POLITICAL CONSEQUENCES OF POPULATION CHANGE

Population change has important consequences for all phases of social life, including productivity, military power, life-styles, and individual freedom. The dire warnings about overpopulation make it easy to forget that until about 1900 there was much concern, especially in the United States, about reaching an optimum level of population. *Optimum population* refers to the theoretical point at which population is exactly right for full development of natural resources and economic potential. Obviously, it is possible for a country to have too few people to fill its labor needs. However, it would be impossible to define the point at which it has exactly the right number of people, since the need for labor varies with the type of industrial system and the level of prosperity. The same is true of military power; types of weapons strongly influence how many soldiers are needed.

Population and military power

Population is only one factor in military power, but an important one. The power of Rome depended on its system of government and the development of its military strategy. However, one of the most important decisions of Rome was to extend citizenship to conquered provinces so that it would have enough people to swell the size of its army and navy.

Militarists have always understood the importance of population. One reason Napoleon opened orphanages in France was so that more of the babies would grow up and add to French military power. Mussolini in Italy and Hitler in Germany encouraged population growth for the sake of national power. Mussolini gave prizes to women with the largest numbers of children. Hitler encouraged a high birthrate, even out of wedlock.

There is no Napoleon, Hitler, or Mussolini today, but anxiety over population is still with us. Probably no country that feels itself surrounded by potential enemies would welcome the prospect of a shrinking population. The Soviet Union, worried over the hugh population of China, follows a pronatalist policy, granting allotments to families with children and providing nursery care to working mothers. France, although not as anxious about invasion as in the past, follows a pronatalist policy of family allotments that has helped to reverse the population decline it experienced between the two World Wars (Bourgeois-Pichot, 1974, pp. 545–591). Israel, worried over Arab power, encourages immigration. On the other hand, a population that is sick or starving is a liability rather than an asset. Today, education and technology have become much more important than mere numbers of people.

Population and life-styles

A nation's entire life-style can be affected by overpopulation. In countries where increased population simply means increased poverty, people suffer need as population grows. Surplus children from rural areas must go to the cities to find ill-paid jobs or to beg or steal; some women turn to prostitution. When these conditions are

Figure 17-1 Communist China's huge, well-trained population is seen as a military threat by the Soviet Union. This may help explain a Russian pro-natalist policy. (*Eastfoto*)

combined with knowledge of a better life in the outside world, revolutionary potential grows. In discussing collective behavior, we noted that revolutions start among people who have been led to expect a better life.

In affluent countries, overpopulation affects life-style in an entirely different way. People realize that it is more important to ensure a productive and rewarding life for a few children than to produce many children with no chance for the future. Women's lives are no longer completely absorbed by family duties. They become free to compete for positions of status in the world and to mobilize safeguards for their rights. Such devices as late marriage, celibacy, and infanticide are no longer needed to control population. Contraception and abortion are used instead. A two-child family becomes the norm, and the couple with ten or twelve children is no longer praised.

Partly because people in the well-populated but affluent parts of the world are less absorbed in family relations than before, they become more concerned with individual fulfillment. Some become ambitious for success in their chosen occupation. Others devote their lives to the pursuit of pleasure. While interesting careers and wealth are available to the few, increased bitterness and alienation result for the many envious poor. Physical poverty is generally not as bad as in the early days of the industrial revolution. However, spiritual poverty may be greater—the feeling of worthlessness experienced by those who feel left out.

Population and national development

Developing countries with strong leaders have given high priority to industrialization. They want to raise the standard of living and to avoid famine. Modern agricultural methods must replace inefficient methods of the past, and new crops must be tried. The *green revolution*—marked improvement in types of crops and agricultural methods designed to avert famine—becomes a necessity. Only the countries that launch successful programs of development can feel secure against famine or revolution. Although overpopulation is a problem in most developing countries, many African and Latin American nations think population increase is necessary for economic growth (Ehrlich and Ehrlich, 1970, pp. 248–249). Brazil, rightly or wrongly, believes that its rapid development depends on continued population growth. The thinly populated Republic of Ireland is the only European country to have experienced a century-long population decline. It wants more people, especially those in the prime years of life. It is during these prime years that many of Ireland's own people have emigrated to the United States. Although over half as large as England, Ireland's population is only 3 million, about one-fifteenth that of England. Population and national development will be discussed further throughout this chapter.

Population and freedom

The denser a population becomes, the more people interfere with each other's freedom. Real-estate values increase, so that people must live on small lots or in apartments. Children have less room to roam. Building codes become necessary so that one person's property does not lessen the value of a neighbor's. Crime rates, fire hazards, and the possibility of accidents all increase, so that more rules and regulations become necessary. These changes occur so gradually in the industrialized parts of the world, that they are hardly seen as a threat to freedom.

In much of the developing world, it is possible that personal liberty will have to be sacrificed for the sake of survival. If two countries, A and B, both population giants, have hungry but increasing populations and both embark on birth-control programs, they might well be watched by other hungry countries. Country A, trying to change gradually, continues to retain many of its old traditions, gives due regard to the property rights of its upper classes, and retains political liberties. The population problem is handled by education and persuasion. Contraceptive devices are made available, and men are paid small sums of money or given free radios if they will agree to have vasectomies. In a few cases, overly eager promoters deceive them as to the nature of the operation, but usually the procedures are fair and honest. After many years of grappling with the population problem, however, country A finds that its population is increasing more rapidly than ever before and that nutrition has improved little if at all.

Country B, on the other hand, undergoes a drastic revolution. The old property-owning class is wiped out. The ruling political party takes full control; it mobilizes the people into enormous labor brigades and turns their energy to land reclamation, water control, and irrigation projects. Thus food production is vastly increased. To control population, people with too many children are labeled a disgrace to their country and prevented from becoming leaders. After many years of these policies, country B, which seemed at first to have been in even more serious trouble than country A, is feeding its people adequately and experiencing high morale. It has none of the constitutional liberties considered essential in the Western world. However, its people, never having known such liberties, seem not to notice their absence.

Which of these two countries will serve as a model for other countries trapped in poverty? Countries A and B are only slightly fictionalized descriptions of India and China, except that in 1975 India's constitutional liberties were restricted temporarily, allegedly to speed up social progress. Unfortunately, in crisis situations, national survival wins out over individual liberties. If population pressures lead to serious internal crises, might not much of the world follow the example of China? If property-owning classes prevail, populations will be mobilized by military dictatorships rather than communist parties. In either case, personal liberties are sacrificed.

In this book *An Inquiry into the Human*

Prospect (1974), Robert Heilbroner asks pessimistically whether a future world, faced with the problems of economic survival, may look upon freedom as a luxury it can no longer afford. Heilbroner's feelings are inspired as much by the problems of energy, environmental deterioration, growing shortages of resources, and nuclear proliferation as by population. Is population growth a problem that will be solved in due time, or is it an ongoing crisis, threatening massive famines, environmental destruction, and possibly revolution and war? Is it a crisis that demands international action, or must each country be left to cope in its own way?

POPULATION GROWTH: THE CRISIS VIEW

At first glance, statistics seem to argue that population growth is a crisis. The twentieth century started with 1,650 million people on our planet; it will end with about 6,500 million, an increase of approximately 400 percent. The twenty-first century will probably see that figure grow to 13 billion, *minimum (UNESCO Courier,* 1974a, pp. 15–19). No one knows for sure how many people the earth can support. Some say it is already overpopulated; others guess that it may be possible to feed 15 billion. Still others think new technologies might enable us to support as many as 50 billion. No one, however, would assume that present rates of increase can go on forever. Eventually, there would be no more standing room.

Resources

Those who view the population explosion as a crisis justify their view in terms of resources. The exhaustion of resources is more of a problem today for the industrialized than for the industrializing nations. The United States, with 6 percent of the world's population, is said to use about 40 percent of its resources. However, if the developing countries are to support their people, they too will have to depend on increasing industrialization. The cost of fuel and fertilizer, and in many cases of water supply, is increasing. This makes it unlikely that developing countries will be able to pay for the technology needed to improve agriculture enough to keep pace with population growth. If we imagine an admittedly impossible situation in which the entire world's population was also to be equipped with automobiles, motorcycles, campers, snowmobiles, motor boats, air-conditioned homes, and all the appliances middle-class American families use, the earth would be rapidly exhausted regardless of population growth.

Although occasional local crises develop, the world has been able to depend on the food-

Figure 17-2 Hydroelectric power stations for industrialization in developing countries. An industrial economy, it is hoped, will feed the fast-growing population and raise the standard of living. (*Eastfoto*)

Population trends and consequences

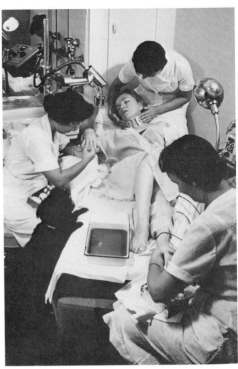
(a)

Figure 17-3 *(a* and *b)* The energy used by this typical beauty spa and suburban home could power *(c)* a shantytown of the developing world. [*(a) Life Magazine; (b) Michael Hayman, Photo Researchers, Inc.; (c) Georg Gerster, Rapho/Photo Researchers, Inc.*]

(b)

(c)

surplus countries, mainly the United States and Canada, to handle emergencies. What would happen if both the United States and Canada should have crop disasters at the same time? There is very little accumulated surplus in the world, almost no "bank supply" of food on which to draw.

The world cannot always depend on good growing weather. In the early 1970s, a famine spread through most of the Sahel region of Africa, in the territory dividing the Sahara Desert from the fertile regions to the south. In ordinary times, rainfall in this region is adequate to provide forage for camels, goats, and even cattle. During years of good rainfall, however, the animal and human population increased past the ability of the region to support them; then tradegy struck in the form of drought and famine. Could it be that the same tragedy will occur on a continentwide or even a worldwide scale? Those who see population growth as a crisis recognize the world's need to be prepared for emergencies.

In addition to the loss of priceless resources, land is being overworked, overgrazed, or turned over to housing, industrial facilities, roads, or airport runways. Increasing pollution goes on at the same time. Sometimes it destroys water supplies, sometimes it ruins agricultural land; always it threatens health.

The malnutrition cycle

René Dumont tells of a world plan, developed by the Food and Agriculture Organization in 1962, calling for a 3.8 percent growth in agriculture in the developing world to eliminate hunger. Because the goal was not met, a revised estimate in 1970 called for a 4 percent annual increase in farm production. The next four years saw a 1 percent increase in food supply and a 2.5 percent increase in population (Dumont, 1974, pp. 13–15). The 2.5 percent increase means a rapid rise in population and an even larger number of children to support. In Guatemala, for example,

45 percent of the population was fifteen years of age or younger in 1970. Such conditions can result in a *cycle of malnutrition*—a situation in which the malnutrition of one generation contributes to malnutrition in the next generation. Children who suffer malnutrition, especially protein deficiencies at an early age, may have mental and physical impairment throughout life. They, in turn, will be less able to care for their own children (see the insert "Maria's Children" on page 484).

Population and international ethics

There are certain ethical implications to the population explosion. When developed countries increase their population, they increase pollution and use up natural resources. When developing countries increase their population, they may do so at the cost of the health and welfare of the children they have produced. Some people advocate coercive measures, such as withholding aid from countries that make little effort at population control (Ehrlich, 1968, pp. 6–7). The assumption is that governments can control the breeding habits of their people.

OTHER PERSPECTIVES ON POPULATION GROWTH

One cannot help but be startled by the picture of the human population increasing so fast that it eats up any possible increases in food production. The world is not one political unit, however, but well over one hundred. Each country has its own interest regarding population trends. Also, ethnic groups within countries have special points of view, and so, for that matter, do individuals. For this reason, people have conflicting views on the population problem. Some call it a crisis, others see it largely as a temporary multiplier of other problems. Still others even call it a "nonproblem" (or a false problem with imperialist overtones), the real problem being development (Freeman and Berelson, 1974, p.

Maria's children   J. MAYONE STYCOS

A typical illustrative case of malnutrition is that of Maria, a young widow from El Salvador with five young children, who she boasts are very good and do not complain of their hunger.

My children don't ask for food if I haven't sold anything during the day. They don't bother me with "Mama, I'm hungry. Mama, I'm hungry." Of course, when meal time comes they begin to come around and the little girl says, "Are we going to eat today, Mama?"

"No," I say.

"Why not?"

"I have no money today." Then later she says to me, "Mama, if there's nothing today, then we're not going to eat."

"That's right."

"Oh well, then, I'm not going to ask any more."

They are good children. They accept it.

From J. Mayone Stycos, "Latin American Overpopulation Shoves Thousands to Margin of Life," copyright © 1974, Smithsonian Institution, from *Smithsonian Magazine*, April 1974, p. 79.

---

36). Those holding the last view contend that the developed nations want the developing nations to hold down their population as a substitute for giving them the aid they need. They accuse the developed world of expecting developing countries to "contracept their way to prosperity," an obvious impossibility. Not only do most developing countries need industrial and agricultural advancement, but they must contend with the traditional attitudes of their people regarding fertility.

Traditional values

Many of the traditional values that support the idea of large families are summed up in the following statement from Kofi Sefa-Boakye, a student from Ghana:

In countries with low life expectancy, it is hard to predict whether little Kwadwo or little Kofi will survive. So in order not to gamble, children should be many to even out inevitable losses.

Children in underdeveloped countries are economic assets rather than economic burdens—and in the struggle to wrest a living from the soil, the bigger the family the better. (Sefa-Boakye, 1973, p. 1)

In many developing countries, family survival is a sacred value. Many children are regarded as a sign of the father's virility and of the blessing of the gods or saints. These emotional considerations are essential to understanding the problem of population control in most developing countries.

Individual versus societal interests

Certain families believe that many children could be considered an asset. The head of a large household in many developing countries has both prestige and a feeling of security. Mahmood Mamdani, in the study of one Indian village in the Punjab, shows that there is only one possible route to economic and status improvement for village families: have many sons, who can either

Sources of change

484

work the land or migrate to the city and send back money from wages (1973). From the national viewpoint, such a policy breeds disaster. For some families, it means economic salvation.

Ethnic groups and political power

Arab people living in the state of Israel are increasing their population rapidly. Israel, concerned over this trend, is encouraging the growth of its own population through immigration and a higher birthrate (Friedlander, 1974, pp. 42–96). In the Soviet Union, there is some concern over the rapid increase of Asians compared with the slower increase of European people. In the United States, black leaders have accused white society of encouraging birth control mainly for the sake of holding down the black population. American Indians are generally pleased to see their numbers growing again after centuries of decline; their leaders are the last to welcome zero population growth. No one takes pleasure in being one of an endangered species. (See the insert "Where Population Spells Power.")

National interests

Since the world is politically fragmented, each country tries to pursue its own interest in population, just as individuals and ethnic groups do.

Where population spells power

America may yet have a 51st state. And if Larry R. Stuck of the University of Alberta is right, the new territory won't be Puerto Rico or even New York City. Stuck foresees the creation of a Navajo state consisting of land taken from Arizona, New Mexico, and Utah (*Human Organization*, Winter, 1971).

The Navajos are one of the largest and most powerful American Indian tribes—and population has been the key variable in the rise of Navajo political and economic power. In 1868, the tribe numbered 8,000. In the 1930s, the Navajos numbered over 48,000, and today the number has grown to 125,000. Their rate of growth has been 2 percent per year, nearly twice that of the entire Indian population and over twice the annual rate for the nation as a whole.

[Population and labor force have attracted industry.] According to a General Dynamics Corporation ad that appeared in several newspapers, the Navajo attracts business "by offering a pool of fast-learning people whose natural intelligence exceeds their formal education." . . .

Recently congressmen, senators, governors, and local politicians have almost trampled each other trying to be "the best friend of the Navajo people" and by obtaining federal and state aid for the tribe. . . .

There are important broad implications in the story of the Navajo tribe. Since Navajo political and economic power is based to a large extent on an increasing population, their success may provide justification for the rejection of birth control programs by certain population groups. Some minorities view such programs as attempts to limit and control "dangerous" ethnic groups. Some Latin Americans have denounced birth control as a "U.S. plot" to weaken their countries. And it is doubtful that the Navajo tribe would be in its present position of power had modern family planning advisers been sent to the reservation back in 1868.

From "How the West is Being Won." Published by permission of Transaction, Inc., from *Society*, vol. 10, no. 2, copyright © 1973 by Transaction, Inc.

National interest in India and China calls for strict control. In certain other countries, immediate interest favors population growth, regardless of the worldwide situation. In the International Population Year, 1974, a variety of opinions was expressed at a United Nations meeting on population. The Soviet delegate pointed out that the Soviet Union and some of the communist countries of Eastern Europe had instituted policies designed to increase the birthrate, such as free, good-quality nursery care and maternal leaves from work. He complimented Czechoslovakia for increasing its birthrate from a very low 14.9 per thousand to a moderate 17.8 in a period of five years. The Soviet Union, he claimed, was also succeeding in increasing its birthrate (Urlanis, 1974, pp. 26–27). At the same time, he felt that many overcrowded countries of Western Europe and the developing world should cut back their birthrates. His reasoning was that both the Soviet Union and Czechoslovakia needed more people for development, while such countries as West Germany, the Netherlands, and Belgium do not. In the developing world, a reduced birthrate is needed to release workers and especially women for national development. However, when birthrates are low, he stated, they have to be raised to ensure an adequate labor supply in the future.

Brazil, whose population is growing by more than 3 percent per year, also argues that it needs more people and that a growing population is an incentive to development. Environmentalists are deeply concerned over the rapid destruction of much of the great Brazilian rain forest. Brazil, however, could easily ask why there was no protest when the United States destroyed its vast forests for the sake of rapid development. At an earlier 1974 meeting of the U.N. General Assembly, the Chilean delegate stated that the problem of population growth was "artificially emphasized by developed countries as an excuse for them to escape their obligations to the international community" (*UNESCO Courier*, 1974a, pp. 7–8). He called for more financial and technical aid to cope with the problems of development. Solving these problems, he said, would make it much easier to support Latin American populations.

Distribution of income

Some of the communist states believe that the major problem is distribution of wealth, not population. Russia's low birthrate is a result of education, urbanization, industrialization, and housing shortages, not of government propaganda. Communist China employs measures that drastically restrict family size, but population control is not given as an excuse. Instead, China speaks of giving men and women more time to serve the country and of preserving the health and well-being of mothers and children.

Regional Attitudes

Africa cannot speak with one voice any more than other continents can. Still Maaza Bekele, an Ethiopian educator, expresses a fairly common view in her resentment of any interference with the "rebuilding" of African population:

The decimation perpetrated during the slave trade in the 17th and 18th centuries, military engagements which attempted to ward off impendiing colonization in the 19th century, the subsequent exploitation of African labor, the introduction of new diseases from Europe and the spread of locally endemic diseases through the migration set in motion at that time, all contributed to an absolute decline in the number of African people over a period of 200 years. Thus the percentage relative to the rest of the world was quite dramatically lowered. It is only since the beginning of this century that the rebuilding of African population has begun. (1974, pp. 42–43; reproduced from the *UNESCO Courier,* May 1974)

India, with a larger population than the entire

continent of Africa in only a fraction of the land area, wants to limit population. The Indian government has been engaged in family planning campaigns for many years, but it is still not satisfied with its progress.

However, statistics on the world increase in population say too little about specifics. Some countries need population control desperately; others can see actual advantages to increase.

POPULATION AND POLICY

Years ago, it was taken for granted that nothing could be done to control population short of total celibacy; otherwise the decision was in the hands of God. Many people still take this point of view, especially in rural Latin America and many Moslem countries, which see birth control as a way of interfering with God's will. In most of the world, however, these older attitudes are gradually giving way. Even where the norms uphold maximum reproduction among rural people, the educated, urban populations are very interested in controlling births. Religious barriers to change are by no means firm. Catholics in the United States have almost the same attitudes toward birth control as do Protestants, and Catholic Poland has one of the lowest birthrates in the world. In fact, in 1965 it dropped to 6.5, well below the amount needed to sustain population. Many Moslems consider reproduction the will of Allah. Still, Egypt is embarking on a birth-control program, and so is mostly Moslem Indonesia. An important question is, "What is the effect of government-sponsored birth-control programs?" Whatever it may be, there is little doubt that other factors are more important than government policy.

Birth control without government policy

The long-term downward trend in birthrate in the United States and Western Europe came about long before any government advocated birth control. The factors most responsible were (and are) education, urbanization, industrialization, and opportunities for upward mobility. When people see that their chances of advancing themselves and their children depend on limiting family size, they will practice birth control. Richard Critchfield gives an account of villagers in Thailand (1976, pp. 1, 4). A mother who was asked whether she wanted more children than the two she already had answered "no." Most rural Thais would say "yes," but she explained her reason. The village now had a school, which her children could attend in order to advance in the world. Although the school was free, the cost of paper, pencils, clothes, and books was such that she could not afford to send more than two children. This Thai village provides one small example of what has gone on in much of the industrialized world. However, demographers are not sure whether this natural tendency to reduce the birthrate will always be sufficient. The period after World War II witnessed a "baby boom" in parts of the world that had had falling birthrates. Japan, which was highly praised for its declining birthrate, has had an upturn in the 1970s. The government may have to exert more pressure, rather than leaving the decision entirely to individuals. Two policies are open to governments: *pronatalist* or *antinatalist*. Antinatalist policies use persuasion, manipulation, and even coercion. Pronatalist policies are sometimes not recognized as such and are very common in countries that do not actually intend to increase their birthrates.

Pronatalist policies

As we have seen, the Soviet Union, Czechoslovakia, France, and a few other countries (Greece, Hungary, Rumania, and Poland) with low birthrates have used policies that encourage an increase. Many other countries use some of the same policies, but not for the same reason. The most common pronatalist policies are financial allotments to families on the basis of how many children they have, income-tax exemptions on the basis of family size, and day-care facilities for infants and children of working women. These policies are often intended more as humanitarian measures than as ways of increasing the birthrate.

In the United States, for example, federal income taxes fall more heavily on single people than on married people or on parents with dependent children. For the poor, direct help in the form of AFDC (Aid to Families with Dependent Children) is given through welfare agencies. Neither the amount saved in taxes nor the amount given in AFDC is enough to meet the needs of children, so it would be silly to say that women have children just to save on income tax or to collect AFDC. However, these policies probably encourage fertility to a slight degree, since people know that at least some money is available. To suggest cutting out tax exemptions, AFDC, or whatever child-care facilities we have would seem inhumane. It would amount to penalizing children for having been born. For humanitarian reasons, then, most industrialized countries employ policies that are pronatalist, whether intended as such or not. At the same time, many governments have family-planning

policies and free birth-control clinics, which are clearly intended to be pronatalist. Bernard Berelson finds that most developed countries favor a slight increase in birthrate. Reasons range from problems of labor supply to simply preventing declines in population. Nations are no happier than individuals or ethnic groups to see themselves as endangered species (Berelson, 1974, pp. 771–789).

Antinatalist persuasion

The U.S. Population Commission recommends no really coercive population policies for the United States. It does suggest education regarding family planning—which would be a way of encouraging the use of birth control. Several countries of the developing world—such as South Korea, Taiwan, India, and Ceylon—have launched extensive campaigns of persuasion. In Latin America, Colombia, Panama, and Trinidad have at least launched national family-planning programs. Others, such as Mexico, have approached the matter cautiously, promoting the idea of family planning for the sake of health and family well-being but not launching major campaigns for population control.

Recent reports indicate that Communist China is very interested in population control, is willing to admit the fact, and is fairly coercive in its

Figure 17-4 This ad for family planning can be found throughout India. (*Paolo Koch, Rapho/Photo Researchers, Inc.*)

Table 17-1

Country	Percent increase per year	Time required to double population
Costa Rica, Kuwait, Liberia	3.8	16 years
East Malaysia, Colombia, Ecuador, Mexico, Dominican Republic	3.6	17 years
Philippines, Thailand, Panama, Honduras	3.2	19 years
Libya, Sudan, Tunisia, Kenya, Peru, El Salvador, Nicaragua	3.0	20 years
Indonesia, Iran, Ghana	2.9	21 years
Brazil	2.8	22 years
India	2.6	24 years

Source: *UNESCO Courier*, May 1974.

approach (Han Suyin, 1974, pp. 52–55). Its population increase is now a fairly rapid 1.5 percent per year, but this is below the world average and well below the 3 percent common in most developing countries.

Antinatalist coercive policies

Kingsley Davis, a strong believer in zero population growth (ZPG), suggests that coercive measures will eventually have to become the rule throughout the world. A country could "permit each couple a maximum of two children, with possible state license for a third. Additional pregnancies beyond the limit would be interrupted by abortion" (1973, pp. 15–19, 28). Any further offenses against population control would result in sterilization. Such policies sound harsh, but, says Davis, "by definition, population control and reproductive freedom are incompatible. . . . "

To date, few have taken Davis's advice. Critchfield mentions that in Indonesia, officials have sometimes ordered women with more than two children to go to the clinic for an intrauterine contraceptive device (1976, p. 1). The women have obeyed, but the policy seems to depend on local officials. The federal government propa-gandizes against more than a two-child family, but it has taken no coercive action.

India is considering mandatory sterilization after a couple has had two children. The Indian state of Maharashtra has finally begun to use coercion, but it allows three children rather than two (see the insert "Coercive Birth Control in Maharashtra"). It should be noted, however, that compulsory sterilization rouses strong protests. The political defeat of Indira Gandhi in early 1977 resulted largely from her high-handed political policies but partly also from her government's strong support of compulsory sterilization.

D. N. Pai, the "father of vasectomy" in India, and an advocate of coercive antinatal policies, has a strong argument on his side. It seems doubtful that the prosperity that has brought voluntary birth control to the developed countries can come to the developing world. There, the choice seems to lie between coercive government policies and even more hunger than at present. Death rates are already rising in Bangladesh, as Malthus predicted. Statistics indicate that death rates may begin to rise in many parts of the world. The United Nations, in 1974, estimated the rates of population increase shown in Table 17-1 and projected how long it would

Coercive birth control in Maharashtra   SHARON ROSENHAUSE

"We have laws against air pollution. Why don't we have laws against people pollution?"

That's the rhetorical question of Dr. D. N. Pai, who calls himself the "father of vasectomy." Pai is the family planning director in Bombay, the capital of Maharashtra State, where the government has ordered compulsory sterilization—the first in the world to do so. . . .

Family planning is a sensitive issue here—on religious, social, and economic grounds. It is widely acknowledged that India's efforts to control population growth have failed. There are now 610 million Indians, and the population grows by 14 million a year.

Nationally, there is now an aggressive family planning campaign, largely identified with Sanjay Gandhi, [former] Prime Minister Indira Gandhi's son.

While Prime Minister Gandhi has voiced doubts about compulsory sterilization, officials in Maharashtra say the state government would not have passed the law without a "green light" from the national government.

In this male-oriented society, the responsibility for sterilization is the man's. If for health reasons he could not have a vasectomy, the wife would be sterilized. . . .

An exception [to the three-child rule] permits a couple with three children of the same sex to have a fourth child. But that is the final try. The reason for the exception is the importance of a son in Indian society. For instance, among Hindus, the dominant religious group, funeral rites are performed only by a son.

Perhaps to emphasize previous failures and to dramatize the difficulties of family planning in India, Pai recalled the time when the rhythm method was in vogue [sexual abstinence during the days when the wife is most likely to conceive]. Women were given necklaces to count the days. Red beads indicated dangerous days and green beads safe days.

"The beads were found around the necks of their babies," he said, shaking his head in frustration. "This is an illiterate country." Pai is convinced that only compulsion will work in this poor, uneducated, rural, overpopulated nation.

"It's a question of survival. We want to improve the standard of living and eradicate poverty," he said.

Pai, who studied medicine in Bombay and earned a master's degree in public health from Harvard, dismissed the argument that compulsory sterilization violates individual rights.

"An individual doesn't have the right to defecate in the road," he said. "Society has rights. The greatest global problem today is the number of people. You just can't go on adding any number of children.

"It's not that there are no children. There are so many children who are miserable. It should be considered immoral to bring an unwanted child into a home of misery. It's hell to see a young child starve to death. You come here and see a sea of poverty.

"Our human values are distorted. Only 0.01 percent of the people enjoy individual liberties. Go to a slum area. What liberties do they have?"

From Sharon Rosenhause, "India Taking Drastic Birth Control Step," *Los Angeles Times*, September 20, 1976, Part I, pp. 1, 10–11. Copyright Los Angeles Times.

take for the population to double (*UNESCO Courier*, 1974a, p. 8).

DEMOGRAPHY OF THE UNITED STATES

The United States once had one of the fastest-growing populations in the world. Today, however, this country is approaching phase 4 of demographic transition. In 1972, for the first time in American history, the number of children per family declined to 2.03. This figure is slightly below the theoretical replacement level of 2.11, (Rosenthal, 1973, p.9), the point of *zero population growth* (ZPG). Since not all children mature and produce children of their own, slightly more than two children per family are needed to maintain the native-born population. (In the United States, the population is swelled by about 400,000 immigrants per year.) A slightly later U.S. Census Bureau report indicated that births per woman had declined even more by 1975, to 1.9. At first glance, it would seem that the problem of United States population growth had been resolved in favor of a stationary or even declining population. Such figures seem strange, since the United States population increased by 24 million during the 1960s and was continuing to increase in the 1970s. One reason for the apparent contradiction lies in the age of different parts of the population.

Are figures deceiving?

The birthrate may be deceptive, even if the death rate remains almost unchanged. Nearly all children are born to women between fifteen and thirty-nine years of age. If an unusually high percentage of the population falls into that age range, then the population could increase even if most women had only two children. This is the situation in the United States for the 1970s and 1980s. By 1970, there were more people in the group aged twenty to twenty-four than in any older group; an even larger group was between the ages of fifteen and nineteen and still more were aged ten to fourteen. Another large but declining block was the five- to nine-year age group. By 1970, there was a drastic decrease in the number of children aged four or less, which foretells fewer potential parents in the 1990s. From now until the 1990s, the United States population can easily be maintained even with a very low birthrate, as indicated in the gap between birthrate and death rate (see Table 17-2, page 492). If the birthrate should increase, another baby boom would result (Freeman and Berelson, 1974).

As of the mid-1970s, family size in the United States had declined drastically. People were marrying later, and there were more women than usual in their late twenties and early thirties who had had no children at all, although many of them still planned to have families (Sklar and Berkov, 1975, pp. 693–700). Since predictions on population are often risky, alternative projections are often made (see Table 17-3). It could be that much publicity about birth control, together with a downturn in the economy in the 1970s, resulted in a decline in family size that will be only temporary. Present figures indicate an eventual leveling off of the population, but one can never be sure. Infant death rates are low enough so that Americans do not feel compelled to have extra children for the sake of survival (see Table 17-4). The logical answer about the future would be that all the factors equated with low birthrate—education, urbanization, job opportunities, high costs of raising children, secularization, persuasion, and the availability of contraceptives and abortion—are at work. Therefore, the long-range downturn in population growth should continue. Ironically, though, most of these factors were already at work before the postwar baby boom of the 1950s.

Immigration

Migration has an indirect effect on world population, since people who migrate to another coun-

Table 17-2 Birth and Death Rates, 1950—1973

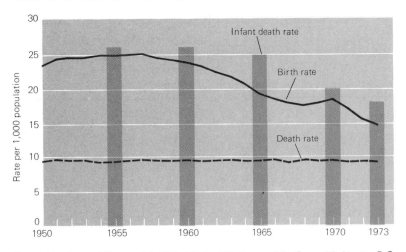

Source: *The Statistical Abstract of the United States, U.S. Bureau of the Census,* Washington, D.C., 1976, p. 52.

Table 17-3 United States Population—Projections to 2050

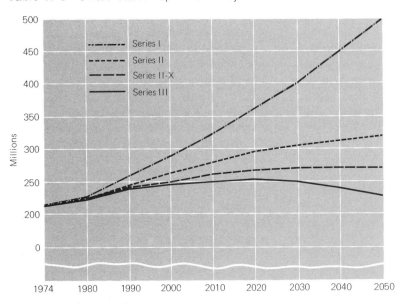

Note: Because predicting the future is always uncertain, there are several projections, assuming low, intermediate, and high birth rates. As of the late 1970s, the second lowest projection seems most probable.
Source: *The Statistical Abstract of the United States,* 1976.

Sources of change

Table 17-4 Infant Death Rates, Developed and Underdeveloped Lands

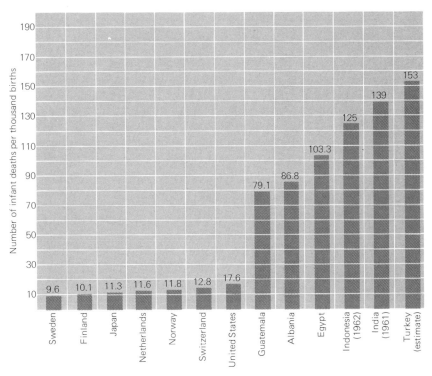

Note: All figures are for the 1970s except where otherwise specified. High death rates among infants and children encourage people in some countries to have many children so that some will survive.
Source: *U.S. Fact Book: The Statistical Abstract of the U.S. Bureau of the Census,* Grosset and Dunlap, New York, 1976, p. 839.

try sometimes change their breeding habits. In internal migration from farms to cities, the effect is just as great. Throughout history, as rural people have migrated to the cities, their birthrates have declined.

The United States has always been a land of immigrants. Peak immigration occurred between 1901 and 1910, when 8.7 million immigrants entered a country whose population was less than 92 million. The United States population had increased by nearly 10 percent in ten years through immigration alone. Even now, immigration is an important factor in United States population, amounting to about 400,000 persons per year plus at least once again this number entering the country illegally.

After 1900, restrictions on immigration favored Europeans and excluded Asians. However, by the 1970s, the immigration from Asia exceeded that from Europe (see Table 17-5). In 1972, there were 384,685 legal immigrants to the United States. Of these, Europe contributed 90,000; Asia, 121,000; North America, 144,000; South America, 19,000; Africa, 7,000; and Australia and New Zealand, 2,000. Of the Asian immigrants, 29,000 were from the Philippines, and about two-thirds that number each came from China, India, and Korea. Of the North American immigrants, 64,000 came from Mexico and 61,000 from the West Indies. During the same year, 1,304,000 nonimmigrants were admitted from Mexico, either as laborers with

Population trends and consequences

Table 17-5 Immigrants to the United States, 1972

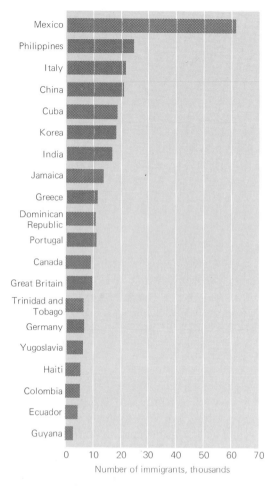

Number of immigrants, thousands

Note: Sources of current immigration to the United States are ranked in descending order. Black: top ten countries of origin, Western Hemisphere. Color: top ten countries of origin, Eastern Hemisphere. Source: Kingsley Davis, "The Migration of Human Populations," copyright © 1974 by Scientific American, Inc., from *Scientific American*, vol. 231, September 1974, p. 102; all rights reserved. Based on data from the U.S. Department of State, 1973.

temporary permits, as students, or as tourists. Most of the tourists returned to Mexico, although each year a certain number remain in the United States. The U.S. Census Bureau has no official estimate of how many aliens remain. We can only say that total immigration is higher than the official figures show, with illegal immigrants entering from many parts of the world.

Age and sex composition

Population pyramids are convenient graphs for showing the age and sex distribution of a population at a particular time. The population pyramids in Table 17-6 show the age and sex composition of the United States population in 1950 and 1970. Males are shown on the left side of the center line and females on the right. Ages are indicated in five-year increments except for those eighty-five and over, who are grouped together. If both the death rate and the birthrate were consistently high or consistently low, the population pyramid would actually be pyramidal in shape. But in fact, the 1950 pyramid is somewhat out of shape because of the low birthrate of the 1930s. The 1970 figure is more complex. It shows a shortage in the age component of those born in the 1930s, a bulge for those born in the 1950s, and a shrinkage in

Figure 17-5 This immigrant Turkish worker in Germany is one of many to settle in the industrialized West. Others include Algerians in France, and Indians and Pakistanis in Great Britain. (*Peter Arnold, Photo Archives, © Gerhard Gscheidle*)

Sources of change

Table 17-6 Population by Age and Sex, United States, 1950 and 1970

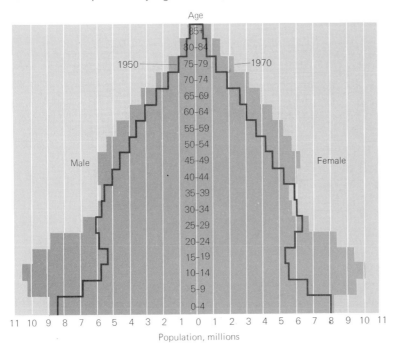

Source: U.S. Bureau of the Census, *Current Population Reports:* Estimates of the Population of the United States and Components of Change by Age, Color, and Sex, 1950 to 1960," series P-25, no. 310; "Preliminary Estimates of the Population of the United States, by Age and Sex, April 1, 1960, to July 1, 1971," series P-25, no. 483.

birthrate starting about 1960 and becoming more marked in the latter half of the 1960s. The early 1970s would show a continued decrease in number of children under five years of age.

In all but the earliest years of life, the female population is slightly larger than the male population. The reason is that the death rate, or *mortality rate*, among males is higher than among females at all ages, with female life expectancy averaging about six years more than that of males. The major reason is that more males than females die prematurely of diseases and heart attacks. Deaths in war make a minor difference, as do accidental deaths and even suicides. Table 17-7 (page 496) shows some of our major health problems but says little about male-female differences in life expectancy. Slightly more males than females are born in a

country in which maternal and infant care are good. Otherwise, live births are about even, since more males than females are stillborn if maternal care is not good. As early as World War I, Great Britain reported a greater proportion of male births during the war years. At first the reason seemed mysterious, as though nature were attempting to provide more soldiers. Actually the reason was that more attention was being given to maternal and infant care than in previous years. Therefore, more boys were being born alive and surviving.

Differential birthrate

Differential birthrate refers to differences in birthrate with respect to location (rural or urban), religion, social class, and racial or ethnic group.

Population trends and consequences

Table 17-7 What's Killing Us? Death Rates from Most Major Killers except Cancer Continue to Decline

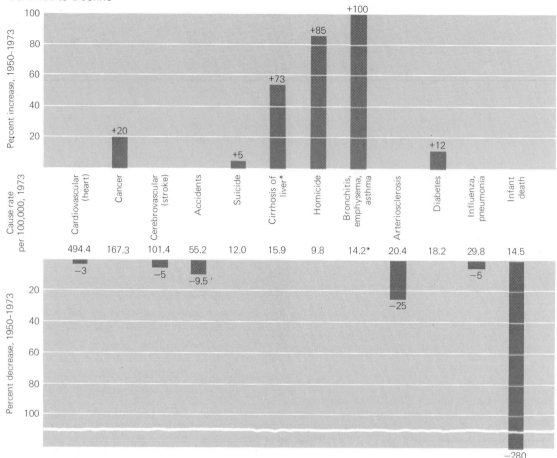

*Deaths from emphysema and other respiratory diseases are associated with cigarettes and air pollution; cirrhosis of the liver is associated with heavy use of alcohol.
Source: Data for all causes except emphysema, U.S. Bureau of the Census; data for emphysema, *Scientific American*, August 1974, p. 46.

Birthrates have always been higher among rural than among urban people. In the past, they were considerably higher among Catholics than non-Catholics, but that differential has almost disappeared. Poor people have more children than middle-class people. Birthrates are also higher among black than white Americans, so that the black population rose from 10.5 to 11.2 percent of the total during the 1960s. (In colonial times, the black population had been approximately 20 percent of the total, but it fell off in the nine-

teenth century because of white immigration and a very high death rate among black people.) Today, black and white birthrates are becoming more equal than in the past. In 1957, 160 children were born per thousand black women aged fifteen to forty-four. By comparison, there were 118 births per thousand white women in the same age group. In 1970, both rates had declined. The black rate dropped even more than the white, probably because of more widely available advice on contraception. The figures were 115 births per thousand black women and 82 births per thousand white women. There is still a differential, but it is declining. Surveys indicate that black women are just as interested in birth control as white, although until recently many have been less informed on the matter (Westoff, 1974, p. 749). Even now, abortions are not as readily available to black women because of the high costs.

Changes in differential birthrates: Social class

There is reason to believe that both well-educated and less-educated people agree more on family size today than in the past. According to a 1969 Gallup Poll, 46 percent of the public approved of only one- or two-child families; 23 percent approved of three children, and only 18 percent approved of more than three (9 percent gave no opinion). In the same survey (with a slight contradiction), 20 percent of the public approved of four or more children as the "ideal number"; but of those under 30, only 12 percent did so. Catholic opinion varied from general national opinion only slightly, with 23 percent approving of four or more children. Of those with less than a high school education, 31 percent considered a family of four or more to be ideal. High school graduates were one percentage point below the national average in approval of a four-child family. College students were well below the national average, with only 12 percent calling four or more children ideal (*Salt Lake Tribune*, 1973).

Given the number of people who consider more than two children the ideal, it seems unlikely that we have reached zero population growth. (There could be a difference between stated values and actual fertility rate.) Economic concerns motivate many people to keep family size to a minimum. Ironically, however, such concerns are stronger among the well-to-do because they are the ones most determined to provide opportunities for mobility for their chil-

dren and to live well themselves. Today as in the past, poor people have more children than middle-class or upper-class people; this increases the difficulty of rising out of poverty. One study concludes that children in a family of four or more have a 10 percent less chance than others in their socioeconomic class of becoming professional persons or technicians and a 21 to 23 percent greater chance of becoming unskilled laborers (Preston, 1974, pp. 492–506). Other studies show that the reasons for little upward mobility are partly connected with health. Since the family with many children, unless it is far more affluent than the average family, cannot provide the best-quality food and health care, illness is more common, death rates are higher, and IQ scores are lower (Wray, 1971, pp. 403–506).

Probable results of slower population growth

An obvious result of the slower population growth is that the young will make up a smaller percentage of the population. As is already happening, school systems will not have to keep growing larger. There will be no disproportionate numbers of young people entering the labor market, which should eventually improve the employment situation for the young. There will also be a smaller percentage of people in those years of life (the late teens and early twenties) when delinquency and crime rates are highest. Therefore, the crime rate might level off.

The aged may grow as a political force, since a larger proportion of the population will be interested in the issues of pensions, forced retirement, medical care, and other concerns of the aged. Larger proportions of people in the middle and later years of life could possibly have a conservative influence on life-styles.

Smaller family size will make it possible for more parents to help their sons and daughters through college, so the proportion of college graduates may increase. The trend toward

Jacques Danois/Unicef Photo

John Weisblat/Unicef Photo

Sharp contrasts exist between affluent countries with housing codes and developing countries where the poor build huts of any materials available. In the poorest places of all, many people sleep in the streets.

greater equality for women should continue. With smaller families, women will spend less of their lives raising families and more time in occupational roles.

A demographic change from a moderate to a low birthrate is sure to result in a few temporary dislocations, for example, among primary and secondary school teachers. Ideally, one would like the population to stabliize, with a more or less constant number of children at the base of the pyramid in each five-year period. Such a situation would probably help stabilize the economy and make school, job, and social security demands far more predictable than they are now. This is one of many reasons why the United States Commission on Population and the American Future calls for zero population growth (1972). The belief today is that population problems in the United States are not severe enough to warrant antinatalist government policies. There is little doubt, though, that the worldwide trend is toward greater government regulation. For many developing areas, such policies are crucial. For the United States, the policy of free choice seems adequate for the moment. Still, a new baby boom would probably lead to new policies, such as financial incentives to limit family size to two children and possible financial penalties for more. As we have noted, increasing populations may limit individual freedom in many ways.

SUMMARY

Although some people think of the United States as too crowded, its population density of about 65 per square mile is very low compared with nearly 1,000 per square mile in England, the Netherlands, and Belgium or nearly 2,000 in Bangladesh. The world population explosion is quite recent, although there have always been places where the population was hard to feed. In general, people have always wanted large families so that at least some of their children would survive them. Exceptions to this rule have occurred only among people with so little food that they have tried to keep down population by *infanticide* or crude attempts at contraception.

Thomas Malthus is famous for his *population theory*, stated in 1798. He predicted a *geometric progression* in population growth and an *arithmetic progression* in increasing food supply. The result would be starvation unless such growth were stopped by wars or epidemics, which, together with famine, he called "positive controls." Malthus doubted that "preventive controls" (late marriage or celibacy) would work. He was partly right. Densely populated but wealthy countries seem to be able to support their people. However, conditions in poverty-stricken, densely crowded parts of the developing world cause many people to take his warnings seriously.

Europe had been undergoing a rapid population increase in the century before Malthus, even though far more "preventive controls" were used than were generally admitted: late marriage, celibacy, infanticide, and the placing of infants in foundling homes in which nearly all of them died. Eventually, however, such practices were largely abandoned and Europe was able to support its increasing population, largely because of having access to the resources of the New World and particularly to its new food crops, potatoes and corn.

We are greatly concerned about *demography* today. Europe and most areas of European settlement have passed through four (possibly five) phases of *demographic transition*, from high birth and death rates to something approaching population stability, with low birth and death rates. Sweden is the best example of a country with population stability. Germany and Poland are in roughly the same phase, and the United States and the European part of the Soviet Union are approaching it. A question is whether the developing countries will be able to achieve a similar stability before mass starvation occurs.

Population trends affect all aspects of society.

Sources of change

Military power is served by large populations, provided they are well fed and equipped. Life-styles are influenced by breeding habits. Poverty is common for large families, especially in developing lands. National development can be retarded if birthrates are so high that nearly half the population consists of children. Overpopulation may also threaten liberty. Starving countries are inclined to take dictatorial measures to increase production and to ration goods. Population growth also threatens natural resources. Societies are vulnerable to famine if no food reserves exist in case of drought or other natural disaster. There is little or no planning for such disasters today. All countries are looking for the *optimum population* to fit their needs.

The hundred or more independent countries of the world do not agree about population policies. In some countries, traditional values demand many children. Sometimes ethnic minorities can gain political power as their numbers increase. Nations may increase their labor supply and their military and economic importance because of growing populations. Some ideologists in developing lands claim that the real problem is the distribution of wealth, not population.

Regardless of views about population, trends are difficult to control. In developed countries, people generally want small families; large families interfere with other pursuits and ambitions. The governments of most industrialized countries also favor small families, although for humane reasons, they give aid to children of poor families—a policy that can be interpreted as *pronatalist*. Several of the less developed countries (e.g., South Korea, Taiwan, India, and Ceylon) use intensive campaigns of *antinatalist persuasion* to keep the birthrate down, but with only fair results. In a few cases (e.g., parts of India and Indonesia) governments have turned to *coercive antinatalist policies*, including sterilization.

In the United States, the problems of population growth are not as severe as in many parts of the world, because the birthrate has declined sharply. However, the population is increased by a sizable immigration, both legal and illegal. European immigration is declining as a percent of the total, but immigration from Asia and Latin America is increasing.

In predicting future population, one must analyze *population pyramids* and *differential birthrates*. Because of the large numbers of young people in the reproductive years of life, a new United States population boom is possible. Several demographers have worried about the possibility, but as of the late 1970s, no such boom seemed to be under way.

The United States population is aging because people are living longer and fewer babies are being born. As in all countries with good health care, the female population here is larger than the male population. Birthrates continue to be somewhat higher among poor people in rural areas than among the well-to-do and the urbanites, but these differences are declining. The black birthrate is higher than the white, but this difference, too, is declining.

A slowdown in birthrates is already bringing a reduction in school populations, and eventually a smaller group will be entering the job market each year. This should eventually improve employment prospects. Although a lower birthrate may create problems for people going into teaching or child care, it is expected to benefit the standard of living. The U.S. Commission on Population and the American Future advocates no further increase in population. It hopes for population stability or *zero population growth*, achieved by persuasion, contraceptives, and abortions.

Study guide

Terms to know

Pronatalist policies
Antinatalist policies
Infanticide
Malthusian population theory
Geometric progression
Arithmetic progression
Demography

Demographic transition
Birthrate
Death rate
Optimum population
Green revolution
Malnutrition cycle

Antinatalist persuasion
Coercive antinatalist policies
Zero population growth (ZPG)
Population pyramid
Differential birthrates

Names to know

Thomas Malthus
William L. Langer
Robert Heilbroner

Kingsley Davis
Paul Ehrlich

Self-test

Part I. Multiple Choice. Select the best of the four alternative answers:

1 Which of the following countries has a population density of about 1,000 people per square mile? (**a**) Belgium, (**b**) Canada, (**c**) France, (**d**) Bangladesh.

2 Malthus's major conclusion is that (**a**) countries should practice pronatalist policies, (**b**) population tends to outrun food supply, (**c**) food supply increases faster than population, (**d**) preventive controls will solve most population problems.

3 According to Malthus, which of the following is *not* considered among the "positive controls" on population? (**a**) pestilence, (**b**) famine, (**c**) celibacy, (**d**) war and vice.

4 Demography is the study of (**a**) social change, (**b**) birth control, (**c**) democratic government, (**d**) population.

5 The fourth phase of demographic transition is most closely approximated by (**a**) Italy, (**b**) Sweden, (**c**) Czechoslovakia, (**d**) China.

6 The phase of demographic transition in which birthrates begin to decline is the (**a**) first, (**b**) second, (**c**) third, (**d**) fourth.

7 A point at which population would be just right for full development of natural resources and economic potential is known as (**a**) optimum population, (**b**) balanced population, (**c**) potential population, (**d**) ultimate population.

8 For national survival in the face of possible starvation, which of the following is most likely? (**a**) decrease in personal freedoms, (**b**) decline of government control, (**c**) increase in personal freedoms, (**d**) return to a free-enterprise economic system.

9 The "green revolution" (**a**) has made hunger unlikely in any part of the world, (**b**) refers to new crops and farming methods, (**c**) has failed to develop new varieties of grain, (**d**) is most successful in the poorest countries.

10 Of the following, the least likely to reduce the world's resources is (**a**) industrialization, (**b**) highly mechanized agriculture, (**c**) simple, nonmechanized farming, (**d**) increasing affluence.

11 The use of coercive antinatalist measures by industrialized nations assumes that (**a**) poor countries should be starved out of existence, (**b**) poor countries will not need help, (**c**) the United States will rescue poor countries, (**d**) governments can control the breeding habits of their people.

12 Regarding fertility, developing countries have to contend with (**a**) industrial development, (**b**) agricultural development, (**c**) traditional attitudes, (**d**) a and b above.

13 An insert about the Navajos says their population increase means more (**a**) alienation, (**b**) political power, (**c**) lawlessness, (**d**) desertion of the tribe.

14 In 1970, the number of children aged four or less in the United States dropped sharply. This statistic may foretell what in 1990? (**a**) fewer potential parents, (**b**) more potential parents, (**c**) an increased crime rate, (**d**) a population boom.

15 One obvious result of slower population growth would be (**a**) more intelligent children, (**b**) a larger proportion of middle-aged and elderly people, (**c**) an end of pollution problems, (**d**) all the above.

Part II. True-False Questions

1 Each year, world population increases by about 80 million.

2 Malthus contended that population increases by arithmetic progression while food supply increases by geometric progression.

3 Famine in Europe was reduced in the 1700s by the introduction of potatoes and corn from the New World.

4 A declining death rate has been a more important factor than a rising birthrate in today's population explosion.

5 If present trends in birthrate continue, a population increase of between 60 and 80 percent can be expected in the industrialized world by 2050.

6 The first country to require sterilization after the third child was the Soviet Union.

7 Increasing fuel, fertilizer, and water costs make it doubtful that agriculture can keep up with population growth in the developing countries.

8 Historically, infanticide was used to keep down populations in some parts of the world, but not in Europe.

9 Food production in the developing countries is increasing at a steady, dependable rate equal to that of population increase.

10 Maria's children do not complain of hunger.

11 African nationalists agree that Africa needs to limit population growth severely.

12 In some countries, governments encourage people to have more children in order to increase the labor supply and possibly military power.

13 Education, urbanization, industrialization, and opportunites for upward mobility are all associated with family planning.

14 Whether they intend to encourage more births or not, most governments employ pronatalist policies for humanitarian reasons.

15 Females tend to have a higher mortality rate than males at all ages of life.

Questions for discussion

1 What are the advantages and disadvantages of achieving zero population growth (ZPG)? In arriving at ZPG, will any social institutions be modified or altered?

2 Argue the views of Malthus on population. Has modern productivity proved him wrong, or are

his views still to be taken seriously?

3 Overpopulation poses many problems for a society. Identify as many of them as possible.

4 Many countries still want at least a moderate increase in population. Do they have a moral right to follow policies leading to population increase? Do such policies make sense socially and economically?

5 There are many connections between a nation's birthrate and economic development. What are some of them? Discuss those you identify in terms of cause and effect.

6 Forced sterilization as a means of population control is a highly controversial idea. What moral, legal, religious, or ethical arguments could be used for or against such a plan?

7 As the industrialized countries reduce their birthrates, one result is fewer children and more elderly people. What are the possible social consequences of such a demographic change?

8 If the population pyramid of a country shows half its population to be less than twenty years of age with very few people surviving past the age of fifty, what could you guess about the development, social norms, standard of living, and occupations of most of the people?

Projects

1 Many jobs are concerned with trends in population growth and decline: city planning, energy engineering, water conservation, real estate, and education among others. Arrange an interview with people holding some of these jobs. Ask them how they compile figures to try to predict population trends in their area. How are their jobs affected by population trends?

2 Prepare a collage of scenes that you feel depict overpopulation or the results of overpopulation. Use clippings from newspapers, magazines, and travel advertisements.

3 Make a survey of family plans among unmarried people of ages eighteen to twenty, asking them how many children they think they would like to have. Compare this with a survey of married people in the reproductive years of life, who already have at least one or two children. How many children does the latter group consider ideal?

  a Compare the two groups. If there are differences, try to explain the reasons for them.

  b On the basis of what you have learned, would you expect the United States birthrate to continue to be low, or would you expect a minor increase in the near future?

Suggested readings

Azumi, Koya: "The Mysterious Drop in Japan's Birth Rate," *Trans-Action*, vol. 5, May 1968, pp. 46–48. Why did the birthrate plunge by more than 25 percent in 1966 and then return to normal the next year? The answer is a good example of the unexpected in human behavior and also illustrates cross-cultural differences.

Davis, Kingsley: "The Migration of Human Populations," *Scientific American*, vol. 231, September 1974, pp. 93–105. What caused extensive migrations in prehistoric times and what causes them now? Why have European countries that used to export people now become importers of people? Are modern migration policies wise and humanitarian, or are they aimed at exploiting cheap labor? A distinguished sociologist investigates all these questions.

Ehrlich, Paul: "Population Control," *Saturday Evening Post*, Fall 1972, pp. 8–12. An outspoken advocate of attempts to impose birth control in poor countries pleads also for economic policies that will help such countries. If people no longer fear childhood death, they may decide that large families are unnecessary.

Hauser, Philip M.: "The Census of 1970," *Scientific American*, vol. 225, July 1971, pp. 17–25. What is the course of internal migration in the United States from region to region and within metropolitan areas? Hauser presents a rundown of the 1970 U.S. Census Bureau report, the last thorough report available. (Hauser is a sociologist who specializes in demography.)

Myrdal, Gunnar: "The Transfer of Technology to Underdeveloped Countries," *Scientific American*, vol. 231, September 1974, pp. 173–182. A distinguished scholar and humanitarian argues that industrial nations have a moral obligation to help the poorer nations develop technologically. He also argues that a better life in the poorer nations will give them a motive for birth control.

Pohlman, Edward, and Daniel Callahan: "Food Incentives for Sterilization. Can They Be Just?" *The Hastings Center Reporter*, vol. 3, February 1974, pp. 10–12. Is it ethical to give food to the hungry only if they agree to sterilization? Yes, says Pohlman. No, says Callahan. Read their arguments.

UNESCO Courier: "And Tomorrow How Many?" May 1974. An entire issue of *UNESCO Courier* devoted to facts about population growth and opinions as to what to do.

UNESCO Courier: "World Population Year," July–August 1974. A second issue devoted to the problems of population. Many articles warn of disaster. A few take the opposite position. Other articles outline policies in China, Ghana, Indonesia, and Latin America.

Key to questions. Multiple Choice: 1-a; 2-b; 3-c; 4-d; 5-b; 6-c; 7-a; 8-a; 9-b; 10-c; 11-d; 12-c; 13-b; 14-a; 15-b. True-False: 1-T; 2-F; 3-T; 4-T; 5-F; 6-F; 7-T; 8-F; 9-F; 10-T; 11-F; 12-T; 13-T; 14-T; 15-F.

18
URBANIZATION

This chapter describes the processes of urban growth, the social changes involved in urbanization, and problems and policies regarding the cities. After reading it, you should be able to:

1 Understand how modern industrial and transportation systems have promoted urban development.

2 Recognize the problems resulting from the high cost of city government, urban decay, and the flight from central cities of middle-class and wealthy residents as well as businesses.

3 See the patterns of racial segregation in major cities and how certain government policies have contributed to segregation.

4 Assess the costs and benefits of urban-renewal plans, model cities, and new towns.

5 Examine the effects of urbanization on personality and mental health.

6 Recognize the many factors that must be considered before dreams of a bright urban future can be fulfilled.

7 Make a carefully reasoned decision about whether to live in a rural area, small town, suburb, or city.

People have moved from farms and villages to towns and cities for thousands of years. However, this movement was given its greatest push by the industrial revolution, which began in England in the 1760s. The industrial revolution was the change in production from hand labor to machinery and from work in the home to factory work. Increasing numbers of agricultural workers—freed from farm labor by more efficient agricultural methods—flooded the cities, looking for work in factories and mills. This urbanization, or massive shift from rural to city life, increased cultural diverstiy and speeded up cultural change. Before, people's patterns of social interaction were limited to family, kinship, and neighborhood groups. Now, they included thousands of other people from all walks of life—from different social-class, racial, ethnic, and religious backgrounds.

Because of the greater social diversity of urban life, city dwellers have more life-styles from which to choose than those who live on farms. On the other hand, those who live in cities often feel trapped by the people who always surround them and the many rules and regulations that restrict their lives. Deviance is more common in the city, and, except in the case of crime, is more tolerated. In rural communities and small towns, deviant behavior was discouraged by parents and other relatives and by neighborhood gossip; the very phrase "alternate life-style" was meaningless.

Modern urban life intensifies the general shift of society from mechanical solidarity to the organic solidarity of which Durkheim spoke (see Chapter 1). People are less alike, less bound by tradition, more differentiated in occupations and ways of life, yet highly interdependent economi-

cally. Urbanization also fosters the growth of secondary-group relationships. Primary relationships continue, but they occupy a smaller part of one's life than in the past. The change to modern urban-industrial society has been characterized by Ferdinand Tönnies (1957) as a shift from a folk society characterized by primary relationships, informality, and little competition, which he called *gemeinschaft*, to business-oriented society, or *gesellschaft*. In gemeinschaft society, people struggle with nature to wrest a living from the soil; in geselleschaft society they compete with each other. Gesellschaft society is contractual, time-centered, and fast-moving.

These contrasts have always set urban life apart from rural life. However, in the past, only a small percentage of people were urban; all societies were overwhelmingly rural. (See Table 18-1, page 509, for the modern contrast.) Since agricultural methods were inefficient, most people had to work on farms to produce enough food. Slow transportation made it difficult to supply the cities; for this reason, the cities were relatively small. Sanitation was so bad that epidemics frequently wiped out large percentages of urban populations. There are equivalent problems of supply, sanitation, and pollution today, but they no longer restrict cities as severely as in the past. Major ancient cities ranged in size from 50,000 to a million or more, whereas the population of modern cities may reach 10 million.

Since industrialization is spreading to the developing parts of the world, urbanization is a worldwide phenomenon. Kingsley Davis reports that world population is today 39 percent urban. This may seem a low figure to people in the United States, which is over 70 percent urban, but it represents a drastic change. In 1850, no

(a)

(b)

Figure 18-1 With urbanization, (a) small-town life has given way to (b) a more competitive, faster-moving existence. [(a) Carl Weese, Rapho/Photo Researchers, Inc.; (b) Hugh Rogers, Monkmeyer]

single country was as urbanized as is the world as a whole today (Davis, 1972, p. 47). If the present trend were to continue unchanged, which Davis realizes is impossible, the entire world would be urban by 2031.

EFFECTS OF THE INDUSTRIAL REVOLUTION

Since 1698, a number of Englishmen had tinkered with the idea of using steam power for pumping water out of mines. Then, in 1769, James Watt developed a two-piston steam engine using a double-action principle. Before many years, another tinkerer fitted this type of engine to a moving device that clanked down the streets at the frightening speed of 3 miles per hour. In Scotland, someone placed such a device on tracks, and in the United States another inventor succeeded in putting steam power into

Table 18-1 Changes in Farming, 1940—1974

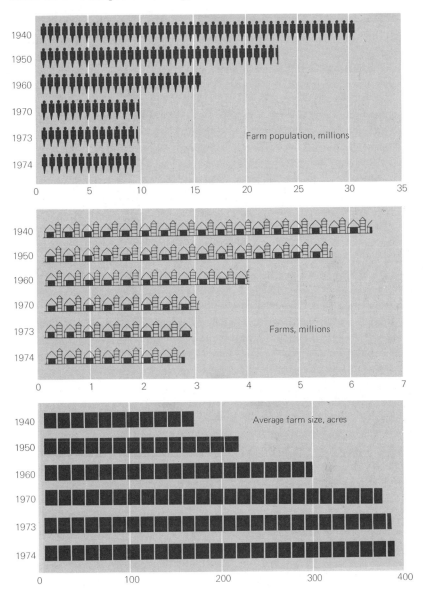

Note: A sharp decline in the percentage of people needed in agriculture is one of many reasons for the urban trend of the modern world.
Source: *Statistical Abstract of the United States Bureau of the Census,* U.S. Government Printing Office, Washington, D.C., 1976, p. 628.

ships. The age of railroads and steamships was under way, vastly increasing commerce and thereby increasing the size of cities. Railroads, and coal and iron deposits, began to dictate where cities would be located and what their patterns of growth would be.

Table 18-2   Concentric Growth

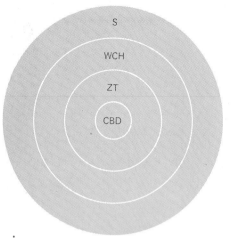

Key: CBD = central business district; ZT = zone in transition; WCH = working-class homes; S = suburbs.

Table 18-3   Sector Development

Patterns of urban growth

Old cities had grown in haphazard ways, sometimes around castles, more often around harbors and seaports or along rivers. Streets were nar-

row, cobblestoned affairs, winding and zigzagging past buildings that closed in upon them, making carriage and wagon traffic slow and impractical. Cities favored with a location along navigable waterways grew easily and prospered, while others were more restricted in growth potential.

With the coming of railroads, cities began to stretch out along new axes. Where raw materials were available, huge steelworks, along with all kinds of factories using steel, sprang up. Workers swarmed into the cities from the countryside, building cheap houses near the smoky factories at the edge of town. Wealthy people, who once lived in the center of town, began to move toward the suburbs and ride the commuter trains to town. The cities grew mightily, sometimes in several directions, along the original river or seacoast and along the new railroad tracks.

Toward the end of the nineteenth century, another revolutionary device was invented—the internal combustion engine. It, too, was fitted with wheels and was soon seen wheezing along roads, frightening horses. The horses had reason to be frightened, for they were looking at their replacement. The automobile enabled the city to spread out in all directions. By the time sociologists began drawing up patterns of urban growth, the automobile was already leaving its mark on the city. Urban growth was first represented by concentric circles or zones, of the type drawn by Ernest Burgess of the University of Chicago. (See Table 18-2.) According to the *concentric-zone theory*, cities develop by expanding outward from a central core in a series of concentric circles.

The central part of the city, or *central business district*, was built up for business and light industry, making it undesirable for residences. The first ring of houses and apartments close to the city center was not very desirable either and eventually became slums that were rented by the poorest people. These areas were called *zones in transition*, on the assumption that they were gradually changing from residential to commercial and industrial use. In the United States, such areas were first inhabited by immigrants from overseas. More recently, black people from the rural South or Puerto Ricans have moved into them. Although they were originally called foreign enclaves, they are now referred to as ghettos. Whatever they are called, however, they are the areas having the poorest city services, the highest rates of illness, and the worst infestations of rats (see the insert below, "Civil Rats").

Beyond the slum area were low-cost dwellings for working-class people, and beyond them, higher-priced suburbs. Variations on this scheme were suggested. Some pointed out that particular sectors of the city continued to be of high residential value, and that well-to-do people who had once inhabited a given sector continued to move outward in the same direction as the houses close to the city center decreased in value. (See Table 18-3.)

Another picture of the city stressed the idea that sometimes a number of communities had grown together, so that the city had several centers—the *multiple-nuclei theory* (Table 18-4). In all cases, natural features of the terrain—such as lakes, rivers, and hills—interfered with the theoretical scheme of development, as did

---

Civil rats

This summer, when 130 officials of twenty cities gathered in the gentleman farmers' community of Warrenton, Va., to discuss the results of the first year of the $15 million Federal anti-rat program, there was a distinct air of optimism. "It was almost evangelism," reports Robert Novick, head of the U.S. Bureau of Environmental Management. "They believed they were doing a job and meeting the needs of the people."

The officials may have been satisfied, but among the nation's slum dwellers—who each year suffer 14,000 bites, 6,000 cases of disease and an incalculable number of electrical fires, all caused by rats—the mood is much less exuberant. For the fact is that while city health officers have been busy poisoning rats in countless numbers, the urban rat population has continued to rise, encouraged by failure of other city services—notably poor garbage collection.

In New York, for instance, where garbage carpets the alleyways and vacant lots of the slums, the proportion of rat infested buildings increased from 8.5 percent to 18.5 percent in one year's time. (Boston has a similar record, and Washington, D.C.'s is even worse.)

"We know we can go in and kill the rats," says Novick, who administers the aid project for some 25 cities around the country. "But they rebound unless you take away the food and harborage, and this really hasn't been tried." Federal officials, in fact, are so desperate to show results (each year the anti-rat program gets a rough going over in Congress where wags refer to it as the "civil rats bill") that they are talking of withholding money from cities that cannot get their trash under control. . . . Novick estimates that there are at least 300 cities with critical rat problems, but at the moment there is money enough to fund Federal programs in only 25.

City residents, moreover, are no longer unique in their concern with the rat problem. There are indications that the rats are now moving out into the suburbs. . . .

Table 18-4 Multiple Nuclei: City Growth around a Number of Business Centers (B), with a Confused Pattern of Residential Values

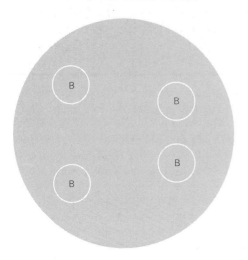

such ecological factors as railroads, steel mills, garbage dumps, and sewage disposal plants.

What eventually happened, though, was that all the big cities began to expand in a leap-frogging manner, with new centers growing up in all areas. The situation has been referred to as an *exploding metropolis*, sometimes unpleasantly compared with a growing cancer. Since automobiles and highways made it possible to commute long distances to work, there was no barrier to expanding outward, as there had been when growth mainly followed rivers and railroad lines. Not only did metropolitan areas expand in all directions, but they began to grow together. New descriptions were found, including such words as *urban sprawl*, *strip cities*, and *megalopolis*, along with more formal terminology from the U.S. Census Bureau.

Urban terminology

The word *city* has become rather vague in its meaning, which is one reason why media accounts often give conflicting views about the size and population of cities. One may read in the newspaper that New York City has 11 or 12 million inhabitants, then consult an almanac and find the figure to be about 7.9 million. The difference is the distinction between the political and the ecological city. The *political city* is the area within the city limits governed as part of the urban unit. The *ecological city* includes the political city plus its surrounding environment. *Human ecology* refers to the relationships between people and their environment, both the natural environment and the alterations in the environment brought about by human activity: roads, railroads, industry, parks, and even housing areas. *Ecological city*, then, is a rather vague term, referring to all the area that can be considered part of the city's ecology and that is economically dependent on the city.

Urban sprawl describes the ugly, haphazard way in which most cities have grown outward, with unsightly factories, slag heaps, billboards, and junkyards interspersed with residential areas. *Strip cities* are cities that grow together in lines for many miles, often along rivers or seacoasts. The hundred miles or more of coast separating Los Angeles from San Diego is rapidly becoming one vast strip city. *Megalopolis* refers to the most far-reaching, densely populat-

Figure 18-2 Urban sprawl has turned many areas into eyesores. Conservationists and urban planners are trying to control it. (*Hugh Rogers, Monkmeyer*)

Figure 18-3 Our highway systems have created suburbs and, ultimately, strip cities. (*Motor Vehicle Manufacturers Association*)

ed urban areas, such as the one extending along the eastern seaboard of the United States from Boston southward as far as Virginia, or the Ruhr Valley region of Germany. Sometimes this term is used more loosely to describe any case in which big cities have grown together. The U.S. Census Bureau uses more exact terms than these for describing urban areas and urbanization. The 1970 census rated the United States population as 73.4 percent urban and 25.5 percent rural. The definition of *urban*, however, includes many residents who probably do not consider themselves urbanites. In 1970, 68.6 percent of the United States population lived within *Standard Metropolitan Statistical Areas* (SMSAs)—central cities with a population of 50,000 or more, together with the surrounding area that is economically integrated with the city. The Census Bureau's definiton of *urban* also

includes any other towns having at least 2,500 inhabitants. Table 18-5 (page 514) shows a growth in urbanization in all parts of the country between the census years 1960 and 1970.

A special report by the Census Bureau in early 1976 indicated that metropolitan areas had grown by only 3.4 percent since 1970, whereas rural areas had grown by 5.5 percent—the first reversal of the tendency for metropolitan areas to grow at the expense of rural areas. The Census Bureau also released a report on what it called *Standard Consolidated Statistical Areas* (SCSAs) which were listed rather than defined (United Press, February 8, 1976). Such areas generally include clusters of cities and constitute more or less the same things as a megalopolis. The statistics for SCSAs (in millions) are as shown in Table 18-6.

Since they describe areas that are linked together by common industries, highways, and public services, these figures are more significant that statistics that include only persons living within particular city limits.

Limits of growth

Will urban growth go on indefinitely? Actually, there have been signs of a slowdown for a number of years. Such big cities as New York, Chicago, Philadelphia, Los Angeles, and especially San Francisco have lost population in their central areas, although the suburbs surrounding them continue to grow. The latest census report indicates that in many cases, growth has slowed even in the suburbs, with rapid urban growth reported mainly in Florida, Texas, and Colorado in the years since the 1970 census. Even in the period 1960 to 1970, the rural decline was slower than in the past, and 65 percent of the towns in the 10,000 to 50,000 range showed substantial gains (Wrigley, 1973, pp. 55–59). The 1970s have shown further gains for small towns, with more gaining than losing population.

The metropolitan areas have apparently become less attractive than in the past for two

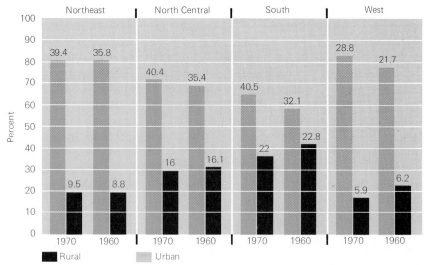

Table 18-5 United States Rural and Urban Population, 1960 and 1970, Millions

	Northeast	North Central	South	West
1970 Urban	39.4	40.4	40.5	28.8
1960 Urban	35.8	35.4	32.1	21.7
1970 Rural	9.5	16	22	5.9
1960 Rural	8.8	16.1	22.8	6.2

■ Rural ▨ Urban

Table 18-6 Standard Consolidated Statistical Areas

	Population (in millions)
New York City region	17.2
Los Angeles region	10.
Chicago	7.6
Philadelphia	5.6
Detroit	4.7
San Francisco Bay area	4.6
Boston	3.9
Cleveland	2.9
Houston	2.4
Miami	2.2
Seattle	1.8
Cincinnati	1.6
Milwaukee	1.6

Source: U.P.I., February 8, 1976.

reasons: decline in the quality of life in the cities and rising costs of urban living.

METROPOLITAN PROBLEMS

The metropolitan areas continue to grow, although at a reduced rate. It is not to be assumed that urbanization will reverse itself to such a degree that giant cities will become a thing of the past. However, many of them are faced with great problems.

The quality of life

Although living conditions in metropolitan areas differ greatly depending on geographic region and social class, it is possible to make certain generalizations: There is a positive correlation between size of city and crime rate (see Table 18-7, page 516). In nearly all cities, ghetto areas are seriously depressed. People who can afford to do so usually leave the central city and settle in the suburbs. Yet even the suburbs become congested. They are often poorly planned and they present serious transportation problems for those who must work in the city; the costs of police and fire protection, water, sewage, garbage, and energy rise rapidly; and there is often heavy smog.

Opinions about the quality of life vary considerably. The *Report of the National Advisory Commission on Civil Disorders* warned that the rot of our central cities would continue and increase the chance of renewed riots in the future (1968). Popular magazines frequently use the term *crisis* when referring to our cities. Leonard Duhl, in the introduction to a collection of generally pessimistic essays on the cities says, "It is one thesis of this book that the crisis of urbanization of America is the crisis of size, of complexity, and of the large and varied administrative structures that are around us" (1969). Edward Banfield takes the opposing view: that

cities represent a major material improvement over the past, that congestion is actually decreasing as people move to the suburbs, and that even slum areas are not as bad as they were years ago (1974). Motion pictures made about 1900 clearly reveal that the cities were at least as dingy then as they are now. Yet we have come to expect more than maintenance of the status quo. Furthermore, urban redevelopment programs often displace poor people from their homes without giving them suitable places to go. The victims of this process may be white, black, or members of another minority group, but they are always poor. Among them are the aged, whose hold on life sometimes depends on sticking to the familiar and not being disturbed (see the insert on page 517 "Elderly Who Are Hard to Relocate").

The nation was startled in 1974 to learn that its largest city, New York, was facing bankruptcy. Over the years, the city had shouldered the burden of staggering welfare costs—continuing its historical role of provider for large numbers of immigrants, especially those coming from Puerto Rico. It had also supported a large program of

Figure 18-4 Some believe that the city attracts the very rich and the very poor: the rich because they can live anywhere, the poor because they have nowhere else to go. (a) Park Avenue, in Midtown New York City, lined with luxurious high-rises. (b) Upper Park Avenue, in the slum of Harlem. [(a) and (b), Joan Roth]

(b)

(a)

Table 18-7 Violent Crime in Metropolitan and Other Areas

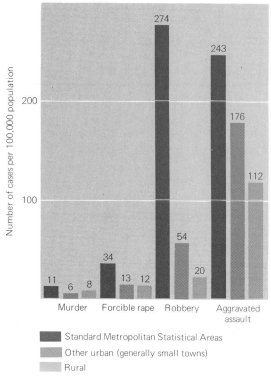

Source: *U.S. Fact Book: The Statistical Abstract of the U.S. Bureau of the Census,* Grosset and Dunlap, New York, 1976, p. 150.

public services. By financial sleight of hand, it was able to delay the crisis for years by borrowing on the future. But eventually credit ran out. The city avoided defaulting on its debts only after receiving loans from labor unions and finally promises of financial aid from the federal government. The problems of New York have been more severe than those of most cities, but many others also have money troubles.

One solution to these financial problems has been to raise taxes while also cutting back on such services as police and fire protection. This could have the unfortunate effect of driving businesses from the city to escape high taxes, thus lowering city revenues even further, which in turn could prompt others to leave.

By maintaining moderate interest rates on suburban home loans, the Federal Housing Administration has—without meaning to—aided the flight of the urban middle class to the suburbs. Their policy has benefited middle-class whites but has been bad for poorer people, both black and white, who cannot afford suburban housing and whose dwellings generally cannot qualify for loans.

The housing problem

As interest rates and construction costs rose sharply in the 1970s, the hope of owning a house in the suburbs, which has always been part of the American dream, began to fade for many. Just what the effect of rapidly rising homeowning costs will be on metropolitan areas is hard to judge. Perhaps greater congestion will pay economic dividends. Apartments, townhouses, and condominiums are cheaper to build than separate dwellings. Their service costs—such as heating, water, and sewage disposal—are also much lower.

Americans prefer to live in their own homes. City planners and architects had assumed that more people would buy townhouses in the early 1970s than actually did, so that in some places they became hard to sell. At the same time, individual houses sold very rapidly, and a housing shortage developed. By the mid-seventies, even multiple-unit dwellings were hard to find, despite the fact that their prices had doubled over five or six years.

SOCIAL-CLASS DIVISIONS

In recent decades, medium- to high-income city dwellers have generally moved out of American cities to the suburbs, while the poorest people have remained near metropolitan centers. But this has not always been the case. Many cities offer attractive houses, apartments, and multiple-family dwellings near their central areas, especially as a result of urban redevelopment.

Also, not all suburbs are middle class; some are poor. Nevertheless, the pattern for many years has been the concentration of poverty in central cities and of greater affluence in the suburbs.

The problem of social-class segregation is largely one of racial segregation. Despite the progress that black Americans have made in the last twenty years, they make up a far greater proportion of the nation's poor than their numbers in the population warrant. Furthermore, and contrary to the age-old stereotype of black Americans, they are more highly urbanized than whites (see Table 18-8). Hence, large areas of urban slums are almost entirely black; the residents are trapped in their ghettos, without the income needed to move out. The following statistical description of Chicago gives a good idea of the changes that have come about as more affluent people have moved to the suburbs (De Vise, 1974, pp. 38–45).

The poor are concentrated in the political city of Chicago, the middle and upper classes in the

Table 18-8 Population Changes in Metropolitan Areas by Race, 1950—1970

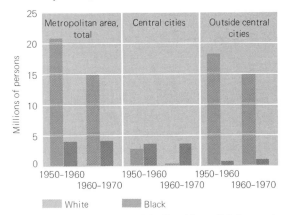

Source: *The Statistical Abstract of the United States, U.S. Bureau of the Census*, Washington, D.C., 1976, p. 3.

Elderly who are hard to relocate

A university anthropologist says a 72-year-old man would rather live in a cockroach-infested hotel and eat eggs, beer and ice cream than live in a nursing home.

The man described by Paul Bohannan of the University of California, Santa Barbara, is one of hundreds who may be forced out of old hotels when redevelopment of downtown San Diego starts.

Bohannan, who has been studying the 16-square-block area of San Diego for two years, said "even though San Diego has been very good about setting up relocation services for the elderly, there is probably no way these particular people can be relocated into the kind of housing they prefer."

The researcher says a subculture of "invisible elderly" all across the nation is dedicated to life style of self-reliance and self-direction rather than the comforts and regulations of a nursing home.

"Sure they want better food," he said, "but not by giving up their freedom to decide on the course of their lives."

Many people want to help these elderly out of their situation in the wrong way, according to Bohannan. "We must not close these places . . . or at least we must find these people suitable housing."

United Press in *San Francisco Chronicle*, July 5, 1976. Reprinted with permission of United Press International.

Urbanization

517

surrounding suburbs. The city contains 90 percent of the blacks living within the Chicago metropolitan area, 64 percent of the unemployed, 85 percent of the welfare recipients, and 76 percent of those whose mother tongue is Spanish (largely Puerto Ricans, whose presence reminds us that other minority groups besides blacks also experience high rates of poverty).

During the period 1960–1970, 220 factories, 760 stores, and—along with them—229,000 jobs moved out of Chicago into surrounding areas. The loss amounted to 14 percent of the jobs available in Chicago. Meanwhile, the well-publicized "white flight" was taking place. During that decade, 500,000 whites moved out of the city, while over 300,000 blacks moved in. Statistics of this type are common for Northern cities.

Because of deterioration, abandonment, and replacement with other land use, the city lost 140,000 private housing units while gaining 19,000 public housing units. The area outside the city gained 350,000 housing units and an estimated 500,000 jobs. Since there were fewer jobs in the city in 1970 than there had been in 1960, more people commuted out of the city for jobs in the suburbs and fewer commuted into the city.

The South Bronx

Dial Torgerson describes what he considers the most hopeless slum area of New York City, the South Bronx (1973, pp. 16–17). This area has 136 juvenile gangs, the highest crime rate in New York City, and 20,000 drug addicts. One store owner reported being burglarized a hundred times in a fifteen-year period. The population is steadily declining as young people grow up and move out. The saying among the Puerto Ricans, who make up 65 percent of the population (the other 35 percent is black), is *sal si puedes* ("get out if you can"). The process of abandonment is speeding up, and the most alert and ambitious are the first to sell out and leave.

Chicago's East Woodlawn

The process that has occurred in the South Bronx has also occurred in Chicago's East Woodlawn, which had 60,000 residents in 1960 but only 35,300 in 1970. The exodus was largely among people aged twenty to forty-four, those able to get out and find housing and possibly jobs elsewhere. Even though an estimated $35 million has been spent to improve the area, the deterioration has continued.

To the west is West Woodlawn, also a black community but one in which more of the housing units are occupied by stable working-class owners and where the rate of abandonment is much lower. To the south is a higher-income area, and to the north the University of Chicago. At first glance, the location near the university would seem to be favorable. However, crime, vandalism, and deterioration have driven away those people who once gave the area a sense of community.

Urban decay and abandonment are good examples of self-fulfilling prophecies. Banks and lending agencies, deciding that certain areas no longer offer safe investments, *redline* them—that is, draw a red line around the areas marked for no further investment of funds. It then becomes impossible to obtain improvement loans in these areas. Property is no longer improved or even properly maintained, and the prophecy of deterioration is fulfilled.

It would be a mistake to assume that all slum areas decline in the same way or at the same rate as those just mentioned. Torgerson points to the large, crowded Bedford-Stuyvesant area in New York as a cause for encouragement. As in West Woodlawn, many of the people own their own homes and have an interest in keeping the community in good repair. A Bedford-Stuyvesant Restoration Corporation was created in 1966 to help finance repairs at low interest rates and to promote such community services as health and child care. What is needed to infuse a sense of hope into slum areas, a Ford Foundation report concludes, is community interest and participation as well as help from governmental and financial agencies. Equally important are a stable working-class population and a high level of home ownership.

URBANISM AND RACE RELATIONS

The hatreds arising from racial discrimination—especially housing policies that excluded minorities—fueled the urban riots of the 1960s described in Chapter 11. Whites who had fled to the suburbs tried to keep blacks out by passing seemingly nondiscriminatory laws which in fact tended to exclude blacks. Laws regulating minimum building size were passed to keep prices too high for blacks to pay. Legal ploys were used to prevent whites from selling property to blacks—this is no longer allowed. Suburban dwellers did, and still do, put up strong opposition to public housing projects in the suburbs, for such projects, intended for the poor, are heavily black. Real-estate brokers have also contributed to discriminatory housing patterns, often steering black clients away from white neighborhoods to areas that are already black. They also engage in the destructive but lucrative practice of *block busting*, in which one or two black families are helped to move into an all-white block in order to frighten white homeowners into selling their houses quickly at low prices.

Housing in ethnic neighborhoods is often inexpensive enough to be within the means of blacks. Yet white ethnics make a determined effort to keep their own neighborhoods to themselves. This is partly because of their ethnocentric attitudes and racial bias but also because they are acquainted with one another, have a sense of community, and share common local customs (Novak, 1971, pp. 282–286).

Peter Binzen notes in his study of Kensington, a blue-collar neighborhood in Philadelphia (1970, p. 230), that poor white areas of the city also have inferior schools, poor housing conditions, and inadequate city services. The white ethnics are inclined to say, "We're getting along

without help, why can't they?" They generally fail to understand that urban blacks suffer certain disadvantages that white ethnics do not: much greater prejudice and discrimination and far fewer jobs for the unskilled than existed in the days when large numbers of Italians, Poles, Irish, Greeks, Czechs, and others arrived in the United States as immigrants. Binzen reports many remarks by the people of Kensington (largely Irish, Italian, and Polish) which show their absorption in the problem of black-white relations. For example, "Kensington has a wonderful future as long as it remains all white" (1970, p. 230).

Black suburbs?

Despite white resistance, during the 1960s and 1970s black people began to move to the suburbs. Usually they moved into poorly built houses that were little better than the housing they left. While 750,000 black people moved to the suburbs in the 1960s, 3.4 million moved to the cities (*Newsweek*, 1971b, p. 53), greatly increasing urban crowding. Although the movement to the cities has declined in the 1970s, the central areas of Northern American cities remain black. In some cases, as in Washington, D.C., and Newark, New Jersey, blacks are the majority.

Ecological change

The desertion of cities by business and industry, the white flight to the suburbs, and the deterioration of housing have made a radical ecological change, leaving some urban areas almost vacant. The U.S. Department of Housing and Urban Development (H.U.D.) at one point acquired over 100,000 housing units through default on payments. At present, H.U.D. is interested in selling its houses at extremely low cost to people who will promise to live in them and improve them. The term *urban homesteading* has been used to describe this effort to infuse new life into abandoned urban areas.

A reversal of trends?

The city retains certain powerful attractions—theaters, museums, libraries, and the like—plus the dynamic, stimulating rhythm of life that can exist only in an urban environment. Have people begun to return to the cities? In fact, thousands have taken advantage of the bargain prices of abandoned but basically sound houses to enable them to move back to the city. The "push" of the suburbs is often more responsible for this move, however, than the "pull" of the city. Our suburbs have become so stretched out that driving distances from city to suburb are prohibitive. Prices in the suburbs have also skyrocketed, making the city once again a possible alternative. The return to the city is a mere trickle compared with the mass exodus of the 1950s and 1960s, but it is sociologically interesting. How are young white couples received when they move into mostly black areas? Do blacks flee whites the way whites have fled from blacks? Does the return of the white middle class help or harm the black community? (See the insert "New Urbanites.")

Whatever the prejudice of blacks against whites, they do not panic, sell, and run. In a few cases, for homeowners, property values improve and black people may make a profit. As a general rule, however, the blacks lose again. If they rent, their rents go up; if they live in a building designated as "rehabilitated," they are evicted. What consideration has been given black people and the poor when the federal government rather than private enterprise has had a hand in urban redevelopment?

GOVERNMENT POLICIES

As early as the 1930s, the solution for urban problems was thought to be federally funded housing units, particularly in the inner city. Although over a million such housing units still exist, they represent a very low rate of public housing compared with that of most European countries. Conservative and business opposition to public housing has been strong, not only because it removes a large and profitable sector of the building industry from private initiative but also because it is considered socialistic. Consequently, public housing has generally been made available only to the very poor, those whose housing would compete little if at all with private industry. Strict income limits have been

---

New urbanites   DIAL TORGERSON

. . . A new story of the slums is taking place slowly, a block at a time, sometimes scarcely noticed in the city where it is happening. The scene is strangely reminiscent of an earlier scene:

The first white family to move into a black neighborhood is called a blockbuster. Sometimes the process is called reverse blockbusting.

The first families in are those which blend well. They are relaxed about matters of race and class, a bit bohemian perhaps—musicians or artists, or maybe a long-haired lawyer with a store-front civil rights practice. Their block is sometimes called the frontier.

Once the first white family is in, the realtors bring in other middle-class whites. See, they say, the first family is already there. The ice is broken. The second family is easier to sell.

Some of the realtors are the sons and daughters of the real estate people who brought the first black families to the same blocks 20 years ago.

"We were the first middle-class family on this block," said Jean Lewton, whose block is on 10th St. in Washington's Capitol Hill district. "Our black neighbors thought we must be poor whites to want to live here."

Their red-brick home is three stories high, 17 feet wide and 40 feet deep, with a little garden at the rear and black-painted wrought iron at the entry stairs.

Outside the tree-lined street is aglare in the brilliance of high-powered street lights Washington hopes will reduce crime—lights that make it look as though someone were getting ready to shoot a movie. A young white mother wheels her baby in a stroller, and four black youths pass, each in a hat of brazen eccentricity, gossiping loudly.

"A realtor brought us here in 1967 and showed us a rehabbed (rehabilitated) house down the street," Mrs. Lewton recalled. "It turned out a speculator had fixed it up and no one lived there. They wanted us in so they could sell other houses here to middle-class people."

In 1967 the "restored area"—a realtor's term for white—stopped at 6th St., two blocks from the Library of Congress complex. The house on 10th St. was deep in a ghetto stretching east toward the Potomac.

"We were living in Pimit Hills, in Virginia, in a ticky tacky tract an hour from Washington at rush hour," Mrs. Lewton said. "Our neighbors were blue-collar workers and army sergeants, and none of the women could talk about anything but babies and diapers.

"We were 26 and 30, and making $10,000 a year. All we could afford was $18,500. That's what we paid for this place."

"It was tough the first three years," said Val Lewton, a tall, sandy-haired man who is an artist and an exhibits designer for the Smithsonian Institution.

"The sound at night was a constant CRASH. . . ." In 1968, after the assassination of Martin Luther King, riots swept the black areas of Washington. Flames glowed in the sky above the Shaw and Cardozo ghettos to the north of Capitol Hill.

An army weapons carrier parked in front of the Lewton home, machine guns on the street, while peace was restored. Property values dropped in the area after the riots. One result: more young whites bought in quickly to take advantage of bargain prices.

Now 10th St. is 60% white. . . . Lewton paints in his downstairs studio and rides his bike to work. Mrs. Lewton is associate editor of a weekly newspaper. The Lewton's house is now worth twice what they paid for it, and they did most of the work themselves. One down the block, completely restored, sold for $65,000. . . .

What happens to blacks in a neighborhood where the first whites begin to appear?

They don't flee in panic as did their white predecessors in the same blocks a generation ago. If they own their own homes, they may sell, take the cash and move to the suburbs, now newly opened to black buyers. Or they may stay, as did many in Capitol Hill, suddenly a new minority.

But suppose they live in a rooming house and are evicted by the middle-class pioneers? Where do they go?

They move into places already too crowded—places like Cardozo.

When private enterprise evicts, those evicted are on their own. No agency aids or even counts them. There are, in fact, few statistics to reflect the changes brought by reverse blockbusting. . . .

From Dial Torgerson, "Middle Class Returning to Inner Cities," *Los Angeles Times*, July 16, 1973, Part I, pp. 1, 18, 20. Copyright Los Angeles Times.

set to determine eligibility. Poor screening of applicants, however, has resulted in a heavy concentration of problem families in public housing—those with alcohol and drug problems, absent fathers, psychopathologies, and the like (Fuerst, 1974, pp. 48–53). The projects have been huge, institutionlike buildings whose forbidding appearance suggests the grim lives of the people inside. A study by the New York City Police Department showed that the rate of serious crimes committed in housing areas increases with the number of floors in a building. In 1971, in three-floor walk-up apartments, there were 30 serious crimes per year per 1,000 families. In buildings of more than thirteen floors, there were 68 serious crimes per 1,000 families (Rosenthal, 1972, p. 41). The concentration of multiproblem families in large buildings has speeded deterioration and vandalism. It has led all who have alternative possibilities to avoid public housing.

Urban renewal

The *urban-renewal* program was started by the federal government in 1949 to improve the appearance of cities, promote trade and commerce, provide better housing, and replace slums (Glazer, 1965, pp. 194–204). Since each city was encouraged to develop its own renewal plan, local politicians made the major decisions, sometimes giving higher priority to civic grandeur than to providing good public housing. Considerable improvements began to appear nevertheless. Blighted areas were torn down and replaced with new business buildings, cultural centers, and sometimes good housing. The people who had lived in the vanished slums, however, could not always afford to live in the new buildings. When slums are torn down, slum dwellers must look for low-rent housing—that is, other slums—somewhere else. Black leaders have called urban renewal "black removal."

Herbert Gans documents a case of urban renewal in Boston, in an area referred to as a slum and inhabited mainly by people of Italian descent (1962). The result was a serious dislocation of community life. Gans questions the use of the word *slum* to describe the area. He suggests that this word be used only in cases where living conditions result in high drug use, crime, violence, and unsafe streets. None of these conditions had existed in the Boston area. It was a place in which large families could afford to live comfortably; none of them thought of their area as a slum.

As a result of strong criticism of past policies, urban-renewal programs have been geared toward less disruption of local communities. An effort has also been made to provide housing for the poor people who are displaced. Priority is also being given to attracting the middle class back to the cities.

Model cities

In 1966, the federal government launched what it called the *Model Cities Program*. This program was to help redevelop urban areas while avoiding some of the problems created by earlier urban-renewal problems. Under the Model Cities Program, residents of areas to be redeveloped had to be consulted. The projects had to show potential benefits to those people, who, if they had the necessary skills, were to be hired to work on redevelopment projects. The number of existing housing units before and after redevelopment was to remain the same. Altogether, 150 Model Cities grants were made before the program ended in 1975.

The typical Model Cities Program included rehabilitation loans to homeowners, health centers, housing inspection and park maintenance, schools, and retraining programs (Post, 1973, pp. 13–15). Federal funds for such projects became scarce early in the Nixon administration, when the federal government started a policy of *revenue sharing*, turning over to the cities direct grants not tied to federal projects such as urban renewal or Model Cities. The same philosophy continued under the Ford administration, result-

A portion of the vast area known as "megalopolis" is shown in this aerial view of Long Island, New York.

ing in greater local control over urban-renewal projects. Whether the aims of the Model Cities Program will be carried out in the future depends increasingly on local power distribution. If financial and real-estate interests dominate the city, renewal projects will probably resemble earlier urban-renewal attempts. If poverty areas exert strong enough pressure, concessions like those of the Model Cities Program will have to be made. The increased voting power of blacks and the prominence of a number of black mayors makes the second possibility more likely than in the past. The cities face such a severe shortage of funds, however, that redevelopment programs will suffer unless Washington develops a bold new approach.

New towns

In the 1960s, the federal government also launched a new towns program. This program had objectives similar to those of Model Cities, but with more emphasis on self-contained communities with shopping areas, places of employment, schools, and recreation areas. When the government reduced its activities in urban planning during the Nixon and Ford administrations, most new towns, such as Rustin, Virginia, and Irvine, California, were taken over by private entrepreneurs. Several new towns have become places of beauty and convenience, but they do not provide low-cost housing for poor or even lower-middle-class families.

New towns have been much more prominent in Europe than in the United States. In Europe, they have been designed to relieve urban congestion, prevent ugly and unplanned urban sprawl, create adequate parks and green areas, and provide houses at various price ranges for people of different incomes. Stockholm has enjoyed the benefit of careful urban planning for many years, with well-coordinated new towns surrounding the central city. Finland is particularly noted for urban planning that does not interfere with the country's natural beauty. Since

World War II, England has built a large number of new towns. The best known are a series of communities surrounding London, separated from the great city by a greenbelt of farms and parkland. The new towns are based on the assumption that there are built-in disadvantages to urban life, and possibly even to the types of people produced in urban areas. Therefore, the new towns have tried to combine the advantages of the city with the pleasures of rural and small-town life.

THE URBAN TYPE

Aversion to city life existed long before the present pattern of urban decay. The urban personality, in the opinion of early Americans, had a certain sophistication but was neither as honest and straightforward as the rural personality nor as hearty and virile.

The antiurban bias

Morton and Lucia White (1964) document a long history of antiurban bias coming not only from the general public but from leading American intellectuals: Jefferson, Emerson, Melville, Hawthorne, Dewey, Park, and Cooley, among others. Public-opinion surveys in the 1970s have revealed some strange contradictions. Of one sample polled, 56 percent (largely urban) expressed a "great deal" of satisfaction and 32 percent a "fair amount" of satisfaction with their present neighborhoods. In reply to another question, asking where they would like to live if they had their choice, a majority preferred a small town, a village, or a rural area. William Watts and Lloyd Free (1973, pp. 82–84) see this reply as an indication of the enduring American myth "that true happiness is to be found only in the country, close to nature." Cross-tabulation of their findings seems to support the existence of this myth. Whereas only 40 percent of city dwellers said they wanted to stay in the city, 90 percent of rural residents said they wanted to stay in the country. Black urbanites were less happy with the city than whites, with 26 percent wanting to move to the suburbs, 11 percent to small towns or villages, and 30 percent to rural districts. In spite of their generally poor neighborhoods, however, 32 percent of black adults and 39 percent of black young people preferred to stay in the city.

New York City and antiurban bias

When New York City was on the verge of bankruptcy in 1974–1975, antiurban bias burst forth with much emotion and resentment. Russell Baker (1975, p. 6), a New Yorker writing a weekly column for *The New York Times Magazine*, describes the situation. He holds that the alleged reason for the country's lack of sympathy toward New York was its "financial irresponsibility." However, the city had actually not lived beyond its means more than many other American cities, and its deficit spending could not even be compared with that of the federal government. Baker concludes that the reason for the hostility was envy of the rich and successful of New York, combined with distaste for New York's very poor. There was almost no awareness that the majority of New Yorkers work hard for a modest living, just as other people do.

Baker notes particularly the American ethic regarding life's losers: they are lazy and deserve what they get.

Thus, the city that to many people symbolizes America, that has welcomed generations of immigrants and has treated them better than most cities would do, receives little sympathy. Baker finally suggests, rather sarcastically, that all New York's poor be given bus tickets to Washington, D.C., where the federal government that preaches to New York about fiscal responsibility could take care of them. This is not to suggest that New York or any other city has a perfect record, but there are no easy solutions to urban problems. Great cities exist because economic need has created them, and antiurban bias will not cause them to go away.

Conflicting studies of the urban personality

The urbanite, according to some sociological views, devotes more of his or her time to secondary and less to primary relationships, is

Figure 18-5 The new satellite town of Täby, Sweden. Swedish urban planning has had great influence in the United States. (*Swedish Information Service*)

highly competitive (unless a dropout), is in a rush, and manages to adjust to noise and congestion at a certain psychic cost. Georg Simmel (1962, pp. 151–165) concluded that the urbanite is therefore rather blasé, not feeling or showing emotions as strongly as does the rural person, developing a hard shell as a defense against the many shocks of the city. Urban dwellers, said Simmel, sharpen their wits but let their emotional natures suffer. Louis Wirth (1938, pp. 3–24), writing in the 1930s, gave a similar picture of the urban personality. He spoke of fragmented social relationships; short, superficial friendships; and alienation from others.

Attempts have been made to study the urban

personality more scientifically than either Simmel or Wirth did. Interestingly, the results have been quite inconsistent. The famous *Mental Health and the Metropolis: The Midtown Manhattan Study* by Leo Srole (1962, chaps. 7, 8) and associates would lead to the conclusion that this fast-moving, noisy, congested part of urban America is psychologically destructive. On the other hand, a much more recent study by John Collette comes to a directly opposite conclusion for city life in general (see the insert "Urban Stress Good for Us, Expert Says"). Srole and Collette agree that wretched poverty is bad for us, but Collette, at least, considers rural poverty even worse than urban poverty. Evidence from different parts of the world suggests that highly urbanized countries can be relatively free of pathologies. The Netherlands and Belgium are among the world's most crowded countries, yet their people generally enjoy good mental, physical, and economic health. The most crowded

Figure 18-6 Two conflicting views of the urban personality: (*a*) tense, impersonal, and competitive; (*b*) aware and involved in community activities. [(*a*) Rapho/Photo Researchers, Inc.; (*b*) Charles Harbath, Magnum]

(a)

(b)

Davy Crockett may have been the king of the wild frontier but he might have lived longer and happier if he'd been headquartered in downtown Manhattan.

So said Dr. John Collette, 34, a University of Utah medical sociologist completing a massive study of urban stress.

"Davy Crockett led a more painful life, with vermin, rotten teeth, probably had ulcers, and more than likely was asthmatic," Collette said, adding that the loner is the man with the greatest propensity for physical and mental ills.

"We have an antiurban bias. Everybody knows—it's part of our folk knowledge—that life was better 50 years ago on the farm than it is today in the city. Which, if we stop to think about it, is absolute nonesense." . . .

For one thing, although the incidence of mental disorder is higher in large urban areas, it isn't found where you might expect it. Collette said crowding inside the home tends to alleviate the effects of crowding outside. In other words, a crowded tenement is more healthy psychologically than a swank bachelor apartment.

In terms of physical health, the results are in favor of urban living. There are fewer maladies per capita as the density of the urban area increases, and again fewer as the size of the household community increases.

Density tends to bring better medical care; crowding involves people in the social relationships necessary to both physical and mental health.

"Some kind of relationship is better than none at all," Collette said. He said social isolation is the best predictor he has found of alcoholism, drug use and psychological disorder.

He ridicules "pop sociologists and doomsday philosophers" who sell books predicting that urban populations are reaching "critical limits" which will result in social catastrophe.

Their criteria, he says, are based on studies of animals forced to live in overcrowded environments—animals who have developed deviant behavior such as cannibalism and homosexuality—and those criteria have no relevance to human beings.

"We can say that it's unhealthy to live in a large, crowded urban area, but at the same time, that's where you find the best entertainment, that's where you find the best medical care, that's where you find the best cultural relief—none of which are of particular interest to rats."

From a UPI dispatch datelined Salt Lake City, printed in the *Los Angeles Times*, Oct. 24, 1974, Part I, p. 32.

Warning: Dr. Collette's conclusions are based in part on a lengthy study of the cities of New Zealand, which may bias his conclusions. Nevertheless, he questions the basis of much traditional and unproved bias against city living.

place on Earth is Hong Kong, famous for both poverty and vice. Yet, incredibly, well-organized Chinese families remain together and retain their traditional culture, while inhabiting "less than 3.7 square meters of living space per capita" (Behrman, 1976, p. 29).

Several studies conclude that cities do not necessarily foster pathology and alienation. Claude Fischer (1973, pp. 311–326) hypothesized that if city life were actually as Wirth describes it, cities would produce people with a sense of powerlessness, social isolation, and alienation. He found a slight, but only very slight, difference in favor of more rural settings where isolation was concerned, but none whatever for powerlessness. He concluded that there is no significant difference between urban and rural personality when people of the same social class are compared.

John Kasarda and Morris Janowitz (1974, pp. 328–339), making a similar study in England, came to roughly the same conclusions. They were particularly interested in whether city dwellers develop as strong a sense of community as those living in small towns. They concluded that there is little difference between the two. The important variable is length of residence; people who live in an area long enough tend to develop a sense of community.

Much antiurban bias results from social problems within the city, especially poverty, blighted central areas, and urban sprawl. In drawing comparisons between cities, Stanley Milgram (1970, pp. 1461–1468) notes that some city dwellers have a lot of civic pride and hence high morale. In such cases, people may gain rather than lose psychologically by living in the city. Although noise, congestion, and ugliness can harm the personality, these qualities do not have to be part of city life. Since rural life is no longer possible for most Americans, our job is to improve cities rather than to flee them.

URBAN PLANS AND PROSPECTS

Planners draw up pictures of cities of the future that are designed in new and beautiful ways. Growth is controlled. Central cities are surrounded by greenbelts. Thoroughfares connect the cities with outlying new towns. Beautiful though the dream is, William H. Whyte (1968, pp. 135–151) points out certain difficulties. In the first place, building costs are so high that we cannot bulldoze present cities and start over again. Second, says Whyte, these designs call for a level of beauty and elegance that excludes the poor from the cities. A more modest plan for

housing is needed. It should be based on utility and economy rather than an artist's dream of gleaming perfection. Finally, we do not have the government machinery for controlling urban growth. Without the necessary government restraints, urban expansion inevitably means real-estate speculation, exorbitant land costs, and destruction of valuable farm land. Although the U.S. Supreme Court in 1975 ruled that cities have a right to limit their growth rate by restricting the numbers of new housing units built, this ruling has been largely neglected. People still equate growth with progress and prosperity.

Accomodating the poor

The crowding of the poor into crumbling neighborhoods competes with unplanned urban sprawl as the greatest barrier to making cities places of beauty, safety, and convenience. It might yet be possible, however, to make public housing work, provided the units are small and designed for both lower- and middle-income persons. In 1970, the federal government began experimentally to pay housing allowances to the poor, leaving it up to them to find their own dwelling places. In 1975, this became official policy. When poor people are free to find their own housing, a certain amount of dispersal results, although housing has to be limited to areas of cheap housing. This approach creates no new houses, however, so that it is not very helpful in cities with housing shortages.

Although many of the abandoned houses and other buildings in urban areas can be rehabilitated, most of this sort of thing is done by private investors. This is true of the previously described young white couple who moved into a black ghetto in Washington, D.C. The result could be the same as that of so many of the earlier urban-renewal projects—providing more housing for middle-income people but less for the poor. It is possible, though, that declining areas could be improved if low interest rates and long payment terms were available. Local community organizations, such as the one in Bedford-Stuyvesant, could organize to promote these efforts.

Energy and environmental considerations

Ironically, just as it becomes clear that impersonal housing projects for the poor result in more crime and pathology, environmentalists argue in favor of clustering all people closer together. Artists' sketches of cities of the future show clusters of homes, apartments, or condominiums. Clustering holds down the costs of heating and lighting, and it simplifies water and sanitation services. Although the separate, individually owned home remains the American dream, mounting costs are making it much more difficult to acquire. The result will probably be a gradual increase in townhouses, apartments, and other multiple-family dwellings. Economics will to some degree force us to do what makes good sense in terms of environmental protection and energy conservation. Many examples from the Model Cities Program, new towns, and even resort areas show that cluster dwellings can be very attractive. No one, however, wants to see more of the massive structures that marked the early days of federal housing for the poor.

Today the housing shortage is growing, even though our population is increasing more slowly than in the past. This is true because more of our population is elderly, and households headed by the elderly usually consist of only one or two persons. More people than ever before are living alone, and more couples are not having children. A statistical illustration comes from the Southern California Association of Governments, which expects a 17.4 percent population increase in the next fifteen years but a 21.4 percent increase in housing demand (Seidenbaum, 1976, p. 1). The smaller household would seem to argue in favor of more apartments and condominiums rather than the old-fashioned family home. If central cities could

again be made livable, they could provide environmentally sound housing for the small household and save the money and energy involved in millions of miles of commuting. Such a plan would also cut down on auto pollution.

Meeting multiple needs

Whatever form housing takes in the future, the problems of existing cities will not go away, and the 140 million residents of Standard Metropolitan Statistical Areas will not be easily displaced. New forms of urban planning and urban renewal will be necessary. Probably some of the ideas of Model Cities and new towns will be revived. To prevent further physical decay and psychic alienation, the needs of all classes must be served. William Whyte quotes a statement from Samuel Pepys Cockerell, a London planner of 1790, whose guidelines for city planning have largely been ignored—to the detriment of our great cities (Whyte, 1968, p. 259):

> The master plan should embrace housing units for all classes. The focal points should be the residential squares and their gardens; the projects should be planned so that their edges blend with the existing neighborhoods, the plan should be amenable to step-by-step development so that each part may be complete in itself. . . .

As Whyte adds: "Those who would draft guidelines for modern project planning could hardly be better."

SUMMARY

Cities with populations into the hundreds of thousands existed in ancient history. But only the *industrial revolution* and increased agricultural efficiency made possible the giant size of modern cities. The transition to *urbanism* means a change in the style and pace of life from rural, folk society to modern business and contractual societies. Tönnies gave the name *gemeinschaft* to the older form of society and *gesellschaft* to the society that replaced it. Only in modern times have a majority of people been urban or suburban dwellers.

The industrial revolution was characterized by a series of inventions that necessitated heavy industry at or near urban centers and that speeded the pace of transportation. At first, the new cities grew along rivers, coasts, or canals, but then they expanded outward along railroad lines. Finally, the automobile age made it possible for cities to expand in all directions.

Ernest Burgess theorized that cities tend to grow in outward circles, or *concentric zones*, with business and financial buildings at the center (the *central business district*). This center is ringed by a *zone in transition*, in which light industry competes with residential use. The result is a decline in residential values and the appearance of tenement houses, cheap hotels, and vice. Beyond the zone in transition, a zone of acceptable homes for working-class people continues to exist. Beyond this lie the more desirable green suburbs. Some cities have grown in a more complex manner than that described by Burgess, either from a number of original centers (*multiple nuclei*) or tending to spread outward in rich, poor, and middle-class sectors. In recent times, all major cities have tended to expand outward in a manner described by the term *exploding metropolis*.

The *political city*—the area within the city limit—is surrounded by a much larger area that depends on it economically and is known as the *ecological city*. *Urban sprawl* is a term describing the spread of cities in an unplanned manner, with an ugly mixture of land use. A similar term, *strip city*, describes an urban area that extends great distances along a coastline or river. A *megalopolis* is a vast area in which many cities have grown together, as in the area from Boston southward to Virginia or the Ruhr Valley of Germany. All people living in *Standard Metropolitan Statistical Areas* (SMSAs) or areas dominated by a city of at least 50,000 are classified as urban by the U.S. Census Bureau. Over 73 percent of the United States population lives in SMSAs. The Census Bureau also considers Standard Consolidated Statistical Area (SCSAs), or clusters of SMSAs. By the late 1970s, for the first time in many decades, metropolitan areas were ceasing to grow at the expense of rural areas.

Metropolitan problems have contributed to a recent slowdown in the rate of metropolitan growth. At least one authority, Banfield, argues that the quality of cities is improving and only *seems* worse because of our rising expectations. Most authorities, however, point to rising tax rates, crime rates, the flight of more affluent people and many businesses to the suburbs, poor black ghettos, and deteriorated and abandoned housing as signs of an unhealthy condition in many major cities.

Modern American cities have become sharply divided between the poor—largely black—who live in decaying areas near urban centers and the middle class and rich—largely white—who move to suburbs. The poorest areas are characterized by vandalism and abandonment. Certain sectors of Chicago and New York provide good examples. Sometimes *redlining* or *blockbusting* help to create slums. Occasionally community action with outside financial help has halted urban decay, as in New York's Bedford-Stuyvesant district. Government-supported Federal Housing Administration loans have helped the middle class move to the suburbs, and government public housing projects have helped concentrate the very poor in huge, centralized housing units. The Department of Housing and Urban Development has recently tried a policy of selling abandoned homes very cheaply to *urban homesteaders* in an attempt to return financially independent people to the central city. An example of a return to a Washington, D.C., neighborhood is given as a success story of such a policy, but it is too early to say whether any major movement back to the central cities is under way.

Urban-renewal projects have often improved

the appearance of downtown areas and restored trade and business values. Often, though, they have replaced cheap housing units without providing for the poor who have been displaced. The *Model Cities Program* attempted to improve the treatment of the poor when urban redevelopment took place, but it was largely abandoned during the Nixon-Ford administrations. *Revenue sharing* was then introduced. *New towns*, usually private developments, have been built in a few cases. These are free of slums and urban blight, but they are too costly for the poor. Several European countries, most notably Sweden and Finland, have long been developing new towns to provide housing for all social classes.

Although America has always shown a bias against city living, there are differences of opinion over whether such a bias is justified. Some sociologists (Wirth and Simmel) and a leading psychologist (Srole) have concluded that urbanism has a bad effect on the human personality. Fischer, on the other hand, finds no significant personality difference between urbanites and small-town people. Collette presents good evidence that urban life is actually good for people. Milgram concludes that the problem is one of *type of urban community*, not urbanism itself. He finds that some cities seem to develop civic pride and high morale.

Some enthusiastic urban planners look forward to an age of gleaming cities with none of the present problems. The trouble, as William H. Whyte points out, is that we must live with our present cities in the meanwhile. We also have the problem of providing for all social classes, protecting the environment, and conserving energy and resources. Housing shortages are acute at present because of high building costs and the tendency of nearly all people to want homes of their own. Under the circumstances, there are strong economic and environmental arguments for condominiums and other types of cluster living, but Americans continue to have a strong preference for single-family houses.

Study guide

Terms to know

Industrial revolution
Urbanization
Gemeinschaft
Gesellschaft
Concentric-zone theory
Zone in transition
Central business district
Multiple nuclei
Exploding metropolis
Political city

Ecological city
Human ecology
Urban sprawl
Strip cities
Megalopolis
Standard Metropolitan
   Statistical Areas (SMSAs)
Standard Consolidated
   Statistical Areas (SCSAs)

Redlining
Blockbusting
Urban homesteading
Urban renewal
Model Cities Program
Revenue sharing
New towns

Names to know

Ferdinand Tönnies
Georg Simmel
Louis Wirth
Leo Srole

William H. Whyte
Nathan Glaser
Herbert Gans
Ernest Burgess

John Collette
Stanley Milgram

Self-test

Part I. Multiple Choice. Select the best of the four alternative answers:

1 Movement from rural areas to urban ares (**a**) is unique to modern times, (**b**) was given its greatest push by the industrial revolution, (**c**) advanced rapidly as a result of the age of discovery, (**d**) has been a rapid development since ancient times.

2 Who described the change to modern urban-industrial society as a shift from folk society to gesellschaft? (**a**) Louis Wirth, (**b**) Ernest Burgess, (**c**) Georg Simmel, (**d**) Ferdinand Tönnies.

3 Which of the following factors did not dictate where cities would grow? (**a**) population growth, (**b**) railroads, (**c**) navigable rivers and seaports, (**d**) iron and coal.

4 According to the concentric-zone theory of urban growth, the zone in transition is undesirable for residences because (**a**) it is the financial center of the city, (**b**) the rent is too high, (**c**) it is an area of urban blight, (**d**) it is given over mainly to parks and recreational areas.

5 The haphazard outward growth of cities, often mixing land use in strange ways, is most precisely known as (**a**) urban sprawl, (**b**) strip cities, (**c**) megalopolis, (**d**) SMSA.

6 A special U.S. Census Bureau report in early 1976 indicated that metropolitan areas are no longer (**a**) experiencing more crime than rural areas, (**b**) growing at the expense of rural areas, (**c**) showing decay around the urban core, (**d**) having serious financial problems.

7 A result of rising taxes and simultaneous cutting back on city services is (**a**) flight of businesses from the city, (**b**) lowered city revenues, (**c**) appeals for federal assistance, (**d**) all the above.

8 Which of the following seems to express American preference in housing? (**a**) joint dwellings, (**b**) townhouses, (**c**) individual homes, (**d**) all are equally well liked.

9 The Kenwood-Oakland district, the South Bronx, and Chicago's East Woodlawn have all experienced (**a**) rapid growth since 1960, (**b**) moderate growth since 1960, (**c**) steady housing loss since 1960, (**d**) steady improvement in quality of life since 1960.

10 Wirth concluded that the urban personality is one based on (**a**) fragmented social relationships, (**b**) enduring friendships, (**c**) strong feelings of social belonging, (**d**) all the above.

11 Of the following, which represents a *push* factor in returning people to the city? (**a**) close proximity to city attractions; (**b**) exciting city life; (**c**) theaters, museums, and libraries; (**d**) skyrocketing prices of suburban housing.

12 When whites move into black neighborhoods, (**a**) blacks move away in panic, (**b**) black homeowners tend to remain in the neighborhood, (**c**) whites don't stay too long, (**d**) blacks burn crosses in the lawns of the whites.

13 The urbanite is rather sharp of wit but blasé, not feeling or showing emotion as the rural person does, according to (**a**) Wirth, (**b**) Srole, (**c**) Simmel, (**d**) Tönnies.

14 What types of arguments favor considerable clustering together of people? (**a**) environmentalist, (**b**) criminologist, (**c**) psychological, (**d**) sociological.

15 Milgram found that by living in the city, people with great civic pride and high morale (**a**) lose psychologically, (**b**) become neurotic, (**c**) become alienated, (**d**) gain psychologically.

Part II. True-False Questions

1 In gemeinschaft society, people compete with nature to wrest a living from the soil.

2 Ancient cities, which were not plagued with problems of air pollution, were able to sustain populations even larger than those of modern cities.

3 One of the first descriptions of urban growth was the concentric-zone theory of Ernest Burgess.

4 The phenomenon of communities that have grown together is known as the political city.

5 The ecological city includes the political city and its surrounding environment.

6 Metropolitan areas are becoming less attractive as living places because of the quality of life and high crime rates.

7 According to Paul Bohannan, the "invisible elderly" are dedicated to a life of dependence and assistance.

8 Recently, the general pattern of American cities has been for those with low to median incomes to leave the cities and for the wealthy to·live in the central cities.

9 All major American cities have been able to retain at least a small majority of whites in their population.

10 Those who can afford to live elsewhere tend to avoid public housing.

11 Criticism of urban renewal has centered on the tendency to displace poor people.

12 New towns typically provide low-cost housing for the poor.

13 Public housing policies have tended to concentrate the poor in urban areas rather than in the suburbs.

14 Claude Fisher found that people of the same social class had personalities that varied according to rural or urban residence.

15 Housing shortages have increased through the 1970s, even though our population is increasing more slowly than in the past.

Questions for discussion

1 Many factors have contributed to urbanization. List as many of them as possible. Which seem to have had the greatest influence in making people change from rural to urban living?

2 Describe the relationship of the city to technology. Where is most technological research conducted? What kinds of technology are first applied in urban areas? Are urban people generally quicker than rural people to adopt new technologies?

3 What does your city or town look like? Is it an example of urban sprawl? If so, why? Are there identifiable ethnic villages in your city or town? Can you see evidence of your town's having developed through concentric zones?

4 What is the history of your city or town? Why did it develop where it is? Do the original reasons for its development still exist?

5 Does your city have building codes that are rigidly enforced? Are zoning laws enforced, or are they ignored by people with influence? Have there been any urban-renewal projects? Who has benefited and who has paid?

6 How do you feel about urban personalities? Do you agree with Simmel, Wirth, and Srole? Provide some examples to back up your position. Think over your experiences of urban living and discuss the extent to which you have an "urban personality."

7 What would be your design for a perfect city? Think of size, location, population density, transportation, building codes, zoning, and industry for the city's support. If financial factors demanded the cutting of certain costs, where would you cut?

8 Deterioration of inner cities is a concern of all major cities. What are some of the factors that contribute to deterioration? What might be done to prevent this decline?

9 Whose responsibility is it to save the cities if they cannot meet their costs? The city itself? The state? The federal government? Discuss the advantages and disadvantages of federal support of financially jeopardized cities.

Projects

1 Arrange an interview with a member of your city planning commission or try to get a member to speak to the class. Try to get a picture of future plans and find out whether any attempts are being made to prevent urban sprawl. To what degree are special interests able to get permits for building contrary to zoning laws and urban plans?

2 Take a tour of your city. Identify (or even take pictures of) zones in transition. What physical features have prevented the city from growing outward in perfect concentric circles? Is there a marked pattern of racial segregation within the city?

3 Interview or invite to class a real-estate broker who concentrates on the more expensive areas of town and another realtor (preferably black) from a poorer area of town. Try to find out whether any redlining is done. (Legally, a realtor must show properties to people regardless of race.) Ask the black realtor whether any cheating occurs.

Suggested readings

Fuerst, J. S.: "Class, Family, and Housing," *Society*, vol. 12, November–December 1974, pp. 49–53. Should public housing be abandoned because so many public housing units deteriorate? No, says Fuerst. Minor changes in policy could make public housing a success. We must start by not stigmatizing occupants of public housing.

Glasgow, Robert W., and Herbert J. Gans: "The Ayn Rand Syndrome: A Conversation between Herbert Gans and Robert W. Glasgow," *Psychology Today*, March 1970, pp. 58, 62. Sociologist and urban planner Gans states that people he has interviewed show only minor interest in the things most planners think of first: urban design, orderly land use, and even open space. What are people interested in, then? The answers Gans gives involve many dimensions of social relationships and human needs, not mere architecture.

Hartman, Chester: "The Politics of Housing: Displaced Persons," *Society*, vol. 9, July–August, 1972, pp. 53–56. By the late 1960s, over a million houses had been demolished for urban renewal, mainly those of the poor. Were the people living in them relocated or merely pushed out? Read a description of the pushing-out process.

Hollister, Rob: "The Politics of Housing: Squatters," *Society*, vol. 9, July–August, 1972, pp. 49–52. What happens when people occupy vacant buildings illegally? Hollister describes such occupancy in England and Ireland, then gives details of "Operation Move-In" in New York.

Nieburg, H. I.: "Crime Prevention by Urban Design," *Society*, vol. 12, November–December 1974, pp. 41–48. Is it possible to design housing areas and cities in such a way as to minimize burglary and vandalism? Nieburg contends that it can be done but that present-day methods contribute to crime.

Sternlied, George, and James W. Hughes: "New York: Future without a Future?" *Society*, vol. 13, May-June 1976, pp. 18—23. Will New York City be able to solve its financial problems? Are the problems of New York City mainly those of city expansion and suburb versus central city, or are they symptomatic of a gradual decline of the Northeastern seaboard? Are central cities in general losing some of their former functions? These are the questions pursued by the authors in an article written during one of New York's financial crises.

Turner, John F. C.: "A New Universe of Squatter-Builders," *UNESCO Courier*, June 1976, pp. 12–14. What happens when there are no government housing projects and the poor are left to build their own shacks? Turner concludes that in many Latin American squatter settlements, the houses begin as deplorable slums but gradually improve under the care of their owners. In American federal housing projects, housing units are good at first but rapidly deteriorate.

Key to questions. Multiple Choice: 1-b; 2-d; 3-a; 4-c; 5-a; 6-b; 7-d; 8-c; 9-c; 10-a; 11-d; 12-b; 13-c; 14-a; 15-d. True-False: 1-T; 2-F; 3-T; 4-F; 5-T; 6-T; 7-F; 8-F; 9-F; 10-T; 11-T; 12-F; 13-T; 14-F; 15-T.

THE INTERDEPENDENT WORLD

This chapter notes how the processes of social change, previously described, affect the entire world. After reading it, you should be able to:

1 *Understand the degree to which the world has become interdependent and developed similar trends and problems.*

2 *Be aware of the contrasts between rich and poor nations.*

3 *Recognize how cultural changes affect the pace of life, time consciousness, and the shift to universalistic norms.*

4 *Understand how social change affects personalities, social stratification, and race and sex inequality.*

5 *See similarities and differences between the impact of education in developing lands and industrialized lands.*

6 *Recognize how the problems of poverty, overpopulation, and resource exhaustion have become international.*

7 *Recognize the need for further steps toward international economic cooperation.*

The last two chapters have shown us an increasingly crowded and urbanized world. Population is growing much faster in the developing countries than in the highly industrialized ones. In many cases, the same is true of the rate of urbanization. It is no coincidence that population trends and rates of urbanization are similar in many parts of the world. All nations are in some ways more alike than they once were. This is true regardless of differences in ideologies, forms of government, levels of education, and levels of industrial development. Nations have become more alike than in the past because they trade with each other more and copy each other's industrial and technological ideas and educational systems. Every aspect of sociology can be illustrated in all parts of the changing world. New trends are affecting the patterns of culture and socialization, types of stratification, minority-group relationships, family systems, the position of women, religions and ideologies, the types of work people do, and even deviant behavior.

The previous chapters have concentrated mainly on the United States, occasionally drawing examples from other societies. Here, we will discuss the world as a whole, stressing the developing nations of Latin America, Africa, Southeast Asia, and the Middle East. First, we intend to show the interdependent nature of the modern world—that is, how events in one country can have powerful effects on others. Second, we will show that the sociological concepts previously studied are applicable in all societies. A look at the developing world reviews for us the basic concepts of sociology in a new setting and shows how they can be used. Finally, since the developing nations are undergoing the strongest conflicts between old ways and new, they show clearly many of the processes and results of cultural change.

Starting with the theme of *interdependence*, everyone can think of examples: oil depletion and dependence upon the OPEC nations, or reliance on international cooperation in shipping, air travel, and the control of drugs. World interdependence is not limited to mineral resources or transportation, however. It also concerns perhaps the most basic commodity—food. This is shown in the insert on pages 538–539 "Changing Food Chain Forges Nation to Nation," about what at first seems an unimportant product—anchovies.

BASIC CULTURAL CHANGES

The above report shows how the policies of one country, unknown even to its own citizens, can have considerable effect on other nations. Food supply is mainly a matter of economics. Still, it shows dramatically how all nations have come to depend on each other for supplies that are held by only a few. This interdependence is the result of diffusion from one culture to another of ideas, products, techniques, and people themselves. It leads to such radical changes that traditional cultures are hardly recognizable. It also leads to population growth that further increases the need for national exchange of products, techniques, and ideas.

Time-consciousness

New attitudes toward time are learned slowly. However, with increasing trade and industrialization, the pace of life becomes calculable and predictable. Factories, loading docks, trucks, and buses begin to maintain schedules and people are expected to work by the clock. The feeling of timelessness, widespread in the developing world, is challenged by the clock-centered Western world. To the American or European businessperson, keeping someone waiting for an appointment is unacceptable. In the developing countries, to rush a person is just as bad. If a person has an appointment but is engaged in conversation with friends, it is considered rude to rush him simply to be on time (Hall, 1959, pp. 15–30). The appointment can wait; everything can wait. However, the clock gradually becomes master as the demands of an international market increase.

Calculability

Production was once largely a matter of subsistence. The family grew corn or millet, or raised sheep or goats, to supply its own needs. Societies that relied on such a subsistence pattern did not use the types of calculations and predictions that farmers in our society would make. Edward

T. Hall illustrates the difference in attitudes:

> I remember an American agriculturalist who went to Egypt to teach modern agricultural methods to the Egyptian farmers. At one point in his work he asked his interpreter to ask a farmer how much he expected his field to yield that year. The farmer responded by becoming very excited and angry. In an obvious attempt to soften the reply, the interpreter said, "He says he doesn't know." The American realized something had gone wrong, but he had no way of knowing what. Later I learned that the Arabs regard anyone who tries to look into the future as slightly insane. When the American asked him about his future yield, the Egyptian was highly insulted since he thought the American considered him crazy. To the Arab, only God knows the future, and it is presumptuous even to talk about it. (1959, p. 11; © 1959 by Doubleday and Company, Inc.)

Hall's statement was made in 1959. Obviously, with all the planning being done by the

---

Changing food chain forges nation to nation   ROBERT A. JONES

After two years the anchovies have returned off the coast of Peru, millions of them teeming in the warmth of the South Pacific, and in this capital [Washington, D.C.] and a dozen others men with slide rules are measuring the repercussions.

In all, the figuring of the Department of Agriculture is that the anchovy return is grim news for the United States farmer but good news for the world's poor. The people of underdeveloped countries may eat better in the coming years.

In Chicago, the anchovies have also had an impact. The price of soybeans plummeted and, in one of the tiny, precise calculations that have become a fixture in the agricultural market, the otherwise bleak cattle market was judged to have brightened a bit.

But more importantly, reaction to the reappearance of the small fish, which are ground up and fed to cattle, suggests the volatility of a new world food market that in the last two years has undergone vast changes. Events that were formerly disconnected or at best of minor importance have now become critical to the world food supply, and relatively small declines in production have caused stunning impacts in prices.

Two years ago the anchovies disappeared from their traditional feeding grounds next to Peru. Some say the waters were overfished; others believe the anchovies just decided to go somewhere else for a while. In any case, Peru stopped exports.

For livestock operators around the world, who were trying to meet unprecedented demands for meat, that meant a protein substitute had to be found, and American soybeans were the answer. The price of soybeans doubled, then tripled.

For many underdeveloped countries which had relied on American soybeans as an important source of protein, the scramble for supplies to feed cattle meant their own people would not be fed. The per bushel price went far above what many of the world's poor could afford to pay.

The story of the anchovies and other stories like it have led some agricultural economists to believe that something fundamental has happened to the world food supply system.

"It appears to me that we are experiencing one of those epic times of change in agriculture," said Don Paarlberg, chief economist of the U.S. Department of Agriculture. "It is obvious that we are at some kind of a hinge point."

Resting on that hinge point, Paarlberg and other economists have observed, is a delicate balance between the prosperity of the American farmer on one hand and the threat of famine in a growing number of underdeveloped countries on the other.

The issues are often clouded, but in many cases they come down to this: a surplus of food that would assure supplies to the poor would simultaneously cause financial ruin for the farmers who produced it.

An internationally controlled food reserve has been suggested to purchase stocks in the event of a surplus and to sell them during shortages. But thus far the United States has refused to participate, since the very instrument that would alleviate famine would also, the government believes, depress farm prices.

And increasingly, the United States, which controls a larger share of the world's exportable food than the Arabs of exportable oil, appears to be moving toward a greater use of its position on a number of fronts.

In one instance, critical supplies of wheat were denied to the Chilean government under Marxist President Salvador Allende even though Chile offered to pay cash.

Shortly after Allende was overthrown, the United States approved the wheat sale and offered the country credit for the purchase. . . .

From Robert A. Jones, "Changing Food Chain Forges Nation to Nation," *Los Angeles Times*, April 17, 1974, Part I, pp. 1, 22. Copyright Los Angeles Times.

Egyptian government and with its heavy dependence on agriculture, it must now look to the future as Western governments do. This change in thinking has come to all societies. At least among the leaders of the society, cultural attitudes have to change to make modern production and sales possible.

Margaret Mead (1955, pp. 194–202) provides another example of the ways in which food and culture are related and how changing one involves changing another. In many lands, certain foods have been preferred or even regarded as sacred. The impact of modernization often changes these values. People turn to growing crops that can be sold for money. A frequent result, according to Mead, is poorer nutritional standards. Cash crops are grown, and the diet depends more and more on refined bread and grains bought at the market. The products lack the nutrients of traditional foods. However, a

gain is made to balance the loss: many more products are available. Whatever the results, traditional cultures change once they become part of the money economy.

Figure 19-1 At this nuclear power plant in India, scientists are learning how to use radioisotopes to preserve food and tracing techniques to locate sources of water. Such studies, it is hoped, will help provide more food and water for India. (*David Channer, Nancy Palmer*)

Universalistic norms

Another basic cultural change is the movement away from *particularistic* norms and toward *impersonal* norms. Many cultures of Africa and Asia have taught a value system that puts one's own group of relatives and other villagers in a special position. Such norms are particularistic—that is, they apply to particular situations, places, and people (Fallers, 1955). One is expected to give preference to relatives and neighbors in all ways, including jobs. As new national standards are accepted, norms become more *universalistic*—that is, the same norms apply to all situations, places, and people regardless of relationship, race, or religion. Universalistic norms correct old injustices, but they are more impersonal. Those who accept the new, impersonal values live in a new social system. They have entered the rush of the modern bureau-

cratic world. They no longer work just to survive. They work to turn out a product for the market as efficiently as possible. This is what Weber called the *rationalization of production*. Along with these changes, they move into the world of secondary relationships—of business and contracts—and deemphasize the world of primary relations: kinship, ancestors, and tradition.

CHANGING SOCIALIZATION

As the developing nations have begun to adopt Western traits, their socialization patterns have also changed. Old values, loyalties to chiefs and patrons, old handicrafts, and tales and mythologies are still taught by the grandparents, but they are taken less seriously by the young. In the older way of life, when time seemed infinite and did not matter, mothers had time for carrying water, grinding grain, chatting at the village well, and nursing infants whenever they seemed hungry. All rituals for protecting the health of the child (whether scientifically valid or not) were carefully observed, as well as ritual protection from witches and the evil eye. Old women and local healers were called on for advice. The children of one mother were the children of the whole village.

Today, most countries have children's bureaus, which are trying to encourage sanitation and to discourage such customs as swaddling infants (wrapping them almost like mummies) (Mead, 1955, pp. 213–217). Immunizations and medical clinics have prevented millions of infant and child deaths. At the same time, some of the patience and close relationships have disappeared, and some of the new practices introduce problems avoided by the old (see the insert "Bottle Babies of the Third World," page 542).

Role change in the developing world

As socialization patterns change, so do roles. At one time, roles were assigned mainly on the basis of age and sex. Household tasks were given to women and the work of farming belonged to men. There was no chance for a better job but also no confusion about what role to play. Authority, too, was related to age and sex. Young men waited until age brought them prestige; the aged were dominant and honored. Today, the leaders of society increasingly ignore the old.

Alex Inkeles has studied the ways in which both life-style and personality change as a culture becomes modernized (1969, pp. 208–225). The countries included in this study are Argentina, Chile, Nigeria, Israel, and Bangladesh. Inkeles found that a *modern personality type* could be found in each of these. It arose mainly through education but also partly through urbanization, factory work, or both. In all cases, the modern personality type could be identified by its willingness to accept new ideas; its loyalty to

leaders of modern governments, schools, and labor unions; and a break with elders and traditional leaders. The new personality accepts science and medicine. It is less fatalistic than the old and holds ambitions for the next generation. The new personality limits family size, is time-conscious, and is interested in national and world affairs rather than just village gossip. Inkeles does not imply that all the people have changed their attitudes; only the leaders have done so. He has found some disorganization and anomie among those people who cling to the past and in very small tribes that have been swamped by the encroaching world. However, he does not think anomie is typical of most people in developing nations.

Briefly, then, Inkeles's optimistic conclusion would be that the developing world will eventually resemble the industrialized world in education, employment, and mobility. Along with this change will come increased education and income. In this view, the world is seen to be coming together sociologically as well as culturally and commercially.

Role conflict

It is inevitable that the new roles should clash with the old. An extreme case of such role conflict is drawn from a description of the chief of a small tribe in Uganda in the 1950s, before the end of British colonialism:

In Uganda, for example, if we were to visit a chief, we might find him attending a committee meeting, helping to work on a budget for the coming fiscal year. If we ask for an appointment, we will be received in a modern office equipped with typewriter, telephone, filing cases, and the other apparatus of modern bureaucracy. If by chance we had called on another day, our chief would have been unavailable. He would have been meeting with his clan mates in the thatched hut of a paternal uncle, and

Bottle babies of the Third World   LEONARD SANTORELLI

A revolution without guns, flags, nor slogans is profoundly changing the lives of many women and children in the Third World. It is the switch from breast to bottle-feeding.

The switch has freed Arab, African, and Asian women, especially city dwellers, from the home and enabled them to take jobs, often overcoming deeply ingrained cultural taboos to do so.

But it has also brought in its wake a pitiful tool of malnutrition and disease among infants whose mothers used dirty water in the mixture or cut down on milk powder to make the packet last longer.

The bottle is already firmly established in many cities and towns and is slowly taking hold in rural areas. Clearly, Western ideas on female emancipation and even on what constitutes a shapely figure are key factors.

But controversy has also been stirred by the role of the firms that sell the milk products. Attention has focused on their sales techniques in places where water is scarce, conditions unhygienic, and costs of products high.

A look at the background in the bottle-vs.-breast debate in Asian and African cultures shows that the bottle has gained a firm foothold, breaking down strong cultural and practical barriers in the process.

Many Asian women, for instance, thought they would lose the love and respect of their infants if they went on the bottles. . . .

Western ideas have had a big influence. One Kenyan social worker blames the "prudery" brought to Africa by colonial missionaries and doctors who discouraged the exposing of women's breasts and public feeding of babies.

The Western practice of putting a baby in a crib, he adds, instead of its mother's bed where it had a constant supply of milk has broken down feeding patterns, and often causes the mother's milk to dry up prematurely.

Even so, many Kenyan women will pay up to a third of their annual income on a product they could produce themselves, and officials of international agencies in Nairobi say one of the reasons is that they believe this is the "modern way, the way of the white man." . . .

From Leonard Santorelli, "Babies of 3rd World Switched to Bottles," Reuters dispatch in *Los Angeles Times*, November 4, 1976. Part I-A, p. 6.

---

the talk would have been of genealogical refinements and the wishes of ancestors. If we are invited to have tea at the chief's house in the evening, we will be introduced to his several wives, and this may surprise us because we have heard that he is a pillar of the local Anglican parish and a patron of the Boy Scout Troop. (Fallers, 1955; reproduced by permission of the American Anthropological Association from *American Anthropologist,* **57**: 290, 1955)

The socialization problems, role conflicts, and struggles between different sets of values that exist in industrialized nations obviously penetrate all areas of the world. One could easily imagine updating Fallers's description of the African chief as he socializes his son into his roles. The son will still be taught to look to his native villages and relatives for support. However, he will be told that it is much more important to become a good administrator of the new independent regime, to be loyal to the central government and the

Figure 19-2 (*a*) A Westernized middle-class family of Africa. (*b*) A worker in an African textile factory. The working class is now moving toward a Western life-style. The gap between the two classes is great. [*(a) Fujihira, Monkmeyer; (b) United Nations*]

bureaucracy, and to acquire a car rather than a ceremonial headdress as his new status symbol.

STRATIFICATION SYSTEMS

One cannot speak of a chief without thinking of stratification, prestige, and social class. All but a few remote, simple hunting tribes have strong differences in social class. We have noted that social-class lines tend to harden as societies move from hunting or simple gardening to more advanced agriculture and as organization shifts to cities and administrative districts. It is only with the movement to industrialism that some reversal of the trend occurs (Lenski, 1961a, pp. 389–432). The rich may become richer than ever, but the poor receive welfare or unemployment insurance.

Rigidity of stratification systems

Much of the developing world has firm social-class lines, with more poor people (peasants) and a smaller middle class than in the United

States, Europe, or Japan. To the lower classes, the stratification system may be something to be endured. A housemaid will hope that her children will find as steady work as she has found. A second possibility is that the housemaid may hear about the life-style of other countries and become discontented. If so, she may try to socialize her children into success values so that, through education, they can do better than she has done. Or, finally, her discontentment, and that of many others like her, may lead to revolutionary views. This was the case in China, Cuba, and Vietnam. We will recall that revolutions are most likely when a better future seems possible. It is this hope for the future, sometimes referrred to as *the revolution of rising expectations*, that helps make much of the developing world unstable.

Although there are upper classes in all countries, the developing countries are overwhelmingly lower class in income. This contrasts with the industrialized countries, which are mainly

Rich-poor gap dominates world poll

The highest crime rates in the Free World are found in Latin America, Africa, and the United States.

North Americans and Western Europeans generally enjoy their jobs, while people in the developing countries overwhelmingly do not.

By 9 to 1 the people of the world favor increased conservation of animals and fish.

These findings of the "first global public-opinion survey" were summarized to the Senate Foreign Relations Committee Monday by pollster George Gallup and Kent H. Collins of the Kettering Foundation.

During the survey 10,000 individuals were interviewed in some 70 nations comprising nearly two-thirds of the world's population. Communist nations and others with restrictions on public opinion surveys were excluded.

Gallup also wrote an article for the October issue of *Reader's Digest* describing the survey's results.

Gallup testified that "nearly half the people of the world are engaged in an unending struggle for survival."

"In the planning stages of this global survey it was hoped that somehwere in the world a nation would be found whose people are poor but happy," Gallup said. "We didn't find such a place."

Gallup said the dominant factor in the 18 volumes of findings was the economic gulf between the "have" and the "have not" nations.

Two-thirds of those polled in Latin America, Africa, and the Far East said they worry "all" or "most of the time" about meeting family expenses, Gallup reported.

Although North Americans and West Europeans "complain about making ends meet, three out of four of those interviewed admit that they worry 'almost never' or 'only part of the time' about finances," he said.

In the United States, Collins said, 87% were opposed to any further population growth, and in Western Europe 75%.

But, he said, in Africa 65 percent favored increased population and in Latin America about 63 percent did.

Other findings from the 2½ year survey:

—If given the opportunity, more than 20% of the population of Latin America would emigrate to other countries.

—The great majority of the rural populations of underdeveloped countries yearns to move to the big cities, while more than half the people in developed countries would prefer to live in small towns, villages, or rural areas.

—On the average, people from the richest countries, those who live in North America, Australia and Western Europe, are more content with their family life, their countries, their communities, their education and with themselves.

By majorities ranging from 60% in Great Britain to 93% in Africa, the people in every country polled except one, Japan, believe in God or a universal spirit, and claim to belong to a church, religious group or faith.

Among the advanced nations, it is only in the United States, Canada and Italy that the majority believe in life after death, or in the kind of God that observes, punishes, or rewards humans for their actions.

United Press International in *Los Angeles Times*, Part I, p. 4, Sept. 21, 1976 (Times Wire Services).

middle class or have a fairly well-paid working class. Except for the oil-rich countries of OPEC, the developing lands sell cheap goods and buy expensive goods. The work is harder and less satisfying than in the industrialized countries. Two-thirds of the people worry all or most of the time about meeting family expenses. (See the insert "Rich-Poor Gap Dominates World Poll.")

A growing middle class?

In the developing countries, how will wealth be distributed? Will there be a sizable middle class? Wilfred Malenbaum (1973, pp. 30–45) projects an economic growth rate of about 3.8 percent per year for developing nations. This is the same rate as the one he sees for the most highly industrialized countries. One would think the growth rate would be higher for developing countries, since they have so much further to go, but the effective rate is actually lower. In many cases, rapid population growth in developing countries eats into the economic gain, although it does not cancel out the gain entirely. Other observers comment that the changes in cultural values and personality described earlier can be translated into trade and industrial development. People become disciplined to factory routines and move to urban centers. Family influence and tribalism decline (Moore and Feldman, 1960).

Continuing gulf between rich and poor

Others are by no means sure that things are improving. Christopher Chase-Dunn (1975) questions whether gains are made through investments by foreign (mainly multinational) corporations. After studying statistical data from several developing nations, he shows that foreign investments benefit the industrial world but not necessarily the poor of developing lands. Mining industries are developed first, because they are most helpful to foreign investors. The

miners themselves earn little. Transportation lines are also opened, more to serve foreign capital than to develop the country. Chase-Dunn concludes that the effect is to make the wealthiest 5 percent of the country slightly richer and the lower half of the population even poorer relative to the rich.

Gunnar Myrdal (1974, pp. 30–45) explains why many developing countries show this very unequal distribution of wealth. The traditional systems have always given high status to upper classes and castes, princes, chiefs, lineage heads, and the like. Foreigners have found it easiest to deal with these upper classes because they are educated. The upper classes, in turn, build on these advantages. They are the best people to deal with because of their class position. Therefore they are given favors that make them even stronger and wealthier. Consider also the role of the self-fulfilling prophecy. The lower classes are seen as incompetent and are given only the most menial jobs. As a result, they cannot develop any competence—they have the same problem as many minority groups in the United States, and a much lower life expectancy (see Table 19-1, page 546).

Because of the relationship between foreign investors and native leaders, the investors are detested by those at the bottom of the social ladder. Sometimes they are hated more than the native upper class itself.

Effect of multinational corporations

Even with the problems of foreign investment, we might think that new industries would open up jobs for a rising middle class. Given the stress on education in developing countries, this would seem especially likely. The long-term result might be that social classes everywhere would someday parallel those of the United States and other Western nations: more white-collar jobs, more efficient farming and fewer farm laborers, and better factory jobs. What is happening now, though, is that the old middle class of shopkeep-

Table 19-1 Life Expectancy

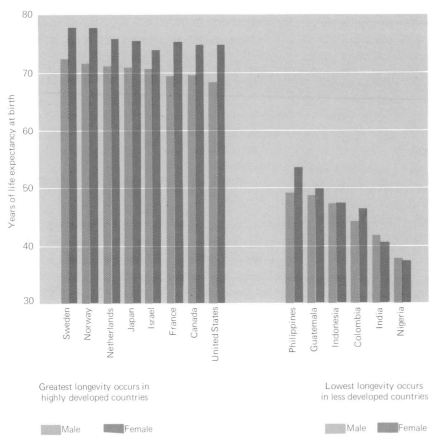

Note: Life expectancy is a fairly good gage of general well being, which is minimal in many of the less industrialized countries.
Source: *U.S. Fact Book: The Statistical Abstract of the U.S. Bureau of the Census*, Grosset and Dunlap, New York, 1976, p. 839.

ers and artisans is often ruined by the competition of major department stores from overseas, such as Sears-Roebuck. At the same time, there is a problem for native managers in the multinational corporations. Often the higher levels of management are open only to people from the incoming country; the host country is excluded. A study of 1,851 managers of United States corporations with large overseas payrolls found that only 1.6 percent of important executives were recruited in the host country. This raises problems since multinational corporations are growing rapidly. Judd Polk, senior economist of the U.S. Chamber of Commerce, predicts that by 2000 A.D. a few hundred global companies will hold assets of over $4 trillion and own 54 percent of the world's production goods (Barnett and Muller, 1974, p. 26). If these multinationals continue to import their management, there may still be a sharp division between classes. Social-class differences, then, may not decline as much as they have in the United States. (Table 19-2 shows United States investments in foreign countries.)

Sources of change

Table 19-2 United States Investments Abroad

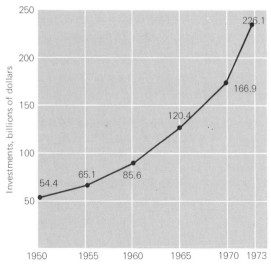

Note: Investments abroad reflect the growth of multinational corporations, whose effect on developing nations is not entirely beneficial. Source: *U.S. Fact Book: The Statistical Abstract of the U.S. Bureau of the Census*, Grosset and Dunlap, New York, 1976, p. 799.

THE TREATMENT OF MINORITIES AS A WORLD PROBLEM

The reasons for treating minority groups differently are similar in many parts of the world. Occasionally, prejudice has developed because of political and economic rivalries, leading to war and continuing bitterness. Greece and Turkey, for example, had to resort to population exchanges to get rid of Greek minorities in Turkey and Turkish minorities in Greece. Previously, they had had incessant war. Sometimes minorities are seen as strangers in the host country, with primary loyalties to their own groups. This is true of the Chinese in Southeast Asia, Indians in Africa, or Gypsies in many parts of the world.

Perpetuation of outcaste status

Generally, discrimination against minorities parallels the treatment of black people in the United States. Economic, political, and legal policies have placed minorities in an inferior position. That position is seen as inevitable and even as deserved. Long periods of discriminatory treatment have harmed the self-concept of minority-group members. Often a violent reaction seems necessary. People who have been treated as inferior must prove to themselves and to the world their right to equality. A good example is the society of South Africa.

Apartheid in South Africa

The black people of South Africa are a minority in a special sense. They outnumber the whites by more than three to one, but they are treated as a minority. They are forbidden to vote in elections; limited mainly to menial jobs on farms, in factories, and in mines; segregated into housing areas outside the major cities; and, as yet, have been given no hope of equality.

Worldwide changes, however, have their effect. The free countries of Africa have protested continuously in the United Nations. South African teams have been barred from the Olympic Games because of their complete segregation of sports events. Increasing pressure against South Africa may be having its effect. On September 24, 1976, the South African government announced a relaxation of its *apartheid* (extreme segregation) policies in sports. It is now possible for blacks, coloreds (people of mixed race), and Indians (who have migrated from India in considerable numbers) to compete against white teams (*Los Angeles Times*, September 24, 1976, p. 1). The announcement of this limited change in sports policies came on the same day as a major demonstration by black students in Johannesburg protesting discrimination.

A more important sign of change is a shift in the opinion of whites, probably, according to opinion research, caused by increasing worries about their future. (See the insert on pae 548: "Majority of Whites Would Ease South African Race Laws.") The change of opinion signals a split between the average white people and the ruling Nationalist Party, which has long worked for the policy of *apartheid.*

The interdependent world

Majority of whites would ease South African race laws

More than half of all white South Africans would support major changes in the race laws, including integration of sports, theaters, universities and churches, a national survey showed Monday.

The survey, commissioned from a private company by the Afrikaans-language newspaper *Rapport*, showed that the all-white electorate would back the scrapping of many laws regarded as planks of the government's policy of apartheid.

A majority of whites questioned favored abolition of the Immorality Act, forbidding interracial sex, and of the Mixed Marriages Act.

Almost 71% favored abolition of the pass laws that require all blacks to carry passes showing whether they are authorized to be in a particular area. But the question carried the proviso that the alternative was the carrying of identity documents by all races.

More than 57% favored abolition of job reservation, which reserves certain jobs for whites only.

About 56% believed universities, now segregated, should be open to all races; 53% want the same for theaters, 60% for ambulance services, 55% would approve open churches, and 65.6% would support racially mixed sports teams at club level. The latter are still forbidden despite a recent easing of apartheid in sports.

The survey showed there was still opposition to some changes.

Fewer than 42% of the whites questioned thought there should be one class of taxi for all races—at present blacks can only use taxis marked "second class"—and 47.4 percent favored unrestricted possession of property by all races.

The survey followed a recent poll published by the West German newspaper *Allgemeine Zeitung* indicating that whites would still follow South African Prime Minister John Vorster if he announced radical liberalization of race policies.

From Reuters Dispatch, "Majority of Whites Would Ease S. Africa Race Laws," in *Los Angeles Times*, November 2, 1976, Part i, p. 2.

Although we have focused on South Africa, racism is not confined to any one country or continent. It is part of a worldwide tradition, declining but not dead. Intergroup antagonism is strong between Malays, Chinese, and Indians in Malaya. In much of Latin America, Indians are the outcastes of society, looked down upon by the mixed-blood mestizos and people of purely European descent. In Brazil and in the Caribbean countries that also had had African slaves, there is a strong correlation between race and poverty. Black people and Indians can be accepted into society if they have enough education and income, as shown by the saying "Money whitens." However, they are generally born poor and find it hard to improve their social-class position.

The female minority

Throughout most of the developing world, most women are still keeping house, carrying water, and constantly bearing children. Although a few of them work, a study by Harold Wilensky (1968) concludes that this is a result of industrialism alone. The men and women of these societies have not had their consciousness raised regarding female equality. In some countries (Sweden and Israel in particular), child-care centers and other adjustments help lighten the housework of working women. In general, though, the work role is simply added to the housekeeping role. Thus, the total workload for women is generally heavy.

In areas of life other than work, women of the developing world have had even more disadvantages than Western women. However, a growing trend toward equal education for both sexes and new ideas about female roles have begun to make a difference. Kenya is one example of the coming change. It is a complex culture with a blend of Christian, Hindu, and tribal attitudes toward the positions of men and women. The insert "A New Law for Kenya:

A new law for Kenya: Equality for wives   DIAL TORGERSON

The law would revise the traditional system by which women, their children and their possessions all belong to the husband—a custom under which the widow cannot inherit and is herself inherited. In much of Kenya a widow becomes an additional wife of her late husband's brother.

The fact that the law gives women equality and rights never dreamed of in traditional African society has brought bitter complaints from many men. But what has brought the most furious criticism is the fact it would make adultery a crime punishable by six months in jail. Adultery is commonplace at present and there is little penalty. . . .

The furor over the erring husbands has distracted attention from the fact that the new law is a carefully thought-out piece of legislation, almost 10 years in the planning, which would bring order to the chaotic intertwining of traditional, religious, and secular marriage laws in Kenya.

Kenyans, living in an interracial culture of mixed levels of modernity, get married five different ways—in Christian, civil, Hindu, or Islamic cermonies, or in what is called a "customary marriage," in which each tribal group has its own way of observing a marriage. The Islamic and customary marriages may be polygamous.

The new law says nothing against polygamy but would require that all marriages be registered as the first step in guaranteeing women certain basic rights.

Wives would have the legal right to inherit their husbands' estates. No girl (or boy) could be forced into marriage by the family. No spouse could legally inflict corporal punishment on the other. Possessions would be community property, or the wife could hold title to her own property. She could borrow and sue.

Traditional African society had a way of caring for everyone. "Who was ever abandoned back home?" asks a new citizen of booming Nairobi. But the breakdown of the old culture in the big city makes the new law a necessity. . . .

Mary Onyiego, bright, modern and well educated, got the first divorce (in 1971) in which a woman won the children, support, and half the house. She had kept the hospital records of every beating and receipts for all the bills she had paid—which was every one that was paid.

"He was a college graduate, and I thought he'd be different." Ms. Onyiego said. "But he blamed me for having daughters instead of sons—and he was a biologist! He came from a tribal society, and when it came to things like that, he thought the way his father did."

From Dial Torgerson, "Plan for Equality for Wives Sets Off Uproar in Kenya," *Los Angeles Times,* Sept. 26, 1976, Part I-A, p. 1. Copyright Los Angeles Times.

The interdependent world

549

Equality for Wives'' is as informative about traditional practices as it is about the female equality in marriage that is yet to come. Such changes are occurring in urban areas of much of the Middle East—Turkey, Iran, and Egypt, for example—countries striving to become modern.

DEVIANT BEHAVIOR

Deviant behavior is inevitable in any society. However, in older cultures with unitary customs, the informal controls of public opinion kept most people in line. Small tribal groups such as Eskimo or Pygmies needed no legal formalities. With social change and contact between cultures, new and often more permissive norms are created. In many cases (Saudi Arabia is an extreme example), the customs of foreigners are looked upon

Figure 19-3 (*a*) On January 27, 1977, former premier Kakuei Tanaka of Japan (*right*) went on trial, accused of accepting $1.66 million in bribes from the Lockheed Aircraft Corporation. (*b*) Daniel J. Haughton (*right*), chairman of Lockheed, with Senator Frank Church, chairman of the Senate Subcommittee on Multinational Corporations. [*(a) United Press International; (b) Wide World Photos*]

(a)

as deviant, whether they concern equality for women, new fashions, or the freedom of young people to date and marry without consulting elders or marriage arrangers. Among the unemployed and the poor in the cities, theft and prostitution are increasing. In part, this is necessary for survival; in part, it is a result of anomie. When old norms are undermined but new ones are not yet integrated into the culture, there is no longer a strong feeling of right and wrong.

Deviance at the higher levels of society is influenced by the interrelationships of the modern world. The narcotics trade is international, and so is the smuggling of weapons and archaeological treasures. Bribery also becomes international, with multinational corporations such as Lockheed Aircraft paying bribes for contracts and other favors. Tax evasion is another case in which international cooperation helps the deviant avoid tax laws. One of the methods of illegal tax avoidance is "laundering" money.

Perhaps the oldest dodge used by individuals and corporations who want to evade taxes—or conceal unreported income—is simply to "launder" the cash in offshore tax havens. Gulf Oil corporation admitted it had made 5.4 million dollars in illegal campaign contributions by funneling the money through a Caribbean subsidiary, intended for stateside pols. The IRS believes U.S.-based mobsters are doing much the same thing—setting up a corporation in a tax haven, funding it with cash from gambling,

(b)

narcotics or prostitution, and then *secretly* reinvesting the money in U.S. real estate. The mobsters win both ways: not only is their dirty money now invested in clean enterprises, but their offshore firms can claim nonresident tax benefits. (*Newsweek*, 1976c, p. 54; copyright © 1976 by Newsweek, Inc. All rights reserved. Reprinted by permission.)

The chapter on deviant behavior described international terrorism. This is becoming more and more common as new political ideologies become international. Members of the Palestine Liberation Organization have sometimes seized Israeli hostages. Especially notable was the murder of the Israeli team in Munich during the 1972 Olympics. Many of the terrorists were killed, but a few who escaped were given a hero's welcome on their return. The passengers of an airliner were hijacked in 1976 and taken as hostages to Entebbe, Uganda. They were later freed by a daring Israeli raid at the Uganda airport. In an age of sophisticated weapons and many revolutionary causes, such terrorism constantly threatens international peace.

Figure 19-4 A peasant women tending a poppy farm in Turkey. The derivative of the poppy is opium. (*b*) A United States Customs agent searching a ship locates 17 pounds of smuggled opium. [*(a) Editorial Photocolor Archives; (b) United Press International*]

EDUCATION FOR DEVELOPING LANDS

Like Americans, the people of developing countries look to education to help social problems and provide upward mobility. However, education brings with it certain problems. Speaking particularly of Kenya but presenting widely applicable views, Ronald Dore (1975, pp. 7–11) states that in 1960, about 13 percent of the children received seven years of education, which prepared them for white-collar jobs by Kenyan standards. By 1970, 60 percent were finishing about the same amount of schooling, but there were jobs for only about 15 percent of them—that is, jobs that literate people wanted to perform. The problem, as Dore explains it, is that education has been seen mainly as a matter of status and as a "bridgehead to modernity"; but there is a gap between education and economics. The economic structure can absorb only a few literate people. Education has, indeed, moved some people into good jobs with acceptable incomes. Those with advanced education can earn an income that is twenty times higher than that of the uneducated. However, those with only a few years of schooling advance little if at all.

The problem of informal education

Thomas LaBelle and Robert Verhine (1975, pp. 161–183), writing on Latin America, present other problems of education. The cost of education has increased rapidly there. This stems partly from the feeling that education is a key to economic growth and partly from the high birthrate. Further, as job opportunities increase, so do the educational requirements for them. When this happens, higher education is needed, as well as schools for more people. The suggested alternative is an apprenticeship program of *informal education*, outside the school system, for improving crafts, skills, and agriculture. There are several places where such training can be helpful. Still, LaBelle and Verhine point out that informal education has very little effect in helping people get better jobs.

Elitist attitudes

Conflict theory, as presented in Chapter 12, states that many occupational groups require advanced education to preserve their position and screen new people. In Latin America, this function of education is much stronger than in the United States. The aristocratic tradition has strongly influenced schooling and employment for elite jobs. As a result, the only path to higher status is through the formal school system, not the alternative programs of informal apprentice training. One possibility is to combine primary education with apprenticeship training. LaBelle and Verhine think this combination might work, especially for independent farmers. However, it will not be accepted by the cultural system as a substitute for more training in traditional schools. As always, traditional cultural values have a strong impact on new possibilities. Also, as in the advanced industrial nations, the developing world has strong feelings of class difference about which schools are the golden door to elite positions.

RELIGION IN CHANGING SOCIETIES

In Chapter 14, we noted that in the United States, religious attendance, emotionality, and otherworldly emphasis differ with social class. For most Americans, however, religious affiliation is linked with class only in the minor divisions between denominations and sects. In some other societies, religious practices are much more divided. In Indonesia, rich people feel themselves to be better Muslims than the poor people of the interior, who recognize spiritual beings that were worshiped before the conversion to Islam (Geertz, 1957, pp. 421–437). In India, rituals and attitudes toward the major gods vary greatly with caste (Beals, 1962, pp. 45–49). Low-caste people are more easily converted to another religion than high-caste people.

Oscar Lewis (1966, pp. 19–25) states that in very poor urban areas of Latin America, the poorest people are alienated from all the institutions of society, including the church. They may revere particular saints and observe holidays, but they have little contact with the church as an institution. In the United States, those who do not attend church show little or no animosity toward it. Many developing lands, in contrast, have proclerical and anticlerical parties. In Latin America especially, those parties try to influence the government and gain religious control in education. The long-term trend is toward more state control and less church control.

Major and minor traditions

In many parts of the world, major religions—such as Christianity, Islam, or Buddhism—coexist with minor religions of particular tribes or regions. Vine Deloria (1974), a leader of American Indian causes, sees the major religions as imperialistic. They try to convert all people and do not recognize the equality of minor religions. Tribal religions have tended to be absorbed into the major religions. In Africa, by a slow process of diffusion, they are gradually being absorbed by Islam. Earlier, Christianity made great inroads, but anti-Western feelings have slowed its growth.

Religion and technological change

All religions, major and minor, must adjust to a world very different from the one in which they arose. Secularism and science have great influence, although less in the developing nations than in those that are industrialized. Although science may weaken religion in some ways, it also brings about new possibilities for spreading it. Just as Americans can watch televised sermons, listen to tape-recorded messages, or attend drive-in churches, so can Moslems listen to the call to prayer from a radio or even a helicopter rather than merely from the muezzin's tower. They can also travel great distances to make their pilgrimage to Mecca—in throngs that Mohammed never dreamed of. There are few better examples of the impact of technology on religion, or of bringing far places of the world together, than that of the modern pilgrimage to Mecca. We can also see that old religious practices create new problems. (See the insert "Jets Bringing More Pilgrims to Jam Mecca," page 544.)

WORK IN THE DEVELOPING WORLD

We have noted that workers are far less satisfied in the developing countries than in the highly industrialized nations. Part of the reason is that the income gap between rich and poor is greater.

Figure 19-5 A public school in Mexico. The curriculum, nineteen months long, links education to the practical problems of rural life. (*United Nations*)

Even more serious, most of the developing countries have chronic unemployment. Partly because of changing farm methods and partly because of overpopulation in rural areas, people flock to the cities to look for work. Once there, they usually find only part-time work or must peddle goods or sell lottery tickets on the streets.

New industries introduced through foreign investment supply some types of jobs but tend to reduce others, especially native handicrafts. The multinational corporations import labor-saving machinery into countries already suffering from severe unemployment. Although they pay workers slightly better than native employers would pay them, the multinationals do not help the labor situation (Barnett and Muller, 1974, pp. 149–150). Whenever profits can be increased with labor-saving technology, the work force is reduced.

As in the United States, workers organize and enter the power conflict. Given the high inflation of the last few years, workers must demand big increases to hold their own. And even in countries with strong labor unions—such as Argenti-

---

Jets bringing more pilgrims to jam Mecca WILLIAM J. COUGHLIN

Modern technology is helping to bring an ancient religion to new heights.

Not long ago, a Bedouin elder who lives in southern Jordan described to a friend the arduous pilgrimage he made more than 30 years ago to Mecca.

The round trip to the holy city, 700 miles to the south, took him three months by camel, he said. He was one of fewer than 50,000 Moslems who made the annual pilgrimage, or haj, from abroad that year.

This year, at the peak of the pilgrimage, as many as 31,700 pilgrims a day arrived at Jidda on jet airliners which brought them from as far away as Taiwan to this Red Sea port which is the entry point for Mecca, 40 miles away. . . .

Every Moslem is expected to make the journey at least once during his lifetime, after which he is called Hajji and is much respected by his fellows. The Great Mosque in Mecca . . . is the chief goal of the pilgrimage. There, in the central courtyard of the mosque, is the holiest shrine in Islam, the Kaaba.

This is a cube-shaped building—kaaba means cube in Arabic—about 33 feet by 40 feet which holds in a silver ring on its south wall the famed black stone, which Islam teaches was given to Abraham by the angel Gabriel.

The Kaaba is covered by a black brocade cloth, known as a kiswa, which has texts from the Koran embroidered on it. Pilgrims walk or run seven times around the Kaaba, praying and reciting verses from the Koran and end by touching or kissing the stone, or at least the glass covering it.

Many are seriously injured or even trampled to death in the crush around the Kaaba at the height of the haj. . . .

The health of the pilgrims is one of the major problems faced each year by the Saudi government. The world cholera epidemic of 1865 began at the haj, killing about 15,000 of the 90,000 pilgrims, before spreading to Egypt, where there were 60,000 deaths, and then to Europe and America, where another 200,000 persons died in large cities alone.

Excerpted from William J. Coughlin, "Jets Bringing More Pilgrims to Jam Mecca," *Los Angeles Times*, March 11, 1973, Part I, pp. 1–2. Copyright Los Angeles Times.

Fiji contract talks

Sva, Fiji—Gold miners here are seeking a 30-minute midday sex break.

The miners believe this is the best time for sex, their union secretary, Navita Ragona, said Friday.

The demand is one of a number of issues the 1600-strong union is discussing with a mining company at Vatukuola.

Ragona said a man has a sexual obligation to his wife and if he goes home exhausted at 5 p.m. he cannot fulfill it. The union wants the sex break added to a normal lunch break.

After lunch and a short rest, a man is in prime mental and physical condition to meet his sexual obligations, Ragona said.

The union proposes to limit the sex break to married men. What he termed "alternative arrangements" would have to be made to compensate bachelors. "We don't want to overdo this," Ragona said.

Reuters Dispatch, "Fiji Contract Talks: Miners Ask 30-Minute Sex Break After Lunch," in *Los Angeles Times*, Jan. 25, 1975, Part I, p. 13.

---

na, Mexico, and Brazil—unions represent only a small percentage of the working class. The unorganized workers are victims of galloping inflation.

Whatever the problems of labor, collective bargaining is widespread throughout the world. This results in higher wages and higher prices for goods imported from lands in which labor was once cheap—Japan, for example. These developments may lead to more similarity among world cultures than existed in the past—a major theme of this chapter. However, local points of view still emerge, showing a certain persistence of cultural differences. Note that in the insert "Fiji Contract Talks," the gold miners are negotiating for a "fringe benefit," but one that is not yet demanded by the A.F.L.-C.I.O.

The brain drain

A different labor problem exists in the developing countries at the highest levels of employment. Some upper-class people receive a very good education, sometimes in universities in their own countries and sometimes abroad. In many cases, both the native-trained and those trained abroad are hired away by the major industrial countries or by multinational corporations, leaving a shortage of talent for local governments and business enterprises. This problem is known as *the brain drain*. The result is to further concentrate the leadership of science and industry in the areas where it already exists.

URBANIZATION IN WORLD PERSPECTIVE

Movement to the city is worldwide, since the city is where the opportunities are. In the developing countries, some parts of cities are very squalid. Still, even these areas are better than the rural areas left behind. In this respect, the movement to the city in the developing nations resembles the movement of black Americans to Northern cities between 1940 and 1970.

Some cities of the developing lands are growing much faster than American cities. As they grow, they show some of the same traits in exaggerated form: a wide gap between rich and poor, housing problems, social-class division,

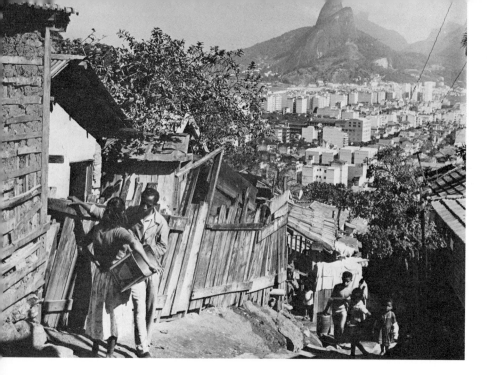

Figure 19-6 The *favelas,* or slums, of Rio de Janeiro, stand on hills surrounding the glittering central city. (*Mann, Monkmeyer*)

racial and ethnic segregation, and pollution of air and water.

Shantytowns

In one respect, cities in developing lands, especially in Latin America and South Africa, differ from American cities. Typically, the poor are not crowded into the inner cities. They live on the fringes of town, sometimes on land claimed by squatter's rights. Here, the dispossessed poor from farm areas build their unsightly shacks of tin and tar paper. Sometimes, as in Peru, they organize for mutual help and gradually improve their lot (Mangin, 1967). In some ways, they could be compared with the immigrants who have settled in American cities, living in squalor but hoping to do better than in the areas they left behind. In much of Latin America, there are no building restrictions. This makes housing for the poor unsightly, but it also means people can have shelter they could not afford under other conditions.

A case study: Mexico City

Built on the site of the old Aztec capital of Tenochtitlán, Mexico City dominates the high central plain of Mexico. It is hard to find a more beautiful setting for a city, standing well above the tropical heat and surrounded by volcanic mountains. Mexico City has beautiful monuments, parks, museums, old Spanish churches, places of entertainment, and elite shopping and residential areas. From the center of the city, all seems prosperous, active, and rushed. Around the fringes of the city, however, are the slums of the poor, usually people who have recently moved in from the rural areas.

Mexico City is interesting and beautiful enough to attract a heavy tourist trade. However, it is no more immune to the problems of pollution than are the highly industrialized cities of the United States. Its high plain (*altoplano*) is really a high valley, surrounded by mountains that often trap smog. The population of Mexico City is about 4 million, but if surrounding areas are included, it is over 7 million. Automobile, truck, bus, and motorcycle traffic is heavy. As a result, pollution has been described by one UNESCO expert as a hundred times the tolerable level. Breathing the air is "equivalent to smoking two packs of cigarettes a day" (Newsweek, August 27, 1973, p. 88). Perhaps no city gives a better picture of some of the ironies of modern development, with rapid progress leading to new types of problems.

CONCEPTUALIZING THE CHANGES

The changes described in the previous pages conform to some of the models of society mentioned in the first chapter. In Durkheim's analysis, the changes are from stable societies with closely binding norms to societies with a different basis for solidarity. They approximate Durkheim's phrase "organic solidarity," in that the division of labor is increasing so that villages are no longer self-dependent but must rely increasingly on the outside world. What is questionable about the idea of organic solidarity is whether such societies have developed new norms that are acceptable to their people. Strong social-class barriers continue to exist, even though the ideological trend of current social movements is in the direction of equality.

Certainly, the emerging nations of the world can be seen in conflict perspective, either Marxist or non-Marxist. Social-class divisions are wide and not disappearing; yet there are generally provisions for a certain amount of health care and education, there are labor unions, and in some cases there are growing numbers of white-collar workers. Such improvements may prevent the ultimate class struggle foreseen by Marx.

According to research done by John Kautsky (1967), it is generally true, as Marx would have predicted, that communist parties grow with industrial development—but only to a point. In countries that are somewhat industrialized but have lagging economic development and alienated work forces, communist parties are strong. However, the communist movement tends to lose its hold if the economy develops well enough to provide for workers and if educational opportunities and laws on wages, hours, and working conditions keep the people from feeling alienated. Given all these "ifs," it is risky to predict the political future of a developing nation.

Even if no Marxist class struggle occurs, there is still a chance for the kind of non-Marxist conflict outlined by Lewis Coser (1956). In fact, this is already happening. Organizations of labor, minority groups, peasants, independent businesspeople, and government bureaucrats struggle to influence policy decisions. Multinational corporations with heavy investments also take part, trying to get all the favors possible.

Finally, the developing world can be seen in cultural-evolutionary terms. First, it is easy to judge progress ethnocentrically, saying that the more closely a developing country comes to resemble our own, the more progress it has made. We must realize, though, that along with industrial progress has come the ability to pollute the earth and to destroy it in war. Also, while we can buy more things and live more comfortably than ever before, crime, mental illness, and general unhappiness are very much with us. Finally, even if industrialism does mean higher levels of production, this does not necessarily mean higher standards of living for all people. The population increase may wipe out production gains, or wealth may be so unevenly distributed that only a small upper class profits.

The change in production methods in both developing and industrially advanced nations means changing possibilities as far as the quality of life is concerned. The possibilities are much greater than ever before—for better health, sanitation, education, and income. However, there are also other, less optimistic possibilities—war, exhaustion of resources, and the pollution of the earth beyond the point of health or even survival. In this sense more than any other, the world has become interdependent. Its very survival depends on increasing cooperation in the use, preservation, and sharing of resources. Any system that causes wealth to flow to developed countries at the expense of developing countries does not serve the common good. Neither do policies that restrict food production or monopolize industrial resources. Despite its differences, the world has become in some ways united into one economic community. As such, it can survive only if it is able to unite into one sociological community as well.

SUMMARY

The nations of the world have grown increasingly *interdependent*, with mutual needs and concerns. Cultural differences remain, but sweeping changes have been brought about by modern science and industry. Thus, most of the themes developed in earlier chapters apply to the entire world, including the developing nations.

The developing countries are becoming geared to a worldwide culture. This culture is characterized by an increasing tempo of life, more *time-consciousness* and *calculability*. Also, *universalistic norms* are replacing the *particularistic norms* and values that favored relatives or other villagers.

Cultural change has affected socialization patterns. No longer are sex and age the sole criteria of roles in life. People are freed from traditional customs and the older generation. However, they must now prepare for more of job possibilities and needs. Role confusion results. Inkeles finds, however, that people in the developing nations who display *modern personality traits* are fairly well adjusted psychologically. The modern personality accepts change, takes an interest in events beyond the local village, follows modern leaders, and seeks education.

In spite of cultural changes, stratification systems are generally more rigid in the developing lands than in the highly industrialized nations. Some people accept social inequality; others try to improve their position. Still others think that the only real improvement lies in revolution. The desire for a more comfortable life has been whetted by awareness of the outside world—this is the *revolution of rising expectations.*

Production in developing countries is increasing, but population is keeping pace. Although a small middle class exists, its development may be hampered by the policies of *multinational corporations.* The multinationals lead in the development of such countries, but they follow policies that help themselves more than the native populations. Leadership jobs are usually filled by people from the highly developed countries.

The treatment of minorities is a problem in all parts of the world. South Africa, with its policy of *apartheid*, is described to exemplify racial problems. Even here, though, international pressures for equality may be having some effect. Opinions are changing in favor of decreased segregation. The minority status of women is changing in most places throughout the world. Kenya, a land of polygyny and male dominance, is described to show changing relationships between men and women.

All countries experience deviant behavior. However, in small tribes and villages, people were once kept in line by gossip and ridicule. With increasing urbanization and more anonymous populations, deviant behavior increases. Multinational corporations trying to win contracts in foreign lands have created new types of white-collar crime such as the bribing of foreign officials. Other forms of deviance on an international scale are drug smuggling and terrorism.

Education has spread greatly in the twentieth century. It is seen as the salvation of the developing countries. Public education has grown, but leadership positions still go to those who have been educated at elite colleges. Such education is available only to the rich. Basic education in agriculture and mechanical arts often lags because it lacks the prestige of liberal education. Some people have suggested the alternative of *informal education*. Religions also change. Social-class conflicts between rich and poor are often reflected in attitudes toward the major churches. The worldwide religions—such as Christianity, Islam, and Buddhism—tend to grow at the expense of small tribal religions. *Secularization* challenges religious worship today.

The problems of workers in the developing lands are similar to those of Western workers a generation or two ago. Pay scales are low and unemployment is chronic, although labor unions and higher wage demands are becoming increasingly common. The multinationals tend to hire the best talent away from local governments—a problem known as *the brain drain*.

The developing nations are now urbanizing at a more rapid pace than the developed lands. People are drawn to the cities by declines in farm jobs and hopes of better opportunities. In many places, the poor build shantytowns around the edges of cities. Living conditions are bad, but it is easier to eke out an existence there than in the rural areas that are being abandoned. Cities in developing lands have many of the problems found in American cities—segregation of rich and poor, noise and congestion, and environmental pollution.

Changes in the interdependent world could be thought of in Durkheim's terms as a movement toward organic solidarity. It may be more accurate to think of the world in terms of the conflict perspective, torn between the rich lands and the poor and between upper classes and lower. Finally, the change can be looked upon as a type of cultural evolution in which the whole world moves from an agricultural to an industrial level. The change promises far less poverty and sickness, but it also poses problems of resource exhaustion, pollution, and war.

Study guide

Terms to know

Interdependence
Time-consciousness
Calculability
Particularistic norms
Universalistic norms

Rationalization of production
Modern personality type
Revolution of rising expectations
Cumulative causation
Multinational corporation

Apartheid
Informal education
Brain drain

Names to know

Edward T. Hall
Margaret Mead
Alex Inkeles

Gerhard Lenski
Gunnar Myrdal

Self-test

Part I. Multiple Choice. Select the best of the four alternative answers:

1 Which of the following produce significant cultural changes in developing countries? (**a**) diffusion of ideas, (**b**) diffusion of products, (**c**) diffusion of technology, (**d**) all the above.
2 A news item on the subject of anchovies illustrates the idea of (**a**) economic interdependence of nations, (**b**) how food surpluses would benefit everyone, (**c**) why United States farming interests favor storing surplus food, (**d**) all the above.
3 Modernization has turned people in less developed countries to the production of "cash crops" and therefore caused a decline in nutritional standards, according to (**a**) Lloyd Fallers, (**b**) Margaret Mead, (**c**) Bert Farkle, (**d**) Edward Hall.
4 Alex Inkeles found that a modern personality type developed as a result of what two forces? (**a**) socialization and nationalism, (**b**) education and nationalism, (**c**) education and urbanization, (**d**) factories and internalization.
5 The modern personality type is distinguished from the old in *all but one* of the following ways: (**a**) an interest in government, labor, and education, (**b**) willingness to accept new ideas, (**c**) allegiance to elders and tribal leaders, (**d**) an interest in urban and national affairs more than in the village.
6 In average income, the developing countries could be compared with which social class? (**a**) the middle class, (**b**) the lower class, (**c**) the upper class, (**d**) the lower middle class.
7 Edward Hall's account of a conversation with an Egyptian farmer indicates that the farmer would have problems as a modern producer because of a failure to (**a**) work hard, (**b**) save, (**c**) calculate future probabilities, (**d**) plant the right kind of seed.
8 The African chief described by Fallers (**a**) has several wives, (**b**) is a pillar of the Anglican Church, (**c**) discusses with his clanmates the wishes of ancestors, (**d**) all the above.

9 According to Chase-Dunn, which industry is promoted first in developing countries? (**a**) transportation, (**b**) mining, (**c**) manufacturing, (**d**) tourism.

10 Dealing with upper-class people and thus making them even more elite by giving them special favors is an example of (**a**) equalizing opportunities, (**b**) cause and effect, (**c**) cumulative causation, (**d**) necessary and sufficient cause.

11 In many developing countries, the greatest hostility is directed against (**a**) foreign investors, (**b**) indigenous upper classes, (**c**) welfare programs, (**d**) educational programs.

12 According to a 1976 opinion poll, how many white South Africans would favor major changes in race laws? (**a**) virtually none, (**b**) less than half, (**c**) a majority, (**d**) virtually all.

13 What African country in 1976 passed its first law stating that women and their children were no longer the possessions of their husbands? (**a**) South Africa, (**b**) Kenya, (**c**) Rhodesia, (**d**) Liberia.

14 The practice by major industrial countries and multinational corporations of hiring trained professionals and leaving a shortage of talent for local governments and businesses is known as (**a**) calculability, (**b**) cumulative causation, (**c**) the brain drain, (**d**) expropriation.

15 What city is cited as an example of rapid progress leading to new types of urban problems? (**a**) Calcutta, (**b**) Cairo, (**c**) Katmandu, (**d**) Mexico City.

Part II. True-False Questions

1 As universalistic laws and bureaucracies are established, they conflict with older, particularistic values.

2 An example of giving a job to the most qualified person rather than to a friend or relative would be an example of upholding a particularistic value.

3 Inkeles concluded that the developing world will eventually resemble the industrialized world in education, employment, and mobility.

4 In the developing countries, the people work less and are more satisfied than people in the industrialized countries.

5 By 9 to 1, the people of the world favor increased conservation of animals and fish.

6 Chase-Dunn concluded that in developing countries, the lower classes lose income as development takes place.

7 Multinational corporations reserve the highest management positions for the people of the countries in which they invest.

8 *Apartheid* is the policy of extreme segregation and unequal treatment of blacks in South Africa.

9 The fact that there are now women in the labor forces of developing countries has resulted from the women's liberation movement, not necessarily from the presence of industry.

10 In older villages with old traditions and customs, crime rates are high because there are not enough police.

11 As Dore points out, schools in the developing countries sometimes prepare more people for white-collar jobs than can be employed.

12 In tradition-directed societies, religious practices are the same for all social classes.

13 Modern technology has done very little to bring more people into contact with religion.

14 The world's nations have become more interdependent because of the need to use, preserve, and share the earth.

15 If industrialism means higher levels of production, then production necessarily means higher standards of living.

The interdependent world

Questions for discussion

1 In the text, several examples are given of world interdependence, especially in raw materials, markets, and trade. What other examples of interdependence can you name?

2 Are you a modern personality, according to Inkeles's definition? Do you know people who do not meet his criteria of modernity? In what way?

3 After reading the paragraph on the role conflict of an African chief, try to imagine some of the other types of role conflict that would arise among people changing from tribal to modern society. Picture yourself as a wife with modern ideas married to a tradition-oriented man, or as a son or daughter with modern ideas who is living in the household of tradition-oriented parents.

4 "The great majority of the rural populations of underdeveloped countries yearn to move to the big cities. . . ." Why do you suppose this is true? What would you lack in rural districts that rural Americans have?

5 Gunnar Myrdal explains the increasing gap between rich and poor as the result of a type of cumulative causation. In this case, the idea is that if you are wealthy, you will receive special favors that will help you become wealthier. Explain why this cumulative causation comes about in the developing world. Are there any similar cases in the United States?

6 Why would you expect to see increased deviant behavior in countries changing from traditional to modern ways? (Remember that what is acceptable in one country might be considered deviant in another.)

7 If you had to describe developing nations using one social model, which would you choose—organic, conflict, or evolutionary—and why?

8 The insert "Rich-Poor Gap Dominates World Poll" presents a variety of attitudes from around the world. Compare, to the average views expressed here, your own position on financial worries, attitudes about population, belief in conservation, desire to emigrate from your country, desire to move to a big city, belief in God, and belief in an afterlife.

Projects

1 To clarify differences in attitudes between Americans and people in less industrialized countries, question people who have traveled abroad considerably. This may involve inviting an outside speaker to class. Possibly some students in the class have had enough experience abroad to speak on the subject and answer questions. A person who was born in one of the developing countries or who lived there a long time will be able to give much better answers to questions than a casual tourist.

2 The United Nations, although weaker and more divided than its founders had hoped, is still an important force regarding international differences and agreements. Study at least two aspects of the United Nations:

a The specialized agencies—such as the Food and Agriculture Organization, UNESCO, the International Labor Organization, and the International Monetary Fund—to see what they do to promote international cooperation.

b The current debates in the General Assembly. These will acquaint you with the points of view of the Soviet bloc, Israel, the Arabic countries, and the poor countries of the Third World.

3 If time permits, stage in class a model General Assembly in which some of the current international conflicts are debated. Students can represent enough conflicting nations to dramatize international differences and gain insight into different viewpoints and vested interests.

Suggested readings

Bose, Nirmal Kumar: "Calcutta: A Premature Metropolis," *Scientific American*, vol. 213, September 1965, pp. 91–102. What happens when a city grows to enormous size without the benefit of the industrial revolution? In Calcutta "the collision of the traditional society with the forces compelling urbanization and industrialization is harsher by virtue of the fact that the city possesses no more than the rudiments of the technological apparatus that makes life possible [for cities of such a size]."

Davis, Kingsley: "The Urbanization of the Human Population," *Scientific American*, vol. 213, September 1965, pp. 40–53. Why has the movement to the cities become worldwide? What are the growth patterns of cities as industrialism increases, and what are the limits of growth? Why is urbanism more rapid in the developing nations than it was at the same phase of technological advancement in the fully industrialized countries? A leading expert on population and urbanization answers these and other questions.

Horowitz, Irving L.: "Capitalism, Communism, and Multinationalism," *Society*, vol. 11, January–February 1974, pp. 32–43. Horowitz discusses how multinational corporations have begun to link East to West, supplying consumer goods to the Soviet bloc in return for essential raw materials. "When internationalism finally did make its move," says Horowitz, "it did so in corporate rather than proletarian guise."

LaBelle, Thomas J., and Robert E. Verhine: "Nonformal Education and Occupational Stratification: Implications for Latin America," *Harvard Educational Review*, vol. 45, May 1975, pp. 16–183. What are your chances of "making it" in Latin America if you have the required education but did not go to the "right" schools? Why is it hard to promote some of the types of practical training that are so badly needed?

Marx, Leonard H.: "Politics of World Information," *Society*, vol. 12, September–October 1975, pp. 26–29. Communications technology can bring the world closer together than ever before. Can we prevent censorship from curbing these possibilities? Why does the world need open communication?

Newsweek, editors: "To Have and Have Not," *Newsweek*, September 15, 1975, pp. 37–41. What is the strategy of the poorer Third World countries to try to get a larger share of wealth? Parts of the Third World are so poor that they might more accurately be called the Fourth World. Which countries are progressing and which are not? This article concerns a mission of former Secretary of State Henry Kissinger, but problems and viewpoints have not changed since his time.

Pogrund, Benjamin: "South African Abyss," *The New Republic*, September 25, 1976, pp. 11–15. Pogrund, a South African journalist temporarily in the United States, shares the concern of many others about the need for racial equality in South Africa and Rhodesia. Why does he think the South African government secretly wishes for majority (black) rule in Rhodesia?

Rosen, Steven J.: "Rightist Regimes and American Interests," *Society*, vol. 11, September–October 1974, pp. 50–61. "The underlying purpose of American imperialism is nothing less than keeping as much as possible of the world open for trade and investment by the giant multinational corporations," says Rosen. What does he mean by American imperialism? On what evidence does he base his conclusion about national favors for multinational corporations?

Key to questions. Multiple Choice: 1-d; 2-a; 3-b; 4-c; 5-c; 6-b; 7-c; 8-d; 9-b; 10-c; 11-a; 12-c; 13-b; 14-c; 15-d. True-False: 1-T; 2-F; 3-T; 4-F; 5-T; 6-T; 7-F; 8-T; 9-F; 10-F; 11-T; 12-F; 13-F; 14-T; 15-F.

GLOSSARY

Achieved status A status or social position attained through effort.

Achievement motivation The urge, hope, and knowledge to reach socially approved goals.

Active crowd Participants in a mob, riot, panic, or other social disorder.

Adaptive traits Traits that make it possible for a species to adjust well to its own particular environment.

Adult socialization Any form of socialization that occurs after the period of adolescence.

Ageism A pattern of stereotyping, prejudice, and discrimination against aging.

Agencies of socialization Officially, the family, the school, and the church. Unofficially, includes the media, peer group, and many other influences from outside the home.

Alienation The feeling of not belonging; having no sense of meaning, no power, and no emotional ties.

Altruistic suicide According to Durkheim, suicide committed for the sake of others.

Anomic suicide According to Durkheim, suicide committed by those who feel "anomic," or "separated from the norms" of society.

Anomie According to Merton, a split between societal goals and the ability to reach them. According to Durkheim, separation from the norms or having norms that are inappropriate to the society.

Anthropology A social science that deals with the total range of human cultures. Focuses on preindustrial societies and on the development of the human species.

Antinatalist coercive policies Government policies to limit family size by law, with additional pregnancies terminated by abortion.

Antinatalist persuasive policies Government policies designed to limit family size through campaigns of public education and persuasion.

Apartheid The policy of extreme racial segregation of South Africa.

Arithmetic progression An increase in the base figure by 1: 1, 2, 3, 4, etc.

Ascribed status A status acquired at birth or assigned at various stages in the life cycle.

Aspiration gap The difference between the job one would like and the job one must often accept. Occurs as certain job categories become oversubscribed.

Association An organized group of any kind, either formal or informal. Often applies to clubs, lodges, public-service groups, and groups pursuing particular causes.

Atonement In terms of punishment, a chance for individuals to repent and make themselves acceptable to a god or gods.

Authoritarian personality According to Adorno and associates, a personality that shows a great deal of prejudice and hostility, observes pecking orders, and cannot tolerate compromise or conflicting opinions.

Authority Power that is recognized as legitimate or legal.

Automation The use of machinery, instructed by self-correcting computers, to do the actual work. The human worker watches to see that nothing goes wrong.

Average (mean) A figure found by adding the total quantities being considered and dividing by the number of cases.

Aversive therapy A systematic attempt to change behavior to acceptable patterns through deprivation or punishment.

Behavior modification The theory that human behavior can be changed (modified) through a system of rewards and punishments.

Birthrate The number of live births per 1,000 population per year.

Blaming the victim Holding depressed minority groups or unfortunate individuals responsible for their problems.

Blockbusting Moving one or two black families into an all-white block in order to frighten white homeowners into selling their houses quickly at low prices.

Boundary maintenance mechanisms Methods used by a subcultural group to keep its members separate from outsiders.

Bourgeoisie According to Marx, the owners of mines, factories, railroads, and other means of production and distribution of goods.

Brain drain The practice, by industrialized nations or multinational corporations, of hiring away the best-educated people of the developing world. This leaves a shortage of talent for local governments and business enterprises.

Bureaucracy According to Weaver, a hierarchy of positions, with each person a specialist in a particular job, in which status is attained through ability alone.

Calculability The possibility of establishing predictions and plans for the future.

Career mobility The capacity for social mobility through a change in occupation.

Caste A social-class system that allows no movement from one class to another. See also **open-class system**.

Casual crowd A collection of people who happen to be at a particular place at the same time.

Catastrophe A sudden, drastic event or series of events that cause a profound change in a culture.

Central business district The central park of the city, consisting of business and light industry.

Central tendency The tendency for statistics to cluster at or near one point rather than being distributed at random.

Closed shop A company in which all workers are required to join the union before being hired. See also **union shop**.

Cognition The process of gaining knowledge through both observation and reasoning.

Cohabitation Living together without being married.

Coleman report Produced for the U.S. Department of Health, Education, and Welfare in 1966. Concluded that the home is the most important factor in determining academic success.

Collective behavior Relatively spontaneous actions of groups of people to relieve feelings of dissatisfaction and anxiety.

Commune A form of social organization resembling an extended family, in which family functions are shared.

Concentric-zone theory According to Burgess, a pattern of urban development in which cities expand outward from the central business district in a series of concentric circles.

Conflict groups Groups whose norms differ from those of the larger society and which struggle for cultural survival within the larger society.

Conflict model A model of society that stresses internal conflicts and disagreements rather than unity and that sees the essential character of society as the outcome of such conflict. See also **unitary model**.

Conflict theory of education States that "professionalization," or upgrading of requirements for jobs, is an attempt to screen out those seen as unfit and to increase the prestige of the job.

Conformist According to Merton, the person who succeeds in reaching goals by honest means.

Contaminative exposure In prisons and mental institutions, a process whereby staff members try to dredge up an inmate's secrets through conversation.

Control In a scientific experiment, a technique for eliminating or minimizing the effect of all variables but one.

Conventional crowd An audience or group of people at an orderly meeting.

Convergence theory The theory that people take part in crowd behavior mainly because they came together as a result of personal attitudes and predispositions.

Correlation The tendency of two phenomena to be related.

Cosa Nostra ("Our Thing") A nationwide, organized criminal structure within the United States, also known as the Mafia.

Counterrioters People who talk to excited groups, urging them to be calm.

Countervailing power A power that opposes other sources of power.

Credential society A society in which various occupational groups have tried to professionalize themselves by setting up rules to determine who is competent and socially acceptable.

Crimes for fun Crimes perpetrated primarily by middle-class people as a game, including especially automobile theft, shoplifting, and computerized crime.

Crimes without victims Crimes in which no one is preyed on by another.

Crisis According to Erikson, a turning point in life, not necessarily a time of peril.

Crowd A temporary, unstructured collection of people who are aware of each other and influenced by each other.

Crowd contagion Crowd characteristics such as heightened suggestibility, lack of reflection, and milling behavior.

Cultural base A culture's state of development at the time under consideration.

Cultural complex An interrelated set of cultural traits.

Cultural diffusion The transmission of cultural traits from one culture to another.

Cultural dynamics Cultural change; also the reasons for change and the consequences of it.

Cultural evolution See **social evolution**.

Cultural lag A situation in which social change lags behind the possibilities opened by technological change.

Cultural relativity The tendency to look at other people and customs in the context of their own cultures, not by the viewer's standards. See also **ethnocentrism**.

Cultural trait The smallest detail of a culture.

Culture The pattern of life shared by the members of a society, including knowledge, belief, art, morals, law, custom, etc.

Cumulative causation The process of using social position and wealth to gain more social position and wealth. Applies especially to the upper classes of developing nations in their relationship with foreign economic interests.

Death rate The number of deaths per 1,000 population per year.

Demographic transition Historical changes in birthrate and death rate.

Demography The study of population.

Dependent variable A phenomenon that appears to be caused, wholly or in part, by one or more other phenomena. See also **independent variable.**

Destiny control Control of one's future. Ideas of destiny control range from the feeling of personal control of one's destiny to the feeling of being a pawn of forces beyond control.

Deterrent In terms of punishment, the view that the punishment of a criminal will be a warning to others and will restrain them from crime.

Deviant behavior Behavior that varies markedly from the norms that are acceptable to a society.

Dialectic In terms of the Marxist conflict model of society, the clash of opposite forces that arises at each stage of history.

Differential association The association of people, in different degrees, with normative and deviant influences.

Differential birthrate Differences in birthrate with respect to location (urban or rural), religion, social class, and racial or ethnic group.

Disablement In terms of punishment, the view that the criminal must be made incapable of committing any more crimes.

Discovery Finding something new or finding new uses for tools, objects, or ideas already in use.

Discrimination A system of unequal treatment toward objects of prejudice.

Disengagement theory The view that loss of roles and social relationships occurs inevitably among the aged and is agreeable to them because they wish to withdraw from many commitments and obligations.

Distortion of scale A visual representation of statistics that makes the figures appear to be more drastic than they actually are.

Ecological city The political city plus its surrounding suburban environment.

Economics A social science that concentrates on wealth and income and their distribution.

Efficiency engineer A person who analyzes industrial processes to try to determine the most efficient methods for workers to use. Most typically, breaks down all operation into the simplest possible movements. Sees people as interchangeable parts of a machine.

Egalitarian family Family in which both spouses have relatively equal rights and responsibilities.

Egalitarian movements Social movements that try to gain equality for particular groups.

Egoistic suicide According to Durkheim, suicide committed by those who are isolated from or have the weakest ties to society.

Emergent-norm theory The theory that crowds develop their own norms as they form.

Empiricism The study of observable facts and of things as they are.

Ethnic group A group whose culture is sufficiently different in beliefs, values, and customs so that its members feel an ingroup identity which sets them apart from others.

Ethnic succession in crime The conclusion that the social environment in certain areas is a significant factor in socializing into delinquency, regardless of the ethnic groups that live there.

Ethnocentrism The tendency to see and judge other people and customs from the viewpoint of one's own culture. See also **cultural relativity**.

Euthanasia Termination of a patient's life in order to prevent unnecessary suffering.

Experiment A trial to test a hypothesis.

Exploding metropolis Pattern of urban growth in which new centers grow up in all areas.

Exploitation According to Marxist theory, the process whereby rich take advantage of the poor, working them hard and paying them little.

Expressive crowd People who are expressing their emotions in a group setting.

Fads Extremes of fashions, quickly adopted and quickly dropped.

Fashions The customs of dress, speech, music, art, and other interests that are widely accepted by leading elements of society.

Folkways Customs which are considered normal or right because people are used to them.

Formal organization An organization in which rules and duties are officially prescribed and enforced.

Frustration-agression theory The theory that aggression is caused by frustration, or the blocking of people's paths toward their goals.

Function The consequences of a social structure, or the purposes it serves.

Functional analysis of sex-role inequality The idea that sex roles change only in a society whose interests are served by such change.

Gemeinschaft Folk society characterized by primary relationships, informality, and little competition. See also **gesellschaft.**

Generalized belief A belief widely held in society or other social groups.

Generalized other According to Mead, the social rules or the voice of society that we internalize during the socialization process.

Generational mobility Movement of a person to a different social class from that to which his or her parents belonged.

Geographical determinism The theory that cultural differences are caused by geographical environment.

Geographical races Classification of races by region of origin, as European race, Australian race (Aborigines), or East Asian race. Also the evolution of races as a result of prolonged geographical separation.

Geometric progression A doubling of the base figure: 1, 2, 4, 8, etc.

Gerontologist A specialist in the problems of aging.

Gesellschaft Businesslike, time-oriented, fast-moving society in which people compete with each other. See also **gemeinschaft.**

Grade inflation The trend toward more permissive high school and college grading standards.

Green revolution Beginning of marked improvement in types of crops and agricultural methods in developing lands, with hope of averting famine.

Group An aggregate of two or more persons held together by a common focus of interest and interaction.

Hawthorne effect The tendency for experimental results to be influenced by the fact that subjects realize they are part of an experimental study.

Hereditary theory of crime A theory holding that criminality is an inherited trait and that criminals are throwbacks to an earlier stage in human evolution.

Hospice In Great Britain, a place devoted exclusively to the care of the dying.

Human ecology The relationships between people and their environment, both natural and artificial.

Human relations approach In industrial relations, an attitude that sees the worker as a human, social, and intelligent being rather than a robot. Is concerned with both productivity and worker satisfaction.

Hyphenated   Americans Polish-Americans, Greek-Americans, Italian-Americans, etc. According to Novak, these Eastern and Southern European ethnic groups in the United States feel that they are not fully accepted as Americans but are thought of as "hyphenated."

Hypothesis A tentative idea about the relationship between phenomena.

"I" According to Mead, the subjective and creative

part of the personality; the part that creates meaning. See also **"me."**

Id According to Freud, that part of the personality consisting of untamed vital energy and the center of such drives as sex and aggression.

Idealized norms Stated norms of a society. See also **real norms**.

Ideal type A typical pattern of institutions and groups of people, built up from many observational studies.

Identification The process by which one imaginatively places oneself in the role of someone else and takes on the traits of that person.

Ideological conservative One who may approve liberal policies but rejects the idea of a welfare state. See also **operational liberal**.

Ideology A body of ideas that provide a rationalization for a particular way of life or social system, such as capitalism, socialism, democracy, or dictatorship.

Independent variable A phenomenon that appears to be a cause or partial cause of one or more other phenomena. See also **dependent variable**.

Indeterminate sentence A sentence giving a maximum and minimum number of years for a particular offense, depending on whether the convict is considered ready for release.

Industrial revolution Beginning in the 1760s, the change in production from hand labor to machinery and from work in the home to factory work.

Infanticide Killing of babies.

Influence Power to sway the opinions or actions of others, often subtly and without legal sanction.

Informal education An apprenticeship program outside the school system for improving crafts, skills, and education; a suggested alternative to traditional education in the developing countries.

Informal organization An organization with no formal rules and with fairly flexible duties and expectations.

Informal structure A group in which social relationships lack formal rules and authority but are bound by primary characteristics and informal rules.

Ingroup Any group to which we belong. See also **outgroup**.

Inner-directed personality According to Riesman, a personality with strongly internalized attitudes, values, and standards of behavior. See also **other-directed personality.**

Innovator According to Merton, a person who succeeds in reaching goals by devious means without getting caught.

Insanity According to American law, usually the inability to distinguish right from wrong.

Intensification An almost ritualistic way of preserving loyalty to one's own culture, traditions, and identification group. See also **nativism**.

Interactionism The view that the group is an entity in itself but that individual group members are still capable of individual autonomy. See also **nominalism** and **realism**.

Interdependence In international affairs, the increasing reliance of countries on each other for social, political, and economic reasons.

Internalization The absorbing of attitudes and beliefs and making them one's own.

Invention Combining objects or ideas in new ways.

Iron law of oligarchy The theory orginated by Robert Michels, that leadership groups in all organizations become entrenched, resisting competition and change.

Jencks report A report which concludes that social-class position, education and occupation of parents, cultural background, and genetic differences are the important factors in determining who will do well in school. Proposes, as a reform of the reward structure, more nearly equal pay for all jobs.

Job satisfaction A feeling that one's job is interesting and worthy of respect and not simply a source of income.

Katba Marriage arranger in Egypt.

Kibbutz A communal system found in many parts of Israel.

Labeling theory The theory that labeling people as deviants causes them to take on a deviant self-identity.

Latent function The unnoticed, often unwanted result of social structures and policies. See also **manifest function**.

Latent functions of education Functions other than the overt, stated ones. Latent functions of education include increasing the gap between social classes, increasing class prejudice, acting as a marriage market, cohabitation on college campuses, creation of youth subcultures and student activism.

Legal paternalism Relative to women, the assumption of the courts that women are more childlike than men and more easily reformed.

Legal responsibility In cases of crime, personal accountability in the eyes of the law, which can be established only if criminal intent is proved.

Legitimization The process of making a political regime seem rightful to the people and in accord with law and custom.

Life chances Collectively, the opportunity to lead a long and rewarding life—with education, a good income, and interesting experiences—and to guarantee the same to one's children.

Looking-glass process According to Cooley, the process of looking at other people and using their responses to establish a self-concept.

Looking-glass self According to Cooley, the self-concept formed from interpreting others' reactions to us.

Loosely structured society A society with wide differences of opinion on norms, in which the government permits free expression of beliefs.

Lower class (underclass) Economically the poorest social class. Occupationally often unemployed or underemployed. Also frequently characterized by feelings of hopelessness and alienation.

Lower lower class The lowest level of the community social system; mostly unskilled and sometimes on welfare; in many cases, psychologically alienated.

Lower middle class In the community social system just below the upper middle class. Composed mainly of white-collar workers and skilled laborers with good jobs. Also includes poorly paid business and professional people.

Lower upper class In the community social system, just below the upper upper class. Consists mainly of newly rich people.

Mafia Originally, Sicilian outlaw organizations. In the United States, crime organizations still having Sicilian members and following a few Sicilian traditions. More loosely, the term is applied to any crime organizations among distinct ethnic groups.

Mala in se One of two types of forbidden acts, "evil in itself." See also **mala prohibita**.

Mala prohibita One of two types of forbidden acts, those that are "evil because prohibited." Opposite of **mala in se**.

Malnutritron cycle A situation in which the malnutrition of one generation contributes to malnutrition in the next, since the older generation lacks the energy needed to care for the young.

Malthusian population theory View that unless checked, population would increase geometrically while the food supply increased only arithmetically, resulting in starvation.

Managerial revolution According to Burnham, the takeover of industry by trained managers.

Manifest function The intended, obvious result of ideas, policies, and social structures. See also **latent function**.

Manifest functions of education The most obvious, openly stated functions. These include providing workers, helping to promote equal opportunity, encouraging upward mobility, and teaching a common culture.

Marginal adaptation The process by which people who live on the border between the two cultures find a niche for themselves in the dominant culture.

Mass hysteria A form of collective behavior characterized by a belief that something in the environment has the power to threaten or destroy.

Matriarchy A society ruled by women.

Matrilineal society A society in which descent is traced through the mother's line.

Matrilocal Family system in which a married couple live in the household or near vicinity of wife's mother.

"Me" According to Mead, the objective side of personality, consisting of all the internalized training, habits, conventions, attitudes, and behaviors. See also **"I."**

Mechanical solidarity A unitary model that compares members of society to the identical products of a machine. See also **organic solidarity**.

Median In a series of statistics, the midpoint, with half the figures on one side and half on the other.

Megalopolis The most far-reaching, densely populated urban areas; *megalopolis* is sometimes used to describe areas where large cities have grown together.

Middle class Includes both the upper middle class (business, professional, and managerial) and the lower middle class (white-collar workers, skilled laborers, and poor business and professional people).

Middleman One who buys goods from a supplier and then sells them to the public, or one who transports goods from a source to other suppliers.

Minimal families Families with very few functions, as in the Israeli *Kibbutz*, where children are reared by specialists rather than by parents.

M'Naghten Rule The rule that a person must be incapable of distinguishing right from wrong in order to be absolved from legal responsibility for his or her actions on grounds of insanity.

Mobililization In collective behavior, spreading propaganda, notifying potential activists, and trying to get community support.

Mode The item in a series of statistical data that occurs most often.

Model A simplified way of thinking about a complex subject. See also **conflict model, organismic model, symbolic interactionism, and unitary model.**

Model Cities Program Urban-renewal program launched by the federal government in 1966. Included rehabilitation loans to homeowners, health centers, housing inspection and park maintenance, schools, and retraining programs.

Modern personality type According to Inkeles, a personality type characterized by a willingness to accept new ideas; loyalty to leaders of modern governments, schools, and labor unions; and a break with elders and traditional leaders.

Mores The rules that are considered essential to the survival of a society.

Movements of world rejection Social movements whose members feel discontent with the world as it is and decide to prepare for a better world to come or to develop little utopian societies of their own.

Multinational corporation A corporation with branches and major economic interests in foreign (particularly developing) countries.

Multiple nuclei According to one theory of urban growth, several communities around which a city develops.

Mortification The process of stripping the inmate of a total institution of self-respect and status so as to create a complete break with the past.

Nativism A strong attempt to preserve one's native culture. See also **intensification**.

Negative (passive) euthanasia The removal of life support from terminal patients. See also **positive euthanasia**.

Neurosis A form of mental illness in which the patient does not lose contact with reality. See also **psychosis.**

Neurosurgery Surgery on the brain in order to remove tumors or other physical abnormalities within it.

New towns Self-contained communities with shopping areas, places of employment, schools, and recreation areas.

Nominalism As applied to social groups, the view that the group exists in name only; that the whole is equal to the sum of its parts. See also **interactionism** and **realism**.

Normative inconsistency Situations in which two conflicting norms or values are both held.

Norms (moral) Rules of right and wrong.

Norm of evasion A custom or type of behavior that is widely accepted even though it defies the stated moral norms of society.

Norms (statistical) An average of what "everyone does."

Nuclear family Parents and children alone, living in their own separate household.

Nurturant behavior The need for someone to care for.

Observational study Research through direct observation of people.

Old age The time when people abandon the occupational roles they have long held, whether or not they are still able to function.

Open-class system A social-class system in which, ideally, there are no barriers to prevent a person from moving freely from one class to another. See also **caste**.

Operational liberal A liberal attitude toward the actual procedures and aims of social welfare policies. See also **ideological conservative**.

Optimum population The theoretical point at which population is exactly right for full development of natural resources and economic potential.

Organic solidarity   A unitary model that sees people becoming more and more interdependent, since they follow specialized lines of work and need others to provide the goods and services they no longer provide for themselves. See also **mechanical solidarity**.

Organismic model   A unitary model that compares society with a living organism in which all parts tend to serve the whole.

Organization   Any social unit that coordinates the activities of its members. See also **formal organization** and **informal organization**.

Organization men   According to Whyte, the middle- and upper-level employees of big organizations; seen as having no freedom, spontaneity, creativity, or minds of their own.

Orgiastic crowd   A crowd that has gotten completely out of hand as occasionally occurs at parties or victory celebrations.

Other-directed personality   According to Riesman, the personality with weakly internalized attitudes, values, and standards of behavior who looks to others for standards of right and wrong. See also **inner-directed personality**.

Outgroup   Any group to which we do not belong. See also **ingroup**.

Parkinson's law   The theory that bureaucracies always grow larger, whether they need to or not.

Participant-observer study   Research in which the observer becomes part of the group under study.

Particularistic norms   Norms that apply to particular situations, places, and people. See also **universalistic norms**.

Party   According to Weber, the ability of prestigious groups to exercise power and influence the social and political system.

Patriarchal   Family rule by the senior male member.

Patrilineal   Pertaining to descent traced through the father's line.

Patterned behavior   Behavior repeated often enough to be characteristic of individuals or societies under a given set of circumstances; includes customs of speech and dress, gestures, salutations, manners, beliefs, attitudes, skills, and work habits.

Peer groups   Any group of status equals.

Perspective   A particular point of view we adopt in looking at society.

Pogrom   The destruction or massacre of helpless populations.

Political city   The area within the city limits governed as part of the urban unit.

Political crimes   Crimes against the state, including subversive, terroristic, or treasonable acts or the flagrant misuse of power.

Political science   A social science that concentrates on power and how it is distributed and used.

Political socialization   The process of internalizing poltical values.

Polyandry   A form of marriage in which a woman has more than one husband.

Polygyny   A form of marriage in which a man has more than one wife. See also **polyandry**.

Population pyramid   A graph that shows the age and sex distribution of a population at a particular time.

Positive euthanasia   The administeration of a drug to terminate a patient's life in order to prevent or end suffering. See also **negative euthanasia**.

Positive reinforcement   Any reward or desired experience that helps strengthen desired behavior.

Power   The ability to cause others to do what we want; in some cases, the ability to help sway the decisions of industry or government.

Power elite   According to Mills, the very rich who control the major corporations and are closely linked to the government and the military.

Precipitating incident   The event that touches off a form of collective behavior.

Prejudice   Negative attitude toward a person or group, not based on experience.

Prestige   Standing or esteem in the eyes of others.

Preventive custody   The detention of people not for acts they have committed but for acts they are believed likely to commit.

Primary groups   Groups characterized by face-to-face interaction and intense feelings of belonging and intimacy. See also **secondary groups**.

Privilege system   The granting of small extras to well-behaved inmates of total institutions.

Professionalization   The attempt by certain occupational groups to set high standards in order to upgrade themselves socially for more prestige.

Professional thief   One who finds crime a means to a livelihood, accepts the self-image of thief, and even rationalizes such a choice of livelihood.

Proletariat   According to Marx, the working class, which does not own the means of production.

Pronatalist   In favor of a large number of births.

Protean man   According to Lifton, a personality that changes rapidly so as to adapt to changing conditions.

Psychology   A social science that concentrates on personality traits and their development, emotionality, aggressiveness, and the individual's ability to deal with reality.

Psychosis   A severe form of mental illness in which the person loses contact with reality. See also **neurosis.**

Psychosurgery   Brain surgery that is intended to alter behavior.

"Pygmalion effect"   The effect of the expectations of others on one's performance. High expectations promote high achievement; low expectations, low achievement.

Race   Inherited physical differences in groups of people of different geographic origins.

Radical movements   Social movements designed to effect basic changes in the social system.

Random sample   A selection of persons at random on the assumption that the right percentage of each category of people will be polled.

Rapport   In an observational study, the ability to be accepted by others as trustworthy and understanding.

Rationalization   The process by which a person finds socially acceptable, plausible, but untrue explanations for actions.

Rationalization of production   Finding the most efficient ways of turning out a product for the market. According to Weber, a dominant concern of modern societies.

Reaffirmation of the norms   In terms of punishment, the view that people punish others to prove to themselves that their ways are right.

Realism   As applied to social groups, the view that the group has a real existence, an identity of its own. See also **interactionism** and **nominalism.**

Real norms   The actual behavior of people within any given society. See also **idealized norms.**

Rebel   According to Merton, a person who values some social norms and rejects others. May use both honest and dishonest means to reach goals.

Recidivism   Repeated convictions for crime.

Reciprocal roles   Roles that depend on one another for definition and fulfillment.

Redlining   The process by which banks and lending agencies decide that certain urban areas are no longer a safe investment.

Rehabilitation   The theory that a person (usually a criminal) can be changed and made an acceptable and functioning member of society.

Relative deprivation   Deprivation by comparison with the wealth or status of others.

Rentier class   According to Pareto, the landowning class, which would be replaced by the speculator class. See also **speculator class.**

Representative sample   Selection of a mix of all segments of the population in proportion to the actual number of people taking part in the activity being studied.

Repression   The process of driving a thought from the conscious mind so that it will no longer be remembered.

Retreatist   According to Merton, one who values neither success goals nor the honest means used by others to reach those goals.

Retribution (revenge)   In terms of punishment, the view that society should treat the criminal as the criminal has treated the victim.

Revenue sharing   Policy begun by the Nixon administration of giving the cities direct grants.

Revolutionary movements   Social movements that aim at overthrowing existing political systems and power structures.

Revolution of rising expectations   The hope for a better future for oneself and one's family. A term applied particularly to developing countries.

Ritualist   According to Merton, one who gives up hope of success but remains scrupulously honest.

Role   The behavior expected of the person who has a particular status.

Role conflict   A form of role strain that results from the conflicting demands of a particular role.

Role distance   According to Goffman, the desire

for a personal identity apart from the identity given by a role.

Role loss The result of encouraging or forcing people to retire (relatively) early and completely.

Role sets Roles acted out in relationship to a number of other people.

Role strain Problems that arise in coping with roles.

Role taking The imaginative taking of a different role so as to reach a sympathetic understanding of that role.

Romantic myth The idea that one can find a perfect mate and that once this has happened, there are no problems in marriage.

Rumor A form of communication that arises whenever people want to know what is happening but where there is little dependable information.

Scapegoat A person or group blamed (usually unjustly) for the troubles of society.

Scientific method The systematic pursuit of knowledge, faithful to facts and cautious about conclusions. Includes hypothesis, research design, interpretation of facts, publicizing of results, and testing of validity.

Secondary groups Groups created for specific purposes and interested in their members mainly for their contributions to those purposes. See also **primary groups**.

Segmental unemployment Unemployment in certain sections of the country and parts of the economy.

Self-concept Our idea of what we are like.

Sexism A pattern of stereotyping, prejudice, and discrimination against people on the basis of their sex.

Sexist hypothesis As applied to law, the theory that in legal cases, women, as the "weaker sex," should be treated differently from men.

Significant others Those who have an important influence on our thoughts, emotions, and actions.

Single-culture traditions The educational tradition in the United States which proceeds as though all children were of Anglo-Saxon descent.

Skidder A person born to a fairly high status who is slipping or feels that his or her personal status is threatened.

Sociability The interaction with others for the pleasure of their company and to fulfill one's psychological needs.

Social class One level in a class system made up of people who are roughly equal (and think of themselves as more or less equal) in income, education, occupation, prestige, and social influence.

Social control The maintenance of order and observation of the norms of society.

Social Darwinism An adaptation of Charles Darwin's concepts of evolution, struggle, and the "survival of the fittest" to human societies. States that through a competitive struggle, superior persons rise to the top and become the upper classes of society, while the "unfit"—the poor or disabled—are eliminated.

Social distance The degree to which people are accepted or rejected in social relationships.

Social evolution The theory that human societies evolved in a series of stages—moving from "savagery" to "barbarism" to "civilization"—and that they will continue to evolve.

Social institution An organized pattern of behavior, thought, and custom designed to meet certain basic needs of a society.

Social interaction The process by which people and groups influence each other—by talking, teaching, helping, changing attitudes, or rousing emotions.

Social invisibility The quality of not being noticed by the rest of society and being known by very few other people.

Socialization The process that links together the individual and the culture and during which the individual absorbs the values, folkways, and mores of the society, but in a manner permitting a distinctive personality.

Social movements The longest-lasting form of collective behavior, designed to create or resist changes in attitudes, behavior, and institutions.

Social register A list of all the people acceptable in the highest social circles in the United States or a particular community.

Social structure The total pattern of organization of a society, including established customs, laws, and institutions.

Social (vertical) mobility Downward or upward movement within the social-class structure.

Society An organization of people or other forms

of life living within a particular territory, persisting through generations, and relatively independent of other societies.

Sociology The scientific study of society; of groups, institutions, and organizations; and of the interrelationships between members of societies.

Speculator class According to Pareto, the enterprising business class, which would replace the *rentier* class. See also **rentier class**.

Split labor market A condition in which minority groups are hired for lower pay than the majority will accept. Also, a condition in which minority groups are the only ones that hold certain menial jobs.

Spurious relationship A relationship that appears to be real but is not.

Stages in dying According to Kübler-Ross, denial, anger, trying to bargain for more time, depression, resignation.

Standard Consolidated Statistical Areas (SCSAs) Clusters of cities; loosely equivalent to megalopolises. See also **megalopolis**.

Standard Metropolitan Statistical Areas (SMSAs) Central cities with a central population of 50,000 or more together with the surrounding area that is economically integrated with the city.

Status Position one holds in society. Also, esteem and recognition, which take different forms in different societies.

Status inconsistency Two or more forms of status that sometimes cause people to experience stress and desire change.

Stereotype A standardized and oversimplified description applied to groups of people.

Stigmatize To mark a person as deviant and set that person apart in the public mind as socially unacceptable.

Stratification The ranking of people in a society in layers of wealth and power.

Strip cities Cities that grow together in lines for many miles, often along rivers or seacoasts.

Structural conduciveness According to Smelser, a trait of a society whose structure includes many conflicting interest groups that make themselves heard, communicate with each other, and may clash.

Structural crystalization A definite, unchanging status or social-class position.

Structural functionalism A unitary model that analyzes society in terms of the structures and functions of its customs and institutions.

Structural strain The strain that occurs when parts of the social system do not—or do not seem to—work properly or mesh with other parts.

Subculture A group within a society which defines its norms somewhat differently. *Subculture* is also sometimes used to describe minor cultural variations.

Subordinate Of lower rank and with little or no power. See also **superordinate**.

Subterranean values Hidden values of middle-class society, shown in leisure activities.

Superego According to Freud, the aspect of the personality that has internalized the norms of society and will feel guilt if they are violated.

Superordinate Superior in rank and power. See also **subordinate**.

Swinging The process by which married couples switch mates for sexual encounters with the full knowledge of all partners.

Symbolic interactionism A model of society (following G. H. Mead) that stresses the importance of human interaction through symbols, mainly language. This model stresses the idea that the ability to interact in symbols leads to the development of human intellect and the growth and transmission of culture.

Syndicate As used with regard to deviant behavior, a general term for organized crime. Synonymous with *Cosa Nostra* and *Mafia*.

Synthesizing Bringing together many types of findings and fitting them into a coherent whole.

Theory A logically consistent and scientifically acceptable general principle that explains the known facts and the relationships between them.

Tightly structured society A society (1) in which most people agree on norms and values, (2) which has strong traditions, and (3) in which there is little conflict over laws and social institutions.

Time-consciousness The perceptions that make it possible to calculate and predict the pace of life in a manner adaptable to modern industrial society.

Total institutions Those institutions that totally control their inmates' lives, regulating all their activities without their consent or even their knowledge of what will happen to them from day to day.

Tracking The placing of public school students in different ability groups, or tracks.

U-curve A statistical pattern. As applied to prisons, the tendency of prisoners to believe in societal norms at the beginning and end of their sentences, but to hold to them far less strongly in the middle of their sentences.

Unconscious mind According to Freud, that part of the mind which contains all the the thoughts, memories, and emotions of which the individual is unaware.

Union shop A company in which workers are required to join the union only after being employed for a certain period of time and after a majority of the workers have called for a union.

Unitary (solidarity) model A model of society that stresses a common core of beliefs and traditions which hold society together. Without being unrealistic, it stresses the positive aspects of society. See also **conflict model**.

Universalistic norms Norms that apply to all situations, places, and people regardless of relationship, race, or religion. See also **particularistic norms**.

Unmeltable ethnics Ethnic groups that have not blended into the general American population as well as other ethnic groups.

Upper lower class In the community social system, just below the lower middle class. Consists of poorly paid semiskilled or unskilled workers who are employed most of the time and not on welfare.

Upper middle class In the community social system, just below the lower upper class. Consists largely of business, professional, and managerial persons.

Upper upper class The top level of the community social system, consisting of solid, reputable people who have been well-to-do for several generations.

Urban homesteading The effort to infuse new life into abandoned urban areas by having government agencies sell homes at low prices to people who agree to live in and improve them.

Urbanization A massive shift from rural to city life.

Urban renewal Attempts by the government to improve the appearance of cities, promote trade and commerce, provide better housing, and replace slums.

Urban sprawl An ugly, haphazard pattern of city growth.

Values Attitudes and standards of judgment about what things are important, desirable, and right.

Vision quests In American Indian cultures, lonely journeys made by the future leaders of tribes during their youth in search of spiritual guidance.

Voluntary association Any association in which membership is voluntary. Most commonly applied to an informal group that promotes friendly ties (a club, a lodge) or that pursues what the members consider good causes.

WASP White Angle-Saxon Protestant.

Welfare state A state in which the government regulates or provides for a variety of goods and services that were once the responsibility of private citizens.

White-collar crime According to Sutherland, the type of crime learned by respectable people as they work for organizations that routinely violate the law. Generally also considered to include embezzlement and similar crimes contrary to the interests of organizations.

Worker participation Giving workers a voice in policies and procedures on the job.

Working class People holding jobs that involve a few easily learned manual skills.

Working-class authoritarianism The theory that the working class may be especially likely to follow national leaders blindly, to be suspicious of foreigners and foreign governments, and to be unwilling to hear both sides of an argument.

Work-related leisure The influence of occupation on the choice of leisure activity, on the amount of money available for leisure activity, and on the friends available to participate.

Zero Population Growth (ZPG) A policy aimed at reproducing no more than the number of people needed to replace those who have died.

Zone in transition In the concentric-zone scheme, the first ring of housing close to the city center; a zone gradually changing to commercial and industrial use.

Bibliography

Adams, Robert Lynn, and Robert Jon Fox: "Mainlining Jesus: The New Trip," *Society*, **9**:50–56, Feb. 1972.

Adams, Samuel Hopkins: "The Juke Myth," *Saturday Review*, **38** (part 2): 13, 48, 49, Apr. 2, 1955.

Adorno, T. W., Elsie Frenkel-Brunswick, D. J. Levinson, and R. N. Sanford: *The Authoritarian Personality*, Harper, New York, 1950.

Allport, Gordon W.: *The Nature of Prejudice*, Addison-Wesley, Reading, Mass., 1954.

Alpern, David A.: "A Skyjacking for Croatia," *Newsweek*, Sept. 20, 1976, p. 25.

Alter, Robert: "A Fever of Ethnicity," *Commentary*, **53**:68–73, June 1972.

Anderson, Robert T.: "From the Mafia to Cosa Nostra," *American Journal of Sociology*, **71**:302–310, November 1965.

Anderson, William A., Russell Dynes, and Enrico Quarantelli: "Urban Counterrioters," *Society*, **11**:50–65, March-April 1974.

Apsler, Robert, and Henry Friedman: "Chance Outcomes and the Just World: A Comparison of Observers and Recipients," *Journal of Personality and Social Psychology*, **31**:887–894, 1975.

Asbel, Bernard: *The New, Improved American*, Dell, New York, 1965.

Asch, Solomon: "Opinion and Social Pressure," *Scientific American*, **193**(5):31–35, 1955.

Associated Press Dispatch: "Egypt's Matchmakers," *Los Angeles Times*, part 1, Apr. 4, 1972, p. 17.

———: "Wealth Education Survey Puts Jews, Catholics Ahead," *Los Angeles Times*, part 5, Oct. 19, 1975, p. 11.

———: "Young People Tending to Stay Single," *Los Angeles Times*, part 1, Jan. 7, 1975, p. 5.

———: "Pope's Birth Control Ban Blow to Church Growth," *Los Angeles Times*, part 1, Aug. 24, 1976, p. 1.

Atchley, Robert T.: "Retirement and Leisure Participation: Continuity or Crisis?" *The Gerontologist*, Spring 1971, pp. 13–17.

Azumi, Koya: "The Mysterious Drop in Japan's Birth Rate," *Trans-Action*, **5**:46–48, May 1968.

Bacci, Massimo Livi: "Italy," in Bernard Berelson (ed.), *Population Policy in Developed Countries*, McGraw-Hill, New York, 1974.

Baker, Paul T.: "Racial Differences in Heat Tolerance," *American Journal of Physical Anthropology*, **16**:283–306, September 1958.

Baker, Russell: "Richly Deserved," *The New York Times Magazine*, Sept. 7, 1975, p. 6.

Bakersfield Californian: "Son of Atheist Denied Eagle Rank," Nov. 14, 1970, p. 7.

Baltzell, E. Digby: "The American Metropolitan Upper Class," in E. Digby Baltzell (ed.), *Philadelphia Gentlemen*, Free Press, New York, 1951.

Bandura, Albert, and S. A. Ross: "Transmission of Aggression through Imitation of Aggressive Models," *Journal of Abnormal and Social Psychology*, **63**(3):575–582, 1961.

Banfield, Edward C.: "A Critical View of the Urban Crisis," *Annals of the American Academy of Political and Social Sciences*, **405**:7–14, January 1973.

———: *The Unheavenly City Revisited*, Little, Brown, Boston, 1974.

Barclay, Allan G., and D. R. Cusumano, "Testing Masculinity in Boys without Fathers," *Trans-Action*, **5**:33–35, December 1967.

Barnett, Richard J., and Ronald E. Muller: *Global Reach: The Power of the Multinational Corporations*, Simon and Schuster, New York, 1974.

Barnouw, Victor: *An Introduction to Anthropology*, vol. 2, *Ethnology*, Dorsey Press, Homewood, Ill., 1975.

Beals, Alan R.: *Gopalpur: A South India Village*, Holt, New York, 1962.

Beauvoir, Simone de, *The Coming of Age*, Putnam, New York, 1974.

Becker, Howard S.: "Whose Side Are We On?" *Journal of Social Problems*, **14**:239–247, Winter 1967.

Behrman, Dan: "Hong Kong: The Most Urban Place on Earth," *UNESCO Courier*, June 1976, p. 29.

Bekele, Maaza: "Population Growth or Economic Growth?" *UNESCO Courier*, May 7, 1974, pp. 42–43.

577

Belfrage, Cecil: *The American Inquisition, 1945-1960*, Bobbs-Merrill, New York, 1963.

Bell, Carolyn Shaw: "The Urban Poor," *Current History*, **64**:253–257, June 1973.

Bellamy, Edward: *Looking Backward*, Random House, New York, 1951.

Benet, Sula: "Why They Live to Be 100 or Even Older in Abkhasia," *The New York Times Magazine*, Dec. 28, 1971, p. 3.

Berelson, Bernard (ed.): *Population Policy in Developed Countries*, McGraw-Hill, New York, 1974.

Berg, Ivar: "Rich Man's Qualifications for Poor Man's Jobs," *Trans-Action*, **6**:45–50, March 1969.

———: *Education and Jobs: The Great Training Robbery*, Praeger, New York, 1970.

Berger, Bennet M.: "Almost Endless Adolescence," in Dennis H. Wrong and Harry L. Gracey (eds.), *Readings in Introductory Sociology*, Macmillan, New York, 1972.

Berger, Henry W.: "Organized Labor and Imperial Policy," *Society*, **10**:94–98, November-December 1972.

Berreman, Gerald B.: "Caste in India and the United States," *American Journal of Sociology*, **66**:120–127, July 1959.

Bettleheim, Bruno: *Children of the Dream*, Macmillan, New York, 1969.

Binzen, Peter: *Whitetown U.S.A.*, Random House, New York, 1970.

Bird, Caroline: *The Case Against College*, Bantam Books, New York, 1975.

Birmingham, Stephen: "The Clubs Griffin Bell Had to Quit," *The New York Times Magazine*, Feb. 6, 1977, pp. 20, 68–69.

Blake, Judith: "Population Policy for Americans: Is the Government Being Deceived?" *California Monthly*, **53**:20–28, October 1969.

———, and Kingsley Davis: "Norms, Values, and Sanctions," in Robert E. L. Faris (ed.), *Handbook of Modern Sociology*, Rand McNally, New York, 1964.

Blau, Peter, and Otis Dudley Duncan: *The American Occupational Structure*, Wiley, New York, 1967.

———, and Richard Scott: *Formal Organizations*, Chandler, San Francisco, 1962.

Blumer, Herbert: "Collective Behavior," in A. M. Lee (ed.), *New Outline of Principles of Sociology*, Barnes and Noble, New York, 1955.

———: "Sociology as Symbolic Interactionism," in Arnold Rose (ed.), *Human Behavior and Social Processes*, Houghton Mifflin, Boston, 1962.

Boesel, David, Richard Berk, W. Eugene Groves, Bettye Edison, and Peter H. Rossi: "White Institutions and Black Rage," *Trans-Action*, **6**:24–31, March 1969.

Bohannon, Laura: "Shakespeare in the Bush," *Natural History*, **75**:28–33, August-September 1966.

Bonacich, Edna: "A Theory of Ethnic Antagonism: The Split-Labor Market," *American Sociological Review*, **35**:547–559, October 1972.

———: "A Theory of Middleman Minorities," *American Sociological Review*, **38**:583–593, October 1973.

———: "Advanced Capitalism and Black/White Relations in the United States: A Split-Labor Market Interpretation," *American Sociological Review*, **41**:34–51, February 1976.

Bordes, François: "Mousterian Cultures in France," *Science*, **134**:803–810, Sept. 22, 1961.

Bose, Nirmal Kumar: "Calcutta: A Premature Metropolis," *Scientific American*, **213**:91–102, September 1965.

Bottomore, T. B.: *Elites and Society*, Penguin Books, Baltimore, 1966.

Bourgeois-Pichot, Jean: "France," in Bernard Berelson (ed.), *Population Policy in Developed Countries*, McGraw-Hill, New York, 1974.

Bowers, Faubion: "Homosex: Living the Life," *Saturday Review*, **55**:23–28, Feb. 12, 1972.

Bowles, Samuel: "Getting Nowhere: Programmed Class Stagnation," *Society*, **9**:42–49, June 1972.

Bowman, Charles T., and Terry H. Morlan: "Revised Projection of the U.S. Economy to 1980 and 1985," *Monthly Labor Review*, **99**:9–21, March 1976.

Brandes, Stanley H.: "Social Structure and Interpersonal Relations in Navánogal," *American Anthropologist*, **75**:750–765, June 1973.

Briggs, Jean L.: "Kabluna Daughter: Living with Eskimos," *Trans-Action*, **7**:12–24, June 1970.

Brinton, Crane: *The Anatomy of Revolution*, Norton, New York, 1938.

Bronfenbrenner, Martin: "The Japanese Howdunit," *Trans-Action*, **6**:32–36, January 1969.

Brown, Warren: "Why Hair Has Become a Four-Letter Word," *Avant-Garde*, May 1970.

Bruyn, Severyn: "The Methodology of Participant Observation," *Human Organization*, **22**:224–235, Fall 1963.

Buckingham, Walter: *Automation*, Mentor Books, New American Library, New York, 1963.

Burger, Robert: "Commercializing the Aged," *The Nation*, **210**:557–560, May 11, 1970.

Burger, Warren E. "No Man Is an Island," address to the American Bar Association, Feb. 21, 1970; reprinted as "A Typical American Prison" in Gary E. McCuen (ed.), *America's Prisons*, Greenhaven Press, Anoka, Minn., 1971.

Burnham, James F.: *The Managerial Revolution*, John Day, New York, 1941.

Campbell, Angus: *White Attitudes toward Black People*, Institute for Social Research, Ann Arbor, Mich., 1971.

Campbell, Anna Montgomery: *The Black Death and Men of Learning*, Columbia University Press, New York, 1931.

Caplan, Nathan: "Delinquency and Perceived Chances for Conventional Achievement," paper presented at the American Sociological Association Convention, Montreal, August 1974.

Caplovitz, David: *The Poor Pay More*, Free Press, New York, 1963.

Carden, Maren Lockwood: *The New Feminist Movement*, Russell Sage Foundation, New York, 1974.

Catton, William R., Jr.: "The Wildland Recreation Boom and Sociology," in Theodore B. Johannis, Jr., and C. Neil Bull (eds.), *The Sociology of Leisure*, Sage, Beverley Hills, Calif., 1971.

Chambliss, William J.: "The Saints and the Roughnecks," *Society*, **11**:24–31, November–December 1973.

Champion, Dean J.: *The Sociology of Organizations*, McGraw-Hill, New York, 1975.

Chang, Dae H., and Warren B. Armstrong: *The Prison: Voices from the Inside*, Schenkman, Cambridge, Mass., 1972.

Chase, Stuart: *The Most Probable World*, Penguin Books, Baltimore, 1969.

Chase-Dunn, Christopher: "The Effects of International Economic Dependence on Development and Inequality: A Cross-National Study," *American Sociological Review*, **40**:720–730, December 1975.

Chicago Sun-Times: "The Case of Kenneth Donaldson," Dec. 25, 1976.

Chomsky, Noam: "The Fallacy of Richard Herrnstein's IQ," *Social Policy*, **3**:19–25, May–June, 1973.

Clark, Dennis: "The Passion of Protracted Conflict," *Trans-Action*, **7**:15–21, March 1970.

Clark, Matt, Susan Agrest, Mariana Gosnell, Dan Shapiro, and Henry McGee: "A Right to Die?" *Newsweek*, Nov. 3, 1975, pp. 58–69.

Clinard, Marshall B.: *Sociology of Deviant Behavior*, Holt, New York, 1963.

Cloward, Richard A., and Lloyd E. Ohlin: *Delinquency and Opportunity*, Free Press, New York, 1961.

Cohen, Albert K.: *Delinquent Boys*, Free Press, Chicago, Ill., 1955.

———, and James F. Short: "Crime and Juvenile Delinquency," in Robert K. Merton and Robert Nisbet (eds.), *Contemporary Social Problems*, 3rd ed., Harcourt Brace Jovanovich, New York, 1971.

Cohen, David K.: "Public Schools: The Next Decade," *Dissent*, **18**:161–170, April 1971.

Cohen, Shelly: "Cultists Receive Help," *Bakersfield Californian*, July 31, 1976, p. 4.

Coleman, James S., et al.: *Equality of Educational Opportunity*, U.S. Department of Health, Education, and Welfare, Washington, D. C., 1966.

Coles, Robert, and Harry Huge: "Black Lung: Mining as a Way of Death," *New Republic*, **160**:17–22, Jan. 25, 1969.

Collins, Randall: "Functional and Conflict Theories of Educational Stratification," *American Sociological Review*, **36**:1002–1018, December 1971.

Commager, Henry Steele: "The School as Surrogate Conscience," *Saturday Review*, **2** (part 1):54–57, Jan. 11, 1975.

Commission on Population Growth and the American Future: *Population and the American Future*, Signet Books, New American Library, New York, 1972.

Conant, Ralph W.: "Rioting, Insurrection, and Civil Disobedience," *American Scholar*, **37**:420–433, Summer 1968.

Cook, Fred J.: *The Nightmare Decade*, Random House, New York, 1971.

Cooley, Charles Horton: *Social Organization: A Study of the Larger Mind*, Free Press, New York, 1956.

———: *Human Nature and the Social Order*, Schocken, New York, 1964.

Cooper, Richard T., and Paul E. Steiger: "Occupational Health Hazards—A National Crisis," *Los Angeles Times*, part 1, June 27, 1976, pp. 1, 22–23, 26.

Coser, Lewis: *The Functions of Social Conflict*, Free Press, New York, 1956.

———: "Social Conflict and the Theory of Social Change," *British Journal of Sociology*, **8**:198, September 1957.

Cosmopolitan: "Love, Marriage, and Independence" (a review of Dorothy T. Samuels' *Love, Liberation, and Marriage*, Funk and Wagnalls, 1976), February 1977, pp. 49, 179.

Coughlin, William J.: "India Tide Runs against Christianity," *Los Angeles Times*, section F, July 18, 1971, pp. 1–2.

———: "Jets Bringing More Pilgrims to Jam Mecca," *Los Angeles Times*, March 11, 1973, part 1, pp. 1–2.

Cousins, Norman: "Nagasaki's Magic Mountain," *Saturday Review*, **37**:22–24, Jan. 9, 1954.

Cowley, Susan Cheever: "Moon Rising," *Newsweek*, May 26, 1975, p. 63.

Cressey, Donald: *Theft of the Nation*, Harper and Row, New York, 1969.

Cressey, Paul Frederick: "Chinese Traits in European Civilization: A Study of Diffusion," *American Sociological Review*, **10**:595–604, October 1945.

Critchfield, Richard: "Population Growth Darkens World Outlook," *Los Angeles Times*, part 7, Feb. 1, 1976, pp. 1, 4.

Cummings, Elaine, and William Henry: *Growing Old*, Basic Books, New York, 1961.

Davidson, Sara: "The Rush for Instant Salvation, *Harper's*, **243**:40–43, July 1971.

Davies, James C.: "Toward a Theory of Revolution," *American Sociological Review*, **27**:5–19, February 1962.

Davis, Alan J.: "Sexual Assaults in the Philadelphia Prison System and Sheriff's Vans," *Trans-Action*, **6**:8–16, December 1968.

Davis, Kingsley: "Adolescence and the Social Structure," *Annals of the Academy of Political and Social Sciences*, **236**:8–16, 1944.

———: *Human Society*, Macmillan, New York, 1949.

———: "The Urbanization of the Human Population," *Scientific American*, **213**:40–53, September 1965.

———: cited in "Rural Earth," *Scientific American*, **227**:47, October 1972.

———: "Zero Population Growth: The Goals and Means," *Daedalus*, **102**:15–19, Fall 1973.

———: "The Migration of Human Populations," *Scientific American*, **231**:93–105, September 1974.

———, and Wilbur E. Moore: "Some Principles of Stratification," *American Sociological Review*, **10**:242–249, February 1945.

Deegan, Mary Jo: "Reversing Roles in the 'Meat Market,'" *Society*, **11**:11, November–December 1973.

Deloria, Vine: *God is Red*, Grosset and Dunlap, New York, 1974.

Dennis, Jack: "Who Supports the Presidency," *Society*, **13**:48–53, July–August 1976.

Denzin, Norman K.: "The Self-Fulfilling Prophecy and Patient-Therapist Interaction," in Stephen P. Spitzer and Norman K. Denzin (eds.), *The Mental Patient: Studies in the Sociology of Deviance*, McGraw-Hill, New York, 1968.

———: "Children and Their Caretakers," *Trans-Action*, **8**:62–71, July–August 1971.

DeVise, Pierre: "The Wasting of Chicago," in Grant S. McClellan (ed.), *Crisis in Urban Housing*, Wilson, New York, 1974.

Dibble, Vernon K.: "The Garrison Society," *New University Thought*, **5**:106–115, Special Issue 1966/67.

Dillman, Don A., et al.: "Increasing Mail Questionnaire Response," *American Sociological Review*, **39**:744–756, October 1974.

Distefano, M. K., Jr.: "Changes in Work-Related Attitudes with Age," *Journal of Genetic Psychology*, **114**:127–134, 1969.

Dore, Ronald P.: "The Future of Formal Education in Developing Countries," *International Development Review*, **17**(2):7–11, Summer 1975.

Douglas, Mary: *Purity and Danger*, Praeger, New York, 1966.

Drabek, Thomas E., and Enrico L. Quarantelli: "Scapegoats, Villains, and Disasters," *Trans-Action*, **4**:12–17, March 1967.

Duberman, M.: "The Case of the Gay Sergeant," *The New York Times Magazine*, Nov. 9, 1975, pp. 16, 17ff.

Dubin, Robert: "Industrial Workers' World: A Study of the Central Life Interests of Industrial Workers," in Ervin O. Smigel (ed.), *Work and Leisure*, College and University Press, New Haven, Conn., 1963.

Du Bois, Cora: "The Basic Value Profile of American Culture," *American Anthropologist*, **57**:1232–1239, December 1955.

Duhl, Leonard J. (ed.): *The Urban Condition*, Simon and Schuster, New York, 1969.

Dumont, René: "A World Gone Mad," *UNESCO Courier,* January 1974, pp. 13–15.

Dundes, Alan: "The Number Three in American Culture," in Alan Dundes (ed.), *Every Man His Way: Readings in Cultural Anthropology*, Prentice-Hall, Englewood Cliffs, N.J., 1966.

Durkheim, Émile: *The Rules of the Sociological Method*, George E. G. Catlin (ed.), Macmillan, New York, 1938.

————: *The Division of Labor in Society*, Free Press, New York, 1947.

————: *The Elementary Forms of the Religious Life*, Free Press, New York, 1965.

————: *Suicide*, John Spaulding and George Simpson (trans.), Free Press, New York, 1966.

Dye, Thomas R.: *Power and Society*, Duxbury, North Scituate, Mass., 1975.

Dynes, Russell, and Enrico L. Quarantelli: "What Looting in Civil Disturbances Really Means," *Trans-Action*, **5**:9–14, May 1968.

Eckhardt, Kenneth: "Divorce, Visibility, and Legal Action: The Duty to Support," *Social Problems*, **15**:470–474, Spring 1968.

Ehrlich, Paul R.: "World Population: A Battle Lost?" *Stanford Today*, series 1, January 1968, pp. 6–7.

————: "Population Control," *Saturday Evening Post*, **244**:8–12, Fall 1972.

————, and Anne H. Ehrlich: *Population, Resources, Environment*, Freeman, San Francisco, 1970.

Encyclopedia of Sociology, Dushkin, Guilford, Conn., 1974. (With a preface by Gayle Johnson, pub.)

Erikson, Erik H.: "Identity and the Life Cycle," *Psychological Issues*, **1**:(1):18–164, Spring 1959.

Erikson, Kai T.: "A Comment on Disguised Observation in Sociology," *Social Problems*, **14**:366–370, Spring 1967.

Esposito, John C.: *Vanishing Air*, Grossman, New York, 1970.

Fairlie, Henry: "In Defense of Big Government," *New Republic*, **174**:24–27, Mar. 13, 1976.

Fallers, Lloyd A.: "Role Conflict of an African Chief," *American Anthropologist*, **57**:290, 1955.

Fannin, Leon, and Marshall Clinard: "Differences in the Conception of Self as a Male among Lower- and Middle-Class Delinquents," *Social Problems*, **13**:205–214, Fall 1965.

Faris, Robert: "Reflections on the Ability Dimension in Human Societies," *American Sociological Review*, **26**:835–843, December 1961.

Fendrich, James, and Michael Pearson: "Black Veterans Return," *Trans-Action*, **7**:32–36, March 1970.

Ferree, Myra Marx: "The Confused American Housewife," *Psychology Today*, **10**:76–78, 80, September 1976.

Festinger, Leon: "Cognitive Dissonance," *Scientific American*, **207**(4):93–98, October 1962.

————, Henry W. Riecken, and Stanley Schacter: *When Prophecy Fails*, University of Minnesota Press, Minneapolis, 1956.

Firestone, Harold: "Cats, Kicks, and Color," in Howard S. Becker (ed.), *The Other Side*, Free Press, New York, 1964.

Fischer, Claude S.: "On Urban Alienation and

Anomie," *American Sociological Review*, **38**:311–326, June 1973.

Fong, Stanley F. M.: "The Assimilation of Chinese in America," *American Journal of Sociology*, **71**:265–273, November 1965.

Form, William H.: "The Internal Stratification of the Working Class: System Involvements of Auto Workers in Four Countries," *American Sociological Review*, **38**:697–711, December 1973.

———, and Joan Rytina: "Ideological Beliefs in the Distribution of Power in the United States," *American Sociological Review*, **34**:19–30, February 1968.

Fortune, magazine: "The Case of the G. E. Babies," January 1954, p. 95.

Frazier, E. Franklin: *Black Bourgeoisie*, Free Press, New York, 1957.

Free, Lloyd A., and Hadley Cantril: *The Political Beliefs of Americans*, Rutgers University Press, New Brunswick, N.J., 1967.

Freeman, Jo: "Growing Up Girlish," *Trans-Action*, **8**:36–43, November–December 1970.

Freeman, Ronald, and Bernard Berelson: "The Human Population," *Scientific American*, **231**:36, September 1974.

Freud, Sigmund: *Civilization and Its Discontents*, Hogarth, London, 1949.

Friedan, Betty: *The Feminine Mystique*, Norton, New York, 1963.

Friedlander, Dov: "Israel," in Bernard Berelson (ed.), *Population Policy in Developed Countries*, McGraw-Hill, New York, 1974.

Fromm, Eric: *Escape from Freedom*, Holt, New York, 1941.

Fuchs, Victor R.: "Differences in Hourly Earnings between Men and Women," *Monthly Labor Review*, **94**:9–15, May 1971.

Fuerst, J. S.: "Class, Family, and Housing," *Society*, **12**:48–53, November–December 1974.

Fullan, Michael: "Industrial Technology and Worker Integration in the Organization," *American Sociological Review*, **35**:1028–1039, December 1970.

Galliher, John F.: "The Protection of Human Subjects," *American Sociologist*, **8**:92–99, August 1973.

Gallup Opinion Index, Report No. 104, Princeton, N.J., February 1974; Report No. 105, March 1974.

Gans, Herbert J.: *The Urban Villagers*, Free Press, New York, 1962.

———: "The Uses of Poverty: The Poor Pay All," *Social Policy*, **2**:20–31, July–August 1971.

Garbarino, Merwyn S.: "Seminole Girl," *Trans-Action*, **7**:40–46, February 1970.

Gaylin, Jody: "Don't Blame the Divorce Rate on Working Wives," *Psychology Today*, **10**:17, July 1976a.

———: "Jobs Cool Student Protest," *Psychology Today*, **10**:30, July 1976b.

Geertz, Clifford: "Ethos, World View, and the Analysis of Sacred Symbols," *Antioch Review*, **17**(4):421–437, Winter 1957.

Gerrard, Nathan L.: "The Serpent-Handling Religions of West Virginia," *Trans-Action*, **5**:22–28, May 1968.

Gingold, Judith: "Battered Wives," *Ms.*, August 1976, pp. 51–54.

Glaberman, Martin: "Unions versus Workers in the Seventies," *Society*, **10**:85–89, November–December 1972.

Glaser, Daniel, and John R. Stratton: "Measuring Inmate Change in Prison," in Donald R. Cressey (ed.), *The Prison*, Holt, New York, 1961.

Glasgow, Robert W., and Herbert J. Gans: "The Ayn Rand Syndrome: A Conversation," *Psychology Today*, **3**:58–62, 80–82, March 1970.

Glazer, Nathan: "The Renewal of Cities," *Scientific American*, **213**:194–204, September 1965.

———, and Daniel P. Moynihan: "Why Ethnicity," *Commentary*, **58**:33–39, October 1974.

Gleason, Ralph J.: "Like a Rolling Stone," *American Scholar*, **36**:555–563, Autumn 1967.

Glick, Paul C., and Arthur J. Norton: "Frequency, Duration, and Probability of Marriage and Divorce," *Journal of Marriage and the Family*, **30**:307–317, May 1971.

Gmelch, George J.: "Baseball Magic," *Trans-Action*, **8**:39–41, June 1971.

Goffman, Erving: *The Presentation of Self in Everyday Life*, Anchor Books, Doubleday, Garden City, N.Y., 1959, pp. 18–19.

———: *Asylums: Essays on the Situation of Mental Patients and Other Inmates*, Anchor Books, Doubleday, Garden City, N.Y. 1961a.

———: *Encounters*, Bobbs-Merrill, Indianapolis, 1961b.

———: "The Inmate World," in Donald R. Cressey (ed.), *The Prison*, Holt, New York, 1961c.

Goldberg, Philip: "Are Women Prejudiced Against Women?" *Trans-Action*, **5**:28–30, April 1968.

Goldfarb, Ronald: *Jails: The Ultimate Ghetto of the Criminal Justice System*, Anchor Books, Doubleday, Garden City, N.Y., 1975.

Goldman, Ralph M.: "Life-Span Educational Insurance: A Proposal," *Educational Record*, **51**:60–65, Winter 1970.

Goleman, David: "We Are Breaking the Silence About Death," *Psychology Today*, **10**:44–47, September 1976.

Goode, Erich: "Social Class and Church Participation," *American Sociological Review*, **31**:102–111, February 1966.

———: "On Behalf of Labeling Theory," *Social Problems,* **22**:570–583, June 1975.

Goode, William J.: "Marital Satisfactions and Instability: A Cross-Cultural Analysis of Divorce Rates," *International Social Science Journal*, **14**:507–526, June 1962.

———: "Family Patterns and Human Rights," *International Social Science Journal*, **18**:41–56, Spring 1966.

Goodman, Ellen: "Police Use of Sexual Decoys: Equal 'Justice' in Hot Pants," *Los Angeles Times*, part 2, July 30, 1976, p. 4.

Goodman, Paul: *Growing Up Absurd*, Random House, New York, 1960.

Gouch, E. Kathleen: "The Nayars and the Definition of Marriage," *Journal of the Royal Anthropological Institute of Great Britain and Ireland*, no. 89, pp. 23–34, 1959.

Gouldner, Alvin: *Pattern of Industrial Bureaucracy*, Free Press, New York, 1954.

Gray, Betty MacMorran: "Economics of Sex Bias," *The Nation*, **212**:742–744, June 1971.

Gregg, Gary: "Private Research and Public Policy: An Uncertain Marriage," *Psychology Today*, **10**:13–14, August 1976.

Griffin, John H.: *Black Like Me*, Houghton-Mifflin, Boston, 1961.

Gusfield, Joseph R.: "Social Structure and Moral Reform: A Study of the Women's Christian Temperance Union," *American Journal of Sociology*, **61**:221–232, November 1955.

Haak, Ronald A.: "Co-opting the Oppressors: The Case of the Japanese-Americans," *Trans-Action*, **7**:23–31, October 1970.

Haley, Alex: *Roots*, Doubleday, Garden City, N.Y., 1976.

Hall, Edward T.: *The Silent Language*, Premier Books, Doubleday, Garden City, N.Y., 1959.

———, and William F. White, "Intercultural Communication," *Human Organization*, **19**(1):5–12, Spring 1960.

———, and Elizabeth Hall, "How Cultures Collide," *Psychology Today*, **10**:66, 68, 74, 97, July 1976.

Han, Suyin: "The Chinese Experiment," *UNESCO Courier*, July–August 1974, pp. 52–55.

Harper, Dean, and Frederick Emmert: "Work Behavior in a Service Industry," *Social Forces*, **42**:216–225, 1963.

Harris, Anthony R.: "Imprisonment and the Expected Value of Criminal Choice," *American Sociological Review*, **40**:71–87, February 1975.

Hartman, Chester: "The Politics of Housing: Displaced Persons," *Society*, **9**:53–56, July–August 1972.

Hauser, Philip M.: "The Census of 1970," *Scientific American*, **225**:17–25, July 1971.

———: "The Chaotic Society," *American Sociological Review*, **34**:1–19, February 1969.

Haythorn, William H., And Irwin Altman, "Together in Isolation," *Trans-Action*, **4**:18–22, January–February 1967.

Heilbroner, Robert: "The Future of Capitalism," *Commentary*, April 1966, pp. 23–35.

———: *Between Capitalism and Socialism*, Random House, New York, 1970.

———: *An Inquiry into the Human Prospect*, Norton, New York, 1974.

Heller, Celia S.: "Chicano is Beautiful: The New Militancy and Mexican-American Identity," *Commonweal*, Jan. 23, 1970, pp. 454–458.

Hendin, David: *Death as a Fact of Life*, Norton, New York, 1973.

Herberg, Will: *Protestant-Catholic-Jew*, Doubleday, Garden City, N.Y., 1955.

Herchoff, Alan C., and Kurt W. Back: *The June Bug*, Appleton, New York, 1968.

Herman, Arthur S.: "Manpower Implications of Computer Control," *Monthly Labor Review*, **93**:3–8, October 1970.

Herrnstein, Richard J.: *I.Q. in the Meritocracy*, Little, Brown, Boston, 1973.

Herskovitz, Melville J.: *Cultural Dynamics*, Knopf, New York, 1964.

Herzberg, Frederick: *Work and the Nature of Man*, Mentor Books, New American Library, New York, 1973.

Heussenstamm, F. K.: "Bumper Stickers and the Cops," *Trans-Action*, **8**:32–33, February 1971.

Hill, Herbert: "Anti-Oriental Agitation and the Rise of Working-Class Racism," *Society*, **10**:43–54, January–February 1973.

Hills, Stuart: *Crime, Power, and Morality*, Chandler, Scranton, Pa., 1971.

Hjelle, Larry A., and Daniel Ziegler: *Personality: Theories, Research, and Applications*, McGraw-Hill, New York, 1976.

Hobart, Charles W.: "Commitment, Value Conflict, and the Future of the American Family," *Journal of Marriage and Family*, **25**:405–412, December 1963.

Hochschild, Arlie Russell: "Disengagement Theory: A Critique and a Proposal," *American Sociological Review*, **40**:553–569, October 1975.

Hodge, Robert W., Paul M. Siegel, and Peter H. Rossi: "Occupational Prestige in the United States, 1925–1963," *American Journal of Sociology*, **70**:286–302, November 1964.

———, and Donald G. Treiman: "Class Identification in the United States," *American Journal of Sociology*, **73**:535–547, March 1968.

Hodgson, Godfrey: "Do Schools Make a Difference?" *Atlantic Monthly*, March 1973, **231**:37–46.

Hoebel, E. Adamson: *The Cheyennes: Indians of the Great Plains*, Holt, New York, 1960.

Hollings, Ernest F.: "The Rural Poor," *Current History*, **64**:258–260, June 1973.

Hollingshead, August B., and Frederick C. Redlich: "Social Stratification and Psychiatric Disorders," *American Sociological Review*, **18**:163–168, February 1953.

Hollister, Rob: "The Politics of Housing: Squatters," *Society*, **9**:49–52, July–August 1972.

Holmes, Lowell D.: *Anthropology*, Ronald Press, New York, 1965.

Hoover, Eleanor: "Unemployment Rated Major Mental Problem," *Los Angeles Times*, part 1, Sept. 4, 1975, pp. 1, 220.

Horn, John L.: "Intelligence—Why It Grows, Why It Declines," *Trans-Action*, **5**:23–31, November 1967.

Horowitz, Irving L.: "Capitalism, Communism, and Multinationalism," *Society*, **11**:32–43, January–February 1974.

Horton, John: "Order and Conflict Theories of Social Problems," *American Journal of Sociology*, **71**:701–713, May 1966.

House, James S.: "Political Alienation in America," *American Sociological Review*, **40**:123–147, April 1975.

Houseman, John: "The Men from Mars," *Harper's*, **197**:74–82, December 1948.

"How the West Is Being Won," *Society*, **10**:16, January–February 1973; review of a study by Larry R. Stucki.

Howard, John: "The Making of a Black Muslim," *Trans-Action*, **4**:15–21, December 1966.

Howells, William: *The Heathens: Primitive Man and His Religions*, Doubleday, Garden City, N.Y., 1962.

Hsu, Francis L. K.: "American Core Value and National Character," in Francis L. K. Hsu (ed.), *Psychological Anthropology*, General Learning Press, Morristown, N.J., 1972, pp. 241–262.

———: *The Ancestors' Shadow: Family and Religion in China*, Natural History Press, Garden City, N.Y., 1967.

Huff, Darrell: *How to Lie with Statistics*, Norton, New York, 1954.

Huizinga, Johann: *Homo Ludens: A Study of the Play Element in Culture*, Beacon Press, Boston, 1955.

Hunt, Morton: "The Future of Marriage," in Harold M. Hodges, Jr. (ed.), *Conflict and Consensus*, Harper and Row, New York, 1973, pp. 264–274.

Huntington, Ellsworth: *The Mainsprings of Civilization*, New American Library, New York, 1959.

Hutchins, Robert M.: *The Learning Society*, Praeger, New York, 1968.

Hyatt, James C.: "Productivity Push: Firms Seek to Upgrade White Collar Output, but Task Is Difficult," *Wall Street Journal*, April 25, 1972.

Illich, Ivan: *Deschooling Society*, Harrow Books, Harper and Row, New York, 1971.

Inkeles, Alex: *What Is Sociology?*, Prentice-Hall, Englewood Cliffs, N.J., 1964.

———: "Making Man Modern: On the Causes and Consequences of Individual Change in Six Countries," *American Journal of Sociology*, **75**:208–225, September 1969.

International Labor Office: *Labour and Automation*, Bulletin No. 5, "Automation and Nonmanual Workers," Geneva, 1967.

Jackson, Donald: "Justice for None," *New Times*, Jan. 11, 1974.

Jencks, Christopher, et. al.: *Inequality: A Reassessment of the Effects of Family and Schooling in America*, Basic Books, New York, 1972.

Jensen, Arthur B.: *Educability and Group Differences*, Harper and Row, New York, 1973.

Johannis, Theodore B., Jr., and C. Neil Bull: *Sociology of Leisure*, Sage Publications, Beverly Hills, Calif., 1971.

Johnson, Benton: "Do Holiness Sects Socialize in Dominant Values?" *Social Forces*, **30**:309–316, May 1961.

Jones, Robert A.: "Changing Food Chain Forges Nation to Nation," *Los Angeles Times*, part 1, April 17, 1974, pp. 1, 22.

———: "Short-Handle Hoe: A History of Agony for Dubious Advantages," *Los Angeles Times*, part 2, April 14, 1975, pp. 1–2.

Kadushin, Alfred: "Is the Child Really Father of the Man?" *Trans-Action*, **5**:6, June 1968; review of a study by Alfred Kadushin.

Kagan, Jerome: "What Is Intelligence?" *Social Policy*, **4**:88–94, July–August 1973.

Kamerman, Sheila B.: "Needy American Women, Waiting for Equity," *The New York Times*, Feb. 19, 1977, p. 23.

Kanter, Rosabeth M.: "Communes," *Psychology Today*, **4**:55–58, July 1970.

———: *Commitment and Community: Communes and Utopias in Sociological Perspective*, Harvard University Press, Cambridge, Mass., 1972.

Karnow, Stanley: "Anti-Semitism on the Rise?" *New Republic*, **171**:12–14, Dec. 14, 1974.

Kasarda, John D., and Morris Janowitz: "Community Attachment in Mass Society," *American Sociological Review*, **39**:328–339, June 1974.

Kautsky, John H.: "Communism and the Comparative Study of Development," *Slavic Review*, **26**:13–17, March 1967.

Kellogg, Mary Alice: "Counter-Culture Kids," *Newsweek*, Mar. 29, 1976, p. 59.

Kelly, J. R.: "Everyman as Sociologist: Comments on Scribner's Publication of Selected Writings of the Founders of Sociology," *America*, **132**:441–442, June 7, 1975.

Kenyatta, Jomo: *Facing Mount Kenya*, Vintage Books, Random House, New York, n. d. (orig. pub. 1938).

Kerchoff, Alan C., Kurt W. Back, and Norman Miller: "Sociometric Patterns in Hysterical Contagion," *Sociometry*, **28**:2–15, March 1968.

Kinsey, Alfred, et al.: *Sexual Behavior in the Human Male*, Saunders, Philadelphia, 1948.

Kissler, Charles A.: "Conformity and Commitment," *Trans-Action*, **4**:32–35, June 1967.

Knoke, David, and Michael Hout: "Social and Demographic Factors in American Political Party Affiliations, 1952–1972," *American Sociological Review*, **39**:700–713, October 1974.

Kochman, Thomas: " 'Rapping' in the Black Ghetto," *Trans-Action*, **6**:26–34, February 1969.

Kohn, Melvin L.: "Social Class and Parent-Child Relationships," *American Journal of Sociology*, **68**:471–480, June 1964.

———: "Bureaucratic Man: A Profile Portrait and an Interpretation," *American Sociological Review*, **36**:461–476, June 1971.

———, and Carmi Schooler: "Occupational Experience and Psychological Functioning," *American Sociological Review*, **38**:97–118, February 1973.

Komarovsky, Mirra: *Blue-Collar Marriage*, Random House, New York, 1962.

———: "Presidential Address: Some Problems in Role Analysis," *American Sociological Review*, **38**:649–662, December 1973.

Kübler-Ross, Elizabeth: *On Death and Dying*, Macmillan, New York, 1969.

Kutscher, Ronald E.: "Revised B.L.S. Projections to 1980 and 1985: An Overview," *Monthly Labor Review*, **99**:5, March 1976.

LaBarre, Weston: "Professor Widjojo Goes to a Koktel Parti," *The New York Times Magazine*, Dec. 9, 1959, pp. 17, 42, 44, 47.

LaBelle, Thomas J., and Robert E. Verhine: "Nonformal Education and Occupational Stratification: Implications for Latin America," *Harvard Educational Review*, Vol. 45, May 1975, pp. 161–183.

Lamb, David: "Zaire's Leader Presides as a God-

Chieftain," *Los Angeles Times*, part 1, April 1, 1977, pp. 1, 24.

Langer, William L.: "The Black Death," *Scientific American*, **210**:113–118, February 1964.

———: "Checks on Population Growth: 1750-1850," *Scientific American*, **226**:93–99, February 1972.

Langone, John: *Vital Signs*, Little, Brown, Boston, 1974.

Lapham, Lewis H.: "Belonging: The Officer Corps," *Harper's*, **243**:73–76, July 1971.

Laslett, Peter: "The World We Have Lost," in Eric and Mary Josephson (eds.), *Man Alone*, Dell, New York, 1962.

Lasswell, Harold D., Daniel Lerner, and C. Easton Rothwell: *The Comparative Study of Elites*, Hoover Institute Studies, Series B, No. 1, Stanford, Calif., 1952.

Lee, Richard Borshay: "Eating Christmas in the Kalihari," *Natural History*, **78**:14ff, December 1968.

Lenski, Gerhard: *Power and Privilege: A Theory of Social Stratification*, McGraw-Hill, New York, 1961a.

———: *The Religious Factor*, Doubleday, Garden City, N.Y., 1961b.

———: "Some Correlates of Religious Interest," *American Sociological Review*, **72**:533–544, 1953.

Leo, John: "Northern Ireland: A Land of Warring Christians," *Time*, Dec. 30, 1974, p. 30.

Leonard, George: "Language and Reality," *Harper's*, **249**:46–48, November 1974.

Lévi-Strauss, Claude: "The Family," in Harry L. Shapiro (ed.), *Man, Culture, and Society*, Oxford University Press, New York, 1971.

Levinger, George, "Sources of Marital Dissatisfaction among Applicants for Divorce," *American Journal of Orthopsychiatry*, **36**:803–807, October 1966.

Levinson, Andrew: "The Rebellion of Blue-Collar Youth," *The Progressive*, **36**:38–42, October 1972.

Levitan, Sar A.: "The Poor: Dimensions and Strategies," *Current History*, **64**:241–246, June 1973.

Lewis, Lionel S., and Dennis Brissett: "Sex as Work: A Study of Avocational Counseling," *Social Problems*, Summer 1967, pp. 8–18.

Lewis, Oscar: *The Children of Sanchez*, Random House, New York, 1961, introduction.

———: "The Culture of Poverty," *Scientific American*, **219**:19–25; October 1966.

Liebow, Eliot: *Tally's Corner: A Study of Negro Streetcorner Men*, Little, Brown, Boston, 1967.

Lifton, Robert J.: *Thought Reform and the Psychology of Totalism*, Norton, New York, 1961.

———: *History and Human Survival*, Random House, New York, 1970.

Lincoln, C. Eric: *The Black Muslim in America*, Beacon, Boston, 1961.

Linton, Ralph: *The Study of Man*, Appleton, New York, 1936.

Lipset, Seymour Martin: *Political Man*, Anchor Books, Doubleday, Garden City, N.Y., 1963.

———: "Education and Equality: Israel and the United States Compared," *Society*, **11**:57–66, March–April 1974.

———, and Reinhard Bendix: *Social Mobility in Industrial Societies*, University of California Press, Berkeley, 1960.

———, and Earl Raab: "An Appointment with Watergate," *Commentary*, **56**:35–43, September 1973.

Lofland, John A., and Rodney Stark: "Becoming a World Saver: A Theory of Conversion to a Deviant Perspective," *American Sociological Review*, **30**:862–875, December 1965.

Look magazine: "The American Family" (complete issue), Jan. 26, 1971.

Los Angeles Times: "Atheist Couple Vow Battle to Keep Child," part 1, Nov. 10, 1970, p. 15.

———: "Egypt's Matchmakers," part 1, Apr. 4, 1972, p. 17.

———: "Pope's Birth Control Ban a Blow to Church Growth," part 1, Aug. 24, 1976a, p. 1.

———: "South Africa Eases Sports Segregation at All Levels," part 1, Sept. 24, 1976b, p. 1.

———: "Wealth, Education Survey Puts Jews and Catholics Ahead," part 5, Oct. 19, 1976c, p. 11.

Lowinger, Paul: "The Detroit Case of Psychosurgery," *New Republic*, Apr. 13, 1974, pp. 17–19.

Lundberg, Ferdinand: *The Rich and the Super-Rich*, Lyle Stuart, New York, 1968.

Lundberg, George: *Can Science Save Us?* Longmans, Green, New York, 1961.

McCormack, Patricia: "Professor Calls Inflation of Grades a Problem," *Bakersfield Californian*, Jan. 16, 1977, p. 46.

McPhail, Clark, and David Miller: "The Assembling Process: A Theoretical and Empirical Explanation," *American Sociological Review*, **38**:721–735, December 1973.

McQueen, Stuart: *The Family in Various Cultures*, Lippincott, Chicago, 1952.

Mace, David, and Vera Mace: *Marriage East and West*, Dolphin Books, Doubleday, Garden City, N.Y., 1960.

Macklin, Eleanor: "Going Very Steady," *Psychology Today*, **8**:53–59, November 1974.

MacMahon, Brian, and Jacob J. Feldman: *Infant Mortality Rates: Economic Factors*, National Center for Health Statistics, Washington, D. C., 1972.

Macoby, Eleanor F.: "Moral Values and Behavior in Children," in John A. Clausen (ed.), *Socialization and Society*, Little, Brown, Boston, 1968.

Maguire, Mary: "Nearly Extinct Species Dwell in Dwindling Mansions of the Very Rich," *Los Angeles Times*, part 1, Jan. 11, 1977, p. 5.

Malenbaum, Wilfred: "World Resources for the Year 2000," *Annals of the American Academy of Political and Social Sciences*, **408**:30–45, July 1973.

Mamdani, Mahmood: *The Myth of Population Control: Family, Caste, and Class in an Indian Village*, Monthly Review Press, New York, 1973.

Mangin, William: "Squatter Settlements," *Scientific American*, **217**:21–29, October 1967.

Mankoff, Milton: "Power in Advanced Capitalist Society: A Review Essay on Recent Elitist and Marxist Criticism of Pluralist Theory," *Social Problems*, **17**:418–430, Winter 1970.

Mann, Michael: "The Social Cohesion of Liberal Democracy," *American Sociological Review*, **35**:423–439, June 1970.

Mark, Vernon H.: "Brain Surgery in Aggressive Epileptics," *Hastings Center Report,* **3**:1–5, February 1973.

Martinez, Al: "The American Dream—Has It Survived?" *Los Angeles Times*, July 2, 1976, pp. 1, 3, 24–25.

Martinez, Thomas M.: "Advertising and Racism: The Case of the Mexican-American," in Edward Simmon (ed.), *Pain and Promise: The Chicano Today*, Mentor Books, New York, 1972.

Martinson, Robert: "The Paradox of Prison Reform," *New Republic*, April 1, 8, 15, and 29, 1972 (a series of four articles).

Martz, Larry, Rick Thomas, and Bernard Krisher: "The Embattled Businessman," *Newsweek*, Feb. 16, 1976, pp. 36–39.

———, ———, and Henry McGee: "Payoffs: The Growing Scandal," *Newsweek*, Feb. 23, 1976, pp. 26–33.

Marwell, Gerald: "Why Ascription: Parts of a More-or-Less Formal Theory of the Functions and Dysfunctions of Sex Roles," *American Sociological Review*, **40**:445–455, August 1975.

Marx, Karl: *Capital*, Ernest Untermann (ed.), Modern Library, New York, 1906.

———, and Friedrich Engels: *The Communist Manifesto*, Samuel H. Beer (ed.), Appleton, New York, 1955.

Marx, Leonard H.: "Politics of World Information," *Society,* **12**:26–29, September–October 1975.

Matza, David, and Gresham Sykes: "Juvenile Delinquency and Subterranean Values," *American Sociological Review*, **26**:712–719, October 1961.

Mayer, Allan J.: "The Computer Bandits," *Newsweek*, Aug. 9, 1976, pp. 60–61.

Mead, George Herbert: *Mind, Self, and Society*, University of Chicago Press, Chicago, 1934.

Mead, Margaret: *Cultural Patterns and Technical Change*, New American Library, New York, 1955.

———: "Future Family," *Trans-Action*, **8**:50–53, September 1971.

Meisler, Stanley: "Folk Singers a Thorn in Spain's Side," *Los Angeles Times*, part 1, Sept. 25, 1976, p. 10.

Merriam, Eve: "A Wasp Hymn," *New Republic*, **161**:24, July 12, 1969.

Merton, Robert K.: *Social Theory and Social Structure*, Free Press, New York, 1949.

Michels, Robert: *First Lectures on Political Sociology*, Alfred de Gracia (trans.), University of Minnesota Press, Minneapolis, 1949.

Michener, James A.: *Hawaii*, Bantam, New York, 1961 (orig. Random House, New York, 1959).

Milgram, Stanley: "The Experience of Living in Cities," *Science*, **167**:1461–1468, March 1970.

———: *Obedience to Authority*, Harper and Row, New York, 1974.

Miller, Stuart C.: "Our Mylai of 1900," *Trans-Action*, **7**:19–28, September 1970.

Miller, S. M.: "The Credential Society," *Trans-Action*, **5**:2, December 1967.

Miller, Walter B.: "White Gangs," *Trans-Action*, **6**:11–26, September 1969.

Mills, C. Wright: *The Power Elite*, Oxford University Press, New York, 1958.

Miner, Horace: "Body Ritual among the Nacirema," *American Anthropologist*, **58**(3):503–507, June 1956.

Mintz, Morton, and Jerry S. Cohen: *America Incorporated*, Dial, New York, 1971.

Mitford, Jessica: "Kind and Usual Punishment in California," *Atlantic*, **227**:45–52, March 1971.

Mock, Carol: "Sharp Rise Found in Female Family Heads," *Los Angeles Times*, part 1, Aug. 8, 1974, p. 24.

Moore, Wilbert, and David Feldman: *Labor Commitment and Social Change in Developing Areas*, Social Science Research Council, New York, 1960.

Moran, Robert D.: "Reducing Discrimination: Role of the Equal Pay Act," *Monthly Labor Review*, **93**:30–34, June 1970.

Morris, Marian Gennaria: "Psychological Miscarriage," *Trans-Action*, **3**:8–13, January–February 1966.

Mueller, Charles W., and Weldon T. Johnson: "Socioeconomic Status and Religious Participation," *American Sociological Review*, **40**:785–800, December 1975.

Murdock, George P.: *Social Structure*, Macmillan, New York, 1947.

———: "How Culture Changes," in Harry Shapiro (ed.), *Man, Culture, and Society*, Oxford University Press, New York, 1971.

Murton, Tom: "Too Good for Arkansas: One Year of Prison Reform," *The Nation*, **210**:12–17, Jan. 12, 1970.

Myrdal, Gunnar: *Objectivity in Social Research*, Pantheon Books, Random House, New York, 1969.

———: *The Challenge of World Poverty*, Pantheon Books, Random House, New York, 1974.

———: "The Transfer of Technology to Underdeveloped Countries," *Scientific American*, **231**:173–182, September 1974.

Nader, Ralph, and Mark Green: *Corporate Power in America*, Grossman, New York, 1973.

Nagel, Stuart S.: "The Tipped Scales of American Justice," *Trans-Action*, **3**:3–9, May–June 1966.

———, and Lenore J. Weitzman: "The Double Standard of American Justice," *Society*, **9**:18–25, March 1972.

Nagel, William G.: *The New Red Barn: A Critical Look at American Prisons*, Walker, New York, 1973.

Nakamura, Hajime: *Ways of Thinking of Eastern Peoples: India, China, Tibet, Japan*, Philip P. Wiener (trans. and ed.), East-West Center Press, Honolulu, 1968.

National Advisory Commission on Civil Disorders, *Report*, Bantam Books, New York, 1968.

Nelkin, Dorothy: "Invisible Migrant Workers," *Society*, **9**:36–41, April 1972.

———: "The Science Textbook Controversies," *Scientific American*, **234**:33–39, April 1976.

Nelson, Bryce: "Citizens Protest Paperwork Avalanche," *Los Angeles Times*, part 1A, Feb. 25, 1976, pp. 1–2.

Nelson, Harry: "Psychosurgery Raises Ethical, Moral Issues," *Los Angeles Times*, part 6, Apr. 14, 1974, p. 5.

Newsweek: "The Case of Harry X," July 27, 1970a, p. 48.

———: "A Matter of Life and Death," Aug. 17, 1970b, pp. 64–66.

———: "What It's Like on the Auto Assembly Line," Sept. 14, 1970c, p. 81.

———: "Civil Rats," Sept. 21, 1970d, p. 90.

———: "The Youthful Suicides," Feb. 15, 1971a, pp. 70–71.

———: "Where the Blacks Are," Feb. 22, 1971b, p. 53.

———: "The American Jew Today," March 1, 1971c, pp. 56–58, 62–64.

———: "Living with Crime U. S. A.," Dec. 18, 1972, pp. 31–34.

———: "The Untouchables," Apr. 2, 1973, p. 88.

———: "The Ex-Con's Unhappy Lot," Feb. 24, 1974, pp. 84–85.

———: "The Embattled Businessman," Feb. 16, 1975a, pp. 56–60.

———: "How's Your Sex Life?" Sept. 1, 1975b, p. 57.

———: "Big Government," Dec. 15, 1975c, pp. 34–46.

———: "The Gospel behind Bars," Mar. 29, 1976a, pp. 48–49.

———: "Who Needs College?" Apr. 26, 1976b, pp. 60–64.

———: "Washing Dollars," June 28, 1976c, p. 54.

———: "The Hunger Lawyers," Aug. 2, 1976d, p. 41.

———: "The Exorcists," Aug. 23, 1976e, p. 57.

———: "Getting Your Head Together," Sept. 6, 1976f, pp. 56–62.

Nieburg, H. I.: "Crime Prevention by Urban Design," *Society*, **12**:41–48, November–December 1974.

Novak, Michael: "White Ethnics," *Harper's*, **243**:17–27, September 1971.

———: *The Rise of the Unmeltable Ethnics*, Macmillan, New York, 1972.

———: "Millions Settle for 'Downward Mobility,'" *Los Angeles Times*, part 9, August 14, 1975, p. 5.

———: "The Family Out of Favor," *Harper's*, **252**:37–44, April 1976.

O'Connor, Connie: *The Leisure Wasters*, Barnes, New York, 1966.

Offir, Carole Wade: "Field Report on Mental Patients," *Psychology Today*, **8**:61–72, October 1974.

Oran, Daniel: "Judges and Psychiatrists Lock Up Too Many People," *Psychology Today*, **7**:20–22, 27–28, August 1973.

Paddock, Richard C.: "U.S. Drug Firms' Kill and Injure Many in Latin America, Scientist Charges," *Los Angeles Times*, May 27, 1976, p. 5.

Paige, Jeffery M.: "Political Orientation and Riot Participation," *American Sociological Review*, **36**:810–820, October 1971.

Palson, Charles, and Rebecca Palson: "Swinging in Wedlock," *Society*, **9**:28–38, February 1972.

Pareto, Vilfredo: *The Mind and Society*, vols. 1 and 2, Harcourt Brace Jovanovich, New York, 1935.

Parker, Tony, and Robert Allerton, *Courage of His Convictions*, Hutchinson, London, 1962.

Parkinson, C. Northcote: *Parkinson's Law and Other Studies in Administration*, Houghton-Mifflin, Boston, 1957.

Peñalosa, Fernando: "Recent Changes Among the Chicanos," in Edward Simmon (ed.), *Pain and Promise: The Chicano Today*, Mentor Books, New York, 1972, pp. 72–78.

Perry, Wingfield: "The Night of Ageism," *Mental Health*, **58**:13–20, Summer 1974.

Pettigrew, Thomas F.: "Not Exactly Black or White," *Society*, **10**:12, March 1972.

———: "Busing Is Made Scapegoat," *Los Angeles Times*, part 7, Sept. 21, 1975, pp. 3–4.

Petroni, Frank A.: "Teenage Interracial Dating," *Trans-Action*, **8**:54–59, September 1971.

Pfeiffer, Eric, and Glenn C. Davis: "The Use of Leisure Time in Middle Life," *Industrial Gerontology*, **9**:37–39, Spring 1971.

Piaget, Jean: *Judgment and Reasoning in the Child*, Harcourt Brace Jovanovich, New York, 1938.

———: *The Moral Judgment of the Child*, Free Press, New York, 1948.

Pitt-Rivers, Julian: "Race, Color and Class in Central America and the Andes," *Daedalus*, **96**:642–659, Spring 1967.

Playboy: "What's Really Happening on Campus," **23**:28–30ff, October 1976.

Pogrund, Benjamin: "South African Abyss," *New Republic*, **175**:11–15, Sept. 25, 1976.

Pohlman, Edward, and Daniel Callahan: "Food Incentives for Sterilization: Can They Be Just?" *Hastings Center Report*, **3**:10–12, February 1974.

Pope, Liston: *Millhands and Preachers*, Yale University Press, New Haven, Conn., 1942.

———: "Religion and the Class Structure," *Annals of the American Academy of Political and Social Sciences*, **56**:84–91, March 1948.

Porter, John: "The Future of Upward Mobility," *American Sociological Review*, **33**:5–19, February 1968.

Post, Dudley: "Requiem for Model Cities," *New Republic*, **168**:13–15, Apr. 14, 1973.

President's Commission on Income Maintenance: *Poverty amid Plenty*, U.S. Government Printing Office, Washington, D. C., 1969.

Preston, Samuel H.: "Differential Fertility and Racial Trends in Occupational Achievement," *American Sociological Review*, **39**:492–506, August 1974.

Psychology Today: "Stress and Longevity: The Thriving Top Executives," August 1974, p. 30–31.

Reckless, Walter C., and Simon Dinitz: "Self-Concept as an Insulator against Delinquency," *American Sociological Review*, **21**:744–747, December 1956.

Report of the Commission on Obscenity and Pornography, Bantam Books, New York, 1970.

Report of the National Advisory Commission on Civil Disorders, Bantam Books, New York, 1968.

Report to the Federal Trade Commission: "The Split-Labor Market on the Navajo Reservation," *The Trading Post System on the Navajo Reservation*, Los Angeles Regional Office, June 1973, pp. 47, 52, 54.

Reuters dispatch: "Fiji Contract Talks: Miners Ask 30-Minute Sex Break After Lunch," *Los Angeles Times*, Jan. 25, 1975, part 1, p. 13.

———: "Majority of Whites Would Ease South Africa Racial Laws," *Los Angeles Times*, Nov. 2, 1976, part 1, p. 2.

Rhodes, A. Lewis, and Charles B. Nam: "The Religious Context of Educational Expectations," *American Sociological Review*, **35**:253–267, April 1970.

Rice, Berkeley: "Messiah from Korea: Honor Thy Father Moon," *Psychology Today*, **9**:36–47, January 1976.

Ridgeway, James: "The Cops and the Kids," *New Republic*, **159**:11–14, Sept. 7, 1968.

Rieslow, Harry W.: "Social Experimentation," *Society*, **12**:34–41, July–August 1975.

Riesman, David: *The Lonely Crowd*, Doubleday, Garden City, N.Y., 1953.

Ritzer, George: *Social Relations: Dynamic Perspectives*, Allyn & Bacon, Boston, 1974; "A Case Study in Deprivation," quoted from Files of the Office of Economic Opportunity, pp. 339–342.

Rivlin, A. M.: "Social Experiments: Their Uses and Limitations," *Monthly Labor Review*, **197**:28–35, June 1973.

Robinson, Donald W.: "An Interview with Christopher Jencks," *Phi Delta Kappan*, **54**:255–257, December 1972.

Roethlisberger, F. L., and W. J. Dickson: *Management and the Worker*, Harvard University Press, Cambridge, Mass., 1939.

Rollins, Boyd C., and Kenneth L. Cannon, "Marital Satisfaction over the Life Cycle," *Journal of Marriage and the Family*, **36**:271–282, May 1974.

Roof, Wade Clark: "Traditional Religion in Contemporary Society," *American Sociological Review*, **41**:195–208, April 1976.

Rosen, Steven J., "Rightist Regimes and American Interest," *Society*, **11**:50–61, September–October 1974.

Rosenhan, David L.: "On Being Sane in Insane Places," *Science*, **179**:250–258, Jan. 19, 1973; and **180**:385–389, Apr. 27, 1973.

Rosenhause, Sharon, "India Taking Drastic Birth Control Step," *Los Angeles Times*, part 1, Sept. 20, 1976, pp. 1, 10–11.

Rosenstone, Robert A.: "The Times They Are A-Changin'," *Annals of the American Academy of Political and Social Sciences*, **382**:123–144, March 1969.

Rosenthal, Jack: "Housing Study—High Rise, High Crime," *The New York Times*, Oct. 26, 1972, p. 41.

———: "Each Change Has Vast Impact," *The New York Times*, part E, May 7, 1973, p. 9.

Rosenthal, Marilyn: "Where Rumor Raged," *Trans-Action*, **8**:34–43, February 1971.

Rosenthal, Neal H.: "The United States Economy in 1985: Projected Changes in Occupations," *Monthly Labor Review*, **96**:24–26, December 1973.

Rosenthal, Robert, and Lenore F. Jacobson: *Pygmalion in the Classroom*, Holt, New York, 1968.

———, and ———: "Teacher Expectations for the Disadvantaged," *Scientific American*, **218**:19–23, April 1968.

Rossi, Peter H., E. Waite, C. E. Bose, and R. E. Burk: "The Seriousness of Crime: Normative Structure and Individual Differences," *American Sociological Review*, **39**:224–237, April 1974.

Ruby, Michael, et al.: "I Say to Them, Go to Hell," *Newsweek*, June 28, 1976, p. 49.

Rudé, George: *Paris and London in the Eighteenth Century: Studies in Popular Protest*, Viking, New York, 1971.

Russell, Candayce Smith: "Transition to Parenthood," *Journal of Marriage and Family*, **36**:294–301, May 1974.

Rytina, Joan Huber, William H. Form, and John Pease: "Income and Stratification Ideology: Beliefs about the American Opportunity Structure," *American Journal of Sociology*, **35**:703–716, April 1970.

Sage, Wayne: "Crime and the Clockwork Lemon," *Human Behavior*, September 1974.

Salt Lake Tribune: "Gallup Poll: Few Favor Large Families," Feb. 5, 1973.

San Francisco Chronicle: "The Laws Cops Rarely Enforce," Aug. 20, 1976.

Santorelli, Leonard: "Babies of Third World Switched to Bottles," *Los Angeles Times*, Nov. 4, 1976, part 1A, p. 6.

Saylin, Mary: "ACLU Seeks to End Victimization of Rape Victim during Rape Trial," *ACLU Open Forum*, June 1974, pp. 2, 5.

Schafer, Walter E., Carol Olexa, and Kenneth Polk: "Programmed for Social Class: Tracking in High School," *Trans-Action*, **7**:39–46, October 1970.

Schneier, Edward V.: "White-Collar Violence and Anti-Communism," *Society*, **13**:33–37, March–April 1976.

Schrag, Peter: "The Forgotten Americans," *Harper's*, **239**:17–24, August 1969.

———: "America Needs an Establishment," *Harper's*, **251**:51–54, December 1975.

Schudson, Michael: "Family Stages," *New Republic*, **170**:27–28, Feb. 16, 1974.

Schuman, Howard: "Sociological Racism," *Trans-Action*, **7**:44–48, December 1969.

Scientific American: "Epidemic Hysteria," **216**:58, February 1967.

———: "Underdevelopment in the U.S.," **227**:45, August 1972.

———: "The Sane and the Insane," **228**:46, 48, March 1973.

Sciolino, Elaine: "Tilling the Soul," *Newsweek*, June 23, 1975, pp. 61, 63.

Sefa-Boakye, Kofi: "Why the Pill Won't Work in the Third World," *Los Angeles Times*, section G, Jan. 7, 1973, p. 1.

Seidenbaum, Art: "Dream House Becoming a Nightmare?" *Los Angeles Times*, part 6, Feb. 6, 1976, p. 1.

Sewell, William H.: "Equality of Opportunity for Higher Education," *American Sociological Review*, **36**:793–809, October 1971.

Senters, Jo M.: "A Function of Uncertainty and Stakes in Recreation," in Theodore B. Bohannis, Jr., and C. Neil Bull (eds.), *Sociology of Leisure*, Sage, Beverly Hills, Calif., 1971.

Shapiro, Harvey D.: "Do Not Go Gently . . . ," *The New York Times Magazine*, Feb. 6, 1977, pp. 36–41.

Shaw, Clifford, and Henry D. McKay: *Juvenile Delinquency and Urban Areas*, University of Chicago Press, Chicago, 1942.

Sheppard, Harold L., and Michael Philibert: "Employment and Retirement: "Roles and Activities," *The Gerontologist*, **12**(part 2):29–35, Summer 1972.

Shills, Edward A., and Morris Janowitz, "Cohesion and Disintegration in the *Wehrmacht* in World War II," *Public Opinion Quarterly*, **12**:280–294, 1948.

Shiloh, Ailon: "Sanctuary or Prison: Responses to Life in a Mental Hospital," *Trans-Action*, **6**:28–35, December 1968.

Simmel, Georg: "The Metropolis and Mental Life," in Eric and Mary Josephson (eds.), *Man Alone*, Dell, New York, 1962.

Simmons, J. L.: "Public Stereotyping of Deviance," *Social Problems*, **13**:223–232, Fall 1965.

Simmons, Roberta, et al.: "Disturbance in the Self-Image at Adolescence," *American Sociological Review*, **38**:553–568, October 1973.

Simmons, William L.: *Eyes of the Night: Witchcraft among the Sengalese People*, Little, Brown, Boston, 1971.

Simon, William, and John Gagnon: "Psychosexual Development," *Trans-Action*, **6**:9–17, March 1969.

Simoons, Frederick J.: *Eat Not This Flesh: Food Avoidances in the Old World*, University of Wisconsin Press, Madison, 1961.

Simpson, Ida Harper: "Patterns of Socialization into Professions: The Case of Student Nurses," *Sociological Inquiry*, **37**:47–54, Winter 1967.

Simross, Lynn: "Invitation to an Unearthly Kingdom," *Los Angeles Times*, part 4, Oct. 31, 1975, p. 1.

Sinclair, Upton: *The Jungle*, Viking, New York, 1965 (orig. pub. 1906).

Sinha, Surajit: "Religion in an Affluent Society," *Current Anthropology*, **7**:1–5, April 1966.

Skinner, B. F.: *Beyond Freedom and Dignity*, Bantam Books, New York, 1972.

Sklar, June, and Beth Berkov: "American Birthrate: Evidence of a Coming Rise," *Science*, **189**:693–700, August 1975.

Smelser, Neil J.: *Theory of Collective Behavior*, Free Press, New York, 1962.

Smith, Alexander B., and Harriet Pollack: "Crimes without Victims," *Saturday Review*, **54**:27–29, Dec. 4, 1971.

Smith, M. Brewster: "The Revolution in Mental Health Care—A Bold New Approach," *Trans-Action*, **5**:19–23, April 1968.

Smith, Thomas S.: "Structural Crystallization, Status Inconsistency, and Political Partisanship," *American Sociological Review*, **34**:907–921, December 1969.

Society: "Not Exactly Black or White," **9**:10, 12, March 1972; summary of research by Angus Campbell.

———: "Reversing Roles in the 'Meat Market,' " **11**:11, November–December 1973.

———: "Marriage and Family," **11**:7, March–April 1974; review of a study by William Ronco.

———: "Working Women," **11**:6, March–April 1974.

———: "The Hidden Proletariat," **12**:12–14, May–June 1975; editorial.

———: "Women in Science," **13**:9, September–October 1976; review of a study by Ruth Hubbard.

Speich, Don: "Growing Grade Inflation in High Schools Reported," *Los Angeles Times*, part 2, Jan. 16, 1977, p. 1.

Spilerman, Seymour: "The Causes of Racial Disturbances: Tests of an Explanation," *American Sociological Review*, **36**:427–443, June 1971.

Srole, Leo, et al.: *Mental Health and the Metropolis: The Midtown Manhattan Study*, McGraw-Hill, New York, 1962.

Steadman, Henry, and Joseph Cocozza: "We Can't Predict Who Is Dangerous," *Psychology Today*, **8**:32–35, January 1975.

Steffens, Lincoln: *The Autobiography of Lincoln Steffens*, Harcourt Brace Jovanovich, New York, 1931.

Steinbeck, John: *The Grapes of Wrath*, Viking, New York, 1939.

Stern, Philip M.: *The Rape of the Taxpayer*, Vintage Books, Random House, New York, 1974.

Sternlied, George, and James W. Hughes: "New York: Future without a Future?" *Society*, **13**:18–23, May–June 1976.

Strauss, Anselm: "Chronic Illness," *Society*, **10**:37–40, September–October 1973.

Strauss, Murray A.: "Leveling, Civility, and Violence in the Family," *Journal of Marriage and the Family*, **36**:13–29, February 1974.

Stuckey, William: "Navajo Medicine Men," *Science Digest*, September 1975, pp. 35–37.

Stycos, J. Mayone: "Latin American Overpopulation Shoves Thousands to Margin of Life," *Smithsonian*, April 1974, p. 79.

Sumner, William Graham: *Folkways*, New American Library, Mentor Books, New York, 1960.

Sutherland, Anne: "Gypsies: The Hidden Americans," *Society*, **12**:27–33, January–February 1975.

Sutherland, Edwin H., and Donald Cressey: *Principles of Criminology*, 6th ed., Lippincott, Chicago, 1960.

Sykes, Gresham: *Crime and Society*, Random House, New York, 1967.

———: "New Crimes for Old," *American Scholar*, **40**:592–598, Autumn 1971.

Symmachus, Quintus Aurelius: quoted in Hendrik Willem van Loon, *Tolerance*, Garden City Publishing Company, Garden City, N. Y., 1927, p. ii.

Szasz, Thomas S.: "The Ethics of Addiction," *Harper's*, **244**:74–79, April 1972.

Tawney, R. H.: *Religion and the Rise of Capitalism*, Harcourt Brace Jovanovich, New York, 1928.

Taylor, Edwin F.: "The Looking-Glass World of Testing," *Today's Education*, **66**:39–44, March–April 1977.

Teevan, James V., Jr.: "Reference Groups and Premarital Sexual Behavior," *Journal of Marriage and the Family*, **34**:283–291, May 1972.

Terkel, Studs: *Working*, Avon, New York, 1974.

Thomason, Dan: "Medicaid Abuse Is about as Old as the Program," *The New York Times*, Sept. 5, 1976.

Thomasson, Richard F.: "Religion Is Irrelevant in Sweden," *Trans-Action*, **5**:22–28, May 1968.

Thompson, Warren S.: *Population and Progress in the Far East*, University of Chicago Press, Chicago, Ill., 1959.

Time: "The Berrigan Brothers: They Rob Draft Boards," June 7, 1968, p. 62.

———: "The New Sociology," Jan. 5, 1970a, pp. 38–39.

———: "The Blue-Collar Worker's Lowdown Blues," Nov. 9, 1970b, pp. 68–70.

———: "The Shame of the Prisons," Jan. 18, 1971, pp. 46–55.

———: "Crime in America," June 30, 1975, pp. 10–24.

———: "The Soweto Uprising: A Soul Cry of Rape," June 28, 1976, pp. 29–30, 33, 34.

Times Wire Services: "Rich-Poor Gap Dominates World Poll," *Los Angeles Times*, Sept. 21, 1976, p. 4.

Toffler, Alvin: *Future Shock*: Bantam, New York, 1970.

Tönnies, Ferdinand: *Community and Society*, Michigan State University Press, East Lansing, 1957.

Tocqueville, Alexis de: quoted in Richard P. Taub and Doris I. Taub: *American Society in Tocqueville's Time and Today*, Rand McNally, Chicago, 1974, p. 479.

Torgerson, Dial: "Parental Pressures Differ Around the World," *Los Angeles Times*, part 1, Jan. 4, 1973a, pp. 1, 18, 19.

———: "Urban Wastelands: Isles of Hopelessness," *Los Angeles Times*, part 1, July 15, 1973b, pp. 1, 16–17.

———: "Middle Class Returning to Inner Cities," *Los Angeles Times*, part 1, July 16, 1973c, pp. 1, 18, 19.

———: "Firing Squad Ends Issue of Women's Lib," *Los Angeles Times*, Mar. 29, 1975, pp. 1, 5.

———: "Plan for Equality for Wives Sets Off Uproar in Kenya," *Los Angeles Times*, part 1A, Sept. 26, 1976, p. 1.

Trans-Action: Roundup of Current Research, "Some People's Children," **4**:3–4, January–Feburary 1967a.

———: "Christian, Love Thy Neighbor," **4**(9):10, September 1967b, synopsis of a study by Gordon W. Allport and J. Michael Ross.

———: Roundup of Current Research, "The Religious Delinquents," **5**:6, December 1967c.

———: "New Determinants of Political Affiliation," **5**:5–6, January–February 1968; synopsis of a study by Morris Janowitz and David Segal.

———: Roundup of Current Research, "Little People of America," **6**:6–7, March 1969; a review of a study by Martin S. Weinberg.

———: Roundup of Current Research, "When Factories Shut Down," **8**:14, January 1971a.

———: "Does Staying in School Up Earning Power?" **8**:6, February 1971b; synopsis of a study by W. Lee Hansen, Burton A. Weisbrod, and William S. Scanlon.

Treiman, Donald J., and Kermitt Terrell: "Sex and the Process of Status Attainment: A Comparison of Working Women and Men," *American Sociological Review*, **40**:174–200, April 1975.

Troeltsch, Ernst: *The Social Teaching of the Christian Churches*, Oliver Wyon (trans.), Macmillan, New York, 1931.

Trombley, William: "S. F. Minority Pupils Killed with Kindness, Study Says," *Los Angeles Times*, part 1, Oct. 5, 1975, p. 3.

Tumin, Melvin: "Some Principles of Stratification: A Critical Analysis," *American Sociological Review,*" **18**:387–393, August 1953.

Turbo, Richard: *An Act of Mercy: Euthanasia Today*, Nash, Los Angeles, 1973.

Turner, James S.: *The Chemical Feast*, Grossman, New York, 1970.

Turner, John F. C.: "A New Universe of Squatter-Builders," *UNESCO Courier*, June 1976, pp. 12–14.

Turner, Ralph U., and Lewis M. Killian, *Collective Behavior*, Prentice-Hall, Englewood Cliffs, N. J., 1972.

UNESCO Courier: "And Tomorrow How Many?" May 1970, entire issue.

———: "Population Growth or Economic Growth?" May 1974a, pp. 7–8.

———: "Shocking Picture a Century from Today," May 1974a, pp. 15–19.

———: "Time Clocks of Doubling Populations," May 1974a, p. 8.

———: "World Population Year," July–August 1974b, entire issue.

United Press International Dispatch: "Syphilis Study

of 600 Blacks Called Racist," *Los Angeles Times*, part 1A, May 13, 1973, p. 6.

———: "Urban Stress Good for Us, Expert Says," *Los Angeles Times*, part 1, Oct. 24, 1974, p. 32.

———: "Florida Leads in Urban Growth," *Bakersfield Californian*, Feb. 8, 1976, p. 3.

———: "Elderly Who Are Hard to Relocate," *San Francisco Chronicle*, July 5, 1976.

———: "Medical Students Poorly Educated on Aging," *Bakersfield Californian*, Sept. 18, 1976, p. 6.

United States Budget in Brief, Fiscal Year 1976, U. S. Government Printing Office, Washington, D. C., 1976.

United States Commission on Population and the American Future: *Population and the American Future*, U. S. Government Printing Office, Washington, D. C., 1972.

U'Ren, Richard C.: "West Point Cadets, Codes, and Careers," *Society*, **12**:21–29, May–June, 1975.

Urlanis, Boris: "The Hour of Decision," *UNESCO Courier*, July–August 1974, pp. 26–27.

U. S. News and World Report: "Population Slowdown: What It Means to U. S.," Dec. 25, 1972, pp. 59–62.

———: "America's Jails: How Bad Are They? What's Being Done?" June 23, 1975, p. 56.

Vener, Arthur M., and Cyrus S. Stewart: "Adolescent Sexual Behavior in Middle America Revisited," *Journal of Marriage and Family*, **36**:728–735, November 1974.

Verlarde, Albert J., and Mark Warlick: "Massage Parlor," *Society*, **11**:63–74, November–December 1973.

Walker Commission Report: *Rights in Conflict*, New American Library, New York, 1968, p. 231. (Report of Daniel Walker and the Chicago Study Team to the National Commission on the Causes and Prevention of Violence.)

Wallich, Franklin: *The American Worker: An Endangered Species*, Ballantine, New York, 1972.

Wall Street Journal: "The Economy Doesn't Need More People," Apr. 22, 1970.

Walster, Elaine: "Importance of Physical Attractiveness in Dating Behavior," *Journal of Personality and Social Psychology*, **4**:508–510, 1966.

Warner, W. Lloyd, Marchia Meeker, and Kenneth Eells, *Social Class in America*, Harper and Row, New York, 1960.

———, and Leo Srole: *The Social Systems of American Ethnic Groups*, Yale University Press, New Haven, Conn., 1945.

Waters, Harry F.: "What TV Does to Kids," *Newsweek*, Feb. 21, 1977, pp. 62–70.

Watts, William, and Lloyd A. Free (eds.): *State of the Nation*, Universe, New York, 1973.

Weber, Max: *The Protestant Ethic and the Spirit of Capitalism*, Allen and Unwin, London, 1930.

———: *The Theory of Social and Economic Organization*, Free Press, New York, 1947.

———: *Essays in Sociology*, H. H. Gerth and C. Wright Mills (eds. and trans.), Oxford University Press, New York, 1958.

Weiss, Robert S.: "The Fund of Sociability," *Trans-Action*, **6**:36–43, July–August 1969.

Wellford, Charles: "Labeling Theory and Criminology: An Assessment," *Social Problems*, **22**:332–345, February 1975.

Westoff, Charles: "The United States," in Bernard Berelson (ed.), *Population Policy in Developed Countries*, McGraw-Hill, New York, 1974, pp. 731–759.

White, Morton, and Lucia White: *The Intellectual versus the City*, Mentor Books, New American Library, New York, 1964.

Whorf, Benjamin Lee: *Language, Thought, and Reality*, Wiley, New York, 1956.

Whyte, William H., Jr.: *The Organization Man*, Simon and Schuster, New York, 1956.

———: *The Last Landscape*, Doubleday, Garden City, N. Y., 1968.

Wilensky, Harold L.: "Women's Work," *Industrial Relations*, **7**:235–248, May 1968.

Williams, Walter, and John W. Evans: "The Political Evaluation: The Case of Head Start," *Annals of the American Academy of Political and Social Sciences*, **38**:118–132, September 1969.

Wilson, James: "The Bureaucracy Problem," *The Public Interest*, (6):3–9, Winter 1967.

Winter, J. Alan, Jerome Rabone, and Marc Chesler: *Vital Problems for American Society*, Random House, New York, 1968.

Wirth, Louis: "Urbanism as a Way of Life," *American Journal of Sociology*, **44**:3–24, July 1938.

Wiseberg, Laurie S.: "The Statistics Jungle: Measuring War, Plague, Fire and Famine," *Society*, **12**:53–60, July–August 1975.

Wolfenstein, Martha: "The Emergence of the Fun Morality," *Journal of Social Issues*, **7**(4):10–15, Winter 1951.

Wood, Harold: "Future Labor Supply for Lower-Level Occupations," *Monthly Labor Review*, **99**:22–31, March 1976.

Woodward, Kenneth, and Phyllis Malamud: "The Parent Gap," *Newsweek*, Sept. 22, 1975, p. 54.

———, and Laurie Lisle: "Divorced Catholics," *Newsweek*, Aug. 16, 1976, p. 72.

Wray, Joe D.: "Population Pressure on Families: Family Size and Child Spacing," in *Rapid Population Growth*, National Academy of Sciences, Johns Hopkins University Press, Baltimore, Md., 1971.

Wright, Richard: "The Ethics of Living Jim Crow," in *Uncle Tom's Children*, Harper and Row, New York, 1937.

Wrigley, Robert L., Jr.: "Small Cities Can Help Vitalize Rural Areas," *Annals of the American Academy of Political and Social Sciences*, **405**:55–59, January 1973.

Yablonsky, Lewis: "The Anticriminal Society: Synanon," *Federal Probation*, **26**:50–57, September, 1962.

Yankelovich, Daniel: *The New Morality: A Profile of American Youth in the '70s*, McGraw-Hill, New York, 1974.

———: "What the Voters Want," *New Republic*, Oct. 23, 1976, pp. 16–19.

Yee, Albert H.: "My Teacher Doesn't Like Me," *Trans-Action*, **7**:10, 12, July–August 1970.

Yinger, Milton: *Society Looks at Religion*, Macmillan, New York, 1973.

Yorburg, Betty: *The Changing Family*, Columbia University Press, New York, 1973.

Young, Pauline V.: *The Pilgrims of Russian-Town*, University of Chicago Press, Chicago, Ill. 1932.

Zimbardo, Philip G.: "Pathology of Imprisonment," *Society*, **9**:4–8, April 1972.

Zurcher, Louis A., Jr.: "The Friendly Poker Game: A Study of an Ephemeral Role," *Social Forces*, **49**:173–186, December 1970.

Name index

Name index

Subject index

Subject index

Palestine Liberation Organization, 252, 551
Parenthood and social class, 337
　(See also Family; One-parent families)
Participant-observer studies, 40—41
Particularistic norms, 540
Party in Max Weber's analysis, 150
Patriarchal family, defined, 328
Patrilineal, defined, 328
Patrilocal family, defined, 325
Patriot, 15
Patterned behavior:
　defined, 6
　in education, 7
　in fighting insurgents, 13
　in institutions, 7
Patterned social relationships, 12
Peer group:
　defined, 98
　in socialization, 98, 102—103
Peninsulares, 158
Personality, 124
Perspectives, sociological, 12—20
Peru, 538
Philadelphia, old upper class, 154—155
Political affiliation:
　new determinants of, 417
　variables in, 414—415
Political boss, latent functions of, 22—23, 26
Political city, defined, 512
Political machine, latent functions of, 22—23, 26
Political mood of American public, 435—437
Political power, 413—443
　associations and, 425—426
　corporate, 418—421
　countervailing, 423, 425—427
　distribution of, 411
　division of, 413
　labor unions and, 421—425
　movements and, 426—427
　sources of, 418—427
Political science, 12
Political socialization, 413—417
　defined, 413
　in later life, 414—417
　in school, 414
　social class differences, 414
　in U.S. and England, 414
Polyandry:
　defined, 330, 334
　Tibetan, 330
　Toda, 330
Polygamy (see Polygyny)
Polygyny, 330—331, 334
　Arabic, 330
　Kenya example, 331
　Koranic rules regarding, 330
Population, 474—505
　conflicting views regarding, 481—487
　controls: in Europe, 1750—1850, 476
　　Malthusian, 475
　densities compared, 475
　growth rate table, 489
　growth rates as crisis, 481—483
　historical increases in, 475
　and international ethics, 483
　and malnutrition, 483
　and military power, 478
　and national development, 479—480

Population:
　and national interest, 485—486
　and political power, 485
　pyramids, 494—495
　and resources, 481
　U.S., 492—499
　　age and sex composition, 494
　　differential birthrates, 495—497
　　policy regarding, 500
　　projections, 492
　world, projections to 2000, 481
　　(See also individual countries)
"Positive controls" on population, 476
Positive reinforcement, 274, 282, 284
　defined, 274
Postindustrial age, 168
Power:
　abuse of, 243
　　(See also Political power)
　defined, 150, 418
Power elite, 171
Poverty:
　and race:
　　percent in poverty, by race, 201
　　Spanish surnamed, 201
　rural, 170—171
Precipitating incidents in collective behavior, 307
Prejudice, 180—191
　authoritarian personality and, 185
　defined, 180
　and discrimination, 180—182
　economic and political explanations, 185—191
　frustration and, 185
　and interaction, 183—184
　rationalization of, 182
　sterotypes and, 182—183
Prejudiced personalities, 185
President's Commission on Income Maintenance, 227
Prestige, 151
Primary groups, 130—136
　defined, 130
　functions of, 130—131
　moral neutrality of, 131
　　Mafia, example of, 133
　　Synanon, example of, 132
　secondary settings of, 135—136
Prison, simulated experimentally, 275—278
Prisoners as guards, 277
Prisons, 270—295
　behavior modification attempts, 282—284
　brutalizing effect, 276—277
　conditions, 279—281
　inmate-staff conflict, 272
　labeling hypothesis and, 278
　mortification and will breaking, 273
　new convicts preyed upon, 273
　"pathology of," 276—277
　privilege system, 274
　rehabilitation, 281
　Swedish, 282—284
Professional thief, 257—259
Professionals, dual loyalty, 452
Proletariat, 164
Pronatalist policies, 487—488
Prophetic function of religion, 390—391
"Protean man," 115
Protestant Ethic, 393, 462

Psychology, 12
Psychosurgery, 282—283
Public housing policies, 520, 522
Pueblo Indians:
　cultural adaptation to environment, 66
　family system, 328
　language, 73
Puerto Ricans, 201, 518
Public opinion polls, 42
Punishment, theories of, 271—272
Puritans, 164, 355, 393—394
"Pygmalion effect" in education, 364, 365

Quality of life, urban, 514
Questionnaires as research technique, 42—43

Race:
　defined, 417
　as factor in political affiliation, 417
　as physical adaptation, 179—180
Racial and ethnic minorities, 178—209
　Black identity, 197—199
　East Asians, 188, 196
　Jim Crow laws, 191
　meaning of race, 179—180
　prejudice, racial and ethnic, 182—192
　race: and busing issue, 192
　　and poverty, 201
　sterotypes, racial and ethnic, 182—183
　　(See also Black Americans; Discrimination; Prejudice)
Racial segregation, urban, 517—519
Racism and caste, 159
Ramayana, 332
Random sample, defined, 42
Rape, 214—215
Rapport, defined, 38
Rats as urban problem, 511
"Raza, la," 197
Reaffirmation of norms as theory of punishment, 271
Realism (of group), 127—128
Rebels (Merton's analysis), 251—252
Redlining, 518
Reference groups, 98, 141
Regulatory commissions, 427
Rehabilitation:
　as rationale for punishment, 272
　U-curve in, 279
Relative deprivation, 247—248
Religion, 383—411
　as "American way," 386
　contradictory functions of, 386—393
　conversion, 399—402
　denominations, sects, cults, 395—399
　in developing nations, 552—553
　as divisive force, 387
　and group emotions, 384, 386
　latent functions, 393—395
　major and minor traditions, 553
　manifest functions, 383—386
　Marxist view, 391
　and philosophy, 383
　and population policy, 475, 487
　and prejudice, 394—395
　in prisons, 398

Subject index